FACE PROCESSING

FACE
PROCESSING

PSYCHOLOGICAL, NEUROPSYCHOLOGICAL, AND APPLIED PERSPECTIVES

GRAHAM HOLE
VICTORIA BOURNE

OXFORD
UNIVERSITY PRESS

OXFORD
UNIVERSITY PRESS

Great Clarendon Street, Oxford OX2 6DP

Oxford University Press is a department of the University of Oxford.
It furthers the University's objective of excellence in research, scholarship,
and education by publishing worldwide in

Oxford New York

Auckland Cape Town Dar es Salaam Hong Kong Karachi
Kuala Lumpur Madrid Melbourne Mexico City Nairobi
New Delhi Shanghai Taipei Toronto

With offices in

Argentina Austria Brazil Chile Czech Republic France Greece
Guatemala Hungary Italy Japan Poland Portugal Singapore
South Korea Switzerland Thailand Turkey Ukraine Vietnam

Oxford is a registered trade mark of Oxford University Press
in the UK and in certain other countries

Published in the United States
by Oxford University Press Inc., New York

© Graham Hole and Victoria Bourne, 2010

British Library Cataloguing in Publication Data

Data available

Library of Congress Cataloging in Publication Data

Data available

Typeset by MPS Limited, A Macmillan Company
Printed in Great Britain by
CPI Antony Rowe, Chippenham, Wiltshire

ISBN 978-0-19-923570-4

1 3 5 7 9 10 8 6 4 2

acknowledgements

Before we begin, we would like to acknowledge those people who have helped in the production of this book. Thanks to our editor, Caroline Davidson; reviewers Olivier Pascalis and two others; Peter Hancock, Sal Navarro, Chris Thompson, and Philippe Schyns for their generous help with some of the images in this book; and to the following colleagues who helped us by reading drafts of various chapters: Nicky Brace, Sanjeedah Choudhury, Gini Harrison, Graham Pike, Matei Vladeanu, and Dan Wright.

figure acknowledgements

Every effort has been made to contact the copyright holders of figures in this text. Any copyright holders we have been unable to reach or for whom inaccurate information has been provided are invited to contact Oxford University Press.

I Introduction © Timewatch Images/Alamy

1.1 Reproduced with permission from the British Journal of Psychology, © The British Psychological Society.

1.2 Reproduced with permission from the British Journal of Psychology, © The British Psychological Society.

1.3 © Graham Hole

1.4 © Graham Hole

1.5 Reproduced from Valentine, T. (1991). A unified account of the effects of distinctiveness, inversion and race in face recognition. Quarterly Journal of Experimental Psychology, 43A, 161–204. Copyright © 2010 Taylor & Francis Group.

1.6 Getty Images/cartoon with kind permission of Sal Navarro, © Sal Navarro

1.7 Reproduced from Valentine, T., & Endo, M. (1992). Towards an exemplar model of face processing: the effects of race and distinctiveness. Quarterly Journal of Experimental Psychology, 44A (4), 671–703. Copyright © 2010 Taylor & Francis Group.

1.8 Reprinted by permission from Macmillan Publishers Ltd: Nature Neuroscience (Leopold, D.A., O'Toole, A.J., Vetter, T., & Blanz, V. (2001). Prototype-referenced shape encoding revealed by high-level after effects. Nature Neuroscience, 4(1), 89–94), © 2001.

2.1 © Graham Hole

2.2 WireImage/Getty Images

2.3 © Graham Hole

2.4 WireImage/Getty Images

2.5 © Graham Hole

2.6 Reprinted from: Tanaka, J.W., & Sengco, J.A. (1997). Features and their configuration in face recognition.

Memory and Cognition, 25 (5), 583–592, copyright 1997, Psychonomic Society Publications.

2.7 Reproduced with permission from: Collishaw, S.M., & Hole, G.J. (2000). Featural and configurational processes in the recognition of faces of different familiarity. Perception, 29, 893–909, © Pion Limited, London.

2.8 © Graham Hole

2.9 Reproduced with permission from: Hole, G.J., George, P.A., Eaves, K., & Rasek, A. (2002). Effects of geometric distortions on face-recognition performance. Perception, 31(10), 1221–1240, © Pion Limited, London.

2.10 © Graham Hole

2.11 Reproduced with kind permission of Philippe Schyns, University of Glasgow, © Philippe Schyns.

2.12 Reprinted with permission from Dakin, S.C., & Watt, R.J. (2009). Biological "bar codes" in human faces. Journal of Vision, 9(4):2, 1–10. © Association for Research in Vision and Ophthalmology (ARVO), 2009.

2.13 Reprinted with permission from Dakin, S.C., & Watt, R.J. (2009). Biological "bar codes" in human faces. Journal of Vision, 9(4):2, 1–10. © Association for Research in Vision and Ophthalmology (ARVO), 2009.

2.14 © Graham Hole

2.15 Reproduced with permission from: Brooks, K.R, & Kemp, R.I. (2007). Sensitivity to feature displacement in familiar and unfamiliar faces: beyond the internal/external feature distinction. Perception, 36, 1646–1659, © Pion Limited, London.

2.16 Reproduced with permission from: Stephan, B.C.M., & Caine, D. (2007). What is in a view? The role of featural information in the recognition of unfamiliar faces across viewpoint transformation. Perception, 36, 189–198, © Pion Limited, London.

2.17 Reproduced with kind permission of Peter Hancock, University of Stirling. © Peter Hancock.

2.18 Reprinted from Burton, A.M., Jenkins, R., Hancock, P.B.J., & White, D. Robust representations for face recognition. Cognitive Psychology, 51, 256–284, copyright 2005, with permission from Elsevier.

3.1 Reproduced from Young, A.W., et al. (2002). Facial expressions of emotion: Stimuli and tests (FEEST). Bury St. Edmunds: Thames Valley Test Company. Publisher : Thames Valley Test Company.

3.2 Reprinted with permission from: Calvo, M.G., & Lundqvist, D. (2008). Facial expressions of emotion (KDEF): Identification under different display-duration conditions. Behavior Research Methods, 40(1), 109–115. Copyright 2008, Psychonomic Society Publications.

3.3 Reprinted from: Cognition, 110, McCullough, S. and Emmorey, K., Categorical perception of affective and linguistic facial expressions, 208–221, copyright 2009, with permission from Elsevier.

3.4 Reprinted from: International Journal of Psychophysiology, 29, Surakka, V. and Hietanen, J.K., Facial and emotional reactions to Duchenne and non-Duchenne smiles, 23–33, copyright 1998, with permission from Elsevier.

3.5 Blau, V.C., et al. The face-specific N170 component is modulated by emotional facial expression. Behavioral and Brain Functions, 2007, 3:7. Copyright Blau et al.

3.6 Reprinted from: Brain Research, 1254, Morel, S., Ponz, A., Mercier, M., Vuilleumier, P. and George, N., EEG-MEG evidence for early differential repetition effects for fearful, happy and neutral faces, 84–98, copyright 2009, with permission from Elsevier.

3.7 Reprinted from: Neuroimage, 30, Fitzgerald, D.A., Angstadt, M., Jelsone, L.M., Nathan, P.J. and Phan, K.L., Beyond threat: Amygdala reactivity across multiple expressions of facial affect, 1441–1448, copyright 2006, with permission from Elsevier.

3.8 Reprinted from: Neuropsychologia, 45, Habel, U., Windischberger, C., Derntl, B., Robinson, S., Kryspin-Exner, I., Gur, R.C. and Moser, E., Amygdala activation and facial expressions: Explicit emotion discrimination versus implicit emotion processing, 2369–2377, copyright 2007, with permission from Elsevier.

4.1 Reprinted with permission from Wollaston, W.H. (1824). On the apparent direction of eyes in a portrait. Philosophical Transactions from the Royal Society of London, Series B, 114, 247–256. © Royal Society of London, 1824.

4.2 Reprinted with permission from: Dal Martello, M.F., & Maloney, L.T. (2006). Where are kin recognition signals in the human face? Journal of Vision, 6, 1356–1366. © Association for Research in Vision and Ophthalmology (ARVO), 2009.

4.3 Pittenger, J.B., & Shaw, R.E. Ageing faces as visceral-elastic events: implications for a theory of nonrigid shape perception. Journal of Experimental Psychology: Human Perception and Performance, 1(4), 374–482, 1975. American Psychological Association. Adapted with permission.

4.4 Ramanathan, N., & Chellappa, R. (2006). Modeling age progression in young faces. IEEE Computer Vision and Pattern Recognition (CVPR), vol. 1, 387–394. © 2006, IEEE.

4.5 Reprinted with permission from Burt, D.M. and Perrett, D.I. (1995). Perception of age in adult Caucasian male faces: computer graphic manipulation of shape and colour information. Proceedings of the Royal Society of London, B, 259, 137–143. Copyright Royal Society of London, 1995.

4.6 Reproduced with permission from the British Journal of Psychology, © The British Psychological Society.

4.7 Reproduced with permission from the British Journal of Psychology, © The British Psychological Society.

4.8 Reprinted with permission from: Apicella, C.L., Little, A.C., & Marlowe, F.W. (2007). Facial averageness and attractiveness in an isolated population of hunter-gatherers. Perception, 36, 1813–1820. © Pion Limited, London.

4.9 Reprinted by permission from Macmillan Publishers Ltd: Nature (Perrett, D.I., May, K.A., & Yoshikawa, S. (1994), Facial shape and judgments of female attractiveness, Nature, 368, 239–242), © 1994.

4.10 DeBruine, L.M., Jones, B.C., Unger, L., Little, A.C., & Feinberg, D.L. Dissociating averageness and attractiveness: attractive faces are not always average. Journal of Experimental Psychology: Human Perception and Performance, 33(6), 1420–1430, 2007. American Psychological Association. Reprinted with permission.

4.11 Reprinted with permission from DeBruine, L.M. (2004). Facial resemblance increases the attractiveness of same-sex faces more than other-sex faces. Proceedings of the Royal Society of London, Series B, 271(1552), 2085–2090. Copyright Royal Society of London, 2004.

5.1 © Graham Hole

5.2 Reproduced with kind permission of George Mather, University of Sussex. © George Mather.

5.3 Reproduced with kind permission of Professor Izumi Ohzawa, from the original concept by Fergus Campbell and John Robson (1964). © Izumi Ohzawa, 2009.

5.4 Reprinted from deHeering, A., Turati, C., Rossion, B., Bulf, H., Goffaux, V. & Simion, F. (2008). Newborns' face recognition is based on spatial frequencies below 0.5 cycles per degree. Cognition, 106, 444–454, copyright 2008, with permission from Elsevier.

5.5 Reprinted by permission from Macmillan Publishers Ltd: Nature Reviews Neuroscience (Johnson, M.H. (2005). Subcortical face processing. Nature Reviews Neuroscience, 6, 766–774), © 2005.

5.6 Reprinted from Johnson, M.H., Dziurawiec, S., Ellis, H., & Morton, J. (1991). Newborns' preferential tracking of face-like stimuli and its subsequent decline. Cognition, 40(1–2), 1–19, copyright 1991, with permission from Elsevier.

5.7 Valenza, E., Simion, F., Macchi Cassia, V. and Umiltà, C. Face preference at birth. Journal of Experimental Psychology: Human Perception and Performance, 22(4), 892–903, 1996. American Psychological Association. Reprinted with permission.

5.8 Simion, F., Valenza, E., Macchi Cassia, V., Turati, C. & Umiltà, C. (2002). Newborns' preference for up-down asymmetrical configurations. Developmental Science, 5(4), 427–434, copyright 2002, with permission from Wiley. Turati, C., Simion, F., Milani, I. & Umilta (2002). Newborns' preference for faces: what is crucial? Developmental Psychology, 38(6) 875–882. American Psychological Association. Reprinted with permission.

5.9 Reprinted from: Macchi Cassia, V., Turati, C., & Simion, F. (2004). Can a non specific bias toward top-heavy patterns explain newborns' face preference? Psychological Science, 15, 379–383, copyright 2004, with permission from Wiley.

5.10 Reprinted from Turati, C., Bulf, H., & Simion, F. (2008). Newborns' face recognition over changes in viewpoint. Cognition, 106(3), 1300–1321, copyright 2008, with permission from Elsevier.

5.11 Reprinted from Humphreys, K., Gosselin, F., Schyns, P.G., & Johnson, M.H. (2006). Using "Bubbles" with babies: a new technique for investigating the informational basis of infant perception. Infant Behavior and Development, 29(3), 471–475, copyright 2006, with permssion from Elsevier.

6.1 Reproduced with permission from the Journal of Neuropsychology, © The British Psychological Society.

6.2 Reprinted from Diamond, R., & Carey, S. (1977). Developmental changes in the representation of faces. Journal of Experimental Child Psychology, 23, 1–22, copyright 1977, with permission from Elsevier.

6.3 © Graham Hole

6.4 Reprinted from Freire, A., & Lee, K. (2001). Face recognition in 4 to 7-Year-olds: processing of configural, featural, and paraphernalia information. Journal of Experimental Child Psychology, 80, 347–371, copyright 2001, with permission from Elsevier.

6.5 Reprinted from de Heering, A., Houthuys, S. & Rossion, B. (2007). Holistic face processing is mature at 4 years of age: evidence from the composite face effect. Journal of Experimental Child Psychology, 96, 57–70, copyright 2007, with permission from Elsevier.

6.6 Reprinted with permission from: Mondloch, C.J., Le Grand, R., & Maurer, D. (2002). Configural face processing develops more slowly than featural face processing. Perception, 31, 553–566. © Pion Limited, London.

6.7 Chang, P.P.W., Levine, S.C., & Benson, P.J. Children's recognition of caricatures. Developmental Psychology, 38(6), 1038–1051, 2002. American Psychological Association. Reprinted with permission.

7.1 © Victoria Bourne

7.2 Reproduced from M.F. Bear et al., Neuroscience: exploring the Brain, 3rd edn. pp. 11–13. Baltimore, MD: Lippincott, Williaims & Wilkins, 2006.

7.3 Reproduced from Marotta, J.J., Genovese, C.R., & Behrmann, M. (2001). A functional MRI study of face recognition in patients with prosopagnosia. Neuroreport, 12(8), 1581–1587. Baltimore, MD: Lippincott Williams & Wilkins.

7.4 Reprinted from: Cortex, 36, Mattson, A.J., Levin, H.S. and Graman, J., A case of prosopagnosia following moderate closed head injury with left hemisphere focal lesion, 125–137, copyright 2000, with permission from Elsevier.

7.5 Reproduced from Marotta, J.J., Genovese, C.R., & Behrmann, M. (2001). A functional MRI study of face recognition in patients with prosopagnosia. Neuroreport, 12(8), 1581–1587. Baltimore, MD: Lippincott Williams & Wilkins.

7.6 © Victoria Bourne

7.7 Adapted and redrawn by permission of Oxford University Press Inc. Central Nervous System, Structure & Function Fig. 2.28 © 2002 by Oxford University Press, Inc.

7.8 © Graham Hole

7.9 © Victoria Bourne

8.1 Reprinted by permission from Macmillan Publishers Ltd: Nature, 410, Le Grand, R., Mondloch, C.J., Maurer, D. and Brent, H.P., Neuroperception - Early visual experience and face processing, 890–890, 2001, © 2001.

8.2 From Bookheimer, S.Y., Wang, A.T., Scott, A., Sigman, M., & Dapretto, M. (2008). Frontal contributions to face processing differences in autism: Evidence from fMRI of inverted face processing. Journal of the International Neuropsychological Society, 14(6), 9. © Cambridge University Press.

8.3 From Bellugi, U., Lichtenberger, L., Jones, W., Lai, Z., & St George, M. (2000). The neurocognitive profile of Williams syndrome: A complex pattern of strengths and weaknesses. Journal of Cognitive Neuroscience, 12, 7–29. Copyright MIT Press Journals.

8.4 Reprinted from: Schizophrenia Research, 87, Kee, K.S., Horan, W.P., Wynn, J.K., Mintz, J. and Green, M.F., An analysis of categorical perception of facial emotion in schizophrenia, 228–237, copyright 2006, with permission from Elsevier.

8.5 Reprinted from: Schizophrenia Research, 55, Loughland, C.M., Williams, L.M. and Gordon, E., Visual scanpaths to positive and negative facial emotions in an outpatient schizophrenia sample, 159–170, copyright 2002, with permission from Elsevier.

8.6 Reprinted from: Schizophrenia Research, 100, Fakra, E., Salgado-Pineda, P., Delaveau, P., Hariri, A.R. and Blin, O., Neural bases of different cognitive strategies for facial affect processing in schizophrenia, 191–205, copyright 2008, with permission from Elsevier.

8.7 Reprinted from: Biological Psychiatry, 63, Fu, C.H.Y., Mourao-Miranda, J., Costafrecla, S.G., Khanna, A., Marquand, A.F., Williams, S.C.R. and Brammer, M.J., Pattern classification of sad facial processing: Toward the development of neurobiological markers in depression, 656–662, copyright 2008, with permission from Elsevier.

8.8 Reprinted from: Psychiatry Research, 127, Horley, K., Williams, L.M., Gonsalvez, C. and Gordon, E., Face to face: visual scanpath evidence for abnormal processing of facial expressions in social phobia, 43–53, copyright 2004, with permission from Elsevier.

8.9 Reprinted from: Brain Research, 1118, Kolassa, I.T. and Miltner, W.H.R., Psychophysiological correlates of face processing in social phobia, 130–141, copyright 2006, with permission from Elsevier.

9.1 Reprinted from: Brain Research, 1123, Latinus, M. and Taylor, M.J., Face processing stages: Impact of difficulty and the separation of effects, 179–187, copyright 2006, with permission from Elsevier.

9.2 Reprinted from: Neuroimage, 36, Jacques, C. and Rossion, B., Early electrophysiological responses to multiple face orientations correlate with individual discrimination performance in humans, 863–876, copyright 2007, with permission from Elsevier.

9.3 Tanaka, J.W., Curran, T., Porterfield, A.L., & Collins, D. (2006). Activation of preexisting and acquired face representations: The N250 event-related potential as an index of face familiarity. Journal of Cognitive Neuroscience, 18(9), 1488–1497. Copyright MIT Press Journals.

9.4 Reprinted from: Brain Research, 1115, Itier, R.J., Herdman, A.T., George, N., Cheyne, D. and Taylor, M.J., Inversion and contrast-reversal effects on face processing assessed by MEG, 108–120, copyright 2006, with permission from Elsevier.

9.5 Reprinted from: Trends in Cognitive Sciences, 4, Haxby, J.V., Hoffman, E.A. and Gobbini, M.I., The distributed human neural system for face perception, 223–233, copyright 2000, with permission from Elsevier.

9.6 From Dekowska, M., Kuniecki, M., & Jaskowski, P. (2008). Facing facts: Neuronal mechanisms of face perception. Acta Neurobiologiae Experimentalis, 68(2), 229–252. Reproduced with kind permission from the Nencki Institute of Experimental Biology.

9.7 Reprinted from: Neuroscience and Biobehavioral Reviews, 33, Minnebusch, D.A. and Daum, I., Neuropsychological mechanisms of visual face and body perception, 1133–1144, copyright 2009, with permission from Elsevier.

9.8 Reprinted from: Neuroimage, 34, Passarotti, A.M., Smith, J., DeLano, M. and Huang, J., Developmental differences in the neural bases of the face inversion effect show progressive tuning of face-selective regions to the upright orientation, 1708–1722, copyright 2007, with permission from Elsevier.

9.9 Reprinted from: Brain Research, 1143, Devue, C., Collette, F., Balteau, E., Dequeldre, C., Luxen, A., Maquet, P. and Bredart, S., Here I am: The cortical correlates of visual self-recognition, 169–182, copyright 2007, with permission from Elsevier.

9.10 © Victoria Bourne

9.11 Reprinted with permission from: Webster, M.A., & MacLin, O.H. (1999). Figural aftereffects in the perception of faces. Psychonomic Bulletin & Review, 6(4), 647–653. Copyright 1999, Psychonomic Society Publications.

9.12 Reprinted with permission from: Fang, F., & He, S. (2005). Viewer-centered object representation in the human visual system revealed by viewpoint aftereffects. Neuron, 45(5), 793–800. © Association for Research in Vision and Ophthalmology (ARVO), 2005.

9.13 Reprinted from: Neuroimage, 37, Furl, N., van Rijsbergen, N.J., Treves, A. and Dolan, R.J., Face adaptation aftereffects reveal anterior medial temporal cortex role in high level category representation, 300–310, copyright 2007, with permission from Elsevier.

9.14 Reprinted from: Robbins, R., McKone, E., & Edwards, M. Aftereffects for face attributes with different natural variability: Adapter position effects and neural models. Journal of Experimental Psychology-Human Perception and Performance, 33(3), 570–592. 2007.

American Psychological Association. Reprinted with permission.

9.15 Reproduced from Darlington, C.L. (2002). The Female Brain. London: Taylor & Francis Group.

9.16 Reprinted from: Evolution and Human Behavior, 25, Penton-Voak, I.S. and Chen, J.Y., High salivary testosterone is linked to masculine male facial appearance in humans, 229–241, copyright 2004, with permission from Elsevier.

9.17 Reprinted from: Evolution and Human Behavior, 30, Rupp, H.A., James, T.W., Ketterson, E.D., Sengelaub, D.R., Janssen, E. and Heiman, J.R., Neural activation in women in response to masculinized male faces: mediation by hormones and psychosexual factors, 1–10, copyright 2009, with permission from Elsevier.

10.1 Diamond, R., & Carey, S. Why faces are and are not special: an effect of expertise. Journal of Experimental Psychology: General, 115(2), 107–117. 1986. American Psychological Association. Reprinted with permission.

10.2 Reprinted from: Vision Research, 37, Gauthier, I. and Tarr, M.J., Becoming a "greeble" expert: Exploring mechanisms for face recognition, 1673–1682, copyright 1997, with permission from Elsevier.

10.3 Reprinted from: Cognition, 103, Robbins, R. and McKone, E., No face-like processing for objects-of-expertise in three behavioural tasks, 34–79, copyright 2007, with permission from Elsevier.

10.4 © Victoria Bourne

10.5 Reprinted from: Neuropsychologia, 41, Duchaine, B.C. and Weidenfeld, A., An evaluation of two commonly used tests of unfamiliar face recognition, 713–720, copyright 2003, with permission from Elsevier.

10.6 Reprinted from: Neuropsychologia, 41, Duchaine, B.C. and Weidenfeld, A., An evaluation of two commonly used tests of unfamiliar face recognition, 713–720, copyright 2003, with permission from Elsevier.

10.7 Reprinted from: International Journal of Psychophysiology, 65, Marzi, T. and Viggiano, M.P., Interplay between familiarity and orientation in face processing: An ERP study, 182–192, copyright 2007, with permission from Elsevier.

10.8 Reprinted from: Neuroimage, 29, Itier, R.J., Latinus, M. and Taylor, M.J., Face, eye and object early processing: What is the face specificity?, 667–676, copyright 2006, with permission from Elsevier.

10.9a Reprinted from: Cognition, 68, Kanwisher, N., Tong, F. and Nakayama, K., The effect of face inversion on the human fusiform face area, B1–B11, copyright 1998, with permission from Elsevier.

10.9b Reprinted from: Neuroimage, 17, Andrews, T.J., Schluppeck, D., Homfray, D., Matthews, P. and Blakemore, C., Activity in the fusiform gyrus predicts conscious perception of Rubin's vase-face illusion, 890–901, 2002, with permission from Elsevier.

10.10 Reprinted by permission from Macmillan Publishers Ltd: Nature Neuroscience, 2, Gauthier, I., Tarr, M.J., Anderson, A.W., Skudlarski, P. and Gore, J.C., Activation of the middle fusiform 'face area' increases with expertise in recognizing novel objects, 568–573, © 1999.

10.11 Reprinted from: Neuropsychologia, 44, Steeves, J.K.E., Culham, J.C., Duchaine, B.C., Pratesi, C.C., Valyear, K.F., Schindler, I., Humphrey, G.K., Milner, A.D. and Goodale, M.A., The fusiform face area is not sufficient for face recognition: Evidence from a patient with dense prosopagnosia and no occipital face area, 594–609, copyright 2006, with permission from Elsevier.

10.12 From: Tsao, D.Y., Freiwald, W.A., Tootell, R.B.H., & Livingstone, M.S. (2006). A cortical region consisting entirely of face-selective cells. Science, 311(5761), 670–674. Reprinted with permission from AAAS.

11.1 Reproduced with kind permisson of the Home Office.

11.2 © Graham Hole

11.3 © Graham Hole

11.4 © Graham Hole

12.1 Reprinted with permission from: Bar-Haim, Y., Saidel, T., & Yovel, G. (2009). The role of skin colour in face recognition. Perception, 38, 145–148. © Pion Limited, London.

12.2 Reprinted from: Michel, C., Rossion, B., Han, J., Chung, C-S. and Caldara, R. (2006). Holistic processing is finely tuned for faces of one's own race. Psychological Science, 17 (7), 608–615, copyright 2006, with permission from Wiley.

12.3 © Graham Hole

12.4 Reprinted with permisssion from: MacLin, O.H., & Malpass, R.S. (2003). The ambiguous-race face illusion. Perception, 32, 249–252. © Pion Limited, London.

12.5 Sporer, S.L. Recognizing faces of other ethnic groups: an integration of theories. Psychology, Public Policy and Law, 7, 36–97, 2001. American Psychological Association. Reprinted with permission.

12.6 Reprinted from: Behavioural Processes, 73, Dufour, V., Pascalis, O., & Petit, O. Face processing limitation to own species in primates: a comparative study in brown capuchins, Tonkean macaques and humans. 107–113, copyright 2006, with permission from Elsevier.

13.1 © Graham Hole

13.2 Bruce, V., Henderson, Z., Greenwood, K., Hancock, P., Burton, M., & Miller, P. Verification of face identities from images captured on video. Journal of Experimental Psychology: Applied, 5, 339–360, 1999. American Psychological Association. Reprinted with permission.

13.3 It has been impossible to trace a copyright holder of the photograph of Edwin Bush, but the publisher would be happy to acknowledge the omission at the earliest opportunity. The Idenikit picture is reproduced with permission from The National Archives.

13.4 Reprinted from: Wells, G.L. and Hasel, L.E. (2007). Facial composite production by eyewitnesses. Current Directions In Psychological Science, 16 (1), 6–10, copyright 2007, with permission from Wiley.

13.5 Reproduced with kind permission of Charlie Frowd, University of Central Lancashire. Copyright Charlie Frowd.

13.6 Reproduced with kind permission of Chris Solomon. Copyright Chris Solomon.

13.7 Reproduced with permission from Legal and Criminological Psychology, © The British Psychological Society.

13.8 Bruce, V., Ness, H., Hancock, P.J.B., Newman, C., & Rarity, J. Four heads are better than one: combining face composites yields improvements in face likeness. Journal of Applied Psychology, 87, 894–902, 2002. American Psychological Association. Reprinted with permission.

13.9 Reprinted from: Brace, N., Pike, G., Kemp, R., Turner, J., & Bennett, P. (2006). Does the presentation of multiple facial composites improve suspect identification? Applied Cognitive Psychology, 20, 213–226, copyright 2006, with permission from Wiley.

13.10 Reproduced from Frowd, C., Bruce, V., Ross, D., McIntyre, A., & Hancock, P.J.B. (2007c). An application of caricature: how to improve the recognition of facial composites. Visual Cognition, 15(8), 954–984. Copyright © 2010 Taylor & Francis Group.

A1 © Graham Hole

A2 Bourne, V.J. (2008). Examining the relationship between degree of handedness and degree of cerebral lateralization for processing facial emotion. Neuropsychology, 22(3), 350–356. American Psychological Association. Reprinted with permission.

A3 Reprinted from: Clinical Neurophysiology, 112, Oostenveld, R. and Praamstra, P., The five percent electrode system for high-resolution EEG and ERP measurements, 713–719, 2001, with permission from Elsevier.

A4 Reprinted from: Neuroimage, 32, Boutsen, L., Humphreys, G.W., Praamstra, P. and Warbrick, T., Comparing neural correlates of configural processing in faces and objects: An ERP study of the Thatcher illusion, 352–367, 2006, with permission from Elsevier.

A5 Reprinted from: Neuroimage, 32, Schiltz, C. and Rossion, B., Faces are represented holistically in the human occipito-temporal cortex, 1385–1394, 2006, with permission from Elsevier.

A6 © Graham Hole

contents

introduction

Like many aspects of visual perception, our ability to process facial information is so quick and apparently effortless that most people take it for granted. Yet if you think about it, on the basis of a brief glance at a face you can usually tell the age, gender and emotional state of the person; whether or not you have seen them before; and, if you know them, who they are, and what their relationship is to you. In the case of a familiar face, you can access your knowledge about them (such as their occupation, interests, likes and dislikes) and, in many cases, you can remember their name. All this can be achieved on the basis of a particular view of that person's face, a view that you may never have encountered before. We can remember faces over protracted periods of time: one of us (Graham Hole) recently met a friend whom he hadn't seen for 25 years, but mutual recognition occurred without any difficulty, despite the ravages of age having altered both faces considerably since the last meeting.

All of this is remarkable enough, but we can also do it incredibly quickly. 'Event-related potential' (ERP) studies measuring the brain's electrical activity in response to visual stimuli suggest that it takes only 130 milliseconds for the visual system to detect that a face is present in a scene, as opposed to some other kind of object (Jacques and Rossion, 2006). Familiar face recognition is truly wonderful: in experiments that require a decision to be made about whether each face shown is familiar or unfamiliar, participants generally take less than a second to decide that they do not know a face. That's pretty fast, when you think of how many faces we have encountered in our lifetime.

This book is an introduction to the scientific research that has been conducted on face processing in an attempt to find out how we manage to achieve these amazing feats. There has been a massive amount of research on faces. Typing 'face recognition' into our library's search engine gave us 111,079 published journal articles and book chapters within the area of psychology. Restricting the search to 'face recognition in 2009' produced 7,813 articles and chapters—and at the time of writing, we are only three-quarters of the way through the year.

Why is there this huge interest in the scientific study of faces? Part of the reason is because faces are incredibly important to us. We use faces for a wide variety of purposes. As alluded to above, they enable us to recognize people, and to assess their emotional state. Their face tells us whether they are male or female, young or old, attractive or not so attractive. On the basis of a person's face, we make inferences about their character. And we do all of this incredibly quickly and easily. Even young babies show an impressive degree of competence at performing many of these tasks.

Another reason for the huge amount of research is because face processing attracts interest from a wide variety of disciplines. In terms of 'pure' science, faces are of interest to psychologists, neuropsychologists and computer scientists, all of whom are trying to get to grips with how face processing is achieved. Cognitive psychologists are interested in face processing as an information-processing problem: for example, what information do people extract from faces in order to recognize them, and how do they use this information? Social psychologists want to know how facial properties such as gender, race and attractiveness influence the interactions between individuals. Developmental psychologists attempt to discover how face processing develops through the lifespan: how does experience interact with the abilities that we possess at birth, in order to arrive at the high level of expertise with faces that is shown by adults? Neuropsychologists are mainly concerned with finding out about the underlying brain structures and processes involved in face processing. Evolutionary psychologists are involved in trying to find evidence of adaptive design, not just in the face itself, but also in the responses to it that are made by others. Computer scientists are busily engaged in trying to build computer systems that can match the human visual system in terms of its ability to find faces rapidly and efficiently in a scene and then decide whether or not they are familiar. For the latter, faces are interesting from a theoretical point of view because object recognition is an extremely challenging problem for computers to tackle, and face recognition is the object recognition task *par excellence*: faces are all variations on a common theme, whose bottom halves wobble and move about while we talk and show expressions. From a computer science point of view, if you can crack the problem of recognizing faces reliably, then the rest of object recognition will be simple in comparison.

Faces are fascinating for their own sake, but they are also very important from an 'applied' point of view. For better or worse, faces provide the primary means of identifying people. Lawyers, judges and police officers need to know how much faith we can place on eyewitnesses' descriptions of criminals, and how well suspects can be recognized if they are apprehended. Curiously enough, the legal systems in almost all countries have never seriously researched these issues, relying instead on common sense and experience. These are no substitute for empirical research, as we shall see, and a major branch of 'applied' psychological research has concerned itself with investigating the (un)reliability of identification of unfamiliar faces. Also, of course, research into face recognition by computer scientists has potential practical uses. At the moment, if you are a terrorist

or a criminal, the ubiquitous CCTV cameras merely record your face, for security personnel to scrutinize at some point. How much better would this system be if the cameras were connected to a computer that recognized your face, matched it to its database of known villains, and then called the police?

Neurologists and clinicians are faced with patients who display impairments in processing faces for one reason or another; perhaps a better understanding of how faces are recognized might help us to develop remedial training in order to compensate for these deficits. From the point of view of applied social psychology, our difficulties in recognizing individuals from other races probably contribute to the development of hostilities between groups and ultimately, perhaps, racist attitudes (because 'they' all look the same).

So you can see that an understanding of how faces are processed is not only intrinsically interesting, but it could change the world, hopefully for the better. (There is, of course, the possibility that we'll end up living in a dystopia where computerized face recognition systems mistake us for similar-looking undesirables, and prevent us from getting on a plane, entering a supermarket or filling our car with petrol. If there's one thing that a knowledge of psychology teaches you, it's that *no* system can ever be 100% reliable. Life in the future may involve having to put up with automatic misidentifications as well as identifications.)

Thinking about it, given all this interest in faces, it's surprising there aren't even more publications on faces every year! When we originally envisaged writing this book, it was going to be a little book (of about 80,000 words) that briefly surveyed our current knowledge of face processing, on the basis of psychological, neuropsychological and 'applied' research. It quickly became apparent that was going to be an impossible endeavour—as you can see, the book has ended up quite a bit tubbier. Even so, we

FIGURE I © Timewatch Images/Alamy

'Good-bye, till we meet again!' she said as cheerfully as she could.

'I shouldn't know you again if we did meet,' Humpty Dumpty replied in a discontented tone, giving her one of his fingers to shake; 'you're so exactly like other people.'

'The face is what one goes by, generally,' Alice remarked in a thoughtful tone.

'That's just what I complain of,' said Humpty Dumpty. 'Your face is the same as everybody has – the two eyes, so – ' (marking their places in the air with this thumb) 'nose in the middle, mouth under. It's always the same. Now if you had the two eyes on the same side of the nose, for instance – or the mouth at the top – that would be some help.''

(Lewis Carroll, 1871).

haven't managed to do more than give a selective review of some of the topics that are interesting in face-processing research. There are important topics that we haven't covered at all, such as the effects of facial disfigurement; face processing in relation to communication (such as its role in normal conversation, non-verbal communication and lip-reading); the social psychology of the character attributions that are made in response to faces; and computer science models of face processing. Most of the other topics that we've covered could have been expanded to fill an entire book in their own right, and space has necessarily precluded dealing with them in as much detail as we would have liked. To this end, we've also tended to focus on more recent research, at the expense of discussing older studies. However, we hope that this book serves as an entry into an area of research that both of us have found consistently fascinating. Each chapter contains suggestions for further reading, so that you can explore the topics that we cover in greater detail. Here is a brief overview of the contents of the book.

Chapter 1 deals with some highly influential theories of face processing, theories that have both summarized and integrated research findings as well as stimulating huge amounts of research in their own right. These provide a framework for understanding how the material covered in the following chapters fits together.

Chapter 2 deals with the 64,000-dollar issue in face-processing research: how do we recognize faces? There are all sorts of difficulties involved in this. Firstly, changes in lighting, perspective and expression mean that we virtually never see the same view of a face twice, and yet we take all this variability in our stride (at least, we do with

familiar faces—as we shall see, we're not so good at coping with these kinds of change when it comes to recognizing faces that we've seen only once or twice before). Another complication is that faces all look pretty similar to one another. The basic problem of face recognition was nicely formulated by Humpty Dumpty in *Through the Looking Glass, and What Alice Found There* (see Figure I):[1]

Chapter 2 reviews what we know about how faces are encoded and stored in memory. Here we introduce a concept that will recur throughout the book: the idea that the 'configural' properties of faces (the spatial interrelationship between the facial features) are very important for face processing.

As well as recognizing faces, we also use them to assess people's emotional state. Chapter 3 reviews psychological and neuropsychological research on how facial emotion is processed by the brain. How accurately can we perceive emotions from faces, and is emotion processing the same across all cultures? How does emotion processing change with age? This chapter also discusses the issue of whether identity and emotion are processed independently of each other, or interactively. A long-held view has been that face processing is 'modular', in the sense that there are separate systems for processing 'invariant' aspects of faces (e.g. their identity) and 'variant' aspects (such as the emotion that they are displaying). Chapter 3 reviews more recent research suggesting there may more 'cross-talk' between these processes than was hitherto believed.

Chapter 4 looks at other social functions of faces. For example, we are very sensitive to where other people are looking (including whether they are looking at us). We are also very

---

[1] After writing this, we discovered that other face researchers have also used this quote from *Through the Looking Glass*—namely Gauthier et al (1999) and Larner (2004). This just illustrates our point, that face processing is a heavily researched area. Larner suggests that Humpty Dumpty is an early case of prosopagnosia ('face blindness'; see Chapter 7).

good at determining someone's sex and age, and surprisingly accurate at deciding whether someone is related to us. Faces are also an important factor in attractiveness. Much of the research on these topics has been conducted within the framework of evolutionary psychology, attempting to show that our face-processing abilities—and indeed our faces themselves—have been shaped by natural selection.

Chapter 5 considers research on the development of face processing in infants. How well can babies recognize faces? The traditional reason for looking at infants' perceptual abilities was to see how much was 'innate' (based on systems that had been built into the infant brain by natural selection) and how much was due to subsequent experience. Modern conceptions of perceptual development regard it as an *interaction* between innate biases to attend to certain aspects of the environment, and the experience obtained as a result. Much of Chapter 5 is relevant to a longstanding question that we will cover at length in Chapter 10: are faces 'special', in the sense of involving dedicated perceptual systems? Early research suggested that newborn babies have a predisposition to look at faces as opposed to other objects. However, whether this necessarily implies that they are 'hard-wired' to respond to faces has been questioned by recent research.

Chapter 6 reviews research on face recognition in older children, focusing on two issues. Firstly, are young children poorer at recognizing faces because they process faces in a qualitatively different way from adults, relying more on a 'piecemeal', feature-based processing than on the configural processing used by adults? Although this idea of an 'encoding switch' remains popular, we will show how more recent research fails to support it. Secondly, how much reliance should be placed on children as eyewitnesses? From a legal point of view, this is a very important question, given the importance of eyewitness identification for apprehending criminals.

Chapter 7 deals with the clinical neuropsychology of face recognition. What can we learn about normal face recognition by looking at people who experience severe difficulties in processing faces? 'Prosopagnosia'— popularly referred to as 'face blindness'—is a fascinating disorder in which there is a selective impairment in recognizing faces, without any significant impairment in other aspects of perceptual processing. This chapter reviews what we know about its neuropsychological basis: which brain structures are essential for normal face recognition, and what precisely is the nature of the underlying processing deficit in prosopagnosia?

In Chapter 8, we discuss developmental neuropsychological disorders of face processing. As well as autism and Williams syndrome, schizophrenia, depression and social phobia can all affect how well people process faces. Trying to identify the nature of these impairments is important in its own right, but it may also give us an insight into 'normal' face processing. Studies of the deficits in face recognition displayed by adults who experienced visual deprivation as young children have raised awareness of the role of early visual experience in the normal development of face recognition.

Chapter 9 covers the cognitive neuroscience of face recognition. Until relatively recently, neuropsychology had to rely on what could be inferred about 'normal' brain functioning from studying brain-damaged individuals. The advent of *in vivo* imaging techniques has changed all that. Positron emission tomography (PET), computed tomography (CT), magnetic resonance imaging (MRI) and functional MRI (fMRI) enable us to look inside the normal healthy brain, and permit us to relate structure and function in ways that would have been undreamt of even 20 years ago. As well as imaging techniques, the development of powerful computers has meant that we are able to interpret the complex electrical activity produced by the brain, in the form of ERPs and magnetoencephalography (MEG). This chapter looks at what has been found out from using these techniques. In this chapter we also review what is known about hormonal influences on face processing.

Chapter 10 is devoted to a single topic that has been of interest to psychologists and neuropsychologists for decades: are faces a 'special' class of stimulus, as far as the brain is concerned? Have we evolved structures and processes specifically to deal with processing faces, or are our face-processing abilities merely the result of our extensive experience with them? This question has been tackled from a number of standpoints, and has generated very heated debate. We'll review psychological, neuropsychological and neurophysiological evidence on the issue.

The final three chapters approach faces from an 'applied' perspective. Whereas 'pure' research has tended to focus on studying how we manage to recognize familiar faces, 'applied' research has been more concerned with our inability to remember unfamiliar faces. This is vitally important because, as we shall see, misidentifications are a major cause of miscarriages of justice. Chapter 11 deals with various factors that are known to affect the reliability of face recognition by eyewitnesses. These can be divided into two broad types: estimator variables (factors that are intrinsic to the witness themselves, such as their personal characteristics, their stress levels, and how good a view they had of a criminal's face); and system variables (the properties of the legal system, such as the length of the delay between witnessing a crime and being interviewed about it, the procedures used for conducting identification parades, and the nature of any feedback given to witnesses about their identification performance). This chapter also briefly covers the issue of individual differences in face recognition.

Chapter 12 is devoted to a single, very important, issue in applied research on face processing: why is it so hard to recognize faces of racial groups other than our own? The 'own-race' bias in recognition is a highly reliable phenomenon, but it is still not clear why it occurs. Various explanations have been proposed to account for it, ranging from it being due to a lack of perceptual expertise with other-race faces, to it being due to more social–psychological factors. Chapter 12 reviews these theories and the evidence for and against them.

Finally, Chapter 13 looks at issues surrounding the use of technology as an aid to identifying unfamiliar faces. How useful are identity cards as a means of verifying the identity of an unfamiliar person? Can faces be recognized reliably from CCTV images? And why do 'face reconstruction systems' such as Photofit and E-Fit generally produce such disappointing likenesses of faces?

Thus, the first six chapters deal primarily with face processing from the perspective of psychological research; Chapters 7–10 focus mainly on the neural machinery that underlies face processing; and the last three chapters cover 'applied' issues, which are extremely important given the great weight attached to eyewitness identification as a means of catching criminals. (We could have included two extra sections, by dividing the 'psychological perspectives' section into 'adult' and 'developmental' perspectives, and by including an additional section on computer science—but that would have left us with a book title that we would have struggled to remember, let alone fit on the spine of the book.)

To some extent, these three sections capture a 'cultural' difference amongst researchers on face processing: each group has its own methods and preoccupations. However, we do not want to overemphasize the differences between these approaches—quite apart from the fact that many groups are interdisciplinary, many researchers successfully straddle one or more fields. Psychological, neuropsychological and applied approaches are highly complementary, and, as you will see throughout the book, each approach generally has something very useful to say about most topics. Reflecting this, we've tried to keep each chapter as self-contained as possible, in the interests of readability, but inevitably there is some overlap between chapters. Therefore, each chapter contains cross-references to relevant material on that topic in other chapters, where appropriate.

PART I

PSYCHOLOGICAL PERSPECTIVES

MODELS OF HUMAN FACE PROCESSING

As mentioned in the Introduction, we can recognize familiar faces rapidly and reliably. We also use faces for a diversity of other purposes, such as determining the person's emotional state, age and gender. How do we achieve these feats of face processing? And how are all these different types of processing related to one another? This chapter will outline the most influential models of how face processing is achieved. Chapter 2 will then discuss what we know about the 'front end' of face processing, specifically in relation to face recognition: exactly what information does the brain extract from a face in order to recognize it?

1.1 The Bruce and Young (1986) model of face processing

The most influential theory of face processing was put forward by Vicki Bruce and Andy Young in the mid-1980s. Derived in part from a previous model by Hay and Young (1982), it was based on what was known at the time about face processing from cognitive psychological research, neuropsychological studies, and diary studies in which participants recorded any failures of recognition that they experienced (Young et al, 1985a).

Bruce and Young's model has two major features. Firstly, it proposes that face processing involves a set of largely distinct processes, in acknowledgement of the fact that faces provide information for a number of different purposes. Faces are used as a basis for individual recognition; perception of the owner's emotional state, age and gender; and, especially in noisy conditions, facial movements are used as an aid to comprehending speech. The Bruce and Young model suggests that the brain handles these processes more or less separately. As we shall see, this is consistent with neuropsychological data suggesting that identity, expression and speech processing can all be impaired independently of one another (see Chapter 3). Secondly, the model suggests that face recognition occurs in a number of discrete, successive stages. This reflects the fact that in everyday life, as well as in experiments, face recognition can fail at various points. Sometimes on seeing a face, we get a feeling of familiarity from it, but nothing more. On other occasions, we know who the person is (we can access semantic information about them, such as 'She's one of my students', 'She owns a budgie' and 'One of her hobbies is taxidermy'). Sometimes we get as far as remembering their name as well.

1.1.1 The types of information obtained from faces: pictorial versus structural codes

Bruce and Young suggested that there are seven different types of information (or information 'codes', as they called them) that are extracted from faces. One important distinction they made was between 'pictorial' and 'structural' codes for faces. **Pictorial codes** contain information about the details of the specific image that is being inspected, as well as the face depicted within it. **Structural codes** are more abstract: they contain the information necessary to recognize a face, despite changes in lighting, pose, expression, etc.

Evidence for the existence of these two kinds of code comes from two experiments by Bruce (1982). In the first, she showed her participants a set of unfamiliar faces, and then tested their ability to recognize them. Performance was best when exactly the same images were used at presentation and test. Participants were slower to respond and made more errors if the images changed in pose or expression, and performance was impaired even more if both changes were made together. Bruce argued that when the images are identical at presentation and test, participants can use both pictorial and structural codes to do the task: they can remember specific aspects of the particular images that they saw (pictorial codes) as well as aspects of the face itself (structural codes). When pose and/or expression are changed, only structural codes remain available for use.

Bruce found that changes to pose and expression affected unfamiliar face recognition the most, but also had some effect on *familiar* face recognition. When she repeated the experiment with familiar faces, she found that changes in pose or expression did not affect accuracy, but did increase response times slightly. She reasoned that participants already have well-developed structural codes for known faces that should enable them to compensate for any changes in view. As viewing identical images nevertheless

facilitates responding, this condition must be providing additional information to participants, in the form of pictorial codes. As Bruce and Young point out, experiments in which pictorial codes can be used tell us something about picture memory but little about real-life face recognition. It is therefore unfortunate that, even today, so many studies persist in using the same face images throughout an experiment.

What is the nature of the structural codes that underlie face recognition? This is a core issue in face processing research, and one that we shall discuss at length in Chapter 2 (and indeed, throughout the whole book). When Bruce and Young devised their model, it was already known that familiar and unfamiliar face recognition probably involved different types of information. Unfamiliar face recognition is more viewpoint-specific, much more closely tied to the particular view or views of the face in question. As shown by 'applied' research on eyewitness performance, unfamiliar face recognition is fairly 'fragile' and unreliable as a result (see Chapters 11, 12 and 13). In contrast, familiar face recognition is more viewpoint-independent, much more tolerant of changes in terms of properties such as pose, expression and illumination.

Structural codes enable us to know whether or not a face is familiar. **Visually derived semantic codes** and **identity-specific semantic codes** provide information about the meaningfulness of a face. Visually derived semantic codes were devised to account for the fact that even an unfamiliar person's appearance provides us with some information about them, such as their age and gender. Facial appearance also leads us to make inferences about the person's personality, such as whether they are conscientious or extrovert (e.g. Little and Perrett, 2007). Identity-specific semantic codes are derived from familiar faces, and provide us with information that is specific about that person (their occupation, interests, friends, etc.). In contrast to visually derived semantic codes, identity-specific semantic codes have an arbitrary relationship with the face: you have to know the person concerned in order to access the information.

Name codes contain the information about the person's name. Bruce and Young argued that names were distinct from other identity-specific semantic information, firstly because we can know someone without ever having known their name, and secondly because forgetting names that we do know (while remaining able to recognize their owners' faces) is a common memory failure in both normal and brain-damaged individuals.

Bruce and Young identified two other types of code: **expression codes**, which provide information on the person's emotional state; and **facial speech codes**, movements of the lips and tongue that affect the perception of heard speech. Bruce and Young's view was that these two types of code had little to do with recognition. From a logical standpoint, we might well expect recognition to involve different representations from expression and facial speech analysis: identity must be based on invariant aspects of a face, whereas by their very nature, expressions and talking involve changes to the shape and position of the facial features.

1.1.2 The structure of the Bruce and Young model of face processing

Face processing involves generating and accessing these codes; these are the *products* of face processing. Bruce and Young's model consisted of a set of *processes* that enabled these codes to be obtained. Figure 1.1 shows the model. Each box represents a functionally separate processing

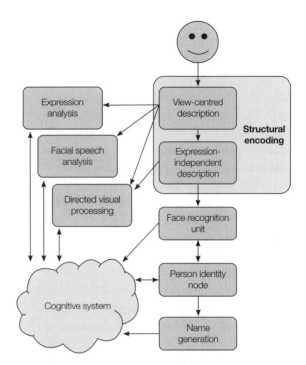

FIGURE 1.1 The Bruce and Young (1986) model of face recognition.

module, and the arrows represent the flow of information between modules.

In Bruce and Young's model, the process of recognition proceeds as follows. First, a face undergoes a process of encoding that produces a **representation** of it. (A representation is a description of a stimulus in the brain that makes certain information explicit.)[1] Bruce and Young's **structural encoding** phase involves the construction of a number of representations, each serving different purposes. They suggested that highly viewpoint-specific representations were used for expression analysis and analysing

---

[1] The map of the London Underground is an excellent example of a representation. Its purpose is to make it clear on which tube lines stations are present, and where they are on the network in relation to one another. It is therefore designed to make this topological information very obvious to the viewer (i.e. explicit). Other information (such as the geographical distances between the stations) is discarded. In the same way, face representations need to make explicit whatever information is best for discriminating between faces: just having a faithful and complete 'picture in the head' of a face would not be very helpful for this task.

facial speech, and separate, more abstract, expression-independent representations were used for recognition.

As we said above, if the face is unfamiliar, its representation will be heavily tied to the particular view of it that is being encountered at that moment. If the face is a familiar one, the initial representation will activate a **Face Recognition Unit (FRU)** for that face. There is a separate FRU for each face that we know. FRUs are quite abstract in nature: they are activated by any view of the particular face that they relate to. Activation of a FRU gives rise to a feeling of familiarity: it signals that the face is one that is known, but nothing more than that.

The next stage in the Bruce and Young model involves **Person Identity Nodes (PINs)**. These were originally conceived to be repositories of semantic information about a person (the 'identity-specific semantic codes' mentioned above), but this idea was revised on the basis of subsequent experimental findings. Instead, PINs became envisaged as 'modality-free' gateways to semantic information, in recognition of the fact that faces are not the only means by which we recognize someone: we can use names or voices, for example. An FRU stimulates the PIN with which it is associated. The PIN, in turn, activates a **Semantic Information Unit (SIU)** (not shown in Fig. 1.1) that contains information about the face's owner, such as their occupation, relationship to us, age, etc. Finally, the SIU might activate the associated **Name Unit** that contains the person's name.

Two other aspects of the model remain to be discussed. The 'cognitive system' includes various features that are related to face processing but not contained within the rest of the model. For example, it contains other aspects of memory that are relevant to knowing a person but are not essential for identifying them. It also contains decision-making and attentional systems. The cognitive system is responsible for the pictorial and visually derived semantic codes. It is not clear why Bruce and Young thought that directed visual

processing (selective and strategic attention to the visual appearance of a face) should be a separate module from the rest of the cognitive system. Perhaps they wanted to draw attention to its importance in real-world face recognition. As they conceded, this part of the model was quite vague (and has received comparatively little attention since). However, it shows that Bruce and Young were very aware that 'face processing' is not a passive process; people will often use strategies to try to encode faces and to recognize them subsequently, both in experimental situations and in real life. You have probably experienced situations in which you have seen someone, and are not sure whether you know them, or are uncertain about whether they really are the person you initially thought they were. As Young et al (1985a) pointed out, making decisions in these circumstances is quite often based on deliberative reasoning, taking things such as context and clothing into account when coming to a conclusion ('That does look very much like my mum, but it can't be her, because she wouldn't be here in this circus at this time in the evening, wearing a leotard, and as far as I know she isn't a trapeze artist'). Laboratory studies have traditionally underplayed these 'metacognitive' aspects of face processing. In contrast, a major preoccupation in 'applied' research has been to understand how eyewitnesses decide whether or not they have seen a face before, and to identify sources of non-facial information that might affect these decisions (see Chapter 11).

1.1.3 **Evaluation of the Bruce and Young model**

This model has been enormously influential in face-processing research, and remains widely used nearly a quarter of a century after it was first formulated. It has made a major contribution to the development of face-processing research by providing a theoretical framework within which to organize what was known about face processing at the time (and most of what's been discovered since). How has it stood up in the light of subsequent research?

Its proposal that recognition occurs in successive stages was well supported by research at the time. Evidence for this came originally from diary studies, such as the one by Young et al (1985a). They asked people to record any failures of person recognition that they experienced in their everyday lives. The results were consistent with the idea that recognition proceeds from a sense of vague familiarity through to knowing something about the person, and then ultimately recalling the person's name. Failures of recognition seemed to occur at each of these stages. For example, Young et al's diarists recorded situations in which they failed to recognize a familiar person altogether; situations in which they had a sense of familiarity about a face, but had no idea who the person was; and situations in which they knew who the person was, but couldn't remember their name. Phenomena that would be at odds with this sequential process (such as knowing someone's name, but having no idea of who they were) were never recorded.

Laboratory studies are also broadly consistent with the model: in experiments that measure participants' reaction times to make various decisions about faces, people are quicker to decide whether or not a face is familiar than they are to retrieve semantic information about it, which in turn is accomplished more quickly than recalling the person's name (Young et al, 1986b). Bruce and Young (1986) cited numerous other experimental studies that supported the model's organization of modules. However, the model's explanation for why it is takes longer to name a face than to retrieve other semantic information about it has been questioned. According to the Bruce and Young model, this occurs because names are linked only indirectly to FRUs: they can only be accessed once other semantic information has been retrieved, via the PIN. Rahman et al (2002) have provided event-related potential (ERP) data that cast doubt on this interpretation, and which are more consistent with the idea that accessing

semantic information and retrieving names are handled by independent processes operating in parallel with each other.

What about Bruce and Young's claim that face processing consists of a set of independent processes, so that face *identification* is independent of face *classification* on the basis of characteristics such as expression, facial speech and gender? Initial evidence seemed to support this argument in the case of expression, but was less clearcut in the case of gender perception. For example, Bruce (1986) conducted three experiments examining the effects of familiarity on the speed with which participants could make various judgements about faces. Participants had to perform one of three tasks for a set of faces: judge each face's emotional expression (decide whether or not it was smiling); decide whether each face was male or female; or decide whether each face was intact or scrambled (i.e. whether it had had its internal features rearranged). The faces were well known to half of the participants and wholly unfamiliar to the rest. Familiarity had no effect on decision times for the expression judgement task. It did have small but statistically significant effects on the other two tasks. Bruce suggested that although identity, gender and emotional expression were processed in parallel, familiarity with a face could sometimes aid the processing of its other attributes. For example, a face's gender would normally be determined by processing its shape; but if the face was androgynous, this processing would be slower, and in these circumstances familiarity with the face might speed the decision process.

Ganel and Goshen-Gottstein (Goshen-Gottstein and Ganel 2000; Ganel and Goshen-Gottstein, 2002, 2004) have questioned the 'parallel routes' hypothesis. They accept that there is fairly good evidence that expression, lip-reading and identity are processed independently of one another (but see Schweinberger and Soukup [1998] and Ganel and Goshen-Gottstein [2004] for evidence that the processing of expression and identity may be somewhat more interrelated than was at first thought). Neuropsychological research suggests that following brain damage, some patients can no longer recognize faces but can still identify emotional expressions, whereas other patients have lost the ability to recognize emotions but can still recognize faces. This complementary pattern of impairments is called a **double dissociation**, and it is good evidence that the two processes are handled by independent brain systems. (However, see Chapter 3 for a qualification of this statement and Chapter 10 for a discussion of double dissociations.) A similar double dissociation has been found for lip-reading (Campbell et al, 1986). We will be covering the neuropsychological underpinnings of different aspects of face processing in greater detail in Chapters 7, 8 and 9, so we won't discuss these issues further here.

However, Ganel and Goshen-Gottstein have challenged the view that identity and gender are processed independently. As they point out, the neuropsychological evidence is less convincing for this assertion: only a single dissociation has been demonstrated (a patient who could no longer recognize faces but who could still tell whether they were male or female), and this might be explained by arguing that gender determination is simply easier than face recognition. Ganel and Goshen-Gottstein have also queried the validity of the behavioural data that have been used to support the parallel-routes hypothesis.

A familiar face that has been seen recently is responded to more quickly than one that has not been encountered for a while: this is an example of **repetition priming**. Bruce and Young originally suggested that repetition priming occurred because the first exposure to a face left the relevant FRU in a heightened state of readiness to respond to that face subsequently.[2] If gender and expression perception are handled separately from face recognition, they should have no effect

on FRUs, and hence should not produce repetition priming: having seen a face recently should make it easier to recognize it, but should not facilitate making decisions about its gender or expression. Support for this prediction came from A. W. Ellis et al (1990). Their first experiment had two phases. First, participants classified a set of famous faces by occupation (actor, sportsperson or politician). These faces were then shown again, mixed with famous faces that had not been seen earlier, plus wholly unfamiliar faces. One group of participants had to decide as quickly as possible whether or not each face in the second phase was familiar; another group decided whether each face was smiling or unsmiling; and a third group decided whether each face was male or female. Repetition priming occurred only for participants performing the familiarity task, and not for those who made decisions about expression or gender.

In a second experiment, participants saw famous and unfamiliar faces in phase one and decided whether they were smiling or unsmiling. This facilitated making familiarity decisions about the famous faces when they were shown again in phase two. However, having seen a face in phase one had no effect on making a decision about its expression when it was seen again in phase two. There was also no effect of familiarity on expression perception: participants not only showed no repetition priming for expression judgements, but they were also no quicker to make these decisions about famous faces than they were to make them about unfamiliar ones. A third experiment produced similar results for gender processing: making gender decisions about faces in phase one did not facilitate making gender decisions about them when they were seen again in phase two, but did facilitate recognizing them.

Ellis et al drew three main conclusions. The first was that repetition priming occurs

---

[2] As we shall see in the next section (1.2), it is now thought that repetition priming actually reflects strengthening of the links between a FRU and its associated PIN. However, this does not affect the current discussion, because both explanations require FRUs to be involved for repetition priming to take place.

automatically for familiar faces (i.e. it does not matter whether a face is processed for identity, expression or gender during the initial encounter, it will still act as a prime for itself). The second was that repetition priming occurs only within the system that processes identity: FRUs have to be involved for priming to take place, and priming therefore does not occur for judgements about gender or expression. The third conclusion was that familiarity with a face does not aid the processing of its expression or gender.

Goshen-Gottstein and Ganel (2000) have suggested that the results of Ellis et al's third experiment (showing an absence of priming for decisions about gender) are somehow an artefact of having included the hair in the photographs of men and women that were used as stimuli. They found that when the hair was deleted (so that participants were forced to attend to the face itself in order to determine its gender, rather than merely looking at the hair), repetition priming did occur—implying that gender and identity processing were linked.

In defence of the parallel-routes hypothesis, it could be argued that repetition priming occurs fairly late in the sequence of processing, and that gender and identity are processed independently in earlier stages. Ganel and Goshen-Gottstein (2002) therefore used a different technique: the **Garner interference paradigm**. This works as follows. Suppose you want to know whether two properties of an object are processed independently of each other. First you measure how quickly and accurately participants can make judgements about each of the two dimensions in question, when the other dimension is kept constant. Then you measure speed and accuracy for each dimension again, but this time allowing the other dimension to vary randomly. If speed and accuracy suffer, interference has occurred: the two dimensions are not processed independently of each other, and are said to be 'integral'. If there is no effect on speed and accuracy, the two dimensions are independent, or 'separable'.

Ganel and Goshen-Gottstein found that participants were slightly slower and less accurate

to make identity judgements (decide whether or not faces were famous) when the faces varied in gender than when they were all the same gender. Likewise, if the task was to decide the face's gender, performance was worse when the faces were a mix of famous and non-famous faces than when they were all famous or all non-famous. In Garner's terms, identity and gender are thus not wholly separable dimensions.

Baudouin and Tiberghien (2002) have also queried the independence of gender and identity. Their participants searched for a target face amongst successively presented distractors. The target face was actually an androgynous blend between a male and female face. When participants were encouraged to think the target face was male, by labelling it 'John', participants took longer to reject male distractors than they did to reject female ones; labelling the same face 'Mary' produced the opposite effect. Ease of identification of a face is thus affected by its perceived gender. Finally, in the course of a study that was concerned primarily with the effects of orientation on face processing, Stevenage and Osborne (2006) found that familiarity affected performance on a gender-discrimination task. If the faces consisted only of the internal features, when the faces were near-upright participants were quicker to judge their gender when the faces were familiar than when they were unfamiliar. (See also Stevenage et al [2005] for further data at odds with the idea that structural encoding and familiarity are independent stages.)

Ganel and Goshen-Gottstein suggest that, contrary to the Bruce and Young model, gender is handled within the FRUs, not separately from them. At present, the most reasonable interpretation of the data is that the idea of parallel processing routes may need to be qualified somewhat: identity, gender and emotion are handled fairly independently, but there does seem to be some degree of interaction between the processes involved. As Baudouin and Tiberghien (2002) point out, gender is in most cases a stable trait of an individual, so therefore it might make sense for gender to affect FRUs. In contrast, expressions are intrinsically variable and hence potentially less useful as a guide to identity, although, as Bruce and Young (1986) pointed out, information about characteristic expressions could aid recognition in some circumstances (for example, Harrison Ford's characteristic crooked half-smile). This speculation is supported by Kaufmann and Schweinberger (2004), who demonstrated that familiar faces are recognized faster if they show their characteristic expressions.

The idea of parallel routes certainly does not have to be discarded just yet. Balas, Cox and Conwell (2006) found that personal familiarity with faces led to participants being significantly quicker to make identity and gender decisions about them in a face-matching task, and to a small extent familiarity might have even facilitated decisions about whether they were upright or upside-down. However, Balas et al's suggestions for how familiarity might exert these effects would not require any substantial revision of the Bruce and Young model. One possibility is that processing strategies might be different for familiar and unfamiliar faces, so that participants attend to different parts of the face. With unfamiliar faces, participants might rely on facial properties that are generally reliable guides to the attribute in question (such as gender) but which are harder or more time-consuming to extract. Alternatively, familiarity might change a participant's criterion for making a decision: for example, if familiarity is determined rapidly, this information could be used to decide that less information has to be acquired from a familiar face before a decision is made about its gender.

1.2 **The Interactive Activation and Competition (IAC) model**

The most recent version of the Bruce and Young model is the **Interactive Activation and Competition (IAC)** model (e.g. Burton, 1998; Burton and Bruce, 1993; Burton et al, 1990, 1999a). This started out as an attempt to make a computer simulation of the Bruce and Young model, but has effectively superseded it. Computer simulations are useful in cognitive psychology because they require a model to be more precise; models that consist of boxes connected by arrows can sometimes conceal a fair amount of vagueness about how the processes involved actually operate in practice. The IAC model has built on the strengths of the original Bruce and Young model, but is more specific about how FRUs and PINs work.

1.2.1 **The structure of the IAC model**

Figure 1.2 shows the main features of the IAC model. The principal components are FRUs, PINs and SIUs, all connected together with two-way excitatory links. Units within a pool (e.g. within the pool of FRUs, or within the pool of PINs) compete with one another, in an inhibitory fashion. As in the original Bruce and Young model, there is one FRU and one PIN for each person known to us. When we see a familiar face, it activates the FRU for that person's face. This in turn activates the PIN for that person. PINs can also be activated by other means, such as by names (Name Input Units; NIUs) or voices (Voice Recognition Units). If a PIN exceeds a certain threshold level of activation, it signals familiarity. Semantic Information Units (SIUs) code information about known individuals, such as their occupation, nationality, likes and dislikes, etc. Many SIUs are shared between individuals. For example, there will be many people that activate the SIUs for 'British', 'actor' and 'appeared in Coronation Street'.

To illustrate how the model works, let's suppose we see a picture of Paul McCartney. This will activate the FRU for McCartney, which will then activate the PIN for him. At this stage, we would know we had seen a familiar face. The PIN could alternatively have been activated by a Voice Recognition Unit that had responded to hearing McCartney sing, or by a NIU that had been

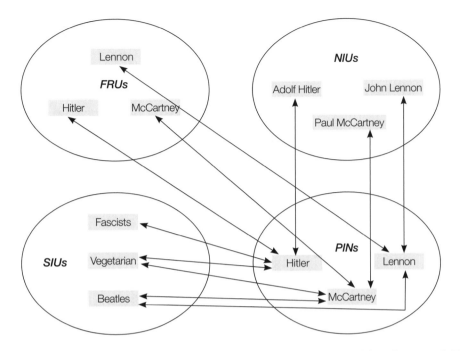

FIGURE 1.2 The Interactive Activation and Competition model of face recognition (adapted from Burton et al, 1990).

activated by hearing or reading McCartney's name. The activated PIN then stimulates the relevant SIUs: 'British', 'Liverpudlian', 'singer', 'one-time member of the Beatles', 'vegetarian', etc. Many of these SIUs are shared by John Lennon and the other two Beatles (e.g. 'Liverpudlian', 'ex-Beatle', 'fabulously rich'), and one or two are shared with Adolf Hitler (e.g. 'vegetarian' and 'lived in Germany for a while').

1.2.2 The IAC model and priming effects

The IAC model accounts for priming effects in face recognition quite nicely. It explains repetition priming as being due to a strengthening of the link between the FRU and PIN for a particular person (Fig. 1.3, (a)). Seeing McCartney's face activates both his FRU and his PIN. The links between them are strengthened so that less activation from the FRU is now required before the PIN reaches its threshold and signals familiarity.

Thus, a subsequent presentation of a picture of McCartney will activate his PIN more easily. This explanation fits well with observed features of repetition priming: it is long-lasting, and, although it is strongest when the same picture is seen twice, substantial priming still occurs with different views of the same face (Bruce and Valentine, 1985; A. W. Ellis et al, 1987).

The model also explains three other aspects of repetition priming. Firstly, priming is domain-specific: names do not prime faces, and faces do not prime names (Burton et al, 1998; A. W. Ellis et al, 1987, 1996). This makes sense, as presenting a name should have no effect on the strength of the FRU–PIN links that underlie repetition priming. Secondly, repetition priming occurs only with familiar faces and not with unfamiliar ones (A. W. Ellis et al, 1987, 1996). This would be expected, because unfamiliar faces have no FRUs and PINs to activate.

Thirdly, repetition priming occurs only if prime faces are recognized spontaneously. Brunas-Wagstaff et al (1992) asked participants to identify

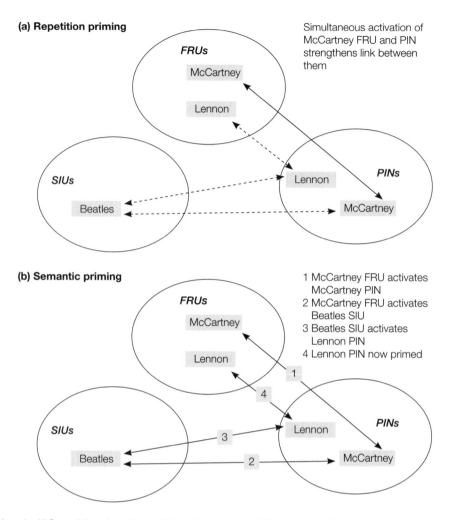

FIGURE 1.3 How the IAC model explains face priming effects: (a) repetition priming; (b) semantic priming.

each face in a set of celebrity faces. These were then shown again, mixed with unseen celebrity faces and wholly unfamiliar faces. The usual repetition priming effect was found (i.e. quicker responses to the celebrity faces that had been seen earlier), but this occurred *only* for faces that had been recognized spontaneously in the first phase: if a participant had required a prompt in order to identify a face (either the name, or semantic information about the person), that face did not prime its subsequent recognition. Steede and Hole (2006) used a

different method to demonstrate the importance of explicit recognition for repetition priming. They produced faces that consisted of the top half of one famous face and the bottom half of another, and asked participants to identify the top half. Such composites are very difficult to recognize explicitly (the **composite face effect**; see Chapter 2). Steede and Hole found that they also failed to act as primes for the complete versions of the celebrities' faces. However, sometimes participants did manage to recognize the top half of the composite; in these circumstances repetition priming occurred, at comparable levels to those obtained with isolated half-face primes. Again, the IAC can account for these findings: spontaneously recognized faces and half-faces will generate FRU activity, which in turn will lead to FRU–PIN link strengthening, whereas unrecognized faces will not. Composite faces either fail to activate their FRU altogether (because the composite is effectively treated as a new, unfamiliar face) or fail to activate it sufficiently for it to strengthen its link with its associated PIN.

The IAC model also does a good job of explaining **semantic priming** (also known as **associative priming**; see Fig. 1.3, (b)). Suppose you see McCartney's face, followed by John Lennon's. McCartney's face activates his FRU and PIN; the PIN activates the SIUs for McCartney. Many of these SIUs are shared by Lennon (e.g. 'British', 'Liverpudlian', 'Beatle'). These SIUs then send activation to Lennon's PIN. This PIN now needs less activation from Lennon's FRU before it fires off. The other Beatles also share many SIUs with McCartney, and so they would be primed too. However, McCartney would not prime Adolf Hitler because McCartney and Hitler have very few SIUs in common. Again, this explanation fits well with the known properties of semantic priming. Firstly, semantic priming can occur across stimulus domains (so that names prime faces, and vice versa). Secondly, semantic priming is short-lived. This is because PIN activation is eliminated by recognizing other people, due to the inhibitory competition between units within the PIN pool.

1.2.3 Evaluation of the IAC model

Given that it is an elaboration of the Bruce and Young (1986) model, the IAC model is of course consistent with the same body of empirical data from psychological and neuropsychological research. It additionally makes predictions about how faces, voices and semantic information should interact with one another, and these are consistent with what has been found from research on priming phenomena. What the IAC model fails to do is to provide much detail on the 'front end' of face perception: it begins by assuming that a face has already been successfully encoded and matched to some kind of internal representation in order to produce FRU activation. But how exactly is that achieved? The question of how faces are encoded and stored in memory is the subject of the next chapter.

1.3 The Multidimensional Face Space model

Valentine's (1991) **Multidimensional Face Space (MDFS)** model tries to explain how we represent faces in memory. Despite its rather intimidating name, the basic idea is quite simple: each face is stored in terms of its values on a wide range of different facial dimensions. An example may help to understand how this works. Suppose we encoded faces purely on the basis of nose length. Some individuals would have a nose that was much longer or shorter than average, but most people would have noses that were around the average. Each person would amount to a dot along a line from tiny nose to gigantic nose, with average nose length in the middle. This would be a one-dimensional face-space model. Now suppose we added a second dimension, for example eye separation. Again, this varies between the two extremes of beady-eyed and sheep-like, with most people having eye separations around an average value. We could now represent each individual in terms of both their eye separation and their nose length. Figure 1.4 shows such a 'two-dimensional' face-space. Add another dimension, such as 'mouth width' and we now have a

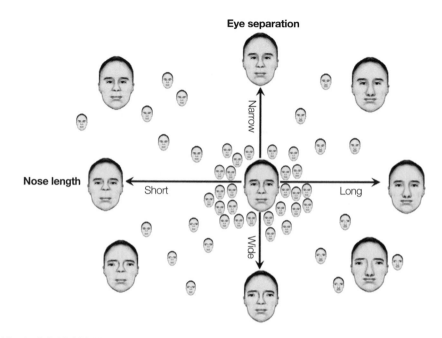

FIGURE 1.4 Valentine's (1991) Multidimensional Face Space (MDFS) model. Each face is represented as a point in MDFS in terms of its values on two dimensions: eye separation and nose length.

three-dimensional face space.[3] We could go on adding dimensions (e.g. 'eye size', 'chin curvature', 'nose width' and so on) to produce a multidimensional face space. It becomes impossible to visualize this, but the principle is the same: each face ends up as a unique point within this space.

1.3.1 **Exemplar versus norm-based versions of the MDFS model**

There are two different versions of Valentine's model. In the **norm-based** model, each face is encoded as a 'vector' that shows its direction and distance from an 'average', 'norm' or 'prototype' face. In other words, faces are represented in terms of how much they deviate from an average face. In

the **exemplar-based** model, each face is encoded as a single point in multidimensional space, without reference to any norm (Fig. 1.5).

It has been surprisingly difficult to decide which of these two versions of the model is correct because they tend to make the same predictions about human face recognition (Lewis and Johnston, 1999a). In addition, whenever any data are obtained that seem to support one of the models, advocates of the other model have always been able to account for those results too.

In both models, faces are unevenly distributed in face space. In the norm-based model, this is because most faces are fairly typical, and so they deviate little from the norm. Consequently, the region around the norm will be densely populated,

---

[3] For simplicity's sake, we have used the lengths of different features as our 'dimensions' here, but the MDFS model does not actually specify what the dimensions consist of, and they could be other, more complex aspects of faces. Valentine (1991) deliberately refrained from speculating on which dimensions were used, merely suggesting that they were whatever dimensions served to discriminate between faces. Chapter 2 discusses findings that are relevant to this issue.

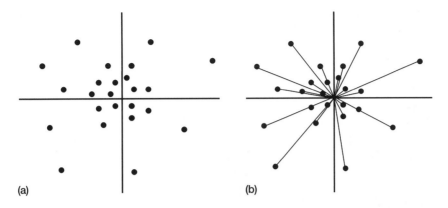

(a)   (b)

FIGURE 1.5 The two versions of Valentine's (1991) Multidimensional Face Space model. (a) In the exemplar-based version, each point represents a face. (b) In the norm-based version, each vector represents a face, encoded with respect to its deviation from a norm (average) face.

whereas the outer regions of face space will be sparsely populated with faces that are very different from average. The exemplar-based model predicts exactly the same arrangement, but for different reasons. Although there is no explicit norm, there is a location in face space that has the highest density of faces. This arises from the fact that most faces are fairly typical, and so they occur within the same area of face space; atypical (distinctive) faces are out on the edges of face space with few neighbours. In both models, ease of recognition is determined by the proximity of neighbouring faces in face space: two faces that have similar vectors (in the case of the norm-based model) or that are close together (as in the exemplar-based model) will be more easily confused than faces that are far apart in face space.

1.3.2 Phenomena explained by the MDFS model

Regardless of which version of the theory you subscribe to, the MDFS model provides plausible explanations for a number of phenomena in face recognition. For example, it has long been known that **distinctive** faces are recognized better than less distinctive faces (e.g. Bruce et al, 1994; Going and Read, 1974; Johnston and Ellis, 1995; Valentine and Bruce, 1986b; Valentine and Endo, 1992). Interestingly, they are also classified as 'faces' more

slowly in a face/non-face classification task, in which participants see faces and scrambled faces (Valentine and Bruce, 1986b). The explanation for distinctiveness effects is that, by virtue of being typical, undistinctive faces are all crowded together near the centre of face space, and so they are easily confused with one another. Because distinctive faces are unusual, they are relatively isolated in face space, which makes them less likely to be confused with other faces. This makes distinctive faces easier to recognize (because they have fewer neighbours to act as competitors), but also means that they are harder to classify as faces (because they are less similar to other faces).

The MDFS model can also account for **caricature effects** (see the extensive review in Rhodes, 1996). Professional caricaturists grossly distort the proportions of a face, yet the person depicted usually remains easily recognizable (Fig. 1.6). To investigate this in a more systematic way, researchers have used computer-based caricature programs. These distort a given face systematically with respect to an 'average', or 'norm', face. In a **positive caricature**, each difference between the particular face and the average is exaggerated by a certain amount. For example, suppose that, compared with the average face, a person's eyes were slightly closer together, their nose was slightly longer, and their mouth was slightly wider. In a 10% caricature, the eye separation would

(a)   (b)

FIGURE 1.6 This caricature of Prince Charles by the American cartoonist Sal Navarro is instantly recognizable, despite the fact that the facial proportions are actually quite different from those of Charles' real face. (Left: © Getty Images. Right: © Sal Navarro. The authors are very grateful to Sal Navarro for granting us permission to use his cartoon; see http://www.salnavarro.com for other celebrity caricatures by this artist.)

be decreased by 10%, the nose would be lengthened by 10% and the mouth would be widened by 10%. **Anti-caricatures** can also be produced, in which all of the differences between a face and the average are reduced by a certain proportion.

In the case of line drawings of faces, positive caricatures are recognized *better* than the original faces from which they are derived, and anti-caricatures are recognized worse (Benson and Perrett, 1994; Rhodes et al, 1987). This led to the idea that caricatures might act as 'super-portraits': it was originally suggested that positive caricatures were more effective input for the visual system than undistorted faces, because they emphasized whatever aspects of the face were being used for recognition. More recent research has not supported this idea, however. For photographic-quality caricatures, positive caricaturing has much smaller effects on the speed or accuracy of recognition, and these caricatures are also rated as poorer likenesses of the faces concerned than are undistorted versions (Benson and Perrett, 1991; Kaufman and Schweinberger, 2008). This is possibly because line drawings are fairly impoverished stimuli compared with photographs, so there is more scope for caricaturing to produce an effect with drawings.

There are competing norm-based and exemplar-based accounts for caricature effects. Rhodes (e.g. Rhodes et al, 1987; Rhodes and Tremewan, 1994) favoured a norm-based explanation for caricature effects. She suggested that a caricature exaggerates the differences between the original face and the norm face: essentially the caricature is encoded as a vector with the same direction as the original face (thus preserving the face's identity), but with a greater magnitude.

Lewis and Johnston (1998, 1999a,b) proposed a modified version of an exemplar-based MDFS. They suggested that instead of faces being represented as points in face space, they are represented as

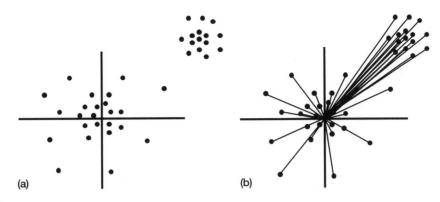

FIGURE 1.7 Valentine and Endo's (1992) two alternative MDFS explanations for the 'other-race effect'. (a) Exemplar-based explanation: other-race faces form a dense cluster of 'distinctive' faces in face space because they are encoded using inappropriate own-race dimensions. (b) Norm-based explanation: other-race face vectors are all in similar directions, because encoding is with respect to an inappropriate own-race norm. This makes it difficult to discriminate between them.

regions (called **Voronoi cells**). For each known individual, there is a region in face space, and if an input face matches any facial representation within this region it is accepted as being that person's face.[4] This allows for the fact that different views of an individual can all be perceived as being instances of that person (as long as they fall within certain limits of likeness to the person concerned). Typical faces have smaller Voronoi cells than distinctive faces. Lewis and Johnston suggest that caricature effects occur because each Voronoi cell is not symmetrically arranged around the best likeness of the face to which it belongs. As a consequence of the mathematics behind the construction of Voronoi cells, they end up being irregularly shaped. An image produced by caricaturing is actually closer to the centre of a Voronoi cell—and hence further away from competing representations of other faces— than is a faithful representation of that person's face.

Another phenomenon that has been explained in terms of Valentine's model is the **other-race effect**: the fact that we are better at recognizing faces of our own race than faces of other races. (We shall discuss this at greater length in Chapter 12.) Valentine (1991) suggested that each person has their own personal multidimensional face space,

within which are represented all of the faces that they know. This face space is developed in the course of their lifetime of experience with faces. Most of these faces will be from their own race, and so the dimensions by which faces are encoded will be ones that are optimal for distinguishing between own-race faces. These dimensions are not necessarily the best ones for discriminating between faces from another race.

Valentine and Endo (1992) proposed two alternative accounts for the other-race effect (Fig. 1.7). In terms of a norm-based MDFS model, one possibility is that other-race faces might be encoded in terms of an inappropriate norm, one that is suitable only for one's own race. As a result, other-race faces all give rise to vectors in a similar direction, which are difficult to distinguish between. In an exemplar-based model, encoding other-race faces on dimensions appropriate to own-race faces results in the other-race faces ending up as a cluster of 'highly distinctive' faces in face space. This cluster is located well away from the cluster of typical own-race faces, and so the other-race faces are seen as 'distinctive'. However, because other-race faces are tightly clustered together, it is difficult to discriminate between them.

---

[4] Tanaka et al (1998) have proposed a similar model, based on what they term 'attractor fields'.

On the basis of a series of experiments on the other-race effect, Valentine and Endo (1992) concluded that a norm-based model could be used to explain it, but they favoured an exemplar-based interpretation for a number of reasons. These included parsimony of explanation: at the time, they felt there were no data on face-processing that required the existence of a norm to be invoked. (As we shall see shortly, more recent research suggests otherwise.) A second reason was that exemplar-based models had been used in other areas of research on concept representation. Valentine and Endo also felt that the exemplar-based model avoided the tricky problem of how an other-race norm could develop from extensive experience with other-race faces. At what point would an individual switch from inappropriately encoding other-race faces with respect to an own-face norm, to encoding them with respect to an appropriate other-race norm? And what would happen to existing representations of familiar other-race faces when this encoding switch occurred? Valentine and Endo suggested that an exemplar-based model could sidestep this problem: as people became more expert at recognizing other-race faces, they could use selective attention to focus more on the dimensions that were appropriate to recognizing other-race faces.

1.3.3 **Face adaptation effects and the MDFS model**

Most recently, strong support for norm-based MDFS models has come from experiments on **face identity adaptation effects**.[5] Leopold et al (2001) produced artificial faces that were at opposite points in multidimensional space (Fig. 1.8). Thus, if 'Adam' had a nose that was larger than average, his **anti-face** ('anti-Adam') had a nose that was smaller than average by a corresponding amount, and so on for all facial dimensions. At test, participants were presented with a set of faces that consisted of blends ('morphs'), to varying degrees, between each target face and the average face of the distribution. These are anti-caricatures: a morph that consists mainly of the average face (in Leopold et al's terms, one that has a low 'identity strength') should be harder to recognize than one that consists mainly of the target face (i.e. one that has a high 'identity strength').

Thresholds for correct identification of target faces (i.e. the amount of identity strength required) were measured under two conditions: after adaptation to an anti-face, and in the absence of adaptation. Five seconds' exposure to an anti-face increased participants' sensitivity to the corresponding target face. In other words, after adaptation, morphs that were objectively closer to the average were now seen as looking *less* like the average face and *more* like the appropriate target face. Similar exposure to the average face or to an unrelated anti-face did not produce these effects (i.e. exposure to 'anti-Mark' did not affect sensitivity to morphs between 'Adam' and the average face). Furthermore, the appearance of the average face was also systematically affected: exposure to an anti-face made the average face look more like that anti-face's target face, and vice versa. These findings seem to be explained best by a norm-based model of face space; so far, at least to our knowledge, no-one has attempted to account for them in terms of an exemplar-based model.

1.4 **Conclusion**

Our understanding of human face recognition has deepened greatly over the past three decades, since research on face recognition really began in earnest. There has been a huge amount of research on the topic in that period,

---

[5] Research on face adaptation effects is also covered in Chapter 9.

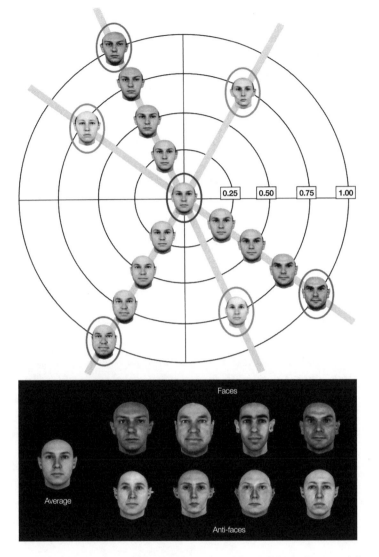

FIGURE 1.8 Examples of the computer-generated faces used by Leopold et al (2001). Along each line are shown a set of 'morphs' (blends) of varying degrees between a target face and the central average face, plus an 'anti-face', which has complementary facial properties to its corresponding target face. (Reprinted by permission from Macmillan Publishers Ltd: Leopold, D. A., O'Toole, A. J., Vetter, T. & Blanz, V. (2001). Prototype-referenced shape encoding revealed by high-level after effects. *Nature Neuroscience*, 4(1), 89–94. © 2001)

from a wide variety of disciplines. Theories of how different stages of face processing relate to one another, such as Bruce and Young's (1986) model, and Burton et al's IAC model, and theories about how faces are represented in memory, notably Valentine's (1991) Multidimensional Face Space model, have been very important in this. Like all good theories, they have had two functions: they have helped

to organize and make sense of the empirical data that have been collected, and they have generated further research by making testable predictions about how face processing should operate. However, none of them tackles the really big question: precisely what information is extracted from faces in order to recognize them? Both the Bruce and Young model and the IAC model assume that this has already been accomplished somehow. Valentine's model talks about faces having been encoded on various 'dimensions', but does not deal with the issue of exactly what these dimensions consist of. In the next chapter, we shall discuss this issue at great length. We'll examine what's known about how people recognize faces, and end with a discussion of some theories of how faces might be encoded, that could serve as the 'front end' of the models discussed in this chapter.

SUMMARY

- The Bruce and Young (1986) model, and its more recent incarnation, the Interactive Activation and Competition (IAC) model, postulate that face recognition involves a number of stages, from initial familiarity through to naming a face.

- The principal components of the IAC model are Face Recognition Units (FRUs) (activated by familiar faces), Person Identity Nodes (PINs) (activated by faces, voices or names) and Semantic Input Units (SIUs) (containing semantic information about the person).

- The IAC model explains both repetition priming (enhanced responding to a face following a previous encounter with it) and semantic priming (enhanced responding to a face following exposure to a related face).

- Valentine's Multidimensional Face Space (MDFS) model attempts to explain how faces are encoded in memory. It has been used to explain numerous phenomena, such as enhanced recognition for distinctive or caricatured faces, and the 'other-race effect'.

- There are competing versions of the MDFS model. 'Norm-based' versions suggest that faces are encoded in terms of their deviations from an average, 'norm', face. 'Exemplar-based' versions suggest that faces are merely encoded as points in MDFS, without there being any explicit norm.

- Deciding between the two versions of the MDFS model has been extremely difficult because they make similar predictions about face processing, but data on face adaptation effects seem to be explained best in terms of a norm-based model.

FURTHER READING

Bruce, V. (1988). *Recognizing Faces.* Hove: Erlbaum. This book is now over 20 years old, and a huge amount of research on face processing has been conducted since. However, it is a superb exposition of Bruce's ideas, and the early research that supported them. A classic work that is still essential reading for anyone seriously interested in face processing.

Valentine, T. (ed.) (1995). *Cognitive and Computational Aspects of Face Recognition.* London: Routledge. A collection of chapters written by experts in this area that is possibly a little dated now, but still worth looking at.

Wenger, J. and Townsend, J.T. (2001). *Computational, Geometric, and Process Perspectives on Facial Cognition: Contexts and Challenges.* Hove: Erlbaum. A collection of sometimes quite 'technical' papers dealing with mathematical and computational models of face processing.

2

THE NATURE OF FACIAL REPRESENTATIONS

What information is extracted from a face in order to recognize it? This issue has been the subject of a huge amount of research in the past 30 years or so, but remains unresolved. We now know that faces are not perceived as collections of isolated parts, but as **configurations**—the whole is definitely more than the sum of its parts. This chapter is devoted to reviewing psychological research on how we recognize faces; later chapters will deal with other aspects of face processing included in Bruce and Young's (1986) model, such as expression analysis and the processing of age and gender.

2.1 **Computational and psychological approaches to face recognition**

There are two complementary strategies for tackling the question of how we recognize faces. One is to take a **computational approach** (Bruce, 1988; Marr, 1982). In order to recognize a face, we could ask: what exactly does the visual system need to compute, and why? We could look at the problems that this task poses for the visual system, try to work out what would be a good way to tackle them, and then check whether these methods work reliably in practice. Computer scientists have come up with many different techniques for finding faces in a scene, or for matching one view of a face to other views of the same person. (For an excellent review of face recognition from the perspective of computer science, see Zhao et al [2003]). However, it's important to bear in mind

that finding an effective method and determining whether humans actually use it are conceptually quite distinct issues. As Marr pointed out, the same computational task (in this case, face recognition) could be achieved by various different methods, or **algorithms**. Even if some of these methods work reliably, this doesn't mean that they are necessarily the ones used by humans (see Hancock et al, 2000).

We can also look for what Marr called **constraints**, limitations on what can happen in the visual input. Due to alterations in viewpoint and illumination, an almost infinite number of images could belong to a single object in the visual field. Figure 2.1 illustrates this in the context of faces.

One of Marr's great insights was to notice that the natural world places lots of constraints on what can happen in an image, and these make object identification a more tractable problem than it would be otherwise. For example, because natural lighting tends to come from above, the

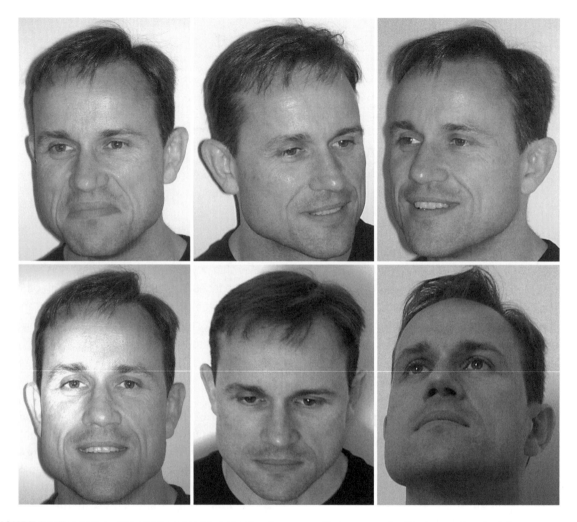

FIGURE 2.1 The complexities of face recognition. Familiar face recognition copes well with changes to orientation, expression and illumination conditions.

visual system can make certain assumptions about the shape of objects, based on shading information. The task of image segmentation (knowing which parts belong to the same object, and which belong to other objects) is facilitated by the fact that parts of a given object tend to be more similar in colour, brightness, texture, and so on to one another than to parts of adjacent objects. These problems affect face recognition as well, of course.

The second approach is one that has been used extensively by psychologists. One way to find out how something works is to see how it copes (or doesn't cope) with various manipulations of the input to the processes concerned. As we shall see, some manipulations disrupt recognition severely (such as turning a face upside-down or turning it into a photographic negative) and others affect it very little (such as vertically stretching a face so that it is three times as high as it is wide). Examining the visual system's response to such manipulations might give us some useful clues about what facial information is being used in order to identify a face.

2.2 Constraints on face processing

Face perception can be aided by high-level knowledge that a face is being looked at, as opposed to some other kind of object. Faces all share the same basic configuration of features (two eyes above a nose, which in turn is above a mouth), their so-called **first-order relational** properties. Individual faces differ from one another in terms of their particular arrangement of features, or **second-order relational** properties (Diamond and Carey, 1986). To some extent, knowing that you are looking at a face might simplify the problem of coping with perspective transformations (Troje and Bülthoff, 1998). For example, if you see a face in three-quarters view, the part that is farthest away from you may well be hidden by the nearer parts, but knowing that faces are reasonably symmetrical could enable you to calculate eye separation from a wide variety of viewpoints. We can also assume that the hidden eye is fairly similar in shape to the one that we can see.

Some facial features are fixed, others are mobile. Eye separation is a good candidate for a facial **primitive** (a basic building block for face processing) because it is fixed and changes little (at least, not during adulthood). Perhaps it is no accident that the contrast between the pupil and the white of the eye is so marked, even in people with dark skin. As Carbon and Leder (2005) point out, this make eyes ideal for indicating that a face is present, and showing how it is currently aligned horizontally. Nose length is fixed, but prone to changes in apparent length due to perspective changes. (If I tilt my head back or forwards, my nose looks shorter to someone facing me than if I look straight at them.) Mouths are worst of all because of their mobility and elasticity. As we shall see, the relative importance of different facial features for recognition is consistent with this line of reasoning.

2.2.1 The effects of photographic negation

Another constraint seems to be that, as with the environment in general, the visual system assumes a face is lit from above. This seems to be the main reason why faces in photographic negative (i.e. where the dark parts are light, and vice versa) are so hard to recognize, as in Fig. 2.2, (a) (Galper, 1970). The main consequence of turning a face into a negative (a process referred to as 'negation' or 'contrast reversal' in the literature) is probably to disrupt the processes that calculate **shape from shading** information (Hill and Bruce, 1996; Johnston et al, 1992).[1] Evidence for this is that normal faces that are lit from below (such as when you hold a torch under your chin) are harder to recognize than top-lit faces, and negative faces that are lit from below are somewhat *easier* to recognize than top-lit negative faces (Johnston et al, 1992). The effects of negation show that faces are processed not just as two-dimensional (2D) patterns, but as three-dimensional (3D) shapes, notwithstanding the fact that we can recognize faces as easily from photographs as we can in real life.

(a) (b)

FIGURE 2.2 Faces are hard to recognize (a) in photographic negative and (b) as line drawings. (WireImage/Getty Images)

---

[1] Negation also disrupts pigmentation information, for example making dark hair look light, and this may be another factor in why face recognition is so difficult with these kinds of stimulus. Evidence on the role of pigmentation in face

Further evidence consistent with the idea that the visual system uses 3D shape information comes from studies demonstrating that we are not very good at recognizing faces from line drawings, unless the drawings contain some shading information (Bruce et al, 1992; Davies et al, 1978; Rhodes et al, 1987) (Fig. 2.2, (b)). As Burton et al (1999a) and Dakin and Watt (2009) have pointed out, the difficulties posed by negative, bottom-lit and line-drawn faces tell us that the basis for face recognition is unlikely to consist of simple measurements between edges in the face, as these would be unaffected by such manipulations.

Overall, the existence of constraints on facial appearance means that the problems involved in recognizing faces become merely very difficult, rather than insoluble! Many computerized face recognition systems achieve recognition with the aid of knowledge that they are dealing with a face, and humans may do the same.

2.3 Effects of image manipulations on human face recognition

Early studies on face recognition tended to envisage faces as collections of isolated features, and tried to see whether some features were more important for recognition than others. This was done by selectively obscuring different parts of the face, and measuring how much this affected recognition accuracy. Most studies agreed on a **feature salience hierarchy** in which the most important region was the upper part of the face,

especially the eye region, then the nose and, least of all, the mouth (e.g. Chung and Thomson, 1995; Goldstein and Mackenberg, 1966; Haig, 1985, 1986; Shepherd et al, 1981). This hierarchy is reflected in studies of visual fixation patterns while faces are being inspected (e.g. Barton et al, 2006). Bindemann et al (2009) recorded eye movements in response to faces displayed at various orientations in depth, from profile through to frontal views. In common with visual stimuli in general, initial fixations were towards the geometric centre of the stimulus. However, this generally coincided with the eye region, which also remained the prime target for fixations during the time the face was displayed.

We are certainly able to recognize faces on the basis of information from individual features: incomplete or scrambled faces can be recognized at well above chance levels (e.g. Collishaw and Hole, 2000). However, research during the past two decades has focused more on how the visual system uses the face's overall configuration as a guide to identity. There are numerous demonstrations that we are sensitive to the spatial interrelationship between the facial features, as long as the face is upright.

2.3.1 The Face Inversion Effect

Yin (1969, 1970) is credited with being the first researcher to draw attention to the fact that faces are much harder to recognize when they are turned upside-down. You might think this is pretty obvious, but the important point is that face recognition seems to be *disproportionately* affected by inversion, compared to recognizing other types of objects. Yin looked at the size of the inversion effect for faces, houses and pictures of stick men in motion. The

recognition is mixed. Kemp et al (1996) manipulated pigmentation and negation independently in colour photographs of faces, and found that only negation significantly impaired recognition. Faces that were reversed in colour but not brightness remained recognizable, implying that negation exerted its effects primarily by disrupting shape-from-shading information. However, Russell et al (2006), and Russell and Sinha (2007) have demonstrated that surface texture, skin pigmentation and skin reflectance may be more important in face recognition than was originally thought.

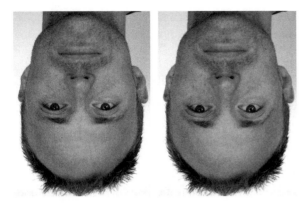

FIGURE 2.3 Inversion makes it hard to detect spatial distortions.

difference between performance with upright and inverted stimuli was much greater for faces than for these other stimulus types, a finding that has been used as support for the argument that faces are 'special' as far as the visual system is concerned (see Chapter 10 for a detailed discusssion of this issue).

Subsequent research has shown that inversion appears to interfere with our sensitivity to the fine-grain spatial interrelationships between facial features: in other words, it affects configural processing while leaving featural processing relatively unimpaired (e.g. Bartlett and Searcy, 1993; Freire et al, 2000; Leder and Bruce, 2000; Rhodes, 1988; Rhodes et al, 1993). Look at the two upside-down photographs in Fig. 2.3. They appear to be quite similar, but when you turn them the right way up, you can see that in fact they are quite different.

Barton and colleagues (2001) presented participants with three photographic-quality images at a time, and asked them to decide which was the odd one out. On each trial, the manipulated face had been subjected to either a configural change (to eye separation or mouth position) or a featural change (an alteration to the brightness of the eyes or lips). Barton et al also varied the exposure duration for which the faces were displayed, and showed the images upright or upside-down. The effects of inversion were non-existent for eye brightness; quite small for eye separation; and much larger for mouth position, especially at brief exposure durations. Inversion also affected perception of mouth colour to some extent. Barton et al suggest that this is due to the eye region naturally being more salient in a face, because, if participants knew that the only changes were going to be to the mouth, the inversion effect for mouths was eliminated. The results are consistent with the idea that inversion results in faces being processed by a piecemeal, feature-by-feature strategy that starts with the eye region.

The effects of inversion are not all-or-nothing. Numerous studies have looked at the effects of face rotation at orientations other than 180 degrees and found that performance seems to get progressively worse (slower and/or less accurate) as one moves away from the upright (e.g. Valentine and Bruce, 1988). Orientation changes seem to affect configural processing more than featural processing (Collishaw and Hole, 2002; Schwaninger and Mast, 1999). At first sight, the fact that recognition gets progressively worse as orientation changes might be taken as evidence that upright and inverted face processing differ only quantitatively (i.e. in degree) rather than qualitatively (i.e. in the sense of involving different types of processing).[2] However, this isn't necessarily the case. Perhaps rotated faces need to be subjected to a process of **normalization** that rotates them back to upright before they can be matched to standardized (upright) internal representations on the basis of their configural properties: as the degree of rotation increases, this

---

[2] A number of researchers (e.g. Riesenhuber et al, 2004; Sekuler et al, 2004; Yovel and Kanwisher, 2004) have argued that there are no qualitative differences between upright and inverted face processing. We concur with Rossion's (2008) view that the great majority of evidence supports the idea that upright and inverted faces *are* processed in qualitatively different ways, and that the few studies to the contrary are methodologically flawed in various ways.

process takes longer and becomes less precise (Rock, 1988).

2.3.2 The Thatcher Illusion

Look at the upside-down photographs in Fig. 2.4. Casual viewing suggests they are fairly similar. If you look closely, you might notice that one of them is slightly different to the other. Now turn the book upside-down, so that the faces are the right way up. You should now immediately notice that one of the faces is normal, and the other one is rather grotesque. This is an instance of the **Thatcher Illusion**, devised by Peter Thompson (Bartlett and Searcy, 1993; Boutsen and Humphreys, 2003; Lewis, 2001; Murray et al, 2000; Sturzel and Spillmann, 2000; Thompson, 1980).

The grotesque image looks that way because the eyes and the mouth have been inverted with respect to the rest of the face. You notice this discrepancy straight away when the face is upright, but not when it is upside-down (Carbon and Leder, 2005), because inversion has reduced your sensitivity to the spatial interrelationship between the features and the rest of the face. As with the Face Inversion Effect, the Thatcher Illusion appears to be progressively affected by rotation of the stimulus away from upright, rather than being an 'all-or-none' phenomenon (Edmonds and Lewis, 2007).

2.3.3 The Composite Face Effect

Yet another powerful demonstration of our sensitivity to the configural properties of upright faces comes from the **Composite Face Effect (CFE)**, first demonstrated by Young et al (1987). If the top half of one face is joined to the bottom half of a different face, it gives rise to an impression of a new, whole face; it is very difficult perceptually to isolate either half and identify it. However, if the face is turned upside-down, it becomes much easier to see it as two separate halves. The CFE also disappears if the two halves are upright but misaligned. Figure 2.5 shows the CFE with faces in frontal view, but it also persists if the faces are rotated in depth (i.e. from profile through to frontal views; McKone, 2008).

What this tells us is that if faces are upright and the parts are reasonably aligned with one another into a normal facial configuration, then a form of configural processing is automatically evoked which binds all of the face parts together into a whole, or 'gestalt'. Young et al (1987) initially demonstrated the CFE with famous faces, but it

FIGURE 2.4 A demonstration of the Thatcher Illusion. These two photographs look similar when they are upside-down, but very different when they are the right way up! (WireImage/ Getty Images)

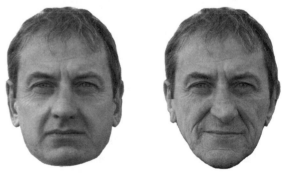

FIGURE 2.5 A demonstration of the Composite Face Effect. These two faces share the same top half, but have different bottom halves. When shown upright, configural processing makes it difficult to see that the tops are identical; inversion makes this task much easier.

is also found with wholly unfamiliar faces, using a matching paradigm in which participants have to decide whether or not two top halves come from the same face while ignoring their differing bottom halves (Hole, 1994). This suggests that the effect is primarily a perceptual (encoding) phenomenon, rather than involving face memory. Not only are the halves of composite faces difficult to recognize consciously, but they also fail to act as **repetition primes** for the faces from which they were taken (Steede and Hole, 2006), suggesting that the visual system treats composite faces as 'new' faces at a very fundamental level. The new configuration appears to change the appearance of the constituent features themselves.

2.3.4 **Whole-over-part advantages**

Tanaka and Farah (1993) showed that facial features are recognized better if they are seen within a facial configuration than if they are presented by themselves. In one condition, Tanaka and Farah asked their participants to learn a series of pairings between facial features and names; for example, the participants learnt that a particular nose belonged to 'Larry'. At test, participants were shown pairs of features and had to decide which one they had seen before. For example, they saw two noses, Larry's and a previously unseen distractor, and had to decide which of the two was Larry's. A second condition was identical to this, except that the noses were embedded within a face. Thus, participants learnt that a given face was 'Larry', and then at test had to decide which of two faces was Larry. The clever twist is that in this condition the test faces were always identical except for the target feature (e.g. the nose). In effect, this condition was much the same as the first: it still involved participants remembering individual features, except now they were embedded in a facial context (a background pattern that was constant for both targets and distractors). A third condition was identical to the second, except that the faces were scrambled.

Participants remembered the target stimuli better if they were whole faces than if they consisted of isolated features or scrambled faces, even though, in all cases, all that differed between targets and distractors were individual features. In other words, recognition of 'Larry's nose', for example, was aided by being shown within the context of a face. On the strength of these results, Tanaka and Farah argued that face recognition involved **holistic** processing that caused faces to be encoded as indissoluble wholes rather than as a collection of separate features.

In an extension of this paradigm, Tanaka and Sengco (1997) examined the effects of modifying the face's configuration between learning and test (Fig. 2.6). As before, features were recognized better if they were presented within a facial configuration than if they were presented in isolation. However, features that were learnt within an 'eyes far apart' configuration were recognized less well if the configuration at test was an 'eyes close together' version of the same face, or vice versa. Tanaka and Sengco claim that this is further evidence that faces are processed holistically: because individual features are not processed independently of one another, changes to the facial configuration affect the appearance of the constituent parts. These effects disappeared if the test stimuli were displayed upside-down to preclude configural processing. Similar results were not found for the recognition of houses and their parts (windows and doors), implying that the whole-to-part advantage may be specific to faces.

2.3.5 **Configurations and prototype effects**

Further evidence for the existence of configural processing comes from a set of experiments by Bruce et al (1991). Participants first rated a set of 50 unfamiliar faces for apparent age and masculinity/femininity. These faces were computer generated, and consisted of five variants around each of ten unseen **prototype** faces. All of the faces within each set of five had exactly the

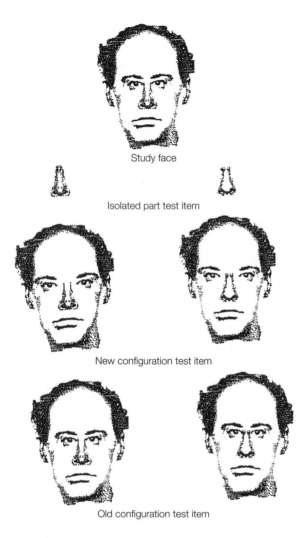

Study face

Isolated part test item

New configuration test item

Old configuration test item

FIGURE 2.6 Example of stimuli from Tanaka and Sengco's (1997) study. A nose learnt in a study face (top) is recognized better when it is presented in the original facial configuration than in a new configuration, which in turn is better than trying to recognize the nose in isolation.

same features, but in slightly different positions. After the rating procedure was completed, participants were given a surprise memory test; on each trial, they were shown two faces and asked to pick the one that they had seen previously. The 'new' face in each case was a novel configuration of the same features as in the other faces.

Two principal findings emerged. Firstly, participants were extremely good at identifying the particular configurations they had seen earlier. This is another demonstration that face recognition can be based solely on configural information. The second finding, shown by other experiments in the same paper, was that if participants were shown the prototypical configurations (from which the variants in each set were derived) they falsely believed they had seen them before. Somehow the participants had extracted the prototypical configuration from all of the variants on it that they had seen. Accuracy was reduced by inverting the faces, consistent with the idea that configural processing was involved in these effects as opposed to generalized pattern-matching abilities.

Cabeza and Kato (2000) investigated the false recognition of prototypes using prototypes that were either averages of the configurations of their donor faces, or constructed by combining different features from them (i.e. the eyes from one face, nose from another, and so on). Both types of prototype were falsely recognized as faces that had been seen before, suggesting that face processing involves features as well as their configuration. Presenting the stimuli upside-down reduced the number of false recognitions for configural prototypes, but not for featural prototypes. This is another demonstration of the selective effects of inversion on configural processing.

2.4 The relationship between featural and configural face processing: the 'dual-route' hypothesis

All of the above techniques show that we are much more sensitive to the configural information in a face when it is upright than when it is upside-down.

Upright faces appear to be processed all of a piece, in a holistic fashion, whereas inverted faces are processed in a more time-consuming 'piecemeal', feature-by-feature manner. Many researchers have suggested that featural and configural processing represent two different routes to face recognition (e.g. Bartlett and Searcy, 1993; Cabeza and Kato, 2000; Collishaw and Hole, 2000; McKone, 2004; Moscovitch et al, 1997; Rhodes et al, 1993; Searcy and Bartlett, 1996; Sergent, 1984).

Collishaw and Hole (2000) looked at the relationship between configural and featural processing by examining the effects of applying various manipulations to faces (inversion, blurring and scrambling) either separately or in various combinations (Fig. 2.7). They reasoned that, if configural and featural processing were the principal ways in which faces could be recognized, recognition should still be possible after any one of these manipulations had been applied; each of them affects only one route to recognition, leaving the other route available. Scrambling and inversion both make it hard to extract configural information from faces, but leave featural information relatively unaffected. Conversely, blurring degrades featural information, but leaves the configural information largely intact (at least, at the moderate levels of blur used by Collishaw and Hole).

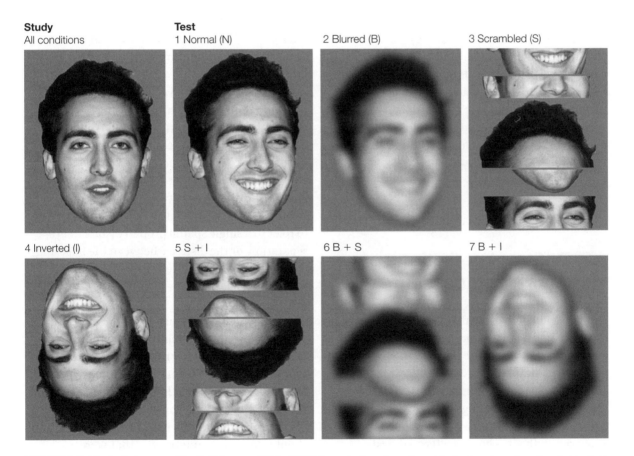

FIGURE 2.7 Manipulations used by Collishaw and Hole (2000) for selective disruption of featural and configural routes to face recognition. (Reproduced with permission from: Collishaw, S. M. & Hole, G. J. (2000). Featural and configurational processes in the recognition of faces of different familiarity. *Perception*, 29, 893–909. © Pion Limited, London)

The results showed that participants were quite good at recognizing faces that had been blurred, *or* scrambled, *or* inverted. They were also about as good at recognizing faces that had been scrambled *and* inverted as they were at recognizing faces that had been subjected to just one of these two manipulations. This is presumably because scrambling and inversion both disrupt the same process (i.e. configural processing). However, combining scrambling or inversion with blurring led to chance performance: the scrambling or inversion disrupted featural processing, and the blurring disrupted configural processing, leaving participants with little information to use as a basis for recognition.

As we shall see, the idea that there are two complementary routes to recognizing faces (configural and featural processing) is a useful way of thinking about face recognition. For example, it helps to explain some of the inconsistencies in research investigating which cerebral hemisphere is most important for face recognition, if one envisages the left and right hemispheres as being responsible primarily for featural and configural processing respectively (see Chapters 7 and 9).

2.5 Different definitions of 'configural' processing

This is a good point at which to mention that there is some degree of ambiguity and confusion associated with use of the term 'configural' processing. Maurer et al (2002) suggest there are three types of configural processing. One version involves detecting the basic configuration common to all faces, of two eyes, above a nose, above a mouth. This has been termed **first-order relational** processing. A second type of configural processing is Tanaka and Farah's (1993) **holistic** processing. They claimed that the visual

system processes faces as indissoluble wholes, rather than as collections of individual features. The data from their studies on whole-over-part effects, described above, certainly support the idea that facial features are normally processed in a highly interdependent way, rather than as separate parts.

The third type of 'configural' processing refers to a form of processing that makes use of the fine-grain spatial interrelationships between facial features. While all faces share the same basic 'first-order relational properties', they differ subtly in the precise spatial interrelationships between these features; individual faces vary in terms of their **second-order relational** properties (Fig. 2.8). When most researchers talk about 'configural' processing, they probably have in mind a form of processing that uses this second-order information in order to identify individual faces.

The relationship between 'holistic' and (second-order) 'configural' processing is not very clear, although as Bartlett et al (2003) point out, 'holistic' processing has connotations of involving the entire face whereas 'configural' processing could, in principle, refer to more local spatial relationships, such as between adjacent features. In principle, 'configural' processing could be used to refer to a single spatial property (such as eye separation, or the distance between the nose and the mouth), but most often it refers to multiple spatial interrelationships within a face rather than just one.

Our own hunch is that some form of 'holistic' processing is automatically evoked in response to any stimulus that fits the basic specification of a face. Perhaps this form of processing serves to tell the visual stimulus that a face is present, and thus aids subsequent 'top-down' processing of the face by allowing the use of those assumptions about bilateral symmetry, etc. that were described earlier. 'Holistic' processing probably underlies the Composite Face Effect, as this is not confined to recognition: it affects perception

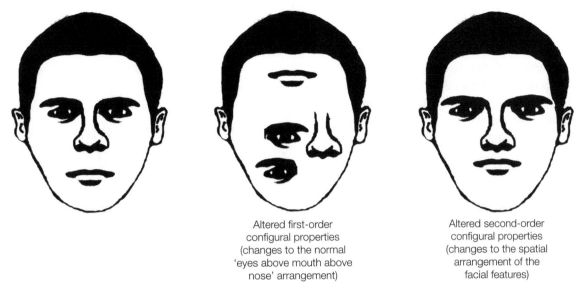

Altered first-order
configural properties
(changes to the normal
'eyes above mouth above
nose' arrangement)

Altered second-order
configural properties
(changes to the spatial
arrangement of the
facial features)

FIGURE 2.8 First- and second-order configural properties of faces.

of emotional expression, gender and age as well. The Face Inversion Effect and Thatcher Illusion probably affect second-order configural processing, as they make it hard to extract the fine details of the spatial interrelationships within a face.

2.6 The properties of configural processing

What precisely does second-order configural information consist of? Numerous studies have shown that we are quite good at detecting small differences to the spatial arrangement of features within an upright face. Haig (1984) performed the first systematic study of this. He produced 39 slightly altered versions of each of 5 faces. On each trial, participants saw one of these faces on a computer screen and had to decide whether it was an original version, or whether it had been modified in some way. Participants were best at detecting

changes in the vertical position of the mouth, followed by the vertical position of the nose, and lastly the vertical position of the eyes. Participants were comparatively insensitive to changes in mouth thickness or head aspect ratio (the width of the head relative to its height). For horizontal eye separation, Haig noted that participants were slightly more sensitive to inwards shifts (detecting a 6% difference on 50% of trials) than outwards shifts (detecting an 8% difference on 50% of trials). Haig must have been on very good terms with his participants: each one completed a total of 39,000 trials spread over 40 sessions!

More recent studies have confirmed that people are quite good at detecting changes to eye separation (Barton et al, 2001; Brédart and Devue, 2006; Brooks and Kemp, 2007; Ge et al, 2003; Kemp et al, 1990). Studies such as these (in particular, Haig's early work) are often cited as demonstrations of our extreme sensitivity to the configural properties of faces. However, this has probably been overstated. In all of these studies, participants were able reliably to detect a difference in eye separation of about 5% of the original interpupillary distance. A well-established finding is that the **just noticeable difference (JND)** for *any* spatial interval judgement (e.g. comparing the length of two lines, or comparing the separation between two dots) is about 5% of the separation being judged. This implies that, although we are pretty good at performing the task of judging eye separation, we do not have any particularly enhanced ability for judging facial spatial properties as opposed to other spatial relations in our environment.

Furthermore, although we are quite good at detecting *differences* in facial configurations, this is not to say that we *perceive* this information accurately, as shown by Schwaninger et al (2003). They asked people to adjust a line on the computer screen to match either the horizontal eye separation of a face, or the vertical separation between its eyes and mouth. In their first experiment, the eye–mouth distance was overestimated by 39% and the interpupillary distance by 11%. In a second experiment, these values were 41% and 16% respectively. There was no effect of inversion on either of these estimates. In contrast, estimates were quite accurate if participants had to adjust the line to match the length of another line.

Thompson (2002) gave participants a piece of paper with two lines drawn on it, and asked them to place a tick on one line to show the length of their own nose and a tick on the other line to show their own interpupillary distance. Participants underestimated their true nose length by 12% and overestimated their interpupillary distance by 32%. The underestimation of nose length in Thompson's study could be explained by perspective-induced foreshortening, but the reasons for the overestimation of eye separation in both studies are not clear.

It is also worth pointing out that, just because we *can* detect small changes to facial configurations, this does not mean this information is actually *used* by the processes that underlie face recognition; as we shall see in the next section, the visual system is actually surprisingly tolerant of major alterations to the configural properties of a face.

2.7 Effects of distortion and caricature on face recognition

Paradoxically, although we are sensitive to the configural properties of faces, we can also recognize faces quite easily despite major perturbations to their configuration, as shown by the studies on **caricature effects** mentioned in Chapter 1. The important point for the present discussion is that caricaturing, even to quite extreme levels (30% in Kaufmann and Schweinberger's 2008 study with photographic-quality stimuli), *does not impair face recognition*. Consequently configural processing must be more sophisticated than is implied by experiments on sensitivity to feature displacements within faces.

Further evidence that configural processing consists of more than merely encoding simple measurements, such as eye separation and nose length, comes from a series of experiments by Hole et al (2002) in which participants saw faces that had been subjected to one of a number of different affine transformations, such as vertical stretching, horizontal stretching or shearing (Fig. 2.9).

All of these manipulations grossly alter the spatial properties of a face. For example, suppose you stretch a face vertically so that it is twice as long as it was originally (while leaving the width unchanged). All of the horizontal dimensions (such as eye separation) are now half of what they were originally, in relation to vertical dimensions such as nose length. Nevertheless, face recognition is essentially unaffected by these distortions: stretched, squashed or sheared faces remain as recognizable as their undistorted counterparts. The only affine transformation that disrupts face recognition is inversion, and yet this merely alters

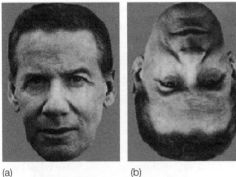
(a)

(b)

(c)

(d)

(e)

(f)

(g)

FIGURE 2.9 Manipulations used by Hole et al (2002) to show that, with the exception of inversion (b), affine transformations do not affect face recognition, as long as they are applied across the whole face. (c) Shearing; (d, e) horizontal stretching by 150% and 200% respectively; (f, g) vertical stretching by 150% and 200% respectively. (Reproduced with permission from: Hole, G. J., George, P. A., Eaves, K. & Rasek, A. (2002). Effects of geometric distortions on face-recognition performance. *Perception*, 31(10), 1221–1240. © Pion Limited, London)

the orientation of the picture with respect to the viewer, leaving it otherwise unchanged. Note that there is an important difference between these manipulations and caricaturing: the distortions produced by caricaturing systematically exaggerate whatever aspects differentiate that face from others. Affine transformations do not do this—they merely distort the face. It is all the more remarkable that the face recognition system is not affected by this.

How does the visual system recover the configural information despite these transformations? There are at least three possibilities. The first is that the visual system might try to match the distorted faces against **deformable templates** of stored faces. Faces could be stored in such a way that they could be stretched and warped to match the input, subject to the constraint that normal topological relations are preserved (i.e. the left eye has to stay on the left of the nose, the right eye has to stay on the right of the nose, and all of these features have to stay above the mouth). It's as if each known face is represented in memory on a rubber sheet that can be distorted to match the visual input. If, once distorted, it matches the input well enough, then the visual system decides that it has recognized the face. Biederman and his associates have investigated a computer implementation of one such **elastic graph matching** system (Lades et al, 1993; Wiscott et al, 1997), and report that it simulates many of the attributes of human face recognition (e.g. Biederman and Kalocsai, 1997; Biederman et al, 1999; Fiser et al, 1996; see also Hancock et al, 1998). However, the problem with this method is that it would work only for familiar faces, because unfamiliar faces would have no templates in long-term memory to be deformed.

The second method, **normalization**, would work with both familiar and unfamiliar faces. The visual system might 'undo' the effects of the transformation, for example unstretching a vertically stretched face back to normal proportions before trying to recognize it. Essentially, the input could be 'cleaned up' before any attempt is made to match it to memories of faces that are stored in a relatively standardized format. This method would work well with both familiar and unfamiliar faces, as long as the visual system had a good enough knowledge of what constitute normal facial proportions.

A third possibility is that no compensations need to be made for facial distortions, because whatever configural information is extracted from faces is unaffected by the transformations. For example, if a face is stretched to twice its normal height, the ratio of horizontal to vertical proportions is disrupted (e.g. eye separation relative to nose length is now wrong) but all horizontal proportions remain constant relative to one another (e.g. if eye separation was twice the width of the mouth, it remains so in the new image).

At present it is unclear which of these three explanations is correct, but unpublished research in our own laboratory suggests that unfamiliar stretched faces can still be recognized easily, which makes an explanation in terms of deformable templates rather unlikely.

2.8 The role of spatial frequencies in face processing

One obvious distinction between features and their configuration is their scale: the structure of features is more fine-detailed than the spatial interrelationships between them. This difference can be expressed in terms of the **spatial frequency** content of a face.[3] Images

---

[3] Spatial frequency refers to how often the intensity changes from bright to dark across the image. Thus, a sinusoidal grating that changed very rapidly from bright to dark and back again over a given distance (say across 10 cm) would have a higher spatial frequency than one that changed only once or twice over the same distance. Spatial frequency is affected by viewing distance: the nearer something is to your eye, the bigger the image it casts on the retina, irrespective of its

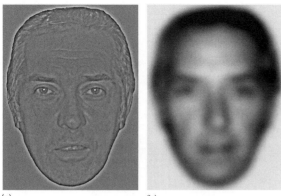

(a)   (b)

FIGURE 2.10 Examples of (a) high-pass and (b) low-pass spatial frequency filtered faces.

can be selectively filtered to retain certain spatial frequencies but not others (Fig. 2.10). For example a **low-pass** filtered image contains only low spatial frequencies; a **high-pass** filtered image contains only high spatial frequencies; and a **band-pass** filtered image contains only frequencies within a certain range, with higher and lower frequencies being removed.

Beginning with Sergent (1986), a number of researchers have suggested that different spatial frequencies might provide useful information for different face-processing tasks. For example, high spatial frequencies provide more information about facial detail and features, so the visual system might use them for tasks such as featural processing and age estimation. Low spatial frequencies convey more information about

the overall shape of the face and the global arrangement of its features; they might be useful for finding faces quickly in a scene, and in order to achieve configural processing for individual identification and the perception of expression (see Ruiz-Soler and Beltran [2006] for a review of research on spatial frequencies in relation to face processing).

Early studies sought to establish whether there was an optimal range of spatial frequencies (SFs) for face recognition, and found that it was most efficient when the face contained spatial-frequency information within a range centred around 8–17 cycles per face width (e.g. Costen et al, 1994, 1996; Fiorentini et al, 1983; Parker and Costen, 1999). More recently, there have been several demonstrations that high SFs are more important for featural processing and low SFs are more important for configural processing of faces (e.g. Goffault and Rossion, 2006; Goffaux et al, 2005). However, the use of SFs by the visual system seems to be heavily task-dependent and much more flexible than was hitherto believed (see review in Morrison and Schyns, 2001).

Oliva and Schyns' **flexible usage hypothesis** (Oliva and Schyns, 1997; Schyns and Oliva, 1999) suggests that different SFs can be used, depending on the nature of the task. Schyns and Oliva (1999) presented participants with hybrid faces very briefly (for 50 milliseconds). These contained the high SFs from one face and the low SFs from another. For example, Fig. 2.11 shows the high SFs from a happy male face and the low SFs from an

actual size. (Think of your thumb and the sun: if you put your thumb near your eye, you can blot out the sun, because although the sun is very much larger than your thumb it is also very much farther away from your eye.) Therefore it is more convenient to express spatial frequency in terms of its rate of change on the retina itself. When we look ahead, we have a field-of-view of about 180 degrees. Thus, a luminance change from bright to dark that occurred once in every degree would have a spatial frequency of 'one cycle per degree of visual angle'. Having said that, in the context of face processing, spatial frequency is often expressed in terms of rate of change per width of face. So, if there were a luminance change that occurred twice across the width of a face, this would have a spatial frequency of two cycles per face width; one that occurred four times would have a spatial frequency of four cycles per face width; and so on. See Chapter 5, section 5.2 for more detail on spatial frequencies, in the context of comparing infant and adult visual performance.

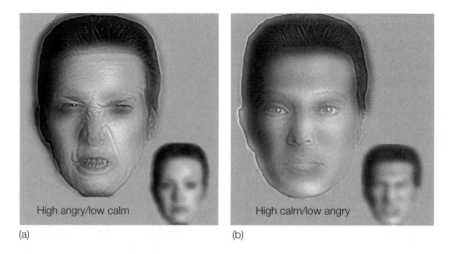

High angry/low calm

High calm/low angry

(a)   (b)

FIGURE 2.11 Two hybrid faces. (a) Face comprises high spatial frequencies (SFs) from an angry male and low SFs from a calm female (as shown in inset). (b) Face consists of high SFs from the calm female and low SFs of the angry male (again, with the low SFs shown in the inset). Close up, you are more sensitive to the high SFs and the faces appear male/angry and female/calm respectively; squint to defocus the image and remove the high SFs, and the faces swap gender and mood. (Reproduced with kind permission of Philippe Schyns, University of Glasgow. © Philippe Schyns)

angry female face. Perception of the face depended on the task: when asked whether or not the face was expressive, participants tended to perceive the high-SF face, whereas when asked to categorize the face as happy, angry or neutral, they tended to perceive the low-SF face.

As Morrison and Schyns (2001) point out, if their flexible usage hypothesis is correct, the claim that recognition is based on SFs of between 8 and 17 cycles per face-width may hold true only under the specific circumstances of trying to recognize a small set of recently learned faces. More research needs to be done, using a variety of face-related tasks, in order to determine more precisely how the visual system uses the information at different SFs.

The orientation of SFs in faces may be an important feature. Dakin and Watt (2009) looked at the effects of filtering faces selectively to remove horizontal or vertical SFs. Figure 2.12 shows the results for two famous faces. Notice that removal of the horizontal SFs makes the faces unrecognizable, whereas removal of the vertical frequencies has much less effect. Dakin and Watt concluded that the

important information for recognition is conveyed primarily in the horizontal structure of faces. Comparison of filtered images of various objects suggested that faces have an unusual structure that can be thought of as a characteristic sequence of light and dark regions as one moves down the face—or, as Dakin and Watt put it, all faces have a characteristic **bar-code** structure, much like the ones found on groceries. Under normal lighting conditions, faces have a distinctive vertical pattern of light and dark regions: foreheads and cheeks are light; eyebrows, eyes and the region under the nose are darker.

Thinking of faces as bar-codes has a number of advantages. Firstly, it provides a way to detect faces quickly and effectively in the environment. Secondly, the large-scale pattern of stripes could be used as a guide to the location of finer-scale stripes. For example, the large-scale pattern shows where the eyes must be. Within this stripe there are finer-scale stripes corresponding to the structure of the eye, although there is much more variability at this level of analysis than at the coarse scale that specifies a 'face' is present.

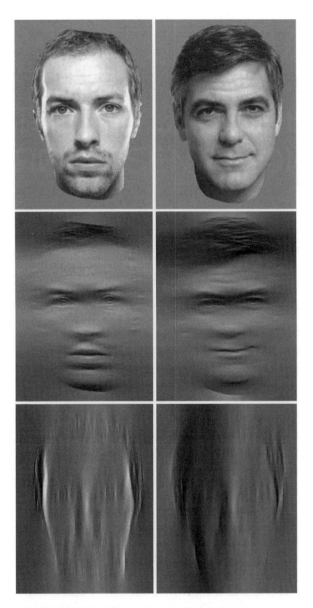

FIGURE 2.12 The differing effects of filtering to remove vertical (middle row) or horizontal (bottom row) spatial frequencies. The crucial information for face recognition seems to be carried in the horizontal spatial frequencies (after Dakin and Watt, 2009).

The bar-code model also neatly explains why inversion and negation impair face recognition: both manipulations produce bar-codes that do not match the specification for a normal face

(Fig. 2.13). An inverted face has the light and dark strips in the wrong order, whereas a negated face has light strips where dark strips should be, and vice versa. Conversely, like human face recognition, bar-codes are not affected much by distortions such as stretching and squashing, minor pose changes or the addition of 'noise' or illumination changes to the image (as long as the illumination comes from above).

2.9 Differences between the processing of familiar and unfamiliar faces

There is considerable evidence to suggest that there are important differences between familiar and unfamiliar face recognition. Consequently, when discussing the results of experiments (particularly those on the structural encoding of faces), we need to be clear about which type of face we have in mind. Unfortunately the term 'familiar' has been used quite loosely to refer to different degrees of familiarity. When some researchers describe faces as being 'familiar', all they mean is that their participants have been exposed briefly to those faces in the course of the experiment. Sometimes researchers use famous faces as 'familiar' faces. Fairly rarely, the faces of personally familiar people (friends and family) are used.

These different types of 'familiar' face are not equivalent. A face that has been encountered only during the experiment itself has no semantic information associated with it (unless the experimenter has asked the participant to learn a name, or some semantic information such as an occupation, for the face). The participant's knowledge of the face's structure is probably based on a very limited number of views of it (in many studies, only a single view). Finally, in most cases, the face has been seen only in static poses. The term

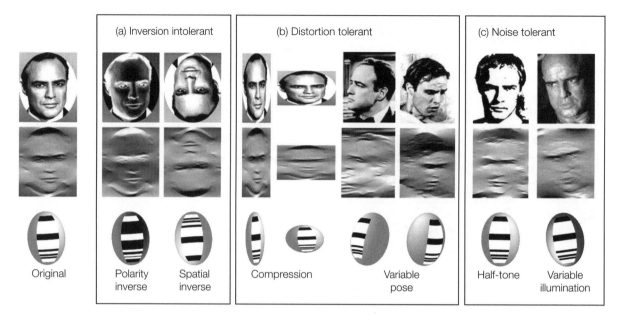

FIGURE 2.13 How Dakin and Watt's (2009) 'bar codes' are affected by manipulations that have been used to study human face recognition. Note that inversion and negation impair recognition and also produce different bar codes to that produced by the original face.

'familiar' is really quite inappropriate for these kinds of stimuli, especially when the same pictures are used throughout the study (recall Bruce's [1982] criticisms of this procedure that were discussed in Chapter 1). It would be more precise to say that these are not 'familiar' faces, but faces with which the participants have been briefly familiarized. The representations underlying recognition of these kinds of faces are likely to be quite different to those for faces with which we are highly familiar.

A personally familiar face has been encountered many times, and for prolonged periods. It has been seen in many different viewpoints and lighting conditions; it has displayed varying emotional expressions; and it has been seen in motion, in colour, in 3D, and at various distances. Semantic information is associated with it. A famous face has some, but not all, of these attributes: millions of people can recognize the face of the actor Keanu Reeves because they have seen it in films and magazines,[4] but relatively few people have actually met him (and even fewer have had repeated interactions with him). Consequently, for most of us, our knowledge of Keanu is based on 2D images of him from magazines, films and television. For some celebrities, such as Che Guevara and Marilyn Monroe, our 'familiarity' with the face may really amount to little more than familiarity with specific 'iconic' images of them. Carbon (2008) made minor changes to faces (such as removing or adding facial hair) and showed that this impaired the recognition of celebrity faces but not faces with which the participants were personally familiar.

---

[4] Millions, but not everyone! Once, in an experiment, we told a participant that she was going to see some famous faces, including Keanu Reeves and Brad Pitt. She looked very puzzled, and eventually asked us why we were going to show her pictures of 'coral reefs' when the study was supposed to be on face recognition. It turned out that she had never heard of Keanu Reeves—or Brad Pitt, for that matter.

How do the representations of familiar and unfamiliar faces differ? One thing is very clear: recognition of familiar faces is much more reliable than recognition of faces that have been encountered only briefly. Familiar face recognition is more tolerant of changes to the input than unfamiliar face recognition. As mentioned above, familiar face recognition is relatively unaffected by changes in pose or expression between presentation and test, whereas both the speed and accuracy of unfamiliar face recognition suffer (Bruce, 1982). As we shall see in Chapters 11, 12 and 13, unfamiliar recognition is highly error-prone, even when the task is merely to try to match two high-quality images of the same person (e.g. Bruce et al 1999, 2001; Henderson et al, 2001; Kemp et al, 1997; Megreya and Burton, 2006a,b, 2007, 2008; see Hancock et al [2000] for an excellent review of the differences between familiar and unfamiliar face processing). For example, in one experiment by Megreya and Burton (2008), participants saw two images of faces, both in frontal views and only slightly different from each other (by virtue of having been taken on different cameras). The task was simply to decide whether or not they showed the same person. Participants were correct on only about 85% of trials. They were little better when asked to match a photograph to a live face that was physically present in front of them. In contrast, familiar face recognition is much more tolerant of changes to the input: for example, we are able to recognize familiar faces well, even if they are shown in poor-quality images such as those produced by many CCTV cameras (e.g. Burton et al 1999b; Liu et al 2003).

There is evidence from both neuropsychology and psychology to suggest that familiar and unfamiliar face recognition are handled by different processes. In patients with **prosopagnosia** (a specific inability to recognize faces; see Chapter 10), a **double dissociation** has been reported, with some patients remaining able to recognize familiar but not unfamiliar faces, and others showing the complementary deficit (e.g. Malone et al, 1982;

Takahashi et al, 1995; Young et al, 1993; see also Chapter 7). In a study of individual differences in normal face recognition abilities, Megreya and Burton (2006b) found that there was no significant correlation between how well participants could match familiar faces and how well they could match unfamiliar faces. However, performance on matching unfamiliar faces was highly correlated with performance on matching upside-down faces (regardless of whether the latter were familiar or unfamiliar). Megreya and Burton suggest that both the matching of upright unfamiliar faces and the matching of upside-down faces are handled primarily by generic (i.e. not face-specific) pattern-matching processes, which are qualitatively different from the processes underlying upright familiar face-matching.

In contrast to our rather poor performance with unfamiliar faces, Tong and Nakayama (1999) suggested that highly familiar faces are highly overlearned, and have **robust representations** in the brain. These are highly flexible representations that are capable of generalizing across different views, lighting conditions and facial expressions. Although just a few exposures to a face can facilitate its processing and make it 'familiar' to some extent, truly robust representations are developed only after many thousands of encounters with a face, under different conditions. Tong and Nakayama examined how familiarity affected people's ability on a visual search task. On each trial, participants searched amongst a set of faces for a highly familiar face (their own) or a stranger's face. Participants found their own face consistently faster than the stranger's face, even when the face sets were presented upside-down or in unfamiliar orientations (such as profile views). As Tong and Nakayama point out, their procedure involved hundreds of exposures to the stranger's face, and yet the advantages in processing speed for the participant's own face persisted; even though the stranger's face had become 'familiar' to some extent during the course of the study, it was still being processed differently to a truly familiar face.

Not only are familiar faces detected more quickly than unfamiliar faces, they are also processed differently once they are found. A number of studies have suggested that familiar face recognition is based more on the inner part of the face (the eyes, nose and mouth region), whereas unfamiliar face recognition relies more on the external features (the hair and face outline). H. Ellis et al (1979) examined how well familiar and unfamiliar faces could be recognized when they were presented as whole faces, faces that consisted only of the internal features, or faces that consisted only of the external features (Fig. 2.14). Overall, familiar faces were recognized better than unfamiliar faces. However, familiar faces were recognized better by their internal features than their external features, whereas unfamiliar faces were recognized equally well in either version. Ellis et al's explanation for these differences was that attention to the internal features during social interactions with familiar people might lead to a better memory for that part of their face.

Similar conclusions were drawn by Young et al (1985c), using a matching task. Participants viewed pairs of faces simultaneously and decided as quickly as possible whether they were images of the same person or different people. Within each pair, one image was a complete face and the other consisted of only the internal features or only the external features. In one experiment the images on 'same' trials came from different photographs of the same person (to preclude simple picture matching). These differed either in terms of pose or expression. Under these conditions, images of familiar faces were matched faster on the basis of their internal features than were images of unfamiliar faces. Familiarity had no effect on how quickly images could be matched on the basis of their external features. Using a similar matching technique, Clutterbuck and Johnston (2002, 2005) confirmed and extended Young et al's results. Their 2005 study showed that a weaker version of the **internal feature advantage** for famous faces could be produced after just ten 2-second exposures to a previously novel face.

Some studies suggest that familiarity enhances sensitivity to the location of the internal features of familiar faces. O'Donnell and Bruce (2001) familiarized their participants with a set of faces and then compared their face-matching performance for these faces to their performance with a set of wholly unfamiliar faces. Horizontal eye displacements were detected better in the familiarized faces than in the unfamiliar faces. No effects of familiarity were found for vertical shifts of the mouth, or for changes in hairstyle, position of hairline, or changes to the chin. O'Donnell and Bruce concluded that familiarization selectively improves processing of the eye region.

Brooks and Kemp (2007) measured the effects of familiarity on people's ability to detect small vertical displacements of the eyes, nose, mouth or ears. Each test face was personally familiar to half of the participants and unfamiliar to the others. On each trial, three photographs of a face were shown. The top one was always unmanipulated, and the task was to decide which of the lower two images did not match the top image. The top image differed in orientation from the lower two, so that this was a test of face matching, not picture

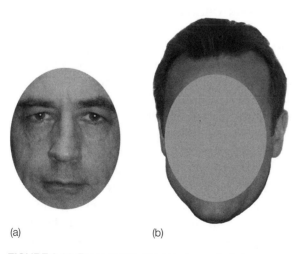

(a)   (b)

FIGURE 2.14 Faces manipulated to show only their (a) internal or (b) external features.

matching (Fig. 2.15). By varying the size and type of feature displacement, Brooks and Kemp were able to work out each participant's threshold for detecting displacements (i.e. the minimum size of displacement that they could reliably detect).

Participants were better at detecting shifts in the vertical position of the eyes or changes to nose length in familiar faces than in unfamiliar ones. Thresholds for eye and nose position were just under 5% of horizontal eye separation. Although, in absolute terms, participants were most sensitive to mouth displacements, no familiarity effects were found with mouths. Neither were they observed for ear position, but this was because participants were unable to perform the task at better than chance levels. On the basis of their findings, Brooks and Kemp suggest that the 'internal features advantage' for familiar faces is limited to the eyes and nose. They suggest that the differential effects of familiarisation on perception of facial features probably arise from differences in their potential value for identification: the eyes and nose are fixed, whereas the mouth is more variable and ears are easily hidden by head movements and hair.

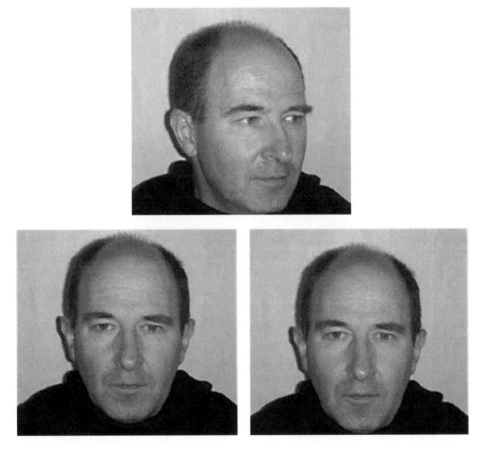

FIGURE 2.15 Example of the stimuli used by Brooks and Kemp (2007). One of the two lower faces is unmanipulated, like the top face; the other has had its eyes shifted upwards by a small amount. (Reproduced with permission from: Brooks, K. R. & Kemp, R. I. (2007). Sensitivity to feature displacement in familiar and unfamiliar faces: beyond the internal/external feature distinction. *Perception*, 36, 1646–1659. © Pion Limited, London)

2.10 **Effects of viewpoint changes on face recognition**

In the normal course of events, we seldom see exactly the same view of a face each time we encounter it. Numerous studies have suggested that viewpoint changes affect face recognition to some extent.

One reason why this might be so is that viewpoint affects the amount of information that is available to the viewer. In principle, a three-quarters view should be recognized most easily, because it provides the most information about a face's 3D structure. Behavioural studies on how well faces can be recognized from different viewpoints have generally found that faces are recognized best in three-quarters views, quite well

in frontal views and most poorly in profile views (e.g. Bruce et al, 1987; Hill and Bruce, 1996; Liu and Chaudhuri, 2002; McKone, 2008; Newell et al, 1999).

Viewpoint effects might occur because information about face parts is harder to extract from some views of the face than others. Stephan and Caine (2007) trained participants to recognize eight previously unfamiliar faces in a three-quarters view, and then tested how well they could recognize these faces in frontal and profile orientations. They also manipulated the information that was available for making these decisions: faces were either intact, or had parts deleted (the eyes, nose or mouth, in various permutations). 'Intact' faces in this experiment consisted of the internal features only (Fig. 2.16).

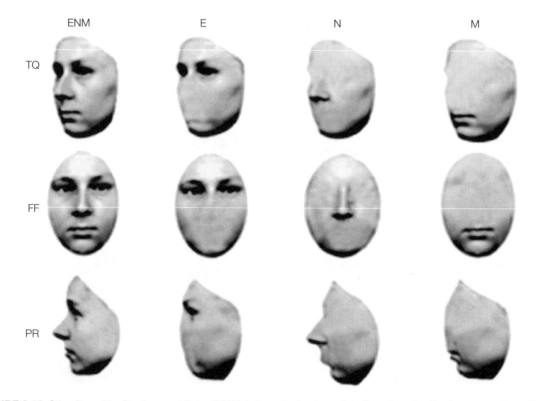

FIGURE 2.16 Stimuli used by Stephan and Caine (2007) to investigate viewpoint effects in unfamiliar face recognition. TQ, three-quarter view; FF, full frontal; PR, profile; ENM, intact faces; E, eyes only; N, nose only; M, mouth only. (Reproduced with permission from: Stephan, B. C. M. & Caine, D. (2007). What is in a view? The role of featural information in the recognition of unfamiliar faces across viewpoint transformation. *Perception*, 36, 189–198, © Pion Limited, London)

At all viewpoints, performance was best with whole faces and at chance for nose-only or mouth-only faces. For part faces, Stephan and Caine found the usual feature salience hierarchy, with eye deletion having the biggest effect on performance. However, 'eyes plus nose' or 'eyes plus mouth' was nearly as good as an intact face, and better than eyes alone, leading Stephan and Caine to suggest that if the eyes and one other feature are available configural processing remains possible. For whole faces, participants showed excellent generalization between three-quarters and frontal views: they were as fast and as accurate to recognize the learnt faces when these were presented in novel frontal views as when they were presented in the original three-quarters views in which they were learnt. In contrast, if the faces were presented in profile view at test, accuracy was significantly reduced. Stephan and Caine suggest this might be because there is more information overlap between three-quarters and frontal views than between either of these and profile views. In particular, more information about the eyes is lost in a profile view (eye separation, eye colour and brow details are all unavailable in profile views).

McKone (2008) performed a series of experiments showing that configural processing for unfamiliar faces was similar for all viewpoints, from frontal through to profile (the Composite Face Effect, for example, was as strong with profiles as it was with frontal views). In contrast, parts-based processing seemed to be poorer for profile faces. McKone suggests that this might be due to the relative lack of exposure to profile views in everyday life, plus the occlusion of facial features that occurs when a face is seen side-on. Because configural processing integrates information from wider regions of the face, it may be able to cope better with viewpoint changes.

Thus, viewpoint effects may occur partly because they affect the information that is *available* from a face. However, they may also occur because of the way in which faces are *represented* in memory. If we can recognize a face easily despite viewpoint changes, it implies that our internal representations might contain information about each face's 3D structure—so that we can generalize from previously seen views to views that we have never encountered before. On the other hand, if viewpoint changes have a marked effect on recognition, this suggests that our internal representations are strongly tied to the original views that we have of faces. In short, knowing about viewpoint independence (or the lack of it) might enable us to determine whether representations of faces are **object-centred** (based on 3D 'models' of faces, independent of the observer's viewpoint) or **viewer-centred** (highly dependent on the observer's particular viewpoint).

Precisely to what extent face recognition is viewpoint-independent has been a source of controversy. As Jiang et al (2009) point out, many of the contradictory findings in this area may simply be due to researchers failing to take into account facial familiarity. There are several lines of evidence to suggest that viewpoint dependence is affected by familiarity.

Firstly, there are data from neurophysiological studies, in which recordings of electrical activity are made from single neurones in monkey cortex, using **microelectrodes**. A variety of cell types have been discovered in the rhesus macaque that respond to faces in some way, and some of these respond preferentially to particular individuals' faces. Of these cell types, some seem to be sensitive to faces in a view-invariant way, whereas others respond only to a specific view or a limited range of views (e.g. Desimone et al, 1984; De Souza et al, 2005; Hasselmo et al, 1989; Perrett et al, 1985, 1991, 1998b).

Secondly, studies of **face adaptation effects** suggest that humans possess both view-independent and view-invariant neurones. After prolonged viewing of an unfamiliar face in one orientation, a frontal or near-frontal view appears to be oriented in the opposite direction (Fang and He, 2005). One explanation for these results is that the face in the original orientation strongly stimulates cells that are selective for that particular orientation, but has no effect on cells that are selective for other orientations. When adaptation stops, the highly stimulated cells are temporarily fatigued and hence fire very little; however, the unstimulated cells continue to fire at their resting rate of discharge. The profile of activity over all of the orientation-sensitive neurones is thus temporarily distorted, and resembles one that would be produced by a face oriented in the opposite direction to the adapting face. Fang and He's data are thus consistent with the idea that at least some cells in the human visual system are viewpoint-selective as far as faces are concerned.

Other studies suggest that adaptation effects persist across viewpoints. Jiang et al (2006) used Leopold et al's (2001) **identity adaptation** technique (see Chapter 1) with adapting faces that were either in the same orientation as the test faces, or in a different orientation. Adaptation effects were obtained in both cases, although slightly attenuated when the adapting and test faces differed in orientation. Jiang et al (2007) replicated and extended these findings. They systematically manipulated the degree of familiarity of the computer-generated faces. In their 'extreme familiarity' condition, participants received 32 5-second exposures to multiple views of the faces concerned. This increased the size of the identity after-effect, and also increased the extent to which adaptation effects generalized across changes in 3D viewpoint.

Even studies that demonstrate clear effects of viewpoint changes between adaptation and test still find a significant degree of transfer between viewpoints. For example, Benton et al (2006) looked at the effects of adaptation using computer-generated faces to which the participants were familiarized during the study. The amount of adaptation decreased substantially as the angle between the adapting and test views increased; when the images were separated by 90 degrees, the adaptation effect was about half of that obtained with identical viewpoints. However, this was still a substantial and significant amount of adaptation; Benton et al's interpretation is that identity encoding is largely viewpoint-dependent, but that there is evidence for viewpoint-invariant mechanisms too.

To date, only one adaptation study, by Carbon et al (2007), has used truly familiar (celebrity) faces, and this found viewpoint independence: adaptation effects were just as strong with different views as when the same view was used at presentation and test.

Thus, overall, the data from a variety of sources imply that both viewpoint-independent and viewpoint-dependent representations of faces exist. This conclusion is also consistent with the results of a functional magnetic resonance imaging (fMRI) adaptation study by Andrews and Ewbank (2004), which looked at how different brain regions responded to being presented with the same images repeatedly. Andrews and Ewbank suggested that viewpoint-invariant and viewpoint-dependent processes have separate anatomical locations. They propose that cells in the fusiform gyrus are involved in processing identity; they are insensitive to changes in image size, but are affected by viewpoint changes. Cells in the superior temporal lobe are involved in detecting changeable aspects of faces that are important for social communication (e.g. expressions and lip patterns); these cells showed an increased response when the same face was shown from different viewpoints and with different expressions.

Representations for familiar faces seem to be more viewpoint-independent than those for unfamiliar faces. One goal for future research is to find out how familiarity produces this change. Recent studies have produced some interesting findings in this respect. Chen and Liu (2009) measured how well participants could match two views of an unfamiliar face, following different types of prior exposure to it. Participants were better at face matching if they had previously seen the face in a variety of different views than if they had seen it in the same view repeatedly. This suggests that seeing a face in different views enhances the ability to generalize to new views of it. If participants saw a face in different poses, they were also better able to cope if changes were made to its expression. However, seeing a face in multiple expressions facilitated recognizing it in a different expression, but did *not* facilitate recognizing it in a different pose. Liu et al (2009) showed that a similar asymmetry occurs in the relationship between changes in pose or illumination. Exposure to different poses helped participants to cope better with illumination changes as well as pose changes. However, seeing a face in a single pose under varying illumination conditions did not help participants to cope with pose changes. Thus, variation in a face *per se* does not produce viewpoint invariance; it looks as though variation in pose is the important factor.

Finally, we mentioned above that knowledge about whether or not face recognition is viewpoint-independent might tell us something about how faces are represented in memory. Can we conclude that familiar face recognition is based on object-centred representations, given that it is relatively viewpoint-invariant? Unfortunately, not! One possibility is that the representations for familiar and unfamiliar faces are not as different as they might at first sight appear: what *looks* like view independence could be achieved if representations for familiar faces were comprised of multiple view-dependent representations (Booth and Rolls, 1998). A relatively small number of **canonical** views (e.g. three-quarters, full-face and profile) would suffice. Perhaps this is how familiarization produces its effects: it simply adds to the number of different viewpoints that are stored for a given face. Ultimately, viewpoint invariance could be achieved in two quite different ways: by matching the input face to a stored 3D 'model' of that person's head, or by matching the input to one of a limited number of view-specific representations of that person's face. Both explanations can account for the same

data at present. However, by postulating that familiar and unfamiliar face processing differ only quantitatively (in terms of the number of view-specific representations available) rather than qualitatively, the 'multiple views' explanation has the advantage of being able to account easily for how unfamiliar faces become familiar ones.

2.11 **Face processing and Principal Components Analysis**

Principal Components Analysis (PCA) is a statistical technique that aims to find a few factors (**eigenvectors**, also often referred to as **eigenfaces** by researchers on face recognition) that account for all or most of the variation within a data set. (For readers with knowledge of statistics, PCA is rather like Factor Analysis.) Each successive eigenvector accounts for progressively less of the variation between faces in a set. Therefore, in practice only the first 15 or so eigenvectors are worth considering.

Different eigenvectors seem to carry information about different aspects of a face. For example, the first one normally accounts for a lot of the variation produced by illumination differences between face images. Gender also gives rise to a large eigenvector. Information that is important for recognition seems to be carried in the later components (O'Toole et al, 1999). Two different images of the same person will overlap in terms of their principal components. Eigenvectors are often displayed pictorially in terms of how they deviate from an 'average' face. Figure 2.17 shows some examples.

In the context of face recognition, PCA has two advantages. Firstly, it is an effective data compression technique. Instead of retaining all of the intensity differences in an image of a face,

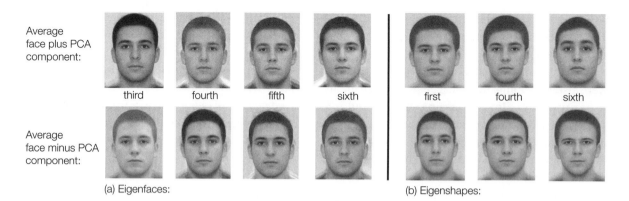

Average face plus PCA component:

third   fourth   fifth   sixth   first   fourth   sixth

Average face minus PCA component:

(a) Eigenfaces: (b) Eigenshapes:

FIGURE 2.17 Some results from Principal Components Analysis (PCA) on 179 key points located on each of 50 young adult male faces (first standardized for expression and interpupillary distance). (a) The third, fourth, fifth and sixth 'eigenfaces', produced by first morphing all faces to the average face shape and then performing PCA on these 'shape-free' images. The top and bottom rows show the average face plus or minus each 'eigenface' respectively. (b) The first, fourth and sixth 'eigenshapes', produced by adding or subtracting shape components from the average face shape. (Reproduced with kind permission of Peter Hancock, University of Stirling. © Peter Hancock)

which would amount to a huge amount of data for each face, PCA reduces each face to just a few values. Secondly, it produces a set of global facial 'primitives' (building blocks) that involve the whole face. (A disadvantage is that, like Factor Analysis in other areas of psychology, the software delivers a set of factors but it's up to the researcher to work out precisely what they represent, which is not always easy!)

PCA has been enormously influential amongst researchers seeking to produce computational models of face recognition. In tests, it has proved to be one of the most successful face recognition systems to date. Precisely how well it compares to human face recognition depends on the particular implementation of it that is being considered: there are many different versions. In addition, it is often combined with other statistical/computational techniques in a bid to improve its performance. Hancock et al (1998) made comparisons between the responses of a PCA system to a set of test images, and human ratings of facial distinctiveness and similarity for those images. There were significant, although small, correlations between

the observers and the PCA system. Hancock et al's conclusion was that PCA responded much like humans do when trying to remember a picture of an unfamiliar face: performance was dominated by details of the individual picture, rather than aspects of the person's appearance. This is understandable, given that PCA is based on very low-level image properties (i.e. the intensity values of pixels in a 2D image), rather than on abstract 3D representations of faces or heads.

2.12 Burton et al's (2005) 'shape-averaging' model of the Face Recognition Unit

The main problem with standard PCA techniques is that they are too sensitive to the effects of superficial image properties such as lighting and pose. Although these provide no information about individual identity, they tend to be quite large in comparison to the intensity changes in an image that are produced by differences between individual faces. Burton et al (2005) circumvent this problem by applying PCA not to an individual image, but to *averages* made up from numerous images of the same person. Their technique involves collecting a set of pictures of a particular face, morphing them to a standardized face shape, and then averaging together these images (Fig. 2.18).

Test images (specific views of faces) are then compared to these **shape-free averages**. In effect,

the test images are compared to a prototype that has arisen from averaging together a number of different instances of a face.

In computer simulations, Burton et al showed that this approach was markedly superior to standard PCA based on individual images. The more images that were averaged together, the better their system performed. With 19-image averages, recognition performance was a creditable 75% correct.

When humans were tested on their ability to identify shape-free averages of famous faces, Burton et al found that the recognizability of the averages improved as the number of faces used for each average increased from three to nine. Even the three-sample averages were recognized fairly quickly and accurately. Thus, even though shape information is held constant in these averages and provides no information about identity, humans find shape-free averages of familiar faces quite recognizable. As a further refinement, Burton et al produced an average of the shape information for each person, and then morphed the shape-free average on to this shape average. These averages were not incorporated into the computer simulation, but in tests with human observers they were recognized faster than individual images of the celebrities concerned.

Burton et al's technique works because the process of averaging images automatically discards any image characteristics that are not diagnostic of the person, such as lighting variations or minor changes in pose. The greater the number of images that are included in the average, the more these 'accidental' image properties are eliminated.

Burton et al's procedure also provides a simple and plausible explanation for how faces are learnt. As we have seen, unfamiliar face recognition appears to involve little more than simple image matching (e.g. Megreya and Burton, 2008). Burton et al's idea is that successive encounters with a particular face lead to the development of a

(a)

(b)

(c)

FIGURE 2.18 Burton et al's (2005) 'shape-free averages', produced by averaging together many different instances of the same person's face, once they have been 'warped' to a standardized shape. (a) Original images; (b) original images warped to a standard face shape; (c) average of standardized images.

progressively more prototypical representation: more instances are simply added into that person's average. By this account, familiar and unfamiliar face recognition are not qualitatively different—it's merely that the representation against which to make a match has been improved. Burton et al's model can also explain the internal–external feature-processing differences that we discussed above: over time, external features vary, but internal ones remain similar and are preserved by the averaging process.

Burton et al confined their technique to analysing frontal views. However, to cope with large variations in pose, they suggest that each familiar face could be represented by a few averages, for example one each for three-quarters, full-face and profile views. In Chapter 1, it was pointed out that one important omission from the Bruce and Young model and its derivatives was a detailed specification of how **Face Recognition Units** actually operate. Burton et al's procedure is an elegant solution to this problem.

2.13 **The role of movement in face recognition**

Finally, in this discussion of how faces are represented in the brain, we should mention the role of motion information. In real life, faces are not static 2D images: they move. Actually, they engage in different types of movement. **Rigid** motion is produced by movements such as head-turns and nods that leave the shape of the face unchanged. **Non-rigid** head movements are distortions of the face that are produced by facial expressions and talking. Do rigid and non-rigid motion facilitate face processing, and, if so, how?

Two main theories have been put forward to account for how motion information might

aid face recognition; see Roark et al (2003) and O'Toole et al (2002) for reviews. The **Representational Enhancement Hypothesis (REH)** proposes that a moving head could provide more information about the 3D structure of a face than can be gleaned from a static image. The **Supplemental Information Hypothesis (SIH)** suggests that moving faces might provide information about the characteristic ways in which people move their heads (their so-called **dynamic facial signatures**—think of Princess Diana's quirky head-tilt or Gordon Brown's chewing-the-cud jaw movements).

Ordinarily, because we are so good at recognizing familiar faces from static images, it is difficult to demonstrate any performance benefits from adding motion information. However, benefits can be detected if faces are degraded in order to make them harder to recognize from static images. This has been done by turning faces into photographic negatives (Knight and Johnston, 1997; Lander et al, 2001); by pixellating them (Lander et al, 2001); or by black-and-white thresholding (Lander et al, 1999).

Many of the findings in this area are consistent with the SIH. For example, the benefits of motion are reduced if its dynamic characteristics are disrupted by showing the video frames in a jumbled order or at a different speed from normal (Lander and Bruce, 2000). In addition, the benefits are seen only for degraded familiar faces that are rated as having 'distinctive', rather than typical, facial movement patterns (Lander and Chuang, 2005). The SIH is also supported by a number of studies showing that participants are able to discriminate between different individuals purely on the basis of their characteristic head movements. For example, Hill and Johnston (2001) 'grafted' different actors' head movements on to a single computer-generated head, thus producing a set of heads that were identical except that each had a unique dynamic facial signature. Nevertheless, participants were able to discriminate between them. Steede et al (2007) used Hill and Johnston's technique with CS, a person who had **developmental prosopagnosia** (see Chapter 7). Although CS was unable to recognize faces from static mages, he was as good as normal participants at learning to recognize faces purely on the basis of their dynamic facial signatures. This is strong evidence that dynamic facial signatures are sufficient for face recognition.

There is somewhat less empirical support for the REH. However, Pike et al (1997) showed that face learning was more accurate if faces were learned from rigid motion sequences than if they were learned as a series of static views. This suggests that rigid motion may facilitate the development of a better structural description of a face than when it is seen statically. Further support for the REH comes from Thornton and Kourtzi (2002), who found that moving faces acted as better primes in a sequential face-matching task than did static faces. This effect cannot be explained by the SIH, because the faces and their movements were unfamiliar to the participants.

2.14 **Conclusion**

Probably the single most important question in face-processing research is: what information is extracted from faces and used as a basis for recognizing them? Research on this issue has progressed through three phases. Initially, faces were conceived of as being collections of features, and research focused on developing 'feature salience hierarchies'. These were important in showing that some parts of the face are more important for recognition than others, but they failed to reflect the fact that faces are *more* than just a collection of isolated components.

The second phase of research has involved an appreciation of the importance of 'configural' processing for recognition purposes. During this phase, there have been numerous demonstrations of the existence of configural processing (using phenomena such as the Face Inversion Effect, the Thatcher Illusion and the Composite Face Effect), and we have developed a greater understanding of the properties of this kind of processing. However, research in this second phase has still been heavily influenced by our subjective impressions of faces as being composed of eyes, noses and mouths. Recent research has started to move away from this way of thinking about faces, and has started to investigate the possibility that facial representations are perhaps quite unlike our introspections. Principal Components Analysis, Burton et al's 'shape-averaging' model, and Dakin and Watt's 'bar-code' model are examples of this latest phase, and probably ultimately hold the key to answering the question of how we identify individuals on the basis of their faces.

SUMMARY

- Faces can be recognized on the basis of their individual features or the configuration formed by these features (the 'dual-route hypothesis'), but configural information seems to be more important for recognition.

- Three different kinds of 'configural' processing have been reported. 'First-order' relations refer to the basic arrangement common to all faces, of eyes above nose, above mouth. 'Holistic' processing binds the facial components into a unified whole, or 'gestalt'. 'Second-order' relations provide information about the configurations of particular faces, and are the key to individual recognition.

- Demonstrations of the importance of configural information for face recognition come from studies of the Face Inversion Effect, Thatcher Illusion, the Composite Face Effect, whole-over-part superiority effects and prototype effects. All of these manipulations suggest that normal face recognition is highly orientation-dependent.

- Although we are good at detecting small changes to the locations of facial features, studies of the effects of caricature and affine distortions suggest that configural processing does not consist merely of a collection of facial measurements.

- Familiar and unfamiliar faces seem to be processed in qualitatively different ways: recognition of familiar faces appears to be based on abstractive and robust representations, whereas unfamiliar face recognition is much more 'image-based'. In contrast to unfamiliar face recognition, familiar face recognition is highly tolerant of changes in viewpoint, expression and lighting.

FURTHER READING

Peterson, M. and Rhodes, G. (eds) (2003). *Perception of Faces, Objects, and Scenes: Analytic and Holistic Processes.* Oxford: Oxford University Press. A collection of papers by experts in this field, many of which deal with configural processing of faces.

Wechsler, H. (2007). *Reliable Face Recognition Methods: System Design, Implementation and Evaluation.* New York: Springer. An in-depth coverage of computer vision systems, as they apply to face recognition. Deals with PCA and many other computational models of face processing. Useful for computer science students, but heavy-going for anyone who is not mathematically minded.

PROCESSING EMOTIONAL EXPRESSION

While much of the research examining face processing has concentrated on the processing of facial identity, identity is only one piece of information that we extract from a face. Another very important piece of information is the emotion being expressed on the face. The ability to interpret an individual's **emotional expression** correctly is really important; is the unfamiliar person walking towards you smiling and looking happy, or do they look angry? You need to interpret this emotional expression accurately in order to decide how best to respond to this person. In this chapter we will examine the processing of emotional expression from a variety of perspectives.

3.1 **What is emotional expression?**

In 1872, Charles Darwin wrote a book entitled *The Expression of the Emotions in Man and Animals.*[1] In this book he aimed to understand '*how far particular movements of the features and gestures are really expressive of certain states of the mind*' (p. 13). Darwin was particularly interested in the **universality** of emotional expression and the interpretation of both facial and bodily emotional expression. In order to achieve this, he observed emotional expression in infants, clinically 'insane' individuals, people from different cultures and animals from various species. He described the following experiment that he conducted:

It fortunately occurred to me to show several of the best plates [*photographs of an old man with various emotional expressions*], without a word of explanation, to above twenty educated persons of various ages and both sexes, asking them, in each case, by what emotion or feeling the old man was supposed to be agitated; and I recorded their answers in the words which they used. Several of the expressions were instantly recognized by almost everyone, though described in not exactly the same terms. (Darwin, 1872, p. 14)

In many ways the questions raised by Darwin are still central to emotion research more than 130 years later. In particular, much research has attempted to determine which emotions form our 'basic' emotions. That is, what are the core emotions experienced, expressed and perceived

---

[1] A full version of this book can be found at http://www.darwin-online.org.uk.

across all ages, cultures and even across different species? One of the pioneers of modern-day emotion research is Paul Ekman, who has contributed greatly to our understanding of the expression and perception of facial emotion.

The issue of the universality of emotional expressions and whether there are universal 'basic' emotions essentially asks one of the most frequently posed questions in psychological research: nature or nurture? If the expression and perception of facial emotion are universal and the same effects are found across a wide range of cultures, this suggests an innate process. In contrast, if there are marked differences between cultures, this suggests that the expression and perception of emotions are learnt.

In a series of experiments in the late 1960s and early 1970s, Ekman and his colleagues examined whether the ability to classify facial emotional expressions varied across cultures. They created a set of stimuli that has been used in much of the emotion recognition research that has been conducted since (Fig. 3.1). Each emotional expression is characterized by a distinct pattern of facial muscular movements. For example, smiling is associated with the contraction of two muscle groups, the orbicularis oculi muscle which lifts the cheeks and creates the 'crow's feet' lines around the eyes, and the zygomatic major muscle which lifts the corners of the mouth.

Ekman and colleagues (1969) showed these stimuli to participants from five different cultures,

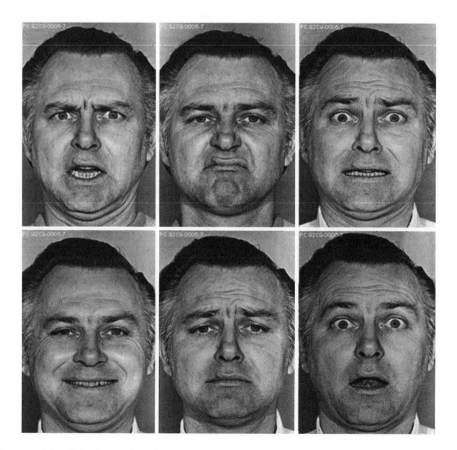

FIGURE 3.1 Images of the six basic emotions (from Young et al, 2002). Top row, left to right: anger, disgust and fear. Bottom row, left to right: happiness, sadness and surprise.

TABLE 3.1 Percentage accuracy for the classification of emotional expression across different literate cultures (data from Ekman, 1972)

Emotion	USA	Japan	Brazil	Chile	Argentina
Anger	69	63	82	76	72
Disgust	82	82	86	85	79
Fear	88	71	77	78	68
Happiness	97	87	97	90	94
Sadness	73	74	82	90	85
Surprise	91	87	82	88	93

all of which were literate cultures: the USA, Japan, Brazil, Chile and Argentina. Participants were shown images of six different facial expressions: anger, disgust, fear, happiness, sadness and surprise. When asked to judge which emotion was being expressed, participants from all of the cultures showed quite high levels of accuracy and there were no significant differences in accuracy across the cultural groups (Table 3.1). This finding was also replicated by Izard (1968, 1971) across a wider range of cultures: the USA, England, Germany, Sweden, France, Switzerland, Greece, Japan and Africa.

There is one major limitation of these cross-cultural studies: all of the cultures examined are literate, well developed and have a great deal of cross-cultural interaction. Ekman and Friesen (1971) therefore extended their work to test people from preliterate and isolated cultures that had virtually no contact with other cultures. They tested people from the Fore cultural group in New Guinea on both their perception and expression of facial emotion. In one experiment they asked their participants to read a short passage that described an emotional scenario and then showed them three faces, each expressing a different emotion. The participants' task was to choose the face that best reflected the emotional content of the story. When compared to the performance

of participants from literate cultures, the Fore participants were in very high agreement for happiness (92%), anger (84%), disgust (81%) and sadness (79%), and relatively high for surprise (68%). Ekman found that fear could easily be distinguished from anger, disgust and sadness, with 80% accuracy. However, the Fore participants frequently confused fear and surprise, and were correct on only 43% of these trials. In another experiment they asked the Fore participants to pose the emotional expression that reflected the emotional content of the story. Participants from the USA were able to classify these posed emotional expressions correctly, apart from confusing fear and surprise.

These early studies led researchers to believe that the processing of facial emotional expressions is universal across different cultures, and therefore innate. However, more recent work suggests that there may be differences in the ability to recognize emotional expressions across different cultures. Indeed, inspection of the Ekman data in Table 3.1 does seem to show some differences across cultures. For example, Japanese participants seem worse at recognizing happiness compared with American and Brazilian participants, whereas Chilean participants appear to be particularly good at recognizing sadness and Argentinians are good at recognizing surprise.

In their review of this field of research, Elfenbein and Ambady (2003) critique much of the work in terms of the stimuli used. They point out that most of the studies use stimuli showing expressions being posed by Americans. It is well known that there are in-group biases in face perception (see Chapter 12); therefore, might some of the differences reported between participants from different cultures actually reflect own-group biases in the processing of facial emotion? Elfenbein and Ambady (2002) conducted a meta-analysis in which they reanalysed data from 97 studies. They found strong evidence for the universality of emotion processing, but they did also find some evidence of an own-group advantage. This own-group bias has been shown experimentally in a study examining emotion recognition in participants from Quebec in Canada and Gabon in

Africa, in which both groups of participants showed an own-group advantage (Elfenbein et al, 2007).

Wickline et al (2009) recently conducted a study in which they attempted to distinguish between cultural and racial group biases in the processing of facial emotion. They conducted their study in America and included four groups of participants: European Americans, African Americans, students from Europe and students from Africa. The participants were asked to classify the emotions expressed on either European American or African American faces. Wickline and colleagues found own-group biases in terms of both culture and race, but the own-culture advantage was larger than the own-race bias. This finding suggests that there is some variability in the processing of facial emotion across cultures.

Darwin also suggested that the universality and innateness of emotional expression could be examined through the study of emotional expression in animals. If animals showed the ability to express and perceive emotions in a similar way to humans, this would provide strong evidence for universality and innateness. A great deal of research has supported the view that animals are able to perceive emotional expression accurately (for a review see Tate et al, 2006). For example, Parr and Heintz (2009) found that Rhesus monkeys are able to match two faces of monkeys expressing the same emotion, even if the identity of the poser varies between the two images. The ability to distinguish between different emotional expressions has also been shown in sheep. da Costa et al (2004) showed sheep pairs of faces, with some being pairs of human faces and the others being pairs of sheep faces, where one was expressing a positive emotion and the other a negative emotion. The sheep preferred to look at the positive emotional expressions on around 80% of trials, and this preference occurred for both sheep and human faces. Such evidence from animal studies provides further support for at least some degree of universality in the processing of facial emotion.

The cross-cultural work on the expression and recognition of facial emotion by researchers such as Ekman and Izard led to the suggestion that there is a discrete number of **'basic' emotions** which are universal. Typically these are recognized as anger, disgust, fear, happiness, sadness and surprise. Although there is a limited number of basic emotions, we experience emotion at varying levels of intensity; we can experience emotions that are blends of the basic emotions; and we may experience different emotions in response to the same stimulus. It is also clear that our ability to recognize the different emotional expressions varies a great deal. Again, look at Table 3.1 in which Ekman (1972) showed that, across all cultures, happiness was recognized with the highest level of accuracy, whereas anger was less well recognized.

More recent evidence has also shown differences between the emotions in terms of how recognizable they are. Montagne et al (2007) showed participants faces in which the intensity of the emotional expression increased from 20% to 100%. This was achieved by morphing neutral faces into emotive faces. So, a 20% intensity face would be 80% neutral and 20% emotive. Like Ekman (1972), they found that happiness was the easiest emotion to recognize; however, they found that fear (not anger) was the least well recognized. Calvo and Lundqvist (2008) showed participants emotional faces for 25, 50, 100, 250 or 500 milliseconds and asked them to decide which emotion was being expressed. The rationale in this study was that, if an emotion is very easy to identify it should be easily and rapidly recognizable. In contrast, if an emotional expression is more difficult to identify then it may take longer. They found that happiness was recognized with the highest level of accuracy, and the performance was near-ceiling even at just 25 ms. In contrast, the negative emotions, particularly fear, were all recognized with lower levels of accuracy and showed marked improvement in accuracy with increased exposure. This difference has also been shown for haptic recognition of facial emotional expression (Lederman et al, 2007) with happiness, sadness and surprise all recognized with above 90% accuracy. Anger and disgust were less well recognized and the recognition of fear was not significantly above chance.

There is considerable evidence showing that happiness is recognized with far greater accuracy than negative emotions, particularly fear. One possible reason for this is that there is only one clearly defined positive emotion, whereas there are a number of different negative emotions. This means that people may get confused between the negative emotions and misclassify them, whereas they are unlikely to confuse happiness with one of the negative emotions. For example, the Calvo and Lundqvist (2008) study found no significant misclassification of happy faces, whereas all of the other emotions showed significant patterns of misclassification (Fig. 3.2). Anger was confused

with disgust, sadness with both fear and disgust, disgust with anger, and fear and surprise were confused with each other. It is therefore possible that happiness is not actually easier to recognize than the other emotions; rather, it is more difficult to confuse with other emotions.

Research has also examined how clear the distinction is between different emotions. The phenomenon of **categorical perception** is well established in psychology and has been shown for a wide range of stimuli. The idea here is to create a set of stimuli where there is a subtle and continuous change between two different categories of a stimulus. For example, a morph sequence might be created showing the change from one emotional expression, such as anger, into another emotional expression, such as disgust (Fig. 3.3). Although the change between the two categories is smooth and continuous, participants tend to still see the faces that are a

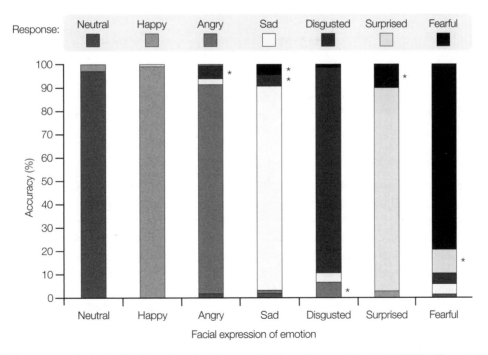

FIGURE 3.2 Accuracy and misclassification of emotional expressions from Calvo and Lundqvist (2008). The asterisks denote significant errors of misclassification.

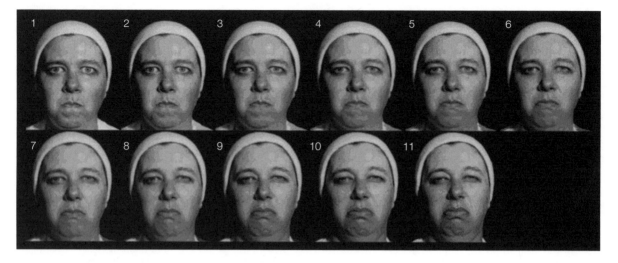

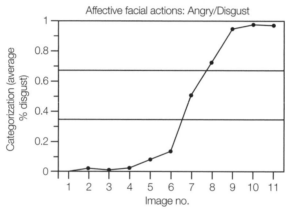

FIGURE 3.3 At the top is a series of 11 images showing a morph sequence between angry (image 1) and disgusted (image 11) facial expressions. The graph below shows the percentage of disgust decisions when shown the anger/disgust images. (Adapted from McCullough and Emmorey, 2009)

mixture of the two expressions as either one or the other. The graph in Fig. 3.3 shows the proportion of 'disgust' decisions made to faces across a sequence of 11 images. You can clearly see that participants classify the face in images 1–6 as expressing anger. There are then two faces (7 and 8) that seem ambiguous. The classification is clearly disgust in images 9, 10 and 11. This clear shift from one categorical decision to the other shows categorical perception. It is particularly important to remember that the change across the different images is continuous; however, the perception of

the emotional expression is clearly categorical and on most images the face is obviously perceived as either one or other of the two categories.

A number of studies have shown the categorical perception of emotional expression (e.g. Calder et al, 1996; Campanella et al, 2002; Etcoff and Magee, 1992; Kiffel et al, 2005; Roberson et al, 2007; Young et al, 1997), and the effect has even been shown in infants as young as 7 months old (Kotsoni et al, 2001). Graham and colleagues (2007) examined the effects of brain damage on the categorical perception of emotional expression.

They tested one patient who had bilateral **amygdala** damage, 13 patients with medial temporal lobe damage, a group of age-matched control participants and a group of younger participants. Three different morph sequences were used: neutral to anger, neutral to fear, and fear to anger. The patient with the amygdala damage was impaired on all of the emotion sequences, relative to all of the other groups, but not on an identity version of the categorical perception task. Because the patient with amygdala damage was less sensitive to the blends of emotions, this suggests that the amygdala is involved in this emotional categorization (more on this later in the chapter).

Research has also examined how much genuine and posed facial expressions differ, and how good people are at distinguishing between them. Porter and ten Brinke (2008) showed participants non-facial images that were disgusting, happy, sad, fearful or neutral, and asked participants to respond to each with either a genuine facial expression, a neutral facial expression, or by masking their instinctive and genuine facial expression. They found that participants were better at falsifying happiness than the negative emotions.

One of the most frequently studied fake emotional expressions is happiness. A genuine smile and expression of happiness is often referred to as a **Duchenne smile**, named after a 19th-century French neurologist and physiognomist who examined the precise muscle movements that formed distinct facial expressions of emotion. Duchenne noted that genuine smiles could be detected on the basis of the contraction of the muscles at the corners of the mouth, which raises them, and the contraction of the muscles around the eyes, which causes the crow's feet around the eyes. In Fig. 3.4 you can clearly see the differences between the faked and the genuine smiles. An eye-tracking study by Williams and co-workers (2001) found that participants were more likely to inspect the crow's feet area of the eyes when looking at a

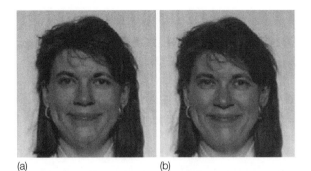

(a)   (b)

FIGURE 3.4 (a) Non-Duchenne smile and (b) Duchenne (genuine) smile. (From Surakka and Hietanen, 1998)

smiling face than when looking at a neutral or sad face. This suggests that we may be predisposed to looking at this area to detect genuine happiness.

There is evidence for us being able to detect the difference between genuine and posed smiles, both explicitly and implicitly. Research has shown that children as young as 6 years old are sensitive to fake smiles, although this sensitivity increases after the age of about 7 years (Gosselin et al, 2002). More recently it has been shown that children as young as 4 years old rate genuine smiles as more authentic than faked smiles, even at a medium intensity of expression (Thibault et al, 2009).

We are even sensitive to the difference between faked and authentic smiles when they are not relevant to the task being completed. Miles and Johnston (2007) asked participants to judge the valence of an emotional word. Each word was preceded by a face that they were told to ignore. The face was expressing either a genuine smile or a posed smile. Even though the facial expression was not relevant, when the smile was genuine the identification of positively valenced words was primed, whereas the posed smiling faces did not cause such a priming effect. Peace et al (2006) found that participants rated a T-shirt more positively when the model wearing it was genuinely smiling than when the smile was posed. This evidence suggests an implicit sensitivity to Duchenne smiles.

3.2 **Are emotional expression and identity processed independently?**

According to the Bruce and Young (1986) model of face processing (see Chapter 1 for a full description), the initial structural encoding of a face is **independent** of the emotion being expressed. Following the structural encoding, processing is then divided into distinct streams, one dedicated to the processing of identity and the other to the processing of facial emotion. This model clearly predicts that the processing of emotional expression and identity are independent, but this suggestion has been questioned in more recent research. Most of these studies use the Garner interference paradigm (see Chapter 1). They present participants with familiar and unfamiliar faces that express varying emotional expressions. The participants have to complete a task that requires them to attend to one property (either identity or emotional expression) while ignoring the other. If the two processes are entirely independent then the ignored property should not influence processing, but if processing systematically varies according to the ignored property then there is evidence for the two systems interacting.

The majority of the behavioural research in this area suggests that the processing of identity and emotion are **interdependent**. Kaufmann and Schweinberger (2004) showed participants images of familiar and unfamiliar faces expressing different emotions and asked them to make a familiarity decision. Emotional expression influenced the recognition of familiar faces, with familiar faces being recognized fastest if they had a happy emotional expression. A similar study was conducted by Lander and Metcalfe (2007). They showed participants famous and unknown faces expressing either a positive, neutral or negative expression. Faces with a

positive expression were judged to be more familiar and faces with a negative expression were thought to be less familiar. A similar symmetrical relationship between facial identity and emotional expression has been shown by Dobel et al (2008). This interaction between identity and emotion has also been shown for recently learned faces (D'Argembeau and Van der Linden, 2007) and for matching unknown faces on the basis of identity (Levy and Bentin, 2008).

Although there seems to be somewhat convincing evidence for an interaction between the processing of identity and emotion, some research has suggested that this relationship may not exist in both directions. Schweinberger et al (1999) morphed faces between different identities while keeping the emotional expression the same, or between different emotional expressions while keeping the identity the same. Reaction times for emotional expression decisions were influenced by the identity of faces, but identity decisions were not influenced by emotional expression. This suggests an asymmetrical relationship between identity and emotional expression processing. Fox and colleagues (2008) found a similar result using an adaptation paradigm. They found that representations of emotional expression were dependent on facial identity, but representations of facial identity were not dependent on emotional expression. That is, the processing of emotional expression was influenced when the identity of the face changed, but the processing of facial identity was not affected by changes in emotional expression.

The relationship between facial identity and emotional expression processing has also been examined using neuropsychological techniques,[2] both by examining the behavioural consequences of brain damage and by electrophysiological or neuroimaging techniques. If the processing of facial identity and emotional expression were entirely independent, they would be expected to be

---

[2] See the Appendix for an outline of these methods.

processed in distinct areas of the brain, whereas if they interacted then some areas of the brain would be expected to be involved in the processing of both identity and expression.

Studies examining the ability of patients to process facial identity and emotional expression following brain damage have provided evidence for a double dissociation (see Chapter 10 for a full explanation of double dissociations). Tranel et al (1988) examined the face-processing abilities of three patients with acquired brain damage. All three were significantly impaired for recognizing familiar faces but were able to recognize facial emotion. Young et al (1993) reported the opposite dissociation, with their patient being impaired for recognizing emotional expression but still able to recognize familiar faces. This double dissociation suggests that different areas of the brain may be responsible for processing facial emotion and facial identity; however, the interpretation of double dissociations is not necessarily this simple (see Chapter 10).

The neuroimaging research examining this question is slightly more mixed than the behavioural evidence. Winston et al (2004) conducted a functional magnetic resonance imaging (fMRI) study and found quite distinct patterns of activation for identity and emotional expression. They repeatedly presented faces where either the identity of the face or the emotional expression changed. Repetitions of identity led to reduced activation in the fusiform gyrus and the posterior superior temporal gyrus, whereas repetition of expression caused a quite different result, with reduced activation in the mid-temporal gyrus. This suggests that distinct areas of the brain are responsible for processing identity and emotional expression, and consequently that these processes are independent.

Not all of the neuroimaging work provides such clear evidence for emotion and identity processing being distinct. Fox et al (2009) showed participants faces that were manipulated in terms of either identity or emotional expression.

They found increased activity in the occipital face area, the fusiform face area and the posterior superior temporal sulcus in response to changes in both identity and emotional expression. However, there were some slight differences in activation. The changes in activation in the posterior superior temporal sulcus were seen only when participants were specifically asked to attend to the faces' emotional expression. They also found specific changes in activation in the middle superior temporal sulcus in response to emotional expression, and in the precuneus in response to identity. Fox and co-workers suggest that the overlapping activation found in the occipital face areas represents the structural encoding of the facial structure prior to any processing of identity or emotional expression. However, they suggest that the activation of the fusiform face area and the posterior superior temporal sulcus shows that the processing of emotional expression and identity cannot be completely independent.

The possible independence or interdependence of the neural processing of facial identity and emotion has similarly been examined using event-related potentials (ERPs), and this work has tended to support the independence of these processes. Münte et al (1998) compared ERP responses when participants were processing either facial identity or facial emotion and found quite different patterns, both spatially and temporally. Responses to identity were evident earlier than responses to emotional expression; identity processing involved more frontal areas; and expression processing involved more occipital areas. This suggests that the processing of identity and emotional expression are independent.

A more recent study by Wild-Wall et al (2008) used an emotion discrimination task, asking participants to discriminate between disgust and happiness when expressed on either familiar or unfamiliar faces. When examining the P300 response over the parietal lobes, they found that the response was larger and slightly earlier for familiar faces expressing happiness than for unfamiliar faces expressing happiness. This distinction suggests an interaction between identity and emotion processing.

Although the Bruce and Young (1986) model proposes that the processing of identity and emotional expression are independent once the basic structural encoding of a face has occurred, the research on this topic is relatively mixed. Neuropsychological evidence, both clinical and neuroimaging, has provided some evidence in support of the processes being independent, but some interaction has also been reported. Stronger evidence for there being an interaction between identity and emotion has been found in behavioural experiments. Although some have shown that there is a symmetrical interaction, others have suggested an asymmetrical interaction with the processing of emotional expression being dependent on identity, but not vice versa. It seems that this issue is still not entirely resolved, but it is possible that the existing models of face processing may need to be adapted to take into account some degree of interrelationship between identity and emotional expression processing.

3.3 Configural and featural information in the processing of emotional expression

We saw in Chapter 2 that two types of facial information can be extracted from faces: featural and configural information. Manipulations that are known to affect these in the context of identification have also been used to examine how configural and featural facial information are used in the processing of facial emotional expression.

One of the most frequently used facial manipulations is inversion. Upright faces tend to be processed primarily on the basis of the configural information contained within them, but when a face is inverted participants are unable to use the configural information and instead rely more on featural information (Yin, 1969; also see Chapter 2). Inversion has also been found to reduce the accuracy of recognizing facial emotional expression. Fallshore and Bartholow (2003) used schematic drawings of faces expressing each of the six basic emotions and found that the ability to accurately identify the emotion expressed was reduced when the faces were inverted. This finding suggests that the processing of facial emotion is also dependent upon the effective processing of configural facial information. However, given that this study used schematic faces rather than photographic images of faces, the conclusions that can be drawn from it may be slightly limited.

Prkachin (2003) also used the inversion effect to examine the role of configural facial information for processing facial emotion, using the Ekman and Friesen (1976) photographic images of the six basic emotions (see Fig. 3.1). Prkachin replicated the finding that inversion reduces accuracy for emotion recognition, but the extent of this impairment varied across the emotions. Inversion impaired the recognition of anger, disgust and fear to a greater extent than it impaired the recognition of happiness, sadness and surprise. When faces were inverted, participants tended to confuse sadness, anger and disgust.

The findings of Prkachin's study support the idea that configural facial information is important for processing facial emotional expression; however, they do suggest that its importance may vary across the emotions. The fact that the recognition of happiness, sadness and surprise was relatively less impaired by inversion (although there was still a significant reduction in accuracy) suggests that these emotions may be processed on the basis of either configural or featural information. In contrast, the strong inversion effects for recognition of anger, disgust and fear suggest that they rely more heavily on configural information.

Lipp et al (2009) also used inversion to examine the role of configural information in the processing of facial emotion, but, rather than using an emotion recognition task, they asked participants to judge how positive the emotive faces were. Happy faces were perceived as being more positive than angry, fearful and sad faces, regardless of orientation. Because inversion did not influence the affective judgement of the faces, the authors suggested that the extraction of the emotive information expressed was not influenced by disruptions to configural facial information.

The inversion effect has also been used in combination with the Composite Face Effect to further understand the distinction between configural and featural facial information for processing emotional expression. In the composite face manipulation, the top and bottom halves of the face each express different emotions. The participant's task is typically to judge whether or not the top halves of the faces presented in a pair are expressing the same emotion. When the top and bottom halves are aligned this is very difficult, because the two halves combine perceptually to give the impression of an intact face. However, when the two halves are misaligned and the configural information is disrupted, this task is far easier (see Chapter 2).

Calder et al (2000) used the Composite Face Effect and found a disruption to emotion recognition comparable to that reported previously for face recognition. They found that participants were slower and less accurate at emotion recognition when the face halves were aligned than when they were misaligned. Inversion disrupted the Composite Face Effect, again replicating the findings from earlier identity recognition experiments. Interestingly, Calder and colleagues also found differences across the six basic emotions in terms of participants' abilities to recognize the emotion being expressed from the top and bottom halves of the faces. Anger, fear and sadness were more recognizable from the top half of the face, whereas happiness and disgust were more recognizable from the bottom half.

Although most of the work examining the contributions of configural and featural information to face processing has concentrated on face recognition, research examining facial emotion processing has provided generally consistent results. It seems that configural facial information is very important for the effective processing of facial emotion, but that emotion processing may also be achieved, albeit more slowly and with less accuracy, via featural information. One particularly interesting finding is that the dependence upon configural facial information and the relative importance of facial features contained in the top or bottom half of a face varies across the different emotions.

3.4 How does the processing of emotional expression change across the lifespan?

3.4.1 Development through childhood

We will see in Chapters 5 and 6 that the ability to process faces and recognize an individual develops a great deal from birth to adulthood. The ability to process facial expressions has also been found to change a great deal during this time. Bornstein and Arterberry (2003) examined the emotion-processing abilities of infants aged 5 months using an habituation paradigm[3] with

---

[3] See Chapter 5 for a full explanation of the habituation paradigm. Briefly, infants are shown a particular stimulus until they are bored with looking at it. When they are shown that stimulus again, if they no longer look at it much this indicates that they can remember seeing it before and are still bored with looking at it. However, if they look at it as much as they would a novel stimulus, this indicates that they do not recognize it and that they are effectively treating it as a new stimulus.

faces expressing happiness and fear. The infants were sensitive to changes in these emotional expressions, indicating that by the age of just 5 months infants have developed basic emotion-processing skills. Peltola et al (2008) showed 7-month-old infants faces expressing either fear, happiness or a novel expression (the poser had a relatively neutral expression, but with their cheeks puffed out with air) and found that the infants looked longer at the faces expressing fear. Such studies suggest that within the first few months of life we are able to process and possibly even discriminate between different emotions.

Most of the research in this area has examined how the processing of emotion develops through childhood and into adulthood. Herba et al (2008) used faces expressing anger, disgust, fear, happiness or sadness to examine the developmental trajectory of emotion processing from 4 to 15 years of age. They also used two sets of stimuli, one of unfamiliar people posing the emotional expressions (the Ekman faces) and the other of people familiar to the children participating in the study. The stimuli were created by morphing between neutral and emotive faces so that, for each emotion, there were four intensities: 25%, 50%, 75% and 100%. All age groups could recognize happiness accurately at all intensities. For recognition of anger, there seemed to be little change across the age groups. However, for recognition of sadness and fear there was a clear improvement with increasing age. The children were less accurate at recognizing anger, disgust and fear from images of familiar faces than from images of unfamiliar faces. Herba and colleagues suggest that children might be distracted by facial familiarity when possessing emotional expression.

An interesting issue is at what age children reach 'adult-like' levels of competence. To address this question, some studies have additionally tested adults and then compared their performance with that of children of varying ages. Thomas et al (2007) tested older children (7–13 years old), adolescents (14–18 years old) and adults (25–57 years old). They created three series of morphs between a face showing a neutral expression or fear, a neutral expression or anger, and between fear and anger. Participants then saw individual faces and had to decide which of the two emotions from within that morph sequence was being expressed. For example, when examining faces from the neutral to fear sequence, they had to decide whether each face was expressing fear or whether it was neutral (even though all faces were morphed combinations of the two expressions).

Thomas and co-workers found that the adults were better at discriminating between emotions within morph sequences than both older children and adolescents. This suggests that the ability to process facial emotional expression effectively does not reach adult-like levels until quite late in the teenage years. However, they did find some differences between the older children and the adolescents which varied across the different emotive sequences. For the fear–neutral and fear–anger sequences they found a linear improvement in performance. For the anger–neutral sequence there was no change between older childhood and adolescence but then a rapid improvement in performance from adolescence into adulthood. This suggests that the ability to process fear and anger may follow different developmental trajectories, with fear developing in a linear manner and anger showing a later, but more marked, developmental trend.

More recently Gao and Maurer (2009) examined the ability to process happiness, sadness and fear in children aged 5, 7 or 10 years and in adults. Again they manipulated intensity by creating morphs between neutral and emotive faces. Children as young as 5 years old were just as good as the adults at recognizing happiness, even at low intensity. When shown a face expressing sadness, all age groups were able to accurately determine that the face was expressive (i.e. not neutral); however, all of the children tended to confuse sad faces with fearful faces. For fearful faces, the children did not reach the same accuracy levels as adults until they were 10 years old, and the youngest group of children tended to confuse fearful faces with sad faces. This study again shows clearly different developmental trajectories across different emotions. The ability to recognize happiness is well developed at an early age, but the ability to recognize fear and sadness develops later in childhood, and younger children tend to confuse the negative emotions.

As we saw in the previous section of this chapter, when processing facial expressions there is a tendency to rely on the configural information contained within a face, although emotional expressions may also be processed using featural information. Durand et al (2007) considered whether there were any developmental changes in the reliance on configural and featural facial information for processing facial emotion. They used both the face inversion and the composite face manipulations with participants aged 5, 7, 9 or 11 years, and adults. The results showed different developmental trajectories across the emotions. For happiness and sadness, performance was high for all age groups and showed little improvement with increasing age. By the age of 7 years, children were processing fear just as well as adults. This occurred by about 9 years for anger and by about 11 years for disgust. Although Durand and colleagues found differences across the age groups in terms of the ability to recognize the different emotions, they found the expected effects of inversion and the composite face effect for all age groups. That is, performance was reduced for all age groups when faces were inverted and when composite faces were aligned. This suggests that the reliance on configural facial information is evident from early childhood.

Some research has also shown that a child's ability to recognize facial expressions may interact with their emotional experiences. For example, Pollak and Sinha (2002) found that children who had been physically abused were more accurate at recognizing anger than children who had not been physically abused. In another study, Grinspan et al (2003) gave children training sessions to improve their ability to recognize emotional expressions. For girls, improved performance with training was associated with reduced social anxiety and increased self-worth. However, for boys, a negative relationship was found, with self-worth decreasing with improved emotion processing. Such studies are important as they show that a child's emotional experiences can influence, or be influenced by, their ability to process facial emotional expression.

3.4.2 **Decline in old age**

Relatively recently, an increasing amount of research has examined how the ability to recognize emotions changes in later life. Isaacowitz et al (2007) asked participants aged 18–85 years to identify, or label, the emotions expressed in both lexical stimuli (words) and facial stimuli. For faces, they found age differences for anger, disgust, fear and happiness; however, the effects were even more apparent for the lexical stimuli and were found for all of the emotions other than fear. This suggests that changes in the ability to process facial stimuli in later life may be stimulus-specific rather than reflecting more general changes in the ability to process emotional stimuli.

Keightley et al (2006) presented younger and older adults with faces and asked them to report the valence of the emotional expression (whether it was positive, negative or neutral). They found no differences between the two groups in terms of accuracy, but the older participants were significantly slower, especially for the negative emotional stimuli. MacPherson et al (2006) used both labelling and matching tasks with emotional faces to examine the effects of ageing on emotion processing and found that the older adults were significantly impaired only for the processing of sadness. They also found the effect with both own- and other-race faces.

A slightly more subtle test of emotion processing was conducted by Bucks et al (2008), who presented participants with ambiguous emotional faces. These were morphs that were created from a mix of 60% one emotion and 40% another. For example, one face might be 60% angry and 40% happy, whereas another might be 60% happy and 40% angry. Participants rated these faces on a 6-point Likert scale. For example, on trials where participants were shown a happy/angry face, they were asked to rate it from very happy through to very angry. Bucks et al found that there was no difference between older and younger participants in their ability to discriminate between positive and negative emotions; however, the older participants were less likely to report anger in the happy/angry faces.

Sullivan et al (2007) compared the emotion-processing abilities of younger and older participants when they were shown full face stimuli or just the eye or mouth regions of the face. The younger participants were significantly better at recognizing fear and anger. This finding is consistent with the research mentioned above, which suggests that the processing of negative emotional expressions is impaired more than that of positive emotional expressions in older people. Sullivan et al also found that the younger participants were more accurate when processing emotion from full faces or eyes alone, but there was no difference between the older and younger participants when processing the mouth region stimuli. They suggest that this finding may reflect a tendency for older participants not to examine the eye region when processing facial emotion. They supported this possibility with an eye-tracking study, in which they showed that younger participants are more likely to fixate on the eye region of the face than older participants and that, for younger participants only, the more they looked at the eyes the more accurate they were.

Other experiments have used a different emotion-processing task and asked participants to rate the emotional intensity of faces (rather than asking them to recognize or identify the emotional expression explicitly). Phillips and Allen (2004) found that older participants rated happy and sad faces as being less intense than younger participants. However, these differences could be accounted for entirely in terms of differences between the age groups in intelligence, anxiety and depression. More recently, Orgeta and Phillips (2008) examined the influence of emotional intensity on emotion recognition in older adults, using facial stimuli with either high- or low-intensity expressions. The older participants were impaired at emotion recognition for sadness, anger and fear across all intensities, but particularly at 50% intensity. However, as with the previous study, they found that these age effects were associated with the participant's general cognitive abilities. The findings from these two studies suggest that decline in older adults' abilities to process facial emotion may reflect a more general decline in cognitive ability or mood effects.

One recent study by Ebner and Johnson (2009) has suggested that previous work examining the effects of ageing on emotion processing may be limited by the tendency to use only the faces of younger people as stimuli. As we will see in Chapter 12, a wide range of own-group biases exist, including an own-age bias. It is therefore possible that the impairments in the processing of facial emotion reported in older adults may actually reflect an own-age bias. To examine this possibility, Ebner and Johnson used faces from both younger and older posers. Older participants were significantly worse than younger participants for both identifying and remembering angry faces, but this impairment was found for both older and younger stimuli. This suggests that the previous findings of age differences in which the faces of younger people were used as stimuli cannot be explained simply in terms of an own-age bias.

A small number of studies have also examined the processing of facial expression in older patients with dementia, specifically **Alzheimer's disease** (AD). Burnham and Hogervorst (2004) gave participants a range of facial emotion-processing tasks. They found that the patients with AD were able to accurately recognize facial expressions and label the emotion expressed. However, when asked to complete a matching task, they were significantly impaired. Henry et al (2008) compared the ability of three groups (patients with mild AD, older and younger control participants) to label the emotion expressed on faces using all six of the basic emotions. Unlike Burnham and Hogervorst (2004), they found that the participants with AD were impaired at labelling facial expressions for all emotions other than disgust. When labelling disgust, the patients with mild AD were just as good as the young control participants.

Garcia-Rodriguez et al (2009) examined how the ability to recognize facial emotion was influenced by giving participants a secondary interference task. When their participants completed an emotion recognition test without a secondary interference task, no difference was found between young, older healthy and older AD participants. However, although the performance of all participants was impaired by the interference task, the magnitude of this effect was far larger for participants with AD. This suggests that the detrimental effect of the interference task on emotion recognition is specific to the effects of AD rather than being a more general ageing effect.

It seems that the ability to process facial emotion does decline in later life; however, this seems to be most apparent in terms of processing negative facial expressions. Indeed, a recent meta-analysis (Ruffman et al, 2008) found that older adults are particularly impaired for the processing of anger, sadness and fear. Why do the changes in later life vary across emotions? One suggestion is that different areas of the brain age and decline at different rates and, therefore, if different emotions are processed in different parts of the brain (an issue that will be discussed in the next section), it is perhaps not unexpected that emotion processing would be differentially affected by increasing age. Indeed, this is the explanation given by Henry et al (2008) to account for disgust processing not

being affected in patients with AD. Although there is no clear evidence to support this possibility, it is discussed in a recent review by Ruffman et al (2008).

3.5 The neuropsychology of emotional expression processing

Where in the brain is facial emotion processed, and are all emotions processed in the same part of the brain? The work covered in this section will discuss various neuropsychological techniques. If you feel the need to recap on these methodologies (or learn them from scratch!) then take a quick look at the Appendix before reading this section. It is also important to note that a great deal of research has examined how neuropsychological processing of facial emotion varies in people with clinical disorders, such as depression, autism and schizophrenia. This clinical evidence is discussed in detail in Chapter 8. The work in the present section considers exclusively 'non-clinical' neuropsychological processing of facial emotion.

3.5.1 Evidence from visual field studies

Visual field studies can easily tell us about lateralization effects. Stimuli presented to the left visual field are initially processed by the right hemisphere, whereas stimuli presented to the right visual field are initially processed by the left hemisphere. Therefore, if there is a difference in performance according to the visual field of presentation, these differences are interpreted as reflecting hemispheric differences. Much of the work done in this area uses either the chimeric faces test or divided visual field paradigms to understand these hemispheric effects. There are two conflicting hypotheses concerning the lateralization of emotion processing: the **right**

hemisphere hypothesis and the **valence hypothesis**.

The right hemisphere hypothesis suggests that the processing of all facial emotions is lateralized to the right hemisphere. This theory has received a great deal of support, especially from studies using the chimeric faces test. A left visual field (right hemisphere) bias has been reported in a large number of studies using positive-emotion chimeric stimuli (e.g. Bourne, 2005, 2008; Compton et al, 2003; Heath et al, 2005; Levy et al, 1983). However, to test the right hemisphere hypothesis properly, it is necessary to show this visual field bias for both positive and negative emotions. Such evidence is easily available. For example, a left visual field bias has been shown for happy and angry chimeras (Ashwin et al, 2005); happy, surprised, sad and angry chimeras (Christman and Hackworth, 1993); and chimeras expressing positive and negative affect (Drebing et al, 1997). The claim that this left visual field bias arises from right hemisphere dominance is supported by evidence from studies of patients who have unilateral brain lesions. Two studies (Bava et al, 2005; Kucharska-Pietura & David, 2003) have shown that patients with left hemisphere lesions show the same left visual field bias as control participants, whereas patients with right hemisphere lesions show no clear visual field bias.

The right hemisphere hypothesis has also been supported by divided visual field studies. A number of studies have shown a left visual field bias for processing facial emotion (e.g. Anes and Kruer, 2004; Basu and Mandal, 2004; Natale et al, 1983; Schweinberger et al, 2003). A recent study by Alves et al (2009) examined different patterns of visual field bias for processing neutral faces and faces expressing happiness, fear, sadness and surprise. They presented two faces in each trial, one to each visual field. The participant's task was to decide to which visual field a target emotion (i.e. one that they had been told to specifically look out for) had been presented. There was a significant left visual field bias for the processing of both happiness and fear. Alves and colleagues also found that there was an overall left visual field bias for processing

emotive faces, but a right visual field bias for processing neutral faces. However, the finding of a left visual field bias for both positive and negative emotions provides support for the right hemisphere hypothesis.

Although the right hemisphere hypothesis seems to have a great deal of support, there is an alternative proposal: the valence hypothesis. This suggests that the processing of positive emotions is lateralized to the left hemisphere, whereas the processing of negative emotions is lateralized to the right hemisphere (Davidson, 1992). These different patterns of lateralization for positive and negative facial emotion have been shown using the chimeric faces test (Adolphs et al, 2001; Jansari et al, 2000), although some have found this pattern only in female participants (Rodway et al, 2003).

Although there is some evidence for the valence hypothesis, the vast majority of the research in this area provides stronger support for the right hemisphere hypothesis. A recent study, which used the chimeric faces test with all six of the basic emotions, directly compared these two hypotheses (Bourne, in press). Bourne found a significant left visual field bias for all six emotions, supporting the right hemisphere hypothesis. However, she did find significant differences in the strength of lateralization across the different emotions. When grouped according to valence, the positive emotions were found to be more strongly lateralized than the negative emotions. Thus, although all emotions may be lateralized to the right hemisphere, this does not necessarily mean that all emotions are processed in exactly the same way or in the same part of the right hemisphere. We shall learn more about this in the next two sections of this chapter.

3.5.2 Evidence from electrophysiological studies

Event-related potentials (ERPs) show us how the brain responds to stimuli by measuring the electrical activity that occurs when a task is completed. In Chapter 9, we will talk a great deal about how there are various ERP responses to faces in terms of processing facial identity, and we will see that there are four main components. The P100 reflects the initial perception of a facial stimulus, the N170 reflects the structural encoding of a face, the N250 reflects the recognition of an individual and the N400 reflects the processing of semantic information associated with that individual (see Chapter 9 for full details).

In terms of processing facial emotion, the main debate centres around the **N170**: is it sensitive to emotional expression and does it respond differently to different emotional expressions? Most of the work on the N170 suggests that it is involved in the structural encoding of a face. If you look back at the Bruce and Young (1986) model, and earlier in this chapter, you will remember that the structural encoding of a face is supposed to occur before any processing of either identity or emotional expression. On this basis, it would be assumed that the N170 should not be affected by emotional expression. A number of studies have shown exactly that (e.g. Bobes et al, 2000; Eimer and Holmes, 2002; Halgren et al, 2000; Herrmann et al, 2002; Krolak-Salmon et al, 2001; Münte et al,

1998). However, more recently there has been an increasing amount of evidence suggesting that the N170 is sensitive to emotional expression.

A number of studies have specifically examined the processing of faces expressing fear and have shown that the N170 response is larger for fearful faces than for neutral faces (Blau et al, 2007; Campanella et al, 2002; Eimer and Holmes, 2002) (Fig. 3.5). This suggests that the N170 is sensitive to the emotional content of a face, or, at least, that it is sensitive to fear. It also suggests that the emotional expression of a face is processed very rapidly, within 200 ms of seeing a face. This is also supported by a study showing an enhanced N170 to fearful faces that had been presented subliminally to participants (Pegna et al, 2008).

Although such research suggests that the N170 is sensitive to fear, this addresses only part of the question. It is important to also consider whether the N170 is enhanced for other emotional expressions and whether the magnitude of this enhancement is the same for all facial emotions. Batty and Taylor (2003) examined ERPs for the processing of all six of the basic emotions. They found that the N170 occurred significantly earlier

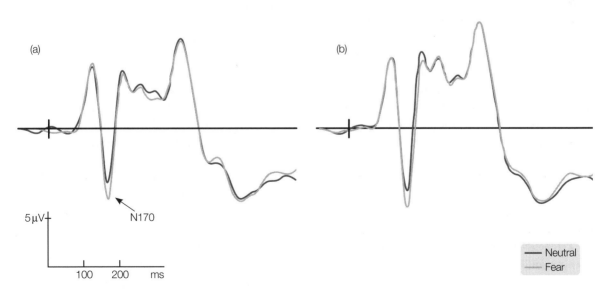

FIGURE 3.5 Demonstration of a larger N170 for faces expressing fear than for neutral faces. (a) Left and (b) right occipitotemporal response. (From Blau et al, 2007)

for positive emotions than for negative emotions. They also found that the N170 was larger in response to fearful faces than to surprised and neutral faces. This suggests that the N170 may be sensitive to the different emotions.

Sprengelmeyer and Jentzch (2006) examined the processing of anger, disgust and fear; however, they also manipulated the intensity of the emotional expression. Faces were presented containing 50% (low intensity), 100% (prototypical) or 150% (caricatured) of the emotional expression. They found no difference in the N170 across the different emotions, but the N170 was larger when the emotional content was more intense. This relationship was particularly evident around the parietal area. This finding suggests that the N170 may not distinguish between different emotions, but that it is sensitive to the intensity of the emotion being displayed on the face. This has been replicated by Utama et al (2009), who used more levels of intensity with happy and disgusted faces. However, Leppänen et al (2007) conducted a similar study and found that the N170 varied according to intensity for fearful faces, but not for happy faces. Consequently it is still relatively unclear how the N170 may be influenced by emotional expression.

Morel et al (2009) showed participants neutral, happy and fearful faces, with each face shown twice. They found that the N170 was larger for the emotive faces than for the neutral face, but only on the first occasion that a face was presented. On the second presentation there was no difference between the neutral and emotive faces. They also found that this effect was slightly more obvious in the left hemisphere than in the right hemisphere (Fig. 3.6). The finding that the N170 is sensitive to emotional expression on only the first presentation of a face may explain why some other studies have failed to find a difference, if they used the same stimuli repeatedly.

Ashley et al (2004) looked at whether there was any interaction between the emotional expression on a face and the face's orientation (upright or inverted). They showed participants neutral,

happy, fearful and disgusted faces. In terms of the N170, there were no overall differences between the emotions, but there was an interaction between emotion and orientation. There was no difference between the four conditions when the faces were upright, but when inverted the neutral faces had the largest response, fearful faces had a slightly smaller response, and happy and disgusted faces had the smallest N170. They found even larger effects in the later ERP components. The P200 was larger for fear than for the other emotions, and the late positive component (LPC) was significantly smaller for disgust at around 300 ms over the right occipital lobe. For inverted faces, the LPC was larger for all of the emotive faces in comparison with the neutral faces.

It still seems relatively unclear how the N170 is influenced by facial emotional expression. There is some evidence that it is at least sensitive to the presence or absence or emotion within a face, or to the intensity of emotional expression. It is less clear whether the N170 differs across emotions, although the strongest evidence comes from an enhanced N170 to faces expressing fear.

3.5.3 Evidence from neuroimaging studies

Haxby et al (2000) proposed a neural model of face processing based on a wide range of neuroimaging studies (for full details see Chapter 9). It contains two systems: the core system, which processes the invariant aspects of a face; and the extended system, which processes the variable aspects. One component of the extended system is the processing of facial emotional expression. According to Haxby, the core system is located mainly in the inferior occipital gyri, the superior temporal sulcus and the fusiform gyrus. The extended system is more widely distributed, with the processing of facial emotion occurring within the **limbic system**, particularly in the amygdala, and the insula which lies in the sulcus between the parietal and temporal lobes.

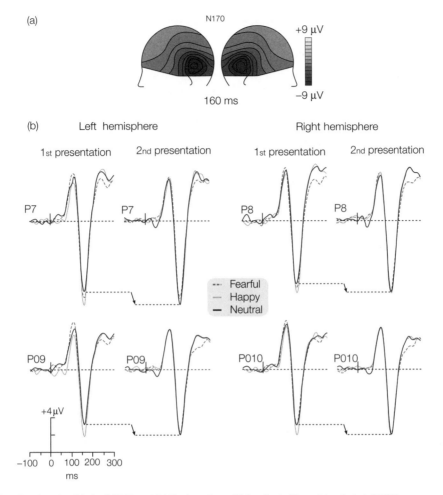

FIGURE 3.6 Graphs showing (b) the N170 and (a) the location of this effect. (From Morel et al, 2009)

Although the fusiform gyrus, often referred to as the **fusiform face area** (FFA), is considered to be part of the core face-processing system, there is some evidence for this area being sensitive to facial emotion. For example, activation in the FFA is higher when processing fearful faces than neutral faces (e.g. Breiter et al, 1996; Morris et al, 1996, 1998; Pessoa et al, 2002; Vuilleumier et al, 2001) and also higher when processing happy faces than neutral faces (e.g. Breiter et al, 1996). Engell and Haxby (2007) asked participants to view faces expressing anger, disgust, fear, surprise or a neutral expression. For all of these emotions, the FFA was more activated when viewing emotive faces than neutral faces; however, there was also activation in other areas of the core system—the inferior occipital gyrus and the superior temporal sulcus. Surguladze et al (2003) examined whether the intensity of emotional expression might influence FFA activation. Participants were shown fearful, disgusted, happy and sad faces with either mild or high intensity of expression. FFA activation was greater for the high-intensity emotions, regardless of the emotion being expressed.

Although there is some evidence for the core system being sensitive to facial emotion, the majority of the research in this area has specifically examined the role of the amygdala. Much of this work was initially inspired by research on patients with damage to the amygdala who showed significantly impaired fear recognition (e.g. Adolphs et al, 1994; Calder et al, 1996). The fMRI research examining the processing of facial emotional expression in participants with no brain damage has largely supported this clinical work, although it has shown that the amygdala may be involved in processing more emotions than just fear.

Fitzgerald et al (2006) showed participants angry, disgusted, fearful, happy, sad and neutral faces, and found significant activation in the left amygdala for all of the emotive conditions (Fig. 3.7/Plate 3.7). The amygdala has also been found to respond to dynamic emotional faces. van der Gaag's (2007) participants viewed movies of faces showing disgust, fear, happiness or a neutral

expression, and then performed three different tasks: passively viewing the face; matching the emotion expressed to another stimulus; or inspecting the face to be able to imitate the emotional expression. The amygdala responded to all of the emotional expressions across all three of the tasks. This provides further evidence for the amygdala being important for the processing of facial emotion. Sergerie et al (2008) recently conducted a meta-analysis of fMRI studies looking at the role of the amygdala in the processing of emotion with a wide range of different stimuli. They found that the amygdala responds to both positive and negative stimuli, and particularly facial emotion.

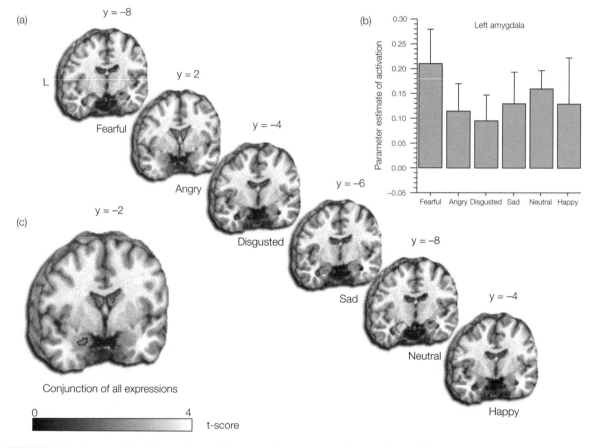

FIGURE 3.7 Left amygdala activation for participants viewing emotive and neutral faces. (a) Location of activation for each emotion; (b) amount of activation in the left amygdala for each emotion; and (c) location of activation when combining all of the emotional expressions. (From Fitzgerald et al, 2006). Please see colour plate section.

The emotional content of a face has also been shown to cause activation in the amygdala when the emotional expression is not relevant to the processing of a face. Two studies (Gur et al, 2002; Habel et al, 2007) showed participants faces expressing anger, disgust, fear, happiness or sadness. In one condition participants were asked to judge the emotional expression (explicit processing), whereas in the other condition they were asked to judge the age of the face (implicit processing). Both experiments found strong activation in the amygdala for the emotion-processing task. For the age judgement task, where the emotional expression was totally irrelevant, there was activation in the amygdala, although it was less apparent than in the emotion task (Fig. 3.8/Plate 3.8). These findings provide strong support for the role of the amygdala in processing facial emotion.

Although the amygdala is clearly very important for the processing of facial emotion, it is by no means the only area of the brain implicated in the processing of emotional expression. As we saw earlier in this section, various areas of the core face-processing system have been found to be sensitive to facial emotion. Another part of the brain that has been examined is the **insula**. A number of studies have shown that the insula is specifically activated when processing facial expressions of

disgust (e.g. Calder et al, 2001; Krolak-Salmon et al, 2003; Phillips et al, 1997, 2004; Sprengelmeyer et al, 1998). It has also been suggested that there may be an anatomical double dissociation between the processing of fear and disgust, with some studies finding unique activation in the amygdala for fear and unique activation in the insula for disgust (Malhi et al, 2007; Phillips et al, 2004).

3.6 **Conclusion**

The ability to recognize facial emotional expressions accurately is vitally important in order to interact with other people. It seems that this ability is relatively universal across a range of different cultures, and consequently it may be innate. It is rather less clear how the processing of facial emotion interacts with the processing of other information that can be gained from inspecting a face. Research examining the interaction between the processing of identity and emotion has not yet produced a clear answer to this question: although the behavioural evidence suggests that there is an interaction, the neuropsychological evidence is less convincing.

This lack of clarity in the evidence raises a really important point to bear in mind when evaluating evidence about the processing of faces. There is such a wide range of information that can be extracted from a face: to what extent is it possible to separate out these different processes? To date, most research has examined the interaction between emotion and identity, but there are other forms of information that may also interact with one, or even both, of these processes. When we look at a face, we also process its sex, attractiveness, race and age, and we may extract more semantic information such as assigning

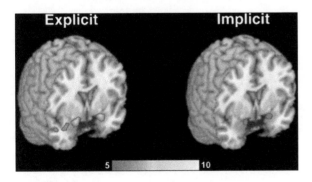

FIGURE 3.8 Amygdala activation when explicitly and implicitly processing facial emotion. (From Habel et al, 2007). Please see colour plate section.

potential personality traits to the person. It is easy to imagine that all of these may interact with the processing of facial emotion.

The capabilities of electrophysiological and neuroimaging techniques have progressed rapidly over the past decade or so, and further improvements are constantly being made to these methodologies. It is perhaps in this area of research that we may be able to tease apart the various processes that occur when viewing a face. Such work will help us to understand further not only the processing of facial emotion, but also how it is integrated into the wider processing of facial information.

SUMMARY

- There are thought to be six basic or universal emotions: anger, disgust, fear, happiness, sadness and surprise. The ability to express and perceive these emotions has been found in both literate and preliterate cultures, which suggests that the processing of these emotions is innate. Some variability across cultures has been reported, however.

- Although the traditional models of face processing suggest that the processing of identity and emotional expression should be independent, more recent research does not necessarily support this. The behavioural evidence strongly suggests that they interact; however, the neuropsychological evidence is less clear and provides some evidence for independence.

- The use of configural and featural facial information for the processing of facial emotional expression is comparable to the use of these types of information for the processing of facial identity.

- There are age-associated changes in the ability to recognize the different emotions. Happiness can be recognized with high accuracy from a very young age and late into old age. In contrast, the processing of negative emotions takes time to develop through childhood and then shows the most apparent decline in old age.

- The neuropsychological processing of facial emotion is thought to occur mainly in the right hemisphere, primarily in the fusiform area, and the amygdala. The processing of facial emotion begins around 200 ms after an emotional stimulus has been presented.

FURTHER READING

Calder, A. J. & Young, A. W. (2005). *Understanding facial identity and facial expression recognition.* Nature Neuroscience Reviews, 6: 641–653. This paper tackles the debate about whether or not the processing of facial identity and expression are independent or not. It provides a comprehensive review of the work in this area; the authors conclude that there is some degree of independence, but that there is also evidence for interactions between the processing of identity and emotional expression.

Elfenbein, H. A., & Ambady, N. (2003). *Universals and cultural differences in recognizing emotions*. Current Directions in Psychological Science, 12(5): 159–164. This paper is a recent review of the research examining whether the recognition of facial emotion is universal across all cultures or whether there is variability. It is particularly interesting as it suggests that both might be true.

Ruffman, T., Henry, J. D., Livingstone, V., & Phillips, L. H. (2008). *A meta-analytic review of emotion recognition and aging: implications for neuropsychological models of aging*. Neuroscience and Biobehavioral Reviews, 32(4): 863–881. This is a meta-analysis paper, taking the findings from a large number of studies and then looking at them in combination to see what the overall findings are from these sources. As well as considering the recognition of facial emotion, it also looks at the recognition of emotion from voices and bodies.

Vuilleumier, P., & Pourtois, G. (2007). *Distributed and interactive brain mechanisms during emotion face perception: evidence from functional neuroimaging.* Neuropsychologia, 45(1): 174–194. This is an excellent review of the neuropsychological evidence about the processing of facial emotion. It is particularly nice as it covers a range of methodologies including single-cell recordings from monkeys, fMRI and ERP evidence.

FACES AS SOCIAL STIMULI

Faces are vitally important for social interaction. The processing of individual identity and emotional expression are such important aspects in this respect that they account for most of this book, but there are other types of information that we glean from faces too. We can readily determine a person's age and gender from their faces, and facial appearance is an important factor in whether we find them attractive.

We also pick up cues from their face that indicate whether they are genetically related to us. Other people's gaze direction serves as a guide to where we should allocate our own attention, and we use their lip movements as an aid to comprehending what they are saying. This chapter will briefly cover each of these topics, and review what we know about how the processing of these facial attributes is achieved.

4.1 Perception of gaze direction, and 'social attention'

A great deal of evidence suggests we are sensitive to where others are looking. We notice whether they are looking at us and, if they are looking somewhere else, we use that as a cue to shift our attention to look at the same thing (for reviews see Emery [2000] and Langton et al [2000]). As Langton (2000) points out, sensitivity to others' gaze direction probably has strong survival benefits: if someone is staring at you, it might be because you are a potential mate, enemy or prey; and if someone abruptly looks elsewhere, it might be because they have detected something that you haven't (a predator, an attractive conspecific, or a precariously balanced large boulder above your head, for example). Gaze also serves communicative functions, for example signalling turn-taking in conversation, and indicating the

referent of a remark (e.g. signalling which one of a number of things you are talking about by means of looking at the thing in question). In fact, probably because of its importance, other people's gaze direction is very difficult to ignore (e.g. Driver et al, 1999; Friesen and Kingstone, 1998; Friesen et al, 2005; Langton and Bruce, 1999), although recent research suggests that this might be true only when the person's face is at the centre of our attention (Burton et al, 2009).

Laboratory-based evidence that our allocation of attention is highly influenced by other people's eye gaze comes from experiments based on **Posner's (1980) cueing paradigm**. This involves responding as quickly as possible to a stimulus that appears on one side of the computer screen or the other. A cue also appears on one side of the screen or the other, shortly before the stimulus is displayed. This cue does not predict on which side the stimulus will appear, but, nevertheless, responses are quicker for trials in which the cue and stimulus occur on the same side, compared with those in which the cue appears on the opposite side to the stimulus. Given that the cues do not predict the location of the stimuli, these orienting effects imply that this attentional system is quite automatic and reflexive in nature. Pictures of faces that are looking in one direction or another function as effective cues in this paradigm (e.g. Driver et al, 1999; Langton, 2000), and are hard to ignore even if they are counter-predictive (i.e. if a face oriented to the right predicts that a stimulus will appear on the left, and vice versa; see Kuhn and Kingstone, 2009). However, cueing effects are by no means confined to faces, as similar effects are obtained with other cues such as arrows (although see Greene et al [2009] for a demonstration of some differences in the neural responses to facial and non-facial cues in the Posner paradigm).

These laboratory studies have all used static, two-dimensional and often schematic faces as their stimuli. As an advocate of **cognitive ethology**,[1] Kingstone (2009) has argued that laboratory studies have opted for impoverished stimuli in the bid for good experimental control, but as a consequence tend to fail to do justice to the rich and sophisticated way in which social attention is influenced in real life. For example, in laboratory experiments using Posner's cueing paradigm, arrows and eyes have similar influences on participants' allocation of attention. However, this is not true for real-world scenes. Birmingham et al (2009) recorded participants' fixation patterns to photographs of naturalistic scenes containing people and arrows (such as on street signs). When people were present in the scene, most of the fixations went to the eyes and very few to the

arrows. Their first fixation was also most likely to be on the eyes, head, or any text that was in the scene. Arrows were not particularly salient even when there were no people in the scene. Birmingham and colleagues claim that their results are consistent with the idea that there are brain mechanisms that are preferentially biased to processing eyes. They conclude that eyes and arrows are not equivalent social cues except in the artificial confines of Posner's cueing experiment.

A fascinating investigation of social attention in more naturalistic settings can be found in a series of studies by a psychologist who is also a magician, Gustav Kuhn. Magicians routinely use misdirection to control the audience's allocation of attention. As Kuhn has explained, a fundamental principle of magic is: 'If you want the audience to look at you, look at them; if you want the audience to look at something else, look at it' (Kuhn et al, 2008). Kuhn's basic technique is to perform magic tricks in various ways, and investigate the effects on the audience's looking behaviour (measured in terms of their eye movements, or in terms of how many of them notice the deception that forms the basis of the magician's trick). For example, misleading looking behaviour (such as looking at one hand in order to divert attention away from what the other hand is doing) can be compared to this action combined with hand-waving (a low-level cue that in itself attracts attention), in order to see how gaze direction and low-level attentional cues interact. These studies are a compelling demonstration of the power of magicians to control where the audience look during a trick, largely by virtue of where the magician looks themselves (Kuhn and Land, 2006; Kuhn et al, 2009).

---

[1] Ethology is the scientific study of animal behaviour under natural conditions, so, by analogy, cognitive ethology is the study of cognition in real-life conditions. Kingstone's arguments for looking at 'cognition in the wild' echo the criticisms of behaviourism made by ethologists in the 1960s and 1970s. The ethologists claimed that many of the conclusions about animal learning were valid only under the artificial and impoverished conditions of the laboratory. It could be argued that much of the 'applied' research on face recognition is in the spirit of cognitive ethology; see Chapters 11, 12 and 13.

4.1.1 **Models of gaze processing**

Two particularly influential models of gaze processing have been those of Baron-Cohen (e.g. Baron-Cohen, 1994, 1995) and Perrett et al, (1992). Baron-Cohen has suggested that social attention is part of a **mind-reading** system which enables us to make attributions about others' mental states. This has four modules. The earliest to develop are the **intentionality detector (ID)**, a primitive mechanism that interprets self-initiated motion as being goal-driven, and the **eye-direction detector (EDD)**, that detects the direction of another person's gaze, based on the position of the iris, and attributes the mental state of 'seeing' to the eyes' owner. By about 9 months, both of these systems are claimed to be fully operational: the infant can interpret another person's behaviour in terms of their goals and desires, and understands that they can see the things to which their eyes are directed. The **shared-attention mechanism (SAM)** develops between 9 and 18 months, and links the ID and EDD. It identifies when the infant and another person are attending to the same thing. This leads to the development, between 18 and 48 months, of the **Theory of Mind mechanism (TOMM)**. The TOMM enables the child to infer someone's mental state from their observable behaviour, and allows the child to create a theory by which other people's behaviour can be predicted and explained. Baron-Cohen claims that the ability to detect eyes and their direction (the EDD) is highly important in the development of Theory of Mind.

Perrett and colleagues (1992) have argued that we do more than merely detect the position of the eyes, as Baron-Cohen suggests. They hypothesize that we might have a **direction-of-attention detector**. This calculates where someone else is looking by combining information from separate detectors that analyse the direction of their eyes, head and body. These detectors are arranged hierarchically, so that eye gaze takes precedence over head orientation, which in turn counts for more than body orientation. This is achieved by having inhibitory connections between the systems; for example, if the head is looking down but the eyes are looking up, the information about head direction is suppressed in favour of the information about eye direction. However, if the eyes are not visible because the person is too far away or their face is obscured, the system will use head orientation to judge the person's direction of attention. If the head is obscured, body orientation is used instead. As we shall see, subsequent studies have suggested that, when both eyes and head are visible, information about both of them is combined, rather than information about head orientation being suppressed.

4.1.2 **How do we know where others are looking?**

To be able to know where someone else is looking, we need to look at the position of their eyes and detect very small differences in pupil position. It has been noted that the marked difference in pigmentation between the sclera (the white of the eye) and the pupil and iris might help in this (Kobayashi and Kohshima, 1997, 2001). Interestingly this is not a trait we share with any of our primate relatives.[2] Watt (1999, cited in Langton et al, 2000) suggested that a simple way of estimating eye position would be for the visual system to compare the reflectance of the parts of the sclera either side

---

[2] In Chapter 1, we suggested that the salience of the pupils might provide an easily detectable metric that would be useful in identity processing. The pupil/sclera contrast could be the outcome of natural selection for both functions (i.e. as an aid to recognition as well as an aid to knowing where someone else is looking, both of which are very important to us as social animals). The puzzle is why it is not apparent in our equally sociable primate cousins.

of the pupil. If the luminance is approximately equal, the person is looking ahead. If the eye moves to the right, the left part of the sclera will produce a stronger luminance signal than the right (and vice versa if the eye moves to the left).

However, the **Wollaston illusion** (Wollaston, 1824; Fig. 4.1) suggests that the processing of gaze direction involves more than simply registering eye position: when judging gaze direction, we take head orientation into account as well. The same eye region seems to face in different directions, depending on the orientation of the head.

Langton (2000) showed participants photographs of heads in which the eyes faced in various directions and asked them to respond as quickly as possible to eye orientation (trying to ignore the head), or vice versa. Sometimes the head and eyes were congruent with respect to orientation (such as when they both faced left, or both faced upwards). On other trials the head and eyes were facing in different directions (such as when the eyes faced to the right but the head was facing to the left, or when the eyes were looking upwards but the head was oriented downwards). Response times

were faster when head orientation and eye direction were congruent than when they were incongruent. Thus, contrary to Perrett et al's model, information about head position is not suppressed when gaze information is available: instead the information from both sources seems to be combined in some way.

4.1.3 The role of the superior temporal sulcus in gaze processing

Perrett et al's (1992) model was based on data obtained from studies recording from responses of single cells in the **superior temporal sulcus (STS)** in monkey inferotemporal cortex. This region seems to be particularly involved in processing information about face viewpoint and gaze direction. Most of the neurones in the anterior part of the monkey STS seem to be selective for face view (Perret et al, 1991), and there are also neurones tuned to specific gaze directions (Perrett et al, 1992). Bilateral removal of the STS can specifically impair gaze perception (Heywood and Cowey, 1992), and, in an imaging study in humans, Hoffman and Haxby (2000) showed that attending to gaze direction activates the STS more strongly than attending to face identity. A functional magnetic resonance imaging (fMRI) study by Engell and Haxby (2007) found evidence of distinct, but overlapping, populations of neurones in the right STS that respond most strongly to expressive faces (showing anger, disgust, fear or surprise), averted gaze, or both; they speculate that their findings might represent the existence of an area in the STS that integrates information about expression and gaze direction. There is evidence of a **double dissociation**[3] between the processing of identity and gaze: Campbell et al (1990) described a patient who was severely impaired at recognizing faces, but relatively unimpaired at gaze

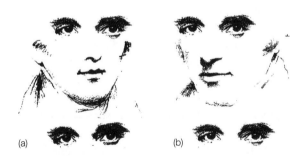

(a) (b)

FIGURE 4.1 Wollaston's (1824) demonstration that head orientation affects perceived gaze direction. The eyes are identical in both images, but (a) appears to look to your right whereas (b) looks straight at you. (From Wollaston, 1824)

---

[3] A double dissociation is strong evidence that two processes are handled independently by the brain; see Chapter 9 for a full explanation.

processing, whereas Perrett, Hietanen, Oram and Benson (1992) described a case with the opposite symptoms (unimpaired at recognizing famous faces, but markedly impaired at gaze processing). Overall, the data suggest that there might be a functionally independent 'gaze detection module' located in the STS.

Bi and colleagues (2009) have recently produced data from humans that are consistent with Perrett et al's model. Bi and colleagues investigated how gaze direction affects the strength of the **face viewpoint after-effect** (see Chapter 2 for more discussion of the face after-effect). After a few seconds of exposure to a face pointing in one direction, a forward-looking face appears to be oriented in the opposite direction. This after-effect occurs regardless of whether the face is upright or upside-down, and is reduced only a little by changing the identity of the face between adaptation and test. However, Bi et al found that if the adapting face pointed in one direction but its eyes remained directed towards the viewer (so that head and eye orientation did not match), the viewpoint after-effect was reduced by about a third—but only if the faces were upright. As Bi and co-workers point out, this reduction is far greater than that produced by changing the identity of the face between adaptation and test.

Bi et al argue that the face viewpoint after-effect is based on selective adaptation of neurones in the STS. The normally strong transfer of the viewpoint after-effect between different people's faces is due to the fact that the STS neurones are generally not sensitive to face identity. The effect of gaze direction on the strength of the after-effect could be explained in two ways. One possibility is that both face viewpoint and gaze direction are processed in the STS. Normally both contribute to the face viewpoint after-effect, but in the present experiment, gaze direction was the same in both the adapting and test stimuli, so only face viewpoint adaptation contributed to the overall effect. Another possibility is that neuronal responses to a face view could be affected by gaze direction; in this case the effect took the form of enhancement, partially counteracting the face view adaptation effect and thus leading to a weaker illusion overall. Bi and colleagues suggest that inversion abolishes the effect because sensitivity to gaze direction is greatly impaired by face inversion; this might lead to less gaze direction-specific adaptation and hence less modulation of the viewpoint after-effect.

4.1.4 The development of gaze processing

Even very young infants show some sensitivity to other people's gaze. Newborns prefer to look at a photograph of a woman with open eyes rather than closed eyes (Batki et al, 2000), and prefer to look at a face with eye gaze that is directed toward them rather than averted away from them (Farroni et al, 2002). Compared to adults, infant preferences may be more influenced by head orientation than eye direction, but nevertheless other people's gaze direction is very important to us from very early on in life (reviews in Doherty et al, 2009; Hoehl et al, 2009). Hoehl et al (2009) conclude that processing the relationship between another person's gaze and an object does not develop until about 3–4 months of age, but thereafter infants use it as a means by which to learn about their environment: looking at where adults look is a potentially effective way of discovering which aspects of the surroundings are most worth attending to.

Doherty et al (2009) tested 2–4-year-olds' ability to judge where someone was looking, in schematic drawings, photographs and real life. They suggest that the ability to judge explicitly what someone else is looking at appears at around 3 years of age. Development of fine-grained gaze judgement was gradual, from chance at 3 years to near adult-like performance at 6 years. Doherty (Doherty, 2006; Doherty et al, 2009) suggests that there are two separate gaze perception systems: a crude one that is present from birth (perhaps based on Watt's luminance mechanism), and a more fine-grained one that emerges at about the age of 3 years (possibly as a consequence of an increasing interest in others' mental states) and then develops slowly from then on. Hoehl et al (2009) also discuss the possibility that the development of gaze perception is handled by different neural systems at different ages; for example, they suggest that the neonatal preference for direct eye gaze might be handled by a subcortical pathway, with the STS supplanting this from 3–4 months of age onwards.

4.2 Age perception

Age is one of the most important attributes of a face. Age estimates are useful to the police, because people are most likely to mention gender and age when describing a face. Many countries have legally enforced age limits for selling alcohol and cigarettes, and prohibitions on having sex with minors. Thus, it is important to know how well people can judge age, and what cues they use in order to do it. It is also important to know how an *individual* face is changed by age. Passport officials are required to recognize someone from their passport photograph even if the passport was issued a long time ago. There are no data on how reliably this can be done. (This is possibly especially problematic in the case of children's passports, as a child's face can change a great deal during the time their passport is valid.) For missing persons investigators who are trying to track down someone who disappeared a long time ago, it would be useful to know what that person might look like now, especially if they disappeared when they were a child. However, despite its importance, age processing has received comparatively little attention by researchers. Space precludes a

detailed discussion of age perception here, so we will confine ourselves to talking about how well people can estimate the age of unfamiliar faces, rather than the effects of age-related facial changes on individual recognition. See M. G. Rhodes (2009) for a review of psychological research on age estimation, and Ramanathan et al (2009) for a review of computer science approaches to modelling the effects of age on faces.

4.2.1 Laboratory studies of age estimation

What information do we extract from a face in order to judge its age? Early research by Pittenger, Mark, Shaw and colleagues (e.g. Mark and Todd, 1983, 1985; Pittenger and Shaw, 1975; Pittenger et al, 1979) focused on head shape, which varies markedly from infancy through to adulthood (Fig. 4.2).

A baby's face is bunched up in the lower part of the head, beneath a large forehead. Compared to an adult, it has large eyes, a small nose and a small chin. By adulthood, the face occupies a much larger proportion of the head. These changes in head shape can be simulated by a mathematical transformation called **cardioidal strain**.

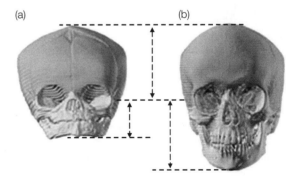

FIGURE 4.2 Craniofacial differences between (a) a newborn and (b) an adult. The newborn's skull has been enlarged to facilitate comparison with the adult's. With increasing age, the face greatly increases in size compared with the cranial vault above it. (From Dal Martello and Maloney, 2006)

Pittenger and his colleagues produced line-drawn profiles that were subjected to varying degrees of cardioidal strain, and asked their participants to rank-order them in terms of apparent age (Fig. 4.3). By this means, they demonstrated that cardioidal strain was a sufficient cue for reliable age estimation.

Subsequent research has shown that **pseudo-cardioidal strain** also affects age estimates: simply moving the internal facial features upwards in a face makes it appear older, and moving them downwards makes it look younger (Bruce et al, 1991; George and Hole, 1995). More recently, Ramanathan and Chellappa (2006) produced a computational model to simulate the facial changes produced by growth. This uses a slightly modified version of the cardioidal strain transformation, whose effects on the face are constrained by normative anthropological data on how face proportions change with age. Figure 4.4 shows some of the results of applying this transformation to children's faces. As you can see, the model's predictions of how the children

would look when they were older are generally quite similar to those children's actual appearance at that age, despite the model's failure to take into account age-related changes in 'puppy fat', skin texture and coloration.

Cardioidal strain is by no means the only cue to age, however. Firstly, it can only be used while the cranium is growing (through childhood and adolescence). As we can estimate the age of unfamiliar adult faces with a high degree of accuracy (Burt and Perrett, 1995; George and Hole, 1995, 2000), there must be other cues that we can use. Secondly, age estimation remains accurate if cardioidal strain is made difficult to extract (for example, by cropping the face so that it consists only of the internal facial features; George and Hole, 1995). It turns out that there are many cues to age, and that we are adept at using any or all of them. (For reviews of age-related facial changes, see Enlow [1982] and Coleman and Grover [2006]. They make depressing reading for anyone over the age of 30.) Accurate age estimation can be achieved on the basis of pigmentation changes in the skin and hair (Burt and Perrett, 1995) and changes to surface texture (such as wrinkling and creasing; George and Hole, 2000; Mark et al, 1980; Montepare and McArthur, 1986), as well as structural changes (such as sagging, due to a decrease in skin elasticity and muscle tone; George and Hole, 2000). Figure 4.5 shows seven composite faces of different ages, produced by Burt and Perrett (1995). Each image was constructed by taking a set of 12 colour photographs of men in that age band, distorting ('warping') each of them to the average shape for that age range, and then taking the average of their colour information. Even in black and white, these seem to do a fairly good job of capturing the age changes that occur through adulthood.

In general, age estimates are to within three years or so of the true age (M. G. Rhodes, 2009), which is remarkable considering that people's physiological and chronological ages do not necessarily correspond closely (some people look older than they really are, and vice versa).

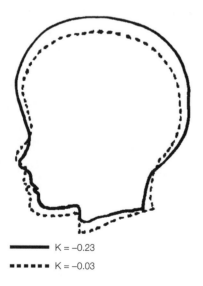

K = −0.23

K = −0.03

FIGURE 4.3 Effects on apparent age of a mathematical transformation called 'cardioidal strain'. A higher strain level (shown by the unbroken line) makes the head profile look younger. (Redrawn from Pittenger and Shaw, 1975)

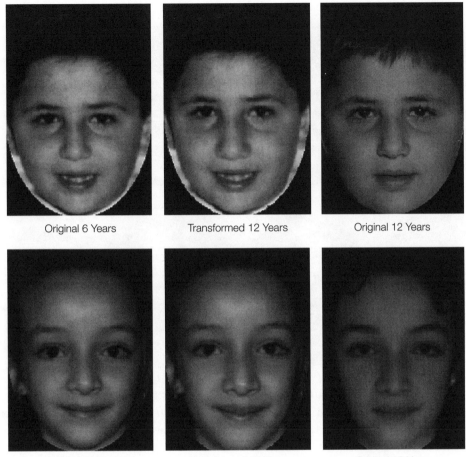

| Original 6 Years | Transformed 12 Years | Original 12 Years |

| Original 8 Years | Transformed 12 Years | Original 12 Years |

FIGURE 4.4 Effects of applying a modified cardioidal strain transformation to 'age' children's faces. (From Ramanathan and Chellappa, 2006)

Manipulations that seriously affect face recognition (inversion [Chapter 2, section 2.3.1] and photographic negation [section 2.2.1]) have very little effect on age-estimation performance (George and Hole, 2000). In fact, George and Hole showed that performance deteriorated markedly only when both configural ('shape') and textural ('surface') information were removed simultaneously (in faces that were negated, blurred, inverted *and* then cropped to reveal only their internal features!). Thus, configural *or* textural information can be enough to permit accurate age perception. This is not to say that these manipulations have no effect at all on age estimates: both Burt and Perrett (1995) and George and Hole (1995, 2000) found that blurring reduced the apparent age of adult faces, an effect that was more pronounced with older faces. This has long been known to photographers: the apparent youthfulness of many an ageing Hollywood star has been maintained by the judicious application of Vaseline to the camera lens in order to defocus the image!

A recent study by Nkengne et al (2008) has drawn attention to the importance of skin cues plus the perceiver's own characteristics as factors affecting the apparent age of women's faces. Rather than manipulate cues to age,

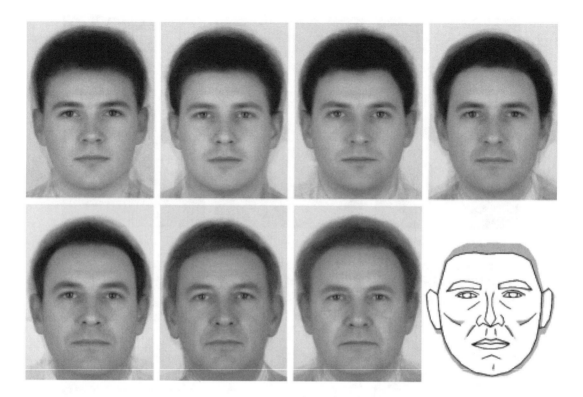

FIGURE 4.5 Face blends. Each is an average of the shape and colour information from a number of faces within the same 5-year age band. From top left to bottom right: 20–24, 25–29, 30–34, 35–39, 40–44, 45–49 and 50–54 years. Bottom right: shaded regions show the differences between the 25–29- and 50–54-year-old average faces. (From Burt and Perrett, 1995)

Nkengne and co-workers simply showed colour photographs of Caucasian women's faces to participants and asked them to estimate each face's age. Each face was also rated on various physical dimensions by a 'trained investigator'. A statistical technique (multiple regression) was then used to see which physical attributes of the faces best predicted the age estimates. The main predictors of perceived age were the eye region (crow's feet, wrinkles and bags), the lips (volume and definition) and skin colour uniformity. However, the relative importance of these cues varied depending on the perceiver's own age and gender. The estimates of participants aged 50 years and over were more influenced by lip definition, lip volume and the extent to which the eyes were open. For participants who were under 50, the presence of dark circles under the eyes,

pronounced nasolabial folds (the creases around the mouth) and brown skin spots were more influential cues.

There are some indications that people are better at estimating the age of faces similar in age to themselves (Anastasi and Rhodes, 2005, 2006; George and Hole, 1995; George et al, 2000). This **own-age bias** (see Chapter 12) in age estimation is given further support by Nkengne et al's study; although, overall, all groups of participants were very accurate, females were better than males (who tended to perceive the faces as being slightly younger than they really were), and younger participants (under 35 years of age) were better than older ones (aged over 50). Attention to different facial cues by different age groups may play a role in this, although why the groups should differ in this respect awaits further study.

4.2.2 **Applied research on age estimation**

'Applied' research on age estimation has focused on assessing the accuracy of age estimates for teenagers and young adults, in order to see whether people can reliably judge whether a young person exceeds the legal minimum age for activities such as drinking, driving, smoking and sex.

Willner and Rowe (2001) investigated how well alcohol-sellers in Wales could decide whether a customer was old enough to buy alcohol (i.e. whether they were over 18 years of age). Sellers were shown photographs of 16-year-old boys and girls and asked to judge their age. Thirty-eight per cent of the boys and 56% of the girls were thought to be aged 18 or older. When some of these children actually attempted to buy alcohol, on most occasions (60% of the time for boys and 70% of the time for girls) they were not asked to produce identification.

There are some suggestions that training can improve age-estimation accuracy, both in the laboratory (Sörqvist and Eriksson, 2007) and in real life via work-related experience (Vestlund et al, 2009). Vestlund and colleagues found that Swedish alcohol salespersons were more accurate at estimating the age of young people than were those in a similarly aged control group. Nevertheless the salespersons still exhibited a bias towards overestimating the age of faces under the age of 20 years (the legal limit for alcohol purchase in Sweden).

In an attempt to assess how well people can determine whether a girl is under the legal age of consent (which is 16 in most countries), Egan and Cordan (2009) examined the effects of alcohol and makeup on the apparent age of young women. Two hundred and forty men and women in bars and cafes were asked to estimate the age and attractiveness of immature and mature female faces. Half of the participants had consumed at least some alcohol. For ethical reasons, all of the stimuli were actually derived from photographs of ten 17-year-old female faces. Four different versions were computer-generated from each face, to give four permutations of age (sexually immature or mature) and makeup (pronounced or not). To produce the different-aged versions, each original face was morphed with two different composites, one produced by averaging together thirteen 10-year-olds' faces, and the other based on thirteen 20-year-olds. Each participant saw all four versions of each face.

The chief findings were that both men and women rated immature faces as more attractive than mature faces. Makeup made the mature faces more attractive, and made the immature faces look older. Alcohol greatly increased the attractiveness of the mature and heavily made-up faces, but it did not affect age estimation. Even heavy alcohol consumption did not interfere with age perception in men, suggesting that this in itself is not a valid defence for having sex with a minor. However, participants consistently overestimated the ages of the faces by 3.5 years on average; the mean age estimates were 18.7 years for the immature faces and 20.4 for the mature faces. This would mean that the 'immature' faces were still judged as being above the legal age of consent. It is possible that this overestimation might stem from the use of computer-generated faces rather than photographs of real minors, so more research is needed to settle the issue of whether people can reliably decide whether a girl is over 16.

Overall, applied research suggests that age-estimation performance, though impressive, is just not precise enough to be used as the sole basis for deciding whether someone is above a legal minimum age (Rhodes, 2009).

4.2.3 **The development of age perception**

Not only are we good at estimating age, but this ability seems to mature quite early. Montepare and McArthur (1986) found that children as young as 2 years of age could use cardioidal strain and wrinkling as cues to age. However, their stimuli consisted of drawings of faces, which might have made these cues more salient to the children. Jones and Smith (1984) selectively masked various regions of photographs of faces and asked children to rank order the faces by age. Four-year-olds were able to order the extremes correctly (the faces of a baby and an older adult) but had problems in ranking mid-range faces (young to older adult faces). Masking the eyes significantly reduced the children's accuracy, but it is not clear whether this manipulation affected the children's ability to estimate age or merely resulted in them paying less attention to the faces.

George and co-workers (2000) examined the age-perception abilities of 4- and 6-year-olds, using photographic-quality stimuli. All but one of the 6-year-olds passed a pre-test which consisted of deciding which of two faces was the oldest. In contrast, only 36% of the 4-year-olds could do so. It was not clear whether the younger children's problems stemmed from difficulties in processing the faces, or difficulties with the concept of 'age' itself. It is known that many 4-year-olds have difficulties with the concepts of 'older' and 'younger' (Kuczaj and Lederberg, 1976). Those 4-year-olds who could pass the pre-test performed as well as the 6-year-olds. Performance was similar with unmanipulated faces and with faces that were manipulated selectively to remove certain cues to age, such as skin texture or cardioidal strain. Thus, like adults, the children were able adaptively to use whatever cues to age were present in the images. Both 4-year-olds and 6-year-olds showed evidence of an own-age age-estimation bias: they were better at age discrimination when it involved children's faces than when it involved those of adults. However, overall the results suggest that children as young as 4 years of age have an impressive ability to estimate age from faces.

4.2.4 Why is age estimation so reliable?

It is tempting to speculate on why age perception is so accurate and so robust. Amongst primates living in social groups, there may well have been strong evolutionary pressures for it to be so. For both males and females, it would be important to mate with an age-appropriate conspecific, one that is not too young or too old to be fertile. Males often need to compete with other males in the group. In deciding whether or not to challenge a more dominant male, it would be helpful to know his age. We would therefore predict that our primate cousins would be good at judging age; however, to our knowledge no studies have yet been conducted on this topic.

4.3 Recognizing the sex of a face

Another important aspect of a face is whether it is male or female. Adults are very good at categorizing the sex[4] of a face, in terms of both the speed and accuracy of responding (e.g. Burton et al, 1993), and this finding has been replicated in children and infants as young as 9 months old (Fagot and Leinbach, 1993). Most of the recent research in this area has focused on two areas. One tries to characterize the physical differences between male and female faces, and identify which of these differences is used as a basis for judgements of a face's sex. The other considers how the categorization of the sex of a face might be integrated into models of face processing and whether or not gender and identity are processed

---

[4] The terms sex and gender are often used interchangeably, although strictly they have different definitions. Sex refers to the biological sex of a person, whether they are chromosomally male or female. Gender refers to a person's sexual identity, which is a more socially constructed property involving a person's degree of masculinity or femininity.

independently of each other. This was discussed at length in Chapter 1 (see section 1.1.3).

4.3.1 **Facial cues to sex**

Male and female faces have been found to differ in terms of their physical structure, such as distances and relative distances between facial features (Burton et al, 1993). Female faces also tend to be shorter and rounder than male faces (Enlow, 1982). Brown and Perrett (1993) found that all facial features contributed to the effective categorization of a face's sex, other than the nose. In terms of their relative importance, the brows and eyes were the most important features, followed by the brows alone, eyes alone, jaw line, the chin, the nose and mouth, and finally the mouth alone. It has been suggested that the importance of the brows and eyes depends on the distance between them, which is shorter in male faces than in female faces. This has been supported in a study that manipulated male faces either to 'masculinize' them by decreasing the distance, or to 'feminize' them by increasing the distance (Campbell et al, 1999a). The masculinized faces were categorized more quickly and accurately.

It has also been suggested that males and females may differ in their facial movements, and that this might aid the categorization of sex. Hill and Johnston (2001) asked their participants to judge the sex of androgynous computer-generated heads that moved in various ways. Participants were able to decide the sex of the face on the basis of facial motion alone, particularly **non-rigid motion** (the movement of the features within the face). Morrison et al (2007) repeated this study, but additionally considered whether these motion cues were related to estimates of facial attractiveness. They replicated Hill and Johnston's results, finding that sex categorization was possible purely on the basis of sex-typical movement. They did not find that facial motion was associated with attractiveness. However, they did report that females tend to show more movement than

males and that females blink, tilt, nod and shake their heads more frequently than males. This suggests that it is not only the difference in facial features between males and females that aid sex categorization, but also the movement of these features (see Chapter 2 for discussion of movement in relation to identity processing).

Although it seems clear that male and female faces differ in terms of their structure and movement, additional cues also aid sex categorization, such as hairstyle and clothing. Studies comparing the processing of male and female faces with and without hair have found that the inclusion of the hair significantly facilitated the processing of the faces' sex (Macrae and Martin, 2007). One study examined how well adults and children could classify sex when these sex-stereotypical cues were removed from the facial stimuli (Wild et al, 2000). When categorizing the sex of adult faces, the adult participants' performance was almost perfect, but for children aged around 7 years performance was not much above chance levels. This suggests that children may be more reliant on sex-stereotypical cues to achieve sex categorization than adults.

Wild et al's study raises an additional issue: we know that male and female adult faces differ, but to what extent do children's faces differ physically according to their sex? On the basis of the skeletal structure of the face, there is little difference between female faces and pre-pubertal male faces (Enlow, 1982). Therefore Wild and colleagues also asked their participants to categorize the sex of children's faces where all sex-stereotypical cues were removed. In this condition, accuracy of classification decreased for all participants. Although performance was still above chance for the adult participants, it was reduced to chance levels for children aged around 7 years. This suggests that children's faces are more difficult to categorize in terms of sex because of the greater facial similarity between male and female children.

The possible roles of facial attractiveness and masculinity/femininity in sex categorization have also been examined. As we shall see below, it has been suggested that attractive faces are more average, or prototypical, than unattractive faces (Langlois and Roggman, 1990) and that this may lead to a processing advantage for them. Indeed, it has been found that sex categorization decisions are faster for attractive faces than for unattractive faces and that the masculinity or femininity of a face facilitates sex categorization (O'Toole et al, 1998). One more recent study examined whether the attractiveness and the masculinity/femininity of a face interact in terms of influencing sex categorization (Hoss et al, 2005). This is particularly important given that attractiveness ratings of females are higher for more feminine faces, whereas for male faces there is a weaker relationship between attractiveness and masculinity (review in Rhodes, 2006). Hoss and colleagues found that attractiveness facilitated sex categorization for both male and female faces, but the effect of masculinity/femininity was more complex. For male faces, being more masculine aided the sex categorization task, whereas for female faces femininity did not influence performance.

4.4 **Facial attractiveness**

Psychological research on facial attractiveness has focused mainly on the determinants of attractiveness, and whether or not attractiveness has any evolutionary benefits.

4.4.1 **The determinants of facial attractiveness**

What makes one face more attractive than another? Facial attractiveness is clearly affected by the properties of the face itself, and also by the characteristics of the perceiver, as not everyone finds the same faces equally attractive. On a wider level, attractiveness is influenced by cultural factors. Other cultures engage in all sorts of practices of self-adornment that many Westerners find unattractive. For example, Maori men in New Zealand have traditionally covered their faces with tattoos. Until the end of the 19th century, young Ainu women of northern Japan had blue lines tattooed between their nose and mouth that looked like moustaches. The Hamar tribe of Ethiopia cut their faces and then rub ash and charcoal into the wounds so that they are left with permanent weals. The Mursi women of southern Ethiopia, and the men of the Kayapo tribe in Brazil, both engage in the practice of inserting large plates into their lower lip.[5]

The diversity of non-Western cultures with respect to facial adornment led Darwin (1874) to conclude that attractiveness was largely culturally defined, and the view that 'beauty is in the eye of the beholder' has persisted to this day. However, in more recent times, research has suggested that, although culture obviously plays an important part in shaping our preferences, there are some universals too. Firstly, cross-cultural studies suggest that different cultures do in fact show considerable agreement about which faces are attractive (review in Langlois et al, 2000; see also Lippa, 2007).

Secondly, preferences for attractive faces are detectable in infants who are too young to have been influenced by their culture. When presented with a pair of faces that differ in attractiveness

---

[5] It should be pointed out that these modifications often serve more functions than merely enhancing attractiveness. For the Mursi, they signify the transition of girls into adulthood; they differentiate the Mursi women from those of adjacent tribes; and they also provide useful revenue from tourists who come from hundred of miles away merely to photograph them (Turton, 2004).

(as judged by adults), infants who are only a couple of days old spend more time looking at an attractive face than at an unattractive face (e.g. Langlois et al, 1987; Samuels and Ewy, 1985; Slater et al, 1998; see Chapter 5 for more detail on the **preferential looking technique**). This preference appears to be based on the internal features of the two faces being compared (Slater et al, 2000), and it is orientation-specific, disappearing if the face pairs are inverted (Slater et al, 2000b).

Three main factors have been proposed to influence judgements of attractiveness (reviews in Rhodes, 2006; Thornhill and Gangestad, 1999): a preference for **averageness** (in the sense that faces are preferred if they are close to the population average); a preference for **bilateral symmetry**; and a preference for **sexual dimorphism** (a preference for feminine traits in female faces and masculine traits in male faces). Other factors also play a role, however, such as skin texture and youthfulness. Let's consider the evidence for each of these influences in turn.

4.4.2 **Averageness**

Any given population of faces can be envisaged as variants around an average, or typical, face. (See the discussion of Valentine's [1991] **Multidimensional Face Space** model in Chapter 1.) Some faces are quite different from average (in one or many aspects), whereas others are very close to it. You would think that attractive faces would be faces that were out of the ordinary, but in fact, attractive faces are *less* distinctive than unattractive faces (Light et al, 1981). Not only this, but, starting with Langlois and Roggman (1990), many studies have demonstrated that average faces are rated as more attractive than less average ones. Langlois and Roggman (1990) produced computer-generated average faces by blending individual faces into a single composite. The composites were rated as more attractive than the faces that had been used to construct them. The more faces that were included in the composites, the more attractive the composites became (up to a maximum of about 16 faces).[6] Figure 4.6 shows images used by Little and Hancock (2002) to replicate this effect.

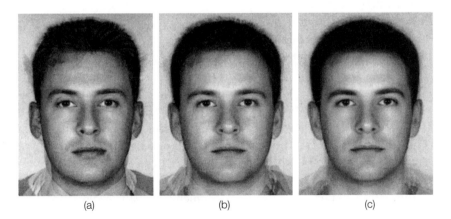

(a) (b) (c)

FIGURE 4.6 Male face composites made by averaging together (a) 3 faces, (b) 6 faces and (c) 12 faces. (From Little and Hancock, 2002)

---

[6] The enhanced attractiveness of composites was described by Francis Galton in 1878–1879. Not having any image-processing software to hand, he produced his composites by making successive exposures onto a single photographic plate. He used the same technique in order to produce various 'archetypes': by averaging together

One problem with composites is that the averaging process produces artefacts that might enhance their attractiveness. It averages away differences in skin texture, leaving the final composite with smooth, unblemished skin (Alley and Cunningham, 1991); it makes the composite more symmetrical than the component faces from which it is derived; and, in early studies, a failure to align feature outlines meant that the composites had larger than normal eyes and lips. However, these factors cannot be the whole explanation for the attractiveness of composites. Firstly, studies using real faces have shown similar effects: average-looking faces are rated as more attractive than distinctive-looking faces (review in Rhodes, 2006). Secondly, even when all of these artefacts are eliminated, composites are still rated as more attractive than their component faces. For example, Rhodes and Tremewan (1996) found similar effects using line drawings of faces (which have no texture to be smoothed by the averaging process).

Little and Hancock (2002) looked at the effects of independently modifying shape and texture information. They asked participants to rate a set of faces for attractiveness that had been modified in one of two ways: either they retained their original texture, but had their shape altered to that of a 12-face composite; or they retained their original shape, but had their texture replaced with that from a 12-face composite (Fig. 4.7). Averageness effects occurred with both types of manipulation, implying that both shape and texture are important for attractiveness, and showing that the enhanced attractiveness of the usual type of composite cannot be due wholly to the smoothing produced by blending.

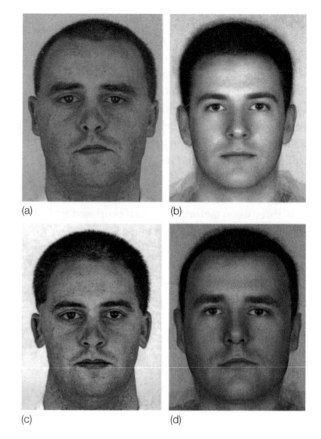

(a)   (b)

(c)   (d)

FIGURE 4.7 Independent manipulations of shape and texture by Little and Hancock (2002). (a) Original face; (b) composite of both shape and texture; (c) texture from original face, combined with the shape of (b); (d) shape from original face, combined with the texture of (b)

Finally, the attractiveness of individual faces can be changed by distorting their configurations towards or away from the average configuration for their sex, to make them look more or less distinctive (e.g. Rhodes and Tremewan, 1996; Rhodes et al, Sumich and Byatt, 1999b; O'Toole et al, 1999).

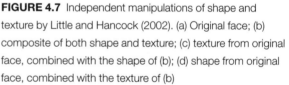

photographs of doctors, he produced a prototypical doctor; by averaging together photographs of soldiers, he produced the prototypical officer and prototypical private; and by averaging together the photographs of various criminals he was able to produce the average 'swindler', 'pickpocket', 'murderer', and so on. (This was at a time when Cesare Lombroso's 'criminal anthropology' was at its height, and it was believed that there were distinct criminal 'types' with characteristic physiognomies.) Galton's (1883) book *Inquiries into Human Faculty* contains a chapter on his work with composites.

An interesting demonstration of the effects of averageness on attractiveness comes from a cross-cultural study by Apicella et al (2007). They compared the effects of averageness on judgements of opposite-sex facial attractiveness in Westerners and in the Hadza, an isolated tribe of hunter-gatherers in northern Tanzania. Apicella et al created four sets of composites (Fig. 4.8): one set for young Hadza men; another set for young Hadza women; a third set for young British men; and a fourth set for young British women. Some of the composites were 'low average' (blends of 5 images) and some were 'high average' (blends of 20 images). Apicella and colleagues found that, for both British and Hadza faces, the British participants showed an effect of averageness: in both cases they rated the 20-face composite as more attractive than any of the 5 face composites. However, the Hadza did this only for the Hadza faces. Apicella et al conclude that a preference for averageness is biologically based, but that relevant experience with faces is necessary in order to develop the 'norm' against which to compare faces. They suggest that the Hadza's lack of preference for the 20-face British composite arises because they have no norm for European faces, due to their lack of contact with white people.

Although averageness is an important factor in attractiveness, it cannot be the sole determinant of it, as shown by Perrett et al (1994). They compared three composites for

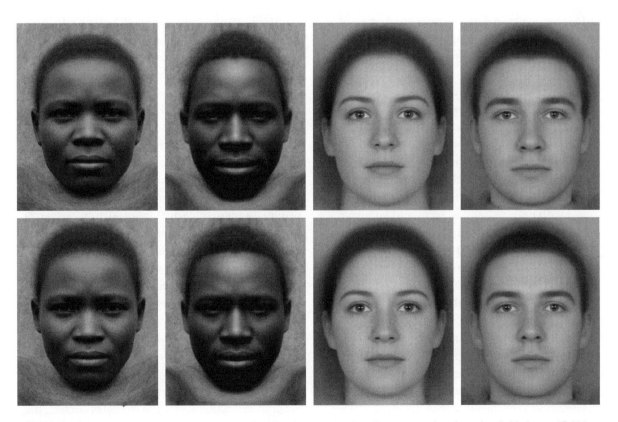

FIGURE 4.8 Top row: female and male Hadza and British 5-face composites. Bottom row: female and male Hadza and British 20-face composites. (Reprinted with permission from: Apicella, C. L., Little, A. C. & Marlowe, F. W. (2007). Facial averageness and attractiveness in an isolated population of hunter-gatherers. *Perception*, 36, 1813–1820. © Pion Limited, London)

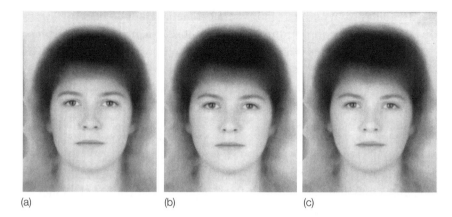

(a)   (b)   (c)

FIGURE 4.9 Composite faces used by Perrett et al (1994) to show that 'average' faces are attractive, but not optimally attractive. (a) Average of 60 female faces; (b) average of the 15 most attractive faces out of this 60; (c) caricature, exaggerating the differences between the average and attractive-average faces.

attractiveness (Fig. 4.9). One was an average of 60 randomly chosen young female faces; one was an average of the 15 most attractive faces of this set; and one was a caricature, produced by exaggerating the differences between the average and attractive-average faces by 50%. The caricatured face was rated as more attractive than the attractive-average face, which in turn was rated as more attractive than the average face. Thus, the average face is certainly attractive, but it is not the *most* attractive face. Similar effects were found with both Caucasian faces and Japanese faces, using Caucasian and Japanese participants.

Rubenstein et al (2002) suggested that Perrett et al's effects could be accommodated by the 'average is attractive' theory if the mathematical average (the one produced by combining a random set of faces) differs from the average that is actually used by the visual system in assessing attractiveness. As people pay more attention to attractive faces (Shimojo et al, 2003), perhaps the *objective* average of faces in the population does not coincide with the average of the faces in the population that have actually been *noticed* by people. In short, the average of face space might be skewed towards attractive faces.

If this explanation is correct, perceived averageness in the population should be biased in the same way as perceived attractiveness: the attractive-average face should not only be rated as more attractive than the average face, but it should also look more 'normal'. DeBruine et al (2007) tested this theory as follows. First, they produced their own versions of Perrett et al's average face and attractive-average face. They measured the differences between these two stimuli, and then exaggerated or minimized these differences to produce a set of 60 caricatures and anti-caricatures on this 'attractiveness' dimension. The positive caricatures thus exaggerate the differences between the average and highly average young Caucasian female faces in one direction, and the anti-caricatures exaggerate it in the opposite direction (Fig. 4.10, (a)).

These images were rated by two separate groups of participants. One group rated them for attractiveness and the other group independently rated them for averageness ('normality'). If the original 'average is attractive' model is correct, the 0% face (the true average face) should be rated both as most attractive and also as most average. If Rubenstein et al's 'biased average' explanation

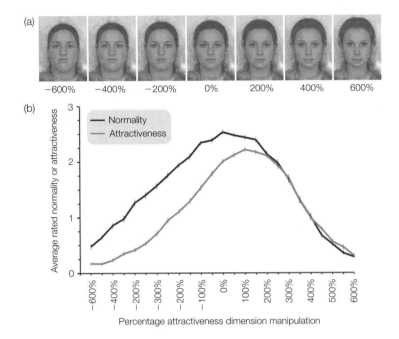

FIGURE 4.10 (a) Examples of some of the stimuli used by DeBruine et al (2007) to challenge the 'average is attractive' hypothesis. The differences were calculated between an average face based on 60 faces (0% here) and the average of the 15 most attractive of those faces. These differences were then added to the average face (positive %) or subtracted from it, to produce the stimuli here. (b) Independent ratings for the 'normality' (0–3 scale from 'very abnormal' to 'very normal') and 'attractiveness' (0–3 scale from 'very unattractive' to 'very attractive') of these faces.

is correct, the face rated as most attractive should also be the face rated as most average, but this face will be one that is shifted along the attractiveness and normality dimensions to the same extent. In practice, contrary to either version of the 'average is attractive' model, the ratings for normality and attractiveness did not coincide (Fig. 4.10, (b)): the face that was rated as most attractive had a more positive value on the 'attractiveness' dimension than the face that was rated as most normal (which was, in fact, the true average, the 0% stimulus).

Other experiments by DeBruine and colleagues also pose problems for the 'average is attractive' theory, at least for female faces. For example, similar-sized deviations in different directions along their 'attractiveness' continuum did not produce equivalent effects on attractiveness, even though the faces concerned were equal amounts away from the average face. Positive deviations

were always rated as more attractive than comparably sized negative deviations.

DeBruine et al favour an alternative explanation, which is that attractiveness is actually determined by a set of dimensions in face space that are independent of averageness. Attractiveness is thus determined not just by how 'different' from average a face is, but also by how different from average it is *in particular ways*. Perrett et al's attractive-average and caricatured faces represent points along these dimensions. Perrett et al (1994) did attempt to identify the ways by which their caricatured-average face differed from the average face: the caricatured face had higher cheek bones, larger eyes and a thinner jaw than the average female face. The female face might be considered an example of **neoteny** (the retention of juvenile characteristics into adulthood). The larger eyes and smaller chin give female faces a juvenile appearance (which in itself has been shown to be attractive; e.g. Cunningham, 1986; Ishi et al, 2004) and make them more 'cute'.

4.4.3 Symmetry

Symmetry also has an effect on attractiveness. Early studies suggested that faces with small amounts of asymmetry were more attractive than perfectly symmetrical ones, whereas more recent studies have found the opposite (review in Rhodes, 2006). Rhodes suggests that the discrepancy arises from the differing ways in which symmetrical stimuli are created. In early studies, they were made by adding together one half of a face and its mirror image. Since faces are usually asymmetrical, this can produce odd-looking faces. More recent studies have produced symmetrical faces by blending the whole face with its mirror image. These look like normal faces, and they are rated as being more attractive than the original faces from which they were derived (e.g. Perrett et al, 1999; Rhodes et al, 1998, 1999a,b).

Further evidence for a role of symmetry in attractiveness comes from studies showing that attractiveness ratings for real faces are correlated with their degree of symmetry, even when the effects of averageness are controlled for (Rhodes et al, 1999b). Rhodes (2006) did a meta-analysis of relevant studies and found that symmetry was related to attractiveness.

One problem is that symmetry is often confounded with averageness, because average faces are fairly symmetrical. Valentine et al (2004) circumvented this problem by using profiles as well as frontal views: the averageness of profiles can be manipulated without affecting their symmetry. Valentine et al found that faces that were morphed towards the average were judged to be more attractive in both profile and frontal views. However, this preference was stronger for frontal views, implying that there are independent influences of averageness and symmetry on perceived attractiveness.

4.4.4 Sexual dimorphism

After puberty, male and female faces are quite different, reflecting the different effects of testosterone and oestrogen on facial development. In males, masculine traits develop, such as a squarer jaw, pronounced brow ridges and a beard. Female faces change more subtly, and as mentioned a moment ago, are somewhat neotenous (they retain juvenile characteristics). Are male faces more attractive if they are more masculine, and female faces more attractive if they are more feminine?

A meta-analysis by Rhodes (2006) confirmed that femininity is attractive for female faces, and masculinity is attractive for male ones. However, the evidence seems more consistent for women's faces. As mentioned above, Perrett et al's (1994) 'attractive-average' composite had more feminine features (a smaller chin and higher cheekbones) than the normal average composite. Other studies have shown that exaggeration of feminine features increases their attractiveness (Perrett et al 1994, 1998a; Rhodes et al, 2000).

For male faces, the effects of masculine traits on attractiveness are less clear-cut. Some studies have shown participants a range of faces that differed in their degree of masculinity and found a preference for slightly feminized male faces (e.g. Little and Hancock, 2002; Perrett et al, 1998a). Rhodes (2006) suggests that these findings are an artefact of using stimuli that are blends between a composite female face and a composite male face. She claims that composite male faces do not capture masculinity very well, as the averaging process removes their coarse skin texture and square jaw.

In studies with real faces, masculinity ratings correlate positively with attractiveness, although the associations are weaker than between femininity and attractiveness (review in Rhodes, 2006). Interestingly, Little et al (2008b) have shown that measurements of symmetry and sexual dimorphism in photographs of real faces are correlated, not just in different races of human (Caucasians and the Hadza tribe) but also in rhesus macaques; in all three groups, symmetrical males had more masculine facial proportions and symmetrical females had more feminine facial proportions. Their work suggests that symmetry and sexual dimorphism are linked traits.

4.4.5 **Skin condition**

Although much less researched than shape-based cues to attractiveness, a fourth factor that influences participants' ratings is skin condition. The public's huge interest in skin-care products would suggest that skin condition is perceived as very important, so it is curious that this variable has not received more attention. The few studies that have been performed suggest that skin coloration affects attractiveness ratings. Fink et al (2001) showed that men's judgements of young Caucasian women's facial attractiveness were influenced by the women's skin texture: homogeneous skin coloration and a slightly reddish skin were most attractive. Fink et al suggested that skin reflected healthy attributes such as good circulation, and that raters were sensitive to this.

As mentioned above, Little and Hancock (2002) produced composites for shape information and texture information separately. Both types of composite were rated as more attractive, less masculine and less distinctive than their component faces. Little and Hancock suggested that the process of composite production smoothes the skin; this effectively feminizes the face, because women usually have smoother skin than men. As we saw above, this smoothing is not the only factor in the increased attractiveness of composites, but it does play a role.

Jones et al (2004) asked participants to rate the attractiveness of photographs of the skin on young Caucasian men's cheeks. Apparent health of skin affected the face's attractiveness, and the ratings for skin attractiveness correlated with ratings of attractiveness for the same faces in their complete versions. Jones et al also produced two versions of each of a set of 97 young male faces. These were identical in terms of shape, but one version was given unhealthy-looking skin and the other was given healthy-looking skin. The latter versions were rated as being significantly more attractive.

Fink, Grammer and Matts (2006) also looked at skin cues in the absence of differences in face shape. They photographed women of different ages, removed any obvious wrinkles and defects, and then superimposed these skin textures on to a standardized computer-generated head. Both the apparent age and attractiveness of these faces varied as a consequence of their skin texture: faces with the more homogeneous skin colour distribution of young women were perceived as younger, healthier and more attractive than the same-shaped faces with the more inhomogeneous skin colour distribution of older women.

Overall, the available data to date thus suggest that skin coloration (more specifically, the apparent smoothness of skin) might convey useful information about attractiveness.

4.4.6 **The evolutionary psychology of attractiveness**

Attractiveness ratings for both sexes seem to be influenced by averageness, symmetry, sexual dimorphism and skin condition. But why is this so? Explanations have centred around the supposed evolutionary benefits of choosing attractive mates (see reviews in Penton-Voak and Perrett, 2000; Rhodes, 2006; Thornhill and Gangestad, 1999). It has been suggested that facial attractiveness has been subject to **sexual selection**:[7] there has been

---

[7] One of the biggest selection pressures on organisms comes from their conspecifics, because they are in direct competition for the same resources, such as food, shelter and mates. Sexual selection refers to the fact that the mating preferences of one sex will strongly affect the reproductive success of the other, and hence will have a strong influence on

a strong evolutionary pressure for us to be able to detect attractiveness, because it is an indicator that the person displaying it has developed normally, is in good health and has a robust immune system (making them resistant to disease, parasites and the like). If faces are a reliable indicator of mate 'quality', it would make good sense to mate with an attractive person, as these traits are likely to be inherited by their offspring. The benefits for the attractive person themself are that it gives them a wider range of mates to choose from. As females invest more heavily in their offspring than males do (in terms of reproductive effort, care-giving, etc.), this would be more of a benefit for women than for men.

How does this explain why averageness is attractive? One possibility is that averageness reflects **developmental stability** (the ability to withstand stress during development). As pointed out by Thornhill and Gangestad (1999), it may also indicate **genetic diversity** (a lack of inbreeding, which may increase disease resistance).

A similar argument has been put forward for symmetry: that it reflects health, vigour and good genes. Like most vertebrates, normally developing humans are largely, although not perfectly, bilaterally symmetrical. There are two different types of asymmetry that are present in populations. **Directional asymmetries** are systematic deviations from symmetry that occur in all members of a population. For example, most people have their heart on the left. It is normal to have these kinds of asymmetry. In contrast, **fluctuating asymmetries** are random deviations from symmetry, perhaps caused by anomalous development or as a result of disease. For example, Quasimodo (at least, in the actor Charles Laughton's version) had a considerable number of fluctuating asymmetries, such as one eye much larger and lower than the other, a lopsided body, and so on. His asymmetries might suggest to Esmeralda that he would not be a good choice for a mate.

Sexual dimorphism is held to affect attractiveness because it correlates with desirable qualities in the two sexes. For men, a high degree of masculinity might reflect their dominance and status. Given that there is some evidence that high testosterone levels are associated with a challenged immune system (reviews in Penton-Voak and Perrett, 2000; Rhodes, 2006), high levels of masculinity might be an example of 'handicapping', like the peacock's tail, showing that this person is such a high-quality mate that he is able to look so masculine despite its disadvantages. A highly feminine woman is likely to be fertile (and young, as women's faces become masculinized to some extent with age, due to declining oestrogen levels). 'Cuteness' in women might elicit protective behaviour on the part of males.

It has been claimed that women's preferences change to some extent depending on where they are in their menstrual cycle. During their fertile phase, they prefer relatively masculine faces (e.g. Frost, 1994; Penton-Voak and Perrett, 2000; Penton-Voak et al, 1999; Perrett et al, 1998a) compared to during the rest of their cycle (see Chapter 9 for more information on how hormones influence face processing). This could be an adaptive reproductive strategy by females: a woman should find masculine men attractive when she is most fertile (so that she gets their good genes), but then she should switch to preferring less masculine men once she is pregnant, as they are likely to be better caregivers than the testosterone-fuelled hunk she mated with.

Lastly, skin colour and smoothness could be indicators of health, disease resistance and freedom from parasites. As mentioned in the section on age perception, skin texture also is

---

their evolution. Sexual selection can be so powerful that it leads to the development of structures and behaviours that are positively maladaptive in other respects. For example, the peacock's tail is a pretty silly thing to have from the standpoint of natural selection, but peahens like it, so sexual selection has led to the development of the tail as it is today.

a good indicator of age. Age and attractiveness are clearly linked. Whatever the merits of elderly partners, from the point of view of reproductive success they are not such a good idea. Perhaps there is an evolutionary basis not just for the ability to detect that a prospective partner is past their prime, but also for finding them less attractive once we have done so.

These hypotheses are entertaining, but a review of the evidence in favour of attractiveness being associated with better health or other desirable attributes (Rhodes, 2006) suggests there is little firm evidence for or against them, and even less evidence that these attributes are heritable (as they would need to be for natural selection to work). To be really sure that something is an evolutionary adaptation, it is necessary to demonstrate that is has been specifically designed by natural selection for that particular function. This is especially difficult to do when a structure has multiple functions so that there are competing selection pressures. Faces are primarily a cluster of forward-facing sensory organs, plus a means of getting food and drink inside the body and words out of it. Selection for efficiency in fulfilling these functions might compete with the need to look attractive to the opposite sex. One would have to show that faces are *designed* by evolution to indicate one's health and the goodness of one's genes, and that others can not only detect this information accurately but also use it as the basis for their mating behaviour.

Such hypotheses are difficult to test in modern societies, because modern healthcare means that any links between health and attractiveness are more difficult to discern. In addition, extrapolating from laboratory preferences to real-world behaviour is a big leap—there are many other factors that influence attractiveness in real life, such as personality (well, one of us hopes that's the case, anyway!). Lippa (2007) analysed the results of a BBC internet survey on sex differences that attracted nearly half a million respondents. When asked to rate their first, second and third most important traits in a partner, the most important attributes listed by men were intelligence, overall good looks, and humour. Facial attractiveness came only fifth (after honesty). For women, the most important attributes in a partner were humour, intelligence and honesty, with overall good looks ranking only eighth and facial attractiveness ranking ninth. Thus, men rated physical attractiveness as more important than did women (43% of men placed good looks amongst their top three traits, compared with only 17% of women), but even for men facial appearance is not the sole determinant of attractiveness.

However, there is some evidence that attractiveness is associated with greater reproductive success (Rhodes et al, 2005): attractive men report having more short-term, but not long-term, partners; and attractive women report the opposite, plus they claim to have begun having sex at an earlier age than unattractive women. Sexual dimorphism showed the clearest association with these measures, although averageness for males and symmetry for women were also associated with them to some extent. Interestingly, for males, attractiveness ratings for faces and bodies did not correlate with each other, but both contributed to self-reported mating success. For females, face and body attractiveness were correlated, but only facial attractiveness was related to mating success. Although these correlations were statistically significant, they were all very small in absolute terms, suggesting that none of these relationships between attractiveness and self-reported mating success is very strong.

Jokela (2009) looked at the fertility rates of 2,241 participants in the Wisconsin Longitudinal Study from 1957 until 2004. Independent raters judged the attractiveness of these individuals from photographs of them as adolescents. Attractive women had more children than unattractive ones (although moderately attractive women had more children than did the highly attractive women), and the least attractive men had fewer children than the rest of the male sample. This could be interpreted as evidence that attractiveness is associated with greater fecundity, but, as Jokela concedes, there are a number of equally plausible alternative explanations for the observed pattern of results.

4.4.7 **Non-evolutionary explanations for attractiveness**

Non-evolutionary explanations for symmetry and sexual dimorphism have not been put forward, to our knowledge. Symmetry might simply have arisen as a natural consequence of having paired sensory organs on the head, but sexual dimorphism is harder to explain. However, an alternative explanation for why averageness is attractive is that it might simply be a byproduct of how faces are represented in memory. Average faces are close to the 'norm' in multidimensional face space (see Chapter 1 for an explanation of the MDFS concept). They are therefore encountered more often than non-average faces. This might affect the ease with which they are processed. Familiarity-engendered **perceptual fluency** of this kind has been shown to affect the attractiveness of non-face stimuli, such as dot patterns (Winkielman et al, 2006), and there is a well-established phenomenon in social psychology research called the **mere exposure effect** (Zajonc, 1968; review in Bornstein, 1989): repeated exposures to all sorts of stimuli (not just faces) tend to increase the amount that people like them.

Thus, average faces could be attractive merely because they seem familiar. There is certainly evidence to suggest that familiarity affects attractiveness ratings for faces. Firstly, a number of studies have shown that attractiveness is positively correlated with familiarity and negatively correlated with distinctiveness (e.g. Light et al, 1981; Peskin and Newell, 2004; Rhodes and Tremewan, 1996; Vokey and Read, 1992). Peskin and Newell also systematically manipulated face familiarity by varying the number of times that each face was seen during the experiment (either once or six times). Increasing the number of exposures led to a small, but statistically significant, increase in the rated attractiveness of the faces. This occurred both for typical and distinctive faces. Secondly, Halberstadt and Rhodes (2000, 2003) showed that the preference for average stimuli is not confined to faces, but extends to images of dogs, birds, watches, fish and cars. This in itself is not strong evidence against an evolutionary explanation, however: it is possible that we possess a mechanism that is designed primarily to find averageness in faces attractive, but that can also be used with other types of stimulus.

However, even the fact that familiarity increases attractiveness could have an evolutionary explanation: the preference may be related to **kin selection** (see following section). DeBruine (2004) manipulated unfamiliar male and female faces by morphing them with either the participant's own face (so that there was a subtle degree of resemblance to the participant) or with an unfamiliar adult's face (Fig. 4.11). The participants were not aware of this manipulation, but it influenced their ratings for the faces. Both same-sex and opposite-sex own-face blends were rated as more average than the corresponding unfamiliar-face blends, so familiarity affected the perception of averageness. If attractiveness was determined primarily by familiarity, the morphing manipulation should have had similar effects on the attractiveness ratings for both same-sex and opposite-sex morphs. However, it did not: own-face blends were rated as more attractive than other-face blends, but *only* when they were the same sex as the participant. This is hard to explain in terms of attractiveness being determined by familiarity, because both same-sex and opposite-sex blends were equally familiar, and so should have produced equivalent effects on attractiveness ratings. However, this result fits well with an evolutionary explanation. Same-sex individuals that resemble you should be found attractive, because they are likely to be your kin. However, to avoid inbreeding, a similar degree of resemblance (and hence, by implication, relatedness) should not be found attractive in members of the opposite sex.

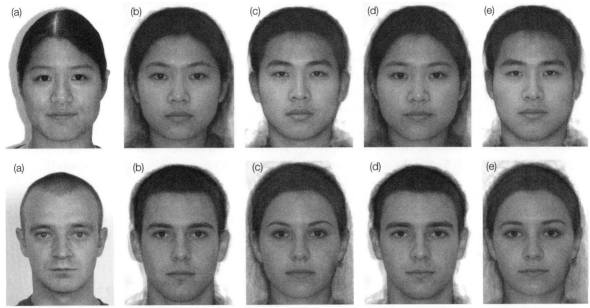

Original | Same-sex composite | Opposite-sex composite | Original-composite blends

FIGURE 4.11 Stimuli from DeBruine (2004). (a) Participant's face; (b) same-sex average face (composite of 20 faces of the same sex and race as the participant); (c) opposite-sex average face (composite of 20 faces of the opposite sex but same race as the participant); (d) a same-sex face with a degree of resemblance to the participant's own face (blend between [a] and [b]); (e) opposite-sex face with a degree of resemblance to the participant's face (blend between [a] and [c]).

4.5 **Kin recognition**

All newborn babies look pretty much the same: pink and crumpled. However, relatives almost invariably comment on how much the baby looks like its father or mother. Can people judge genetic relatedness (of children and adults, as well as babies) with any degree of reliability? And, if so, what facial cues are they using in order to do this?

The importance of being able to recognize kin is explained by Hamilton's (1964) theory of **inclusive fitness** (the basis of Richard Dawkins' [1976] more famous **selfish gene** theory). Hamilton suggested that animals should preferentially help individuals who are genetically related to them, especially close kin. This is because, by helping kin, animals promote the survival and proliferation of the genes that they share with them.[8] The best way for you to pass on your genes is to have children, because each of them will have, on average, 50% of your genes. However, you can also pass on your genes by helping your relatives to reproduce. On average, you share 50% of your genes with a brother or sister, so, if one of them survives to have

---

[8] Evolution can also select for helping non-kin, by virtue of the process of **reciprocal altruism** (Trivers, 1971): basically, I help you now, in return for you helping me at some future time, so that neither of us incurs a net reproductive cost.

a child, on average 25% of your genes will be passed on via them. (In theory, you are therefore better off persuading your brothers and sisters to have numerous children than you are to have just one of your own!) Consequently, it would be advantageous for animals to be able to detect genetic relatedness with others: they should be able to recognize their own kin, and be able to discern different degrees of relatedness in their relatives. This is especially important in the case of rearing children, because they represent a major investment in terms of time and resources, especially for humans. Another important benefit of being able to recognize kin is that it facilitates incest avoidance, and hence avoids excessive inbreeding.

4.5.1 Evidence that people can recognize kin

Numerous studies have shown that people are sensitive to facial cues to genetic relatedness, both in terms of detecting who is related to them, and in terms of being able to tell whether strangers are related to one another (e.g. Alvergne et al, 2007; Brédart and French, 1999; Bressan and Dal Martello, 2002; Bressan and Grassi, 2004; DeBruine et al, 2009; Maloney and Dal Martello, 2006). As well as these behavioural studies, there is now neuropsychological evidence from a fMRI study that different brain regions are activated in response to different types of face, for instance one's own face, and the faces of kin, friends and strangers (Platek and Kemp, 2009).

We seem to assess relatedness on the basis of facial similarity. Maloney and Dal Martello (2006) showed participants 30 pairs of photographs of children. Unknown to the participants, half of the pairs showed siblings and half showed pairs of unrelated children. One set of participants were asked to rate each face pair for 'similarity', with this term deliberately left undefined. Another set of participants decided whether the faces in each pair were siblings or non-siblings. The similarity ratings strongly predicted whether or not pairs would be

classified as siblings: 96% of the variance in kinship decisions was accounted for by the rated similarity between the faces. In other words, when asked to judge 'similarity', observers in effect judged 'relatedness'.

Interestingly, in judging similarity, sex and age differences between the children's faces were ignored. This is not the case for adult faces, where similarity ratings are higher for same-sex sibling pairs than for opposite-sex pairs. Possibly this reflects the increased sexual dimorphism of adult faces (DeBruine et al, 2009).

Determining relatedness to one's children is not a problem for mothers, but paternity is inherently uncertain. It is possible that facial resemblance in children is used by males to reassure themselves that a child is theirs. Research suggests that males are more sensitive to resemblance to their children than are women, and value this resemblance more than women do; conversely, women tend to perceive a resemblance between their child and the father, which is what you might expect if the mother wants to persuade her partner that he really is the father of her child (brief review in Alvergne et al, 2007).

Alvergne et al (2007) point out that previous studies of whether children differentially resemble one or other parent are rather inconsistent in their findings, probably due to various methodological problems. They compared independent judges' evaluations of resemblance between parents and children to the parents' own assessments of how much their children looked like them. There were four different age groups of face, ranging from birth to 6 years of age. For the independent judges, each trial displayed a child's face below three adult faces, one of which was the parent and the other two of which were same-sex distractors. The task was to pick the parent.

Alvergne et al found that, for all age groups, the judges were able to select both of the child's parents at better than chance levels; thus, children do resemble their parents more than they resemble other (unrelated) adults. However, this was moderated by differences in resemblance to one or other parent that depended on the age and sex of the child. For newborns, the judges considered that both sexes resembled their mother more. For girls this persisted into older age groups, but for boys there was a change so that by 2–3 years of age they were considered to resemble their fathers more.

The independent raters' decisions were rather different from those of the parents of the children. Fathers overwhelmingly thought that their babies looked like themselves (although Alvergne et al concede that a weakness of their study was that the fathers were interviewed in the presence of the mothers!). Mothers also considered that their babies resembled their fathers, in line with the idea that a mother's behaviour is designed to reassure their partner that he is indeed the child's father. Two intriguing findings for which Alvergne and colleagues had no ready explanations were that the mothers of older boys thought they looked more like themselves, whereas the raters thought that they looked more like their father; and the mothers of older girls thought that they looked like their fathers, whereas the raters thought they looked more like their mothers. But, overall, the message from this study is that babies' faces do reflect their relatedness to their parents, and even strangers can detect this.

In fact, not only can humans detect relatedness between pairs of individuals from their own species, but they can also judge relatedness between individuals in other primate species too, at better than chance levels (for chimpanzees: Vokey et al, 2004; for chimpanzees, lowland gorillas and mandrills: Alvergne et al, 2009).

Detecting similarity between others must be based on some pretty sophisticated face processing, and is impressive enough,[9] but how do we detect the similarity of our kin to ourselves? Bear in mind that mirrors are a comparatively modern invention, so our ancestors would have had little information about their own facial appearance to use as a basis for evaluating their degree of resemblance to others. Lieberman et al (2007) have suggested we use three lines of evidence to decide that someone is kin: whoever is associated with our mother when we are a baby; the amount of time they have lived with us;[10] and detection of cues to genetic relatedness. One way to detect relatedness is to assess how similar a face is to our close relatives, who presumably look like us. Inspecting our siblings' faces would give us a good idea of what we look like ourselves. Yet, as Bressan and Zucchi (2009) point out, this is still rather uncertain, and any of our ancestors who managed to include information about their own face into their 'kin template' would have been at an advantage. We do have some information about ourselves, even in the absence of mirrors. For example, we can tell our own hair colour and skin coloration, and pools of still water might have provided a mirror of sorts. Therefore, it is possible that kin recognition could be based on **self-referential** cues as well as **family-referential** cues.

Bressan and Zucchi (2009) showed monozygotic and dizygotic twins[11] pairs of

---

[9] It is even more impressive when you consider that the ultimate appearance of an organism (its 'phenotype') is determined only partially by the organism's genetic makeup (its 'genotype'). This is illustrated by identical twins who are usually not perfectly identical despite having identical genotypes. Kinship is thus being detected from phenotypes even though they are imperfect and 'noisy' reflections of their underlying genotypes—a pretty remarkable achievement!

[10] People who have grown up in the same family group tend to avoid mating with one another as adults, even if they are unrelated—the so-called 'Westermarck effect'.

[11] Monozygotic (identical) twins come from the same fertilized egg: they are genetically identical and look very similar to each other. Dizygotic (fraternal) twins each come from a separate fertilized egg; they merely share a uterus and are no more genetically related or similar in appearance than normal siblings.

photographs of same-sex faces. These looked like unfamiliar faces, but one had been blended with a photograph of the participant and the other had been blended with a photograph of the participant's twin (in much the same way as in DeBruine's 2004 study mentioned above, in the context of attractiveness). Each participant was asked to choose which of these two faces they would favour in two different 'pro-social' situations. First, they were asked which one they would help in case of danger. Second, they were asked which one they would encourage their brother or sister to marry. In both contexts, people chose the face blended with their own significantly more than the face that was blended with their twin's face. The same effect occurred with both types of twin.

This study shows two things. Firstly, it shows that people are sensitive to the fact that a face resembles their own face more than if it resembles a same-aged sibling's face. This is all the more remarkable when one considers that the participants who were identical twins were detecting the difference between a face that contains some elements of their own, and a face that contains some elements of their very similar-looking twin. This is an impressive demonstration of our sensitivity to kinship cues in faces. Secondly, it shows that (for hypothetical scenarios at least) a 'stranger' who resembles us is likely to elicit pro-social behaviour more than a stranger who resembles a close family relative. This applies even when the relative is as close as our identical twin (who is as genetically related to us as we are). This latter finding might seem a little odd, but it could be explained by suggesting that twins possess the same kinship detection mechanism as everyone else, even if it is not appropriate to use it in their case.

4.5.2 What facial information is used for kin recognition?

It seems clear that genetic relatedness can be detected on the basis of information provided by the face, but what exactly is this information? Dal Martello and Maloney (2006) reasoned that the visual system should rely on aspects of the face that are largely genetically determined and that remain relatively unchanged during development. As they point out, although the bony parts of both the upper and lower parts of the face are genetically determined to the same degree, the lower face does not reach its final form until early adulthood (recall the differences between a child's skull and an adult's in Fig. 4.2). Therefore, it would make sense for the visual system to focus on the top half of the face when evaluating relatedness, because this is the part that changes the least throughout life. Moreover, within this region, because eye size changes very little during development (at birth, eyes are already 70% of their adult size) it would make sense to pay attention to the eyes. To test these predictions, Dal Martello and Maloney selectively masked different parts of the face in photographs of pairs of children who were either siblings or unrelated to each other. Their first experiment showed that adults' ability to judge the relatedness of these children was almost as good with photographs that showed only the upper half of the face as it was for photographs that showed the whole face. Performance with bottom halves of faces was significantly poorer than in the other two conditions, but still significantly above chance. Contrary to predictions, however, a second experiment showed that selectively masking either just the eyes or the mouth had virtually no effect on people's ability to judge relatedness.

Dal Martello and Maloney conclude that the upper half of the face is most important for judging relatedness, which parallels its importance for individual identification (see Chapter 2). However, they tentatively suggest that identification and kin recognition differ when it comes to the role of the eye region: although the eye region is important for identification, it might not be important for judging relatedness. This looks like another example of the visual system extracting from a face whatever information is most useful for a particular task. As Maloney and Dal Martello (2006) point out, their conclusions are restricted to children's faces; it is possible that different cues might be used for different ages of face, with the upper half being used more for infant and child faces, and the lower half of the face being used more with respect to adult faces, once they have finished growing.

4.6 **Conclusion**

Faces are clearly a rich source of information about their bearer's characteristics, including their age, sex, attractiveness, health, and whether they are genetically related to us. The research on 'social attention' reveals that faces are also informative to us in another way: the direction of their owner's gaze tells us that we are they are interested in us (for good or bad) or that there is something in our environment that they have noticed which might concern us too.

Much of this chapter has centred around the possible evolutionary benefits of certain facial properties, such as attractiveness and relatedness. Study of these topics, more than any others in face-processing research, has been driven by an attempt to demonstrate that we show adaptations for these facial properties. Has sexual selection moulded the appearance of our faces so that they give prospective mates clues to our genetic quality? Has evolution also provided us with the necessary mechanisms to detect this? We clearly can detect family resemblance, not only in terms of being able to assess how

similar our relatives are to one another, but also in terms of how similar strangers are to one another.

The issue of whether we have evolved to detect these properties is difficult to resolve, reminiscent of the wider arguments over whether or not faces are 'special' as far as processing is concerned (see Chapter 10). Do we have special-purpose mechanisms that have evolved specifically to process certain kinds of information from faces, but that can be co-opted into dealing with other kinds of information? Or do we simply have general-purpose processing mechanisms that are not face-specific, but only appear to be so because we are more practised at using them with faces? In the context of attractiveness, are we specialized for detecting it, or is our preference for attractive faces merely a byproduct of how we process stimuli generally? Evolutionary explanations of attractiveness and kin detection are necessarily rather speculative, and much of the evidence supporting them is rather circumstantial. They are also complicated by the fact that the variables discussed in this chapter interact in complex ways. For example, Conway et al (2008) found that gaze direction, sex of face, and expression all interacted with one another; essentially, they found that smiling, opposite-sex faces that looked straight at the viewer were highest rated in attractiveness. Although these results were interpretable in terms of a theory of 'efficient allocation of mating effort', they show how difficult it can be to isolate the factors involved in phenomena such as attractiveness so that they can be manipulated experimentally. However, the research on all the topics covered in this chapter throws up too many indications that natural selection has been at work for these to be dismissed as mere coincidences.

SUMMARY

- From infancy, we are highly sensitive to other people's gaze direction; our allocation of attention is highly influenced by where others are looking.

- Two influential models have been Baron-Cohen's (1994) 'eye-direction detector' (part of his 'mind-reading' model) and Perrett et al's (1992) 'direction-of-attention detector'. The Wollaston illusion suggests that we take head orientation into account when processing eye position.

- The superior temporal sulcus is very important in processing gaze perception; it may integrate information about others' gaze with information about their emotional expression.

- Age perception is an extremely robust ability, based on numerous facial cues to age such as head shape ('cardioidal strain'), wrinkling, sagging and pigmentation changes.

- Applied research on age perception has focused on whether adults can reliably judge the age of minors. It suggests that shopkeepers and bartenders would be wise to ask young people for ID.

- Even young children can reliably estimate age, and show adult-like performance with faces that have been manipulated selectively to remove cues to age. Our expertise in age perception may stem from its evolutionary importance to us, for instance in terms of choosing mates.

- We are very good at telling which sex a person is, probably mainly on the basis of the brow and eye region.

- Three factors have been claimed to influence attractiveness judgements: averageness, bilateral symmetry and sexual dimorphism. These are interrelated to some extent. Skin condition is also an influential attribute.

- Although average faces are attractive, highly attractive faces are not average: computer-generated blends of highly attractive faces are rated as more attractive than blends of average faces.

- It has been suggested that attractiveness is an indicator of a person's state of health and their genetic 'quality'. These evolutionary hypotheses are difficult to test in modern societies, but are supported by a great deal of circumstantial evidence.

- We can detect genetic relatedness between pairs of faces, even when the faces are unrelated to us. Some studies suggest we may even be sensitive to the degree of similarity between other faces and our own.

FURTHER READING

Buss, D. M. (ed.) (2005). *The Handbook of Evolutionary Psychology*. Hoboken, NJ: Wiley. An introduction to evolutionary psychology in general, this is a fascinating set of essays dealing with diverse topics such as the evolution of language, dominance and cognitive biases, as well as attractiveness and kin recognition.

Doherty, M. J. (2009). *Theory of Mind: How Children Understand Others' Thoughts and Feelings.* Hove: Psychology Press. Although we haven't covered it in this chapter, gaze direction is an important aspect of Baron-Cohen's theory that autism represents a deficit in Theory of Mind in children. This book provides a critical review of research in this area.

Fink, B. and Penton-Voak, I. (2002). *Evolutionary psychology of facial attractiveness.* Current Directions in Psychological Science, 11(5): 154–158. A short review of research on atractiveness from an evolutionary perspective.

Hepper, P. (2008). *Kin recognition, functions and mechanisms. A review.* Biological Reviews, 61(1): 63–93. A recent critical summary of research on kin recognition in animals as well as humans.

Rhodes, G. and Zebrowitz, L. (2002). *Facial Attractiveness: Evolutionary, Cognitive, and Social Perspectives.* Westport, CT: Ablex. An edited collection of papers on attractiveness, from a variety of different theoretical viewpoints.

THE DEVELOPMENT OF FACE PROCESSING 1: INFANTS

How does the ability to recognize faces change with age? Apart from its intrinsic interest, studying infants might enable us to find out whether cognitive processes such as face recognition are 'hard-wired' into the nervous system and thus present from birth, or whether they develop as a result of experience. (This is relevant to the issue of whether or not faces are 'special', which will be discussed in detail in Chapter 10.) Studying infants' face perception might help us to decide between these two standpoints. If newborn babies process faces differently to other stimuli, in the absence of

any experience with them, this is consistent with the view that they possess innate mechanisms for dealing with faces. (However, as we shall see, differential processing of faces from birth can also be interpreted in terms of non-face-specific systems too—things are seldom straightforward in psychology!) In this chapter, we'll examine research suggesting that not only do babies seem to be attracted to faces from birth, but they also possess surprisingly sophisticated face-processing abilities, despite the limitations imposed by their immature visual systems.

5.1 Techniques for studying face processing in infancy

The study of face processing in infants began in earnest in the 1960s, for two reasons. Firstly, after decades of behaviourism, there was renewed interest in cognition, and a concomitant interest in how cognition develops. The second reason for a resurgence in interest in infant face processing was that new techniques were developed to examine infant behaviour. Studying infants poses obvious problems. With adults, we normally make inferences about cognitive performance by studying overt behaviour, but that is difficult to do with young babies because they lack control over

their bodies: they can't sit up, let alone press a key on a response pad! However, a number of ingenious behavioural techniques have been devised that capitalize on the fact that even newborns have some limited control over their eye and head movements.

The **preferential looking** technique involves displaying two stimuli to the infant, one to the left and one to the right, and recording how long he or she looks at each one. The assumption is that infants will look longer at the stimulus that they prefer, but this assumption isn't central to using the technique: whatever their motivation for doing so, if the infant looks at one of the stimuli for longer than the other, this implies that they can discriminate between them. (To ensure the preference is not due to extraneous factors such as the infant having a consistent bias towards one side or the other regardless of what appears there, each stimulus is shown an equal number of times on both the left and the right.)

The **habituation** technique is based on the fact that if the same stimulus is presented repeatedly an infant will eventually tire of looking at it and begin to look elsewhere (Fig. 5.1).

Once the infant has habituated in this way, two stimuli are presented: the one to which the infant was habituated, and a novel one. If the infant cannot discriminate between them, he or she is likely to look more or less equally at both stimuli. As far as the infant is concerned, the new stimulus is just another example of the thing that they have become bored with looking at. However, if the infant can tell the difference between the old and new stimuli, they may show dishabituation: they may display renewed interest in the new stimulus, as evidenced by an increase in the amount of time they spend looking at it.

Operant conditioning techniques can also be used with babies. In order to change the stimulus that is being displayed, the baby makes a particular response, such as turning their head to one side or the other, or sucking on a dummy that is connected to a computer via a pressure transducer.

In the past 20 years or so, these behavioural techniques have been supplemented by electrophysiological measurements. It is now possible to perform **event-related potential (ERP)** studies with babies, to see whether their electrophysiological responses to faces and other visual stimuli are similar to those shown by older people. (For more information on ERP research, see Chapter 9.) This technique involves measuring the electrical response of an infant's brain to a pattern (such as a face). The same pattern is presented repeatedly, and EEG measurements are taken each time. Subsequently, computer analysis averages the electrical response over all the trials on which the stimulus was presented. Although the cortical response to any single presentation of the pattern is usually hard to detect because of the presence of random 'noise' in the EEG reading, averaging over a large number of trials makes the 'noise' cancel out, so that any systematic responses to the stimulus are revealed. Typically, ERP studies tend to show evidence of discrimination between visual stimuli at somewhat earlier ages than behavioural studies do.

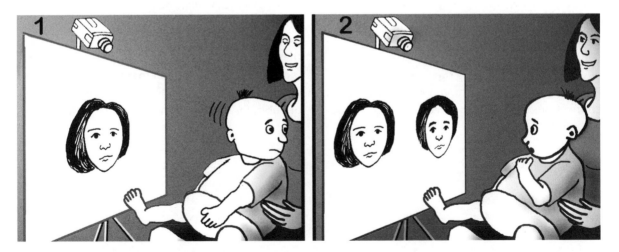

FIGURE 5.1 Using habituation to determine whether babies can recognize faces. (1) The baby is repeatedly exposed to a face until it gets bored with looking at it. (2) The baby is shown the habituated face, plus a novel face. Renewed interest implies the baby can discriminate between them.

5.2 **The infant's visual system**

Before discussing infant face processing, it is necessary to know a little about the nature of the infant's visual system. Human babies are born in a very immature state compared with other mammals, and a great deal of maturation of the nervous system occurs after birth. In fact, neural development is not fully complete until around puberty. The visual system of a newborn baby is very different to an adult's in many ways. The retina undergoes considerable maturation after birth, and takes about four years to reach its adult state. At 15 months of age, the distance between neighbouring photoreceptors in the central area of the retina is twice the comparable value for an adult (Yuodelis and Hendrickson, 1986). The newborn baby lacks full control of its eye movements, so that saccades (large-scale movements of the eyes from one fixation point to another) are poorly controlled, and smooth pursuit movements to track moving objects are impossible (Aslin, 1981; Bronson, 1990). The visual cortex and the 'higher' cortical areas that are involved in processing and interpreting visual information are relatively undeveloped. The cortex develops more slowly than subcortical structures. Consequently, as the infant matures, there is a shift from subcortical to cortical control of processes such as eye movements. During the first six months of life in particular, an enormous number of synaptic connections are formed between neurones, and a large amount of myelination of nerve fibres occurs (something that speeds up nervous conduction considerably).

All of these changes have perceptual consequences. Simply as a result of the cortical and retinal immaturity, one would expect an infant's visual acuity to be much poorer than an adult's. 'Poorer' can be expressed in quantitative terms, and, before we proceed, it is necessary to make a brief digression about how this is done.

Firstly, any pattern, no matter how complex, can be broken down into a set of simple sine waves that change smoothly and repeatedly from dark to light and back again. This process is called **Fourier Analysis**, after the 19th-century mathematician Jean-Baptiste Fourier, who first elucidated it. (Conversely, any pattern can be produced by assembling sine waves, a process known as 'Fourier Synthesis'.) Any visual stimulus can be described purely quantitatively, in terms of four attributes of its constituent sine waves.

The first is **spatial frequency**. This refers to how frequently a sine wave repeats itself per unit distance. A high spatial-frequency pattern might contain 100 cycles (alternations of light and dark) per centimetre, whereas a low frequency pattern might contain only two cycles per centimetre.[1] Look at Fig. 5.2, which consists of four different sine waves. The top left pattern has a lower spatial frequency (a slower rate of change per unit distance) than the bottom right pattern. The second property is **orientation** with respect to vertical: the patterns on the right-hand side of Fig. 5.2 are at different orientations to the patterns on the left-hand side.

---

[1] As mentioned in Chapter 2, in practice it is more convenient to express the unit of distance in terms of 'visual angle', the distance on the retina, expressed in degrees. This is because the effective size of a pattern, and hence its constituent spatial frequencies, depends on not just on its own size, but also on how far away it is from the viewer. Rather than having to give the size of an object *and* its distance from the observer, one merely needs to supply the visual angle that the pattern covers on the retina. Our field of vision is about 180 degrees when we look straight ahead. One degree is divided into 60 minutes, and 1 minute is divided into 60 seconds. Your thumb at arm's length covers about 2 degrees of visual angle; coincidentally, the sun and the moon both cover about half a degree (i.e. 30 minutes). Although they are very different sizes, they are also at very different distances from us!

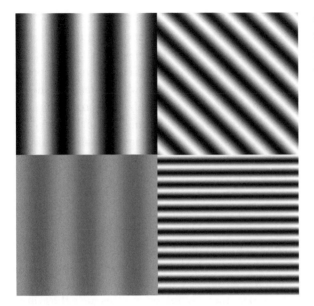

FIGURE 5.2 Patterns differing in spatial frequency, phase, orientation and contrast (for explanation see text). (Reproduced with kind permission of Professor George Mather, University of Sussex. © George Mather)

The third property is **contrast**, the difference between the brightest and darkest parts of a cycle, or its 'amplitude of modulation'. The two patterns on the left-hand side of Fig. 5.2 have the same spatial frequency, but the lower one has much lower contrast than the upper one. The final attribute is **spatial phase**, which refers to the position of the sine wave in relation to some fixed point. If two sine waves are in phase, their peaks and troughs will be in alignment; if they are 180 degrees out of phase (as in the case of the two patterns on the left-hand side of Fig. 5.2), the peaks of one wave would align with the troughs of the other.

This may all seem rather arcane, but it gives us a means to specify the performance of the visual system in quantitative terms. You are no doubt familiar with the conventional eye-chart; this measures our ability to detect fine detail, which is represented by high spatial frequencies. Generally speaking, the higher the spatial frequency, the more contrast we need in order to be able to see it. Once a pattern's spatial frequency exceeds a

certain level, we cannot detect that pattern, no matter how much contrast it has. The photographs in newspapers are based on this principle. If you look very closely, you can see that they are made up of individual black and white dots, but at a distance the separate dots are no longer discriminable, and you perceive unbroken regions of grey. By presenting participants with sine waves that vary in spatial frequency and contrast, it is possible to plot how much contrast is needed in order to perceive each spatial frequency. The resultant plot of contrast versus spatial frequency is called the **contrast sensitivity function (CSF)**.

By looking at Fig. 5.3, you can get some idea of your own sensitivity to different spatial frequencies at various contrast levels. As you move from left to right, the pattern increases in spatial frequency, and as you go from the bottom to the top of the figure, the contrast decreases. The precise effect will vary depending on your distance from the pattern, because changing the viewing distance changes the effective spatial frequency content of the pattern: the closer it is to you, the lower the spatial frequencies become. However, you should notice that the pattern appears to fade to grey earlier on the left and right

FIGURE 5.3 Sinusoidal grating varying in spatial frequency (SF) from left to right (high SFs on the right) and in contrast from bottom to top (high contrast at bottom). (Reproduced by kind permission of Professor Izumi Ohzawa, from the original concept by Fergus Campbell and John Robson [1964]. © Izumi Ohzawa, 2009)

than it does in the middle. This is an illusion, arising from your visual system's differential sensitivity to low, medium and high spatial frequencies. The decrease in contrast from bottom to top is actually the same across the entire width of the pattern, but, because you are less sensitive to low and high spatial frequencies, you need more contrast to see these, compared to the middling spatial frequencies.

If you imagine drawing a line that marks the point at which the sine wave appears to fade to a uniform grey, you should obtain something like the 'adult' curve in Fig. 5.4, which shows the contrast sensitivity functions for an adult, a 1-month-old infant, and a 3-day-old baby.[2]

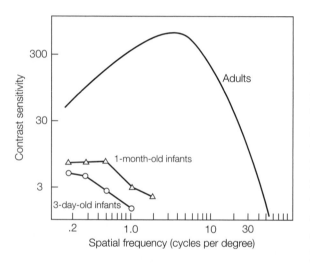

FIGURE 5.4 Contrast sensitivity function at different ages. The horizontal scale shows spatial frequency, ranging from low to high; the vertical scale shows sensitivity (measured in terms of how little contrast is needed to detect a given spatial frequency—thus adults need far less contrast to detect a spatial frequency of 1 cycle per degree than does a 3-day-old baby).

This graph tells us two things: that the baby's CSF is very different from that of an adult, and that there is rapid improvement in sensitivity during the first few months of life. Adults can see much more fine detail than a baby can, and they need much less contrast in order to be able to do so. Adults are most sensitive to spatial frequencies in the range of 3–5 cycles per degree. A 3-day-old baby's peak sensitivity is around 0.1–0.2 cycles per degree, and they cannot even detect frequencies above 1 cycle per degree (Banks and Salapatek, 1981).

Based on knowledge of their CSF, we would predict that faces should look rather different to infants than they do to adults. In particular, infants should be unable to detect much of the fine detail information that we can see in faces, such as details of features, wrinkles, etc., because these are conveyed by the high spatial frequencies. This has recently been confirmed by de Heering et al (2008). By presenting newborns with faces that were filtered to remove certain spatial frequencies, they were able to show that newborns' face recognition is based only on very low spatial frequencies, within the range of 0–0.5 cycles per degree. However, this is still probably good enough for recognition to be achieved: even a newborn baby would be able to make out the basic configuration of a nearby face, and be able to perceive the shape of the person's hair, because this information is present in the low spatial frequencies that an infant can detect (Bartrip et al, 2001).

In short, to a young infant, a face consists of a pasty blob with darker blobs within it representing the eyes and mouth. Figure 5.5 gives some idea of what faces probably look like to a newborn baby at viewing distances of 50 cm and 2 m.

---

[2] You may be wondering how a baby's CSF can be measured. Behaviourally, it can be done by using the habituation technique described earlier. For example, the baby is shown a uniform grey square until it gets bored of looking at it, and then is shown a grating of a certain spatial frequency that has the same average luminance as the grey square. Dishabituation implies that the baby has detected that the new stimulus is different from the grey square. If the baby does not dishabituate, this implies that it cannot detect the grating (i.e. that the grating also appears to be a uniform grey). ERPs can also show whether the baby can detect the difference between two stimuli.

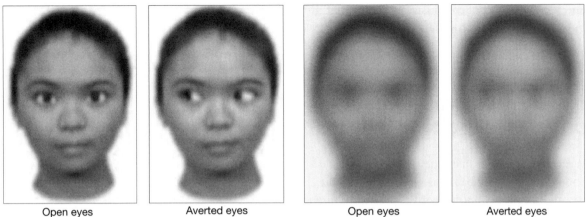

Open eyes	Averted eyes		Open eyes	Averted eyes
(a) at 50-cm viewing distance			(b) at 2-m viewing distance	

FIGURE 5.5 How faces probably appear to a newborn baby at a viewing distance of (a) about 50 cm (the typical distance for face-to-face interaction) and (b) 2 m. Compare the appearance of these images with the schematic faces shown in Fig. 5.6. (Reprinted by permission from Macmillan Publishers Ltd: Johnson, M. H. (2005). Subcortical face processing. *Nature Reviews Neuroscience*, 6, 766–774. © 2005)

We now have a reasonably good idea of what information babies potentially have *available* to them, in order to recognize faces. The data on how well they can actually *use* this information (i.e. how well they can recognize faces in practice) are rather complex. Part of the reason for this may be that studies of infant face processing have often used schematic faces rather than real ones, and in some instances these have not been very life-like. Compare the appearance of the schematic face in Fig. 5.6 with the real faces in Fig. 5.5. For one thing, unless they are badly frost-bitten, real faces do not have black noses! It is known that, in adults, schematic faces are processed in rather different ways from real faces (Leder, 1996), and this may account for some of the inconsistencies in the literature on infant face processing. Schematic faces tend to be much simpler than real faces, and they have much more luminance contrast between their features and the rest of the face. As babies need more contrast than adults in order to see a pattern, this is likely to affect their responses. Evidence for this assertion comes from a study by Maurer (1985), who found that before 4–6

weeks of age babies scanned the internal features of schematic faces more than they scanned the internal features of real faces. Maurer suggested that this is might be because the schematic faces are relatively impoverished, or because their internal features are more prominent than those of real faces. The same explanation would account for the results of a study by Schwarzer and Zauner (2003), who found that 8-month-old babies processed photographs of faces more holistically than they processed line-drawn faces.

There are also difficulties in interpreting the results from behavioural studies involving infants. They can be very difficult people to work with! Most studies lose sizeable numbers of participants either because the infants fall asleep or because of 'fussiness', a euphemism for the fact that the infant was screaming its head off and could not be persuaded to take part in the procedure. The data from the cooperative infants are often 'noisy' and prone to sizeable individual differences. Finally, a failure to find evidence of a discrimination between two faces is open to all the usual interpretational difficulties raised by null results, and it is certainly not conclusive evidence that the baby is unable to discriminate between them.

5.3 Do newborn infants preferentially attend to faces?

With all these points in mind, what do we know about how newborn babies respond to faces? The record for early testing currently stands with Goren, Sarty and Wu (1975), who demonstrated that infants as young as 9 minutes of age preferred to look at moving schematic faces rather than 'scrambled' face patterns that contained the same elements but arranged in a non-face-like pattern. This finding was replicated by Maurer and Young (1983) on babies aged between 12 hours and 5 days, and by Johnson, Dziurawiec, Ellis and Morton (1991), using infants tested within the first hour after birth (Fig. 5.6).

5.3.1 CONSPEC and CONLEARN

Curiously, the preference for moving face-like patterns seems to disappear after 4 weeks: 1-month-old infants appear to show no preference for faces compared to non-face stimuli (Johnson, Dziurawiec, Ellis and Morton, 1991). A preference for faces re-emerges somewhere between 2 and 3 months, but then includes stationary faces as well as moving ones (Maurer and Barrera, 1981; Morton and Johnson, 1991; Turati, Valenza, Leo and Simion, 2005). Inspired by work on 'imprinting' in animals, Morton and Johnson (Johnson and Morton, 1991; Morton and Johnson, 1991) put forward a theory to explain this puzzling developmental trend. They suggested that there are two systems at work. Initially, a subcortical system[3] called **CONSPEC** directs babies to attend preferentially to moving

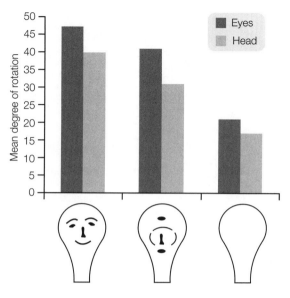

FIGURE 5.6 Extent of newborn eye and head turns in response to different kinds of moving stimulus. (From Johnson et al, 1991, experiment 1)

face-like patterns (specifically, to attend to patterns that have three dark patches, representing the eyes and mouth, within a face outline—a pattern Morton and Johnson termed 'config'). As the baby matures, cortical systems take over, and from around 4 weeks of age a second process, called **CONLEARN**, causes the baby to start to learn about individual faces. The idea is that the subcortical system is 'domain specific', in the sense that it has evolved specifically for the purpose of processing faces. Babies are born with a predisposition to attend to faces and, as a result, they learn about them. The CONSPEC system serves to bias the input to the developing cortex so that it ends up with the neural circuits that will, ultimately, underlie adult face recognition abilities (Johnson, 2001). This is an ingenious and elegant model, but, as we shall see, there are serious problems with it that render it implausible as a complete account of infant face processing.

---

[3] The original location proposed for this subcortical system was the *superior colliculus*, a structure that in adults is involved in controlling eye movements.

5.3.2 **The Linear Systems Model**

Although it would be tempting to conclude from the preferential looking data that infants are born with an innate attraction to faces, there is an alternative explanation: infants might merely have a predisposition to look at complex patterns, which incidentally happen to include faces. An early version of this idea was Banks and Salapatek's (1981) **Linear Systems Model**, which suggested that infants prefer to look at low spatial frequency, high contrast patterns, because these best match the properties of their immature visual systems (see also Kleiner, 1987; Kleiner and Banks, 1987).

This is why Goren et al (1975), Maurer and Young (1983) and Johnson et al (1991) all examined the extent to which newborns looked at 'scrambled' schematic faces. These stimuli were similar to the schematic faces in terms of complexity (spatial frequency content), luminance and contrast, but they lacked the basic 'first order' facial configuration of two eyes above a nose, above a mouth. If this configuration is important, infants should prefer these faces to their scrambled counterparts.

The differences in looking behaviour for scrambled and unscrambled faces are not large, and not all researchers have found them; for example, in three separate studies on infants aged 2 days or less, Easterbrook et al (1999) found a preference for patterned stimuli compared with blank face outlines, but no evidence of a preference for schematic faces over scrambled faces. However, by and large, the research suggests that newborns prefer to look at patterns with a face-like configuration, rather than patterns that contain the same elements but in a non-face-like arrangement. Although the Linear Systems Model can account for many aspects of infants' looking behaviour as far as non-face-like patterns are concerned, it fails to explain this preference. Kleiner (1990) therefore modified the earlier Linear Systems Model by adding a

second stage: she proposed that, if two patterns are similar in terms of possessing the optimal amplitude for the infant, discrimination between them will occur on the basis of their structural properties. This is tantamount to saying that, if two patterns are similar in spatial frequency content, the one that has a face-like structure is preferred. However, it does make the prediction that the infant will prefer a non-face-like pattern over a face, if the former fits the infant's CSF better than the latter.

In a test of this hypothesis with newborn babies, Valenza et al (1996) found that babies still preferred the face-like pattern. Figure 5.7 shows some of the stimuli compared by Valenza and co-workers (1996), using babies aged between 25 and 155 hours. Babies oriented an equal number of times to a 'face-like' configuration and a non-face-like configuration of three dots within a head outline, but they looked at the face-like version for more than twice as long as they looked at the non-face-like configuration. Valenza et al also found that babies preferred to look at a face-like configuration, rather than at a stimulus that was non-face-like but more salient according to the Linear Systems Model (the latter's striped components had a spatial frequency of 0.19 cycles per degree, close to

FIGURE 5.7 Newborn babies prefer to look at the face-like configuration on the left rather than the non-face-like configuration in the middle, even though the two patterns possess similar spatial frequencies. They also prefer the face-like configuration to the pattern on the right, even though the latter's spatial frequency content fits the infant's contrast sensitivity function better. (From Valenza et al, 1996)

the babies' peak contrast sensitivity). Even the revised Linear Systems Model does not account for these results.

5.3.3 **Preference for 'top-heaviness'**

Facial *structure* thus seems to influence babies' looking behaviour. In a series of studies, Turati and her colleagues investigated infants' preferences for structure in greater detail, and consistently found that newborns appear to have a preference for patterns that contain most of their elements in their upper half. For example, Simion et al (2002) tested 1 to 6-day-old babies with non-face-like geometric patterns that contained a preponderance of elements in either their upper or lower half (Fig. 5.8, left-hand pane). In all cases, fixation times were biased towards the stimuli that had most of their elements in their upper half (i.e. those in the extreme left column of Fig. 5.8).

Turati et al (2002) performed three experiments to investigate infants' looking preferences to stimuli that consisted of three dots within a face outline, arranged in various configurations (see Fig. 5.8, right-hand pane). In each case, the infants preferred the 'top-heavy' configurations, but there was no evidence of a preference for a symmetrical 'face' configuration over an asymmetrical configuration of two dots above a single dot. More problematic for Morton and Johnson's theory, infants preferred to look at a non-face-like dot configuration whose dots were all located in the upper half of the face outline, than to look at a face-like configuration whose dots were all positioned towards the bottom of the face outline. In other words, babies' preference for looking at 'top-heavy' patterns seems to be stronger than their preference for looking at face-like patterns.

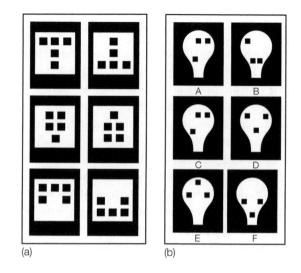

FIGURE 5.8 Newborn infants prefer to look at 'top-heavy' patterns rather than 'bottom-heavy' ones. (a) Stimuli in the left column were preferred to those in the right column (Simion et al, 2002). (b) A was preferred to B; E to F; C and D were fixated equally (Turati et al, 2002).

Three studies by Macchi Cassia et al (2004), using images of real faces, showed that infants preferred upright faces to inverted faces, top-heavy scrambled faces to bottom-heavy scrambled faces, and looked equally often at top-heavy scrambled faces and normal upright faces (Fig. 5.9). Once again, the data are consistent with infants having a preference for top-heavy patterns, rather than for 'faces' *per se*.

Why does the preference for 'top-heaviness' exist? Turati et al's explanation is similar to the one that underlies the Linear Systems Model: babies prefer to look at patterns that they are able to process more easily. Turati et al point out that there are some studies showing that adults are more sensitive to stimuli that fall on the upper half of their visual field rather than the lower half.[4] Perhaps babies also find it easier to detect patterns that fall in the upper half

---

[4] Actually, the findings in relation to adults are more complex than Turati et al suggest. Many studies show a *lower* visual field advantage (reviewed in McAnany and Levine, 2007), and in fact for cartoon face matching Hagenbeek and Van Strien (2002) found a upper right visual field *and* lower left visual field advantage!

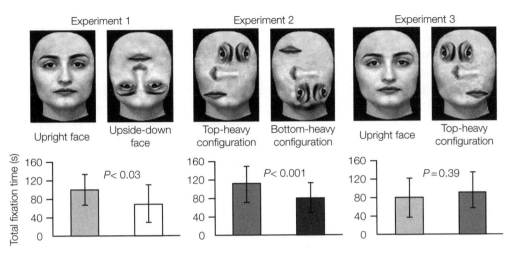

FIGURE 5.9 Total time that newborns spend looking at various facial stimuli. (From Macchi Cassia et al, 2004)

of their visual field. Interestingly, this preference for 'top-heavy' patterns remains detectable in adults: Caldara et al (2006) performed a functional magnetic resonance imaging (fMRI) study using stimuli similar to those used by Simion et al (2002) and Turati et al (2002), and found that curvilinear patterns with most of their elements in the top half produced activation in the right **fusiform face area**, an area known to be heavily involved in face processing (see Chapter 9). Caldara et al suggest that this area might be tuned for geometrical properties that are found in faces, as part of a system that is optimized for rapidly detecting faces in scenes.

Top-heaviness is not the sole factor influencing babies' looking preferences, however: they are also affected by the shape within which the elements are presented. A *post hoc* comparison of data on babies' responses to stimuli like those in Fig. 5.8 suggested that faces and schematic faces were looked at for longer than non-face-like geometric patterns (Simion et al, 2001). This implies that babies' preference for top-heavy patterns is enhanced by the addition of a curvilinear external contour. Furthermore, babies are influenced by the contrast polarity of the stimuli. A normally lit face is light with darker regions around the eyes and mouth due to shadowing. A series of experiments

by Farroni et al (2005) showed that newborn babies prefer to look at faces and schematic faces that have normal contrast rather than ones that have reversed contrast (i.e. rather than schematic faces that consist of black faces with white blobs, or real faces in photographic negative). This result would not be predicted by an explanation of preferences solely in terms of top-heaviness. Farroni et al claim that babies' preferences are for stimuli that share many of the features of faces, rather than being determined merely by a preference for top-heavy patterns.

5.3.4 'Domain-specific' versus 'domain-general' views of infant face processing

There are thus two subtly different conceptions of newborns' face-processing abilities. Morton and Johnson's view is that babies are born with a predisposition to track face-like patterns. The alternative view, held by Turati and her colleagues, is that infants are born with a preference for looking at particular types of pattern, which just happen to include faces (see Chapter 10). Both of these conceptions of development are **neuroconstructivist**; in both cases, specific cognitive abilities such as face recognition are envisaged as developing from the interplay between the infant's proclivity to attend to faces and the experience that the infant obtains as a result. The net result is the same in both cases: babies selectively expose themselves to faces, and as a result they become expert with them.

The difference between the theories is in terms of how specific the mechanisms are that cause infants to attend to faces in the first place. Morton and Johnson's CONSPEC system is **domain-specific**. The claim is that it has been designed by evolution specifically so that babies attend preferentially to faces rather than other stimuli. (At least in their original formulation of their theory, the CONLEARN system was not seen as domain-specific but as a perceptual learning system that just happened to be exposed a lot to faces as opposed to other stimuli, by virtue of the CONSPEC system.) The system envisaged by Turati and others is wholly **domain-general**, in the sense that it is not dedicated to face processing. It arises instead from the basic properties and limitations of the infant's visual system.

In practice, deciding between these alternative conceptions is virtually impossible. The optimal stimulus for attracting a newborn baby's attention appears to be an ellipse that is lighter than its background and contains darker elements arranged so that more of them fall in the upper half of the pattern than in its lower half. To Turati and her colleagues, this is a pattern that just happens to suit the capacities of the infant's visual system; to Johnson and his colleagues, this is a good description of a face.

In real life, of course, the primary caregiver (normally the mother) also has an important role to play in determining what the infant looks at. Bushnell's (1998, 2001) 'sensory-ecology' model highlights the primary caregiver's role as a 'multisensory system' that both engages the infant's attention and—by virtue of being the main source of need gratification for the infant—rewards the infant for attending to their face.

5.4 **Preference for *individual* faces**

The studies just described tell us something about whether newborns prefer to look at faces rather than other patterns. How well can babies distinguish between individual faces? Studies using real people, rather than photographs or schematic faces, suggest that newborns are capable of more than merely orienting towards a moving face: they appear to show a preference for their mother's face compared to a stranger's.

Field et al (1984) found that newborn babies (on average 45 hours old) preferred to look at their mother's face rather than at a similar-looking stranger's. Before testing, these babies had had an average of just 4 hours' total exposure to their mother's face. Bushnell et al (1989) and Pascalis et al (1995) successfully replicated Field et al's findings using 3 to 4-day-old infants, and controlling for the possibility of odour cues from the mother.

Bushnell (2001) performed an interesting observational study to obtain data on how much experience babies need to have with their mother's face in order to show a preference for it compared to a stranger's face. Newborn babies were observed for 3 days, during which their behaviour was time-sampled for four 2-hour periods in every 24 hours. The babies were then tested by showing them their mother's (live) face and a stranger's, and measuring how much time the baby looked at each. For more than 60% of the study period, the babies were asleep; but when they were awake most of their time was spent with their mother. Of this time with the mother, 39% of it was spent looking at her face, and 61% was spent not looking at her.

When tested, there was considerable variability between babies, but overall 22 of 29 babies looked more at their mother than the stranger. There was a significant (0.51) positive correlation between the amount of time they had spent looking at their mother's face during the previous 3 days and the degree of visual preference for her. Again, the

data were very variable: one baby who had only
1 hour of exposure to its mother's face showed a
preference for looking at her, and seven infants who
had between 2 and 5 hours of exposure did not. But
overall, the data suggest that very little exposure to
the mother's face (just a few hours) is required for
most infants to show a preference for her.

Bushnell (2001) also examined how well
infants could tolerate a delay between seeing the
mother's face and being tested with it in a mother–
stranger preference task. The average age of testing
was 45–93 hours after birth. Infants still showed a
preference for the mother's face after a 15-minute
delay since last seeing her, suggesting that they
have some kind of memory for her face.

5.4.1 **The nature of newborn babies'
face representations**

The existence of a preference for individual faces
(specifically, the mother's) poses some problems for
Morton and Johnson's (1991) original formulation
of the CONSPEC theory, because it suggests that
newborn responses to faces are not governed solely
by a subcortical system that merely tracks face-like
patterns. Johnson and de Haan (2001) therefore
revised the theory, suggesting that newborn babies'
preference for individual faces might be due to a
system based in the hippocampus that represents
faces only as isolated stimuli; they claim that an adult-
like system, in which different views of the same face
are related to one another and encoded relative to a
prototype, does not emerge until 3 months of age.[5]

Support for this argument comes from a study
by de Haan et al (2001). They familiarized 1- and
3-month-old infants with four individual faces, and
then gave them a preference test. One of the faces in
the test was a novel face, and the other was either
one of the four familiarized faces or a blend that
was produced by morphing together these four
faces. Both the 1- and 3-month-old infants preferred
to look at the novel face rather than at one of the
four faces to which they had been habituated, but
only the 3-month-old infants preferred to look at a
novel face rather than the blend, implying that they
regarded the morph as a familiar face too.

However, other research suggests that newborn
babies *can* generalize over different views, implying
that their representations of faces do not consist
merely of isolated, unrelated and image-specific
views. In Walton and Bower's (1993) study, newborn
babies (aged between 8 and 78 hours) sucked on
a dummy that was connected to a computer via
a pressure transducer. Sucking controlled the
presentation of photographs of women's faces.
The babies were shown six faces in succession:
four individual faces, a composite of these, and a
composite of four previously unseen faces. (Half
of the babies saw the familiar-face composite
followed by the unfamiliar-face composite, and
the rest saw the two composites in the opposite
order.) Over the course of the entire experimental
session, total looking times to the two composites
did not differ, but the first look at the familiar-face
composite was significantly longer than the first
look at the unfamiliar-face composite,[6] implying

---

[5] This account is consistent with a popular distinction in memory research, between *explicit (declarative)* and *implicit (non-declarative or procedural)* memory systems. Explicit memory requires conscious awareness of a previous experience. Implicit memory involves perceptual or skill learning and does not require awareness of previous experiences. Many researchers have suggested that implicit and explicit memory have separate neural bases, and that implicit memory develops earlier than explicit memory memory. See Rovee-Collier and Cuevas (2009) for an extended criticism of this conception of memory, and in particular a criticism of its implication that babies are somehow 'imperfect' or 'incomplete' adults.

[6] Composites were counterbalanced across babies; in other words, the familiar-face composite that was seen by some of the babies was used as the unfamiliar-face composite for others, and vice versa. Consequently the differences

that the babies were able to distinguish between the two composites in some way. de Haan et al (2001) point out a problem with Walton and Bower's study: because it contained no test of whether the babies were able to discriminate between the faces, it is possible that the babies simply could not discriminate the prototype from the exemplars. Apparent 'generalization' produced by an inability to discriminate between different images is also de Haan et al's explanation for why infants seem to be able to recognize their mother across different views.

This criticism cannot be applied to the findings of Turati et al (2008). They tested babies aged between 12 and 72 hours. Each baby was habituated to one particular view of an unfamiliar woman's face. At test, the baby was shown two faces in a different pose: one was the woman just seen, and the other was a previously unseen woman. Thus, a baby might be habituated to a frontal view of a face, and then shown this face together with a different woman's face, both in three-quarter views (Fig. 5.10). A preference for the novel woman's face would imply that the baby has a viewpoint-invariant representation of the face that was originally seen: the baby has detected that the face to which it was originally habituated is present in the new pairing, albeit in a different pose, and so prefers to look at the face that has not been encountered before. Turati et al found that babies did not generalize between profile views and either frontal or three-quarter views, but they did generalize between three-quarter and frontal views. This generalization did not occur simply because the babies could not discriminate between them: when the babies were habituated to a full-face view and then shown this view paired with a three-quarter view of the same face (or vice versa), they preferred the novel view.

Thus, the weight of evidence suggests that even newborn babies can form fairly sophisticated representations of individual faces that are, at least

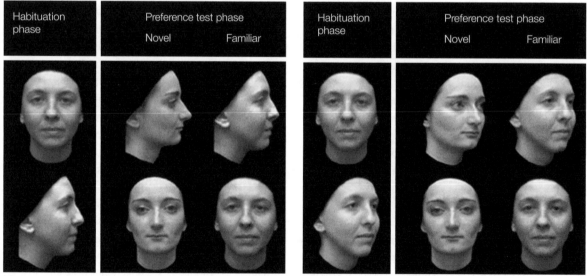

(a)   (b)

FIGURE 5.10 (a) Views of unfamiliar faces between which newborn babies do not generalize, and (b) views between which they do generalize. (From Turati et al, 2008)

in looking time cannot be attributed to differences between the composites themselves in terms of properties such as attractiveness or distinctiveness.

to some extent, viewpoint-invariant (bear in mind that even adults' representations of unfamiliar faces can show viewpoint-dependence; see Chapter 2). This does not fit well with the notion of a simple subcortical 'face-detector' system, such as CONSPEC.

The question then is: where does a newborn baby get its 'knowledge' of faces, in order to make these discriminations? One interesting idea, put forward by Quinn and Slater (2003), is that a baby's representation of faces is based on proprioceptive feedback from moving and touching its own face, while it is still in the womb. After birth, the baby is attracted to configurations that resemble its own face. (See Pascalis and Kelly [2009] for a review of supporting evidence for this theory.)

5.4.2 The role of internal and external features in infant face recognition

What facial information do these young babies use in order to discriminate between faces? Earlier studies, using static schematic faces, suggested that there is a developmental trend in infants' scanning behaviour, reflecting the rapid development of the oculomotor system during the first few months of life. One-month-old babies tend to scan the external edges of faces (and other objects too), whereas older infants are more likely to scan the internal features, especially the eyes (Maurer and Salapatek, 1976). Fixations tend to be very prolonged in younger infants (Aslin and Salapatek, 1975), but by about 3 months of age babies have developed a more adult-like pattern (see Chapter 2), consisting of more extensive scanning accompanied by shorter but more numerous fixations.

Research with realistic face stimuli has tended to support this idea of a developmental shift from an initial reliance on external facial features (head shape and hair) to a later use of information from the internal facial features. For example, in Pascalis et al's (1995) study, the babies appeared to be recognizing their mothers on the basis of hairstyle and/or face shape,

because the preference for the mother's face disappeared when these cues were obscured with headscarves so that only the internal facial features of the two women were visible. Bartrip et al (2001) replicated Pascalis et al's results with 3-week-old infants, but found that slightly older children (about 5 weeks old) were still able to discriminate between their mother and a stranger when both wore headscarves, implying that the older children were able to use internal facial features to recognize faces. When both women wore masks to hide their faces, so that only the external features were visible, only infants over the age of 4 months showed a preference for their mother. Bartrip et al's interpretation of these data was that babies' use of internal features develops faster than their use of external features; however, Bartrip et al also mention that babies found the masks distressing, so perhaps their lack of an apparent preference in the latter condition was also related to this.

More recent studies have provided some evidence that even newborns can use information from the internal facial features. Hunnius and Geuze (2004) performed a longitudinal study of babies' eye movements. Each baby saw two short videos: one of their mother's face that showed her interacting with them in a natural way (i.e. looking, smiling and nodding at the baby), and another showing an animated abstract pattern that was derived from this video and that was intended to be comparable to it in terms of its low-level physical properties. The babies were tested every 4 weeks between 6 and 26 weeks of age. Even at 6 weeks, Hunnius and Geuze found little evidence of a preference for scanning edges: the youngest babies scanned the internal and external features equally, and from 10 weeks on, the internal features were scanned significantly more. This might be because edge preference is strongest at 1 month of age (and so had peaked before Hunnius and Geuze started recording eye movements), or it might be because the internal features of Hunnius and Geuze's stimuli were animated and hence more attention-grabbing to the infants. Another factor might be that the edges of their stimuli were less pronounced than the high contrast edges of schematic faces.

Earlier studies (e.g. Maurer and Salapatek, 1976) suggested that babies paid little attention to the mouth, but Hunnius and Geuze found that the mouth attracted a lot of attention. Even at 6 weeks, the babies spent equal amounts of time looking at the mother's mouth and eyes. By 26 weeks, they were devoting 57% of their time to looking at her mouth and 28% of their time to looking at her eyes. Again this discrepancy with earlier findings might have occurred because the faces were animated, or it might be due to the fact that the videos were silent, so that the mouth movements appeared rather strange to the babies. Between 10 and 14 weeks, the babies changed the way they scanned the faces: there were fewer prolonged fixations; they paid less attention to edges; and they directed more attention to the meaningful parts of the face (the eyes and mouth). Hunnius and Geuze suggest these changes parallel the increase in social interaction with the mother that occurs at 3 months of age.

The idea that young babies are reliant on external features seems at odds with the results of the study by Turati et al (2008) that was mentioned in the previous section. In their work, newborn infants were clearly basing their discriminations solely on the internal facial features, because these were all that were provided (look again at Fig. 5.10). One explanation for the apparent discrepancy between Turati et al's findings and the earlier research is that babies might be influenced by the salience or availability of various facial cues: perhaps if only internal facial features are present, babies can use them as a basis for their discriminations, but if external features are present, these are used in preference. Support for this idea comes from a study on older babies by Blass and Camp (2004). They studied face recognition in 2 to 5-month-old infants, using live faces in an habituation paradigm. Each infant saw a young woman dressed in white, who smiled at the infant,

engaged eye contact with them, and stayed in the room until the infant had habituated to them. She then left the room. One minute later, either she returned, or a different but identically dressed woman entered the room instead. Looking time increased for the novel woman, but not when the original woman returned. This suggests that the infants were able to discriminate between the two women solely on the basis of their faces. Similar results were obtained if the women's hair, ears and neck were hidden from view by a nun's habit, implying that infants at this age are able to use the internal facial features as a cue to identity.

In a second experiment, Blass and Camp habituated the infants to a woman wearing a short curly wig. She then left, and 1 minute later either she or a different woman returned to the room, wearing either the same wig or a long straight wig. The infants remained habituated to the original woman, regardless of which wig she was wearing— implying that they perceived her to be the same person, and that this perception was based on her internal facial features. Interestingly, the infants looked longer at the stranger only when she was wearing the long wig: they did not dishabituate to her when she wore the short wig. This suggests that the infants did not discriminate between the two women on the basis of their internal features.

Blass and Camp suggest that perhaps similarity of internal *or* external features is sufficient for infants to perceive the face as being the same person. They speculate that the infants scanned the new face, and used a single aspect of it (either the internal or external features) to decide within seconds whether or not it was familiar. This interpretation does not seem to account for the results of experiment one, however. In the 'internal features only' condition, when a different woman entered the room she wore the same white habit as the first one; in effect, therefore, their external features were identical. In these circumstances, why didn't the infants treat these women as being the same person? Judging from Blass and Camp's illustrations, the short wig was quite striking, so perhaps it was just much more salient to the infants than the white habit. At any rate, this study shows that infants as young as 8 weeks have the ability to distinguish between two unfamiliar faces solely on the basis of their internal features, even though they are not doing this consistently. This might be the explanation for the apparent inconsistencies between earlier and more recent studies of babies' use of internal and external facial features: perhaps young babies recognize faces on whatever features are most salient to them. When hair is provided as a possible cue for recognition, they readily use it, but when hair is removed (as in Turati et al's study) the internal facial features become more obvious and they are used instead.

Further support for this **cue salience** idea comes from a study by Rose et al (2008), comparing 5-, 7- and 9-month-old infants in terms of their ability to recognize photographs of unfamiliar babies' faces. In Rose et al's first study, each infant was familiarized with a frontal view of a face by repeatedly pairing it with different novel faces until the infant showed a consistent preference for the new face. The infant was then shown two faces. One was a novel view of the familiarized face (either upright and in three-quarter view, or inverted and in a frontal view). The other was yet another novel face, in the same pose as the familiarized face. Recognition in all age groups (5-, 7- and 9-month-olds) was disrupted by inversion to a similar extent, implying that all three age groups were better at recognizing upright faces. However, Rose et al's other experiments suggested that there were age differences in the infants' reliance on internal and external features.

Their second experiment was similar to the first except that only part of the face was inverted at test. For one group, the internal facial features were upside-down at test and the external features remained upright. For the other group, the internal features remained upright and the external features were inverted. All three age groups performed at chance when the internal features were inverted and the external features were upright. However, when the external features were inverted and the internal features were upright, the 7- and 9-month-olds recognized the familiar face but the 5-month-olds did not. This implies that the 5-month-olds were not using the internal features as a basis for recognition.

In Rose et al's third study, the familiarized face was paired at test with a face that had either identical external features but different internal features, or identical internal features and different external ones (all of the faces were upright). When the external features were changed, all age groups paid more attention to the novel face than to the familiarized one. However, when the internal features were changed, the 7- and 9-month-olds showed a preference for the novel face, but the 5-month-olds did not. These results imply that the 5-month-olds were relying more on the external features as a guide to familiarity. Seven- and 9-month olds are more flexible, able to use either internal or external cues to identity as required.

Humphreys et al (2006) used a very different method to investigate the basis of 7-month-old babies' ability to discriminate between their mother and a similar-looking stranger. They employed a modified version of Gosselin and Schyns' (2001) 'bubbles' technique. In the normal version, the participant performs a discrimination task (such as, in this case, discriminating the mother's face from a stranger's), but on each trial only small regions of the face are displayed (Fig. 5.11). These regions vary randomly from trial to trial. Over many trials (about 200 or so), the whole of the face is sampled in this way. It is then possible to work out which of the displayed regions is associated with significantly better performance on the discrimination task. These regions can be considered the 'diagnostic' regions for the task at hand. One advantage of this technique is that it does not involve subjective and fairly arbitrary assumptions by the experimenter about what constitute facial 'features'. Humphreys et al modified the procedure by testing each of 13 babies 20 times and then pooling the data across all the babies to get a large enough sample of data for statistical analysis.

The results showed that the babies looked at different regions of the mother's and stranger's faces. Figure 5.11 shows these as dark patches overlaid on the same face image. For the mother, the babies preferred to look at the right eye and left-hand corner of the mouth (using 'left' and

'right' here to refer to the face from the baby's point of view). For the stranger, they preferred to look at the left eye and parts of the left-hand side of the face. Thus, by 7 months of age, babies appear to be using both 'internal' and 'external' features in order to recognize faces (although, as Humphreys et al concede, obscuring the women's hair with a shower cap may have led to an underestimation of the importance of hairstyle).

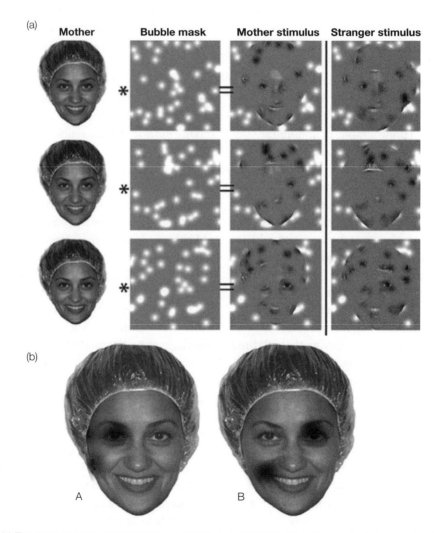

FIGURE 5.11 (a) The 'bubbles' procedure used by Humphreys et al (2006). On each trial, the baby saw two images (one of its mother and one of a stranger) obscured by the same 'bubbles' mask. The regions obscured by the mask varied from trial to trial. (b) The facial regions that were inspected by the infants for longest: A, stranger's face; B, mother's face

5.4.3 **Configural processing in infants**

A longstanding claim has been that children and adults process faces rather differently: whereas adults engage in **configural** processing, children have been thought to process faces more on the basis of their individual features, with an '**encoding switch**' from featural to configural processing taking place in late childhood (Carey and Diamond, 1977; Diamond and Carey, 1977). This hypothesis—and the mounting evidence against it—is reviewed in detail in Chapter 2, but there is now evidence from a number of studies, using diverse techniques, to show that even infants engage in configural processing to some extent.

Firstly, a hallmark of configural processing of faces in adults is the **Face Inversion Effect**: adults find it easier to recognize faces if they are upright than if they are upside-down (see Chapter 2). As mentioned in the previous section, Rose et al (2008) found evidence of an inversion effect in 5-, 7- and 9-month-old infants. Turati et al (2004) found that, under certain circumstances, an inversion effect could be found in 4-month-old infants. They performed two experiments. In both cases, infants were habituated to a three-quarter view of an unfamiliar woman with her hair obscured by a shower cap, so that only the internal features were visible. In the first experiment, an identical photograph was shown at test, paired with a photograph of a different woman in the same pose. Under these conditions, the infants showed a preference for the novel face regardless of the orientation of the test photographs. In the second experiment, the habituation phase consisted seeing a woman's face in a number of different poses. In the test phase, the babies were exposed to this woman's face paired with that of a different woman, both in a new pose that had not been experienced during the habituation phase. Under these conditions, the infants showed a preference for the novel face, but only when the faces were upright. Thus, under conditions that favour face recognition across different views

(rather than picture matching, as in experiment one), 4-month-old infants show an inversion effect.

As Turati et al point out, it would be unwise to draw too strong a parallel with the inversion effect in adults, because an important characteristic of the latter is that face recognition is *disproportionately* affected by inversion, compared with recognition of non-face objects. Nevertheless, their data suggest that, at least by 4 months, babies are better at recognizing faces when they are upright than when they are upside-down.

Another line of evidence for the idea that babies are engaging in configural processing comes from demonstrations of a **Composite Face Effect** in infants. When they are shown faces that are constructed from parts they have already seen, infants seem to perceive these faces as novel faces (see Chapter 2). Cohen and Cashon (2001) habituated 7-month-old infants to two adult female faces. The infants were then tested with one of these faces, a novel face, or a composite face that consisted of the internal features of one of the habituated faces transplanted into the external features of the other one. All of these faces were seen either upright or inverted. The logic behind this study was as follows. All of the *features* of the composite face were familiar to the infants due to habituation, but the *configuration* of the composite was novel. Suppose the infants did not look longer at the composite than at the familiar face. This would imply that they must be processing the face as independent features; in effect the baby has seen all of the features before and is indifferent to the fact that they were originally seen in different faces. On the other hand, if the infant looked longer at the composite than at the familiar face, this would imply that the infant was processing the facial features interactively, rather than in a piecemeal fashion, and was alert to the fact that the configuration was novel. Cohen and Cashon found that infants in the upright condition looked longer at the composite than at the familiar test face. In the inverted condition, they looked longer only at the novel face. This suggests that, like adults, 7-month-olds process the whole face when it is upright, but only its features when it is inverted.

Schwarzer and Zauner (2003) used a similar technique to Cohen and Cashon, but swapped individual features between faces rather than all of the internal features. They habituated 8-month-old infants to two faces, one male and the other female. At test, one group of babies saw faces in which the eyes or the mouth were swapped between faces (e.g. they saw the male's face with the female's eyes); one group saw novel faces; and a third group saw the same faces again. The logic is similar to that of Cohen and Cashon: if the infants process the faces as isolated features, they should not dishabituate to the swapped-feature faces because all of the individual features have been seen before in the habituation phase. However, if the infants process the faces holistically, they should dishabituate to the swapped-feature faces because, from a holistic point of view, these are faces with a novel configuration. In practice, the infants dishabituated to the feature-swapped faces, suggesting that they were processing the faces holistically. Schwarzer and Zauner performed a similar experiment with schematic (line-drawn) faces and obtained different results: the infants dishabituated to swapped eyes, noses and facial contours, but not to swapped mouths. These results imply that, in the case of the schematic faces, the infants were processing the eyes, nose and facial contour as isolated features, whereas the mouth was processed in conjunction with the facial context. Schwarzer and Zauner concluded that the discrepancies between their two experiments arose because line-drawn faces emphasize the individual features to a greater extent than photographs do. Their work suggests that infants have both configural and featural processing modes (like adults), but are biased towards configural processing with real faces.

A third line of evidence for configural processing in infants comes from studies showing that they are sensitive to the spatial arrangement of the facial features (the face's **second-order relational** properties; see Chapter 2). Hayden et al (2007) performed two experiments with 5- and 7-month-old infants, using a modified habituation technique. Each baby saw two versions of a photograph of a woman's face. One was unmodified and the other was distorted by moving its eyes outwards and its mouth downwards. The changes were similar in extent to those used by Mondloch et al (2002) with older children (see Chapter 6), and remained within the range of normal facial variation. In the first experiment, 7-month-olds showed evidence of being able to discriminate between the normal and distorted faces. The second experiment replicated this finding with 5-month-olds, and also showed that no evidence of discrimination was found if the faces were presented upside-down. Thus, not only are young infants sensitive to the second-order relational information in faces, but they are less sensitive to this information when the face is inverted.

One manipulation that has been used as evidence for the orientation specificity of configural processing in adults is the **Thatcher Illusion** (see Chapter 2). Turning the eyes and mouth upside-down with respect to the rest of the face makes the face look grotesque, but only if it is seen upright: the grotesqueness is hardly apparent when the whole image is inverted. Leo and Simion (2009) performed two experiments to investigate how 1 to 3-day-old newborns responded to Thatcherized faces. In the first experiment, half of the babies were habituated to a normal face and then subsequently shown this paired with a Thatcherized version of it. The rest of the babies were habituated to a Thatcherized face and then shown this paired with a normal face. In both cases, the babies showed a novelty preference for the version of the face that they had not seen previously. In other words, newborns can detect the difference between two faces that share the same basic facial plan (i.e. they have the same **first-order configuration** and the same features), but which differ in the precise spatial arrangement of their features (i.e. their **second-order configuration**). The second experiment showed that babies failed to make this discrimination when the faces were presented upside-down. Thus, newborn babies appear to be susceptible to the Thatcher Illusion, and by implication have sensitivity to the second-order relational properties of faces.

Lastly, evidence for the existence of configural processing in infants comes from an ERP study by Scott and Nelson (2006). They recorded ERPs from 4-month-old infants, 8-month-old infants, and adults. Participants were first familiarized with the face of an initially unfamiliar female. They were then shown a series of trials which included that same face; a configurally altered version (whose eyes and mouth had been moved slightly); a featurally altered version (whose eyes and mouth had been replaced with those from another face); and an entirely different female face. The infants also performed a visual paired-comparison task in which looking behaviour was recorded in response to the familiarized face paired with a featurally or configurally altered version. In the adults, the right hemisphere **N170** (one of the ERP components that occurs in response to faces; see Chapter 9) was greater for configural than for featural changes, whereas the left hemisphere N170 showed the opposite pattern. The 8-month-old infants' P400 component (which may be a developmental precursor to the N170) showed similar hemispheric differences to the adults' N170. There were large individual differences in performance, but the behavioural data from the visual paired comparison task suggested that the 8-month-olds, but not the 4-month-olds, could detect both featural and configural changes in faces to some extent.

5.5 Fine-tuning of infant face recognition by experience

Although infants' face-processing abilities are now known to be more sophisticated than was once thought, there is a lot of evidence to show that they are greatly affected by experience with faces during the first year of life (and beyond). Nelson (2001) has suggested that exposure to faces produces **perceptual narrowing**: infants start off with a fairly undifferentiated and crude face-processing system that rapidly becomes fine-tuned so that it is optimized for dealing with the kinds of face that it encounters most commonly (also see Chapter 12).

Research on infants is consistent with Nelson's idea; initially, babies have the ability to discriminate between all sorts of faces, but with increasing age this ability seems to disappear, and they become poorer at discriminating between faces that are different to the ones that they encounter regularly. Kelly et al (2005) measured newborn and 3-month-old Caucasian infants' preferences for looking at own- and other-race faces. Each baby was shown two pairs of unfamiliar faces, one male pair and one female pair. In each pair, one face was a member of the baby's own race (i.e. a Caucasian face) and the other face was either Middle Eastern, African or Asian. Kelly et al simply recorded how much time each baby spent looking at the faces. Newborns showed no preference for looking at faces of their own race, but the 3-month-olds looked significantly longer at the Caucasian faces. Kelly et al (2007) looked at the development of this preference in 3-, 6- and 9-month-old Caucasian infants, using the visual paired-comparison technique. Each infant was habituated to a single face, and then shown a pair of faces in a different viewpoint. One of the faces was novel, and the other was the face that was seen previously. The faces were Caucasian, African, Middle-Eastern or Chinese. The 3-month-old infants showed a preference for the novel face, regardless of race.

The 6-month-old children showed a novelty preference only for Caucasian and Chinese faces, and the 9-month-olds showed a preference only for Caucasian faces. With increasing age, it seems that the ability to differentiate between faces appears to become progressively more restricted to the infant's own race.

Exposure to faces plays a crucial role in the development of these preferences. Bar-Haim et al (2006) examined 3-month-old infants' preferences for looking at African and Caucasian faces. There were three groups of infant. One group comprised Caucasian Israelis. Both of the other groups consisted of racially African infants, but they differed markedly in terms of their exposure to Caucasian faces: one group lived in Ethiopia and had very limited exposure to Caucasian faces, whereas the other group came from families that had recently immigrated to Israel and were living in 'absorption centres'. These centres provided the infants with extensive opportunities to view Caucasian faces. The Caucasian and the Ethiopian African infants showed a preference for looking at faces of their own race, whereas the Israeli African infants looked equally at both races.[7]

Own-race preferences in infants thus appear to be modifiable by exposure to faces of another race. In the normal course of events (or at least, in our evolutionary past, before the advent of multicultural societies), infants would obtain exposure only to own-race faces, and would become skilled at differentiating between these, but at the expense of finding it hard to discriminate between faces from other races. Interestingly, in young infants, the own-race bias in face processing can be overcome by quite limited exposure to other-race faces. Using a visual paired-comparison technique with Caucasian and Asian faces, Sangrigoli and de Schonen (2004) found evidence

for an own-race preference in Caucasian infants at 3 months of age. However, if the infants were habituated to three different Asian faces instead of just one, the own-race bias was eliminated. This suggests that the **own-race bias** is rather fragile at this age, and can be eliminated with surprisingly little experience of other-race faces. Similar conclusions can be drawn from research on **own-species bias** by Pascalis and colleagues (2002), who found that the ability to distinguish between different monkey faces was present in 6-month-old infants, but not in 9-month-olds or adults. However, if the infants were shown pictures of monkey faces between 6 and 9 months of age, they retained their ability to discriminate between monkey faces (Pascalis et al, 2005).

Kelly et al (2005, 2007) support Nelson's (2001) idea that there is a progressive perceptual narrowing of face recognition abilities with increasing age. Newborn infants seem to have a fairly generalized face-processing system at birth, which enables them to discriminate between faces from all races (and even between non-human faces). By 3 months, a preference for own-race faces is beginning to be apparent. This preference is more clearly in place by 6 months of age. Experience with faces increases babies' ability to recognize faces of their own race, but at the expense of reducing their ability to recognize faces of other races. Kelly et al (2007) suggest that the own-race bias seen in adults has its origins in the first year of life. Initially, babies spontaneously attend to faces, which selectively exposes them to faces of their own race. As a result, they become more familiar with faces of their own race, and develop a preference for looking at them. This in turn leads infants to attend to own-race faces more than other-race faces, even if the latter are available. Finally, infants become better at

---

[7] Exposure to faces may also produce a gender bias in face processing. Quinn et al (2002) found that 3 to 4-month-old infants prefer to look at faces of the same gender as their primary caregiver (i.e. female faces if they are raised by a female, or male faces if raised by a male).

recognizing faces of their own group than other groups that are encountered less often.

Kelly et al (2007) relate these findings to Valentine's (1991) **Multidimensional Face Space** model (see Chapter 1). They suggest that the own-race bias seen in adults might be the ultimate consequence of having a modifiable face prototype. This prototype is the average of all the faces experienced during a person's lifetime. As a result it will resemble the race of the faces that are most often seen, and the dimensions by which faces are distinguished will be optimized for distinguishing between own-race faces. An alternative possibility is that there are multiple face spaces, one for each race of face. The face spaces for other races are poorly developed, because people have limited experience with faces of those races.

Humphreys and Johnson (2007) performed a series of experiments on 4- and 7-month-olds and adults, to address the issue of how face space might develop during infancy. Although faces can be conceptualized as 'points' in face space, in practice these points are more likely to be 'regions', to accommodate the fact that we still identify someone despite changes in viewpoint, expression, etc. (for adults, there is generalization across different views of the same face: see Chapter 1, section 1.3.2). Humphreys and Johnson looked at how these regions changed during development. The infants were habituated to a face, and then shown this face together with one of five morphs. Each morph was a blend between the familiarized face and a novel face, to varying degrees. The adults were briefly familiarized with a face, and then given a recognition memory test for the same five morphs that the infants saw. The 4-month-old infants failed to dishabituate to the morphs until they contained 90% of the novel face. The 7-month-olds dishabituated to the morphs once they contained 70% of the novel face. The adults responded to the morphs as 'novel' once they contained 50% of the novel face. These results imply that 'identity regions' in face space become smaller with increasing age, so that there is less likelihood for confusion between similar-looking faces. Again, this appears to be evidence that face-recognition skills are fine-tuned by increasing experience with faces, but that they are not *qualitatively* different from those of adults.

5.6 **Conclusion**

Every aspect of an organism is the outcome of a complex, continuing interplay between a genetic endowment and the environment within which the developing organism finds itself. Face processing is no exception to this rule. Babies are born with a predisposition to track face-like patterns. It is not clear whether this is because they are drawn to 'faces' *per se* or merely to any pattern that has certain physical properties, but the net result is the same: babies spend a lot of time looking at faces, and this leads them to develop expertise at distinguishing between them. There is an interesting parallel between the development of face recognition and the development of language: in the case of language, we are born with the ability to distinguish between all of the speech sounds used in all human languages. As the result of prolonged exposure to one particular language (the one that will become our native tongue), we become more sensitive to the speech sounds that it employs, and lose the ability to distinguish between the sounds used in other languages (review in Werker and Tees, 2005). For example, Japanese babies, but not adults, can distinguish between 'la' and 'ra', a discrimination that is easy for a native English speaker. With faces, newborns can discriminate between faces of different races, or even different species, but experience with their caregivers' faces causes them to lose this ability and become expert with one particular set of faces—those of their own race.

One problem with research on infants is that the great majority of studies have tested babies' ability to recognize static faces, in identical poses, for the initial presentation and at test. This makes it hard to know to what extent the results obtained reflect picture matching rather than face recognition (Turati et al, 2008). In addition, the use of static images is highly unnatural, given the degree of social interaction that would normally occur between a baby and nearby adults. During the past 30 years of research on the cognitive abilities of older children, it has become apparent that it is vital to take account of how the child construes the experimental task; a failure to do so has often led to an underestimation of children's abilities (and we shall see examples of this in the context of older children's face recognition abilities, in the next chapter). What do infants make of the experimental situations in which they are placed? Most studies present them with oddly impassive and static faces, when what they are used to is moving, interacting and animated faces.

Use of static images may also have led to an overestimation of how attention-grabbing faces are to babies: when 5½-month-old babies were shown unfamiliar women performing repetitive actions such as combing their hair, cleaning their teeth or blowing bubbles, the babies remembered the actions better than the women's faces. In fact, with limited exposure time (160 seconds), the babies' memory for the faces was at chance levels (Bahrick and Newell, 2008; Bahrick et al, 2002). Bahrick and Newell (2008) suggest that babies of this age have limited attentional capacity, and so the actions are encoded at the expense of the actors' identities. Most studies of infant perception have sacrificed naturalism for strict experimental control. In doing so, they may have inadvertently overemphasized the salience of faces for young babies.

Nevertheless, babies seem to find faces interesting and, despite their limited visual capabilities, even newborn babies appear to have surprisingly sophisticated face-recognition abilities. Notwithstanding the limitations of their visual systems, they can learn faces rapidly (so that just a few hours of exposure enables them to discriminate their mother's face from a stranger's); they show a degree of viewpoint-invariance; and they are already sensitive to the second-order relational properties of faces. However, as sophisticated as a newborn's face-processing abilities might be, they are still very crude in comparison to an adult's: experience with faces rapidly fine-tunes the immature system, so that it becomes optimized for distinguishing between the kinds of face with which the infant is most likely to come into contact.

SUMMARY

- A variety of techniques (habituation, preferential looking, ERP) enable us to measure babies' face-processing abilities.

- Newborns only 9 minutes old appear to have a preference for looking at face-like patterns (Goren et al, 1975), but why they do so is open to debate.

- 'Domain-specific' conceptions of infants' face processing suggest that there are innate neural systems specifically designed by evolution for face processing; in contrast, 'domain-general' views hold that expertise in face processing arises because faces just happen to be optimal stimuli for the developing visual system.

- Johnson and Morton (1991) proposed that early preferences for looking at faces are based initially on an innate subcortical system called CONSPEC. Later a cortical system called CONLEARN takes over, and infants learn about individual faces. However, more recent demonstrations of individual face recognition in newborns pose problems for the CONSPEC component of this model.

- The Linear Systems Model claims that infants attend to faces merely because faces happen to be optimal stimuli for their immature visual systems, in terms of spatial frequency content and contrast. Research has not supported this model.

- Turati and Simion's research group have shown that the basis for infants' preference for faces might stem from their preference for looking at 'top-heavy' patterns within a curvilinear outline.

- Because babies have much poorer visual acuity than adults, they are probably unable to detect much more than the overall configuration of a face. Nevertheless, they have surprisingly sophisticated face-recognition abilities; for example, newborns show a preference for their mother's face after only a few hours' exposure to it.

- Babies can generalize across different views of the same face, and they show configural processing (as evidenced by their sensitivity to manipulations that affect configural processing in adults, such as the Inversion Effect, Composite Face Effect and the Thatcher Illusion).

- There seems to be a developmental shift from relying on external features (hair and face shape) to using the internal facial features (eyes, nose and mouth). However, to some extent this depends on their salience, and even very young babies can use the internal features alone as a guide to recognition.

- Early experience with faces appears to 'fine-tune' face-recognition abilities: babies initially have the ability to recognize faces of all races (and those of other species too), but lose this ability with increasing experience of own-race faces. This may be the origin, at least in part, of the 'other-race effect' shown by adults.

FURTHER READING

Morton, J. and Johnson, M. H. (1991). *CONSPEC and CONLERN: a two-process theory of infant face recognition*. Psychological Review, 98(2): 164–181. Worth reading, given how influential this theory has been for researchers in this area.

Pascalis, O. and Kelly, D. J. (2009). *The origins of face processing in humans: phylogeny and ontogeny*. Perspectives on Psychological Science,

4(2): 200–209. This is a short review of research on infant processing from an evolutionary perspective.

Pascalis, O. and Slater, A. (2003). *The Development of Face Processing in Infancy and Early Childhood: Current Perspectives*. Hauppauge, NY: Nova Science. This is an edited book containing chapters written by many of the researchers mentioned in this chapter. Highly recommended.

6

THE DEVELOPMENT OF FACE PROCESSING 2: CHILDHOOD

From an 'applied' standpoint, children's proficiency at face recognition has been the subject of controversy for over a century, largely because of concerns in the legal profession about whether children can be competent eyewitnesses. A number of early 20th-century researchers drew very pessimistic conclusions about children's face recognition abilities. Varendonck (1911), for example, after finding that 16 of 18 7-year-olds were prepared to describe their teacher's non-existent beard when trying to remember what he looked like, wrote: 'When are we going to give up, in all civilized nations, listening to children in courts of law?' Had he also tested adults, he may well have obtained similar results, as adult eyewitness performance is often similarly unimpressive (see Chapters 11, 12 and 13). This chapter reviews more recent research on how well children can recognize faces. To what extent does it support Varendonck's views?

6.1 The developmental time-course of face recognition

Although infants show evidence of surprisingly sophisticated face-processing abilities (see Chapter 5), children do not seem to recognize faces as well as adults. It is difficult to be too precise about how much worse children are, as there are no methodologically unproblematic laboratory studies of how face recognition develops with age. A number of early studies investigated this issue by using an 'old/new' discrimination task with children of various ages (e.g. Blaney and Winograd, 1978; Carey et al, 1980; Feinman and Entwistle, 1976; Goldstein and Chance, 1964). In an initial learning phase, participants saw a series of unfamiliar faces for a few seconds per picture. They then saw these pictures again, randomly intermingled with an equal number of new unfamiliar faces, and tried to identify the faces that they had seen before. Unfortunately, as discussed in Chapter 1, by using the same pictures in the learning and test phases, all of these studies confounded *picture* recognition with *face* recognition; we do not know to what extent the participants were remembering the particular images that they had seen before, as opposed to the people depicted within those images.[1]

---

[1] An exception to this generalization is a study by Bruce et al (2000), who administered a battery of face-processing tests to children ranging in age from 4 to 11 years. There was clear evidence of a developmental progression in ability,

The same criticism applies to a more recent study by Lawrence et al (2008). They tested a large sample of 500 children aged between 6 and 16 years, but used the Warrington Recognition Memory for Faces (WRMF) test, a poor choice of test despite its past popularity with neuropsychologists. As an 'old/new' discrimination task, not only does the WRMF use identical images in the learning and test phases, but it encourages the use of pictorial cues because the individuals portrayed in the photographs have distinctive clothing and hairstyles.

A further problem is that most of these researchers used adult faces as stimuli. As described in Chapter 12, there is an ***own-age bias*** in face recognition, so part of any observed developmental trend in face recognition might be attributable to this (Chung and Thomson, 1995). Having said that, Goldstein and Chance (1964) and Feinman and Entwistle (1976) both used children's faces as test stimuli and obtained broadly similar results to researchers who used adult faces.

The results of these laboratory studies are rather mixed. By and large, they suggest that recognition performance improves markedly during early childhood (up to the age of 10 years or so). Thereafter, the rate of improvement flattens off somewhat (e.g. Blaney and Winograd, 1978; Flin, 1980). Carey et al (1980) found a marked improvement in performance from 6 to 10 years of age, and then a period around the age of 12 during which performance seemed to decline, before starting to improve again, up to the age of 16. Lawrence et al (2008) found considerable improvement between the ages of 6 and 10 years,

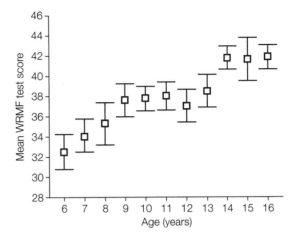

FIGURE 6.1 Mean Warrington Recognition Memory for Faces (WRMF) test scores in relation to age of child. Error bars are ± one standard deviation. (From Lawrence et al, 2008)

no improvement between 10 and 13, but then some further improvement between 13 and 16 (Fig. 6.1).

Not all researchers have found Carey et al's (1980) 'dip' in face recognition performance around puberty (see the excellent reviews of earlier work on this topic by Chung and Thomson [1995] and Flin and Dzurawiec [1989]). For example, Feinman and Entwistle (1976) found that face recognition ability improved from 6 to 8 years of age, but appeared to change very little from age 11 to adulthood. Although Lawrence et al's (2008) results appear to show a 'dip' at around the age of 12, this was not statistically significant. Reviewing earlier studies on the developmental 'dip', Chung and Thomson (1995) noted that only some studies found evidence for it, and also that the age at which it occurred varied quite widely from study to study. Chung and Thomson

with the 11-year-olds showing near-ceiling performance on all of the tests. Bruce et al's tests of face recognition included a simultaneous matching test: three children's faces were shown simultaneously and the participant had to decide which two were images of the same person. This test included triads of images that were identical, identical in pose but not expression, identical in expression but not in pose, or dissimilar in both pose and expression. Unfortunately the data for these conditions were combined to give a single overall face recognition score for each participant, so that the final report provides no information about how well children of different ages can cope with transformations of pose and expression.

claimed that this casts doubts on whether the 'dip' represents a genuine developmental phenomenon. However, the different methods and age ranges used in these studies might give rise to some of the inconsistencies in the findings. In addition, one problem with research in this area is that, for ethical reasons, information about individual children's pubertal status is usually quite vague.

Soppe (1986) investigated age changes on a range of cognitive tasks, and found evidence for a 'dip' at puberty, but only on a task that involved the children trying to identify a previously seen man from a sequentially presented eight-photograph lineup. As the other cognitive tasks that Soppe used showed a more progressive pattern of improvement with age, he concluded that the improvement in face processing followed a distinctive developmental trend, and hence did not merely reflect generalized cognitive development. However, Flin (1985) found evidence of a 'dip' for recognition of stimuli other than faces (flags and houses), implying that it is not face-specific. Soppe's results also seem at odds with the results of a study by McGivern et al (2002). They found a pubertal dip in performance in response times (but not accuracy) using a simple emotion recognition task. Their participants saw a series of briefly presented words and faces, and merely had to decide whether or not each one showed a particular emotion. The fact that similar effects were obtained with both faces and words suggests that something might be happening to children's cognitive abilities at puberty that is not specific to face processing.

Carey's (1981) original explanation for the pubertal 'dip' was that it reflected a change in encoding strategy that was produced by children's need to encode many new faces when they changed from small primary schools to larger secondary schools. Another possibility was that it was a byproduct of the hormonal changes that accompany puberty. However, McGivern et al (2002) cite research suggesting that puberty is associated with a phase of cortical reorganization, especially in the **prefrontal cortex** (a brain region known to be involved in decision-making and other 'higher' cognitive processes). Perhaps information processing becomes temporarily less efficient while this reorganization takes place.

To sum up, laboratory studies in which children try to remember a number of unfamiliar faces have given the impression that development of face recognition is quite protracted: the bulk of improvement occurs before the age of 10 years or so, after which performance continues to improve but at a more modest rate. Full adult performance is reached somewhere in the late teens.

What underlies this extended period of development? As Crookes and McKone (2009) point out, hypotheses about this fall into one of two main camps. **Face-specific perceptual development** theories propose that improvement in face recognition stems principally from the refinement of perceptual mechanisms that are dedicated to faces. (See Chapter 10 for a detailed discussion of the issue of whether or not faces are 'special'.) In principle, younger children's poor performance might stem from limitations at any stage of face processing. It might be that children do not encode faces as effectively as adults; perhaps they do not focus on the facial information that is most effective for remembering faces or for distinguishing between them. Another possibility is that children's storage of faces in memory might be more susceptible to interference from other faces seen afterwards, or it might degrade more quickly than in adults. Yet another possibility is that children may experience problems in accessing their memories of faces.

General cognitive development theories propose that the processes underlying face perception are already well developed in early childhood, and that any observed age-related changes are due to improvements in general cognitive processes, such as attention, concentration explicit memory ability, and an increased ability to use strategies to cope with the peculiar demands of experimental situations.

6.1.1 **The 'encoding switch' model of face processing development**

Most research on children's face-processing abilities has assumed there is 'face-specific perceptual development', and in particular has focused on the idea that children are poorer at recognizing faces than adults because they do not encode them as effectively. H. D. Ellis (1992) described a series of experiments in which 3 to 5-year-old children had to match one view of a face to a different view of the same face that was presented amongst a set of distractors. Simple transformations between the two images in terms of image size, clothing, viewpoint or expression were enough to disrupt performance, even when both images of the target face were in view at the same time. Ellis suggested that young children might have difficulty in extracting facial invariants, aspects of the face that are unaffected by these kinds of transformation.

Pedelty et al (1985) conducted a study suggesting that younger and older children might differ in the amount of information they can encode from a face. They showed their participants (7-, 9- and 12-year-old boys, and a group of young men) all possible pairings of 12 different photographs of boys' faces. Each participant had to rate the faces within each pairing in terms of how similar they were to one another. These ratings were then subjected to a statistical procedure called multidimensional scaling. This extracted three factors that explained most of the variation in the ratings: hair colour, face width and nose-to-lip distance. The fact that the same factors emerged for all age groups implied that all age groups were encoding the faces in qualitatively similar ways. However, whereas the 12-year-olds' and adults' judgements were more likely to be based on all three dimensions, the 7- and 9-year-olds were more likely to use only one or two of the dimensions. This implies that the younger children were encoding less information from faces than the older participants, an idea

that is supported by H. D. Ellis and Flin (1990). They looked at the effects on face recognition performance of two variables (exposure duration and length of delay between study and test) in 7- and 10-year-old children. If the delay between study and test was short, the 10-year-olds' performance was improved by giving them longer to encode the faces; however, the 7-year-olds did not benefit from being given viewing times longer than about 2 seconds. (If tested after a week's delay, however, these age differences disappeared.)

According to these studies, young children are simply less efficient at encoding faces. However, work by Susan Carey's group (e.g. Carey and Diamond, 1977; Diamond and Carey, 1977) suggested that young children and adults encode faces in *qualitatively* different ways. Carey proposed that under the age of 10 years or so, children tried to use information from the individual facial features in order to recognize faces, rather than using configural information like adults. Carey envisaged configural processing as a skill that develops only with extensive experience of faces. She suggested that children lack this experience and so, unlike adults, they are not 'face experts'.

The conclusion that there was an **encoding switch** from **featural** to **configural** processing was based primarily on two lines of evidence. The first came from studies suggesting that children do not show the classic **Face Inversion Effect** to the same extent as adults (see Chapter 2, section 2.3.1). The most popular explanation of the Inversion Effect in adults has been that it arises as a consequence of perceptual expertise. The claim is that prolonged exposure to faces causes people to become adept at extracting the fine-grain configural information that distinguishes one face from another. The penalty for this expertise is that they become reliant on faces appearing in their normal upright orientation; consequently, when an upside-down face is encountered, an adult cannot use configural processing and has to fall back on a less efficient feature-based form of processing.

Carey (1981) argued that, if children are not showing a pronounced Inversion Effect, it must be because they are using a piecemeal, feature-based processing strategy with both upright and inverted faces; they have not yet learned the efficient adult strategy of using configural processing as an aid to recognizing faces.

The second line of evidence came from experiments by Diamond and Carey that looked at how children's face recognition was affected by the addition of **paraphernalia** (hats and scarves, or glasses) to photographs of faces. For example, in Carey and Diamond's (1977) study, children first saw a photograph of a woman and were then presented with a pair of photographs. One was the woman they had just seen, and the other was a picture of a different woman. The children had to decide which photograph showed the woman they had seen earlier. Under the age of about 10 years, children's choices were determined largely by the paraphernalia, rather than the person's face, as shown by their performance when the paraphernalia were misleading. In this condition, the woman who was seen first was wearing a hat and a scarf. When the pair of photographs was presented, only the previously unseen woman was wearing a hat and scarf (Fig. 6.2). In these circumstances, the children were more likely to make a mistake and choose the novel woman as the person they saw earlier—their choices seemed to be based on the paraphernalia rather than the face itself.

As these paraphernalia effects did not occur with faces that were familiar to the children, Diamond and Carey (1977) suggested that even the youngest children's representations of *familiar* faces were similar to those of adults (see Chapter 2). However, Diamond and Carey claimed that for unfamiliar faces it was only by the age of 10 or 12 that children (like adults) were able to form a representation from a single photograph that was sufficient for them to be able to distinguish between a new photograph of this person and a photograph of a different face. Diamond and

(a)

(b)   (c)

FIGURE 6.2 One of the conditions used by Diamond and Carey (1977). After seeing (a), children were presented with (b) and (c), and asked to choose which one was the woman they had seen before. Children tended mistakenly to respond (b) rather than (c), i.e. their choices were based on the paraphernalia (hat) rather than the face.

Carey speculated that '*what develops during the ages from 5 to 12 is a schema for making new faces familiar with greater and greater efficiency*' (1977, p. 19).

In the following sections, we evaluate the evidence for the 'encoding switch' hypothesis: do children really encode faces any differently to adults? It's worth looking in detail at the evidence for this idea because it has been an enormously influential theory. Even recent books and articles often refer to the notion of an encoding switch as if it were a well-established finding. However, as we shall see, there is actually overwhelming evidence against it.

6.1.2 Development of the Face Inversion Effect

As mentioned in Chapter 5, a variety of techniques have been used to show that even very young babies are sensitive to the orientation of a face. Leo and Simion (2009) have demonstrated the **Thatcher Illusion** in newborns; **inversion effects** (in the sense of better discrimination performance with upright faces) have been found in 4-month-olds by Turati et al (2004), and in 5-month-olds by Rose et al (2008). Hayden et al (2007) showed that 5-month-olds were better at discriminating between the normal and distorted versions of the same face if the images were presented upright.

Only a handful of studies have looked specifically at the effects of inversion on face recognition in preschool children. Brace et al (2001) investigated the inversion effect in children varying in age from 2 to 11 years. Each child saw three different views of an unfamiliar target face. After a short delay, there was a series of trials in which the child attempted to pick out the target face from amongst eight distractors, as quickly as they could (Fig. 6.3). On half of the trials the faces were all upright, and on the rest they were all inverted. This procedure was embedded within a story-book format, to engage the children's attention and motivate them to respond as quickly as they could. Although the older children had faster response times overall, all but the youngest children showed a comparable inversion effect: they were significantly slower to find the target face amongst the distractors when the faces were upside-down. Thus, 5-year-olds show the adult pattern of sensitivity to the orientation of faces. The 2 to 4-year-old children showed an 'inverted inversion effect': they were actually faster with inverted faces than with upright ones. Although this could be evidence that 2 to 4-year-olds process faces differently to both younger and older children, Brace et al pointed out that the inverted inversion effect could equally well be explained in terms of age differences in the use of strategies to perform the task.

Sangrigoli and de Schonen (2004) investigated the inversion effect in young children as part of a study of the development of the **other-race effect** (an advantage for processing faces of one's own race compared to those from other races: see Chapter 12).

(a) (b)

FIGURE 6.3 Examples of stimuli used by Brace et al (2001) to investigate the development of the Face Inversion Effect in young children. After exposure to several views of 'Tom' or 'Jamie' (a), children tried to identify him hidden amongst distractors (b).

They used a more conventional two-alternative forced-choice procedure: on each trial, children saw a face for 500 milliseconds, quickly followed by a pair of faces, and chose the one they had seen before. The faces were either Caucasian, like the children themselves, or Asian. In one experiment, Sangrigoli and de Schonen found an inversion effect in 5-year-old children. Three-year-olds did not show an effect of inversion, but this was because their performance with upright faces was very poor; consequently there was little opportunity for inversion to make their performance worse. In another experiment, this problem of 'floor effects'[2] was remedied by increasing the exposure time to one second. This improved the 3-year-olds' performance enough for inversion to make a detectable difference. Now, not only did the 3-year-olds show an inversion effect, but they also showed an 'other-race' effect. They were better at recognizing faces of their own race, and also showed a larger inversion effect for Caucasian faces than for Asian ones. Whereas the older children showed a more pronounced inversion effect, the size of the other-race effect did not change with age. Sangrigoli and de Schonen's interpretation of the latter result is that children as young as 3 years of age already have a well-established face 'schema' or 'prototype' based on the own-race faces to which they have been exposed.

Picozzi et al (2009) looked at whether orientation affected how well 3 to 5-year-olds could recognize various stimuli (faces, side views of shoes and frontal views of cars). They used a two-alternative forced-choice procedure similar to that of Sangrigoli and de Schonen (2004). Although the 3-year-olds performed worse overall than the 4-year-olds, both age groups showed a significant inversion effect for faces but not for side views of shoes. Another experiment found an unexpected sex difference: 3- and 4-year-old boys showed an inversion effect for faces but not for cars, whereas girls showed similar inversion effects for both kinds of stimulus. A third experiment demonstrated an inversion effect in 5-year-old children of both sexes for faces but not for cars. Picozzi et al suggested that sex differences in interest for cars might underlie these effects. The important point for the present discussion is that this study found a Face Inversion Effect in children as young as 3 years of age.

Notwithstanding Brace et al's curious 'inverted inversion effect', the results of the experiments described in this section are consistent in showing that children as young as 3 years of age are showing a Face Inversion Effect. If the standard interpretation of this effect is accepted (i.e. that it occurs because configural processing is used with upright faces to a greater extent than with inverted faces) then children as young as 3 years of age are processing faces configurally, in qualitatively similar ways to adults.

6.1.3 Refutation of the 'encoding switch' hypothesis: paraphernalia revisited

On the basis of their experiments in which paraphernalia such as hats and scarves misled

---

[2] Ceiling and floor effects are the bane of developmental research. To find a difference between two conditions, one of them has to be capable of producing a detectable increase or decrease in performance compared to the other. Ceiling and floor effects can prevent this. In the context of the Face Inversion Effect, if performance with upright faces is already close to chance, it is hard for performance with inverted faces to get much worse. Under these conditions, finding a small difference between upright and inverted performance might mislead a researcher into thinking that there is little difference between the two conditions. These difficulties are aggravated by the problems involved in finding stimuli that are at an appropriate level of difficulty for all age groups in a study: a set of faces that are discriminable for adults might be impossibly difficult to discriminate between for a 3-year-old.

children into choosing a face they had not seen before, Diamond and Carey (1977) concluded that children under the age of 10 years were relying on isolated featural information in order to identify unfamiliar faces. However, as Freire and Lee (2001) point out, children's over-reliance on paraphernalia constitutes a rather indirect demonstration of 'featural' processing. It now seems likely that Diamond and Carey's (1977) results occurred because of an interaction between task difficulty and the children's naivety as participants. Diamond and Carey's stimulus faces happened to be very similar to one another. Unable to tell them apart easily, children probably resorted to using the highly salient paraphernalia as a basis for their choice of photograph at the test phase (Baenninger, 1994; Flin, 1985). Presumably the children could not tell which one of the two faces they had seen before, but did remember that the person was wearing a hat and a scarf. Under these circumstances, a reasonable strategy is to assume that this is the face to choose.

Flin (1985) replicated Diamond and Carey's study, but manipulated the degree of similarity between the faces. She found that 4-year-old children based their decisions on the paraphernalia to a greater extent when the faces were similar than when they were quite dissimilar. Baenninger (1994) modified Carey and Diamond's procedure so that the paraphernalia failed to provide any misleading clues about what the correct response should be. For example in one condition, Baenninger presented paraphernalia in *all* of the photographs in a trial. In another condition, the first photograph showed a person without paraphernalia, but both of the test photographs showed people with paraphernalia. Under these conditions, the paraphernalia provided no misleading indications about which face should be chosen, and the age differences in performance disappeared. Baenninger's conclusion was that any age differences in face recognition ability were more likely to have arisen

from differences in factors such as motivation or attention, than from the children's inability to use configural processing.

Freire and Lee (2001) found that 4 to 7-year-old children could recognize an unfamiliar face solely on the basis of configural information, but this ability was easily disrupted by adding misleading paraphernalia to the image. In their study, each child was told a story involving 'Bob' and shown a photograph of him for five seconds. This was followed by an array of four photographs: one was the image of Bob just seen, and the other three were distractors. The latter were photographs of the same face as Bob, but with the mouths and eyes in slightly different locations within the face, so that they differed from Bob only in their configural properties (Fig. 6.4). The child's task was to decide which of the four faces showed the version of Bob they had just seen. Even 4-year-olds were able to perform this task at above-chance levels, implying that they were able to discriminate between highly similar faces purely on the basis of their configural properties.

To examine the effects of paraphernalia, this procedure was repeated after each child had received extensive training with the task and had reached a criterion level of competence at it. Each child now saw a bare-headed Bob, followed by four test photographs showing some or all of the faces wearing hats. Consistent with Baenninger's (1994) earlier work, Freire and Lee (2001) found that performance was unaffected when all of the test faces wore hats. Thus, when paraphernalia were present but not misleading, children could still use configural information to identify a face. However, performance was markedly affected when only Bob and one distractor wore a hat. Now, two of the distractors looked more like the original bare-headed Bob than did Bob himself. Faced with highly similar faces and misleading paraphernalia, children were prone to make a mistake and choose one of the bare-headed distractors. This effect was more pronounced for the younger children.

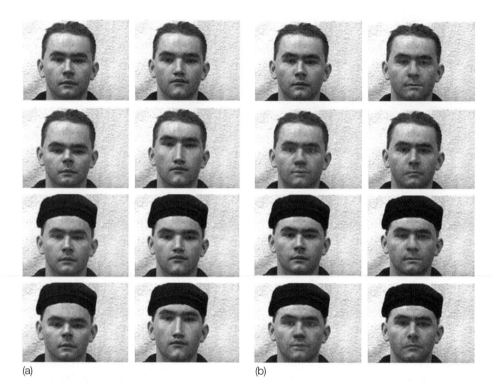

(a)   (b)

FIGURE 6.4 Stimuli used by Freire and Lee (2001). (a) Faces differ configurally; (b) faces differ featurally (in each case, the bottom four faces are the same as the top four, but with the addition of a hat)

Freire and Lee conducted a second experiment that was identical to the first, except that 'Bob' and his 'brothers' differed in terms of featural information: features from different faces were pasted into the same locations within a face, in order to keep the configural properties of the stimulus faces as constant as possible. Performance was better in this study than in the first, implying that it might be easier for young children to learn the features of a face rather than its configuration. However, the effects of paraphernalia on performance were still present, although much less pronounced—and, again, worse for younger children.

Overall, the conclusion that can be drawn from Friere and Lee's experiments is that paraphernalia do reliably impair face recognition performance, especially in the case of younger children; however, this is not evidence that children are processing

faces featurally, because children as young as 4 years of age can use either configural or featural information to recognize faces, even when the faces are highly similar.

In fairness to Diamond and Carey, it should be pointed out that they were aware of the possibility that their results could have been influenced by non-perceptual factors; in fact, they attempted to control for them in some of their experiments by means of explicit instructions, participation in a session in which sample stimuli were constructed, and practice with sample stimuli produced from familiar faces. Because none of these manipulations reduced the effects of misleading paraphernalia on the young children's performance, Diamond and Carey concluded that the effects were based on the children's perceptual limitations. However, there is research suggesting that children are resistant to these kinds of instructions; for example, Davies et al (1988) gave children practice at making a 'not present' response when presented with a target-absent lineup. This procedure failed to prevent the children from making make false identifications when they were subsequently presented with another target-absent lineup in a different context. When the target was absent, an incorrect response was made by half of the 9 to 11-year-olds, and 88% of the 7 to 8-year-olds. Young children seem to have a particularly strong 'urge to please' the experimenter by choosing a face if asked to do so (Davies, 1991; also see Chapter 11, section 11.3.1).

6.1.4 **Direct evidence for configural processing of faces by young children**

Direct tests of whether young children can recognize faces on the basis of their configurations, as well as investigations of whether children's recognition performance is affected by manipulations that disrupt configural processing, have failed to support the 'encoding switch' hypothesis. There is now clear evidence that even very young children can use configural information in the process of encoding unfamiliar faces, although possibly not as effectively as adults. (In fact, as we saw in the previous chapter, there is some evidence for the use of configural processing by infants who are just a few months old.) The current consensus is that children may be less efficient than adults at recognizing faces, but that children and adults probably do not differ qualitatively in the way that they process either familiar or unfamiliar faces.

Some of the earliest evidence for configural face processing came from Diamond and Carey themselves. Carey and Diamond (1994) tested 6- and 7-year-olds to see whether they were susceptible to Young et al's (1987) **Composite Face Effect (CFE)** (see Chapter 2, section 2.3.3). Like adults, these children found it harder to name the tops of composites made up of halves from two different faces when the halves were aligned than when they were misaligned. This effect was

diminished when the composites were presented upside-down. Carey and Diamond concluded that some form of rudimentary configural processing was present even in young children, contrary to the idea of an 'encoding switch' in later childhood.

More recently, de Heering et al (2007) measured the CFE in 4-, 5- and 6-year-olds using an unfamiliar face-matching task. The children had to decide whether two face top-halves were the same or different, ignoring the bottom halves. When the tops were from the same face but the bottom halves were from different faces, the children made more errors (they were more likely to decide incorrectly that the tops were from different faces). This effect occurred only when the tops and bottoms were aligned. Figure 6.5

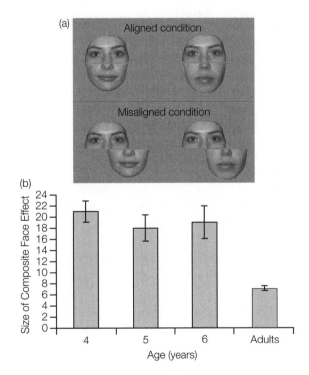

FIGURE 6.5 (a) Examples of the stimuli used by de Heering et al (2007, experiment 2) to study the development of the Composite Face Effect (CFE) in children. (b) de Heering et al's results (the CFE is represented by the difference in accuracy between the 'misaligned-same' and 'aligned-same' conditions).

shows de Heering et al's results, expressed as the difference in accuracy between the 'misaligned same-face' and 'aligned same-face' conditions: the bigger the difference in accuracy between these two conditions, the larger the CFE. All three age groups of children showed similar sizes of CFE. Adults showed a smaller CFE, but this was probably an artefact of the procedure, which allowed all participants unlimited exposure to the faces before they made their response. (Hole [1994] showed that long exposure times tend to reduce the size of the CFE in adults, probably because they use the extra time to engage in feature-by-feature processing of the stimuli before making a response.) Thus, children as young as 4 years of age are processing faces holistically.

Macchi Cassia et al (2009a) examined the CFE in 3-, 4- and 5-year-old children and adults, using pictures of faces and fronts of cars. (The latter were chosen as a class of non-face-like stimuli that varied in terms of their second-order relational properties, such as headlight spacing, size of front grille, etc.) Macchi Cassia et al used a two-alternative forced-choice procedure. A stimulus consisting of the top half of a face was presented briefly, followed by two composite faces shown side-by-side. The two halves of each composite were either aligned or misaligned, and one of the composites contained the same top half as the stimulus that had just been presented. The same procedure was used with composite cars, produced by combining halves from cars that had been divided in half between the windscreen and the bonnet.

Similar effects were found in adults and in 4- and 5-year-olds: a clear composite effect was obtained for faces, but not for cars. Three and a half-year-olds showed the same pattern, but only when the memory demands on them were reduced by modifying the task so that all three images in a trial were displayed simultaneously rather than sequentially. Macchi Cassia et al suggest that by 3 years of age, children are already processing faces differently from other

types of perceptually homogeneous stimuli. As in de Heering et al's study, Macchi Cassia et al found evidence of a decrease in the magnitude of the CFE from 4–5 years to adulthood. Like de Heering et al, they suggest this change might arise from methodological factors, rather than necessarily reflecting any fundamental age-related differences in holistic processing. However, this is something that warrants further research.

Another technique that has been used to demonstrate configural processing in children is the **whole-over-part effect** technique, first used with adults by Davidoff and Donnelly (1990) and Tanaka and Farah (1993). More details of this can be found in Chapter 2, section 2.3.4. Essentially, participants are shown a stimulus consisting of a single facial feature, such as a pair of eyes. They are then shown two stimuli simultaneously, and asked to decide which of these was seen before. In one condition, the two test stimuli consist of isolated features (e.g. one stimulus consists of the eyes that were seen previously, and the other consists of a novel pair of eyes). In another condition, these features are embedded within a face that is otherwise identical for both of the stimuli. If participants are processing isolated features, it should not matter whether the features are presented in isolation or within a face: the face is the same in both test stimuli, and so it amounts to being little more than a constant background pattern that provides no useful information to aid the participant in making their choice. However, if faces are processed configurally, then placing the features within a face effectively produces two different configurations. In practice, adults recognize a feature better when it is embedded within a face than when it is presented in isolation; they benefit from the additional configural information that is available in the whole-face condition. However, this whole-over-part advantage is found only if the faces are presented upright, implying that the emergent configural information that is available from the whole faces is harder to access with inverted faces.

Tanaka et al (1998) demonstrated configural processing in 6-year-old children, using this procedure. Children aged 6, 8 and 10 years were all similar to adults in performing best with upright (but not inverted) whole faces, although the older children were more affected by inversion of the stimuli. The implication is that, like adults, these children were using configural processing for the intact faces, and, like adults, they were sensitive to the orientation of the face, with even the youngest children benefiting from seeing the faces upright rather than upside-down. (See also Seitz [2002], who successfully replicated Tanaka et al's findings with 8- and 10-year-olds.)

In two separate studies, Pellicano and co-workers used Tanaka's procedure with 4- and 5-year-olds, and obtained similar results. Pellicano and Rhodes (2003) showed that recognition of individual facial features (eyes, nose and mouth) was aided by embedding them within an upright face. There was an overall improvement in performance with age (adults were much better than 4- and 5-year-olds, and the two groups of children did not differ from each other). However, the adults and children were qualitatively similar in performance, in the sense that all age groups demonstrated greater accuracy when the target feature was shown in the context of the original face than when it was shown in isolation. Pellicano et al (2006) replicated these effects, but additionally demonstrated that, like adults, 4 to 5-year-olds recognized facial features better when they were embedded in the original face at test than when they were shown in a configurally altered face. Again, this effect disappeared when the faces were inverted. The results suggest that 4 to 5-year-olds, like adults, are sensitive to configural information in upright faces, and respond to it in a qualitatively similar way.

Mondloch et al (2002) looked at the development of face processing in four groups: 6-, 8- and 10-year-old children, and young adults.

They used a modification of Freire and Lee's (2001) procedure, taking a single female face ('Jane') and producing different versions of it (Jane's 'sisters'). There were three conditions (Fig. 6.6). The 'spacing' condition used four faces that varied subtly in facial configuration: the eyes were moved inwards or outwards, and the mouth up and down. In the 'featural' condition, the eyes and mouth were replaced, while trying to retain the original configuration of Jane's face as far as possible. In the 'contour' condition, the internal region of Jane's face was pasted into the external face shapes of four different females. There was also a control condition, using four female faces that were entirely different from one another.

Mondloch et al's participants saw two faces in rapid succession, and tried to decide whether they were the same or different. Each participant saw all three types of face, both upright and inverted. To estimate the magnitude of the inversion effect at each age, Mondloch et al (2002) measured the difference between performance with the upright and inverted stimuli in each condition.

For the adults and 10-year-olds, the effects of inversion were greater for the spacing set than for the featural or external contour sets, suggesting that these age groups were relying on configural processing more for the spacing set than for the other types of stimulus. The 6-year-olds showed some evidence of configural processing, as they performed at above-chance levels of accuracy with the upright spacing set. However, both the 6- and the 8-year-olds showed similar sizes of inversion effect with all three sets of stimuli, implying that they were less able to use the configural information in the upright spacing set. Whereas the 6-year-olds were nearly as accurate as adults with the external contour and featural sets, even the 10-year-olds made more errors on the spacing set than adults.

Mondloch et al's conclusion was that face-processing skills develop with age, improving from 6 to 10 years of age, but that they are not fully adult-like until after the age of 10 years.

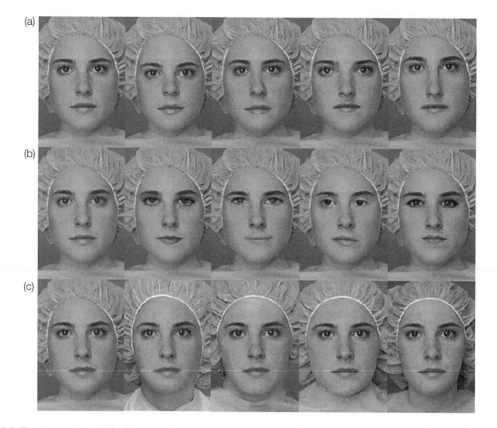

FIGURE 6.6 The faces used in Mondloch et al's (2002) study. 'Jane' (left face in each row) and 'sisters' that differ from her in (a) feature spacing, (b) features and (c) external contour. (Reprinted by permission from: Mondloch, C. J., Le Grand, R. & Maurer, D. (2002). Configural face processing develops more slowly than featural face processing. *Perception*, 31, 553–566. © Pion Limited, London)

They suggest that the slow development of face-processing skills is due to the slow development of **second-order configural processing**, which develops more slowly than featural or external contour processing.

In the previous chapter, it was mentioned that Hayden et al (2007) found evidence of configural processing in 5-month-old infants. Not only were the infants able to detect the differences between faces with normal and altered featural spacing, but this ability was impaired by turning the faces upside-down. The changes in spacing were similar in extent to those used by Mondloch et al (2002). Why then did Mondloch and colleagues fail to find evidence of second-order relational processing until much later in childhood? Hayden et al suggest that perhaps the ability to process faces configurally is initially rather fragile, and is easily disrupted under the more cognitively demanding testing conditions that have been used with older children.

This suggestion is given some support by the results of a set of experiments by Mondloch et al (2004), comparing 8-year-olds and adults on a series of tasks. One experiment tested whether the relatively poor performance of children with configurally altered faces stemmed from problems with encoding or memory. Mondloch et al's (2002) study showed the faces for only 200 milliseconds each, and presented them sequentially. The new experiment used the original stimuli (the spacing, featural and contour sets, displayed both upright and upside-down), but made even fewer demands on memory by presenting the faces simultaneously and for an unlimited length of time. Adults showed a large inversion effect for the spacing set. The 8-year-olds showed a much smaller inversion effect, but it was still larger with the spacing set than with the featural or contour sets. The 8-year-olds' performance on the featural and contour sets was comparable to that of adults.

For the adults, performance on the spacing set was unaffected by increasing the exposure duration. However, this manipulation improved the 8-year-olds' performance compared to that of the children in the 2002 study, suggesting that the 8-year-olds' problems in the latter may have stemmed from difficulties in encoding the faces. Another experiment by Mondloch et al (2004) showed that the 8-year-olds could respond like adults when the spacing manipulations were extreme enough to make the faces appear bizarre. Like adults, the 8-year-olds rated Thatcherized faces and spatially distorted faces as less bizarre when they were inverted. Mondloch et al concluded that young children are sensitive to second-order relations when viewing time is unlimited and the spacing distortions are outside the normal range. However, more extreme testing conditions (sequential presentation of stimuli and brief presentation times) reveal that they are not as sensitive as adults to the configural properties of faces.

On the basis of experiments using the **Thatcher Illusion**, Donnelly and Hadwin (2003) came to similar conclusions: configural processing is detectable in young children, but it is affected by task demands. As explained in Chapter 2 (section 2.3.2), in the Thatcher Illusion the eyes and mouth are placed in the opposite orientation to the rest of the face. The fact that this manipulation is immediately noticeable in upright faces, but hard to detect in upside-down ones, demonstrates that we are comparatively insensitive to the second-order relational properties of inverted faces. The Thatcher Illusion can thus be taken as an indicator of configural processing: if children process faces solely on the basis of their individual features, there should be less difference between their performance with upright and inverted faces (because they are processing both types of face in much the same way). Donnelly and Hadwin showed 6-, 7-, 8- and 10-year-olds, plus a group of adults, ten pairs of photographs of faces on a computer. In each pair, one of the faces was normal and the other was Thatcherized. The task was for the participants to pick out the 'unusual' face. Reaction times to decide were progressively faster with increasing age. However, everyone showed the Thatcher Illusion: all age groups were faster and more accurate in detecting the Thatcherized faces when the test faces were upright than when they were inverted.

To increase perceptual demands, Donnelly and Hadwin ran the experiment again, after degrading the stimuli of experiment 1. The faces were 'thresholded' to just two grey-scale levels, so that they consisted of only a white face with black blobby features and hair ('Mooney' faces, like those in Fig. 9.1). With these stimuli, somewhat different results were obtained. Except for the 6-year-olds, all age groups showed clear effects of the Thatcher Illusion (i.e. they were much better at detecting Thatcherized faces when these were upright). In fact, for all age groups except the adults, performance was at chance with the inverted faces. However, for the 6-year-olds, performance was at chance levels with the upright faces too. Donnelly and Hadwin's conclusion was that configural processing is detectable in 6-year-olds under optimal conditions, but increasing the processing demands reveals that this kind of processing is rather fragile in younger children; with the Mooney faces, configural processing was absent in 6-year-olds, and the data suggested that susceptibility to the Thatcher Illusion increased with age from 8 years to adulthood.

Overall, the impression that emerges from the studies described in this section is that young children are capable of processing faces configurally, but perhaps not as efficiently as adults.

6.1.5 **The internal-feature advantage in familiar face recognition**

Another way in which it has been claimed that adults and children differ is in terms of which facial regions they use as a basis for recognition (see Chapter 2). H. D. Ellis et al (1979) found that adults find it easier to recognize familiar faces from their internal features (eyes, nose and mouth) than from their external features (the face outline and hair). In contrast, for recognizing unfamiliar faces, adults seem to use the external features as much as the internal ones. Young et al (1985c) showed that adults were faster to match whole familiar faces to photographs showing the internal features than to photographs showing the external features alone. These effects did not occur with unfamiliar faces.

As mentioned in the previous chapter, there is some evidence that young infants pay more attention to the external facial features, although to some extent this preference appears to be affected by the relative salience of the internal and external features. A series of studies on older children by Campbell and colleagues (e.g. Campbell and Tuck, 1995; Campbell et al, 1995, 1999b) failed to find the adult pattern in children under the age of 11 years, and claimed that children below that age tend to rely on the external facial features for recognizing both familiar and unfamiliar faces.

If true, this would be evidence of a qualitative difference between children and adults in terms of how they process faces. However, Campbell's studies suffer from a number of methodological problems. Firstly, the stimuli were not very 'clean'. For example, if the sample stimuli depicted in Campbell et al's (1995) article are anything to go by, the 'external' features condition showed upper clothing as well as the external facial features. This may have encouraged the younger children to attend more to the external features than would otherwise have been the case. The stimuli used by Campbell and Tuck (1995) included cartoon characters as well as human faces. Although the cartoon faces were dropped from the subsequent analyses of the results, their highly distinctive external features may again have had an influence on how the youngest children allocated their attention to the stimuli.

A second problem with Campbell's studies is that the faces may not have been very familiar to the children, in which case one would not expect to see an internal-feature advantage. Campbell and Tuck (1995) and Campbell et al (1999b) used adult television celebrities who were assumed to be known to the children—although looking at the very poor recognition rates for most of the human faces in Campbell and Tuck's experiment, this is unlikely to have been the case. As Bonner and Burton (2004) point out, children may find it harder to recognize adult faces than faces of their own age (see the discussion of the **own-age bias** in Chapter 12). Children are also likely to be less familiar with adult celebrity faces. Campbell et al's (1995) study used the faces of schoolmates as 'familiar' faces, and similarly aged children from another school as the 'unfamiliar' faces. However, there was no check on whether the participants actually knew the 'familiar' children—although they attended the same school, they were not necessarily classmates, and without an indication of how large the schools were it is possible that the participants were, again, not actually very familiar with the supposedly 'familiar' faces.

Want et al (2003) found that, for *unfamiliar* faces, children showed the adult pattern of better performance with external features. They showed their participants (5-, 7- and 9-year-old children, and adults) a brief video of an unfamiliar face, quickly followed by a pair of pictures of faces. The task was to decide which of the faces belonged to the person in the video. The faces were either whole, just the inner parts, or just the outer parts. The older the participants, the faster they were overall, but all groups showed the same pattern of being fastest with whole faces, slower with outer parts, and slowest with inner parts. All age groups were more accurate at recognizing whole faces. However, the 5- and 7-year-olds were better at recognizing outer parts than inner parts, whereas the 9-year-olds and adults were equally accurate with inner and outer parts.

More recent studies, using faces that were known to be familiar to the participants, have confirmed earlier reports that older children are generally *quantitatively* better than younger ones (they are faster and more accurate at recognizing faces). However, they have failed to find any *qualitative* differences in performance between children and adults. In Bonner and Burton's (2004) study, 7 to 8- and 10 to 11-year-old children performed a matching task: they saw two faces and had to decide whether or not they were two views of the same person. The faces consisted of either the external features alone or the internal features alone. The faces were either their classmates (and hence personally familiar to them, and similar in age to them) or unfamiliar children from a different school.

Both age groups showed an adult-like pattern of responding. With familiar faces, both groups were more accurate at matching faces on the basis of their internal features than by means of their external features. For unfamiliar faces, the opposite pattern was shown, and matching performance was better with external features. The ability to use external facial features to recognize faces did improve with age: whereas the 7 to 8-year-old children could recognize only 52% of their classmates on the basis of their external features, the 10 to 11-year-olds were able to recognize 77% of them.

Wilson et al (2007a) looked at developmental trends in face identification rather than face matching. Three different age groups of children (5 to 6-, 7 to 8- and 10 to 11-year-olds) were shown pairs of photographs of adult faces. In each pair, one photograph was of an unfamiliar face and the other

was of a member of staff at the child's school. The child had to press one of two buttons, depending on whether the familiar face was shown on the left or the right. Each child saw sets of faces in full face, inner feature or external feature versions. Wilson et al found age differences in overall speed and accuracy (the older children performed better than the younger ones), but all three groups were more accurate with whole faces than with parts, and all three groups were more accurate with internal than external features. In other words, when adult faces used are highly personally familiar to the children, there is no evidence of any processing shift: even children as young as 5 years show an internal-feature advantage for familiar faces.

Ge et al (2008) investigated familiar face recognition in 4-, 8- and 14-year-old children. The children tried to identify ten of their classmates (five boys and five girls) from photographs that showed the whole face, the internal features, the external features, or just the eyes, nose and mouth. Ge et al made sure that each group had equivalent familiarity with the stimulus faces; each of their age groups had been in their school (and hence in contact with the classmates whose faces were used as stimuli) for only one academic year. The results were consistent with those of Bonner and Burton, and Wilson et al: all three age groups were able to recognize their classmates at above-chance levels from just the internal or external features, but all three groups performed better with the internal features than with the external ones. Also consistent with earlier reports (e.g. Hay and Cox, 2000), all three age groups recognized eyes better than other isolated facial features (noses and mouths).

As with the previous studies described, Ge et al (2008) did find evidence of an overall improvement in recognition performance with increasing age. As Ge and colleagues point out, this could be due to a development in face recognition ability, or to a generalized cognitive improvement (for example, improvements in memory or attention). Both the 8- and 14-year-old girls showed an own-gender bias in recognition, whereas only the 14-year-old boys did so. Ge et al suggest that this might reflect the effects of differential experience, in this case with own-gender as opposed to opposite-gender faces.

In summary, like adults, children seem to use internal features for familiar faces, and they rely more on external features for recognizing unfamiliar faces. This adult-like pattern is detectable in children as young as 4 years of age.

6.2 Developmental differences in distinctiveness effects in face recognition

Another way in which children might differ from adults is in terms of how they are affected by the **distinctiveness** of faces. As we saw in Chapter 1 (section 1.3.2), one characteristic of adult face recognition is that distinctive faces are recognized better than ones that are more typical in appearance. These findings have been interpreted in terms of Valentine's (1991) **Multidimensional Face Space** model; the suggestion is that typical faces are densely clustered together in face space, and hence more easily confused than distinctive faces. The latter are located in less densely populated regions of face space.

Naturally distinctive faces may differ from typical faces in all sorts of ways other than just their distinctiveness, such as in attractiveness,

age and health (Rhodes et al, 1987). Therefore, researchers have used caricature-generating computer programs to produce different versions of the same face, that differ systematically in terms of their distinctiveness. **Caricatures** exaggerate any differences between a particular face and the 'average' face. It is also possible to produce **anti-caricatures** that reduce these differences (thus making a face look less distinctive). Compared with the original faces, adults typically find caricatures as easy to recognize as the original faces, and anti-caricatures harder to recognize. Do children respond to caricatures in the same way as adults?

Chang et al (2002) looked at children's responses to photographic-quality caricatures. They used four groups of participants: 6-, 8- and 10-year-old children, and 27-year-old adults. For each age group, Chang et al produced two 'norm' faces (one male and one female) by averaging together facial coordinates for a dozen faces of that age group. Then they produced caricatures and anti-caricatures by increasing or decreasing coordinate values of faces away from these norms. They used –36% and –18% anti-caricatures, veridical (0%) faces, and +18% and +36% caricatures[3] (Fig. 6.7).

In their first experiment, participants were shown the range of caricatures of each face and asked to pick those that were the most and least distinctive versions of that face. All age groups showed similar effects, picking the caricatures as being more distinctive and the anti-caricatures as being less distinctive. As in previous work (Rhodes et al, 1999b), the greater the degree of

---

[3] The caricature program works by exaggerating all of the differences between an individual face and the 'average' face by a given amount. In a 36% caricature, if an individual face's eyes are slightly wider than average, this difference would be increased by 36%; if the mouth is narrower than average, its width would be reduced by 36%; and so on. An anti-caricature works in the opposite way, reducing all of the differences between the individual face and the norm by set amounts.

FIGURE 6.7 Examples of the caricatured faces used by Chang et al (2002). '0%' is the original face. Negative values are anti-caricatures in which differences from the average face are reduced; positive values are caricatures in which differences from average are exaggerated.

caricature, the higher the distinctiveness ratings for the faces. There was an age effect, in that the older the participant, the more consistently they picked the more-caricatured faces. However, at least some of the 6-year-olds showed sensitivity to distinctiveness in faces, although the effects were not as strong as in the older children and adults.

In a second experiment, the same age groups saw faces that were either familiar or unfamiliar to them. They had to identify the faces as quickly as possible, and were also asked to pick the image that they considered to be the best likeness of each face. Although, as might be expected, participants were generally faster the older they were, all age groups showed a distinctiveness effect in the speed and accuracy with which they named faces: caricatures were named faster than

anti-caricatures. In the case of the 'best likeness' judgements, the adults tended to pick the veridical face, whereas the 8- and 10-year-old children tended to prefer anti-caricatures for unfamiliar faces and caricatures for familiar ones. The 6-year-olds showed a non-significant trend in the same direction as the older children.

Chang et al interpreted their results within Valentine's (1991) Multidimensional Face Space model. Like Valentine, they suggest that ease of recognition is related to the density of faces in face space. Typical faces are, by definition, more common, and hence they are densely packed together near the origin of face space. Distinctive faces are less common and therefore more isolated in face space. Trying to recognize a typical face is harder because there is more competition from neighbouring similar faces. As people age, they come into contact with many more faces, and so their face space becomes more densely populated with exemplars. Children have similar face spaces to adults, although much less densely populated, and this explains why they show distinctiveness effects but to a somewhat lesser extent than adults.

6.3 **Effects of delay on face recognition**

All of the studies described so far have examined face recognition over short time intervals. How well can children remember faces over lengthier delays? H. D. Ellis and Flin (1990) tested 7- and 10-year-olds' ability to recognize 20 unfamiliar faces immediately after they were presented, 1 day later or 1 week later. The effects of exposure duration were also examined; in one experiment, each face was shown for 1 or 3 seconds and in a second experiment each face was shown for 2 or 6 seconds. The results were similar in both cases: lengthening the exposure duration improved both age groups' performance. For the older children, performance decreased as the delay between presentation and testing increased. For the younger children, delay had no effect on performance. Ellis and Flin's interpretation was that there were age differences in encoding efficiency, but not in storage; the older children initially benefited from additional exposure time because they could use it to encode extra information about the faces. However, this extra information was lost over time, so that the 10-year-olds' performance declined back to that of the 7-year-olds. One drawback to this study is that it used identical pictures of faces

at presentation and test, so we don't know how well the children were remembering the faces, as opposed to the particular images that they saw.

Cain et al (2005) tested young children's ability to recognize the young adults who had been voluntary caregivers in their class for seven weeks. There were three groups: older toddlers (average age 34 months), younger preschoolers (average age 43.5 months) and older preschoolers (average age 57.6 months). The children's ability to recognize their caregivers was tested by asking them to pick out their caregiver from a lineup of five photographs. This was done twice: once within a week of the caregivers leaving and then again after three months. There were clear age-related increases in performance. The toddlers performed at chance levels on both occasions. After three months' delay, younger preschoolers recognized 43% of their caregivers, and older preschoolers recognized 86% of them. (In fact, half of the older preschoolers showed perfect performance.) In principle, poor recognition performance could be due to children experiencing problems in encoding faces, storing them, or retrieving the information. A notable finding of Cain et al's study was that the length of the delay had no effect on the children's performance: they were no worse after three months than after only a week. Cain et al suggest that this implies that the children's problems arise predominantly at the encoding stage.

One limitation with most behavioural studies of young children's memory for faces is that they require the children to make explicit decisions about whether or not faces are familiar to them. Given their limited language skills, this may result in an underestimation of young children's abilities. Stormark (2004) tested 3-year-old children's ability to recognize children with whom they had shared a nursery school for an average of 13 months, but whom they had not seen for at least 6 months. The children were tested with photographs of current playmates, former playmates and wholly unfamiliar children. The children recognized their current playmates, but failed to show any reliable overt (verbal) recognition of their past playmates. However, the covert measures of skin conductance and heart rate told a different story: both of these measures were different for former classmates than for unfamiliar children (but not significantly different between present playmates and unfamiliar children), implying recognition of past playmates at some implicit level at least.

6.4 'Applied' studies of the development of face recognition in children

We have seen that studies of face recognition in children imply that it undergoes a protracted period of development that is not fully completed until the mid-teens. Yet we have also seen that recent research has failed to show any qualitative differences between children and adults in terms of how they process faces, at least not for children over the age of 5 years or so. In that case, why are children poorer than adults at recognizing faces? The resolution to this paradox may come from studies that have examined how well children recognize faces under less artificial conditions. A somewhat different impression of children's face recognition abilities comes from studies conducted within an 'applied' framework.

Applied research generally measures performance in terms of ecologically relevant measures, such as how well a participant can identify a face from a lineup of several faces after having seen it briefly beforehand (see Chapter 11). Typically, a single target face is encountered during an event of some description (such as a staged crime), and the participant does not expect

to have to recognize it afterwards. The encoding conditions in applied studies are therefore often rather different to those in 'pure' research, where participants usually see a number of faces in the knowledge that they will be expected to recognize them subsequently. Pozzulo and Lindsay (1998) performed a meta-analysis on studies of children that used these kinds of method, and found evidence for age-related changes in both '**hits**' (correct identifications from lineups) and '**false alarms**' (incorrect identifications). However, these two aspects of performance show rather different developmental trends.

With target-present lineups (where the face that was seen originally is shown in the lineup), Pozzulo and Lindsay (1998) noted that although 4-year-olds made fewer correct identifications than adults, adult-like performance was present from the age of 5 years onwards. However, with target-absent lineups (ones that do not contain the face that was seen originally), children as old as 14 years were prone to making more false identifications than adults. Interestingly, Pozzulo and Lindsay noted that children's problems with target-absent lineups persist even when the lineup is presented sequentially rather than simultaneously (a procedure that reduces the number of false identifications in adults; see Chapter 11, section 11.3.3). They are also resistant to various attempts to 'train' older children, for example by giving them practice with target-absent lineups before the main experiment is performed.

The overall impression from 'applied' studies thus differs from that provided by laboratory studies. Laboratory studies focus on correct identifications and, as we have seen, suggest that there is marked improvement up to the age of 10 years. Applied studies suggest that there are two different developmental patterns, one for correct identifications from target-present lineups and a different one for correct rejections with target-absent lineups. Pozzulo and Lindsay

(1998) suggest that these apparent anomalies can be explained by considering the social as well as the cognitive factors involved in the tasks that are set to participants. From a cognitive point of view, applied and laboratory studies differ in the demands that they make. Applied studies normally require one target face to be recognized from a lineup of distractors, whereas to perform well on the 'old/new' discrimination tasks used in many laboratory investigations participants have to remember a number of faces and distinguish these from a number of novel faces. The memory burden is therefore greater in laboratory studies.[4]

Pozzulo and Lindsay suggest that the different developmental patterns for correct identifications and correct rejections in applied studies arise because the former pattern reflects cognitive performance, whereas the latter reflects a combination of cognitive and social factors. Cognitively, children might make more false identifications from target-absent lineups because they have a poorer memory of the face that they saw. Hence, it is easier for children to choose a face from the lineup that roughly matches their hazy memory of the target. However, children's performance is also affected by the **demand characteristics** of the experimental situation; from their point of view, the fact that they are being asked to make an identification strongly implies that the person they saw must be present in the lineup. In these circumstances, perhaps children feel more pressured than adults to attempt an identification, even when they are unsure. This is not too much of a problem if the person that they saw is actually in the lineup, but with target-absent lineups it leads to a false identification.

6.5 Conclusion

Over the past decade or so, it has become clear that children's face recognition abilities are much more sophisticated than was hitherto believed. Claims that children process faces in a *qualitatively* different way from adults have failed to gain much empirical support. Configural processing is clearly quite well developed from very early on in life. The work on babies described in Chapter 5 shows that even they are sensitive to facial configurations to some extent, and, as we have seen, various indicators of configural processing (the Face Inversion Effect, the Composite Face Effect and the Thatcher Illusion) are observable in 4-year-olds.

It is slightly harder to rule out the possibility that there might be *quantitative* differences between children and adults. It is true that children do not seem to show adult-like competence on laboratory tests of face recognition until around the age of 10 years or so. Possibly this is because they are less adept at using the fine-grain configural processing system, as suggested by Carey and Diamond (1977) or Mondloch et al (2002). Certainly, experience does play some role in the development of face processing, as shown by the effects of early experience with faces on the development of the own-race bias (see Chapter 9). However, performance in face recognition experiments also involves many other aspects of cognitive processing, such as the ability to fully understand what is required in order to perform the experimenter's task. One cannot discount the possibility that children's deficiencies might stem more from limitations in memory, attention or motivation (or even meta-cognitive attributes such as choosing which strategy to use) rather than being due to problems with face processing *per se*.

---

[4] It should be noted that, although most 'applied' studies require the participants to remember only one or two faces, these faces often have to be recognized despite changes between study and test in aspects such as pose and illumination, so it could be argued that, compared to many laboratory studies, applied studies are a tougher test of person recognition than laboratory studies that use picture-matching.

Apparent age differences in the effects of experimental manipulations may also occur for methodological reasons rather than because of genuine differences between the age groups involved. Earlier, we referred to the problems of interpretation produced by 'floor' effects, when we discussed Sangrigoli and de Schonen's (2004) study on the development of the Face Inversion Effect. If recognition performance is good with upright faces, inversion can produce a marked impairment. However, if performance is already poor with upright faces, there is little scope for inversion to make things much worse. This factor alone will make younger children appear to show less of an inversion effect than older children and adults; the difference between performance with upright and inverted faces widens with increasing age not because young children are less affected by inverting the faces, but because they are not as good at the task of recognizing upright faces.

Crookes and McKone (2009) suggest that these kinds of effect are pervasive in this area of research. Studies in which the range of performance is limited by floor effects in younger children, but not in older ones, give the impression that performance improves with age. Studies in which the range of performance is limited for the older children, but not for the younger ones, tend to show an apparent *decrease* with age. (An example of this type of study is H. D. Ellis et al's (1993b) investigation of **repetition priming** in 5-, 8- and 11-year-olds. This found that priming effects decreased with age. At least in part, this result might have arisen because the oldest children were already very quick with unprimed faces; consequently, it would have been difficult for them to be much faster with primed faces. In contrast, the younger children were much slower with unprimed faces, and so priming had more scope to exert an effect on their reaction times.) Finally, studies in which there is a reasonable range of performance for both younger and older age groups tend to suggest that there are no age-related changes in performance.

On the basis of the available evidence, we are inclined to support Crookes and McKone's (2009) view that there is little evidence for marked improvements in the accuracy of face processing *per se*, qualitatively or quantitatively, at least not beyond the age of 5 years or so. Any observed improvement could be accounted for by non-perceptual factors. Crookes and McKone concede that there might be age changes in the *speed* with which faces are processed, but more research is required on this.

As long ago as 1993, in a review of research on face memory in children from a predominantly 'applied' perspective, Graham Davies concluded:

> There is perhaps a need for face processing studies to go through the same learning experience as Piagetian researchers have undergone in terms of widening their data base and looking at tasks from a child's perspective before talking confidently of universal rules which can be generalised to the real world... Likewise, most models of face processing treat it as a purely cognitive process divorced from social and affective influences... Theories need to take account of such factors in their basic building blocks; a peripheral box marked 'affective and social influences' just will not do! (p. 151)

For a long time it has been appreciated that Varendonck's (1911) demonstrations of children's fallibility as witnesses were affected by his failure to appreciate the social factors that were operating in his studies. Varendonck was a figure of authority who questioned his young participants in a way that implied he believed their teacher had a beard. They would be unlikely to challenge him on this, even if they clearly remembered their teacher as being clean-shaven. Hopefully, modern children are less in awe of adults. However, as we have seen, even in modern-day research, a failure to consider social factors (in particular, how children might construe experimental situations) may have led to an underestimation of children's abilities. Current research is beginning to show that children are more 'expert' with faces than was originally believed.

SUMMARY

- Children do not perform as well as adults on laboratory tests of face recognition; studies generally find marked improvement up to 10 years of age, and a slower rate of improvement during the teenage years.

- Some studies have found a temporary 'dip' in face-processing performance at puberty, although this may extend to other cognitive abilities too.

- In 'applied' studies, adult-like performance with 'target-present' lineups is present in 5-year-olds, but performance with 'target-absent' lineups does not reach adult levels until the late teens.

- Diamond and Carey (1977) proposed that there was an 'encoding switch' at puberty, from piecemeal processing of faces to a more efficient and adult-like configural mode of processing.

- Evidence for an 'encoding switch' came from studies showing that children showed less of a Face Inversion Effect than adults, and were also more distracted by 'paraphernalia' such as hats, scarves and glasses.

- Subsequent research has failed to support the 'encoding switch' hypothesis.

- Young children are susceptible to the Composite Face Effect, Inversion Effect, the Thatcher Illusion and caricature effects, all of which reflect configural processing.

- Young children can distinguish between faces purely on the basis of subtle configural differences, but may not be as skilled as adults at doing this.

- Like adults, young children recognize familiar faces better from their internal features, and unfamiliar faces equally well from their external features.

- Children and adults do not appear to process faces in qualitatively different ways. Children might possibly be less efficient than adults at encoding faces, but other factors may also influence their performance, such as poorer memory, attention and concentration, and a heightened susceptibility to the demand characteristics within experimental settings.

FURTHER READING

Crookes, K. and McKone, E. (2009). *Early maturity of face recognition: no childhood development of holistic processing, novel face encoding, or face-space.* Cognition, 111: 219–247. An excellent summary and critique of the evidence for age-related development of face recognition abilities, this provides more details of some of the issues discussed in this chapter.

de Haan, M. (2001). *The neuropsychology of face processing in infancy and childhood.* In: C. A. Nelson, M. Luciana and M. L. Collins (eds)

Handbook of Developmental Cognitive Neuroscience, 381–398. Cambridge, MA: MIT Press. Given the fast pace of research in this area, this chapter is already a little dated. However, it remains a clear and comprehensive introduction to research on face processing in children from a neuropsychological perspective.

Pascalis, O. and Slater, A. (eds) (2003). *The Development of Face Processing in Infancy and Early Childhood: Current Perspectives.* New York: Nova Science. A collection of chapters written by various experts in this field, giving more detailed coverage of many of the issues discussed in this chapter.

PART II
NEUROPSYCHOLOGICAL PERSPECTIVES

7

CLINICAL NEUROPSYCHOLOGY OF FACE PROCESSING

Every day most of us see dozens, if not hundreds, of different people. We see both familiar and unfamiliar faces; we may see faces in the environment around us, on television, or the internet or in books, magazines and newspapers. For most of us perceiving these faces is effortless. We may not always be very good at identifying relatively unfamiliar faces (as we will see in Chapters 11–13); however, we rarely look at a face and think: 'Is that the face of my best friend or a pineapple?' Our ability to see a face is so effortless that we take it for granted that we can look around the world and pick a face out in a busy scene, and that we can look at that face and tell whether it is familiar to us, whether they are male or female, and whether they look happy or angry. Imagine if we were not easily able to complete this task. For some people, following a brain injury, these tasks are very difficult. In this chapter we will discuss a number of these patient groups, what they can and cannot process when looking at a face, and also what these patterns of impairment and ability may tell us about 'normal' face processing in individuals without brain damage.

7.1 **Prosopagnosia**

Clinical impairments in the ability to recognize familiar faces were reported as early as the late 19th century (Charcot, 1883; Hughlings Jackson, 1876; Wigan, 1844; Wilbrand, 1892). However, it was not until Bodamer (1947; see Ellis and Florence [1990] for a translation) published a detailed account of three patients who suffered from impaired face processing that the term **prosopagnosia** was coined. The term prosopagnosia (also sometimes called face blindness or facial agnosia) comes from the ancient Greek words *prosopon*, meaning face, and *agnosia*, meaning non-knowledge.

Bodamer's first case study was S, a 24-year-old man who suffered a brain injury that left him blind for a number of weeks. After his sight returned, he suffered from a wide range of neuropsychological impairments, but by far the most pronounced was his inability to recognize familiar faces or process facial expressions. S claimed to be able to visualize faces, but he was able to achieve recognition only through cues such as hairstyle or glasses. S was also unable to distinguish between human and animal faces. Bodamer's second case study was A, who presented very similar symptoms to S. Again, A could achieve face recognition only through non-facial cues. For example, he could recognize a photograph of Adolf Hitler on the basis of his moustache and side parting. The third case study described by Bodamer, that of B, showed very different patterns of face processing impairments and abilities to S and A. One month after he suffered brain damage, just for a few days, he saw all faces as distorted, with some features being either misplaced or rotated within the face in some way.

Bodamer's paper on these three cases of prosopagnosia presented the first systematic study of impairments in face-processing ability. This work inspired the hundreds of papers that have subsequently attempted to understand the way in which brain damage may selectively impair face processing.[1] It was clear from Bodamer's three case studies that the understanding of prosopagnosia would not be an easy task. Each of the three case studies differed, and some cases were quite transitory. What is clear is that the study of prosopagnosia is furthering our understanding of brain–behaviour relationships, the localization of functions in the brain, and how face processing and recognition is achieved in people without brain damage.

7.1.1 What can prosopagnosia tell us about 'normal' face processing?

One of the most influential models of face recognition was proposed by Bruce and Young in 1986 (see Fig. 1.1 and Chapter 1 for a full description of this model). Although this model was designed to explain 'normal' face recognition, much of the architecture was built on the basis of research with prosopagnosic patients.

To recap briefly, in the Bruce and Young model of face recognition there are four principal functional components: structural encoding, face recognition units (FRUs), person identity nodes (PINs) and name generation. When a face is initially encountered it is structurally encoded, which provides a representation or description of the face. This structural code is then compared against all the existing structural codes that are stored within each FRU. If the encountered representation matches a stored representation, that FRU will be activated and the face recognized as belonging to a familiar person. The activated FRU then triggers a PIN, which contains semantic information about the recognized person. Finally, the person's name is accessed.

Young et al (1988) discussed three prosopagnosic patients (PG, RG and LH) who had all suffered from damage to the right side of their brain. All of these patients seemed to be impaired in the structural encoding of faces. Structural encoding deficits have a perceptual basis so the patient may find it difficult even to realize that the stimulus they are looking at is a face. In experiments, such a patient may be unable to distinguish a face from a non-face, such as a scrambled face. Patients with impaired structural encoding are unable to do any further processing of that stimulus, so they cannot make familiarity distinctions and access semantic information or names by examining the person's face. If they were to access any of this information about a person, it would be possible only via non-facial cues such as the person's voice.

Another famous case study is PH, who suffered occipitotemporal lesions following closed head injury (de Haan et al, 1987). He could accurately classify stimuli as faces or non-faces, implying that his structural encoding of a face was unimpaired. However, forced-choice decisions of familiarity

---

[1] One important issue is the specificity of prosopagnosia. Is it really possible to have brain damage that selectively impairs the ability to process and recognize faces, while leaving the processing of all other types of stimuli entirely unimpaired? This issue is discussed, with direct reference to prosopagnosia, in Chapter 10. It is also interesting to note that almost all of the research on face processing in patients with prosopagnosia examines the processing of identity. Very little has considered whether the processing of facial emotion is also impaired in prosopagnosia. To read a case study of the prosopagnosic patient, SC, who suffered from impairments for processing some, but not all, emotional expressions see Stephan et al (2006).

		Case Studies			
		PG	PH	ME	EST
Structural encoding	Can you perceive that this is a face?	✗	✓	✓	✓
Face recognition unit	Do you know whether this is a familiar face?	✗	✗	✓	✓
Person identity node	Do you know whose face this is?	✗	✗	✗	✓
Name generation	Do you know the name of this person?	✗	✗	✗	✗

FIGURE 7.1 Summary of how damage at different stages of face processing can lead to different patterns of ability and impairment. For each stage, the chart shows whether each patient would be able to answer the question successfully (✓) or unable to answer it (✗). The shaded cells represent the unit of processing that is hypothesized to be damaged in each case study.

were at chance level. Although he could see that a face was a face, he was unable to match this structurally encoded representation to those stored in FRUs. This may be explained in terms of his brain damage affecting either the FRUs themselves or the mechanism that allows the matching of the encoded representation to the stored representation in the FRU. PH was also unable to proceed any further with the processing of this face, so he could not access semantic information or names from viewing the face.

de Haan et al (1991) reported the case of ME who was able to identify that a particular stimulus was a face and to make accurate familiarity decisions about faces. This suggests that ME could successfully encode a face structurally and then match that code to a stored FRU to make an accurate familiarity decision. However, ME was unable to recall any semantic information about correctly categorized familiar faces, suggesting PIN impairment. As with all of the previous studies, ME was also unable to complete the subsequent stages of processing and could not recall the names of familiar people on the basis of their face alone.

The final stage in Bruce and Young's model of face recognition is name generation. Flude et al (1989) discussed the case of EST, who suffered from anomia (a problem with word finding), following surgical removal of the left temporal lobe. After

surgery, EST was able to perceive and encode a face correctly (suggesting intact structural encoding), make accurate familiarity decisions (suggesting intact FRUs) and recall semantic information about a recognized familiar face (suggesting intact PINs). His only impairment was in retrieving the name of the person.

One very important aspect of the Bruce and Young model is that it suggests face recognition is a sequential process. It implies that each step of the process must be completed one after the other, and that it is not possible to progress beyond a stage if that stage is damaged. This can clearly be seen in all the case studies discussed above (Fig. 7.1). PG's damage meant that the structural encoding of a face was not possible. Consequently, PG was unable to complete any of the subsequent stages of processing. PH was able to perceive faces as a class of stimulus, but could not make familiarity decisions, which is what one would expect from FRU damage. PH was also unable to retrieve any semantic information about a person or their name. ME was able to perceive a face and say that it was familiar; however, ME could not retrieve any semantic information about the person and was then unable to retrieve their name. This pattern of deficits is consistent with the idea of PIN damage. EST was able successfully to perceive, recognize and even retrieve semantic information about an individual, but could not retrieve a person's name. All of these case studies support the sequential nature of the Bruce and Young model. Note that this does not mean that a prosopagnosic patient with a structural encoding impairment will never be able to recognize a familiar person, retrieve semantic information about them or know their name. It just means that these tasks must be achieved through alternative methods, such as recognizing the person's voice, way of moving or hairstyle, for example.

Bruce and Young's (1986) model of face recognition was based largely on the study of patients with brain injury who subsequently suffered impaired processing and recognition of faces. However, their model considered only the *functional* components that were necessary to recognize a familiar face successfully. The model made no assumptions as to where each of these modules might be localized in the brain. Bruce and Young did, however, acknowledge that various processes within face recognition might be localized and even possibly lateralized to different sides of the brain. We return to this point later in this chapter.

Some researchers have divided prosopagnosia into two distinct types:[2] apperceptive and associative prosopagnosia (see Barton, 2003). *Apperceptive prosopagnosia* is the more severe type of prosopagnosia. These patients are not able to form an accurate facial *percept*. That is, they have problems at the most basic level of visually perceiving faces. If a patient with apperceptive prosopagnosia were shown an array of unfamiliar faces and asked to identify which one was a target face, which was also in full view (as in the Benton Face Recognition Test), they would fail the test

miserably. This type of prosopagnosia may be explained by damage to the structural encoding mechanisms proposed in the Bruce and Young model. A patient with *associative prosopagnosia* is able to perceive a face. If they were shown a face they would be able to state that it was the face of a human and they would probably be able to describe that face, say whether the person was male or female and estimate their age. If they were given the Benton Face Recognition Test, they would probably pass it, although it has been suggested that associative prosopagnosics take an abnormally long time to complete the task to this level (Farah, 1990). The problem for patients with associative prosopagnosia is to *associate* the correctly perceived face with a stored familiar face. This type of prosopagnosia might be explained in terms of damage to the FRU in the Bruce and Young model.

7.1.2 What types of brain damage lead to prosopagnosia?

Prosopagnosia has traditionally been considered to result from *unilateral right hemisphere lesions*, implying that the right hemisphere is primarily responsible for face processing and recognition (e.g. De Renzi et al, 1968; Inoue et al, 2008; Joubert et al, 2003; Schiltz et al, 2006; Warrington and James, 1967; Yin, 1970). De Renzi et al (1994) used magnetic resonance imaging (MRI), computerized tomography (CT) and positron emission tomography (PET)[3] to examine the brain damage of three prosopagnosic patients and found that all had unilateral RH occipitotemporal lesions. They also cite 27 other cases of prosopagnosia that

---

[2] An alternative explanation for prosopagnosia has also been suggested: that it has nothing to do with impairments to face processing at all, but that the behavioural impairments reflect more subtle underlying impairments to the processing of visual stimuli in general. This possibility is discussed in detail in Chapter 10.

[3] The way in which these various neuroimaging methods work and what they show us about the brain is described in detail in the methodological Appendix of this book.

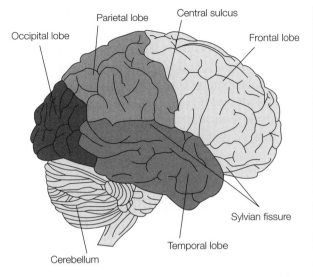

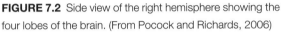

FIGURE 7.2 Side view of the right hemisphere showing the four lobes of the brain. (From Pocock and Richards, 2006)

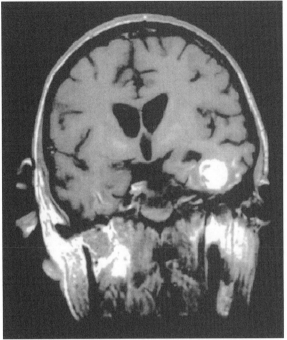

FIGURE 7.3 Unilateral right hemisphere lesion in prosopagnosic patient CR. (Adapted from Marotta et al, 2001)

resulted from unilateral right hemisphere lesions. The right temporal lobe (Fig. 7.2) has been frequently suggested as the primary site of damage in prosopagnosia, and the right inferotemporal region has been proposed as the typical lesion site for prosopagnosia (De Renzi et al, 1991; Landis et al, 1988; Whiteley and Warrington, 1977).

More recently, functional MRI (fMRI) studies have shown specific damage to the right hemisphere in prosopagnosic patients (Marotta et al, 2001; Wada and Yamamoto, 2001). This evidence all seems to suggest that prosopagnosia results from very specific damage to the right hemisphere, probably somewhere in the right temporal lobe (Fig. 7.3). Unfortunately, if you look at a wider selection of prosopagnosic patients, this pattern of unilateral right hemisphere damage is less common than you might expect.

Although prosopagnosia can arise from unilateral right hemisphere lesions, it has been argued that prosopagnosics typically suffer from **bilateral** lesions (Damasio et al, 1982; Meadows, 1974). Damasio and colleagues (1982) re-examined

the causes of prosopagnosia in cases that were originally thought to have resulted from unilateral right hemisphere lesions. Eight cases were examined via autopsy reports and three by CT. All were found to have symmetrical bilateral damage affecting equivalent functional areas. Many of the more recently reported patients with prosopagnosia have been shown to suffer from bilateral lesions (e.g. Barton et al, 2002; Boutsen and Humphreys, 2002; De Gelder and Rouw, 2000a,b; De Renzi and di Pellegrino, 1998; Farah et al, 2000; Sorger et al, 2007). This evidence suggests that both hemispheres play an important role in face processing.

If prosopagnosia can result from bilateral lesions, this suggests that the left hemisphere aids the effective processing and recognition of faces, at least to some extent. Stronger evidence for the involvement of the left hemisphere in face recognition comes from the existence of prosopagnosia resulting from unilateral left

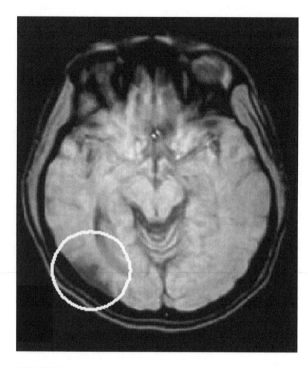

FIGURE 7.4 Unilateral left hemisphere lesion in pro-sopagnosic patient DN. (Adapted from Mattson et al, 2000)

hemisphere lesions (Fig. 7.4). One such example is WJ, a farmer who was prosopagnosic for human faces but remained able to recognize the faces of individual sheep from his flock. WJ suffered from low-density lesions in the left occipital, temporal and frontal lobes, with only very slight damage to the right occipital lobe (McNeil and Warrington, 1993). This suggests that his prosopagnosia is likely to have resulted from the extensive damage to his left hemisphere.

A number of other cases of prosopagnosia arising from unilateral left hemisphere damage have been documented (Barton, 2008; Hamsher et al, 1979; Hécaen and Angelergues, 1962; Meadows, 1974; H. Wright et al, 2006), with damage found in the left occipital lobe (Mattson et al, 2000) and the left temporoparietal region (Benke, 1988). However, it has been noted that cases of prosopagnosia resulting from left hemisphere lesions tend to show more variable symptoms

(De Renzi et al, 1987). Despite this possible variability in symptoms the existence of prosopagnosia resulting from unilateral left hemisphere lesions provides strong support for the involvement of both hemispheres in face processing and recognition.

On the basis of all the case studies presented above, it seems that there is not a simple answer to the question of what brain damage leads to prosopagnosia. In some patients unilateral right hemisphere brain damage is sufficient, in others unilateral left hemisphere brain damage may cause prosopagnosia, whereas in others bilateral damage may lead to prosopagnosia. A distinction has been drawn between prosopagnosia resulting from unilateral and bilateral lesions in terms of the severity of the impairment acquired. It has been suggested that unilateral lesions cause specific and selective impairments in face processing and recognition, whereas bilateral lesions cause more extensive disruption to face-processing abilities (Boeri and Salmaggi, 1994; Warrington and James, 1967). This is a really interesting idea as it suggests that both hemispheres make a distinct contribution to the effective processing and recognition of a face (see Chapter 9 for evidence supporting this idea in non-clinical participants). Consequently, if one hemisphere's face-processing mechanism is damaged, the other hemisphere's intact mechanism may compensate to some extent and enable some degree of residual face-processing and recognition ability. Thus, if unilateral right hemisphere damage occurs, there may be some impairment, but face processing may still be possible (at least to some extent) via the left hemisphere processing mechanisms. In contrast, if bilateral damage is sustained then no such compensation may be possible and the face-processing impairment will be complete.

7.1.3 Is prosopagnosia the result of impaired configural processing?

In Chapter 2 we saw that faces contain two types of information that we use to process and recognize faces: configural and featural facial information. Many prosopagnosics appear to be impaired at processing faces due to difficulties with processing configural facial information. Shuttleworth et al (1982) suggested that, in order to compensate for the inability to process configural facial information, the residual face-processing abilities of prosopagnosics are typically reliant on featural information. This suggestion is supported by many of the reported case studies of prosopagnosics. For example, Duchaine (2000) reported the case of BC who '*reported a feature matching strategy, focusing in particular on the eyebrows, rather than matching facial configurations*' (Duchaine, 2000, p. 80). Similarly Farah et al (2000) reported the case of 'Adam', who was able to use only featural strategies to achieve some degree of face processing. Finally, Saumier et al (2001) reported the case of a prosopagnosic patient whose impairment appeared to stem from an inability to integrate the individual features into a complete facial configuration.

Impaired configural facial information processing and an over-reliance on featural information are frequently found in patients with unilateral right hemisphere lesions. Patient KB suffered unilateral right temporo-occipital lesions and subsequently had prosopagnosia. It was reported that his remaining abilities were reliant on 'local features' (Bliem, 1998). Similarly, the prosopagnosic CR was able to use only featural facial information for recognition following right temporal lobe lesions (Gauthier et al, 1999a; Marotta et al, 1999). Uttner et al (2002) presented two cases of prosopagnosia, both resulting from unilateral right temporo-occipital lesions. Case one '*failed to integrate … [a face's] … features into a whole that represented a specific individual*' (Uttner et al, 2002, p. 933) and reported focusing on the orientation and edges of the mouth to determine emotional expression. Similarly, case two reported using specific and distinguishing features to complete a face-processing task, frequently using the eyebrows as a cue. These verbal reports suggest

that configural processing may be impaired in at least some prosopagnosics and that there is subsequently a greater reliance on the featural information contained within a face to guide processing and recognition. The compensatory strategy of relying on facial features has been reported by a number of prosopagnosic patients (e.g. Baudouin and Humphreys, 2006; Inoue et al, 2008).

These reports suggest that prosopagnosia involves a shift from processing configural information to processing featural facial information. This possibility has been investigated experimentally. An fMRI study of brain activation in prosopagnosics has shown reduced activation in the right hemisphere, specifically in the fusiform face area (where activity would normally increase when processing a face), but increased activation in the posterior left hemisphere (Marotta et al, 2001; see Fig. 7.5/Plate 7.5). This is very different to the pattern that would be found in 'non-clinical' samples. Marotta et al suggest that one possible explanation for this finding is that the processing of configural facial information, normally the more important form of facial information, is impaired by the damage to the right hemisphere. Therefore, any residual face-processing abilities might depend on the undamaged left hemisphere, which may process facial information in a more featural manner.

Direct evidence for the impaired processing of configural facial information in prosopagnosia comes from studies that have used various facial image manipulations. As we saw in Chapter 2, there are a variety of image manipulations that have been shown to impair the processing of either configural or featural facial information disproportionately. For example, inverting or scrambling a face reduces the configural information available within a face, while leaving the featural information relatively unimpaired. In contrast, blurring a face reduces the featural information in it, while leaving the configural information relatively unimpaired. By examining

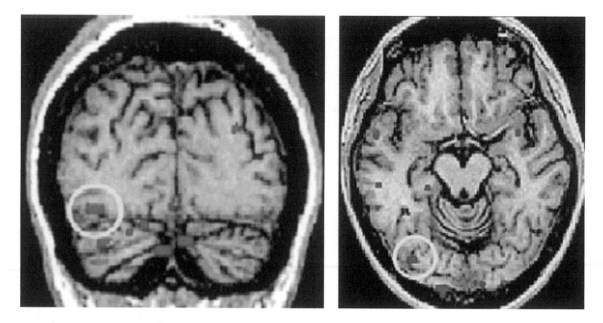

FIGURE 7.5 Left hemisphere face-specific activation in prosopagnosic patient CR during a face-processing task, as shown by fMRI. (Adapted from Marotta et al, 2001). Please see colour plate section.

how these image manipulations affect the face-processing abilities of prosopagnosic patients, it is possible to gain further insights into the importance of configural and featural facial information, and possibly gain some understanding of how these different processing mechanisms might be localized in the brain.

Yin (1970) examined the effect of inversion on face stimuli, comparing the performance of patients with unilateral left or right hemisphere lesions to that of neurologically intact controls. In the upright face condition, patients with right hemisphere lesions performed significantly worse than patients with left hemisphere lesions and control participants. These latter two groups did not differ significantly. This suggests that the right hemisphere damage disrupted the ability to process upright faces on the basis of their configural information, whereas the left hemisphere damage did not. In contrast, when shown inverted faces, the left hemisphere lesion group performed significantly worse than those with right hemisphere lesions and the control

group. Again, the latter two groups did not differ from each other. These results suggest that the left hemisphere damage disrupted the patients' ability to process the featural information on which the processing of inverted faces depends, whereas those with right hemisphere damage remained able to process the featural information contained in inverted faces. The lack of inversion effect in prosopagnosics has been found a number of times (Boutsen and Humphreys, 2002; de Gelder and Rouw, 2000a,b; Farah et al, 1995; Rouw and de Gelder, 2002). The evidence from the inversion effect therefore seems to support the idea that the processing of configural facial information is impaired in prosopagnosia, possibly due to the right hemisphere damage sustained.

Further research has investigated the use of featural information in the residual face-processing abilities of prosopagnosics. If prosopagnosics simply suffer from the inability to process faces via their configural information and are entirely reliant on featural information, they might be expected to show similar performance with both upright and inverted faces (de Gelder and Rouw, 2000a). In practice, a number of prosopagnosics have been shown to demonstrate an **inversion superiority effect**: they have *improved* performance for inverted faces in comparison to upright faces (e.g. AD [de Gelder et al, 1998]; LH [de Gelder and Rouw, 2000a]; HJA [Boutsen and Humphreys, 2002]; CR [Marotta et al, 2002]; RP [Rouw and De Gelder, 2002]).

The inversion superiority effect suggests that the ability to process configural facial information is not entirely absent in these prosopagnosic patients (de Gelder and Rouw, 2000a, 2001). Because inverted faces are processed primarily according to the featural information contained within them, it is not surprising that prosopagnosics are able to process inverted faces. What is particularly fascinating is that their performance is actually *improved* by inversion, in contrast to control participants. This inversion superiority effect has been explained in the following way. When a prosopagnosic patient views an upright face, the patient's damaged configural processing systems automatically try (and fail) to use the configural information that is present in the face. In contrast, when a face is inverted, the configural information is no longer salient, just as in normal individuals. The prosopagnosic is then able to process the face's featural information, without any interference from the impaired configural processing systems. The 'disengagement' from configural processing that is achieved by inverting the face allows the prosopagnosic to concentrate on the featural facial information—the type of information that they are better able to use in order to achieve processing and recognition.

7.1.4 Covert face processing in prosopagnosia

It is clear from all of the evidence discussed above that individuals with prosopagnosia are impaired at overtly processing and recognizing faces. However, some research has examined whether prosopagnosics might be able to process and identify faces *covertly*. That is, although they may report not being able to recognize a face as familiar, at some unconscious level they might in fact detect that the face is a familiar one. This raises a fascinating possibility about face processing in some patients with prosopagnosia: perhaps these individuals are able to process and recognize faces in some sense, but they are just not aware of it. In order to examine this possibility, a number of different methods have been used and each will be discussed separately here.

When participants who have suffered no brain damage see a familiar face, there are some physiological responses that occur automatically and that the person is not even aware of. One of these is the **skin conductance response** (SCR). The SCR technique records subtle changes in the electrical conductivity of the skin. This increases when non-clinical participants view familiar faces (e.g. Shearer and Mikulka, 1996). This technique has been used in a number of studies to examine whether individuals with prosopagnosia show an increased SCR when viewing a familiar face (or at least one that they would have recognized as familiar to them prior to acquiring the brain damage), even though they overtly report that the face is not familiar to them.

Bauer (1984) examined the overt and covert processing of familiar faces in a prosopagnosic patient, LF, whilst measuring SCR changes. LF was shown photographs of faces that should have been familiar to him, either because they were family members or because they were very famous. LF was unable to name any of these faces spontaneously. When shown a face along with five names, one of which was the correct one, LF chose the correct name 20% of the time, that is, at chance levels. However, when LF viewed a face and listened to five names being read aloud, on around 60% of trials the SCR was highest when the correct name was read out. This finding was taken to suggest that, although LF was unable overtly to recognize and name faces that would have been familiar to him before the brain damage, covertly there was some level of recognition that he was unaware of. A similar finding has been reported by Tranel and Damasio (1988), and more recently by Bobes et al (2004), who both found that prosopagnosic patients had an increased SCR when simply viewing a familiar face compared with an unfamiliar face.

The measurement of electrical activity in the brain (event-related potentials; ERPs)[4] has also been used to examine possible covert face recognition in patients with prosopagnosia. In participants without brain damage there are particular patterns of brain activity associated with viewing familiar faces that are different from those associated with viewing unfamiliar faces (see Chapter 9, section 9.2.2, for more details). Research using ERPs with prosopagnosic patients has also suggested that covert recognition is possible in some cases. For example, Renault et al (1989) found a P300 response to familiar faces which suggested covert recognition, even though the patient incorrectly reported that the faces were unfamiliar. Covert processing of facial identity in unfamiliar faces has also been shown in a prosopagnosic patient (Bobes et al, 2003). These authors showed a prosopagnosic patient, FE, pairs of faces that were all unfamiliar and asked him to decide whether the two images were of the same person or not. Overtly, FE was very impaired at this task; however, he showed an enhanced N300 when shown pairs of faces of the same person, suggesting that there was some successful processing of facial identity at a covert level.

Covert processing has also been shown in patients with prosopagnosia using a number of behavioural paradigms. For example, some studies have shown that, when asked to learn names associated with faces that were familiar to

the patient prior to acquiring damage, individuals with prosopagnosia find it easier to learn the correct name of a person than an incorrect one (e.g. Bruyer et al, 1983). de Haan et al (1987) asked prosopagnosic patients to make semantic decisions about famous names, such as classifying them on the basis of their occupation. Simultaneously, a previously familiar face was presented. If the face was from the same category (e.g. both the name and the face were of famous singers), reaction times were faster than if the name and the face had different occupations. Similarly, repetition priming effects have also been shown for individuals with prosopagnosia. Young et al (1988) found that familiarity decisions about names were made faster when the name was preceded by the face of that person than when the name was preceded by the face of a different famous person or an unfamiliar person, even though none of the faces could be recognized overtly.

Recently, Klein et al (2008) examined covert self-processing in a patient. He was asked to make various trait judgements about a number of faces of people he knew well, including his own face. With the other people's faces, his judgements were significantly below chance, however with his own face his responses were accurate. Given that he did not overtly recognize any of these faces, this suggests some covert self-recognition in the absence of covert recognition of other people.

Taken together, evidence from a variety of sources has shown that some prosopagnosic patients can covertly recognize familiar faces even though they overtly report being unable to recognize the same face. It has been suggested that covert recognition may reflect residual processing by the undamaged left hemisphere (Barton et al, 2004). However, covert recognition has not been found in all

---

[4] For a fuller description of what ERPs are and the way in which the various components relate to face processing and recognition, see Chapter 9.

patients with prosopagnosia. This suggests that prosopagnosia is not a unitary disorder, but that there are various subtypes, which may include a distinction on the basis of whether covert recognition is possible or not (see Young, 1998).

7.1.5 **Is it possible to have prosopagnosia without brain damage?**

Although prosopagnosia is traditionally thought to result from acquired brain damage, a number of case studies have been reported in more recent years where patients have significant impairments to their face-processing abilities but no obvious brain damage. This type of prosopagnosia is referred to as either developmental or **congenital prosopagnosia**. There is somewhat less research on the face-processing abilities and impairments for this type of prosopagnosia, however it is a rapidly developing field with the studies helping to increase both our understanding of 'normal' face processing and the ways in which it can be impaired.

A number of studies have attempted to characterize the patterns of impairment and ability in participants with congenital prosopagnosia by using a wide variety of face recognition tests. However, this has proven to be a very difficult task, as the performance of individual congenital prosopagnosic patients varies a great deal. Let us consider the possible face-processing tests in terms of the sequence of processing proposed by Bruce and Young (1986; see above). The first stage of face processing is to encode a face structurally, and the ability to do this is typically assessed by asking participants to classify particular stimuli as familiar. The congenital prosopagnosic Edward, who was studied by Duchaine et al (2006), was unimpaired at identifying facial stimuli and this has been shown in a number of other studies (e.g. de Gelder and Rouw, 2000a,b; Duchaine, 2000; Duchaine et al, 2003). This suggests that patients with congenital prosopagnosia are typically able

to perceive a face. Perceptual processing has also been examined in tasks where participants are asked to distinguish between similar faces or to perform delayed matching of faces. Again, patients typically perform at normal levels for these tests (e.g. Dobel et al, 2007; Duchaine et al, 2007; Humphreys et al, 2006). Tests such as gender discrimination, which requires the perceptual processing of a face without necessarily processing its identity, have been found to be mildly impaired in one case study (Duchaine et al, 2006).

In terms of the recognition of familiar faces, all congenital prosopagnosics show at least some level of impairment. What is interesting is that the extent of the impairment can vary by quite a large amount, from borderline impairment to severe (e.g. Barton et al, 2003; Dobel et al, 2007; Duchaine et al, 2006, 2007; Grueter et al, 2007; Humphreys et al, 2006). Similarly, patients with congenital prosopagnosia tend to have impaired memory for faces (Duchaine et al, 2006, 2007; Grueter et al, 2007). One study asked participants to learn new faces and the names associated with them (Dobel et al, 2007). Four of the patients were able to complete this task, but two showed significant impairment. Finally, the ability to process facial emotion has also been examined. Results here are conflicting, with some congenital prosopagnosics showing no impairment (Duchaine et al, 2007; Humphreys et al, 2006) and others showing significant impairment (Duchaine et al, 2006).

Although there is variability in the processing of faces by patients with congenital prosopagnosia, it seems that most are able to accurately perceive that a particular stimulus is a face, but they are unable to link that face with a stored representation of a known person (which implies that they have an associative type of impairment). The work with patients with acquired prosopagnosia suggests that the impairment may, at least in part, result from the impaired processing of configural facial information. This also seems to be the case for patients with congenital prosopagnosia (Barton et al, 2003; Carbon et al, 2007; Duchaine et al, 2006). Duchaine and colleagues (2006) presented Edward with upright and inverted faces. With upright faces, his performance was significantly worse than that of the control participants. However, his performance did not decrease when the faces were inverted, and his performance with the inverted faces was within the normal range. This suggests that Edward was more reliant on the featural information contained within a face than the configural information. Barton et al (2003) presented three congenital prosopagnosics with faces in which either the configuration was subtly manipulated (by changing the location of the features slightly within the face) or a featural change was made (changing eye colour). All of the patients showed a significant impairment when perceiving changes to the facial configuration. These findings suggest that congenital prosopagnosia, like acquired prosopagnosia, can be the result of the impaired processing of facial configurations. Carbon et al (2007) showed 14 participants with congenital prosopagnosia Thatcherized faces (see Chapter 2, section 2.3.2) and also found evidence for impaired configural processing in these patients.

An important issue within this area of research is what might actually cause congenital prosopagnosia. One of the initial assumptions about congenital proposagnosia was that it did not result from damage to the brain, hence allowing it to be clearly distinguished from acquired prosopagnosia. Neuroimaging[5] studies have recently attempted to address this issue; however, the results are very conflicting. Some case studies have found no anatomical abnormalities (e.g. MZ [Avidan et al, 2005]; GA [Barton et al, 2003]; KM, MT and TM [Humphreys et al, 2006]). However, others have found a wide variety of abnormalities

(e.g. KBN and KT [Barton et al, 2003]). In one very interesting study, Behrmann et al (2007) used MRI to examine the brains of six patients with congenital prosopagnosia. They found that the fusiform gyrus, the part of the brain that is thought to be the area specialized for face processing, was smaller in these patients. Importantly, they also found a relationship between the extent of the face-processing impairment and the size of the fusiform gyrus: the smaller the fusiform gyrus, the more marked the impairment. Further studies have used functional neuroimaging to see whether similar patterns of brain activation occur when congenital prosopagnosics and control participants view faces. Some studies have found very comparable patterns of activation (Avidan et al, 2005; Hasson et al, 2003) using fMRI. However, a study of five congenital prosopagnosics using magnetoencephalography (MEG) found that two showed responses comparable to controls, but that in three the responses did not occur (Harris et al, 2005).

One fascinating study by DeGutis et al (2007) attempted to rehabilitate MZ, a congenital prosopagnosic, by training her for over a year with tasks that required the discrimination of faces on the basis of their configural properties (remember that faces are processed primarily on the basis of the configural information contained within them). Before training, MZ performed poorly on a battery of tests of face processing and recognition, and did not show any brain response or activation in the areas typically associated with face processing. However, after training, her performance on the face-processing measures was within the 'normal' range, and importantly she showed face-selective responses (measured by electroencephalography [EEG]) and face-selective activation (measured by fMRI), particularly in the right hemisphere. This suggests that, with intensive training, some congenital prosopagnosics may learn to process faces to

---

[5] For a fuller description of these various neuroimaging methods, see the Appendix.

a 'normal' level. It also suggests that they may be able to achieve this using the same parts of the brain to process faces that are used in non-prosopagnosic participants.

Another interesting possibility that has recently been suggested is that there may be some genetic component to congenital prosopagnosia and that it may be hereditary. Duchaine et al (2007) examined face-processing abilities in ten members of a family who all reported face recognition impairments. Compared with age-matched control participants, the family members were significantly worse at identifying faces. On the Cambridge Face Memory Test, eight of the family members' scores were significantly below normal. On the Cambridge Face Perception Test, which involves matching faces according to their familiarity, all of the family members showed a significant impairment. Although the family's processing of facial identity was clearly impaired, their processing of facial emotion showed no impairment. Importantly, all family members (with one possible exception) performed at or above normal levels on a range of non-visual cognitive ability tests, so their impairments cannot be explained simply in terms of reduced cognitive ability.

Grueter et al (2007) conducted a similar study, examining face-processing impairments in eight patients with congenital prosopagnosia (taken from seven different families in which multiple members reported difficulties with face processing). Overall the congenital prosopagnosic patients who took part in this study did not show significant impairment on the Warrington Recognition Memory Test for Faces. In terms of recognizing famous faces, two of the participants with congenital prosopagnosia were significantly impaired; the remaining six showed some impairment, but it was not as severe. There now seems to be a fair amount of evidence that, at least in some cases, congenital prosopagnosia is inherited. This suggests a possible genetic basis to the impairment.

7.2 Delusional misidentification syndromes

Following brain damage, some patients suffer from delusions that specifically affect their face recognition abilities. Four types of **delusional misidentification** have been reported: Capgras syndrome, Frégoli syndrome, intermetamorphosis and subjective doubles (Ellis, 1994). Capgras syndrome is the most frequently occurring of the delusional misidentification syndromes. Patients with Capgras syndrome frequently claim that a familiar person, often their partner, close family member or friend, has been replaced by an imposter. Although Capgras syndrome may occur after brain injury, it is reported most frequently in patients diagnosed with schizophrenia and may also occur in patients with dementia. The Frégoli delusion involves a person believing that various different people they interact with are actually the same person in disguise. Intermetamorphosis is a disorder in which patients claim that a stranger's appearance might radically change to take on the physical characteristics of someone else familiar to them. Therefore, the people around them might be able to change identity without any accompanying change in appearance. The delusion of subjective doubles involves the patient believing that they have a double, or *doppelganger*. Although the double has the same appearance as the patient, the delusion typically involves the belief that the double has very different character traits to the patient.

Much of the research on delusional misidentifications has attempted to explain the delusions in terms of the existing models of face processing. With respect to the Bruce and Young model, Ellis and Young (1990) suggested that intermetamorphosis could be explained if the threshold for FRU activation was abnormally low: in these circumstances, an unfamiliar face might falsely activate an FRU and hence be categorized and recognized as a familiar person. Ellis and

Young (1990) also suggested that Frégoli syndrome might result from PIN dysfunction. They suggested that the delusion that a familiar person was disguised as another person could be explained if the PIN system was excessively activated and consequently activating an incorrect person identity in response to a correctly activated FRU.

More recently, Breen et al (2000) have extended the original Bruce and Young model in an attempt to explain the delusional misidentification syndromes (Fig. 7.6). This model follows the same basic structure as the Bruce and Young model in that a face is initially structurally encoded, and this code is then passed on to the FRUs where a familiarity decision can be made before the identity of the person is retrieved via the PINs. However, according to Breen et al's model, there are two outputs from the FRUs. One is to the PINs, whereas the other initiates an affective response to the face. In part, this affective response allows for a distinction between familiar and unfamiliar faces, but it also enables an emotional response to a face. For example, when you see your partner or best friend you are likely to have a positive emotional response, whereas when you see your arch enemy you are likely to have a negative emotional response. This affective response is linked to the unconscious physiological responses (arousal and orienting response) that occur when we view a familiar face, such as the SCR discussed earlier in this chapter.

Breen et al (2000) suggest that the Capgras delusion occurs as a result of damage to the link between the FRU and the affective response, as well as to the affective response itself. Consequently, the patient can view a face, correctly identify it as familiar and decide who the person is, but they have no affective or physiological response to the person. This lack

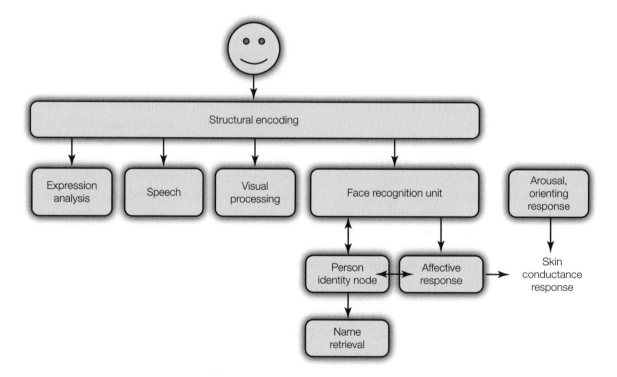

FIGURE 7.6 The Breen et al (2000) model of face processing (see text for a description of the model). (Adapted from Breen et al, 2000)

of response to a familiar face is thought to be the source of the delusion, with the patient trying to reconcile the incongruity between recognizing a familiar face and there being no emotional response to that person to support this successful recognition. This possibility was supported by a study of five patients with Capgras syndrome by Ellis and colleagues in 1997. They gave the patients a number of face-processing tasks, including matching unfamiliar faces, recognizing familiar faces, and retrieving semantic information (occupation) and the names of familiar faces. Most of the patients were able to recognize the faces just as well as non-clinical control participants. However, what was particularly striking about the results was that all failed to show a change in SCR when viewing familiar faces.

Ellis and Young (1990) suggested that the delusional misidentification syndromes and prosopagnosia could be seen as mirror images of each other. Patients with prosopagnosia fail to recognize familiar faces, but may have an appropriate affective response to them, as shown by their covert recognition. In contrast, patients with delusional misidentifications successfully identify a face as familiar, but they suffer from the delusions as a result of a lack of affective response to these faces. This distinction can be explained explicitly in terms of the Breen et al (2000) model. Delusional misidentification occurs as a result of damage to the link from the FRU to the affective response, with the FRU itself and its subsequent links to the PINs being intact. Hence, these patients can identify a face as familiar, but they have no affective response to it. Conversely, associative prosopagnosia (the ability to perceive a face visually without the ability to make a familiarity decision) occurs as a result of disruption, but not complete damage, to the FRU and the links between FRUs and PINs. Hence, the patient is unable to identify a face as familiar, but the slight residual FRU activation successfully feeds into the affective response leading to SCRs and covert recognition of familiar faces.

In addition to improving our knowledge about how faces might be processed and recognized in participants without brain damage, the research on patients with delusional misidentification can also aid our understanding of the neuropsychological mechanisms underpinning face processing. Patients suffering from delusional misidentification typically suffer from unilateral or predominantly right hemisphere damage. For example, patients suffering from Frégoli syndrome have been found to have damage to the right frontal lobe (Box et al, 1999; Feinberg et al, 1999) and those with Capgras syndrome have damage to the right frontal and parietal lobes (Edelstyn et al, 2001). This is perhaps not entirely surprising given the large amount of evidence showing that the right hemisphere is dominant for face processing and recognition. However, what is interesting is how the face-processing abilities of these patients might inform our understanding of the way in which the left and right hemispheres might process facial information differently.

Rapcsak et al (1994) conducted detailed examinations of two patients who both suffered from delusional misidentification following frontal, temporal and parietal right hemisphere lesions, as identified by CT scans. Both of these patients frequently misidentified unfamiliar people as being familiar to them. Rapcsak et al found that both patients completed unfamiliar face-matching tasks on the basis of featural information. This use of featural facial information following unilateral right hemisphere damage might be explained in terms of an over-reliance on the featural processing mechanisms in the left hemisphere. If the patients were relying primarily on featural information to identify familiar faces and an unfamiliar person had a feature similar to that of a familiar person, that feature might falsely activate the FRU for the latter, resulting in a feeling of familiarity, or hyper-familiarity, towards the unknown person. Experiments with patients suffering from Capgras syndrome also support such hemispheric specializations in face processing.

Non-clinical participants typically show a right hemisphere advantage for face-processing tasks. However, individuals with Capgras syndrome have been found to have a left hemisphere advantage for face processing (Ellis et al, 1993a). Again, this is consistent with the suggestion that such patients are processing faces via an alternative featural mechanism that is lateralized to the left hemisphere.

7.3 Face processing in 'split brain' patients

Much of our early understanding of brain lateralization came from the study of so-called **'split brain' patients**. These patients have undergone neurosurgery to sever the **corpus callosum**. The corpus callosum is a large collection of nerve fibres that connect the left and right cerebral hemispheres (Fig. 7.7), enabling information to be passed between the hemispheres.

The split brain operation is very rare and conducted only on patients with very severe epilepsy that has not been alleviated by all other possible treatments.

The study of 'split brain' patients gives us a fascinating understanding of the way in which each hemisphere processes information. Because the corpus callosum has been severed, information can no longer be passed directly between the hemispheres, and each hemisphere effectively processes information as a relatively isolated unit. The research conducted with split brain patients typically presents stimuli to either the left or the right visual field. Information that is presented to the left visual field is processed by the right hemisphere, whereas information that is presented to the right visual field is processed by the left hemisphere (Fig. 7.8). Therefore, if performance is better when a stimulus is presented to the left visual field, this suggests that the right hemisphere is more specialized for processing that type of stimulus. If performance is better when a stimulus is presented to the right visual field, this suggests that the left hemisphere is more specialized for processing that type of information.

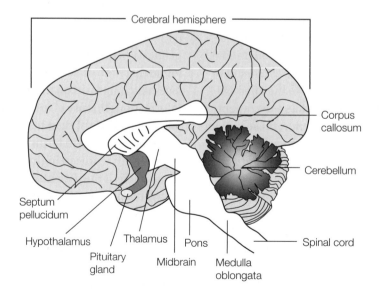

FIGURE 7.7 Midsagittal view of the right side of the human brain showing the relationships of the main structures. (From Pocock and Richards, 2006)

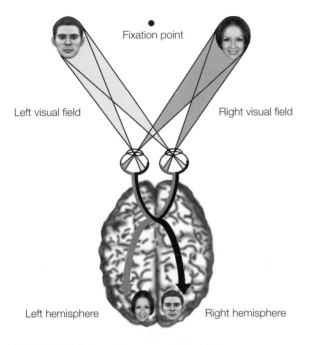

FIGURE 7.8 Schematic representation of the neuroanatomical organization of the visual pathways.

FIGURE 7.9 Example of a vertically split chimeric face stimulus. In this example the face in the left visual field is female and would be processed by the right hemisphere; the face in the right visual field is male and would be processed by the left hemisphere.

Levy et al (1972) examined the face-processing abilities of 'split brain' patients. They showed them a number of faces and later presented them with vertically split chimeric face stimuli, where the face in each half was of a different person (Fig. 7.9). When asked to select which of the two faces they had been shown previously, the face shown in the left visual field was most frequently selected (thus, in Fig. 7.9, the female face would be chosen). This bias towards picking the face presented in the left visual field reflects the right hemisphere's specialization for processing faces.

Although Levy et al (1972) found a right hemisphere superiority for face processing in 'split brain' patients, they suggested that both hemispheres might actually be able to process facial stimuli, but that '*the two hemispheres accomplished the same task by characteristically different strategies*' (p. 74). More importantly, they noted specifically that the left hemisphere '*seemed unable...to recognise or remember a face as a whole, needing instead to pick out some analytical detail*

to which a verbal label could be attached' (p. 74). This observation fits well with the evidence from prosopagnosic patients discussed above, which suggests that the left hemisphere is specialized for processing the featural information contained within a face but not its configural information.

The idea that each hemisphere is specialized for processing different types of facial information has been supported in other studies of 'split brain' patients. Gazzaniga and Smylie (1983) presented blurred faces to each visual field. In these faces, the featural facial information was relatively degraded and the configural facial information relatively intact. When presented to the left visual field (right hemisphere) the patients responded with 85% accuracy, whereas when presented to the right visual field (left hemisphere) accuracy dropped to 30%. This finding is in line with the suggestion that the left hemisphere is specialized for processing featural information and the right hemisphere for processing configural information. The processing of inverted faces, in which the configural information is relatively impaired but the featural information is relatively intact, has been examined in monkeys with split brains by Vermeire and Hamilton (1998). They found a right hemisphere advantage for processing upright faces, but not for processing inverted faces. Again, this finding is consistent with the suggested hemispheric specializations for processing facial information.

Although most of the research on the face-processing abilities of 'split brain' patients has concentrated on the recognition of other people's faces, a small number of studies have examined the patient's ability to recognize their own face. Turk et al (2002) presented patient JW with images of his own face, with images of another highly familiar face, and with a number of morphed images containing varying amounts of each of the two faces. These images were then presented either to the left or the right visual field, and JW was asked whether the face was his, or whether it was the face of the other person. Turk et al found a clear difference in processing between the hemispheres, with a left hemisphere advantage for self-recognition and a right hemisphere advantage for recognizing other familiar people. However, another similar study with a different split brain patient, NG, found a different result (Uddin et al, 2005). These authors observed the expected right hemisphere superiority for processing the faces of familiar people, but found that both hemispheres were equally good at self-recognition. To complicate matters further, studies conducted with another patient, ML, found that the right hemisphere was better than the left at self-recognition (Keenan et al, 2003). The reason for the differences found across these patients is not clear; however, it clearly illustrates the

problems of case study research (see below for a more detailed discussion of these methodological issues).

7.4 Conclusion

In this chapter we have discussed the face-processing abilities of three different groups of brain-damaged patients. As well as giving us a fascinating insight into the behavioural consequences of brain damage, the study of these patients allows us to test some of the predictions made about face processing in non-clinical samples and further understand 'normal' face processing and recognition. First, the study of face processing in patients with prosopagnosia has informed the development of models of face processing and recognition. Second, the study of the sites of damage acquired across the different patient groups has provided invaluable insights into the neuropsychological bases of face processing and recognition. This research suggests that the right hemisphere is dominant for face processing and recognition, but that the left hemisphere is also involved. In fact, each hemisphere may make its own unique contribution to the effective processing and recognition of faces. Although the study of patient groups has undoubtedly expanded our understanding of 'normal' face processing, it is important to acknowledge the limitations of using this evidence and the problems involved in extrapolating the findings from clinical to non-clinical groups.

Other than with the possible exception of the split brain operation, it is almost impossible to know each individual patient's premorbid cognitive abilities, that is, how good they were at face processing and recognition before they acquired their brain damage. Most of the studies assume that a patient's premorbid abilities would be comparable to the norms of the general public and that the patient would have been 'average' prior to the brain damage. However, this is a big assumption and it is not possible to tell whether the patient may have previously been particularly good at face processing, in which case the extent of their impairment might be underestimated, or particularly bad at face processing, in which case the extent of their impairment might be overestimated. Researchers may be able to get around this problem with patients who are undergoing split brain operations by performing extensive cognitive testing before surgery takes place. However, this does not mean that extrapolating from 'split brain' patients is any less problematic. The split brain procedure is a very extreme operation and conducted only as a last resort option when a patient is suffering from severe epilepsy. The very fact that a neurosurgical procedure is necessary means that brain activity is abnormal to begin with. Consequently, it is not possible to claim that a split brain patient's face-processing abilities before their surgery is comparable to 'normal' face processing, as they have suffered for most of their life from a chronic neurological disorder which ultimately was so debilitating that extreme neurosurgery was necessary.

The majority of the research on patients with brain damage is also limited to experiments on single patients, or a very small number of patients. This is problematic as all brains differ slightly, even in people who have not suffered any brain damage. This is true in terms of both the physical structure of the brain and the location for various processing mechanisms. This makes it very difficult to compare the site of damage and subsequent patterns of impairment and abilities across patients. This might also explain why behavioural outcomes can vary so much across patients with apparently comparable damage.

Another limitation of this area of research is that it is very difficult to really understand why particular patterns of impairment and ability occur following damage. One difficulty is working out whether the residual abilities are successfully completed because the part of the brain responsible for carrying out that function is undamaged. It is possible that either behavioural or neurological compensation may enable patients to complete different tasks following brain damage. For example, patients with prosopagnosia often report using alternative cues, such as voice, hairstyle, clothes or makeup, to help them successfully recognize people who are familiar to them. Alternatively, it may be that the brain has reorganized to compensate for the damage acquired, in an attempt to regain lost processing abilities. A possible example of this is the left hemisphere activation that has been reported in some prosopagnosic patients when viewing faces (see earlier in this chapter). Does this left hemisphere activation occur in all people without brain damage, so that this undamaged part of the brain is all that is left to enable face processing in some prosopagnosics? Or is it that the brain has compensated for the damage, by recruiting an alternative and undamaged part of the brain in an attempt to regain some face-processing abilities?

Although there are some relatively major limitations in the use of clinical research to inform our understanding of 'normal' face processing and recognition, it has made a major contribution to our understanding of face processing. Until relatively recently it was very difficult to examine the way in which normal, undamaged brains process information, which is why much of the early neuropsychological research was so dependent upon clinical data. With the development of neuroimaging methods it is now possible to see how brain activity changes when completing various cognitive tasks, and we can consider the extent to which conclusions drawn from studying clinical samples can be verified. This issue is the focus of Chapter 9.

SUMMARY

- Impairments to face processing can occur following unilateral right hemisphere lesions; however, bilateral lesions are a far more common cause of prosopagnosia. In developmental (or congenital) prosopagnosia there is no obvious damage to the brain.

- Patients with prosopagnosia tend to have impaired processing of configural facial information. Instead they rely on processing facial features; this may result in left hemisphere processing of faces.

- Delusional misidentification syndromes are thought to occur as a result of damage to the links between the face recognition unit and the affective response to that face.

- Evidence from 'split brain' patients has shown that both hemispheres are necessary to enable the effective processing of faces and that information is shared between the hemispheres via the corpus callosum.

FURTHER READING

Barton, J. J. S. (2003). *Disorders of face perception and recognition.* Neurologic Clinics of North America, 21(2): 521–548. This paper reviews a range of clinical conditions in which face processing is impaired. It gives a detailed review of prosopagnosia. It also discusses Capgras syndrome and the processing of faces in autism, which we will discuss in the next chapter.

Ellis, H. D. and Lewis, M. B. (2001). *Capgras delusion: a window on face recognition.* Trends in Cognitive Sciences, 5(4): 149–156. This paper provides both a review of the research on Capgras syndrome and a discussion of how these findings have been used to develop models of face processing further. It provides a really clear demonstration of how clinical findings can inform and help to develop models of face processing.

Marotta, J. J., Genovese, C. R., and Behrmann, M. (2001). *A functional MRI study of face recognition in patients with prosopagnosia.* Neuroreport, 12(8): 1581–1587. In this paper, two patients with prosopagnosia are studied and discussed. Their residual face-processing abilities are also examined using fMRI. This is a great paper to read as it shows nicely how case studies have furthered our understanding of face processing.

In addition, take a look at http://www.prosopagnosia.com, a website put together by Cecilia Burman who has congenital prosopagnosia. She gives an excellent description of what it is like to have prosopagnosia and the strategies that she uses to help her recognize people.

8

DEVELOPMENTAL NEUROPSYCHOLOGICAL DISORDERS OF FACE PROCESSING

We are not born with exactly the same face-processing abilities that we have as adults. As we saw in Chapters 5 and 6, although we may have some capability from birth, our quite proficient face-processing abilities as adults are the outcome of a great deal of development too. However, what happens when that development goes wrong? This may occur due to a trauma at birth, a loss of vision, a genetic disorder or neurochemical imbalances. In this chapter we will examine how these varying neurodevelopmental problems affect the ability to process faces, and discuss the neuropsychological mechanisms underlying the development of normal face-processing abilities.

8.1 Face processing following early visual deprivation

The ability to process faces develops over the course of infancy and through childhood and adolescence. As discussed in Chapters 5 and 6, normal development involves experience of viewing faces; however, some children suffer from bilateral congenital cataracts from birth, which greatly reduce the visual input that they receive. This condition tends to be alleviated by removal of the cataracts when the child is around 3–6 months old. Once the cataracts are removed, most children have normal vision. It is therefore possible to examine the effects of **early visual deprivation** on later visual perception, including face perception.

Geldart et al (2002) tested 17 participants, aged from 10 to 38 years, who had suffered early visual deprivation for a minimum of 7 weeks (one was nearly 2 years old when their vision was corrected!). They also tested normally sighted child and adult control participants. Five different tests of face processing were completed: recognition of identity across changes in viewpoint; recognition of identity across changes in expression; recognition of emotional expression; perception of gaze direction; and lip-reading. The participants who had early visual deprivation were significantly impaired on both of the identity recognition tasks, but not on the other three face-processing tasks. Importantly, other than for the one participant who had visual deprivation for nearly two years, there was no relationship between the duration of the visual deprivation and the magnitude of the face-processing deficit. There are two key points to take away from this study. First, it suggests that the neural mechanisms underlying face processing are established within a few weeks of birth. Second, it suggests that not all aspects of face processing are established at this stage, as the processing of identity was impaired but the processing of expression, gaze and lip-reading was not. This implies that these unaffected processes may be dealt with by different neural mechanisms, which either develop later in infancy (after the visual deprivation has been reversed) or which are less dependent on early visual input.

It has been suggested that the deficits in face processing found in participants with early visual deprivation may result from impaired processing of configural facial information. Recall that there are two types of facial information: configural and featural (see Chapter 2). Le Grand et al (2001) examined whether children with early visual deprivation were able to process both of these types of information. They showed participants a face very briefly, for 200 milliseconds, and then showed them three faces, one of which matched the face they had just seen. The participants' task was to decide which of the faces they had just been shown. The faces were subjected to either a configural manipulation, in which the eyes and mouth were moved slightly, or a featural manipulation, in which the eyes and mouth were replaced with others (Fig. 8.1). In comparison to age-matched controls, the children who had early visual deprivation were significantly impaired at detecting the configural changes, but not the featural changes. This finding suggests that the sensitivity to facial configurations, which is central to the ability to process facial stimuli, is established in the first few weeks after birth, but that the development of featural processing occurs later.

The impaired processing of configural facial information in people with early visual deprivation has also been shown in a study by Le Grand et al (2004) which used the composite face effect (see Chapter 2, section 2.3.3). The control participants showed the usual composite face effect; when asked to decide whether the top halves of two faces were the same, performance was better when the faces were misaligned than when they were aligned. This is because aligning the top

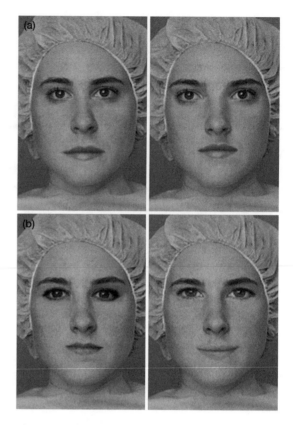

FIGURE 8.1 Examples of stimuli taken from Le Grand et al (2001). The faces in the top row differ only in terms of their configural properties as the eyes and mouth have been moved. The faces in the bottom row differ primarily in terms of their featural properties as the eyes and mouth have been replaced. (Reprinted by permission from Macmillan Publishers Ltd: Le Grand, R., Mondloch, C. J., Maurer, D. & Brent, H. P. (2001). Neuroperception—early visual experience and face processing, *Nature*, 410, 890. © 2001)

and bottom halves elicits holistic or configural processing which makes it more difficult to match the faces on the basis of their top halves. The participants with early visual deprivation showed a very different pattern of performance. The alignment of the two face halves did not cause any impairment to processing. Indeed, they were actually better than the control participants when the face halves were aligned. This is presumably because the visually deprived participants did not merge the two face halves into a complete face and so were able to complete the matching task on the basis of the features contained in the top halves of the faces without interference from the configural percept.

The work with people who had early visual deprivation provides us with a number of important insights into the neuropsychology of face processing. First, it shows that the neural mechanisms are established, at least to some extent, in the first few weeks of life. Second, it shows that facial identity is likely to be processed independently of other facial attributes, such as expression, gaze and lip-reading. At the very least, it shows that these develop later than identity processing. Third, it shows that the ability to process configural facial information is established very early in infancy and that, if the development of this processing mechanism is disrupted, face recognition becomes reliant on the processing of featural facial information instead.

8.2 Autistic spectrum disorders

Autistic spectrum disorders (ASD) include a range of neurodevelopmental conditions, the most common of which are autism and Asperger's syndrome. In ASD, behaviour is characterized primarily by reduced social interaction, a tendency to pay attention to only a very narrow range of interests, and engagement in very repetitive behaviours. Within psychology, much research has concentrated on the lack of **Theory of Mind** in ASD. Theory of Mind is the ability to understand that other people have thoughts, beliefs and emotions. When attempting to understand the mental state of another person, the face and facial expressions provide a great deal

of information. Lots of research has examined the face-processing abilities of individuals with ASD, and some of this research has attempted to use their observed patterns of impairment in order to explain the atypical behaviours found in this group.

8.2.1 Face processing in ASD

Much of the research on face processing in ASD has concentrated on the processing of facial emotion; however, impairments in face processing have been shown across a number of different tasks. Deruelle et al (2004) found that children with ASD were worse than controls on a range of face-processing tasks including recognition of identity, emotional expression, gaze direction, gender and lip-reading. In terms of processing facial identity, Wilson et al (2007b) examined whether children with ASD and normally developing children differed in terms of the information they extracted from a face, by comparing their recognition abilities for the whole face, just the inner face or just the outer face. They found small impairments in face recognition in children with ASD, but all participants showed the adult pattern (see Chapter 2, section 2.9); they were best at recognizing full faces, then inner faces and, worst of all, outer faces.

The perception of gaze direction has also been found to be atypical in ASD. Wallace et al (2006) asked participants to judge the direction of eye gaze in either whole faces or just the eye region. Participants with ASD were able to complete this task successfully. However, the control participants were better at judging averted gaze in a whole face and direct gaze in the eyes only, and this pattern was not replicated in the ASD participants. This suggests that, although accurate gaze perception may be possible in ASD, it does differ from gaze perception in normally developing children. Akechi et al (2009) showed children faces in which the facial expression and the eye gaze were either congruent or incongruent. According to Akechi, when you are angry you are more likely to look directly at whatever you are angry at, whereas with fear you are more likely to look away. So, an angry face looking directly at you, or a fearful face looking away from you, would be a 'congruent' face, whereas an angry face with averted eye gaze or a fearful face that looked directly at you would be 'incongruent'. Akechi and colleagues found that the children from the control group took longer to respond to an incongruent face than a congruent face, whereas children in the autism group were not affected by this manipulation. This finding suggests that children with autism take less notice of eye gaze when looking at faces.

Although impairments in processing identity and gaze direction have been shown in ASD, the majority of the research in this area has examined the ability to process facial emotion. Castelli (2005) found no impairment in recognition of facial emotion across all six of the basic emotions at varying levels of intensity. However, most studies have shown impairments. Humphreys et al (2007) conducted a very simple experiment in which participants were shown faces from the original Ekman set of stimuli (see Chapter 3) that were expressing the six basic emotions: anger, disgust, fear, happiness, sadness and surprise. They found that adults with ASD were particularly impaired at recognizing fear and, to a lesser extent, disgust and happiness. Anger, sadness and surprise showed no impairment. This finding suggests that the impairments to emotion processing in ASD may not be common across all emotional expressions, but rather that particular emotions might be specifically affected.

Wallace et al (2008) considered whether individual facial features might contribute differently to the processing of facial emotion in ASD. When shown complete faces, adults with ASD were significantly worse at recognizing disgust, fear and sadness. They were then shown emotive faces in which sections of the face were revealed one at a time, starting with either the eye area or the mouth area. In the eyes condition the processing of fear was particularly impaired,

whereas in the mouth condition the processing of disgust was impaired. They also found that the ASD participants had a tendency to classify fearful eyes as angry. This suggests that individuals with ASD process facial features in a different manner to control participants. We will return to this issue in the next section.

Clark et al (2008) showed participants faces very briefly, for either 15 or 30 ms. They were given two different face-processing tasks to complete. In one task they were shown emotive faces and had to decide whether the expression was happiness or sadness. In the other they had to decide the sex of a face with a neutral expression. They were also given a non-face task in which they had to decide whether a stimulus was an animal or an object. The participants with ASD were significantly worse on the emotion decision task, but not on the other two tasks. This suggests that their impairment is specific to processing facial emotion. However, remember the study by Deruelle et al (2004) mentioned above, which showed deficits in a range of face-processing skills. The specificity of the face-processing impairment in ASD still seems unclear.

Some research has examined how the social interaction skills of individuals with ASD might be affected by their impaired ability to process facial emotion. Begeer et al (2006) found that children with ASD perform poorly when asked to match pairs of images of smiling and frowning faces. However, they also used a second version with a socially relevant interaction (e.g. being told off or given a sweet). In this version, the performance of children with ASD improved. This suggests that when asked to match faces on the basis of emotional understanding within a social context, the processing of facial emotion can occur in ASD. Teunisse and de Gelder (2001) found that individuals with ASD who had higher social functioning skills were better at emotion processing than those with lower social functioning skills. This finding implies a relationship between the ability to process facial emotion and the ability to interact socially in ASD.

Some research has shown that the impairment in processing facial emotion in ASD might be exaggerated by the frequent use of static images in studies. Tardif et al (2007) used both static images and dynamic images that were moving at different speeds. They found that the impairment in emotion recognition in ASD was reduced when stimuli were shown with slow movements. Back et al (2007) found that accuracy for recognizing emotion in both static and dynamic faces was reduced in adolescents with ASD, but recognition was still above chance levels. Importantly, though, they found that when emotion was shown through dynamic movements in the eye area, performance in the ASD group improved. These studies suggest that recognition of facial emotion in ASD is aided by the movements of facial expressions of emotion.

Some impairment in the processing of facial emotion has also been shown in unaffected relatives of people with ASD. Palermo et al (2006) found that parents of children with ASD were significantly worse than control participants at processing sadness and disgust. The effect was greater for fathers of children with ASD than for mothers. Bolte and Poustka (2003) showed that the magnitude of this impairment increases when there is more than one family member with ASD. The findings of these studies are important as they provide evidence for a genetic basis to ASD and its heritability.

8.2.2 Why is face processing atypical in ASD?

It is clear that, at least to some extent, the processing of faces, and particularly facial expressions of emotion, is atypical in ASD. One interesting question is why this difference might exist. Research has examined two possible differences in processing strategies that might account for this finding. The first is that individuals with ASD might differ in the way that they actually look at faces and the areas that they either concentrate on, or ignore. The second is that they might differ in their processing of configural and featural facial information (see Chapter 2). Each of these theories will be discussed in turn.

Pelphrey et al (2002) tracked the **eye movements** of participants while they looked at faces. They found that participants with ASD were more likely to look at the areas of faces without features, whereas control participants tended to look at the facial features. The methods of viewing faces in the two groups did not change with different instructions. This tendency to avoid looking at facial features has also been shown in children with ASD as young as 3 years of age (de Wit et al, 2008). Atypical patterns of eye movements and fixations when inspecting faces have been found for both familiar and unfamiliar faces (Sterling et al, 2008).

When shown emotive faces, differences in viewing strategies have also been reported. de Wit et al (2008) found that, although children with ASD looked less at facial features, both ASD and control participants had more fixations around the eye area when faces were expressing a negative emotion than when they were expressing a positive emotion. Hernandez et al (2009) recorded the eye movements of adult participants while they were looking at neutral and emotive faces, and reported a similar finding. Both control adults and adults with autism looked more at the eyes than other facial features, but this was less exaggerated in adults with autism. Spezio et al (2007) also found that participants with ASD looked less at the eye region; however, they also found that those with ASD tended to look more at the mouth region.

Speer et al (2007) examined eye movements to faces across two different manipulations: static versus dynamic faces, and isolated versus socially interactive faces. They found differences between participants with ASD and control participants only in the dynamic social condition. The ASD participants looked less at the eye region of faces and more at the body. They also found that this pattern of fixations was more pronounced in ASD participants with poorer social responsiveness.

The research from eye movement studies seems to provide strong evidence that individuals with ASD actively avoid looking at the eyes of others. This may account for both the impaired processing of facial emotion and the reduced or absent social interactions in this group.

An alternative (or possibly complementary) explanation is that individuals with ASD have atypical processing of configural and featural facial information. Recall that in the neurotypical population faces are processed primarily on the basis of the configural information contained within them and that the processing of the featural facial information is secondary (see Chapter 2). However, in individuals with ASD, this may not be the case.

Inversion of a face disrupts the configural information contained within a face and leaves processing reliant on the featural information contained within a face (see Chapter 2, section 2.3.1). In control participants, inversion impairs processing, whereas this inversion effect is not found in participants with ASD (e.g. Hobson et al, 1988; Schultz et al, 2000; Tantam et al, 1989; Wallace et al, 2008). This suggests that face processing in people with ASD is reliant on the processing of featural facial information, rather than configural facial information. However, Lahaie et al (2006) found that inversion increased reaction times and decreased accuracy in ASD participants in a manner similar to that in control participants, suggesting that their processing of configural information is not impaired. Lahaie and colleagues also conducted a second experiment in which they used facial features to prime whole faces. They found that priming from single facial features was significantly greater in participants with ASD than in control participants. Looking at the results of these two experiments in combination, Lahaie et al suggest that there is no impairment in the processing of configural facial information in ASD, but instead they have superiority for processing featural information.

Joseph and Tanaka (2003) asked participants to recognize individual facial features, either in isolation or within a face. They found that control children were better at recognizing a facial feature when it was presented in the context of a whole face than when the feature was presented on its own (see Chapter 2, section 2.3.4). In contrast, children with ASD only had a whole face advantage for recognizing mouths and were particularly bad at processing the eyes stimuli. This finding fits well with the eye-tracking research showing that people with ASD look more at the mouth than the eyes. It also fits well with the conclusions of Lahaie et al (2006) as it suggests that the impairment in configural processing is not absolute and that different processing strategies can be adopted when processing different parts of the face.

Experiments have also examined the processing of faces in which either the high or low spatial frequencies are filtered out (see Chapter 2, section 2.8). These have shown that participants with ASD are impaired at processing facial emotion only when high spatial frequencies are filtered out (Deruelle et al, 2004; Katsyri et al, 2008). This provides further support for the reliance on featural information for effective face processing in ASD as the featural information is contained within the high spatial frequencies. Deruelle et al (2008) replicated this finding for the recognition of both identity and emotion, but not for the processing of gender. This suggests that different facial information might be used for different tasks.

One possible explanation for the lack of configural processing in ASD is that, because of the reduced social interactions with others, the 'typical' face-processing abilities do not develop normally. We will see in Chapter 10 that faces are processed configurally, but other types of stimuli are not. Some people have used this to argue that faces are 'special', but others claim that this is not the case and that the reliance on configural processing occurs only because of the larger amount of experience that we have with faces.

Gauthier et al (2009) suggest that the reliance on featural information for processing faces in ASD can be explained in terms of their lack of expertise for face processing as a result of their reduced social interactions. Support for this idea comes from a study in which participants with ASD showed significant improvement in the processing of configural information from emotional faces following training (Faja et al, 2008). However, children with ASD have also been found to have problems acquiring expertise with Greebles[1] (Scherf et al, 2008). This suggests that children with ASD may have difficulties learning to make fine detail discriminations between very similar stimuli, and provides support for this explanation of the face-processing deficits in ASD.

8.2.3 The neuropsychology of face processing in ASD

Another area of research has considered whether the face-processing deficits of individuals with ASD might be explained in terms of different neuropsychological processing of faces (see Chapter 9 for a discussion of event-related potentials [ERPs] in response to faces in non-clinical participants). In studies using ERPs, the N170 response to faces has been frequently found to be both smaller and later in ASD participants than in controls (e.g. Kylliainen et al, 2006; McPartland et al, 2004; O'Connor et al, 2005). In control participants the N170 response is faster to upright faces than to inverted faces, but this is not found in ASD participants (McPartland et al, 2004). Differences have also been shown in other ERP components, with the P1 being later (O'Connor et al, 2005) and the P400 being absent (Dawson et al, 2002) in participants with ASD. The atypical ERP responses found in people with

ASD have also been found in parents of children diagnosed with ASD (Dawson et al, 2005). Such findings clearly show that the neuropsychological processing of faces differs in individuals with ASD.

Research conducted using functional magnetic resonance imaging (fMRI) techniques have been able to give us a clearer insight into the neuropsychology of face processing in people with ASD. This work has tended to concentrate on two areas of the brain in particular: the **fusiform face area** and the **amygdala**. In neurotypical participants the fusiform face area is one of the main areas that shows activation when processing and recognizing faces, whereas the amygdala is more specifically involved in the processing of the emotional expression of faces (see Chapters 3 and 9 for more details).

Pierce et al (2001) found that, in participants with ASD, activation in response to faces was either reduced or totally absent in the four key areas of the brain associated with face processing: the fusiform face area, the amygdala, the inferior occipital gyrus and the superior temporal sulcus (see Chapter 9). Reduced activation in the fusiform face area, amygdala and posterior superior temporal sulcus has also been found in response to dynamic faces (Pelphrey et al, 2007). Deeley et al (2007) also found reduced activation in the fusiform face and extrastriate areas in participants with Asperger's syndrome, across a range of different emotional expressions and intensities. However, not all studies have shown reduced activation in the fusiform face area in response to faces. Hadjikhani et al (2004) found typical activation in the fusiform face area when processing faces. The authors suggest that the behavioural impairments may result from atypical processing in other areas of the brain that are more involved in the social aspects of face processing.

---

[1] Greebles are a type of non-face stimulus designed to be comparable to faces when participants are trained to become expert at recognizing them. They are discussed in more detail in Chapter 10.

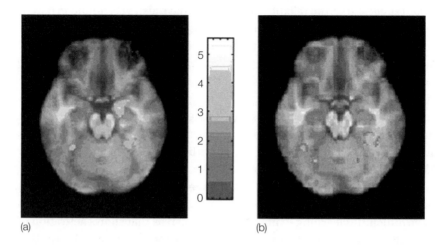

FIGURE 8.2 Patterns of brain activation in (a) control and (b) participants with autistic spectrum disorder (ASD). Both groups show activation in the fusiform face area, but the controls have activation in the amygdala, which is absent in the ASD group. (From Bookheimer et al, 2008). Please see colour plate section.

The atypical brain activation in response to faces in people with ASD has been used to explain their impaired processing of configural facial information and their over-reliance on featural facial information. Hubl et al (2003) found less activation in the fusiform face area in participants with ASD when inspecting faces, but more activation in the medial occipital gyrus, an area more typically associated with object processing. This may explain the advantage for processing featural facial information, as objects are typically processed in a more featural manner than faces. Bookheimer et al (2008) compared patterns of brain activation in controls and children with ASD when matching upright and inverted faces. As expected, the children with ASD were less affected by inversion than the controls. There was little difference between the two groups of children in terms of activation in the fusiform face area; however, there was less activation in the prefrontal cortex and the amygdala in the ASD participants (Fig. 8.2/Plate 8.2). Given that these areas are implicated in social cognition and interactions, the authors suggest that the atypical processing of inverted faces in ASD is due to their problems with the social interpretation of faces.

Ashwin et al (2007) examined activation in the amygdala in response to faces expressing fear. There was bilateral activation of the amygdala in the control participants, but not in the ASD participants. This atypical processing of facial emotion may, at least to some extent, be able to explain the impaired social interactions in this patient group. Hadjikhani et al (2007) looked at whether there is a correlation between brain activation when looking at faces and social interaction skills in ASD participants. Activation in the right inferior frontal cortex was correlated with the extent of the social impairment symptoms. This means that better social interaction skills are associated with patterns of brain activation that are more like those found in control participants. Activation has been found in the amygdala when people with ASD process personally familiar faces, such as their own mother's face, but not when they process unfamiliar faces (Pierce et al, 2004). This suggests that there is an emotional response to familiar faces in people with ASD.

As we saw above, eye-tracking studies have shown that people with ASD tend to avoid looking at the eyes of a face. Dalton et al (2005) conducted

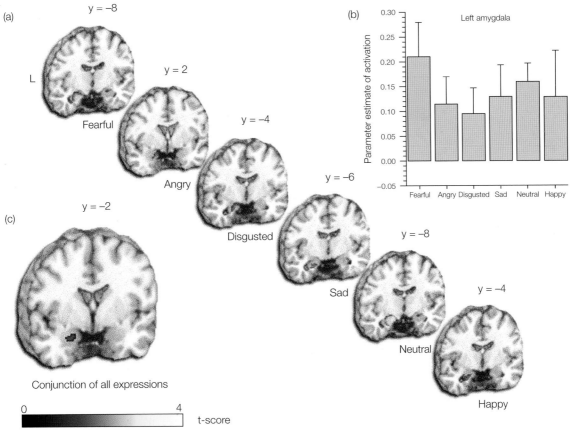

PLATE 3.7 Left amygdala activation for participants viewing emotive and neutral faces. (a) Location of activation for each emotion; (b) amount of activation in the left amygdala for each emotion; and (c) location of activation when combining all of the emotional expressions. (From Fitzgerald et al, 2006)

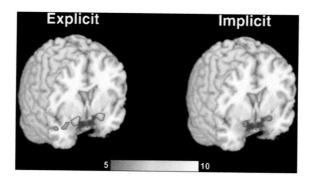

PLATE 3.8 Amygdala activation when explicitly and implicitly processing facial emotion. (From Habel et al, 2007).

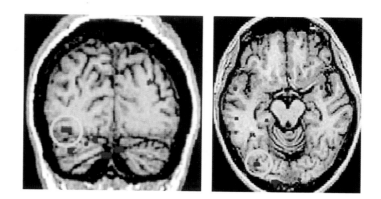

PLATE 7.5 Left hemisphere face-specific activation in prosopagnosic patient CR during a face-processing task, as shown by fMRI. (Adapted from Marotta et al, 2001)

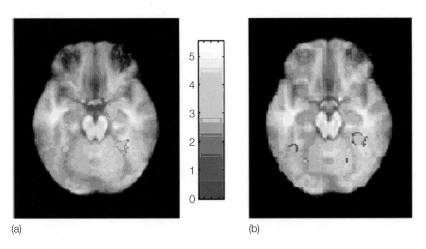

PLATE 8.2 Patterns of brain activation in (a) control and (b) participants with autistic spectrum disorder (ASD). Both groups show activation in the fusiform face area, but the controls have activation in the amygdala, which is absent in the ASD group. (From Bookheimer et al, 2008)

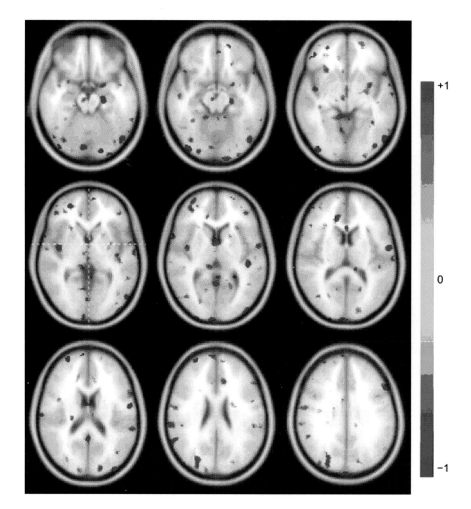

PLATE 8.7 Areas of activation in response to sad faces that distinguish between control and depressed participants. The red areas are associated with activation in the depressed participants whereas the blue areas are associated with activation in the control participants. (From Fu et al, 2008a).

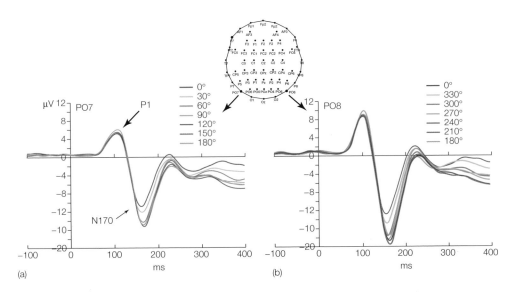

PLATE 9.2 N170 responses to faces at varying orientations from upright (0°) to inverted (180°), measured from occipitotemporal electrodes over (a) the left hemisphere and (b) the right hemisphere. (From Jacques and Rossion, 2007)

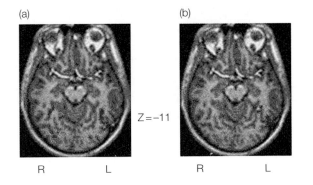

PLATE 9.8 Activation of the fusiform gyri in adult participants in response to (a) upright faces and (b) inverted faces. (Adapted from Passarotti et al, 2007)

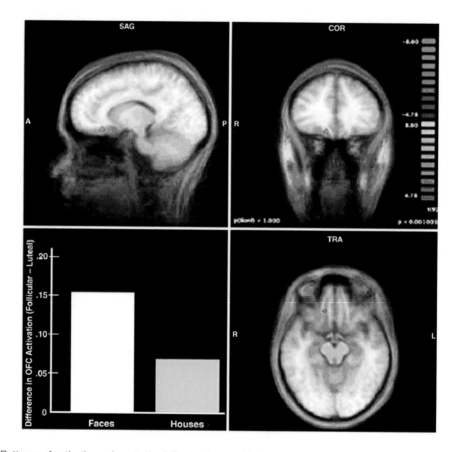

PLATE 9.17 Patterns of activation unique to the follicular phase of the menstrual cycle whilst processing male faces. (From Rupp et al, 2009)

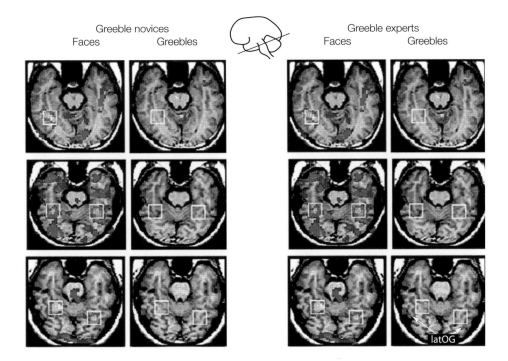

PLATE 10.10 Patterns of activation before and after training. The white squares show the location of the fusiform gyri.

(Gauthier et al, 1999)

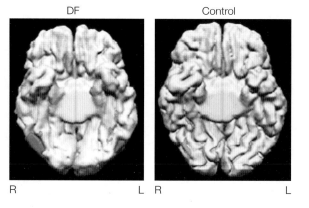

DF   Control

R   L   R   L

PLATE 10.11 FFA activation in a prosopagnosic patient (DF) and a control participant. (From Steeves et al, 2006)

a study in which they used fMRI and eye-tracking techniques simultaneously to investigate face processing in people with ASD. They found a strong positive correlation between the amount of time spent fixating on the eye region of a face and levels of activation in both the amygdala and fusiform face area. Essentially, what this means is that ASD participants with more 'normal' ways of looking at faces have more 'normal' brain activation in response to faces.

8.3 Williams syndrome

Williams syndrome (WS) is a very rare neurodevelopmental disorder that occurs as a result of a chromosomal abnormality. Children with WS tend to have distinctive facial features, are hypersociable, and have a very distinctive cognitive and neuropsychological profile. Although they tend to have some general cognitive impairment, their language skills are unaffected and may even be above average (e.g. Losh et al, 2000; Reilly et al, 1990). Bellugi et al (2000) provide an excellent review of the pattern of impairments and abilities found in people with WS on a wide range of cognitive and neuropsychological tests.

In terms of visual perception, individuals with WS show a marked impairment in the processing of global information and instead concentrate on the local elements of a stimulus (see Bellugi et al, 2000). For example, when shown a letter D that is actually made up of smaller Ys, children with WS tend to reproduce the local elements (the Ys) rather than the global element of the letter D. In contrast, children with **Down syndrome** (a group often used as a control group in WS studies as their IQ scores are roughly comparable) tend to report the global letter D (Fig. 8.3, left). Similarly, when asked to draw an image of an everyday object, such as a house or a bike, children with WS tend to draw all of the correct local elements, but without a clear global organization of these features (see Fig. 8.3, right).

8.3.1 Face processing in individuals with Williams syndrome

Although Bellugi et al's (2000) review found evidence for impaired visual processing of global information in children with WS, they did not find evidence for any impairment in their ability to process faces. A more recent review by Martens et al (2008) presented very mixed evidence for the ability to process faces in WS. Actually, they present the findings of studies showing that individuals with WS are impaired, unimpaired, and even superior at a range of face-processing

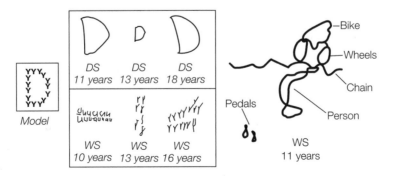

FIGURE 8.3 Examples of drawings from children with Williams syndrome (WS) showing the impaired processing of global information, but the intact processing of local features. DS: Down syndrome. (Adapted from Bellugi et al, 2000).

tasks. The majority of studies seem to show no impairment in the recognition of faces or in the ability to discriminate between faces (e.g. Deruelle et al, 1999; Pezzini et al, 1999; Wang et al, 1995), but rather more interesting findings have been reported in terms of the processing of facial emotion in people with WS.

A number of studies have compared the processing of facial emotion in participants with WS to that of both mental age-matched and chronological age-matched controls. Those with WS perform at a similar level to the mental age-matched controls, but below the level of the chronological age-matched controls. This pattern has been shown for the processing of recognition of emotional expression from whole faces (Gagliardi et al, 2003; Plesa-Skwerer et al, 2006) and when labelling the emotion being expressed in eyes-only stimuli (Plesa-Skwerer et al, 2006). O'Hearn et al (2009) found a slightly more complex pattern of facial emotion-processing skills. They tested memory for emotional faces and contrasted performance for happy and neutral faces. When the performance of the WS participants was compared with that of mental age-matched controls, those with WS were not impaired when remembering the happy faces, but were worse for the neutral faces.

The processing of emotional faces in individuals with WS has been linked to their tendency to be hypersociable. Frigerio et al (2006) asked participants with WS and control participants to rate faces with positive and negative expressions in terms of their approachability. Interestingly, they actually found that the participants with WS gave more extreme ratings for both approachable and unapproachable faces. The faces generally rated as approachable by control participants were rated as even more approachable by WS participants, and vice versa.

Given the unusual processing of global and local information in non-face stimuli in people with WS (see above), a number of researchers have considered whether a comparable atypical

processing of configural and featural facial information also exists. If people with WS tend to ignore the global properties of stimuli and concentrate on the local properties, it might be predicted that they process faces more on the basis of the featural information contained within them, rather than from the configural information that is used by most non-clinical participants.

Tager-Flusberg et al (2003) used the part–whole face-processing task that was developed by Tanaka and Farah (1993; see Chapter 2, section 2.3.4). They found no overall differences between the WS participants and their age-matched controls. Importantly, they found that the WS participants showed an advantage in the whole face condition that was comparable to the control participants. Deruelle and Santos (2009) also found no difference between children with WS and age-matched controls when asking them to identify the emotional expression in upright and inverted faces. These findings suggest that individuals with WS process faces configurally and in a manner that is typical in non-clinical participants.

Other researchers have found differences between control and WS participants in terms of their use of configural and featural facial information. Karmiloff-Smith et al (2004) conducted three experiments that used face inversion and found that participants with WS were less sensitive to inversion than control participants. Nakamura et al (2006) looked at the effects of inversion in a single participant with WS. Not only did they find that he was less sensitive to inversion than control participants, they found that he was actually faster at processing inverted faces than upright faces! This 'inversion superiority effect' has been reported in a number of studies on patients with prosopagnosia (e.g. Boutsen and Humphreys, 2002; de Gelder and Rouw, 2000a; de Gelder et al, 1998; Marotta et al, 2002; Rouw and de Gelder, 2002; see Chapter 7 for full details). This effect is thought to provide strong evidence for face processing being reliant on the featural information, which is not degraded with inversion, rather than configural information. Consequently, there is some evidence that the reliance on local information in non-face stimuli that is shown by people with WS may also be apparent in their reliance on featural information when processing face stimuli.

One area of research has considered whether the patterns of brain activation in WS participants differ from those of control participants when processing faces. Given that there are behavioural differences in the ability to process faces, it is quite plausible that this atypical processing will result from atypical neuropsychological processing. Mills et al (2000) conducted an ERP study in which participants had to decide whether two successively shown faces were the same or different. This was done with both upright and inverted faces. They found atypical ERPs in the WS participants, particularly a small N100 and a large N200. Mills et al suggested that this is evidence for atypical neuropsychological processing of faces in individuals with WS, and that this may be explained in terms of people with WS giving increased attention to facial stimuli.

Evidence from fMRI studies has shown atypical activation in the amygdala when individuals with WS inspect emotive faces. Recall from Chapter 3 that the amygdala is heavily involved in the processing of facial emotion. Meyer-Lindenberg et al (2005) showed images of threatening faces and scenes to participants with WS. They found that, in comparison to the control participants, levels of activation in the amygdala in the WS sample increased when the threatening scenes were viewed, but a decrease in amygdala activation was found when the threatening faces were viewed. This suggests atypical neural mechanisms underlying the processing of faces for social interactions. Haas et al (2009) conducted a fMRI study in which they asked participants with WS to look at faces expressing either happiness or fear. They found that the levels of activation in the amygdala were atypical in both conditions. When

inspecting a happy face there was more activation than was found in control participants, but when inspecting a fearful face there was less activation. The authors interpret this finding in relation to the hypersociability of individuals with WS. They suggest that the increased activation in response to happy faces may increase their attention towards positive interactions, whereas the decreased activation in response to fearful faces may lead to reduced arousal and consequently a less negative interpretation of such faces.

8.3.2 Comparisons between Williams syndrome and autism

Some researchers have compared the face-processing abilities of individuals with WS and autism. This comparison is of interest due to the contrasting social interactions of these two groups. Individuals with WS are hypersociable, whereas those with autism avoid social interactions. Riby and Hancock (2008, 2009a,b) conducted a series of experiments in which they used eye tracking to compare the visual inspection of emotional stimuli in participants with WS and autism. The same overall pattern was found across a range of stimuli: participants with WS spent longer inspecting emotional faces than control participants, whereas those with autism spent less time inspecting emotional faces. This finding fits well with the different patterns of social interactions in these two groups. Given that individuals with WS are hypersociable, they are likely to actively seek out positive interactions, whereas individuals with autism are more likely to avoid any interactions with others.

In a review of the autonomic responses to emotional faces, such as tears, increased heart rate and sweating, Macefield (2009) discussed how these responses differed between people with WS and autism. They concluded that children with WS have reduced autonomic responses to emotional faces whereas children with autism have increased autonomic responses. It is possible that this physiological response may account for the differences in sociability between the two groups. For those with autism, the heightened physiological response may be unpleasant, and therefore social interactions and the inspection of faces are avoided. However, for those with WS, even more interaction may be necessary to produce the autonomic responses typically elicited in normal individuals when inspecting faces or interacting with others.

Two recent studies have examined more directly whether the ability to process faces varies between individuals with WS and autism. Lacroix et al (2009) showed participants emotive and neutral faces and then asked them to complete three different emotion-processing tasks: labelling, matching and identification. They found that those with WS were more impaired at processing facial emotion than the participants with autism. Annaz et al (2009) examined the distinction between configural and featural facial information using Tanaka and Farah's whole–part task (Tanaka and Farah, 1993; see also Chapter 2, section 2.3.4). They compared performance across participants with WS, high functioning autism, low functioning autism and Down syndrome, and found impaired performance for all four groups and atypical developmental trajectories. However, the findings varied across the four groups, suggesting that the underlying problems differ across the four disorders.

8.4 Schizophrenia

Schizophrenia is a chronic neuropsychiatric disorder that is characterized by two classes of symptoms: positive and negative. Positive symptoms are those that are present, such as hallucinations and delusions, whereas negative symptoms are those that are absent, such as a lack of social skills and emotional responsiveness (affect). Individuals with schizophrenia usually suffer from dysfunctional social interactions, and for this reason

a great deal of research has examined the face-processing abilities of this group.

8.4.1 Behavioural studies of face processing in schizophrenia

Much of the research examining face processing in schizophrenia has considered possible impairments in processing facial emotion. Typically these studies have used two different experimental paradigms. The first is simply to present participants with emotive faces and ask them to decide which emotion is being expressed. Many studies using this methodology have shown that schizophrenics are impaired at this task in comparison to control participants (e.g. Kucharska-Pietura et al, 2005; Whittaker et al, 2001). The second methodology is to present participants with pairs of faces and ask them whether the faces are expressing the same emotion or different emotions. Again, a large number of studies using this methodology have shown that schizophrenics are significantly worse at this task than control participants (e.g. Hooker and Park, 2002; Martin et al, 2005). Further studies that have used both paradigms have also shown impaired emotion processing in individuals with schizophrenia for both tasks (e.g. Addington et al, 2006; Penn et al, 2000). This impaired emotion processing has also been found to be associated with poor social skills in patients with schizophrenia (Meyer and Kurtz, 2009).

Kee et al (2006) looked at the categorical perception of emotion in patients with schizophrenia. Full details of this phenomenon are given in Chapter 3, but, briefly, non-clinical participants tend to perceive morphed blends of emotions not as blends, but as one or other of the two emotions from which the morph was made. Kee and colleagues found that this categorical perception was less pronounced in patients with schizophrenia (Fig. 8.4). This suggests that patients with schizophrenia find it more difficult to extract emotional expression from faces in which the expression is ambiguous.

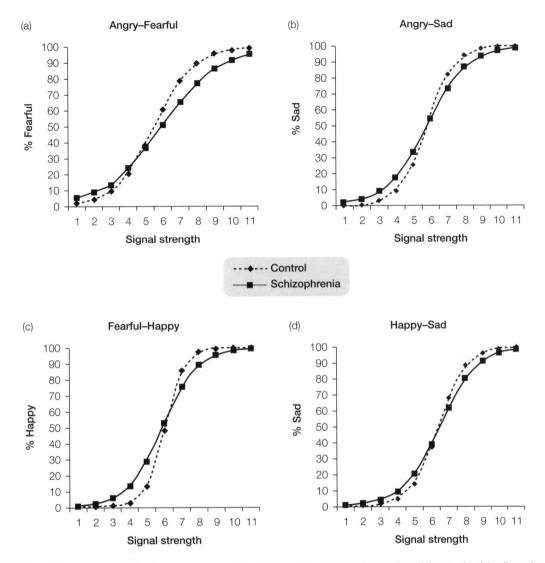

FIGURE 8.4 Categorical perception of emotion in patients with schizophrenia and control participants. (a–d) In all graphs, the patients show a less abrupt transition from perceiving one emotion to perceiving the other, as shown by the shallower line for their data. (From Kee et al, 2006)

A great deal of research has shown that facial emotion processing is impaired in individuals with schizophrenia, but it is less clear whether this dysfunction is consistent across all emotions. One approach is to separate the emotions according to valence, that is, to compare the processing of positive and negative emotions. Brune (2005) showed faces expressing either positive or negative emotions and asked participants to identify which emotion was being expressed. Schizophrenics were more impaired at recognizing the negative emotions than they were at recognizing the positive emotions. Other researchers have suggested that the impairment is even more specific and that the recognition of fear is impaired to a greater extent than any other emotion (Edwards et al, 2001; Hall et al, 2008; van't Wout et al, 2007a). A different finding was reported by Tsoi et al (2008), who found that patients were impaired for processing happy faces and that they tended to over-classify all faces as expressing either fear or sadness. The processing of facial emotion has also been found to vary according to the occurrence of positive and negative symptoms in patients with schizophrenia. The ability to recognize fear is worse in patients with negative symptoms (van't Wout et al, 2007b).

The way in which patients with schizophrenia visually inspect emotional faces also differs from non-clinical controls. Typically their eye movements are found to be far more restricted (Fig. 8.5) and they tend to avoid fixating on the facial features (Loughland et al, 2002). This finding has been reported in a large number of studies

(for a review see Marsh and Williams, 2006). It is possible that this restricted inspection of faces may account for the impaired processing of facial emotion in patients with schizophrenia. If the visual input is restricted or degraded, it is perhaps not entirely surprising that processing is similarly impaired.

There is some recent evidence to suggest that the processing of facial emotion in patients with schizophrenia can be improved. Russell et al (2008) found that after using the Micro-Expression Training Tool,[2] patients were significantly better at emotion processing than patients who had simply inspected emotional faces for the same length of

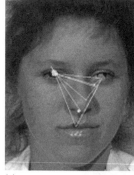 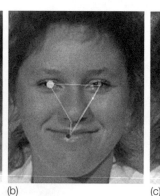 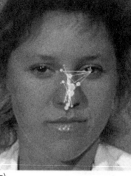 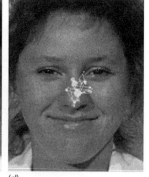

(a)   (b)   (c)   (d)

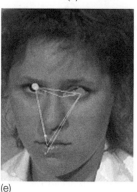 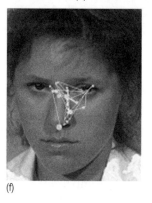

(e)   (f)

FIGURE 8.5 Visual inspection of neutral (a, c), happy (b, d) and sad (e, f) faces for a control participant (a, b, e) and a patient with schizophrenia (c, d, f). (From Loughland et al, 2002)

---

[2] The Micro-Expression Training Tool teaches people how to detect small, unconsciously expressed, emotions. Most of the training techniques of this type help people to distinguish between emotions and to detect very small expressions of an emotion. You can see a demonstration of the Micro-Expression Training Tool at http://www.mettonline.com.

time. After training, the patients were more likely to fixate on the facial features, which would explain their improved performance. This effect lasted for a week, after which it became far less pronounced. Improvement with training has also been reported for other training methods: the Training Affect Recognition programme (Frommann et al, 2003; Wolwer et al, 2005) and Emotion Training (Silver et al, 2004). It therefore seems that the impairments shown in patients with schizophrenia may be reduced with training, which may in turn alleviate some of the behavioural disturbances. Further research is necessary to test this possibility.

Studies have also considered whether individuals with schizophrenia are impaired at processing the identity of faces. When asking participants to discriminate between pairs of unfamiliar faces or to match pairs of unfamiliar faces, schizophrenics show significant impairment (e.g. Kucharska-Pietura et al, 2005; Penn et al, 2000). Schizophrenics are also significantly worse at identifying familiar faces (e.g. Sachs et al, 2004; Whittaker et al, 2001). It therefore seems that the processing of both emotion and identity is impaired in schizophrenia. Deficits in face processing have also been found in more basic tasks such as face detection, face discrimination and working memory for faces (Chen et al, 2009). Because these tasks do not require any interpretation of emotion or identity, this study suggests that there may be quite fundamental impairments in face processing in people with schizophrenia.

A number of studies have examined whether the deficits in face processing in patients with schizophrenia might result from atypical use of configural and featural facial information. Whereas non-clinical participants tend to use configural information, there is a large body of evidence showing that patients with schizophrenia have impaired processing of configural facial information and instead rely on featural facial information. This has been shown using face inversion (Shin et al, 2008),

detection of eye separation (Baudouin et al, 2008) and fractured faces (Joshua and Rossel, 2009). However, Chambon et al (2006) found that, relative to controls, patients with schizophrenia were impaired at the processing of emotion from upright faces but that they showed the same inversion effect. This suggests that configural information is processed to some extent by patients with schizophrenia.

Although it does seem that the processing of facial emotion and identity are impaired in schizophrenia, it has been suggested that these effects may not necessarily result from a face-specific impairment, but rather a more **general cognitive impairment**. For example, it has been suggested that when a face-processing task requires a great deal of attention or memory capacity in order to be completed successfully, patients with schizophrenia show a greater degree of impairment. If simpler tasks are used, such as recognizing familiar faces (Whittaker et al, 2001) or matching faces that are identically posed (Hooker and Park, 2002), performance is improved. Another possibility is that, if schizophrenics have impaired visual processing at a more basic level, this may account for any impairment of face processing. Whittaker et al (2001) gave participants with schizophrenia a range of tests of both face and non-face visuospatial processing. They found that the performance on these two tests was correlated, which suggests that impairments in face processing in schizophrenia may, at least to some extent, be explained in terms of more basic visual processing impairments. It has also been shown that poor error monitoring might contribute to the impairments in face recognition (Silver et al, 2006).

Norton et al (2009) gave participants three different processing tasks, involving facial emotion, facial identity and visual contrast detection. Comparing performance across these three tasks provides an important insight into the interactions between these processes. They found that patients with schizophrenia were worse at discriminating faces with both positive and negative emotional expressions. However, for the processing of fearful faces, performance in the schizophrenic group was predicted by the performance on both the identity and the contrast detection task. This provides strong evidence for the impaired emotion processing found in schizophrenia being, at least in part, caused by more general deficits in face processing or even in general visual perception abilities.

8.4.2 Neuropsychological studies of face processing in schizophrenia

Wynn et al (2008) compared the P1, N170 and N250 responses (see Chapter 9) to faces when participants were making either an emotive or a non-emotive (gender) decision. A non-face task was also included. There was no difference in the P1 or N170 response between the patients with schizophrenia and the control participants. However, the N250 was smaller in the patient group across all three of the tasks. This finding suggests that the basic processing of faces is relatively spared in schizophrenia, but that the later processes are affected. Although Wynn and colleagues found no difference in the N170, two other studies (Lynn and Salisbury, 2008; Onitsuka et al, 2006) reported either reduced or absent N170 responses in patients with schizophrenia when processing emotive faces. Turetsky et al (2007) also reported differences in the N170 between control and patient groups; however, they also found that the N170 was larger (so more like the control group) in patients who reported fewer delusions. This suggests that the magnitude in the reduction of the size of the N170 is associated with the severity of the schizophrenia.

A number of studies have also used neuroimaging methods to see whether individuals with schizophrenia have either structural or functional abnormalities that might explain their impaired face-processing abilities. In non-clinical participants the fusiform gyrus has been shown to be of particular importance for face processing

and has become known as the fusiform face area (FFA) (see Chapter 9 for more detail). The FFA has been found to be significantly smaller in patients with schizophrenia (Lee et al, 2002; Onitsuka et al, 2006). This suggests that the deficits in face processing in schizophrenia may result from a neuroanatomical dysfunction. Further, Onitsuka et al (2006) examined whether the ability to process facial identity and the size of the FFA were correlated in schizophrenics. They found that the greater the reduction in volume, the greater the impairment in face recognition. Namiki et al (2007) reported a similar finding when looking at the relationship between the size of the amygdala and the processing of facial emotion. The amygdala was smaller in the patient group and poorer performance on an emotion-processing task was associated with having a smaller amygdala.

Levels of activation in the FFA have also been found to differ between patients with schizophrenia and control participants. Walther et al (2009) found that activation in the FFA increased in control participants when they were learning faces that they later recalled successfully. This finding was not replicated in the patients with schizophrenia. However, Anilkumar et al (2008) found that, although patients were significantly worse at encoding and recalling faces, there was no difference in brain activity between patients and controls. Similarly, Yoon et al (2006) found no difference in FFA activation between control and patient groups when inspecting faces.

Another area of research has examined activation in the amygdala in response to emotive faces. Gur et al (2002) found reduced activation in the left amygdala and hippocampus in patients with schizophrenia when inspecting emotional faces. Seiferth et al (2009) also found decreased activation in the FFA and left inferior occipital gyrus, and increased activation in the right cuneus, in juveniles with schizophrenia when they processed both positive and negative emotional faces. This decrease in brain activation in response to emotional faces may explain the deficits in the processing of emotion in patients with schizophrenia discussed above. Although these studies have reported reduced activation in patients with schizophrenia, Holt et al (2006) found higher levels of activation in the left hippocampus when patients were viewing neutral, happy and fearful faces, and higher levels of activation in the right amygdala when viewing fearful and neutral faces.

Fakra et al (2008) compared two emotion-processing tasks: labelling and matching. They found no differences in brain activation on the labelling task, but on the matching task the patient group had no activation in the limbic system (which includes the amygdala), whereas there was activation in this area in the control group (Fig. 8.6). Interestingly, they also found that the patients had less activation in the areas of the brain typically associated with configural processing (the FFA) but more activation in

the areas associated with featural processing. This finding fits well with the behavioural work showing that people with schizophrenia tend to use featural facial information and that they are impaired at processing configural facial information.

Other studies have specifically considered the processing of fear in patients with schizophrenia. Hall et al (2008) found that, for the patients with schizophrenia, activation in the amygdala was less for fearful faces than for neutral faces. Interestingly, though, they showed that this resulted from abnormally high levels of activation in response to neutral faces, rather than from low levels of activation in response to fearful faces. This suggests an atypical neuropsychological processing of neutral faces in schizophrenia. Michalopoulou et al (2008) examined whether patterns of activation in response to fearful faces in patients with schizophrenia varied according to the extent of their positive and negative

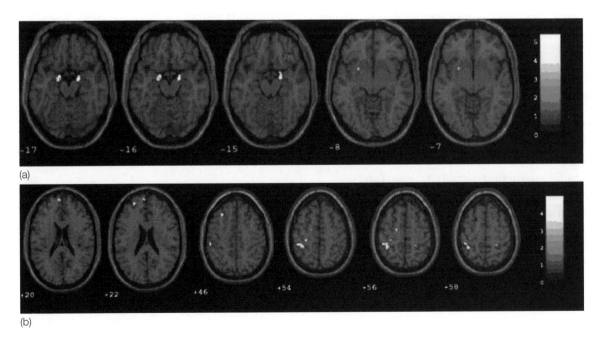

(a)

(b)

FIGURE 8.6 Areas of activation while completing an emotion face-matching task. (a) Images show areas where there is more activation in control participants than in patients with schizophrenia. (b) Images show areas where there is more activation in patients with schizophrenia than in control participants. (From Fakra et al, 2008)

symptoms. They found no relationship with positive symptoms, but there was less activation in the left superior temporal gyrus in patients with more negative symptoms. This makes sense as the negative symptoms involve a lack of affect and social interaction, so it may be that this reduced behavioural experience is associated with the reduced neural activation.

8.5 Depression

Depression is characterized by low mood that affects all aspects of everyday functioning. It is one of the most frequently occurring clinical disorders. According to a report published by the World Health Organization in 2001, depression affects up to 50% of women and 25% of men in the UK. Given the clear relationship between depression and emotion, it is perhaps not surprising that most of the research examining face processing in this group has concentrated on the processing of facial emotion.

8.5.1 Face processing in non-clinical levels of depression

Most of the research in this area has examined face processing in patients with clinically diagnosed depression, but a relatively small amount has considered whether people with mild (non-clinical) levels of depressive symptoms have any impairments in their face-processing abilities. Koster et al (2006) found no relationship between attention towards emotive faces and depressive symptoms in a non-clinical sample. However, van Beek and Dubas (2008) tested children aged 9–15

years and asked them to judge the intensity of emotional expressions. For girls only, anger was interpreted as more intense and joy as less intense, but no relationship was found for boys.

Some small effects of non-clinical depressive symptoms have also been shown in terms of the neuropsychological processing of emotive faces. In an ERP study, Cavanagh and Geisler (2006) found that the P3 response to happy faces was smaller and later in participants with depressive symptoms. Chan et al (2009) looked at the neuropsychological processing of faces in non-clinical participants with high neuroticism scores (i.e. people with a tendency to be nervous, lacking confidence and self-pitying). They thought that this group might be at risk of depression. Differences were found between high and low neurotic participants. When processing fearful faces, participants who were at risk of depression had higher levels of activation in the right fusiform face area and the left middle temporal gyrus. The result was in the opposite direction for those not at risk of depression.

These results suggest that people with non-clinical levels of depression may process facial emotion differently, both in terms of the behavioural and the neuropsychological processing of emotive faces. However, far more research has considered these issues in patients with diagnosed clinical depression.

8.5.2 Face processing in clinical depression

A number of studies have examined the simple recognition of facial emotional expressions in patients with diagnosed clinical depression.[3] Mendlewicz et al (2005) found that patients

---

[3] Some research has also examined face processing in bipolar disorder. In this condition, the patient experiences both depressive and manic episodes. We will not be discussing bipolar disorder in this chapter, but for a review of this research please read Rocca et al (2009).

with depression had a specific impairment for recognizing anger in comparison to control participants and patients with anorexia. A different result was reported by Leppanen et al (2004), who found no difference between controls and patients with depression in the recognition of happy and sad faces, but that those with depression were slower and less accurate at recognizing neutral faces—they were more likely to classify them as emotive, either happy or sad. This finding suggests that the problem with processing facial emotion in patients with depression is that they falsely attribute emotions to neutral faces. However, two studies (Kan et al, 2004; Weniger et al, 2004) either failed to find, or only found very minor, impairments in the recognition of the six basic emotions in patients with depression.

Some more subtle tests of emotion processing have also revealed impairments in the processing of facial emotion in patients with depression. One method is to show participants neutral faces that gradually change into emotive faces. The more emotion shown in the face, the more intense the expression. The participant has to decide as quickly as possible which emotion is being expressed. The key issue here is how much emotion is needed in the face before it can be identified correctly. Using this method, Joormann and Gotlib (2006) found that patients with depression were able to recognize anger and sadness with less intensity, but needed more intensity to recognize happiness. Surguladze et al (2004) showed participants happy and sad faces with different intensities for either 100 milliseconds or 2 seconds. Patients with depression only had quite subtle impairments and were less likely to classify a low-intensity happy face as being happy. In a similar study, Csukly et al (2009) found that patients with depression were impaired at recognizing the emotions when they had low-intensity expressions. It therefore seems that patients with depression may be particularly impaired at processing emotional faces in which the expression is ambiguous and may be misinterpreted.

Yoon et al (2009) compared the processing of facial emotion in patients with depression, patients with social anxiety and control participants. All groups were shown two faces in which the emotional expression was at only 40% intensity. When asked to decide which face in the pair had a more intense expression, there were differences between the groups. Patients with depression less frequently chose a happy face as being more intense than the neutral face, and both patient groups more frequently chose a negative face as being more intense than the positive face. This shows that the interpretation of subtle emotional expressions is atypical in patients with depression.

Two studies have shown that impaired processing of facial emotion occurs in patients with depression, even when the emotion being expressed is not relevant to the task. Ridout et al (2009) showed participants neutral, sad and happy faces, and asked them to make a gender decision. Patients with major depression took significantly longer than controls to make this decision for happy faces, but there was no difference for the neutral or sad faces. However, when they were later given a recognition test, the patients were generally worse at remembering the faces they had seen, regardless of the emotion being expressed. Gilboa-Schechtman et al (2004) asked participants to look at emotive male and female faces. In one task they had to make a gender decision and ignore the emotion being expressed. In the other task they had to ignore the gender of the face and decide which emotion was being expressed. The patients with depression found it difficult to ignore emotional information, even when the emotion being expressed was irrelevant to the task. These findings suggest that the dysfunctional processing of emotional expression is quite fundamental and does not occur only when emotion is being processed explicitly.

Although there is a fair amount of evidence for the processing of facial emotion being atypical in patients with depression, it is not entirely clear whether this occurs because of a specific face-processing deficit or whether it might be explained in terms of wider cognitive dysfunction. Langenecker et al (2005) compared performance across a wide range of cognitive tasks for women with diagnosed depression and women with no such diagnosis. They found that the women with depression were significantly worse at emotion recognition and inhibitory control, an executive function that stops a person responding (often in an inappropriate manner) to stimuli. On all other cognitive tests there were no differences between the two groups of women. This finding shows that people with depression not only have impaired perception of emotional expressions, but they may also respond inappropriately to emotional faces.

Differences in brain activation in response to emotive faces have also been shown in patients with depression. Surguladze et al (2005) showed participants neutral, happy and sad faces, and asked them to decide whether the face was male or female. They found completely the opposite pattern of increasing and decreasing activation between the two groups. When looking at happy faces, activation in the bilateral fusiform face area and right putamen decreased in patients with depression but increased in the control participants. When looking at sad faces, activation in the right fusiform face area, left putamen, and left parahippocampal gyrus and amygdala increased in the patient group and decreased in the control group. This finding suggests that there is hypoactivation (less activation) in response to positive faces and hyperactivation (more activation) in response to negative faces in patients with depression. This finding may account for the negative interpretation bias in this group.

Fu et al (2008a) conducted a similar study in which patients with depression and control participants were asked to make gender decisions about sad faces of varying intensities. These authors attempted to predict which participants had clinical depression and which did not, by using only the patterns of activation across the entire brain in response to sad faces. They were able to predict the patients with 84% accuracy and the control group with 89% accuracy. Figure 8.7/Plate 8.7 shows the areas of activation that were most strongly associated with being either a control participant or a patient with clinical depression. You can clearly see that activation across the entire brain is very different in the two groups.

A number of studies have considered whether these atypical brain activations in response to emotive faces in patients with depression change in relation to improvement in depressive symptoms. Canli et al (2005) found that patients with higher levels of activation in the amygdala in response to emotive faces showed more improvement in their depressive symptoms when reassessed six months later. Returns to more 'normal' patterns of brain activation have also been reported following cognitive behavioural therapy (CBT) (Costafreda et al, 2009). Lower levels of activation in the dorsal anterior cingulate predicted improvement in depressive symptoms in response to CBT (Fu et al, 2008b). Fu et al (2007) also found that the reduced activation in the limbic and extrastriate visual regions of the brain when inspecting happy faces was less severe after eight weeks of treatment with fluoxetine (an antidepressant more commonly known as Prozac). They also found that more change in activation levels was found in those with greater improvement of depressive symptoms. Another antidepressant drug, sertraline, a selective serotonin-reuptake inhibitor (SSRI), has also been found to change brain activations in patients with depression. Sheline et al (2001) found that patients with depression had higher levels of activation in the left amygdala in response to emotive faces. This effect was particularly pronounced for fearful faces. Following treatment with sertraline for eight weeks this hyperactivation reduced bilaterally. It therefore seems that the atypical brain activation found in patients with depression may be relatively transitory and may be found only when patients are suffering from severe depressive episodes.

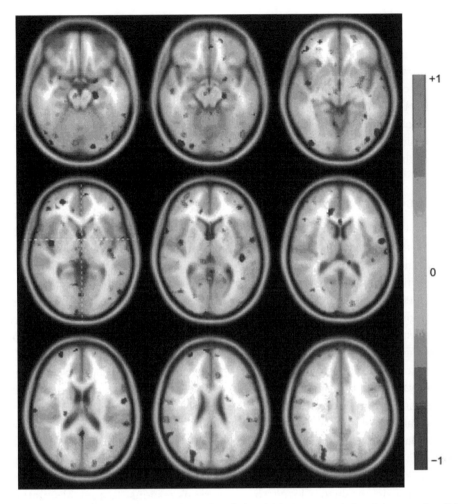

FIGURE 8.7 Areas of activation in response to sad faces that distinguish between control and depressed participants. The red areas are associated with activation in the depressed participants whereas the blue areas are associated with activation in the control participants. (From Fu et al, 2008a). Please see colour plate section.

8.6 Social anxiety

Individuals with **social anxiety** tend to have a great fear of being in social situations and consequently may actively attempt to avoid such situations. This pattern of behaviour has been described as hypervigilance to social interactions and avoidance of social situations. Social anxiety is one of the most common types of anxiety (Kessler et al, 2005). Much of the research in this area has actually examined the relationship between social anxiety and face processing in non-clinical samples. In these studies participants are asked to complete a questionnaire (there are a number of different ones available) that gives them a social anxiety score. The researchers then either look for a correlation between social anxiety and face-processing ability or they divide the participants into low and high social anxiety groups and look for differences in face-processing abilities between the two groups. These approaches are advantageous in that it is very easy to get participants for these studies; however, it is possible that some more subtle effects may be missed in non-clinical samples. Luckily, we have a range of behavioural and neuropsychological evidence from both clinical and non-clinical samples. By looking these different sources of evidence in combination it is possible to gain a better understanding of face processing in individuals with social anxiety.

8.6.1 Face processing in non-clinical social anxiety

Biases in the processing of facial emotion in participants with non-clinical levels of social anxiety have been shown using a variety of methodologies. Yoon and Zinbarg (2007) showed participants emotionally ambiguous faces and found that those with higher levels of social anxiety were more likely to interpret the ambiguous faces as threatening. Silvia et al (2006) asked participants to recognize happy, sad and angry facial expressions. They actually found no relationship between speed of responding and social anxiety when responding to negative emotive faces, but when recognizing happiness, those with social anxiety were slower. Mullins and Duke (2004) found that those with higher levels of social anxiety again took longer to respond to the faces, but they found no differences in reaction times across the emotions when recognizing angry, fearful, happy or sad faces.

D'Argembeau et al (2003) asked participants to learn faces that were expressing either happiness or anger. When asked later to recognize these faces, but with a neutral expression, participants with low social anxiety were better at remembering the happy faces, whereas participants with high social anxiety were just as good at remembering both happy and angry faces. This may indicate that most people have a bias towards remembering positive facial stimuli, but that this bias is absent in people who are socially anxious.

Biases for processing emotional faces in people with social anxiety have also been shown

in children. Melfsen and Florin (2002) showed children aged 6–12 years neutral, happy, angry, disgusted and sad faces very briefly, for just 60 milliseconds. The children then had to decide whether each face was expressing a positive or negative emotion. Those who were socially anxious took longer to make this decision and were far more likely to claim that the neutral faces were emotive.

Although biases have been reported in the processing of emotive faces, one study examined whether there was a relationship between autonomic physiological responses to subliminally presented faces and social anxiety. This is important because the participants, in effect, do not see the faces and they do not need to make a conscious response to a stimulus. Tsunoda et al (2008) measured the galvanic skin response, which gives a physiological measure of emotional arousal. This was significantly higher in response to fearful faces than happy faces in socially anxious individuals than in participants without social anxiety. This suggests that individuals with social anxiety have a pre-attentive bias for processing fearful faces.

Two studies have considered the interaction between face processing in social anxiety and a person's response to a social situation. Leber et al (2009) examined whether being in a socially threatening situation might alter the processing of facial emotion. They asked participants to classify facial expressions of anger, disgust, fear, happiness, sadness and surprise. When participants were in a non-threatening social situation, there was no difference in emotion processing between those with and without social anxiety. However, when in a socially threatening situation, participants with social anxiety were significantly faster at classifying faces as expressing anger, fear or sadness. Heuer et al (2007) showed participants faces expressing anger, happiness or a neutral expression, and asked them to decide whether they would prefer to approach or avoid the face. They found that socially anxious participants were more likely to avoid both happy and angry faces than participants who were not socially anxious. One important point to raise is that both groups of participants gave the emotive faces comparable valence ratings. This suggests that the emotional percept is comparable in the two groups, but that their decision about how to interact with another person differs. The findings of these two studies clearly show how being socially anxious can influence social interactions.

Neuropsychological studies have attempted to understand whether the brain activation in response to emotive faces varies according to social anxiety. Muhlberger et al (2009) measured ERPs in response to faces expressing anger, fear or happiness, and neutral faces. For participants with high social anxiety, the early posterior negativity was larger in response to negative faces, but not to the faces with positive or neutral expressions. In contrast, participants with low social anxiety had a larger late positive potential to emotive faces, regardless of their valence, in comparison to neutral faces. This finding suggests that early neuropsychological processing of emotive faces is influenced by social anxiety.

Given that the amygdala is strongly associated with the processing of emotional faces (see Chapter 3, section 3.5.3), some studies have examined whether this activation varies as a function of social anxiety. Ewbank et al (2009) found different patterns of amygdala activation between socially anxious and non-socially anxious participants, but these effects varied across emotions. In comparison to non-socially anxious participants, individuals with high social anxiety had greater activation in the right amygdala when viewing angry faces and in the left amygdala when viewing fearful faces. Greater activation in the amygdala when processing fearful faces has also been reported in a sample of adolescents (Killgore and Yurgelun-Todd, 2005). Furthermore, activation levels were positively correlated with a range of social measures that reflect social anxiety,

including fear of peer rejection, humiliation, performing in public and separation from loved ones.

8.6.2 Face processing in clinical social anxiety

Biases in the recognition and interpretation of emotive faces have been reported in a number of studies in which the participants were diagnosed with clinical levels of social anxiety. Garner et al (2009) showed faces with ambiguous emotions to patients with generalized social phobia and non-anxious controls. These faces were made from blends of anger and happiness, fear and happiness, or anger and fear. The participants had to decide which emotion they thought the face was expressing. For both of the conditions involving fearful faces, those with social anxiety were significantly worse at discriminating between the emotions than the non-anxious participants. However, for the faces that were a blend of anger and happiness, there was no difference between the two groups. This finding suggests that the processing of fear is specifically impaired in individuals with clinical social anxiety.

A similar study was conducted by Joorman and Gotlib (2006) who presented participants with faces that changed gradually from neutral to emotive, expressing happiness, sadness or anger. They asked participants to respond as soon as they could identify which emotion was being expressed. The crucial factor here is how much of the emotion is needed before a person can identify it. Joorman and Gotlib found that patients with social anxiety required less anger in a face to identify its emotional expression correctly than did patients with depression or control participants. Mohlman et al (2007) used a different methodology in which they asked participants to complete an emotional card sorting task. They found that patients with social anxiety were faster at sorting cards in which faces were expressing anger and were more likely to classify neutral faces as expressing anger.

Exactly the opposite pattern of results was found for the control participants. These two studies suggest that the processing of anger is specifically disrupted in people with clinical social anxiety.

An eye-tracking study has also shown differences in the inspection of emotive faces between patients with social anxiety and control participants (Horley et al, 2004). Those with social anxiety tended to have bigger scanpath lengths (the distance that the eyes move between fixations), which indicated hyperscanning of faces. They also tended not to fixate on the eye region, indicating avoidance of eye contact (Fig. 8.8). This pattern was strongest when the participants were viewing angry faces. Again, this suggests that the processing of angry faces is particularly impaired in this clinical population.

In a study of children diagnosed with clinical social anxiety, Simonian et al (2001) found that the ability to recognize emotional expressions correctly was significantly worse in socially anxious children than in control children. They also asked the children to rate their levels of anxiety before and after completing the emotion recognition task. The children with social anxiety reported a significantly greater increase in anxiety. This anxious response may account for the avoidance of social situations in these groups.

Creswell et al (2008) examined the possible developmental basis of social phobia by examining the processing of emotional faces in infants of mothers with social phobia. They suggest that these infants may be 'at risk' of developing atypical processing of facial emotion and social anxiety in later life. The infants were tested at four different times, between 10 days and 10 months of age. Infants whose mothers

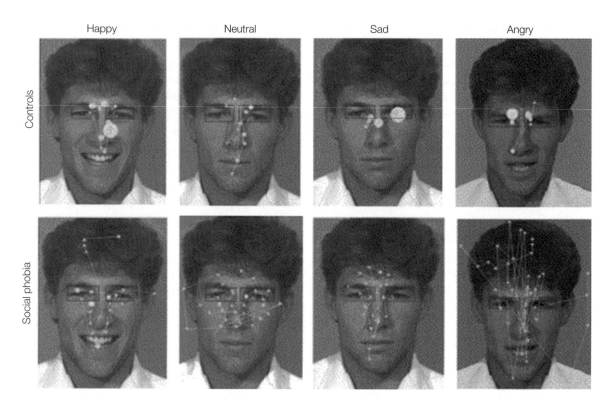

FIGURE 8.8 Scanpaths and fixations on faces from control and socially anxious participants. Larger dot size indicates increased fixation. (From Horley et al, 2004)

suffered from social phobia spent less time looking at fearful faces than did the infants of control mothers. This finding raises two possibilities about the development of emotional face processing and social phobia. First, it may be that there is some genetic basis to the disorder that is passed from parent to child. Alternatively, it may be that the mother's social phobia influences and reduces the infant's exposure to emotive faces, which in turn causes atypical development.

Kolassa et al (2006) found that, relative to spider phobics and control participants, individuals with clinical social anxiety had an enhanced N170 in the right temporoparietal region in response to angry faces (Fig. 8.9). They also found that, for participants with social anxiety only, higher scores on the Fear Survey Schedule (which measures social anxiety, in addition to other anxiety scales) were associated with larger P1 responses. They also replicated this enhanced P1 in individuals with social anxiety in a later study using schematic emotional faces (Kolassa et al, 2007). These very early

neuropsychological responses to emotive faces in people with social anxiety may explain the hypervigilance often reported in these groups.

A large number of studies have used fMRI techniques specifically to examine how activation in the amygdala changes when patients with clinical social anxiety inspect emotive faces. Gentili et al (2008) found that, when processing both emotive and neutral faces, the patient group had more activation in the left amygdala, insula and bilateral superior temporal sulcus but less activation in the left fusiform face area, left dorsolateral prefrontal cortex and bilateral intraparietal sulcus. The authors suggest that the areas of increased activation are those typically involved in processing facial emotion, whereas the areas with decreased activation are involved in attention and processing of non-emotional facial information. They suggest that this pattern may reflect a hypervigilance towards emotive faces, but also a 'wariness' of them. The activation found in the amygdala and prefrontal cortex in response to both positive and negative faces has also been found to occur later in patients with social phobia

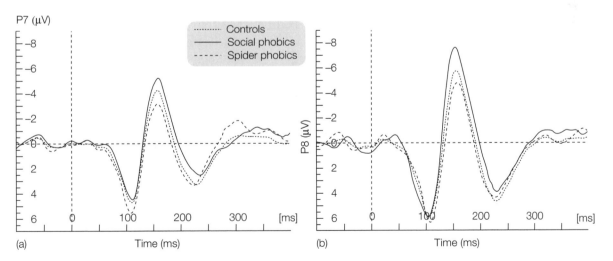

FIGURE 8.9 Emotion identification of angry faces: event-related potentials in response to angry faces over the parietal lobes in (a) the left hemisphere (P7) and (b) the right hemisphere (P8). Note how the N170 response to the angry faces is larger for social phobics than for the other two groups, particularly in the right hemisphere recordings. (From Kolassa et al, 2006)

than in control participants (D. W. Campbell et al, 2007), and to increase in relation to the increasing intensity of emotional expressions (Yoon et al, 2007).

Different patterns of amygdala activation have also been found for patients with social anxiety when processing neutral faces in which no emotion is being expressed. Cooney et al (2006) found a significant increase in activity in the left amygdala in response to neutral faces in participants with clinical social anxiety, but not in the control participants. This finding suggests that even neutral faces are processed as being emotive by individuals with social anxiety. This possibility fits well with the behavioural work discussed above. The extent of the increase in amygdala activation in response to neutral faces has also been found to be associated with the severity of the social anxiety, with patients who suffer from more severe social anxiety showing even greater activation in the amygdala (Phan et al, 2006).

The increased activity in the amygdala in response to faces expressing negative emotions has also been found when the emotional expression was totally irrelevant to the task. Stein et al (2002) showed participants faces expressing happiness, anger, fear or contempt and asked them to decide whether the face was male or female. Even though the emotional expression was not important, participants with clinical social anxiety had significantly higher levels of activation in the amygdala in response to faces expressing anger or contempt.

8.7 **Conclusion**

Although we have discussed face processing in a number of neurodevelopmental and clinical disorders in this chapter, similar impairments have been reported in a range of other disorders. For example, emotion processing is atypical in individuals with neurodevelopmental disorders such as attention-deficit/hyperactivity disorder (Yuill and Lyon, 2007) and Down syndrome (Hippolyte et al, 2009). Negative consequences of harmful experiences in early life have also been shown to influence face processing, as was shown in a study of children with post-traumatic stress disorder following mistreatment (Masten et al, 2008). Finally, although we discussed some clinical disorders, atypical processing of facial emotion has been shown in a number of other conditions including bipolar disorder (Rocca et al, 2009), generalized anxiety (Frenkel et al, 2009), panic disorder (Pillay et al, 2007), obsessive compulsive disorder (Corcoran et al, 2008) and anorexia nervosa (Pollatos et al, 2008).

It seems that face processing, and in particular the processing of facial emotion, is impaired in a wide range of neurodevelopmental and clinical disorders. In all of these, the impairments are not just behavioural. Abnormal patterns of brain activation, in terms of either over- or under-activation, have been reported in all these conditions. One issue that has not been addressed is whether the dysfunctional processing of facial emotion may share common features, or possibly even causal factors, across these disorders. Particularly within the clinical disorders, there is often a high degree of co-morbidity between different disorders. However, much of the existing research has tended to examine each disorder separately. It may be particularly useful to take a wider look at face processing across a number of disorders in an attempt to fully understand the patterns of ability and impairment, the underlying neuropsychological dysfunction and the possible causes of them.

One issue that is particularly relevant is how the behavioural and neuropsychological processing of facial emotion might affect an individual's social interactions. In this chapter we discussed the evidence for such a relationship in autistic spectrum disorders, schizophrenia, depression and anxiety. It therefore seems that the ability to process facial emotions effectively is associated with the ability to interact with others. However, this raises a really important question that has not yet been answered: what is the direction of the relationship between atypical face processing and the development of clinical disorders?

Take, for example, social anxiety. One possibility is that there may be an underlying neuropsychological dysfunction that causes impaired processing of facial emotion. As a consequence of this impairment, the individual may find it difficult to interpret the emotional expressions of others, which makes interactions more difficult and may lead to a fear of social situations. Alternatively, it might be that the individual is fearful of social interactions and consequently has fewer, and poorer quality, social exchanges. This degraded experience with others and the interpretation of faces and emotional expressions may then lead to atypical development of the neuropsychological processing of faces. Indeed, the research on early visual deprivation discussed at the beginning of this chapter highlights how important it is to see faces in order to develop typical face processing. Although the research in this area has begun to identify clearly the neuropsychological and behavioural impairments to face processing, there are still a great many questions that remain unanswered.

SUMMARY

- Children who experience early visual deprivation, and consequently are not exposed to faces in the first few weeks or months of life, have impaired face-processing abilities. This finding clearly demonstrates the importance of seeing and interacting with faces for the behavioural and neuropsychological development of face processing.

- The most obvious impairment in face processing, which was found across all the disorders discussed in this chapter, is in the processing of facial emotion. There is some evidence for other aspects of face processing being impaired, but it is not particularly consistent.

- Control participants tend primarily to use configural facial information, with featural information being secondary. This finding is not observed in autistic spectrum disorder, Williams syndrome or schizophrenia. In all three of these groups, the processing of faces is more reliant on featural information.

- Levels of activation in the fusiform face area are typically lower in people with autistic spectrum disorder, schizophrenia, depression or anxiety. However, a small number of studies have reported increased fusiform face area activation in these groups.

- The levels of activation in the amygdala in response to emotive faces seem to show the most reliable differences in activation across the clinical groups discussed in this chapter. In autistic spectrum disorders, schizophrenia and depression, levels of activation are lower, whereas in anxiety levels of activation increase.

FURTHER READING

Jemel, B., Mottron, L. and Dawson, M. (2006). *Impaired face processing in autism: fact or artifact?* Journal of Autism and Developmental Disorders, 36(1): 91–106. This paper reviews the research on face processing in individuals with autism. Interestingly, the authors conclude that, although there are some obvious impairments in face processing, individuals with autism actually have far better face-processing abilities than is often assumed.

Martens, M. A., Wilson, S. J. and Reutens, D. C. (2008). *Williams syndrome: a critical review of the cognitive, behavioral, and neuroanatomical phenotype.* Journal of Child Psychology and Psychiatry, 49(6): 576–608. This paper reviews the findings of 178 studies on cognitive processing in individuals with Williams syndrome. As well as discussing the impairments and abilities found for face processing, the authors give detailed consideration to a wide range of other cognitive abilities.

Marwick, K. and Hall, J. (2008). *Social cognition in schizophrenia: a review of face processing.* British Medical Bulletin, 88(1): 43–58. This paper reviews both the psychological and the neuropsychological research on the processing of faces in schizophrenia. In particular, it considers how the impairments in face processing, and especially the processing of facial emotion, are implicated in the social interaction difficulties experienced in this group.

Monk, C. S. (2008). *The development of emotion-related neural circuitry in health and psychopathology.* Development and Psychopathology, 20(4): 1231–1250. In this paper the neuropsychology of face processing in anxiety, depression and autistic spectrum disorders is reviewed. Monk proposes a theoretical framework that combines neuropsychological, environmental and genetic components to understand the processing of emotion in clinical populations.

9

THE COGNITIVE NEUROSCIENCE OF FACE PROCESSING

In Chapter 7 we learned a great deal about how faces are processed in the brain by looking at evidence from patients who have suffered from brain damage. In these patients we find out what they can and cannot do in terms of face processing and then link this to the damage that they have sustained. In these studies, it is often assumed (not necessarily correctly!) that the area of the brain that has been damaged is usually involved in the impaired processing. In Chapter 8 we learned about how face processing can be atypical in patients with developmental neuropsychological disorders such as schizophrenia, depression or autism. One problem with both of these sources of evidence is that we cannot be certain that the processing that we observe is the consequence of a brain lesion or atypical development. For a full understanding of how faces are processed in the brain, we need to examine the neuropsychology of face processing in individuals who have suffered neither brain damage nor atypical development.[1] In this chapter we will examine this evidence[2] and, importantly, consider whether it is consistent with the evidence presented in the previous two chapters, or whether it tells a very different story.

9.1 Left or right? Evidence from divided visual field studies

Much of the earlier research examining the neuropsychological processes underpinning face processing in individuals without brain injury used **divided visual field** techniques to assess each hemisphere's capabilities. Facial stimuli that are presented to the left visual field are initially received and processed by the **right hemisphere**, whereas stimuli presented to the right visual field are initially received and processed by the left hemisphere.

---

[1] Note that in this chapter we are concerned with the neuropsychology underlying face detection, structural encoding of faces and the processing of facial identity. A great deal of work has also considered the neuropsychology of processing facial emotion; this is reviewed in Chapter 3.

[2] The methods used in this chapter and a basic guide to neuroanatomy are given in the methodological appendix.

By comparing performance across the left and right visual fields it is possible to examine hemispheric specializations in face processing.

9.1.1 Hemispheric specializations in face processing

A wide range of face-processing tasks have been used within this area of research. Hillger and Koenig (1991) used a same–different task with schematic faces. They first showed a target face centrally and then showed a probe face, in either the left or right visual field. On each trial, participants had to decide whether or not the probe face was the same as the target face. A significant right hemisphere advantage was found for both the same and the different trials, although the magnitude of this effect was larger for same trials than for different trials.

The Hillger and Koenig study can be criticized, however, in terms of both the stimuli and the tasks that were used. Firstly, it is not clear whether schematic faces are processed in the same way as real faces (Leder, 1996). Therefore, any conclusions that can be drawn from such studies are somewhat limited. Secondly, the use of same–different matching paradigms may not be ideal. Such tasks may not reflect face-processing mechanisms, but may instead test the ability to remember a visual stimulus and then decide whether a subsequently presented stimulus is the same or not. These limitations do not mean that these studies are without merit, but the findings do need to be supported by divided visual field studies that use more valid face recognition tasks.

Possibly the simplest and most direct test of face recognition is to present familiar (e.g. famous) and unfamiliar faces to either visual field and ask participants to make a familiarity decision. Such studies have shown a left visual field advantage, indicating a right hemisphere advantage for face recognition (e.g. Young et al, 1985b). This visual field bias has also been shown in infants as young as 4–5 months when distinguishing between their mother's face and the face of an unknown woman (de Schonen and Mathivet, 1990).

The ability of the right hemisphere to distinguish between familiar and unfamiliar faces was examined by Stone and Valentine (2005). They presented participants with pairs of faces. In each pair, one face was famous and the other unfamiliar. Participants were asked which face made the stronger visual percept (i.e. which face was more salient or would be processed preferentially). They found a larger difference between famous and unfamiliar faces presented to the left visual field. This suggests that the right hemisphere is better than the left hemisphere at distinguishing between familiar and unfamiliar faces.

Further evidence for the right hemisphere being particularly important in familiar face recognition comes from a study by Brooks and Cooper (2006). They asked participants to perform two different tasks under divided visual field conditions. One tested for basic level face processing: the ability to distinguish between human faces, animal faces and objects. The other task tested for subordinate-level face processing in which participants saw famous faces and had to decide whether or not they were an actor. Brooks and Cooper found a right hemisphere advantage only for the subordinate-level face-processing task, suggesting that the hemispheric advantage is not simply due to the processing of a facial stimulus *per se*, but is the result of processing a familiar face.

Repetition priming paradigms (see the methodological appendix and Chapter 1, section 1.2.2) have also been used to examine patterns of lateralization for processing facial stimuli. Bourne and Hole (2006) presented participants with faces in either the left or right visual field and asked them to decide whether or not they were famous. This task was then repeated with all faces shown centrally (i.e. not presented unilaterally to one hemisphere). A significant priming effect was found for prime faces presented to the right hemisphere, but not for faces presented to the left hemisphere. One possible limitation with this study is that the same image of the face was used for the prime and the target stimulus. However, this finding has also been replicated, albeit to a slightly lesser extent, by Cooper et al (2007) who used both same and different image pairings as primes and targets.

A right hemisphere advantage has also been found for recently learned faces (Rizzolatti et al, 1971). Buttle and Raymond (2003) compared patterns of lateralization for processing already-known faces (famous ones) and faces that were learned in the laboratory. They presented two faces to participants, one to each visual field, for 100 milliseconds. They then presented a second pair, again with one face to each visual field for 100 ms. Between the two presentations, one of the faces remained the same and in the same location (in either the left or the right visual field). The other face was replaced with a different face, but of the same sex. The participant's task was to decide whether the face that had changed was presented in the left or the right visual field. Performance was more accurate for the famous faces than for the learned faces, but only when faces were presented to the left visual field. This indicates that the right hemisphere is dominant for face recognition, but, more interestingly, that this superiority is more pronounced for previously known faces than for recently learned faces. This raises an interesting question: why would patterns of lateralization differ between already-known and recently learned faces?

One possible explanation for this difference is that we also have a great deal of wider knowledge about already-known faces, such as their name and lots of semantic information about them. It is possible that this additional knowledge may explain the different patterns of lateralization. A number of studies have considered exactly this issue by looking at patterns of lateralization for processing the semantic information, such as name or occupation, associated with faces.

Sergent et al (1992) presented familiar faces to either visual field and asked participants to make an 'occupation' judgement. Participants were both faster and more accurate when faces were presented to their right visual field (left hemisphere) than to their left visual field (right hemisphere). This left hemisphere advantage for processing the semantic information associated with familiar faces is consistent with evidence taken from patients who have had unilateral brain damage (e.g. Sergent and Villemure, 1989; Warrington and Taylor, 1978). However, a more recent replication failed to find any significant hemispheric effects (Kampf et al, 2002) and a study using lateralized semantic priming actually found a right hemisphere advantage (Vladeanu and Bourne, 2009).

Although there is currently no clear evidence for which hemisphere is specialized for processing the semantic information associated with familiar faces, a great deal of evidence from a variety of paradigms shows that the right hemisphere is specialized for processing familiar faces. It is important to note, however, that just because the right hemisphere is specialized for familiar face processing, this does not mean that the left hemisphere is incapable of processing faces effectively. The right hemisphere may be faster and more accurate than the left hemisphere, but most studies have found that left hemispheric processing is still above chance levels (e.g. Ellis and Shepherd, 1975; Hillger and Koenig, 1991; Leehey and Cahn, 1979; Leehey et al, 1978). Furthermore, it is relatively common for research in this area to find hemispheric differences in the speed but not the accuracy of processing (e.g. Bourne and Hole, 2006; Hillger and Koenig, 1991). It is therefore important to remember that the hemispheric effects found are *relative specializations* rather than absolute distinctions.

9.1.2 **Hemispheric specializations in processing featural and configural facial information**

From the research presented above it seems that the right hemisphere is specialized for processing faces, but that processing can also be achieved by the left hemisphere (although possibly more slowly and less accurately). It has been suggested that each hemisphere is differentially involved in face processing and that the hemispheric effects found in this research arise due to the right hemisphere's mechanisms being more specialized and suited to the processing of facial stimuli. In a number of chapters we have discussed the distinction between configural and featural information, and it is this distinction that has been used to explain the differential involvement of each hemisphere in face processing.

As described in Chapter 2 the Face Inversion Effect has frequently been used to examine the role of configural and featural facial information in face processing: upright faces are processed primarily on the basis of the configural information contained within them, whereas the processing of inverted faces is more reliant upon featural information. Rapazynski and Erlichman (1979) presented participants with upright and inverted photographic face stimuli and found a right hemisphere advantage for recognizing learnt, previously unknown, upright faces, but no visual field effect for inverted faces. This suggests that the right hemisphere configural mechanisms are disrupted by inversion. Two other studies have replicated this, finding not only a right hemisphere advantage for upright faces, but also a left hemisphere advantage for inverted faces (Leehey et al, 1978; Rhodes, 1993). In both of these studies, participants were presented with faces unilaterally to each hemisphere and subsequently asked to identify the face from an array of 12 faces containing

the target face and 11 distractors. These experiments provide evidence consistent with the suggestion that there are hemispheric specializations in face processing. There is a right hemisphere advantage for processing upright faces, which are processed primarily on the basis of the configural information contained within them, whereas there is a left hemisphere advantage for processing inverted faces, which are processed primarily on the basis of the featural information contained within them.

Other manipulations of configural and featural facial information have also provided evidence in support of this hemispheric distinction. Bradshaw and Sherlock (1982) manipulated the configural properties of schematic faces by moving target features closer together and found a right hemisphere advantage for detecting this change, thereby supporting the right hemisphere specialization for processing configural facial information. In a second experiment, Bradshaw and Sherlock (1982) manipulated featural facial information by changing the orientation of the nose, represented by a triangle in the schematic faces they used. For detecting this change, they found a left hemisphere advantage, supporting the specialization of the left hemisphere for processing featural facial information. This finding was replicated in a similar study by Parkin and Williamson (1987), using simple line drawings of faces. However, the findings of these studies may be limited by the use of schematic or line-drawn faces (Leder, 1996). The stimuli may have been treated as patterns of geometric shapes, rather than as face stimuli. In addition, the task of detecting the change does not necessarily require activation of face-processing mechanisms. It is quite plausible that the task given was treated as a non-face, pattern-change detection task, rather than as a face-processing task.

A number of other studies have examined hemispheric specializations in face processing using a feature-swapping paradigm. In such experiments participants are shown faces in which one feature has been substituted with a corresponding feature from another face, and have to decide whether or not the face has been changed. The detection of changes to individual features has been found to elicit a left hemisphere advantage (Fairweather et al, 1982; Hillger and Koenig, 1991; Patterson and Bradshaw, 1975; Sergent, 1982). In contrast, a right hemisphere advantage was found when three or four features were changed simultaneously (Hillger and Koenig, 1991; Sergent, 1982). Again, these experiments provide evidence for the right hemisphere being specialized for processing configural facial information and the left hemisphere being specialized for processing featural facial information.

Although the studies discussed so far support the idea that each hemisphere is specialized for processing different forms of facial information, many have some methodological limitations. Firstly, a number of the studies used schematic faces rather than photographs of real faces. It is unclear whether schematic faces elicit face- or object-processing mechanisms. Secondly, the task used is often a 'same/different' paradigm. Again, it is unclear whether it is necessary to use face-processing mechanisms to complete such tasks, particularly with schematic stimuli. Thirdly, manipulations of featural and configural facial information are often examined separately.

All three of these issues have been addressed in a recent study which used a lateralized repetition priming paradigm (Bourne et al, 2009). In this study, photographs of famous and unfamiliar prime faces were presented to either the left or the right visual fields and participants had to make a familiarity decision. The faces were either unmanipulated, blurred (which removes featural information) or had displaced features (which alters their configural information). They were then presented a second time, all presented without any manipulation and centrally. As with previous studies (Bourne and Hole, 2006; Cooper et al, 2007), for the unmanipulated faces priming was found for prime faces presented to the right hemisphere, but not for those presented to the left hemisphere. Blurring did not change the priming from left hemisphere primes, but when presented to the right hemisphere negative priming (an increase in reaction times) was found. Conversely, manipulating the configuration of the features did not change the priming from the right hemisphere primes, but when presented to the left hemisphere negative priming was found.

Effectively, this study shows hemispheric differences in priming when you manipulate a face so that one form of information is degraded to a greater extent than another. For the right hemisphere, disrupting the featural information makes no difference to the priming effect, but disrupting the configural information leads to a significant increase in reaction times (negative priming). For the left hemisphere, disrupting the configural information makes no difference to the priming effect, but disrupting the featural information leads to negative priming.

Taken together, the evidence from divided visual field studies provides a number of insights into the neuropsychology of face processing in 'normal' individuals. They show that the right hemisphere is specialized for processing faces, perhaps particularly in the recognition of familiar faces. However, the left hemisphere is also capable of face processing, just in a different way. The left hemisphere is specialized for processing the (less important) featural facial information, whereas the right hemisphere is specialized for processing the configural facial information.

9.2 Evidence from electrophysiological studies

Electrophysiological studies of face processing examine mainly **event-related potentials**[3] (ERPs) to faces. By measuring the electrical activity in the brain in response to face stimuli, such studies can tell us three important things about face processing. Firstly, they can show how rapidly brain activity occurs in response to faces. Secondly, they can tell us how much brain activity there is, particularly whether there is an increase or a decrease in activity. Thirdly, they can tell us (roughly) where in the brain this activity occurs. Responses to faces can be found as early as 103 ms after viewing a face (the 'P100' response: Herrmann et al, 2005; Marzi and Viggiano, 2007), and, importantly, these responses are unique to faces. However, three components have been identified as particularly important for face processing by Schweinberger and Burton (2003). These components map on to the established models of face processing. The **N170** is thought to reflect the structural encoding of faces; the **N250** may reflect the recognition of individuals (i.e. face recognition units); and the **N400** may reflect the processing of semantic information associated with faces. Each of these will now be discussed in detail.

9.2.1 The N170 component

The N170 has been identified as a key early marker for face processing (Bentin et al, 1996). In addition to being produced by photographic images of faces, the N170 is elicited by schematic faces and drawings of faces (Bentin et al, 1996; Sagiv and Bentin, 2001), Mooney faces (George et al, 2005; although see Latinus and Taylor, 2006) and faces of other species such as apes (Carmel and Bentin, 2002; de Haan et al, 2002; Itier et al, 2006b). Importantly, the N170 is far smaller for non-face stimuli than for faces (e.g. Bentin et al, 1996; Carmel and Bentin, 2002; Eimer, 2000; Itier and Taylor, 2004e; Rousselet et al, 2008). This evidence has been used to suggest that the N170 is particularly associated with face processing rather than being a more general response to visual stimuli (see Chapter 10 for a full discussion of this issue).

Although the N170 appears to be a specific response to faces, a great deal of evidence suggests that it is an early response that reflects the structural encoding phase of face processing. This suggestion is supported by evidence that the N170 response does not vary according to the familiarity of a face (e.g. Bentin and Deouell, 2000; Eimer, 2000; Paller et al, 2000; Rossion et al, 1999a) or the sex of the person (Mouchetant-Rostaing et al, 2000). Consequently, it seems that the N170 is a face-specific response that deals with the structural encoding of a face prior to the processing of familiarity, identity or any other derived information. Unfortunately, not all evidence is consistent with this claim, as the N170 has been found to be larger when a person is viewing their own face than when viewing other faces. This suggests that at least some identity information must be processed at this early stage (Tanaka and Porterfield, 2002).

Most of the research examining the N170 considers its sensitivity to the distinction between *configural* and *featural* information in faces. For a full discussion of this distinction see Chapter 2, but a brief recap will be given here. Faces are processed primarily according

---

[3] See the appendix for details on this methodology. Remember that ERPs are named according to the direction of the potential (Positive or Negative) and the time (in milliseconds) at which the activity peaks after the stimulus presentation. Thus, the P100 is positive modulation 100 ms after presentation and the N250 is negative modulation 250 ms after stimulus presentation.

to the configural information contained within them, that is, the distances and relationships between the features contained within a face. The features *per se* are also processed, but they are probably less important. Various manipulations have been used to alter either the configural or featural information contained within faces, and researchers have then examined how performance changes as a consequence. Similarly, within this area, researchers have considered how the N170 varies according to these manipulations. As with the behavioural research, inversion has been used by a great many researchers to examine the distinction between configural and featural processing. Upright faces are processed primarily on the basis of their configural properties, whereas the processing of inverted faces is more reliant on featural information (Yin, 1969). A large number of studies have shown that the N170 is larger and occurs slightly later when a face is inverted (Fig. 9.1) (Bentin et al, 1996; de Haan et al, 2002; Eimer, 2000; Fleuaris et al, 2008; Ishizu et al, 2008; Itier and Taylor, 2002a, 2004b; Itier et al, 2006a; Latinus and Taylor, 2006; Rossion et al, 1999b, 2000b; Taylor et al, 2001). The effect has also been shown for inverted Mooney faces (George et al, 2005). More specifically, the N170 is delayed by about 30 ms by inversion (Jacques et al, 2007). This larger N170 has also been reported by Anaki et al (2007), who additionally reported that the effect did not vary according to the familiarity of the face.

Another demonstration of configural processing, the Thatcher Illusion (see Chapter 2), has also been found to elicit larger N170 responses (Carbon et al, 2005) and delayed N170 responses over the occipitotemporal region (Boutsen et al, 2006). Similar findings have been reported for faces presented in photographic negative (Itier and Taylor, 2002a, 2004c; Itier et al, 2006a). The N170 has also been found to respond more to the internal features of a face than its external features (Olivares and Iglesias, 2008).

The effect on the N170 of manipulating configural and featural information appears to differ between the left and right hemispheres. Rossion et al (1999b) gave participants a face-matching task using either upright or inverted faces. N170 activity in the right hemisphere varied between upright and inverted faces. This effect was far less pronounced in the left hemisphere. Rossion and co-workers attributed this to the loss of configural information in inverted faces and the specialization of the right hemisphere for processing configural facial information. More recently they examined the response of the N170 at various orientations between upright and inverted (Jacques and Rossion, 2007). As a result of inversion, the right hemisphere N170 was larger, occurred about 10 ms earlier and showed more variability (Fig. 9.2/Plate 9.2). A study on the Composite Face Effect also found an enhanced N170 in the right hemisphere compared with the left hemisphere (Letourneau and Mitchell, 2008).

Scott and Nelson (2006) examined the effects of both configural and featural manipulations and considered how these affected the N170 in the left and right hemispheres. Participants were presented with a series of faces in which either a featural change was made or the configural properties of the face were altered slightly. When a configural manipulation was made, the N170 was enhanced in the right hemisphere, but when the features were manipulated the N170 was enhanced in the left hemisphere.

So, what do we know about the N170 response to faces? It seems to be specific to the structural encoding of faces and is greater in the right hemisphere around the occipitotemporal area (the area where the occipital and temporal lobes meet). The N170 in the right hemisphere is sensitive to manipulations of configural facial information, whereas the N170 in the left hemisphere is sensitive to manipulations of featural facial information. This finding of different hemispheric specializations is consistent with the evidence

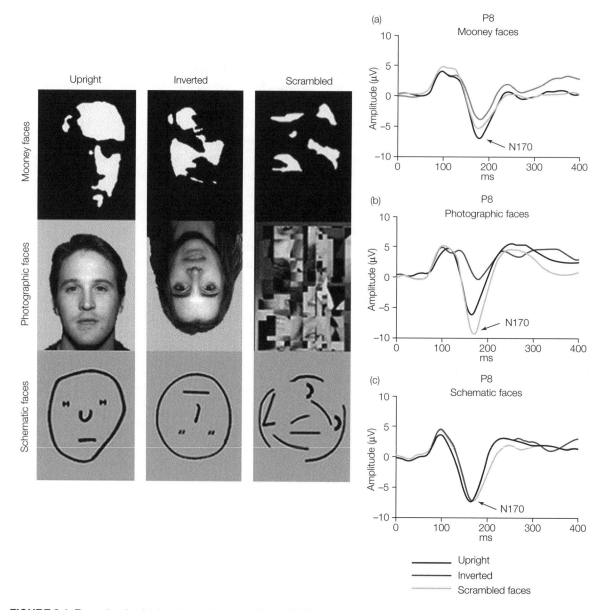

FIGURE 9.1 Example stimuli taken from Latinus and Taylor (2006), showing three different types of facial stimulus and the N170 response to them.

discussed earlier using the divided visual field methodology. Rossion et al (1999b) have suggested that the increase in size and delay in occurrence of the N170 in response to these manipulations might reflect the increased effort required by the brain to achieve the effective processing of degraded face images. Because the right hemisphere is specialized for processing configural facial information, the processing of, for example, inverted faces is more difficult behaviourally, takes longer and requires greater effort for the brain to achieve.

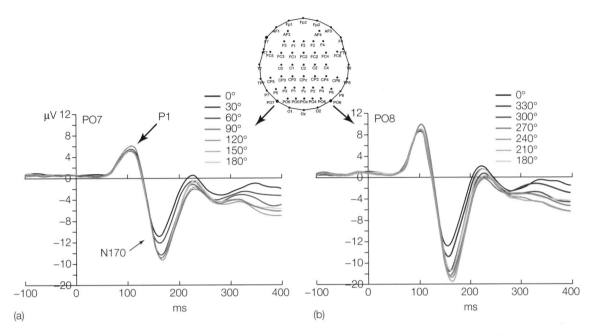

FIGURE 9.2 N170 responses to faces at varying orientations from upright (0°) to inverted (180°), measured from occipitotemporal electrodes over (a) the left hemisphere and (b) the right hemisphere. (From Jacques and Rossion, 2007). Please see colour plate section.

9.2.2 **The N250 component**

The majority of the work on the N250 component shows that it reflects the processing of individual identity. Typically the N250 is found to be larger for familiar than for unfamiliar faces (Begleiter et al, 1995; Pfutze et al, 2002; Schweinberger et al, 1995). The N250 has also been found to increase, across both hemispheres, when learning new faces (Kaufmann et al, 2009). This change in the N250 can occur within a very short period of time. Tanaka et al (2006) conducted an experiment in which they showed participants two faces: their own face and that of an unfamiliar person ('Joe'). Each time they were shown a face, participants had to decide whether the face belonged to Joe or whether it was their own. At the beginning of the experiment the N250 was clearly evident for their own faces, but not for Joe's face. However, by the second half of the experiment, the N250 for Joe appeared (Fig. 9.3). The N250 response to newly learned faces has also been found for faces

a week after they had been learned (Herzmann and Sommer, 2007).

The N250 has also been examined using repetition priming paradigms. In these experiments the ERP is often referred to as the N250r. Schweinberger et al (2002b) recorded ERPs while participants viewed familiar and unfamiliar faces that had just been preceded by a different face, the same image of that face or a different image of that face. They found that the primed familiar faces elicited a significantly larger N250r over the parietal lobes. The N250r has also been found following both intentional and incidental recognition of a prime face (Boehm and Sommer, 2005).

ERPs have been used in an attempt to understand the neuropsychological basis of the own-group bias effects that have frequently been reported (see Chapter 12). In these experiments the N250 has been identified as particularly important. Herrmann et al (2007)

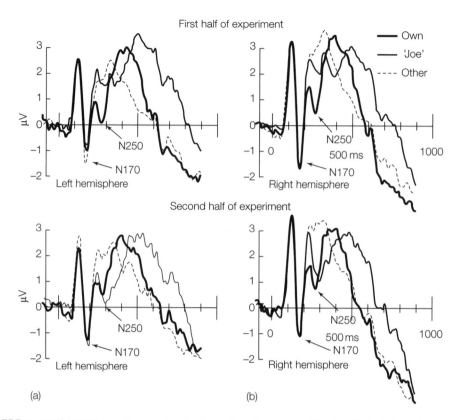

FIGURE 9.3 ERPs to participants' own faces and to the face of another person ('Joe') in (a) the left hemisphere and (b) the right hemisphere. Notice how the N250 is barely evident for 'Joe' in the first half of the experiment, but clearly visible in the second half of the experiment. (From Tanaka et al, 2006)

used a priming paradigm to examine the own-race bias and found that the N250r was significantly reduced in the 'other-race' condition compared with the 'own-race' condition. Tanaka and Pierce (2009) examined whether the N250 could be influenced by training participants to perform at a higher level. They trained participants in two ways: one to distinguish between faces at the basic level (between different races) and the other at the subordinate level (between individuals). They found that this training did not change the N170, but that the N250 increased for subordinate-level decisions.

An increased N250 has also been reported for the own-age bias (Wiese et al, 2008). The N250 response over the right occipitotemporal sites

is larger to own-age faces, but only for younger participants. The authors suggest that this effect arises because the younger participants have easier access to the structural representations of own-age faces.

9.2.3 The N400 component

The N400 component is thought to reflect the processing of semantic information associated with faces. As such, it is not really an ERP in response to the perceptual processing of faces, but in response to the processing of semantic information about that person. This idea is supported by the finding that both names and faces evoke similar N400s (Schweinberger, 1996).

Similarly, as you might expect given that we only have semantic information about familiar faces, the N400 is larger for familiar faces than for unfamiliar faces (Bentin and Deouell, 2000; Eimer, 2000).

The issue of familiarity was further examined by Paller et al (2000). They asked participants to learn 40 faces. Half of the faces were learned with accompanying semantic information, such as their occupation and name. The other half had no such information attached to them, and they were learned simply as faces. After learning the faces, participants had to distinguish between new unseen faces and the old learned faces. Potentials were more positive for the old learned faces than for the new faces. For the named faces this occurred at both anterior (towards the front) and posterior (towards the back) areas, whereas for the unnamed learned faces the difference was evident only in the posterior recordings. This led Paller and colleagues to conclude that the posterior N400 reflects the recognition of a person as familiar and the anterior N400 reflects the retrieval of semantic information about that person.

The N400 has also been examined using semantic priming paradigms. In these experiments the recognition of a familiar face (for example, Prince Charles) is faster if the participant has previously seen a face that is semantically related to it (for example, the Queen). Wiese and Schweinberger (2008) examined the N400 in response to two different types of semantic priming: associative priming (where two people are highly associated with each other, such as being married) and categorical priming (where two people belong to the same semantic category, such as 'actor'). The N400 was found for both types of priming, but it occurred in different places: it was more central and parietal for associative priming and more posterior for categorical priming. Such evidence provides more support for the idea that the N400 reflects the processing of semantic information associated with familiar faces.

9.2.4 **Evidence from magnetoencephalography (MEG)**

The evidence from ERPs has provided a number of insights into how faces are processed in the brain, particularly in terms of the time course of processing. However, one major limitation of the ERP is that, although its temporal resolution is excellent, its spatial resolution is less precise. Although a number of studies, particularly with the N170, identify the right occipitotemporal area as being important for face processing, this is a relatively imprecise estimate. This lack of accuracy has been resolved, at least to some extent, with the development of **magnetoencephalography** (MEG), which provides greater spatial resolution.

Generally the evidence from MEG studies supports the ERP work, with the addition of more information regarding the location of these effects in the brain. Again, MEG studies have shown that faces can be detected and distinguished from other types of stimulus after just 100 ms; these effects occur in the occipital cortex (Susac et al, 2009). The M170, the MEG equivalent to the N170, has received the most attention and provides further evidence for the structural encoding of faces within this timeframe. Firstly, the M170 is larger to faces than to other non-face stimuli such as houses (Hadjikhani et al, 2009; Sterzer et al, 2009). Secondly, when viewing inverted faces the M170 is delayed, although not necessarily different in size (Itier et al, 2006a; Schweinberger et al, 2007). Importantly, Itier et al (2006a) found two distinct site locations for the M170 (Fig. 9.4). One of these, the M170A, came from a bilateral and posterior source. The other, the M170B, was clearly lateralized to the right hemisphere, and more ventral and anterior in location. The location of the M170B corresponds to the fusiform gyrus, and, as we shall see later in this chapter, this area is known to be an important face-processing area in the brain.

ERP and MEG studies have provided conflicting evidence on how the N170/M170

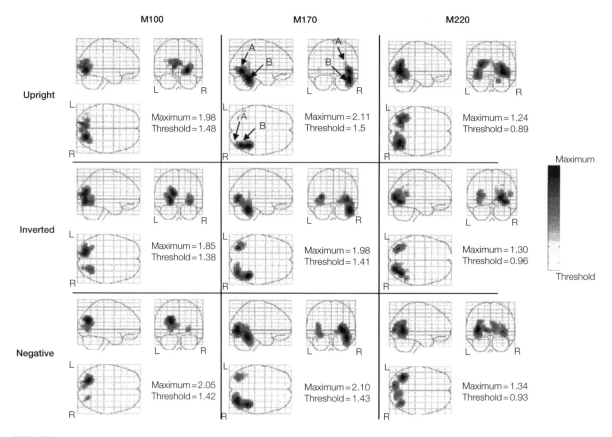

FIGURE 9.4 Source analysis showing the MEG components in response to upright faces, inverted faces and faces presented in photographic negative. (From Itier et al, 2006a)

component responds to familiarity. The majority of the evidence from studies on the N170 suggests that there is no difference between familiar and unfamiliar face processing; however, the evidence from the MEG data is not consistent with this. The M170 is larger in response to personally familiar faces than to unfamiliar faces, particularly over the right hemisphere (Harris and Aguirre, 2008; Kloth et al, 2006), although an M170 in the right fusiform gyrus has also been reported for unfamiliar faces (Deffke et al, 2007). Further evidence for the M170 being sensitive to familiarity comes from a near-perfect relationship ($r = 0.98$) between recognition performance and the size of the M170 response (Tanskanen et al, 2007). It seems, therefore, that the M170 may be sensitive to face familiarity.

9.3 Evidence from neuroimaging studies

Although divided visual field studies have told us a great deal about the lateralization of face processing and electrophysiological studies have provided lots of information about the time course of face processing in the brain, neither has been able to tell us precisely where in the brain the various aspects of face processing occur. Since the mid-1990s methods such as **functional magnetic resonance imaging** (fMRI) have been used a great deal in an attempt to further our understanding of the neuropsychology of face processing.

As we saw in Chapter 1, a number of models have been developed to explain the sequence of processing stages involved in face processing. These have been adapted to take into account evidence from neuroimaging studies. A neural model of face processing was initially developed by Haxby et al (2000), and this has been updated recently (Gobbini and Haxby, 2007).

The neural models of face processing propose two systems that enable effective face processing: the 'core' system and the 'extended' system (Fig. 9.5). The first stage within the core system is the visual perception of the face stimulus. This is thought to occur in the **inferior occipital gyrus** (IOG), which is also referred to as the occipital face area (OFA). This then feeds into the recognition processes, which are further subdivided into two components. First is the processing of invariant aspects of faces. This means the ability to recognize faces in spite of changes to the image in terms of viewpoint, expression, etc. This invariant processing occurs in the fusiform gyrus, which

is located in the temporal lobe and is sometimes referred to as the **fusiform face area** (FFA). The second aspect of recognition is the processing of variable or changeable aspects of the face, such as facial expression of emotion or perception of eye gaze. Processing of these changeable aspects is located in the **superior temporal sulcus** (STS). The STS is the crevice that separates the superior and middle gyri in the temporal lobe.

This core system then feeds into the extended system. The extended system, in some ways, does not reflect face recognition *per se*, but rather the associated processes that we might conduct using facial stimuli. These include the processing of spatially directed attention (e.g. perception of eye gaze), the perception of prelexical speech (e.g. lip-reading), the processing of emotional facial expressions, and the processing of personal identity, semantic or biographical information associated with a face and the name belonging to the person. Each of these is located in different areas of the brain.

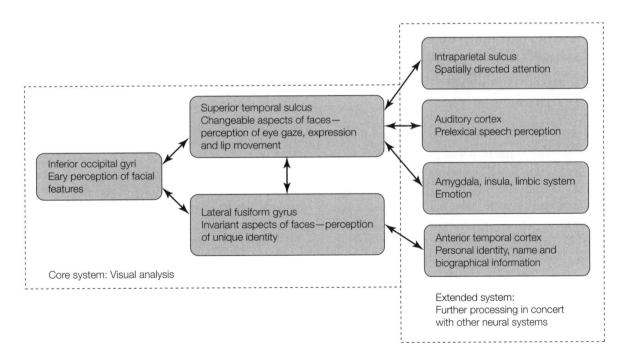

FIGURE 9.5 Neural model of face processing. (From Haxby et al, 2000)

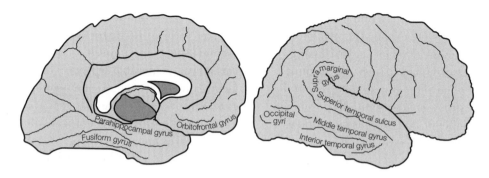

FIGURE 9.6 Main areas of the brain involved in the processing of faces. (From Dekowska et al, 2008)

It is obvious that face processing is not located discretely in one particular part of the brain, but rather distributed across various parts of it (Fig. 9.6). The core processing of the visual percept takes place in the OFA; the processing of identity from invariant aspects of a face takes place in the FFA; and the processing from variant aspects takes place in the STS. The extended system is even more widely distributed across the brain. We shall now discuss each of these stages in more detail.

9.3.1 Neuroimaging studies of face perception

According to the Haxby neural model of face processing, there are two areas responsible for the initial processing of a face: the OFA, which processes the basic visual perception, and the FFA, which processes the invariant aspects of a face and its identity (Fig. 9.7). The role of these two areas has been examined in a wide variety of ways. For example, when simply detecting the presence of a face, FFA activity has been reported (Grill-Spector et al, 2004). Another experiment used Mooney faces. These are not actually faces, but meaningless shapes that can be perceived as being face-like. When these Mooney faces were perceived as faces, FFA activation was found, but when the same stimuli were not perceived as faces there was no FFA activation (Andrews and Schluppeck, 2004). This suggests that the FFA activation is specific to

perceiving a stimulus as a face. In another study, participants were shown line drawings of faces and asked to remember them so that they could draw them later (Miall et al, 2009). During the encoding, activity was found in both the OFA and the FFA.

A great deal of the research examining the visual perception of face stimuli has examined which areas of the brain are active and how this activity changes across different viewpoints. This is important as familiar faces can be recognized even when they are viewed from different angles or with differing facial expressions (i.e. regardless of the changeable aspects of a face). The Haxby model suggests that the OFA and FFA are both implicated in the invariant aspects of face, whereas the STS is sensitive to these changes.

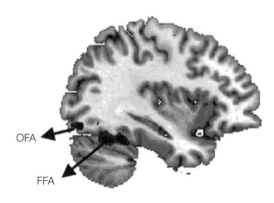

FIGURE 9.7 Location of the occipital face area (OFA) and fusiform face area (FFA). (From Minnebusch and Daum, 2009)

Fox et al (2009) showed participants faces that varied according to either identity or emotion and in which structural changes (physical changes to the face that did not change the identity or emotional expression) were made. They found that the right OFA was sensitive to changes in structure, but not in identity or expression, supporting the idea that the OFA is involved in the early processing of invariant facial information. Other studies have examined patterns of activation when viewing frontal and profile, or semi-profile, images of faces. Chen et al (2007) found no difference in activation in either the FFA or the OFA in response to different views of faces, supporting the view that these two core systems process the invariant properties of a face. They did, however, find differences in activation in brain areas implicated in the extended face-processing system, such as the middle occipital gyrus and the intraoccipital sulci. Andrews and Ewbank (2004) distinguished between the inferior temporal areas, which they found were not sensitive to changes in viewpoint, and the superior temporal areas (including the STS), which they found were sensitive to such changes.

Another study examined differences between viewpoints using a priming paradigm to examine how the brain responds to repetitions of familiar and unfamiliar faces across different viewpoints (Pourtois et al, 2005a). These authors found no difference in FFA activation across different viewpoints, supporting the idea that the FFA is able to process faces even when the facial information varies and suggesting that the integration of facial information across different viewpoint occurs later in processing. Pourtois and

co-workers did, however, find some differences between the processing of familiar and unfamiliar faces. Following the repetition of unfamiliar faces there was a reduction in activity in the medial part of the right fusiform gyrus, whereas following the repetition of familiar faces there was reduced activity in the left middle temporal and left inferior frontal areas.

The early visual perception of faces has also been examined by studying brain activation in response to faces that are perceived without the participants being aware of them. This is an important area of research as the patterns of brain activation in response to faces that participants are not aware of can tell researchers a great deal about the very early stages of face perception. The first key point is that the same network of brain regions is activated when faces are presented, but the participant is not aware of this. For example, Kouider et al (2009) used a subliminal face priming paradigm and found three primary areas of activation, the areas also identified as key in the Haxby model: the OFA, FFA and STS. Morris et al (2007) used 'masking'[4] to make participants unaware of visual stimuli. They found right FFA activation following the masked presentation of faces, but not of objects. Again, this supports the wider evidence showing that the right FFA is specialized for face processing and also suggests that the right FFA is involved in automatic face perception. Large et al (2008) presented participants with a set of four faces and then another set of four faces where one may or may not have been changed in terms of either identity or expression. When the participants detected, or were aware of, a change there was activation in the OFA, FFA and STS. When the change was not

[4] 'Masking' (or more specifically 'backward masking') is a technique used to limit the amount of time for which a visual stimulus can be processed. If a picture is shown very briefly to a participant, you might suppose that they can see it only for the time that it is displayed. However, in practice its effects on retinal photoreceptors might endure for considerably longer. To try to prevent this, masking is used. An image is shown for a very brief amount of time, generally in the order of tens of milliseconds, and is followed immediately by another image, often a 'patterned mask' consisting of random dots or lines, etc. The idea is that processing of the first image is over-written by presentation of the second.

detected, so that the participant was not aware of it, there were changes only in the OFA. This suggests that the OFA is implicated in the pre-conscious processing of faces.

In terms of the visual processing of facial information, another distinction that has been discussed many times throughout this book—and indeed already in this chapter—is between configural and featural facial information. This distinction has also been examined using fMRI methodology.

A number of studies using the inversion effect have found that inversion (which disrupts the processing of configural information and causes the participant to rely more on featural information) leads to decreased FFA activation (e.g. Kanwisher et al, 1998; Yovel and Kanwisher, 2005). Passarotti et al (2007) also found changes in activation to inverted faces in the FFA, particularly in the right FFA (Fig. 9.8/Plate 9.8). This lateralized effect supports the idea discussed earlier in this chapter that each hemisphere is specialized for processing a different type of facial information. The finding that inversion affects the right FFA more than the left FFA is consistent with the suggestion that the right hemisphere is specialized for processing configural facial information whereas the left hemisphere is specialized for processing featural

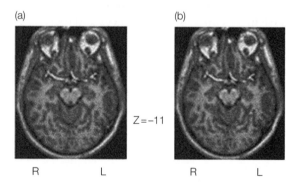

FIGURE 9.8 Activation of the fusiform gyri in adult participants in response to (a) upright faces and (b) inverted faces. (Adapted from Passarotti et al, 2007). Please see colour plate section.

facial information. Furthermore, Passarotti and colleagues found a relationship between the behavioural inversion effect and the changes in right FFA activation in response to inverted faces.

The Composite Face Effect (see Chapter 2, section 3.3.3) has also been used to examine the role of particular brain areas in processing configural facial information. Schiltz and Rossion (2006) found that the OFA and the FFA, particularly the right FFA, were sensitive to this effect and concluded that the right FFA is implicated in integrating facial features holistically in order to form a complete percept of a face.

When attempting to distinguish between the processing of configural and featural facial information, it is particularly important to consider experiments in which manipulations to both forms of information have been conducted, and can consequently be compared. Maurer et al (2007) asked participants to make same–different judgements for faces that were manipulated either configurally, by changing the spacing of the features, or featurally, by changing individual features. They found right FFA activation when faces were being processed, but also found different effects of the two manipulations. A section of the right fusiform gyrus, right next to the FFA, showed increased activity for configural processing, whereas there was left prefrontal activity for featural processing. Again, this finding is consistent with the existence of different hemispheric specializations for processing configural and featural facial information.

Rotshtein et al (2007) also conducted a study where faces were manipulated either configurally (by changing the spatial relations between the features) or featurally (by changing the actual facial features). Like Maurer et al (2007), they also found effects of the spatial manipulation in the right fusiform gyrus, as well as bilaterally in the OFA. Importantly, though, they also found a relationship between the behavioural effects of these manipulations and the changes in brain activation, providing further evidence for these brain areas being implicated in the processing of these types of information.

One final study to be discussed examined this distinction by using a delayed match to sample task (Lobmaier et al, 2008). These authors presented participants with either a blurred face (in which the configural properties were relatively unaffected but the featural information was degraded) or the scrambled features of a face (in which the featural information was unimpaired but the configural information was removed). Participants were then shown an unmanipulated face and had to decide whether or not it was the same as the one they had just seen. The processing of scrambled faces led to left hemisphere activation in the fusiform gyrus, parietal lobe and lingual gyrus, whereas the processing of blurred faces led to bilateral activation of the middle temporal gyrus.

9.3.2 Neuroimaging studies of familiar face recognition

The second aspect of the core system proposed by Haxby et al (2000) is the recognition of facial identity, which is thought to occur in the FFA. This finding has been reported in a wide range of studies (e.g. Grill-Spector et al, 2004; Turk et al, 2005). However, some studies have also found a slightly wider network of activation. Some have found that both the OFA and the FFA are active in the perception of facial identity (George et al, 1999; Hoffman and Haxby, 2000), although it is possible that the OFA activation reflects the early perceptual stages of processing. Others have more generally identified the anterior temporal lobe as the main region of activity during the recognition of a face as familiar (Gorno Tempini et al, 1998; Leveroni et al, 2000). Although these studies seem to find different patterns of activation, they actually report very similar patterns; it may just be the specificity of the activation patterns that varies.

Eger et al (2005) examined the difference between processing familiar and unfamiliar faces, using a priming paradigm in which the prime and target images of a person were either the same or different images of the same person. They found priming effects in the bilateral fusiform gyrus and in orbitofrontal regions, although the right anterior fusiform area was more sensitive to repetitions of familiar faces than of unfamiliar faces.

Other studies have examined the neural activity that occurs when learning new faces and during the subsequent recognition of those faces. Leveroni et al (2000) compared activation for recently learned faces with activation for already familiar (famous) faces. Although the behavioural responses to these two types of familiar stimulus were very similar, the patterns of brain activation were quite different. A far wider pattern of activation was found for the famous faces, with activation in the prefrontal, lateral and medial temporal lobes. It is likely that this wider network of activation can be explained in terms of the additional knowledge that we have stored about already familiar faces, such as biographical information and the person's name, or our emotional response to their face. These possibilities are discussed in more detail later in this section.

The processing of facial identity has been considered in a range of studies contrasting the recognition of familiar faces with the recognition of the participants' own faces. Sugiura et al (2008) presented participants with the names and faces of themselves, a friend and an unfamiliar person. They found no differences in activation across the three conditions for the name stimuli, but differences were found for the face stimuli. The face of a friend or an unfamiliar person led to activation bilaterally in the parietotemporal areas; however, own-face presentations led to activation in right inferior frontal, precentral, supramarginal and bilateral ventral occipitotemporal areas. This suggests that there are networks in the brain specifically dedicated to own-face processing. In a recent meta-analysis of nine studies of own-face processing, it was found that the own-face processing system is bilateral, although more activation occurs in the right hemisphere, and that activation is found in the left fusiform gyrus, bilateral middle and inferior frontal gyri, and right precuneus (Platek et al, 2008).

Devue et al (2007) showed participants images of their own face and the face of a friend. Some of the faces were altered by changing the distance between the eyes. They found that activation during own-face processing occurred in the right frontal cortex and insula (Fig. 9.9). A similar study (Uddin et al, 2005) created a series of morphs between each participant's own face and the face of a person familiar to them. The authors then showed the morphed faces to participants and asked them to decide whether each one looked more like themselves or the other person. They found that when the morph faces contained more of the participant's own face than the other face there was activation in the right inferior parietal lobe, inferior frontal gyrus and inferior frontal gyrus.

9.3.3 Neuroimaging studies of the processing of semantic information and names of familiar faces

Once a face has been recognized as familiar, this information then feeds into the retrieval of semantic or biographical information about that individual and their name. According to the Haxby neural model, this processing is one component of the extended system and is located primarily in the anterior temporal lobe. Work in this area has examined the processing of semantic information and names, both independently of each other and in combination.

Turk et al (2005) used fMRI in an attempt to distinguish between the processing of identity and semantic information. They showed participants images of famous faces. In the identity task participants were also presented with the name of a famous person and asked to decide whether it belonged to the face shown. In the semantic task they were shown the face with an occupation, and had to decide whether or not the occupation

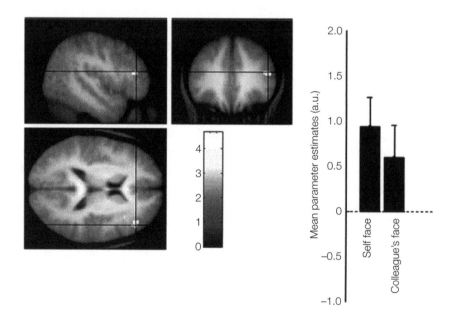

FIGURE 9.9 Activation in the right inferior frontal gyrus that is specific to self recognition. a.u., Arbitrary units. (From Devue et al, 2007)

was the correct occupation for that face. For the identity decisions there was greater activity in the FFA; however, Turk and colleagues did not find any areas that were exclusively activated by the semantic decision, suggesting that this processing was contained within the face recognition areas.

A study by Denkova et al (2006) examined the processing of familiar (famous) faces in terms of whether the participants had any autobiographical memories associated with that famous person (e.g. going to see that person in concert). They suggested that this autobiographical component represents 'pure' semantic information associated with a familiar face. Before being scanned, participants completed an interview in which they reported whether they had any autobiographical memories associated with 116 famous people. Denkova and co-workers found different patterns of activation dependent on personal significance, with the medial temporal lobe showing activation only in response to familiar faces that had personally significant semantic associations.

Other research has examined the processing of visually derived semantics, such as the sex or race of a presented face. Cloutier et al (2008) found left fusiform gyrus activation during a sex classification task, and Elfgren et al (2006) found left posterior medial temporal lobe activation for sex classification for famous faces. Kim et al (2006) examined the own-race bias using fMRI and found that the level of FFA activation was significantly different between own- and other-race faces when the faces were unfamiliar, but for familiar faces there was no difference.

The perception of names of familiar people has been found to elicit anterior temporal lobe activation (Gorno Tempini et al, 1998; Leveroni et al, 2000). This suggests that this area is implicated in the retrieval of semantic information about people, in line with the Haxby model. Some more recent studies have used face learning paradigms to examine the interaction between familiarity, semantic information and name information. Tsukiura and colleagues

(2006, 2008) conducted two such studies. They asked participants to learn either a face with a name, or a face with a name and an occupation (semantic information). Participants were then shown the learned faces and asked to retrieve the associated name. Greater left anterior temporal lobe activation was found for faces where the occupation had already been learned. In another condition, where participants were shown the names and asked to retrieve the faces, there was more right anterior temporal lobe activation if the occupation was already learned. This provides further support for the idea that the anterior temporal lobes are involved in the processing of semantic information associated with individuals.

9.3.4 Neuroimaging studies of the extended face-processing system

In addition to the processing of names and semantic information, the Haxby model includes three further processing components within the extended face-processing system: spatially directed attention, prelexical speech perception, and emotion. Again, each is proposed to be located in different areas of the brain. We discuss each of these in turn.

Spatially directed attention is the perception of another person's head orientation or eye gaze, cues that are used to work out where that person is directing their attention (also see Chapter 4, section 4.1.3). According to Haxby's model, this form of processing is localized to the intraparietal sulcus. Hoffman and Haxby (2000) conducted a study in which participants had to process either the identity of faces or their eye gaze (i.e. pay attention to the direction of the eye gaze). As would be expected, the OFA and FFA were active for the processing of identity; however, the processing of eye gaze elicited unique activation in the intraparietal sulcus.

The role of the intraparietal sulcus in the perception of eye gaze is also supported by a study in which brain activation was compared in response to eye and mouth movements (Puce et al, 1998). There was STS activation for both eye and mouth movements, but intraparietal sulcus activation was specific to the perception of eye movements. This implies that the STS may also be involved in the perception of eye gaze. Indeed, some studies have reported exclusive STS activation in response to eye-gaze perception (Cloutier et al, 2008; Sato et al, 2008), although others have reported both STS and intraparietal sulcus activations for the perception of eye gaze (Hadjikhani et al, 2008). Additionally, it has been found that right STS activation is higher when viewing a face with averted eye gaze (i.e. looking away from the participant) than when viewing a face with the gaze looking directly at the participant (Engell and Haxby, 2007).

The Haxby face-processing model also incorporates the perception of prelexical speech (lip-reading), which occurs in the auditory cortex, an area towards the posterior section of the superior temporal gyrus. Mouth movements that are not speech related have been found to cause activation in the STS (Puce et al, 1998); however, lip-reading when there are no associated speech sounds has been found to elicit activity in auditory areas of the superior temporal gyrus (Calvert et al, 1997; Okada and Hickok, 2009; Wright et al, 2003). Brain activations to lip-reading have been further localized to the left superior temporal gyrus, and the level of activation there has been found to be positively correlated with the behavioural ability to lip-read (Hall et al, 2005).

The final component of the extended face-processing system in the Haxby model is the processing of emotion, which is associated with a distributed network of activation in the amygdala, insula and limbic system. The neuropsychology of facial emotion is discussed in detail in Chapter 3; please refer back to section 3.5 for information about how each of these areas is involved in the processing of facial emotion and how this varies across different emotions.

9.4 Does interhemispheric transfer aid face processing?

We know from work conducted on patients who have undergone the split brain operation that the corpus callosum passes a great deal of information between the hemispheres (see Chapter 7, section 7.3). Given that both the left and the right hemispheres are involved in face processing, albeit to different extents and possibly with different specializations, it seems that **interhemispheric transfer** is likely to occur in order to aid processing. Only a small amount of work has been done in this area of research, all employing two adaptations of the divided visual field paradigm: the redundant targets effect and the within versus across paradigm (see Bourne, 2006).

In the redundant targets effect (Fig. 9.10), stimuli are presented in either the left or the right visual fields in exactly the same way as in the standard divided visual field paradigm. However, an additional condition is added where stimuli are presented in both visual fields. In this condition one of the stimuli is effectively redundant, hence its name. Despite the redundancy of this extra stimulus, reaction times are often faster under such conditions. This is attributed to the recruitment of both hemispheres and the communication between them. In order to validate this methodology, the redundant target paradigm has been tested on split brain patients. Given that these patients do not have an intact corpus callosum and so are not able to easily pass information between the hemispheres, they should have much longer reaction times to redundant target stimuli. This is exactly what has been shown by Corballis (1998). This supports the idea that the faster reaction times in non-clinical participants are the result of interhemispheric transfer of information.

The other test used is the within versus across paradigm (see Fig. 9.10). In this test, participants are presented with two stimuli at the top of the screen, one in each visual field. A third stimulus is also presented at the bottom of the screen, again in

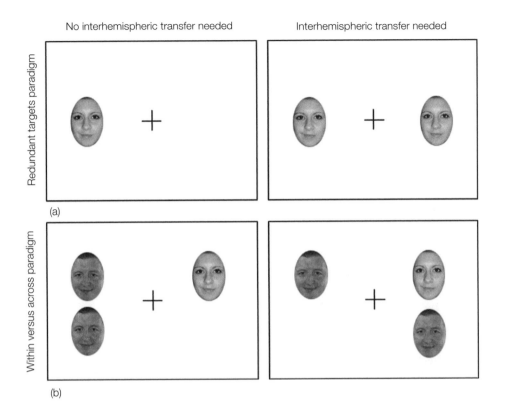

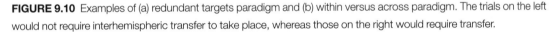

FIGURE 9.10 Examples of (a) redundant targets paradigm and (b) within versus across paradigm. The trials on the left would not require interhemispheric transfer to take place, whereas those on the right would require transfer.

one visual field or the other. The participants' task is to decide whether the stimulus at the bottom is the same as *either* of the two at the top. When the two matching stimuli are presented *within* the same visual field, all of the processing can take place within the same hemisphere. However, when the matching stimuli are presented *across* the two hemispheres, interhemispheric transfer is necessary to complete the task.

Compton (2002) was the first to examine interhemispheric transfer for face processing using the within versus across paradigm. She found an across-hemisphere advantage for processing both facial identity and facial emotion. A more recent study by Compton et al (2005) showed that this across-hemisphere advantage was present only when processing emotive faces (happy and angry faces), but not when processing neutral faces. They

suggested that this was because interhemispheric transfer occurs to aid the processing of complex, but not simple, stimuli. This has also been shown using the within versus across paradigm with non-face stimuli (Weissman and Banich, 2000).

Interhemispheric transfer to aid the processing of emotions has also been shown using the redundant targets effect for both simple emotions (happiness and fear; Tamietto et al, 2006) and more complex emotions (flirting and arrogance; Tamietto et al, 2007). Tamietto et al (2006) raised the possibility that the redundant targets effect may occur due to an image matching advantage, rather than being anything to do with emotion processing specifically. To address this problem, when presenting stimuli in the redundant targets condition they presented either the same two images or images of two different people, one male and one female, who were expressing the same emotion. They found that the size of the redundant targets effect did not change in the second condition. This suggests that the effect arises from the processing of the emotion expressed, rather than because the two images are the same.

Schweinberger et al (2003) used the redundant targets effect to examine interhemispheric transfer for processing of both facial identity and facial emotion. They found an interhemispheric advantage for the processing of familiar (famous) faces, but not for processing of unfamiliar faces or facial emotion. They suggest that this pattern of results occurs because groups of cells (transcortical cell assemblies; Pulvermüller and Mohr, 1996) are formed in the brain, each of which represents people that we know. These cell assemblies are spread across both hemispheres, although they may be distributed asymmetrically, with more in the right hemisphere than in the left. Because we do not have these cell assemblies for unknown people or for perceiving facial emotion that can be expressed by any face, familiar or unfamiliar, the interhemispheric effect is found for familiar face recognition only.

Interhemispheric repetition priming has also been used to examine the role of interhemispheric transfer in face processing. Bourne and Hole (2006) presented faces to either the left or right visual field and asked participants to decide whether or not they were familiar (famous). Participants then saw the same faces a second time and had to repeat the familiarity task. This is known as repetition priming; participants are usually faster in the second trial (see Chapter 1 for an explanation of why this occurs). In this experiment the second face was repeated in either the same visual field (within hemisphere) or the opposite visual field (across hemispheres). In the latter condition, if any priming occurred it would have had to have

been via interhemispheric transfer. There were two primary findings from this experiment. First, interhemispheric effects were found only when recognizing familiar faces, supporting the findings of Schweinberger et al (2003). Second, the interhemispheric priming effect was found to be asymmetrical: more priming occurred from the right to the left hemisphere than from the left to the right. One interpretation of these results is that the 'dominant' right hemisphere helps out the 'less able' left hemisphere when the latter needs to recognize a familiar face. However, the right hemisphere can achieve recognition by itself, quite effectively, without any assistance from the left hemisphere.

9.5 Face adaptation effects

After-effects are ubiquitous in visual processing.[5] Probably the best known is the 'movement after-effect': if you look at motion in one direction for 30 seconds or so and then look at a stationary surface, it appears to move in the opposite direction. Another example is the 'tilt after-effect': staring at a line tilted in one direction makes an upright line appear to be tilted in the opposite direction. Research on after-effects has a very long tradition in psychology, mostly in connection with the low-level processing of basic visual properties such as colour, motion and orientation. However, in recent years it has become apparent that adaptation can occur at a relatively high level as well (for a review see Clifford and Rhodes, 2005). In particular, there have now been many demonstrations that prolonged exposure to a face can alter the perception of that face and others.

---

[5] To see both of the illusions described here, and others, go to http://www.viperlib.com.

9.5.1 **Methods used to study face adaptation effects**

Most of the research on **face adaptation effects** has used one of four basic methods. The first, devised by Webster and MacLin (1999), demonstrates that face perception is subject to 'figural after-effects': after prolonged exposure

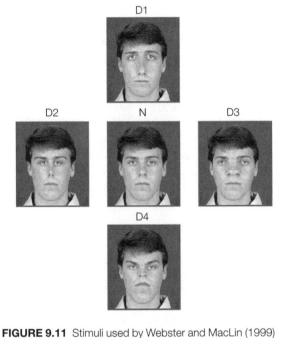

FIGURE 9.11 Stimuli used by Webster and MacLin (1999) to produce 'figural after-effects'. Staring for a few seconds at one of the distorted images (D1–D4) biases perception of the neutral face (N) and any of the other distorted faces

to a grossly distorted face in which the internal features are contracted or expanded, a normal face appears to be distorted in the opposite direction (Fig. 9.11). This type of after-effect generalizes to test faces of individuals other than the one used in the adaptation phase, and hence appears to be largely independent of the identity of the adapting face (Robbins et al, 2007; Webster and MacLin, 1999; Yamashita et al, 2005).

The second technique originates from Fang and He (2005), who showed that exposure to faces oriented at 30 degrees to the left or right caused frontal and near-frontal views of faces to be misperceived as facing in the opposite direction to the adapting face (Fig. 9.12). As with figural after-effects, Fang et al (2007) showed that adaptation still occurred when the adapting and test faces were different individuals (as long as they were not too dissimilar) or if they were of different genders. The effects even transferred between upright and inverted faces, although after-effects were much weaker in these circumstances.

The third technique, devised by Leopold et al (2001), measures the effects of adaptation on the perception of facial identity (see Chapter 1, Fig. 1.8). Leopold et al's procedure was outlined in Chapter 1, in connection with a discussion of Valentine's (1991) 'multidimensional face space' model. Essentially, adaptation to one

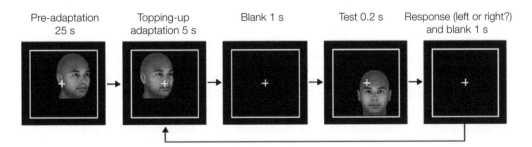

Pre-adaptation 25 s Topping-up adaptation 5 s Blank 1 s Test 0.2 s Response (left or right?) and blank 1 s

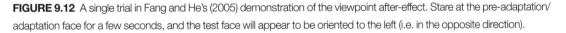

FIGURE 9.12 A single trial in Fang and He's (2005) demonstration of the viewpoint after-effect. Stare at the pre-adaptation/adaptation face for a few seconds, and the test face will appear to be oriented to the left (i.e. in the opposite direction).

identity in face space enhances sensitivity to its complementary 'anti-face'[6] (its opposite, on all of the dimensions used to construct the face space), while leaving other faces unaffected.

A fourth method involves looking at the effects of adaptation on the perception of ambiguous 'morphs' (blends) between two different types of face. This technique has been used to investigate not only identity-specific adaptation, but also the perception of categorical facial attributes such as race and gender. This method is illustrated by Furl et al's (2007) study of adaptation effects on identity and expression perception. Part of their procedure involved adapting participants to a picture of 'Bob' or 'Jim', and then showing them a series of morphs that contained varying proportions of these two faces. Following adaptation to Bob, the morphs that were a mixture of the two faces tended to look more like Jim, and vice versa (Fig. 9.13).

Although the after-effects produced by these four methods have much in common, they are not necessarily always affecting the same neural mechanisms. In the following discussion, if we use the term 'after-effects', you can assume that whatever we are talking about has been found with all four techniques. If we are talking about something that has been found with only one of the methods, we'll refer to that technique in more specific terms.

9.5.2 What can face adaptation effects tell us about face processing?

Face after-effects are thought to reflect selective fatigue of the neurophysiological systems that are involved in face processing. Robbins et al (2007) discuss the issue of underlying mechanisms at length. They conclude that a relatively simple 'opponent-process' model, as has been used to explain many other after-effects, can

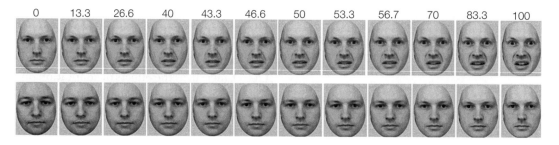

FIGURE 9.13 Top row: morphs between 'neutral Jim' and 'fearful Jim'. Bottom row: morphs between 'Bob' and 'Jim'. The numbers represent the proportion of the right-most face in each of the images to its left. Adaptation to the face at the end of either row will change the appearance of the ambiguous morphs in the middle of that row. Stare at 'Bob' for a few seconds, and the morphs in the middle will look more like 'Jim'. Stare at 'Jim', and the same morphs will look more like 'Bob'. (Adapted from Furl et al, 2007)

---

[6] Don't get confused between 'anti-faces' and the 'anti-caricatures' mentioned in Chapter 1. The best way to think of these two types of face is in terms of Valentine's 'multidimensional face space' model. A given face ('Bob') occupies a particular location in face space. Bob differs from the average (norm) face in terms of various physical measurements. An anti-caricature is a face that occupies a point somewhere on a line between the norm and Bob: it is just a version of Bob that has less of whatever makes Bob look like Bob. In contrast, an anti-face is the *opposite* of Bob in all important respects: it is a face that occupies a point on the opposite side of face space to Bob. It is as if you extended the line that connects Bob and his anti-caricatures to the norm, through the norm and off on to the other side of face space. Thus, Bob might have a long, broad nose. His anti-caricatures have thinner, shorter noses that are closer to the average nose for width and length. Bob's anti-face has a wide, short nose (i.e. the complete opposite of Bob's).

accommodate most of the findings on face after-effects. Figure 9.14 shows the basic idea, using eye height as an example. There are two pools of neurones: 'pool 1' neurones respond to deviations below the norm (i.e. to faces with below-average eye height) and 'pool 2' neurones respond to deviations above the norm (i.e. to faces with above-average eye height). The *appearance* of the face's eye height is determined by the relative activity in these two sets of neurones. In the absence of adaptation, a face with objectively average eye height stimulates both sets of neurones equally, and is perceived as being 'average' or 'normal' in eye height (as in Fig. 9.14a).

Exposure to a face with above-average eye height will strongly stimulate pool 2, but not pool 1. If the exposure is prolonged, eventually the neurones in pool 2 will become fatigued, and hence temporarily less responsive. However, the neurones in pool 1 have not been stimulated, and so they are not fatigued. The effect of the adaptation is to alter the balance of activity between the two pools of neurones. The 'norm', or midpoint on this

particular facial attribute, is shifted away from its usual position. The perceptual consequence of adaptation is that faces look as if their eyes are lower than they appeared before. If participants are asked to decide which of a range of faces has average eye height, they will now reject the pre-adaptation average, because its eyes now appear to be too low. Instead they will choose as the 'average' a face whose eye height is actually *above* average (as in Fig. 9.14b). The opposite holds true for adaptation to a face with below-average eye height: this will make all faces' eye heights seem higher than they really are. Consequently, the eye height of the original average face will now appear to be too high, and the perceived midpoint will be shifted downwards so that a face has to have objectively below-average eye height in order for it to be perceived as 'normal'. Robbins et al suggest that there are many such pairs of pools of neurones, each pair representing a particular facial attribute.

An important issue is whether face adaptation effects reflect the fatiguing of mechanisms that are truly related to face processing, or whether they are

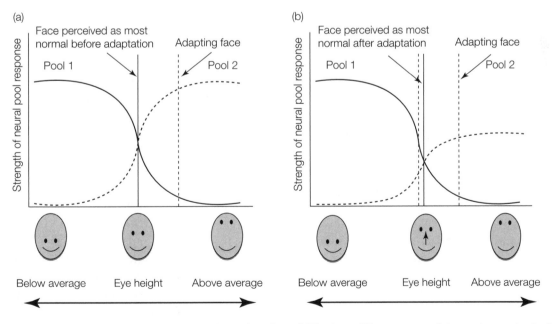

FIGURE 9.14 An 'opponent-process' explanation of face after-effects. (a) The 'normal' face corresponds to equal amounts of activity in neurone pools 1 and 2. (b) Adaptation reduces activity in pool 2, leading to an upwards shift of the midpoint. Now eyes have to be higher in order to appear 'normal', so the eyes in the original average face appear to be too low. (After Robbins et al, 2007)

due to selective fatigue of lower-level mechanisms involved in processing various aspects of the retinal image, such as edges and texture. If face adaptation effects are merely due to low-level adaptation, we would expect them to be tied fairly closely to the characteristics of the adapting stimulus, in terms of features such as retinal location, size and orientation. It is unfortunate that many studies have used identical images in the adaptation and test phases, because this makes it more difficult to rule out the contribution of low-level adaptation to physical properties of the picture (see Chapter 1, section 1.1.1, for detailed criticisms of this practice in face research generally). Nevertheless, there seems to be good evidence that face adaptation effects involve more than just the adaptation of low-level processes. It is true that face after-effects are linked to retinal location to some extent, as simultaneous but opposing figural after-effects can be produced by presenting a stretched face and a contracted face side by side during the adaptation phase. At test, a normal face that is in the same location as the stretched face appears contracted, while, at the same time, a normal face that is in the same location as the contracted face appears stretched (Webster and MacLin, 1999). However, identity-specific after-effects can still be found even when the adapting and test stimuli are presented to different retinal locations, separated by up to 6 degrees (Leopold et al, 2001; but see Afraz and Cavanagh [2008] for some qualifications to this statement).

Further evidence that face adaptation effects are not due solely to low-level adaptation comes from studies demonstrating that they can occur despite large differences in the retinal size of the adapting and test images (e.g. Anderson and Wilson, 2005; Leopold et al, 2001; Rhodes et al, 2004b; Yamashita et al, 2005; Zhao and Chubb, 2001). After-effects also transfer across changes in orientation, both in the picture plane (Leopold et al, 2001; Rhodes et al, 2003; Watson and Clifford, 2003) and in depth (Jeffery et al, 2006; Jiang et al, 2006, 2007). Yamashita et al (2005) looked at how Webster and MacLin's figural after-effect was affected by various differences between the test and adapting stimuli in terms of their physical properties. Manipulations that are known to affect the recognizability of faces (such as photographic negation or mismatches in spatial frequency content) had more influence on the size of the figural after-effect than manipulations that have little effect on face recognition (such as changes in image size, colour or contrast).

All of these manipulations attenuate the magnitude of the after-effects obtained, but do not eliminate them entirely. The implication is that, although face after-effects are probably the net outcome of changes in sensitivity at a number of different levels in the visual system (Robbins et al, 2007; Watson and Clifford, 2003), there is at least some involvement of high-level processes related to face processing.

Adaptation effects provide a useful tool for investigating the neural underpinnings of face processing in humans, confirming and extending many of the findings from more traditional behavioural studies. For example, the issue of view dependence has been addressed (see Chapter 2 for an extended discussion of this topic). Single-cell recording techniques have shown that monkey inferotemporal cortex contains both view-specific and view-independent face-selective neurones. Studies of face viewpoint after-effects suggest that the same is true of humans. As mentioned above, Fang and He (2005) found evidence of viewpoint-dependent face-specific adaptation, implying the existence of view-dependent neurones in humans. However, although both figural after-effects (Jeffery et al, 2006) and identity after-effects (Jiang et al, 2006, 2007) are strongest when the adapting and test faces show identical views, they are still found with different views, albeit reduced in magnitude. This implies that there is some degree of viewpoint independence. Or, looking it another way, at least some of the cells that respond to facial viewpoint are also sensitive to facial structure (and hence identity) to some extent (Fang et al, 2007).

Ryu and Chaudhuri (2006) looked at the effects of face familiarity on Fang and He's (2005) viewpoint after-effect. They familiarized participants with four faces, by presenting them 36 times in various orientations and providing fictional semantic information for them (such as name and occupation). They compared the viewpoint after-effects for these faces with those produced by wholly unfamiliar faces, and found an interesting effect of familiarity. When adapting and test faces were views of the *same* identity, familiarization with the faces made no difference: similar viewpoint after-effects were obtained for both familiar and unfamiliar faces. However, if the adapting and test faces were views of different identities, a viewpoint after-effect was obtained for unfamiliar faces but not for familiar faces. In other words, adaptation to one familiar face in a specific viewpoint does *not* produce an after-effect if the test image is of a different familiar face. Ryu and Chaudhuri's explanation for this result is rather speculative; they suggest that when the test face is a different familiar face to the adapting face it activates semantic information associated with itself, and this interferes with the processing of the viewpoint information. Whatever the explanation turns out to be, it shows the necessity to distinguish between familiar and unfamiliar face processing when talking about after-effects.

Adaptation effects have also been used to investigate the perceptual categorization of faces on various dimensions other than identity. For example, the apparent gender of an ambiguous morph between a male and a female face is affected by prolonged exposure to either of the faces that contributed to the morph: following exposure to the male face, the morph looks more female, and vice versa (Webster et al, 2004). Using this method, similar biases can be produced for race (e.g. whether an ambiguous morph appears to be Japanese or Caucasian) and emotional expression (Fox and Barton, 2007; Furl et al, 2007; Webster et al, 2004). These effects are strongest when the adapting face is the same as one of the

faces in the ambiguous morph that is presented in the test phase; however, they still occur to some extent even when the adapting and test faces are from different individuals (Barrett and O'Toole, 2009; Butler et al, 2008; Fox and Barton, 2007; Webster et al, 2004).

Barrett and O'Toole (2009) showed their participants a set of morphs between a pair of male and female faces that were ambiguous in terms of gender, and asked them to decide whether each one was male or female. If participants had previously been adapted to a male face, the morphs tended to look more female, and vice versa. Comparable effects were obtained when the procedure was used with adult or child faces. These after-effects were due to gender adaptation rather than adaptation to the specific faces that were shown, as the male and female faces used in the adapting stimuli were different to the ones used to produce the morphs. Furthermore, similar effects were obtained when the adapting stimuli were adult male and female faces but the test morphs were children's faces. (Adaptation to male and female children's faces also significantly affected the apparent gender of adult faces, although this effect was weaker.) Barrett and O'Toole's results imply that adaptation was occurring to some aspect of gender that is common to the faces of children and adults, even though they are physically dissimilar in many ways. However, the asymmetry in the cross-age adaptation results suggests that the after-effects were not based simply on the physical properties of the children's and adults' faces, but were affected by the greater *salience* of the gender information in the adult adapting stimuli, given that the gender of children's faces is harder to determine (Wild et al, 2000).

'Category-contingent' face after-effects are an intriguing phenomenon. Simultaneous but opposite figural after-effects can be produced in a set of faces, depending on how they are categorized. For example, following simultaneous adaptation to a male face with increased eye-spacing and a female face with decreased eye-spacing, male faces appear to have decreased eye-spacing and female faces appear to have increased eye-spacing (e.g. Little et al, 2005). After adaptation to upright male faces and inverted female faces, an androgynous face appears female when upright and male when inverted (Rhodes, 2004b). Bestelmeyer and colleagues (2008) measured category-contingent after-effects using male, female and 'hyper-female' faces. The latter looked female, but in structural terms were as different from the female faces as they were from the male faces. Adaptation to male faces did not transfer to female or hyper-female faces, whereas adaptation to female faces transferred to hyper-female faces. This pattern of results suggests that adaptation effects were determined by the perceptual categorization of the face (i.e. whether it looked male or female) rather than by the face's structural properties.

Similar effects have been obtained with other facial categories. For example, Little et al (2008a) have demonstrated category-contingent figural after-effects for race (European versus African), age (adult versus infant faces) and species (human versus monkey). Jaquet et al (2008) showed that simultaneous adaptation to Caucasian and Chinese faces that were distorted in opposite directions resulted in opposing figural after-effects; for example, after simultaneously viewing expanded Caucasian and contracted Chinese faces, the Caucasian faces looked contracted and the Chinese faces looked expanded. As mentioned in Chapter 1, in connection with the discussion of Valentine's 'multidimensional face space' model of face representations, research on adaptation effects in general is consistent with the idea that faces are represented with respect to 'norms' or 'prototypes'. It has been argued that category-contingent after-effects show that there might be separate face spaces, and separate prototypes, for each of the categories concerned (Byatt and Rhodes, 1998; Jaquet et al, 2008; Little et al, 2005). Thus, there might be one face space (and norm) for male faces, and a separate one for females; one face space for

own-race faces, and another for other-race faces; and so on.

Bestelmeyer and colleagues (2009) used category-contingent after-effects as a way of testing Bruce and Young's (1986) claim that expression and gender were processed independently of each other (see Chapter 1, section 1.1.3). Participants were adapted with ten angry faces of one sex and ten fearful faces of the other sex. They were then shown two intermixed sets of morphs, and asked to judge the expression of each morph. One of the sets consisted of morphs between angry and fearful composite male faces, and the other consisted of morphs between angry and fearful composite female faces. Adaptation to angry male faces and fearful female faces made the male morphs look less angry and more fearful, and the female morphs look more angry and less fearful. Adaptation to angry female faces and fearful male faces produced the opposite effects. Thus, expression perception seems to be influenced by a face's gender.

Bestelmeyer et al used the same technique with different-race faces, rather than different genders, and obtained race-contingent expression after-effects; for example, exposure to African angry faces and East Asian fearful faces caused African morph faces to look less angry and more fearful, and East Asian morph faces to look more angry and less fearful. Processing of expression and race seem to be interdependent too. Bestelemeyer et al suggest more work is needed to decide whether these interactions between expression, race and gender occur because all three share some common neural basis, or whether they are processed by distinct, specialized neural systems that nevertheless can interact with one another under some circumstances.

Although studies of face after-effects have already provided a wealth of information about face processing, most of this information has been about the nature of the processing of *unfamiliar* faces. In almost all adaptation studies to date, participants have been either wholly unfamiliar with the faces used, or they have been familiarized with them during the course of the experiment. There are virtually no studies of adaptation effects using real faces that are truly familiar to the participants. This is a serious limitation given that we know there are important differences between familiar and unfamiliar face processing. As mentioned in Chapter 2, even relatively brief periods of familiarization with faces can increase the strength of identity after-effects and increase the extent to which they generalize across viewpoints (Jiang et al, 2007), and we saw earlier how familiarization affected Fang and He's (2005) face viewpoint effect (Ryu and Chaudhuri, 2006). To our knowledge, only one study has used truly familiar faces. Carbon et al (2007) used the Webster and MacLin paradigm with celebrity faces. Adaptation to a set of distorted familiar faces affected the subsequent appearance of undistorted versions of either the same or different images of those celebrities, but did not affect the appearance of unfamiliar faces that had not been seen in the adaptation phase. Interestingly, these identity-specific after-effects were still detectable 24 hours later.

We have explained how adaptation effects might work. They imply that faces are represented in a contrastive fashion. 'Opponent processes' such as this are found throughout the visual system. Why is face perception based on such an apparently unreliable mechanism? There are various possibilities. One is that after-effects are epiphenomenal: they are just a byproduct of the way in which we happen to represent faces in the brain, that is convenient for researchers but otherwise serves no real function. Ordinarily they would not occur, firstly because we would not be staring at an immobile face for an extended period of time and, secondly, because in everyday life faces are so distinct from one another that any small adaptation effects would go unnoticed. A more interesting possibility is that after-effects in general (not just those involving faces) might function to keep the visual system optimally calibrated (Clifford and Rhodes, 2005; Rhodes et al, 2003). For example, if faces were encoded with respect to a 'norm' or 'average' face, it might be advantageous to keep that norm continually updated and fine-tuned so that it is optimized for the population of faces with which it habitually comes into contact.

9.6 How do hormones influence face processing?

Psychoneuroendocrinology (possibly the longest word in this book!) is the study of how **hormones** influence our brain and behaviours. In recent years there has been an increasing amount of attention given to the effect of hormones on our ability to process faces and the neuropsychology underlying these abilities. Although some of this work directly measures levels of hormones in saliva, much of it has used more indirect estimates of fluctuations in levels of hormones.

One of the most frequently used methods in this area is to examine how face perception changes across the menstrual cycle. The menstrual cycle consists of four phases, and levels of oestrogen and progesterone vary within each of these (Fig. 9.15). By comparing performance at different times in the menstrual cycle, it is possible to see how levels of oestrogen and progesterone can influence face perception. The effects of these hormones have also been assessed by examining the effects of taking these hormones artificially, such as in the oral contraceptive pill or in hormone replacement therapy (HRT).

The work examining menstrual cycle effects considers how changes in the 'female' hormones may influence face perception; however, the 'male' hormone, testosterone, has also been examined using other methods. The relative length between the second and fourth fingers, the 2D:4D ratio,

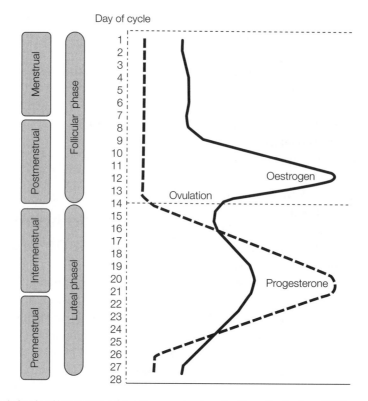

FIGURE 9.15 Changes in levels of hormones across the menstrual cycle. (From Darlington, 2002)

provides a behavioural estimator of prenatal testosterone exposure. A low 2D:4D ratio (less than 1), where the index finger is shorter than the ring finger, indicates higher levels of prenatal testosterone and a more masculine 2D:4D ratio. In contrast, the index and ring fingers being of comparable length, or the ring finger being shorter than the index finger, indicates lower levels of prenatal testosterone and a more feminine 2D:4D ratio (equal to or greater than 1). The relationship between prenatal hormonal exposure and 2D:4D ratio has been shown through the measurement of hormone levels in the amniotic fluid and measurement of 2D:4D ratios later in life (Lutchmaya et al, 2004; Manning et al, 1998). Artificially increased levels of testosterone administered prenatally in rats have also been found to lead to lower 2D:4D ratios (Talarovičová et al, 2009).

9.6.1 Hormonal influences on facial attractiveness

The majority of the work in this area has looked at women's preferences for facial masculinity across the menstrual cycle (also see Chapter 4 for more information about how hormones influence the perception of attractiveness). In these studies women are shown male faces that have been manipulated to look either more or less masculine. A number of studies have shown that during the follicular phase, just prior to ovulation and when oestrogen levels peak, women prefer masculine male faces (Johnston et al, 2001; Penton-Voak and Perrett, 2000). This effect has been shown even after controlling for the perceived attractiveness of the male stimuli (Jones et al, 2005a) and has been shown only for women who are in a relationship (Little et al, 2008b). One problem with menstrual cycle studies is that it is difficult to disentangle the effects of the different hormones. One study (Welling et al, 2008) addressed this by measuring levels of hormones in women's saliva and then testing their preferences for masculine faces at two time points: once when testosterone was high and again when testosterone was low. At both time points, levels of oestrogen and progesterone were constant; thus, any differences can be related directly to the differing levels of testosterone. Welling et al found that, when levels of testosterone were higher, women preferred more masculine faces.

In addition to women preferring more masculine faces in the follicular phase of the menstrual cycle, they have also been found to prefer more masculine bodies (but only for rating the men for possible short-term relationships: Little et al, 2007a), taller males (Pawlowski and Jasienska, 2005) and more masculine voices (Feinberg et al, 2006). Women also prefer more symmetrical faces when fertility is at a peak, although, again, only for judgements of short-term relationships (Little et al, 2007b). Women's perception of facial emotion has also been found to be more accurate during the follicular phase (Derntl et al, 2008; Pearson and Lewis, 2005; Wirth and Schultheiss, 2007).

A relationship between face perception and hormones has also been found for males. In a study that measured levels of testosterone in participants' saliva, Welling et al (2008) found that men were more attracted to more feminine faces when testosterone levels were high. Another study artificially manipulated hormonal levels by means of inhalation and found that men perceived male faces as more masculine after inhaling testosterone, but not after inhaling oestrogen (Kovacs et al, 2004). It therefore seems that hormonal fluctuations can influence face perception in both men and women. Indeed, differences in face perception across the menstrual cycle have even been reported in rhesus monkeys (Gasbarri et al, 2008; Lacreuse et al, 2007).

In addition to hormonal influences on how we perceive faces, it has been shown that hormones are implicated in our own facial characteristics. Penton-Voak and Chen (2004) measured the levels of testosterone in the saliva of men and then created separate composites of those with higher and lower levels of testosterone (Fig. 9.16). They found that the high testosterone composite was rated as more masculine than the low testosterone composite. This suggests that men with higher levels of testosterone have more masculine facial characteristics.

Two studies have examined the relationship between 2D:4D ratios and facial characteristics. One found that more feminine 2D:4D ratios were associated with more feminine facial characteristics, but only in women (Burriss et al, 2007). The other examined the relationship between the 2D:4D ratio and facial asymmetry (Fink et al, 2004), and found that a more masculine 2D:4D ratio was associated with greater facial asymmetry in males, whereas a more feminine 2D:4D ratio was associated with greater facial asymmetry in females. Such findings suggest that hormones not only influence the way in which we perceive faces, but also the actual appearance of our own faces.

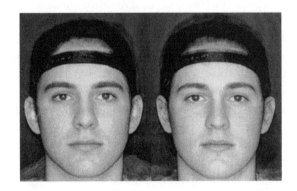

FIGURE 9.16 Composite images of men with higher (left) and lower (right) levels of testosterone. (From Penton-Voak and Chen, 2004)

9.6.2 **Hormonal influences on the neuropsychological processing of faces**

As well as influencing our perception of faces, hormones have been implicated in the neuropsychological processes underpinning face perception. This work has primarily examined variability in lateralization in relation to hormonal exposure. Geschwind and Galaburda (1985) suggested that prenatal testosterone exposure causes the right hemisphere to develop faster than the left hemisphere. This theory can account for why males tend to be more strongly lateralized for face processing (Bourne, 2005, 2008) as well as other right-hemisphere lateralized tasks such as mental rotation (e.g. Johnson et al, 2002) and perception of geometric illusions (Rasmjou et al, 1999).

Again, much of the research in this area has examined differences across the menstrual cycle. Hausmann and Güntürkün (2000) presented faces to either the left or the right visual field. Participants had to decide whether the faces were unmanipulated or whether they had their features distorted and mis-located to create 'monster' faces. They found stronger patterns of right-hemisphere superiority for this task during menstruation than during the follicular stage. Hausmann and Güntürkün suggested that this may occur due to changes in the ability of the non-dominant left hemisphere, leading to more symmetrical patterns of lateralization during the follicular stage. Subsequently they have suggested that the reduced lateralization may actually reflect a decrease in interhemispheric transfer due to increased levels of progesterone (Hausmann, 2005; Hausmann and Güntürkün, 2000; Hausmann et al, 2002).

Bayer and Erdmann (2008) used a divided visual field face decision task to compare patterns of lateralization in three groups of women: those taking oestrogen-only HRT; those taking a combined oestrogen–progesterone HRT; and those not taking HRT. They found the expected right-hemisphere advantage across all groups; however, it was reduced in the oestrogen-only group. The effect of prenatal hormonal exposure, by measurement of the 2D:4D ratio, on lateralization for processing facial emotion has also been examined. Bourne and Gray (2009) used the chimeric faces test (see the methodological appendix and Chapter 3, section 3.5.1 for full details of this test) and found that, for both happy and angry facial emotion, women with lower, more masculine, 2D:4D ratios were more strongly lateralized. This finding fits well with the Geschwind and Galaburda theory that prenatal testosterone is associated with development of cerebral lateralization.

One study has used fMRI further to examine differences in the neuropsychological processing of faces across the menstrual cycle. Rupp et al (2009) asked women to look at a series of male faces to decide whether they could be potential sexual partners. During the follicular phase, in comparison to the luteal phase, activity was increased in the right medial orbitofrontal cortex (Fig. 9.17/Plate 9.17). Rupp et al also ran a non-face condition where participants saw images of houses and decided whether they would rent the house to live in. The activation found was specific to the face task. This neuroimaging study provides strong support for changes in the way in which faces are processed in the brain across the menstrual cycle.

9.7 **Conclusion**

This chapter has reviewed evidence from a variety of sources that have examined the neuropsychology of face processing. One key issue now is to consider these sources in combination. Each method has its own advantages and disadvantages, so it is important to draw evidence from a range of methodologies when attempting to

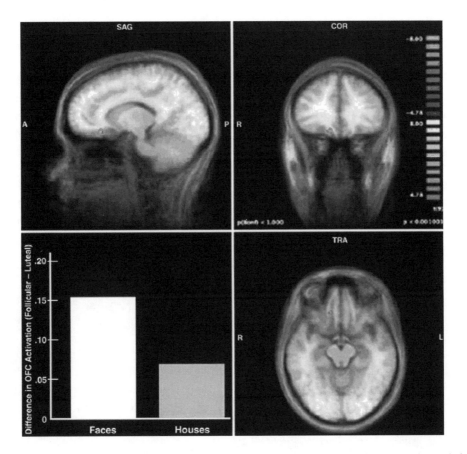

FIGURE 9.17 Patterns of activation unique to the follicular phase of the menstrual cycle whilst processing male faces. (From Rupp et al, 2009). Please see colour plate section.

summarize how faces are processed in the brain. To achieve this, we also need to look outside this chapter and consider the evidence that we discussed in Chapter 7 about impairments to face processing following brain damage.

All sources suggest that face processing is bilaterally distributed but that the right hemisphere is dominant or superior. Prosopagnosia is most common following bilateral brain lesions, and evidence from divided visual field, ERP, MEG and fMRI studies all support this bilateral but asymmetrical distribution of face-processing abilities. There is also consistent evidence across all sources for making a distinction between configural and featural facial

information, and for suggesting that these types of information are differentially lateralized. The evidence from both clinical and non-clinical participants is also consistent with the early incarnations of models of face processing, such as that of Bruce and Young (1986). Evidence supports the sequential nature of face processing, with structural encoding feeding into face recognition and this then being followed by the wider processing of semantic and name information.

One area where the evidence is inconsistent concerns the post-recognition processing of the semantic or biographical information associated with familiar people. The evidence from individuals who have suffered brain damage suggests that this is handled by left hemisphere mechanisms, whereas the studies discussed in this chapter have suggested that a wide range of sites is involved, distributed across both hemispheres. It is likely that the lack of clarity on this area stems from two sources. First, semantic information is not associated exclusively with faces; it is also linked with the individual's name and their voice. Consequently the findings differ according to whether participants are presented with faces, names or voices. Second, there is a wide range of types of semantic information, which may also include names. Semantic information may be the job that someone has, or their favourite food or band. It may also be considered in terms of the semantic associations between individuals (e.g. being married or related). Other research has examined visually derived semantic information, such as sex, race, attractiveness or personality. As well as semantic information being incredibly multifaceted, it is also likely that different aspects interact with one another. Hopefully, over the next few years, the research in this area will be able to tease apart all of these various aspects to further our understanding of the neuropsychology of face processing.

SUMMARY

- Divided visual field studies have shown that both hemispheres are able to process faces, but that the right hemisphere is more specialized for this than the left hemisphere. These studies have also suggested that each hemisphere makes a distinctive contribution to the processing of facial information, with the right hemisphere being specialized for processing configural information and the left for processing featural information.

- ERP studies have told us a great deal about the time course of face processing in the brain and have given us some information about its location. Activity occurs as early as 100 ms after viewing a face (P100). Structural encoding starts at around 170 ms (N170), recognition at 250 ms (N250) and the retrieval of semantic or name information by 400 ms (N400). In terms of localization, the ERP evidence also supports face processing as a bilateral, although more rightwards, processing system in the occipitotemporal region.

- The fMRI evidence suggests a distributed network of activation across the brain, again with more right than left hemisphere activation. The structural encoding of a face is localized to the inferior occipital gyri (or occipital face area). Recognition via invariant facial information occurs in the fusiform gyrus (or fusiform face area), and the wider variant information is processed across a number of brain regions.

- Prolonged exposure to a face affects the subsequent appearance of that face (and others too, depending on the particular adaptation technique that is used). These face adaptation after-effects are a useful tool for investigating the neural representations of faces in normal individuals. In particular they can be used to examine how the brain categorizes faces on the basis of identity, gender, race and other dimensions.

- Interhemispheric transfer has been found for the processing of emotional expression and familiar face recognition.

- Fluctuations in hormonal levels have been associated with both the behavioural perception of faces and the neuropsychological mechanisms underpinning face processing. It is suggested that the changes across the menstrual cycle occur to maximize the chances of conception.

FURTHER READING

Clifford, C. W. G. and Rhodes, G. (eds) (2005). *Fitting the Mind to the World: Adaptation and Aftereffects in High-level Vision.* Oxford: Oxford University Press. This is a collection of papers on high-level adaptation effects, mainly but not exclusively involving faces. The overriding theme of the book is how adaptation might function constantly to 'fine-tune' and calibrate the visual system at all levels.

Dekowska, M., Kuniecki, M. and Jaskowski, P. (2008). *Facing facts: neuronal mechanisms of face perception.* Acta Neurobiologiae Experimentalis, 68(2): 229–252. A good and easy-to-read review article that covers both electrophysiological and fMRI evidence.

Gobbini, M. I. and Haxby, J. V. (2007). *Neural systems for recognition of familiar faces.* Neuropsychologia, 45(1): 32–41. This is the updated version of the Haxby model. Much work was done between 2000 and 2007 using fMRI to examine face processing; this updated model integrates this information to develop the model further. Another interesting development is that this version of the model places more emphasis on social interaction and its implications for face processing.

Haxby, J. V., Hoffman, E. A. and Gobbini, M. I. (2000). *The distributed human neural system for face perception.* Trends in Cognitive Science, 4(6): 223–233. The Haxby neural model of face processing is the primary current model of the neuropsychological processes underlying face perception. This paper gives a detailed explanation of the model and the evidence used to form and support it.

Jones, B. C., DeBruine, L. M., Perrett, D. I., et al. (2008). *Effects of menstrual cycle phase on face preferences.* Archives of Sexual Behavior, 37(1): 78–84. This is a really clear review which not only outlines the research on hormones and face processing, but also discusses why these variations might occur.

ARE FACES SPECIAL?

One of the most widely debated questions in the field of face processing is: are faces special? On one side of this argument, people have claimed that faces are special: that we process faces in a different way from other forms of information; that we use special areas of the brain to achieve this; and that this ability is innate. On the other side, people have argued that there is nothing special about our processing of faces. They claim that we use the same processes and parts of our brain to process faces as we do to process objects, or even language. The argument for faces being special envisages face processing as being **domain-specific**, so the processes and mechanisms used are specific to faces. The argument against faces being special considers face processing as being **domain-general**, so the processes and mechanisms used are general purpose and used to process a range of stimuli. Although this issue has been widely (and heatedly!) argued for a long time, we still do not really know whether or not faces are special. In this chapter we will examine evidence from a variety of sources in an attempt to address this issue.

10.1 **What can we learn from psychological studies?**

Before launching straight into whether there is a particular part of the brain that is specialized for processing faces, we will first consider whether the psychological processing of faces is comparable to the processing of other stimuli. Generally, there is lots of support for faces being processed in a different way to **objects**. As we saw in Chapter 2, there is a great deal of evidence for faces being processed primarily according to the configural information contained within them. In contrast, non-face stimuli tend to be processed more on the basis of their featural attributes. This evidence will be briefly summarized here before considering how it may address the question of whether faces are special. For detailed information about this area of work, refer back to Chapter 2, section 2.4.

Yin (1969) was one of the first to examine the effects of inversion on the ability to process a range of stimuli. He gave participants a recognition task in which they were presented with faces, houses, aeroplanes or stick men figures in either an upright or an inverted orientation. Yin found that each category of stimuli was impaired by inversion; however, inversion reduced face recognition accuracy by 30%, whereas it reduced accuracy for non-face stimuli by only 10%. In his experiments, Yin (1969) obtained verbal feedback from his participants which suggested they used differing strategies to complete the face recognition task. Participants claimed to use holistic, or configural, strategies in the upright face condition, in order 'to get a general impression of the whole picture' (p. 145). In the inverted face condition, and for each type of non-face stimulus in both orientations, participants reported that they used a more feature-based strategy, typically searching for individual distinguishing features.

On the basis of the feedback he received, Yin drew two conclusions. The first was that faces and non-faces employ distinct forms of processing; specifically, he argued that upright faces are processed on the basis of configural information whereas object processing is more reliant on featural processing. Second, Yin proposed that the existence of an exaggerated inversion effect with face stimuli suggests that upright and inverted faces are processed using different types of information: upright faces are processed using holistic, configural information, whereas inverted faces are processed in the featural manner typically used in object processing. This suggestion implies that upright faces are processed predominantly according to the configural information extracted from them, but that this mode of processing is disrupted when a face is inverted, thereby leaving recognition of the face reliant upon the less effective extraction of featural information.

Another manipulation that has been used is to ask participants to base their decisions on either the *whole* of the stimulus or on just *part* of the stimulus. The logic here is that, if faces are processed holistically on the basis of the configural relations between features, performance should be impaired when trying to recognize a person from just one of their features. In contrast, if objects are processed featurally, recognition on the basis of just one feature should be possible. Tanaka and Farah (1993) asked participants to learn either faces or houses. They then asked them to complete a recognition task on the basis of either the entire face or house, or on the basis of an individual feature from it. When recognizing

faces, accuracy was reduced by about 10% for individual features in comparison to the whole face. For houses, the difference was only 2%, and participants were actually slightly better with an isolated house feature than with an entire house. Again, this experiment suggests that faces are processed on the basis of the configural information contained within them, whereas objects—or at least houses—are processed in a more featural way.

Evidence for configural processing of faces also comes from the Composite Face Effect (e.g. Young et al, 1987), the Thatcher Illusion (e.g. Thompson, 1980), blurring or scrambling facial features (e.g. Collishaw and Hole, 2000), photographic negation (e.g. Hole et al, 1999; Kemp et al, 1990), and from substituting facial features and manipulating the relative distances between features (e.g. Freire et al, 2000; Kemp et al, 1990). These effects are explained in detail in Chapter 2, so they will not be repeated here, but suffice to say there is a huge amount of evidence showing that faces and objects are processed differently—faces on the basis of the configural information contained within them, and objects on the basis of their more featural, piecemeal elements.

Surely, if faces and objects are processed using different sources of information, faces must be special? Well, here we come to probably the biggest area of debate within this topic. Diamond and Carey (1986) performed an enormously influential study that has often been cited as evidence that the Face Inversion Effect is the result of **expertise** with faces (see Chapter 6, section 6.1.1). They tested the ability of dog experts (breeders and judges) and novices to recognize photographs of upright and inverted faces and dogs. Both groups showed a large inversion effect for faces; accuracy dropped by 20% when the faces were shown upside-down. The dog breeders showed a similarly sized inversion effect for dogs, whereas for the novices there was no significant difference between their performance with upright and inverted dogs (Fig. 10.1). Diamond

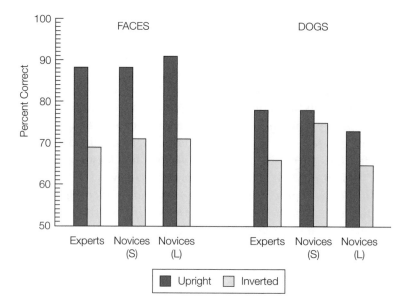

FIGURE 10.1 Accuracy for experts and novices when recognizing faces and dogs in either an upright or an inverted orientation. Novices were given either a smaller (S) or a larger (L) set of dog stimuli. (From Diamond and Carey, 1986)

and Carey's interpretation was that prolonged experience with any homogeneous class of stimuli, where all exemplars share many features, leads to the use of configural processing as a means of distinguishing efficiently between individual examples of that class. However, the penalty for this is a heavy reliance on the stimuli being presented in their usual orientation (i.e. upright). According to this view, faces are 'special' only in the sense that they are a homogeneous class of stimuli with which we have particularly high levels of expertise; in theory, the inversion effect can occur with any class of stimuli, as long as we are expert at recognizing them.

Inversion effects have been reported for individuals with expertise for processing other forms of stimuli. For example, experts, but not novices, show significant inversion effects for handwriting (Bruyer and Crispeels, 1992). However, it is difficult to measure levels of expertise and to control for this within experiments. Therefore, Gauthier and colleagues devised a whole set of novel stimuli called **Greebles**.

Greebles were created by Gauthier and Tarr (1997) to provide a set of stimuli (Fig. 10.2) that were not face-like but nevertheless shared many of the properties of faces. Like faces, Greebles are symmetrical and they all have the same number of features, which always occur with the same first-order relations. There are two different genders, and members of families share some similar characteristics. Finally, and most importantly, once expertise has been gained, it

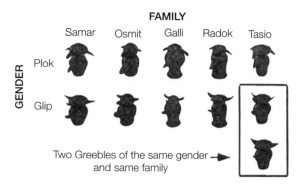

FIGURE 10.2 Some of the Greeble stimuli used by Gauthier and Tarr (1997).

is possible to identify and even name individual Greebles. Consequently, Greebles can be used to examine how people may acquire expertise, and to investigate how the reliance on configural and featural information might change as expertise increases.

Gauthier and Tarr (1997) trained participants to learn the Greebles to such a level that they could identify individual Greebles. They then conducted a series of experiments to determine whether manipulations of configural information would impair recognition of Greebles in the same way that such manipulations impair the recognition of faces. Over ten training sessions, they tested participants' abilities to identify the gender of Greebles, the family to which they belonged, and the identity of individual Greebles. Using both inversion and whole–part manipulations, Gauthier and Tarr found that Greeble experts were more sensitive to these configural manipulations than were novices. Gauthier et al (1998) replicated these findings using inversion and the Composite Face Effect. From this evidence they argued that faces are not special *per se*, it is just that we are especially expert at processing faces and that, as a result of this expertise we use configural information to allow us to make subtle distinctions between them.

One limitation of these early studies by Gauthier and co-workers is that only Greeble stimuli were used. Rossion et al (2002) examined the effects of inversion on both faces and Greebles, for novices and experts. For faces, inversion increased reaction times by about 70 milliseconds. For Greebles, reaction times increased by only 25 ms for novices, but increased by 46 ms for experts. Although the extent of the inversion effect for the Greeble experts was not as pronounced for Greebles as it was for faces, the difference between Greeble novices and experts certainly suggests that we become more reliant on configural information as we become more familiar, or expert, with a particular class of stimuli. Indeed, Gauthier and Bukach (2007) acknowledge that the inversion

effect might be larger for faces than other stimuli, but they argue that this simply reflects our high level of expertise with faces in comparison to other stimuli.

Although the research involving the learning of Greebles provides some evidence for faces not being special, it has been criticized by some research groups. Robbins and McKone (2007) returned to the methods used by Diamond and Carey (1986), and examined the effects of configural manipulations for faces and dogs in both novices and experts. Their experts were show judges, breeders or trainers of Labrador dogs, and only Labrador dogs were used as stimuli. Given that dogs can differ a great deal physically between species, using just one breed reduces the possible variability between individual dogs. This consequently provides a set of stimuli that may be considered to be more comparable to faces in terms of the very subtle information that allows discrimination between individuals. Robbins and McKone also used two control groups, one age-matched to the experts and one consisting of younger individuals.

This careful replication of Diamond and Carey's (1986) experiment failed to reproduce its results; whereas Diamond and Carey found that inversion impaired dog recognition as much as it impaired face recognition (reducing accuracy by about 20%), Robbins and McKone found only a small dog-inversion effect, amounting to a 7% drop in accuracy for experts and a 3% drop for novices. Reviewing other studies that have investigated the inversion effect with non-face stimuli (including cars, Greebles and handwriting), Robbins and McKone concluded that there is an effect of expertise (in that experts with these stimuli show a greater effect of inversion than do novices) but it is typically quite small, and nowhere near as big as the effect of inversion on face recognition. Robbins and McKone suggest that Diamond and Carey's results are anomalous compared with those of other studies. Perhaps they occurred because Diamond and Carey's dog breeders were already highly familiar with the particular photographs used as stimuli in the study; it is possible that, because the breeders were used to seeing these photographs in their normal orientation, inversion had a particularly strong effect on them.

Robbins and McKone (2007) also measured the Composite Face Effect (see Chapter 2, section 2.3.3) in these groups, using horizontally split faces and dogs (Fig. 10.3). Participants saw a pair of stimuli simultaneously (two faces or two Labradors) and had to decide whether the tops were the same or different, ignoring the bottom halves. The tops and bottoms were either aligned or misaligned with each other. Both groups showed the usual Composite Face Effect (worse performance with upright aligned face halves), but no Composite

Same identity aligned

Different identity aligned

Same identity unaligned   Different identity unaligned

FIGURE 10.3 Example stimuli from Robbins and McKone (2007). Top left is an unmanipulated example; top right is an example shown in photographic negative (contrast reversed); and the bottom examples show the composite dog pairs for the various conditions.

Dog Effect was found in either the novices or the experts. At present, the evidence suggests that the Composite Face Effect is confined to faces, rather than occurring with any stimulus class for which participants have expertise.

In a third experiment, Robbins and McKone presented the face and dog stimuli in photographic negative. Again, negation reduced performance for face processing, but had no effect on the ability to process the dog stimuli, for either the novices or the experts.

These three experiments by Robbins and McKone (2007) seem to provide very strong evidence against the expertise hypothesis and in favour of faces being special. After this paper was published there was a rather heated reply from Gauthier and Baukach (2007), who criticized Robbins and McKone's studies on the basis of both their methodology and their statistical analysis, and claimed that these experiments did not allow the expertise hypothesis to be rejected. McKone and Robbins (2007) replied, strongly defending their methods and reaffirming that the expertise hypothesis should be 'put to rest'. If you want to see what an academic argument is like, read these three papers! It is certainly clear that, on the basis of psychological evidence, there is still no clear answer to our question of whether face are special. Maybe we can get closer to an answer by looking at how faces are processed in the brain.

10.2 What can we learn from patients with brain damage?

As we saw in Chapter 7, the ability to process faces can be seriously impaired following certain types of brain damage. By studying patients with prosopagnosia and comparing their ability to process faces with their ability to process other stimuli, it is possible to gain some insight into the specificity of their face recognition deficits. If a part of the brain is damaged and then face processing is impaired, but all other processing remains unimpaired, surely that must be the special part of the brain that is responsible for face processing and nothing else?

10.2.1 Dissociations and double dissociations

Imagine that you are a clinical neuropsychologist and you see a patient who has just suffered brain damage. You give them a wide range of neuropsychological tests and find that they are very impaired at processing faces, but perform normally for all other processing. This is a **dissociation**. You might think that this is evidence for faces being processed in the part of the brain that was damaged, and that the other processes tested are located somewhere else in the brain that was not damaged. However, maybe face processing is just more difficult than the other processes. Perhaps this patient's brain damage means that they can complete easy tasks, but not more complex tasks.

Now imagine that a second patient comes to see you and you give them the same range of tests. This patient is very impaired at producing language, but their performance is normal on all other tests, including the face-processing test. You now have another dissociation: this patient is impaired at language production but not impaired for face processing. If you combine the two dissociations (Fig. 10.4), you can see that one

	Patient 1	Patient 2
Face processing	✗	✓
Language production	✓	✗

FIGURE 10.4 Illustration of a double dissociation (see text for explanation).

patient cannot process faces but can produce language, whereas the other shows the opposite pattern and can process faces but cannot produce language. This is called a **double dissociation**.

Double dissociations are very important in the argument about whether faces are special. If faces are special, patients with prosopagnosia should be impaired at face processing, but unimpaired for processing all other types of stimulus. Additionally, other patients should be impaired for processing non-face objects but unimpaired for processing faces. If these double dissociations are found, they will provide strong evidence for faces being special.

10.2.2 Is there a double dissociation between face and object processing?

The key double dissociation for demonstrating that faces are special would be one between faces and objects. Certainly a number of cases of patients with agnosia, who have impaired object-processing abilities, have been reported to have unimpaired face-processing abilities (e.g. Feinberg et al, 1994; Karpov et al, 1979; McMullen et al, 2000; Moscovitch and Moscovitch, 2000; Moscovitch et al, 1997). Whether there are patients with prosopagnosia who have no problems at all with processing objects is harder to prove. Some patients with prosopagnosia do have some difficulties with object processing (e.g. Farah et al, 1995; Gauthier et al, 1999b; Sergent and Signoret, 1992). However, it is possible that these patients suffered an extreme and wide-ranging brain injury that damaged both the object- and face-processing mechanisms. It is therefore necessary to look for case studies that show that prosopagnosia can exist in the absence of any impairment to object processing.

A large number of studies have provided detailed examinations of the face- and object-processing abilities of patients with prosopagnosia, and some have claimed to find no apparent impairment to object processing (e.g. Bukach et al, 2006; De Renzi and di Pellegrino,

1998; De Renzi et al, 1968; Wada and Yamatoto, 2001). However, the tests of object processing used in these studies are problematic. One frequently used test is to identify different objects, such as a car, a spoon or a raspberry. However, this kind of object-processing task simply requires the identification of the class of object that the exemplar represents. A more valid test, which would also be more comparable to a face-processing task, would be to ask patients to identify particular individuals within a class of stimuli. For example, rather than identifying that it is 'a car', they should be able to identify that it is a Peugeot 206 LX HDI.

This form of **within-class discrimination** has been reported across a wide range of object classes for patients with prosopagnosia. For example, patients have been shown to be able to identify individual cars (Bruyer et al, 1983; Henke et al, 1998; Rossion et al, 2003a), specific places (Bruyer et al, 1983; Evans et al, 1995) and individual pairs of spectacles (Farah et al, 1995). There is also evidence that patients with prosopagnosia can make within-class decisions when naming or identifying flowers (Evans et al, 1995), and fruits and vegetables (Henke et al, 1998; Riddoch et al, 2008). These cases provide strong evidence for a double dissociation between face and object processing.

In addition to finding double dissociations between face and object processing, some researchers have found double dissociations between the ability to recognize human faces and the ability to recognize individual animals. One famous case was WJ, a farmer who was prosopagnosic but able to recognize individual sheep from his flock (McNeil and Warrington, 1993). The same pattern was reported in another farmer who became prosopagnosic but was still able to identify his animals (Bruyer et al, 1983). The double dissociation is completed by a patient who was unimpaired at processing faces, but who could no longer recognize his cows following brain damage (Assal et al, 1984). Such a double dissociation seems to suggest that there is something particularly special about human faces. This possibility is supported by evidence showing that a patient with prosopagnosia was able to match the bodies of humans accurately (Duchaine et al, 2006).

Although the study of face and object processing, and the double dissociations that can arise, seem to provide evidence for faces being special, the argument that the findings are all due to expertise rears its head again. In order to recognize faces we have to make very fine within-class discriminations on the basis of subtle differences in the second-order relations between the facial features. According to the expertise hypothesis, this is why we are so much better at processing faces than other classes of stimulus. Perhaps the brain injuries that lead to prosopagnosia do not damage a 'face' area, but instead damage a part of the brain responsible for making these subtle within-class discriminations. Faces may appear to be selectively impaired only because we rely so heavily on that method of processing.

Some researchers have attempted to address this possibility by training patients with prosopagnosia to become Greeble experts. If prosopagnosia does occur as a result of damage to the area of the brain that enables this specialized form of processing, then a patient with prosopagnosia should not be able to become a Greeble expert. Unfortunately for supporters of the 'expertise' hypothesis, patients with prosopagnosia seem to be able to learn to discriminate between Greebles just as well as control participants (Behrmann et al, 2005; Duchaine et al, 2004; Riddoch et al, 2008). Duchaine et al's (2006) patient, FB, was able to identify and name individual Greebles and identify the family that each Greeble belonged to just as well as the control participants—actually he was far better than two of them. The finding that patients with prosopagnosia can become Greeble experts provides more support for faces being special.

10.2.3 **Is there a double dissociation between different aspects of face processing?**

There seems to be a fair amount of evidence for a double dissociation between face and object processing. However, it is also interesting to consider whether the examination of double dissociations can further our understanding of the different aspects of face processing (for discussion of the psychological evidence for such distinctions in non-clinical participants, see Chapters 1 and 3). Is there any evidence of double dissociations *within* face processing?

A large number of patients with prosopagnosia are impaired across a wide range of face-processing abilities (e.g. Campbell et al, 1990; de Haan and Campbell, 1991; Kracke, 1994). However, these may be patients with damage to a relatively large area of the brain that affects a range of face-processing skills. To address this question properly, it is necessary to look for far more specific impairments to face processing.

Young et al (1993) gave a range of face-processing tests to seven ex-servicemen who all had unilateral brain lesions. They completed two tests of unfamiliar face matching, two tests of familiar face recognition and two tests of emotional expression processing. Five of the participants were significantly impaired at matching and recognizing facial expressions of emotion, but were able to recognize familiar faces and match unfamiliar faces. This finding is not necessarily unexpected when you consider that the Bruce and Young model separates familiarity and emotion processing at a very early stage (although see Chapter 3 for more on this issue). The other two patients were able to identify and match facial expressions accurately; however, one was able to recognize familiar faces but not match unfamiliar faces, and the other was able to match unfamiliar faces but not recognize familiar faces. This study almost suggests a triple dissociation between the processing of unfamiliar faces, the processing of familiar faces and the processing of facial expressions of emotion.

Many of the case study reports of patients with prosopagnosia test a wide range of face-processing abilities. For example, Duchaine et al (2006) found that 'Edward' was able to detect faces and correctly categorize faces, but was extremely impaired at familiar face recognition. He was also impaired at recognizing facial emotion and showed some impairment, although less severe, for processing the gender and attractiveness of a face. It seems that Edward's face-processing abilities were quite widely affected. In contrast, FB (Riddoch et al, 2008) was impaired at recognizing familiar faces but was able to recognize facial emotion accurately, make good age judgements and correctly classify the sex of a face. This pattern has also been shown in other patients with prosopagnosia (Tranel et al, 1988) and there is even one case study reported of a person who was unable to recognize familiar faces but could lip-read accurately (Campbell et al, 1986). Although such evidence is far from showing double dissociations between different aspects of face processing, such evidence tentatively suggests that double dissociations may exist.

10.2.4 Is the existence of face-specific prosopagnosia really evidence for faces being special?

Although the evidence from patients with prosopagnosia is consistent with the notion that faces are special, it is important to be critical when assessing the validity of these studies. In the conclusion to Chapter 7, we discussed a number of limitations that arise from the study of individuals with brain damage. All of these studies are based on administering various tests of face processing to patients and then seeing whether they do well or badly on these tasks. One criticism of this approach is that some of the face-processing tasks may be completed through alternative non-face strategies. For example, if asked to make an age judgement the patient may simply look for wrinkles around the eyes and base their decision solely on this individual piece of featural information. Or if asked to classify the sex of the person, a prosopagnosic might base their decision on hairstyle or evidence of wearing make-up.

Two very widely used tests, the Warrington Recognition Memory for Faces Test and the Benton Face Recognition Test, have been criticized by Duchaine and Weidenfeld (2003). In the Warrington Recognition Memory for Faces Test participants are shown images of 50 men and asked to decide whether they are pleasant or not. After this phase, they are presented with pairs of faces. Within each pair, one face is novel and the other is one they have seen before. The participant has to say which is the face they saw before (Fig. 10.5). Duchaine and Weidenfeld suggest that this test does not necessarily require face-processing skills. It is possible that participants may be achieving 'face recognition' by simply remembering the image or by remembering a particular feature within that image, such as the tie being worn by the poser (see the discussion of 'pictorial codes' in Chapter 1). This problem is nicely illustrated by the case of EP, who was prosopagnosic, but able to perform within normal levels on this test (Nunn et al, 2001). EP reported that he achieved this high level of 'recognition' by using exactly these types of non-facial feature.

FIGURE 10.5 Example pair of faces from the Warrington Recognition Memory for Faces Test. (From Duchaine and Weidenfeld, 2003)

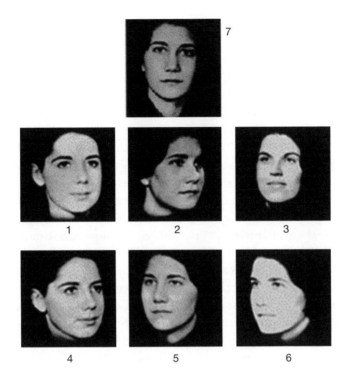

FIGURE 10.6 Example trial from the Benton Face Recognition Test. Participants are asked to decide which three of the lower six faces are the same person as the target face (7) at the top of the display. The correct answer is 2, 5 and 6. (From Duchaine and Weidenfeld, 2003)

Duchaine and Weidenfeld also criticized the Benton Face Recognition Test. This presents the participant with a target face at the top of the display and six faces below it. They have to decide which three faces are alternative views of the target face (Fig. 10.6). With this test, some patients with prosopagnosia can perform very well. There is no time limit on the task and consequently some prosopagnosics achieve scores within the normal range by laboriously using just the shape of the eyebrows and the hairline, and repeatedly cross-checking across the stimuli. It is therefore likely that patients with high scores on this test are achieving them through processing mechanisms that do not require face-processing skills.

10.3 **What can we learn from neuroimaging studies?**

By using modern neuroimaging techniques,[1] such as event-related potentials (ERPs) and functional magnetic resonance imaging (fMRI), it has been possible to examine activation in the brain in response to stimuli. This approach has been used in a great many studies in order to examine whether patterns of brain activation when viewing faces are different from the patterns observed when viewing other stimuli. If these are distinct, this is good evidence for faces being processed in a 'special' part of the brain that is dedicated to face processing.

---

[1] See the methodological appendix for a full description of these methods.

As we saw in Chapter 9, ERPs have been used a great deal in an attempt to locate where in the brain face processing might occur. A great many studies have shown that there is a negative evoked potential that occurs about 170 ms after seeing a face. This is known as the **N170** and is recorded at electrodes placed over the junction where the temporal and occipital lobes meet (Fig. 10.7). It is also stronger over the right hemisphere than over the left.

A huge amount of work has examined the way in which the N170 responds to faces under a wide range of situations. These are reviewed in Chapter 9, section 9.2.1. For the purposes of this chapter we are interested primarily in whether there is an N170 response to stimuli other than faces. If the N170 is evoked only by faces, then this would provide support for faces being special. However, if the N170 is also evoked by non-face stimuli, it may be that faces are not so special.

Bentin et al (1996) were probably the first to report the face N170. They provided some comparisons between face and non-face stimuli and found a strong N170 response for faces, which was reduced slightly for scrambled faces. The N170 to human faces was also significantly greater than the N170 response to animal faces, hands or furniture. This suggests that the N170 component responds to human faces to a significantly greater extent than to other stimuli.

This finding has been replicated in a number of more recent studies. For example, Itier et al (2006b) examined the N170 in response to a variety of stimuli: human faces, just the eyes of human faces, and non-face stimuli (cars, houses and chairs). They also presented their stimuli either upright, inverted, in photographic negative, or both inverted and in photographic negative. They found a strong N170 for human faces and for the eyes of human faces (Fig. 10.8). This was slightly reduced for ape faces, and non-existent for non-face stimuli.

More recently, Itier et al (2007) have even suggested that the N170 is not face-specific, but

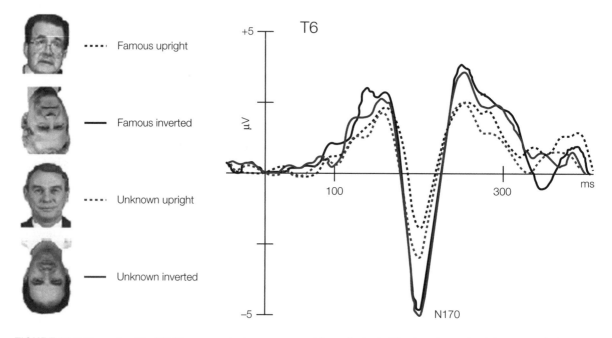

FIGURE 10.7 Example of the N170 response to faces measured from electrode T6, placed over the right temporal lobe. (From Marzi and Viggiano, 2007)

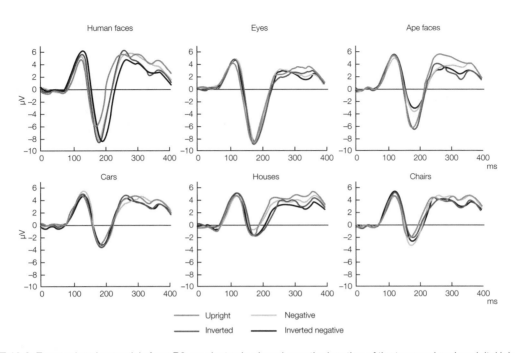

FIGURE 10.8 Event-related potentials from P8, an electrode placed over the junction of the temporal and occipital lobes in the right hemisphere. The negative component seen about 170 ms after the stimulus (the N170) is clear for human faces, eyes and ape faces, but barely apparent for cars, houses or chairs. (From Itier et al, 2006b)

rather eye-specific. They compared the N170 for full faces, eyes only, faces with eyes missing, and houses. All stimuli were also presented in either an upright or an inverted orientation. Itier et al found the largest N170 for the 'eyes only' stimuli, and also found that this response was not affected by inversion. In light of these findings they suggest that it may be the eyes that make faces special.

The N170 component seems to selectively respond to faces. However, supporters of the expertise hypothesis question this. They suggest that the N170 response reflects expertise for making fine-detail discriminations on the basis of second-order relations between features. Tanaka and Curran (2001) recorded ERPs in dog and bird experts, when viewing images of both dogs and birds. They found an N170 when viewing both dog and bird images, but the N170 was significantly larger when viewing the stimulus type for which the participants had expertise.

This seems to provide strong support for the N170 responding to stimuli that you have an expertise for processing.

Rossion et al (2002) further tested this possibility by training participants to become Greeble experts and then measuring their ERPs in response to both faces and Greebles. Before training, the N170 to Greebles was smaller than that for faces and occurred slightly later. After training, the N170 was larger and occurred slightly earlier, in a similar way to the N170 for human faces. Again, this evidence was used to support the expertise hypothesis and the idea that the N170 is not a special response to faces.

As we saw in Chapter 9, there appears to be a part of the brain in the temporal lobes that responds specifically to faces: the **fusiform face area** (FFA). Is this area really activated only in response to faces? If so, this would be strong support for the argument that faces are special.

Alternatively, if the FFA is found to be activated in response to other stimuli, it may be that faces are not so special after all.

In the original paper that identified the FFA (Kanwisher et al, 1997), participants were asked to view faces, faces in profile, scrambled faces, hands, objects and houses while in an fMRI scanner. Kanwisher and colleagues then looked for differences in patterns of activation between the facial stimuli and the other classes of stimulus. In the FFA, they found unique activations in response to faces that did not occur in response to any of the other stimuli. This means that the FFA was actually defined as an area of the brain that responds to faces, but not to other classes of stimuli. This seems to provide very strong support for faces being special; however, a great deal of research has been conducted since then, and the answer may not be quite this simple.

One possible issue to consider is what type of stimuli we use when we say that we have shown participants 'faces'. Faces can come in many forms, and a large number of studies have found FFA activation in response to a wide range of different types of face. Tong et al (2000) performed a series of experiments in which participants were asked to look at a wide range of facial and non-facial stimuli. They found strong evidence for FFA activation in response to faces in a variety of profiles, when just the eyes were shown and when a face was shown with the eyes removed. They also found FFA activation for cat faces, cartoon faces and, to some extent, schematic faces. Although they did find some activation in the FFA to animals, houses and objects, the level of activation was very low and much less than to faces.

The FFA has also been found to respond to line drawings of faces (Spiridon and Kanwisher, 2002) and to Mooney faces (Kanwisher et al, 1998). Andrews et al (2002) used the face–vase illusion (Fig. 10.9) in which participants are shown a stimulus that they may perceive as two faces

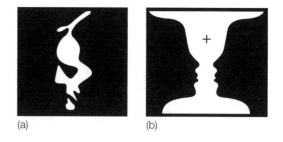

FIGURE 10.9 Examples of some of the face stimuli used. (a) Mooney faces (Kanwisher et al, 1998) and (b) the face–vase illusion. (Andrews et al, 2002)

looking at each other, or as a white vase on a black background. FFA activation occurred when the participants reported perceiving the stimulus as faces, but not when perceiving it as a vase. This is a particularly important finding as the properties of the stimulus were exactly the same in both conditions; it was just the participant's perception that changed. This seems to provide strong support for the FFA being a special face area. Another study used a binocular rivalry paradigm (Pasley et al, 2004) in which one eye saw a face and the other did not. Perceptions tend to alternate, with first one eye's image being perceived and then the other's. When the participant reported seeing the face there was FFA activation, but when they reported seeing the non-face stimulus, there was no FFA activation.

A great many studies have compared activation in the FFA when viewing faces to that produced by viewing a wide range of non-face stimuli. Such studies have reported greater FFA activation in response to faces than in response to letter strings and textures (Puce et al, 1996), flowers (McCarthy et al, 1997), houses (Haxby et al, 1999; Kanwisher et al, 1997; Yovel and Kanwisher, 2004), insects (Rhodes et al, 2004a) and objects (Kanwisher et al, 1997; Rhodes et al, 2004a). Additionally, the difference in FFA activation is greater in the right FFA than in the left (Allison et al, 1999; Kanwisher et al, 1997; McCarthy et al, 1999; Rossion et al, 2000a). This evidence is consistent with the idea that faces are processed predominantly by the right hemisphere.

It is important to remember that at the beginning of this chapter an argument was put forward that faces are special because they are processed using the configural information contained within them, whereas objects are processed on the basis of more featural information. However, when faces are inverted there is a shift from relying on configural information to relying on featural information. Obviously the way in which FFA activation may change in response to manipulations of configural information may also add to the debate about whether faces are special or not. This evidence is reviewed in great detail in Chapter 9 (section 9.3.1), so the key points will be recapped here only briefly. Kanwisher et al (1998) used the inversion effect in this way and found that FFA activation significantly decreased when faces were presented upside-down. Yovel and Kanwisher (2005) also reported a similar finding.

Rossion et al (2000a) showed participants images of faces and houses. They then performed a delayed matching task, using either whole stimuli or just parts (individual features) of the stimuli. The right FFA was active when matching whole faces, but the left FFA was active when matching individual facial features. Matching either whole or part objects did not induce such changes. Yovel and Kanwisher (2004) also used facial and house stimuli, and applied either featural or configural manipulations. They found three times more activation in the FFA for faces than for houses, and found that this did not vary across the tasks. They also found there was less activation in the FFA when viewing inverted faces than when viewing upright faces.

Once again, supporters of the expertise hypothesis disagree that the FFA is a face-specific area, and instead argue that this area is responsible for fine-detail discriminations, which are necessary for distinguishing between faces (Gauthier et al, 1999b, 2000; Tarr and Gauthier, 2000). There is some evidence for this possibility. Levels of FFA activation in response to birds and cars are greater for experts than for novices, particularly so for bird experts viewing birds (Gauthier et al, 2000). Additionally, the FFA has been found to respond more to own-race than other-race faces (Golby et al, 2001). Given that expertise is one of the primary explanations for the own-race bias (see Chapter 12), this provides strong real-world evidence for the FFA being recruited when processing stimuli for which we have expertise.

In order to provide further evidence for the expertise hypothesis, participants have been trained to become Greeble experts, and researchers have then looked at levels of activation in the FFA. Gauthier et al (1999b) found that when participants were unfamiliar with the Greebles, there was no activation in the FFA. After training and acquiring expertise, participants showed activation in the FFA when viewing Greebles, although the levels of activation were still higher for faces than for Greebles (Fig. 10.10/Plate 10.10). This provides more support for the expertise hypothesis. However, other studies have failed to find FFA activation for non-face stimuli with which the participants have expertise (e.g. Grill-Spector et al, 2004), and others have reported very small, but not significant, levels of FFA activation (Moore et al, 2006; Rhodes et al, 2004b).

It is relatively unclear whether the FFA really is specialized for processing faces or whether it is specialized for fine-detail within-class discriminations for classes of stimulus for which we have a particular expertise. Although Gauthier et al (1999b) did find FFA activation for Greeble experts, levels of activation in the FFA were still far higher for faces. Gauthier and Bukach (2007) argue that this finding does not necessarily mean that faces are special, but that we are just are incredibly expert at processing faces and it is difficult to replicate that level of expertise for

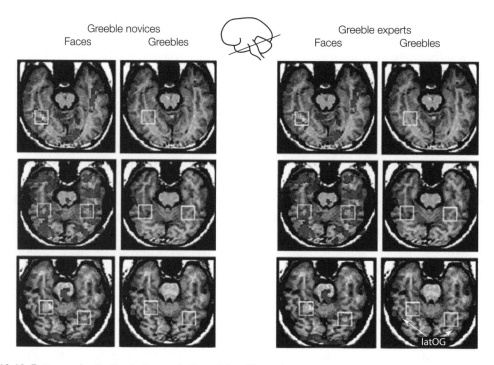

FIGURE 10.10 Patterns of activation before and after training. The white squares show the location of the fusiform gyri. (Gauthier et al, 1999). Please see colour plate section.

Greebles through training in the laboratory. They suggest that, if it were possible to equate the level of expertise across types of stimulus, the levels of activation in the FFA would be similar. This possibility is supported by a correlation between the strength of FFA activation and the level of expertise in dog and bird experts (Gauthier et al, 2000).

It has also been suggested that FFA activation to Greebles may occur because the Greebles are perceived (or learned) as something that is relatively face-, animal- or body-like (Kanwisher and Yovel, 2006). If participants are interpreting the Greebles as animate creatures, this might account for the FFA activation, particularly given that FFA activation has been shown for animal faces and cartoons (Tong et al, 2000). Following on from this, if Greebles are perceived in a 'creature-like' way, it is possible that some of the activation

detected actually comes from the fusiform *body* area, which is adjacent to the FFA (Peelen and Downing, 2005; Schwarzlose et al, 2005). The spatial resolution of fMRI scans is still relatively low, so it is possible that the processing of Greebles may activate areas of the fusiform gyrus other than the FFA, such as the body area, and that due to mis-measurement the activation is classified as being within the FFA (Kanwisher and Yovel, 2006; Rhodes et al, 2004b).

Finally, a small number of studies have examined whether FFA activation occurs in patients with prosopagnosia. McKone et al (2007b) are strong supporters in favour of faces being special and point out that the location of the FFA is consistent with the typical location of the lesion in prosopagnosia. Two patients with prosopagnosia failed to have any FFA activation when passively viewing faces (Kanwisher et al,

1999). Another patient studied by Schiltz et al (2006) had not suffered any focal damage to the FFA, but there was evidence of some low levels of activity when viewing faces. Similarly, Steeves et al (2006) found that DF had FFA activation that was very comparable to the patterns of activation found in control participants (Fig. 10.11/Plate 10.11). However, DF was completely unable to process facial identity, gender or emotional expression. This led the authors to conclude that the FFA is necessary for effective processing of faces, but that it is not the only area responsible and that a wider network of brain areas must be recruited in order to process faces.

10.4 **What can we learn from developmental studies?**

Research with newborn babies and very young infants has also been used in the argument over whether faces are special. If the ability to process faces were innate, the argument for faces being special would be strengthened.

The research on this evidence was covered in detail in Chapter 5, so it will just be summarized here.

Babies that are just a few minutes old do seem to look preferentially at face-like patterns rather than other stimuli (Goren et al, 1975; M. H. Johnson et al, 1991; Maurer and Young, 1983). As these babies would not have had the time or exposure to faces necessary to develop any form of expertise, at first sight it seems to imply that a preference for looking at faces is **innate**. However, it has been argued that this preference might occur because the stimulus faces just happen to possess certain characteristics that are attractive to the neonate (i.e. they are 'top-heavy' patterns that are well suited to the capabilities of the immature visual system) rather than because they are 'faces' *per se* (e.g. Cassia et al, 2004; Simion et al, 2002; Turati et al, 2002). Thus, it seems that the evidence taken from newborn infants cannot really give us a clear answer to the question of whether or not faces are special.

10.5 **What can we learn from animal studies?**

We have reviewed a wide range of evidence from humans in an attempt to discover whether or not faces are special. The final source of evidence that we will consider is research that has been done with monkeys. Just as fMRI has been used to identify the FFA in humans, comparable work has attempted to identify whether there are specific parts of the brain in other animals, particularly monkeys, that are dedicated to face processing. Tsao et al (2003) conducted exactly such a study. Images of monkey faces, human faces, human hands, fruits and human-made objects were shown to both monkeys and humans whilst they

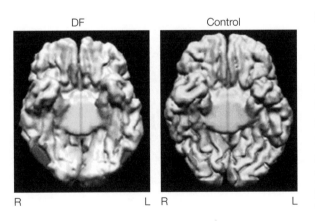

FIGURE 10.11 FFA activation in a prosopagnosic patient (DF) and a control participant. (From Steeves et al, 2006). Please see colour plate section.

were in an fMRI scanner. Face-specific activation was recorded for both monkey and human faces. However, in humans the responses to human and monkey faces were similar, whereas in the monkeys the area of response to monkey faces was larger than for human faces. Most importantly, the activation in the monkeys was found to be in the equivalent position to the FFA in humans.

One major limitation with the fMRI methodology is that it has quite low spatial resolution. fMRI scans show us levels of activation within voxels (like 3D pixels in a digital image), but each voxel contains many thousands of neurones. Ideally, we would examine face-selective activation at a more fine-detail level. This is possible through single-cell electrophysiological recordings in the monkey. In these experiments microelectrodes are placed within the brain. The tips of these electrodes are only about 3–10 micrometres in width. Consequently it is possible to record the changes in electrochemical activity within single neurones.

The ability to record the activity from **single cells** in monkeys allows us to ask an even more interesting question that may help us to establish whether faces are special: do individual neurones respond to individual faces? There are two proposals, first that individual faces are encoded by clusters of cells, and second that individual cells are activated by particular individuals. This second idea is called the **grandmother cell** or gnostic neurone hypothesis (see Gross, 2002). If there is evidence that single neurones respond to faces, or even better to individual faces, this would be strong evidence for faces being special.

In addition to examining fMRI activation when viewing faces in monkeys, Tsao et al (2006) also used this single-cell recording technique. Having identified the area of the brain that responded most selectively to faces, they then used single-cell recording in that area. They found that 97% of the cells in that region responded strongly to faces, but not to other stimuli, such as bodies, fruits, human-made objects and hands (Fig. 10.12).

As well as single cells responding selectively to faces, even more specialization for single neurones has been reported. For example, cells have been found to respond to different facial features (Sigala, 2004). Some cells are

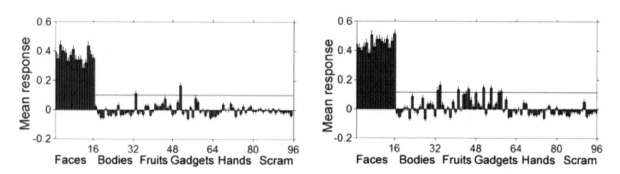

FIGURE 10.12 Responses from single-cell recordings to six different types of stimulus taken from two different monkeys. (From Tsao, D. Y., Freiwald, W. A., Tootell, R. B. H. & Livingstone, M. S. (2006). A cortical region consisting entirely of face-selective cells. *Science*, 311(5761), 670–674. Reprinted with permission from the American Association for the Advancement of Science)

viewpoint-specific, responding particularly to either frontal or profile views (Perrett et al, 1991). Most importantly though, Sugase et al (1999) found evidence for two stages of information processing: processing the type of stimulus (e.g. monkey face, human face or shape) preceded processing about the specific expression or identity conveyed by the face. Such evidence seems to support the suggestion that faces are indeed special.

10.6 **Conclusion**

In this chapter we have tried to establish whether faces are 'special', that is, do we have an innate ability to process faces, do we process them in a special way, and do we process them in a special part of the brain? The evidence seems mixed. We certainly use different information when processing faces than when processing most objects. Does this reliance on processing faces configurally, or holistically, mean that they are special or just that we have developed a special way of achieving a very difficult processing task? Some of the reports from patients with prosopagnosia provide clear double dissociations between face and object processing. Two recent studies in particular provide very strong evidence for face-specific prosopagnosia (Duchaine et al, 2006; Riddoch et al, 2008). Face specificity does seem to be demonstrated through the N170 and

the FFA, but to what extent can these findings be explained in terms of expertise effects?

The expertise hypothesis seems to be the main issue in the argument about whether faces are special or not. It is difficult to disentangle whether all of these face-specific effects are really due to faces being innately special, or whether we are just incredibly good at processing faces because we have so much experience with them. One of the main obstacles here is being able to train participants to have an equivalent level of expertise with a class of stimulus other than faces. Both the behavioural and the neuropsychological evidence from dog, bird and Greeble experts seems to suggest that expertise is important, but the magnitude of the effects found with faces and other expert stimuli are not equal.

Perhaps we don't really need to decide between the two extreme views here. Although the evidence is often presented in a very dichotomous 'for' or 'against' way, it may be possible to reconcile these two approaches within the same framework. There are two possible ways in which this might work. First, it may be that a number of processing mechanisms contribute to the effective processing of stimuli, and that a face-specific mechanism is just one component within this wider structure (see Duchaine et al, 2006). Second, it is possible that we are innately prewired with special face-processing areas of the brain that make us orient towards faces from birth, but that we then develop our high level of expertise over a lifetime of experience with faces.

SUMMARY

- Faces are processed primarily using the configural information contained within them. The processing of other types of stimulus does not depend on this type of information; rather they are processed in a more featural or part-based manner. This distinction between processing styles for faces and other stimuli has been used to suggest that faces are special.

- However, according to the expertise hypothesis, this distinction occurs only because we have a great deal of practice with faces. For example, dog breeders show a dog inversion effect.

- Double dissociations have provided strong evidence that very specific and focal brain damage can impair face processing while leaving all other processing unimpaired. This provides strong evidence for there being a 'special' part of the brain dedicated to face processing.

- Neuroimaging work with non-clinical participants has identified this 'special' part of the brain as the right fusiform gyrus face area.

- However, it has been suggested that activation in this area merely reflects fine within-class discriminations, which are learned through acquiring expertise at processing that type of stimulus.

- Single-cell recordings on monkeys have shown that individual neurones are specialized for processing faces, with there possibly even being specific 'grandmother cells' for particular individuals.

- Whether faces are special or not is still a hotly debated topic and, ultimately, one that is perhaps impossible to resolve conclusively.

FURTHER READING

Duchaine, B., Yovel, G., Butterworth, E. and Nakayama, K. (2006). *Prosopagnosia as an impairment to face-specific mechanisms: elimination of the alternative hypotheses in a developmental case.* Cognitive Neuropsychology, 23(5): 714–747. This paper presents a very detailed case study of a patient with developmental prosopagnosia. Within it, the authors give an excellent summary of the main theoretical viewpoints in the 'Are faces special?' debate and provide strong evidence for faces being special through thorough testing of Edward.

Bukach, C. M., Gauthier, I. and Tarr, M. J. (2006). *Beyond faces and modularity: the power of an expertise framework.* Trends in Cognitive Science, 10(40): 159–166. This paper provides a good overview of the expertise hypothesis and brings together all the evidence in support of it.

McKone, E., Kanwisher, N. and Duchaine, B.C. (2007). *Can generic expertise explain special processing for faces?* Trends in Cognitive Sciences, 11(1): 8–15. This is a great paper to read alongside the Bukach et al (2006) paper as it argues against the expertise hypothesis and outlines the evidence in support of faces being special.

Kanwisher, N. and Yovel, G. (2006). *The fusiform face area: a cortical region specialized for the perception of faces.* Philosophical Transactions of the Royal Society of London.

Series B, Biological Sciences, 361(1476): 2109–2128. An excellent review of the research on the fusiform face area giving a far broader coverage than was possible in this chapter.

Tate, A. J., Fischer, H., Leigh, A. E. and Kendrick, K. M. (2006). *Behavioural and neurophysiological evidence for face identity and face emotion processing in animals.* Philosophical Transactions of the Royal Society of London. Series B, Biological Sciences, 361(1476): 2155–2172. A great deal of work has examined the face-processing abilities of various animals, but particularly monkeys and sheep. These were discussed only briefly in this chapter, but this paper provides an excellent and very thorough review.

PART III

APPLIED PERSPECTIVES

EYEWITNESS IDENTIFICATION EVIDENCE, AND RECOGNITION OF UNFAMILIAR FACES

The research described in Chapter 1 suggests that we are very good at recognizing faces that are familiar to us, despite changes in factors such as illumination, viewpoint and expression. But how well can we recognize a face that we have seen only once before? This issue has obvious practical implications and consequently it has been heavily studied within the 'applied' framework of forensic psychology.[1] This chapter reviews research in this area that has demonstrated the fallibility of eyewitnesses, attempted to identify the factors underlying their unreliability, and sought to discover ways by which these could be overcome.

11.1 The methods by which eyewitnesses identify suspects

A witness to a crime may be asked to identify its perpetrator in a number of ways. One method that has been used extensively in the USA (Dysart and Lindsay, 2007a) is the '**show-up**': if a crime has just happened, the police may apprehend someone in the vicinity whom they think could be the criminal, and ask a witness whether this is the person they saw committing the crime. (In the UK, a distinction is made between 'street identifications' and 'confrontations'; both involve asking witnesses to decide whether or not a suspect is the criminal, but the latter takes place in a police station after a suspect has been arrested.)

---

[1] To some extent, there are two separate, albeit greatly overlapping, cultures of researchers on face recognition: those who perform 'pure' research, primarily out of theoretical interest, and 'applied' researchers who are more interested in its practical importance. The former have tended to study factors affecting recognition of familiar faces, whereas the latter have been more preoccupied with investigating factors that affect recognition of unfamiliar faces. The two groups tend to use different methods of measuring recognition performance. Researchers conducting 'pure' research are normally lab-based and use measures such as reaction times and error rates. In contrast, although the 'applied' group's studies are often lab-based, they tend to use measures that are more ecologically valid, in line with their desire to be able to draw conclusions that are relevant to the legal profession.

A second method is to ask a witness to look through a series of photographs of known criminals ('**mugshots**'), in case the person that they saw is a criminal who is already known to the police. If the police have a suspect, they might set up an **identification parade** or '**lineup**'; the suspect is placed amongst a number of people who match the witness' description of the person that they saw, and the witness has to decide whether that person is present in the lineup, and, if so, try to identify which member of the lineup it is. In practice, 'live' lineups are now rarely used. In the USA, witnesses view a photospread, in which a photograph of the suspect is placed amongst photographs of similar-looking individuals. The photographs are either shown all at once, or one after another. In the UK, the lineup takes the form of a series of videos of moving heads. Each video is seen twice, and then the witness makes their identification.

A witness may also be asked to produce a likeness of the criminal's face, using a **face composite system**[2] such as **E-FIT**, which can be publicized in the hope that someone who knows the criminal will recognize the face and contact the police (see Chapter 13).

Four decades of research have shown that all of these procedures are fraught with problems because people are quite poor at recognizing faces that are unfamiliar to them. The difficulty of recognizing unfamiliar faces has often had serious consequences. Eyewitness identification of a suspect is frequently the major source of evidence against that person, and juries and judges are often heavily influenced by it.

Unfortunately, research has clearly shown that mistaken identifications are not uncommon.

Wright and McDaid (1996) examined real-world lineup performance at two specialist identification suites as well as at ordinary police stations in the Greater London area. Overall, performance was poor: only 40% of witnesses picked the police's suspect from the lineup; 20% picked one of the other members of the lineup (a 'filler'); and 40% chose no one at all. Valentine et al (2003) performed a similar study in London, and obtained almost identical values. An analysis of 461 identification attempts in the USA by Behrman and Richards (2005) found that half of the witnesses identified the police's suspect, and 15% incorrectly identified a filler. Clearly the 15–20% of witnesses who choose a filler are mistaken in their identification, because these individuals are in the lineup merely to act as distractors for the suspect and so are known by the police to be innocent. However, because the police suspect is not always the person who actually committed the crime, it is likely that some proportion of the 40–50% of witnesses who choose the suspect are also mistaken in their identification. In a recent review of studies on eyewitness reliability, Penrod and Bornstein (2007) estimated that identifications from **target-present lineups** (lineups that actually contain the suspect) may be correct less than half the time; about a quarter of witnesses mistakenly choose an innocent person instead. With **target-absent lineups** (ones that do not contain the person originally seen by the witness), about 35–40% of witnesses nevertheless attempt to make an identification.

Considering the extent to which showups are used in the USA, there are surprisingly few empirical studies of how often they give rise to misidentifications. (See Steblay, Dysart, Fulero and

---

[2] The term 'composite' has two different meanings in psychological research on face perception. In laboratory research, it usually refers to faces that are made up of halves from different faces (see Fig. 2.5 for an example), stimuli that are sometimes referred to as 'chimeric' faces. That's how we've used it in this book up to now. In 'applied' research, 'composite' refers to the facial likenesses produced by systems such as Photofit, Identikit and E-FIT. Hence, in this chapter (and Chapters 12 and 13), 'composite' will be used in the latter sense.

Lindsay [2003] and Valentine [2006] for reviews of what little is known.) Some experts believe that the procedure is dangerously suggestive in nature: the witness sees only a single person, and is well aware that the police believe this person to be the criminal. In addition, as Steblay et al (2003) point out, one advantage of the lineup procedure is that it can provide some indication of a witness' reliability: the witness can demonstrate that they are unreliable by choosing an innocent foil instead of the suspect in a target-present lineup, or by making a positive identification from a target-absent lineup. The show-up procedure provides no such protection for innocent suspects.

In some cases, mistaken identification has led to an innocent person being imprisoned for a crime they did not commit, an error that has come to light only with the development of DNA forensic techniques. In the USA, the **Innocence Project** is a non-profit legal clinic that is devoted to exonerating wrongly convicted people by means of DNA testing. To date (February 2010), it reports that 249 convictions have been overturned; more than three-quarters of these involved mistaken identification of the defendant by an eyewitness.

The death of a Brazilian student, Jean Charles de Menezes, was a recent tragic case of misidentification. He was shot on a tube train by the Metropolitan police, who mistook him for Hussain Osman, a would-be suicide bomber known to them mainly from CCTV images. The police subsequently released a composite image of de Menezes and Osman, which they claimed showed how much alike the two men were (Fig. 11.1). This backfired from a public relations point of view, as presenting the two faces in this fashion emphasizes the differences in appearance between them. In addition, unlike the police officers concerned in this incident, the public were able to compare the two faces side by side for as long as they wanted. As we shall see, eyewitness performance is known to be greatly affected by stress, and this must have been an incredibly stressful situation for the police officers concerned,

FIGURE 11.1 Composite image of Jean Charles de Menezes (right) and Hussein Osman (left) issued by the Metropolitan Police to illustrate the similarity between the two men. (Reproduced with kind permission of the Home Office)

given that they believed they were in the presence of a suicide bomber who could blow himself up at any moment. The police officers' misidentification was therefore a terrible mistake, leading to the death of an innocent man, but one that is understandable given what we know about the psychology of eyewitness performance.

11.2 Factors affecting witnesses' performance with lineups

A witness who takes part in a lineup procedure can make one of two kinds of mistake: they can wrongly identify someone as the person that they saw, when in fact the person chosen is innocent (a 'false positive' error); or they can incorrectly decide that the person whom they saw is not present in the lineup (a 'false negative' error). Both types of error are undesirable, because a false identification means that an innocent person might be convicted of a crime they did not commit, whereas a false rejection may result in a criminal being allowed to go free. Consequently there has been a great deal of research examining various factors that influence a witness' performance. These factors can be divided into **estimator variables** and **system variables** (Wells, 1978). Estimator variables are factors that are intrinsic to the person and the situation they were in, such as the age of the witness or the level of illumination at the scene of the crime. It is important to be aware of these factors, and how they might affect witnesses' reliability, but there is little that can be done to change them in practice. System variables concern the procedures that are used to obtain an accurate identification by a witness, such as the way in which a lineup is conducted and how a witness is interviewed. These procedures are potentially under the control of the legal system and could be altered in an attempt to avoid miscarriages of justice from happening.

When asked what factors affect the accuracy of eyewitnesses, people tend to disregard system variables and attach overwhelming importance to estimator variables, especially the characteristics of the eyewitness themselves (Boyce et al, 2007; Shaw et al, 1999). However, research shows that both estimator and system variables are important determinants of eyewitness performance.

11.3 **Estimator variables**

11.3.1 **Individual differences in witness characteristics**

As we have seen in previous chapters, much of the laboratory research in face processing is interested primarily in comparing groups or conditions in response to some experimental manipulation. Probably all published research

will have found some variability *within* groups or conditions. There can be marked differences between participants in terms of their face-processing abilities, but laboratory research tends to treat these individual differences as 'noise', to be eliminated as far as possible. (That is why most studies look for differences, *on average*, between groups of participants.) Surprisingly little work has examined these sources of variability. However, from an 'applied' point of view, it would be highly desirable to be able to predict a witness' reliability on the basis of knowledge of their individual characteristics. In this section, we will briefly summarize 'pure' research on individual differences in face processing, before assessing whether this information would be useful in a forensic context. Could the legal system use information about a witness' age, intelligence and personality in order to decide whether or not they are likely to be a reliable witness?

Sex differences

Probably the most widely researched area of individual differences in face processing concerns sex differences. In laboratory studies, sex differences have been reported on a wide range of cognitive tasks. Males are typically better at visuospatial tasks, and females are typically better at verbal tasks (see Halpern, 2000). However, females have been found to be better on a wide variety of face-processing tests, including detecting a face within a stimulus (McBain et al, 2009), the processing of facial identity (Lewin and Herlitz, 2002; McBain et al, 2009), the classification of facial sex (Cellerino et al, 2004) and perceiving facial emotion (Hampson et al, 2006; also see McClure [2000] for a meta-analysis).

One explanation for these differences is that they might stem from women's superior verbal processing abilities, with women being better at using verbal labels to aid the encoding and processing of faces (Lewin et al, 2001). Lewin and Herlitz (2002) tested this hypothesis by asking men and women to complete a face recognition task and two tests of verbal processing ability. They found that women were better at face recognition than men, but only for female faces, supporting the existence of an own-sex bias in face processing. In terms of the relationship between verbal processing ability and face-processing ability, they did not find a relationship for women, but for men they found a significant positive relationship; that is, for men, the better the verbal processing ability, the better their ability to recognize faces. Therefore, it seems that verbal skills may provide only a very limited explanation of sex differences in face processing.

Another possible explanation for sex differences, not just in face processing but in cognition generally, is the influence of hormones. Performance on cognitive tasks that are typically found to have a male advantage, such as visuospatial tasks, and those that are typically found to have a female advantage, such as verbal tasks, has been found to vary according to exposure to different hormones. For example, increased exposure to oestrogen, a 'female' hormone, tends to result in improved performance on verbal tasks, whereas increased exposure to testosterone, a 'male' hormone, tends to result in improved performance on visuospatial tasks (Schattmann and Sherwin, 2007; Sherwin, 2003). The influence of hormones on face processing has led to a wide range of research on this topic, mainly examining the role of hormones in the processing of the sex and gender of a face, attractiveness, facial symmetry and emotion (see Gasbarri et al, 2008; Jones et al, 2008; Macrae et al, 2002; Oinonen and Mazmanian, 2007). (A detailed review of this issue is given in Chapter 9.)

Are the sex differences in face-processing ability affected by whether the face being processed is male or female? Lewin and Herlitz (2002) found that women were better than males on a face recognition task, but only when the face being recognized was female. For male faces there was no difference between the male and female participants. This finding has also been replicated in a study with children (Rehnman and Herlitz, 2006). Stronger evidence for an own-sex[3] bias in face recognition has been found by Wright and Sladden (2003), who found that each sex was better at recognizing faces of their own sex than of the other sex. However, the opposite relationship has also been reported. Hofmann et al (2006) asked participants to name familiar faces that were expressing different emotions. Female participants were faster at naming male faces, and male participants were faster at naming female faces. This finding therefore suggests an opposite-sex bias for face processing!

Personality

Few studies have examined a possible relationship between face processing and personality. Traditionally personality is seen in terms of the 'big five' personality traits: openness, conscientiousness, extraversion, agreeableness and neuroticism (McCrae and Costa, 1997). However, research directly linking these to face-processing abilities is lacking. There is some research linking face processing with other traits that are sometimes considered to be aspects of personality. For example, individuals who tend to be hostile are biased towards the processing of negative facial emotion (Harrison and Gorelczenko, 1990) and are less accurate at processing facial emotion (Herridge et al, 2004). Furthermore, compared to individuals with prosocial tendencies, individuals with antisocial tendencies are less accurate at identifying fear (Marsh et al, 2007) and sadness (Dolan and Fullam, 2006).

---

[3] For a more detailed explanation of a variety of own-group biases in face recognition, including the own-sex bias, see Chapter 12.

Intelligence

In terms of intelligence, one study examined whether there were differences in the ability to recognize and match facial expressions in patients with varying levels of mental retardation (Hetzroni and Oren, 2002). They found that performance on both tasks was significantly higher for individuals with mild intellectual impairment than for individuals with moderate intellectual impairment. Herlitz and Yonker (2002) considered this relationship in a sample of participants without any intellectual impairment, and found that higher levels of intelligence were associated with higher face recognition abilities, but only for men.

Austin (2005) considered whether there was a relationship between intelligence, emotional intelligence and the processing of facial emotion. As would be expected from the sex differences literature, she found that females performed better than males on two different tests of processing facial emotion. Higher levels of intelligence were associated with higher levels of emotion processing, but this relationship was not found after controlling for the participants' age. This suggests that any apparent relationship between face-processing ability and intelligence may actually be explained in terms of changes in ability through adulthood (the sample comprised participants aged from 19 to 85 years). In terms of a possible relationship between emotional intelligence and the processing of facial emotion, Austin found a positive relationship, but only on one aspect of emotional intelligence: interpersonal emotional intelligence. There was no relationship with intrapersonal emotional intelligence. This suggests that the ability to process facial emotion is associated with the ability to interact with other people but not with the ability to manage and be aware of one's own emotions.

Age

In contrast to these other attributes, the possible effects of the age of a witness have been investigated extensively in both 'pure' and 'applied' settings. Whereas young children and the elderly perform as well as young adults with target-present lineups, both groups are more likely to make false-positive identifications with target-absent lineups.

Pozzulo and Lindsay (1998) conducted a meta-analysis of studies that had looked at children's face identification performance. Four groups of children (4-, 5–6-, 9–10- and 12–13-year-olds) were compared to adults. With target-present lineups, 4-year-olds were poorer than adults at identifying the target, but children over the age of 5 years had similar correct identification rates to those of adults. However, with target-absent lineups, all age groups of children were poorer than adults; even children as old as 12–13 years were significantly more likely to mistakenly select someone from the lineup as being the person that they had seen.

As Pozzulo and Lindsay point out, these results are rather different from those obtained in 'pure' research into children's face recognition abilities, which suggest that adult performance is not reached until about 10–12 years of age (see Chapter 6 on the development of face recognition). Pozzulo and Lindsay suggest that these discrepancies arise because of differences between pure and applied studies in terms of the procedures used and the social demands of the situation.

'Pure' studies of face recognition typically test a person's ability to discriminate between a number of targets and distractors, whereas in an 'applied' study the participant usually has to identify only one previously seen target amongst a handful of distractors. When the target is present in the lineup, applied studies make fewer demands on memory than pure studies, and so one might expect children to do better with this procedure.

A popular explanation for children's poorer performance with target-absent lineups has been that it reflects their response to the social demands of the situation—the child may feel under pressure to make a positive identification. Pozzulo and Dempsey (2006) found that, like adults, children are affected by the instructions given to them: they make fewer false-positive identifications if they are given neutral instructions (which make it clear that the target may or may not be present in the lineup) than after receiving biased instructions (which imply the target is present in the lineup, even if they are not). However, even with neutral instructions, children still make more false identifications than adults. This implies that social compliance is not the only factor at work. Pozzulo and Lindsay (1998) suggest that children's memory limitations may also play a role; children might find it harder to discount possible matches of distractors to the target face because they do not remember the target as well as adults, and hence the faces in the lineup represent more plausible matches to the target for them.

The discrepancies between the results of pure and applied studies imply that the developmental changes being charted by the former are not due simply to improvements in face processing *per se*, but also reflect the development of other aspects of cognition (such as attention, memory and decision-making processes). They also serve to remind us to be wary of assuming that developmental changes in performance are necessarily due to cognitive changes: children's performance may often be influenced by their lack of adults' tacit knowledge that experiments are very strange social settings. Children do not necessarily realize that experimenters often ask their participants to perform odd and apparently arbitrary tasks—such as trying to identify a face that the experimenter knows is not actually present.

At the other end of the lifespan, the elderly have also been shown to be somewhat poorer than younger adults at recognizing unfamiliar faces. In Memon et al's (2003a) study, young adults (aged between 16 and 33) and old adults (aged between 60 and 82) saw two videotaped incidents, one involving a young perpetrator and the other an older perpetrator. The participants were then tested with target-present or target-absent lineups,

after a delay of either 35 minutes or 1 week. There was little difference between the young and old participants with the short delay. However, after a week, the older participants were less accurate. They made more false identifications with the target-absent lineups, especially when the task involved a lineup of young faces. Memon et al suggest that the older adults' difficulties may be related to deficits in **source memory** (memory for the circumstances in which information was acquired), because this is known to decline with age. However, as explained in Chapter 12, an alternative interpretation of the elderly's poor face recognition ability is that it stems from an **own-age bias**: people are better at recognizing faces similar in age to themselves (Perfect and Moon, 2005).

Individual differences and the legal system

Returning to the question posed at the start of this section, is a knowledge of a witness' psychological attributes of any use to the legal system? Probably not. Firstly, they tend to be quite small differences, and hence unimportant in practical terms. Secondly, they are differences between *groups*; although, on average, women might be better at face recognition than men, the distributions of performance overlap greatly, because within each group there is a wide range of ability. Although most men might be worse than most women, nevertheless there are many men who are very good at face recognition, and many women who are very poor at it. Simply by knowing a person's sex, it is not possible to determine with any degree of certainty whether or not they are likely to be good at recognizing faces. Thirdly, as we shall see later in this chapter, there are many other factors that are likely to affect a witness' performance, such as stress—a given witness' performance will be determined by a unique *interaction* of many factors, and so knowledge of just one of these (such as the witness' sex) cannot enable us to decide whether this particular witness is likely to be reliable.

In a brief review of the 'applied' literature on individual differences in eyewitness performance, Wells and Olson (2003) conclude that there is little evidence of any sex differences in the accuracy of eyewitness performance, nor for any effects of intelligence (at least, not amongst people within the normal IQ range). However, as we have seen, there are some suggestions that age may affect performance.

11.3.2 The 'other-race effect' and other in-group biases

People are better at recognizing faces of their own group than those of a different group. Thus, it is harder to recognize faces from a different race to one's own. It is also harder to recognize faces that differ from us in gender or age. These **in-group biases** are such an important aspect of face recognition that we have devoted a separate chapter to them (see Chapter 12).

11.3.3 Duration of the initial encounter with the suspect

All things being equal, the longer the view that someone has of a face, the more likely they are to remember it (e.g. Shapiro and Penrod, 1986). Memon et al (2003b) showed participants a video of a simulated robbery and varied the amount of time for which the robber's face could be seen. When presented with a lineup subsequently, participants who had seen the robber's face in the video for 45 seconds made more correct identifications and fewer false identifications than those who had seen it for only 12 seconds; in the former condition, 90% of participants identified the robber, compared with only 32% of those in the short-exposure condition.

One problem is that stress may cause someone to overestimate the length of time for which they saw the suspect (Loftus et al, 1987). In addition, as Wells and Olson (2003) point out, the extent to which a witness attends to a face is probably

more important than the exposure time *per se*. Often someone will not realize that a crime has been committed until after the culprit has left (for example, in the case of doorstep fraudsters). If so, they may not have paid much attention to the person's face, and may find it hard to recognize as a consequence.

Another difficulty is that, although increased duration is associated with an increase in correct identifications, it may also inflate witnesses' confidence. Some studies have found that increased exposure durations can lead to a greater number of false identifications with target-absent lineups (Shapiro and Penrod, 1986). For example, in Read's (1995) study, participants interacted with a shop assistant for less than a minute, or between 4 and 15 minutes. The long-interaction group performed better than the short-interaction group with target-present lineups, but made more false identifications from target-absent lineups. Read suggested this might happen because witnesses mistakenly use exposure duration as a basis for estimating how well they should be able to remember a face. Those who see the face for longer assume they must therefore have a good memory of the face, and hence show greater readiness to choose someone when presented with a lineup.

11.3.4 Delay between initial encounter and subsequent identification

In an applied context, you might expect that one of the most obvious issues is the extent to which memory of a face declines with the passage of time. Intuitively, one might expect that a witness who saw a criminal a year ago would be less reliable at identifying that person than someone who saw them only yesterday. This rather general statement is probably true. However, after reviewing the literature on the effects of delay on memory for faces, Dysart and Lindsay (2007b) conclude that the precise effects of delay are complex, and that much more research needs to be done on this topic. They argue that it is not possible at present to make any firm statements about the effects of delay. However, they say that there are some suggestions that the effects may differ for showups and lineups. For showups, delays of as little as 24 hours may result in a decrease in correct identifications and a concomitant increase in false identifications. In contrast, lineup identification performance appears to be relatively unaffected by delays unless they are very long (in the order of many months). There are virtually no data on how performance with mugshots is affected by the passage of time.

Deffenbacher and colleagues (2008) are much more optimistic about the possibility of making statements about the effects of delay on recognition performance. Following a meta-analysis of 53 published studies on the topic, Deffenbacher and colleagues concluded that recognition performance follows roughly the same pattern as Ebbinghaus described for verbal material over a century ago: forgetting occurs rapidly soon after exposure to a stimulus, but then the rate of forgetting levels off with the passage of time, to produce a negatively accelerating curve (Fig. 11.2).

Deffenbacher et al use Wickelgren's model of **memory trace decay**. This suggests that the strength of memory for a stimulus is the net result of three factors. The first of these is the strength of the initial memory trace (for example, how well a criminal's face was seen to begin with). The second factor is the extent to which the memory trace is consolidated in memory. Initially, memory traces are very fragile and easily disrupted, but with time they become more robust. The third factor is the extent to which exposure to other similar stimuli interferes with the memory trace (for example, how many other faces are seen between the initial encounter with a criminal's face and the subsequent viewing of it in a lineup or in an array of mugshots). This **retroactive interference** becomes stronger with time, because the longer the delay, the greater the opportunity for encountering stimuli that can interfere with the original memory.

Deffenbacher et al claim that Wickelgren's model simulates the data from several published studies rather well. One practical problem in using this model in a legal context is how one can reliably determine the strength of the initial encoding of the face in question. Deffenbacher et al attempt to tackle this issue by devising a 'best-case scenario'. They used data from a field study of eyewitness performance by bank tellers who believed they had interacted with 'criminals' attempting to cash a cheque (Pigott et al, 1990). Deffenbacher et al argue that the bank tellers were operating under optimum conditions; they were unstressed and had a prolonged (1.5 minutes), undistracted view of the 'criminal' in good lighting conditions. Using Wickelgren's model, Deffenbacher et al estimate that at the time of testing (only 4 hours after the 'criminal's' face had been seen) the strength of the tellers' memory was only 79% of what it had been originally. This value is based on a number of assumptions, but the basic message seems valid— that, all other things being equal, memory for an unfamiliar face is likely to deteriorate very rapidly soon after it has been seen. In this light, it is worth noting that a survey of UK police forces by Pike, Brace and Kynan (2002) found that the median delay between a request for a live identification parade and it actually taking place was ten weeks.

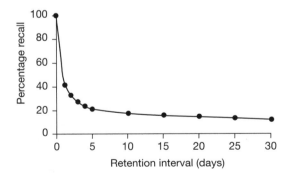

FIGURE 11.2 Typical Ebbinghaus forgetting curve, demonstrating how, with the passage of time, recall declines dramatically at first, but then levels off.

11.3.5 **Witness confidence**

It seems obvious that a witness who claims that they are confident about their memory for faces and events is likely to be more reliable than someone who is uncertain of their testimony. Following the *Neil versus Biggers* (1972) case, the United States Supreme Court recommended that jurors should take account of how confident witnesses seemed to be.[4] In fact, research offers little support for this suggestion; numerous studies have suggested that there is actually very little correlation between a witness' rating of their confidence and their actual accuracy (Bothwell, Deffenbacher and Brigham, 1987). In addition, witnesses tend to be overconfident both for their memory of events and for their identifications of suspects (e.g. Allwood et al, Knutson and Granhag, 2006; Luus and Wells, 1994).

Even worse, a witness' confidence level can be affected by their experiences following the event in question. The legal system would like to establish how confident a witness was at the time they saw a suspect, or at the time that they made an identification from a lineup. In practice, what a witness may provide in court is a retrospective assessment of how confident they were at the time. This memory is not necessarily accurate, because it can be affected by feedback to the witness about their competence that has been provided since the event took place. For example, Wells and Bradfield (1998, 1999) showed participants a target-absent lineup and then gave them either positive or negative feedback about their performance, such as 'Good, you identified the suspect' or 'Oh.

You identified number … The actual suspect is number …'. Participants' subsequent ratings of how confident they had been *at the time of the identification* were increased or decreased according to whether they received positive or negative feedback. Feedback may not only affect the witness' memory of how confident they were when they made their identification, but also their memory of how well they remembered other aspects of the event in question, such as the length of time for which they saw the suspect, how clear a view they had of events, and so on. A recent meta-analysis of 14 studies by Douglass and Steblay (2006) has confirmed that **post-identification feedback effects** are robust and reliable for these factors, which is worrying given that they are likely to have a strong influence on jurors' assessments of a witness' accuracy (e.g. Penrod and Cutler, 1995).

Wells et al (2003) looked at the timing of positive and negative feedback in relation to when witnesses rated their confidence. The biasing effects of feedback on confidence ratings made two days after viewing a staged crime were similar irrespective of whether the feedback was given immediately after the event took place, or two days later. Wells et al's interpretation is that confidence judgements are constructed at the time they are given; when participants are asked to assess their confidence after a delay, they are unable to remember how confident they were originally.

Based on research like this, the British Psychological Society issued a document in 2008 entitled *Guidelines on Memory and the Law*, which contained scientifically based recommendations to the legal profession about what would

---

[4] The *Neil versus Biggers* case centred around assessing the reliability of the evidence from a woman who identified her rapist at a show-up held by the police seven months after she was attacked. The US Supreme Court identified five factors that should be considered in evaluating the reliability of eyewitness identifications: (1) to what extent the witness had the opportunity to witness the criminal act taking place (i.e. could they have obtained a good view of the criminal committing the crime?); (2) the witness' degree of attention; (3) the accuracy of the witness' prior description of the criminal; (4) the witness' level of certainty at the time of the identification; and (5) the length of time between the crime and the identification.

constitute good practice. One of these was that witnesses' assessments of their confidence should be recorded *before* they find out whether they have identified the police's suspect, not afterwards. However, one influence that will be difficult to avoid in practice is that of other witnesses: there are often two or more witnesses to a crime, and they frequently discuss it amongst themselves before being interviewed by the police (Paterson and Kemp, 2006). Skagerberg (2007) has shown that feedback does not have to come from an 'authority figure' such as a police officer or an experimenter for it to be effective. A witness' confidence level can be inflated merely by another witness agreeing with them. In Skagerberg's study, pairs of participants watched a video together of a staged mugging, and then attempted to identify the mugger from a target-absent lineup. About half of the participants agreed on the mugger's identity, and these participants scored higher on a variety of measures than those who disagreed; for example, those who agreed were more certain of their identification, believed they had a better memory for faces that they had seen only once, and believed they had a clearer image of the mugger. Bear in mind that everyone in this study saw target-absent lineups, so that all the identifications that were made were incorrect; even so, as a consequence of apparently confirmatory feedback from a co-witness, a witness' confidence ratings can be boosted.

Brewer and Wells (2006) point out that conventional correlational techniques probably underestimate the strength of any relationship between confidence and accuracy. Using a more sensitive method, they found that confidence estimates made *immediately* after the identification did show some relationship with accuracy. Witnesses who were quick to select someone from the lineup, and who expressed a high level of confidence in their decision, were more likely to be correct than witnesses who were slower and less confident. Similar conclusions were drawn by Behrman and Richards (2005),

who looked at police descriptions of witnesses' behaviour in 461 real-life lineups. In cases where there was corroborating evidence (i.e. where there was independent verification of the accuracy of an eyewitness' decision), 43% of identifications of the police's suspect were accompanied by high confidence, as opposed to only 10% of incorrect identifications.

However, as Brewer and Wells point out, these findings do not in any way contradict the established finding that it is unwise to attach any credibility to a witness' rating in the courtroom of how confident they had been in the past, when they saw the lineup originally. Witnesses' insight into their accuracy appears to decay rapidly with the mere passage of time and, as mentioned above, is highly susceptible to bias from external influences such as lineup administrators.

11.3.6 Stress

There is some evidence that, under conditions of stress, a person's attention becomes narrowed (Christianson, 1992; Easterbrook, 1959). As a result, they may concentrate on events in central vision, and fail to encode information about events or people in their peripheral vision. One version of this theory involves the concept of **weapon focus**: faced with a weapon such as a knife or a gun, a witness may concentrate on this at the expense of encoding information about the person who is wielding the weapon. Loftus et al (1987) tested students' performance as eyewitnesses after they had watched one of two different sets of slides of an interaction between a man and a cashier in a restaurant. In one of the slide sequences, the man handed the cashier a cheque and she gave him some money. In the other sequence, he pulled out a gun and she handed him some money. Eye-movement recordings showed that participants in the gun condition looked at the gun more than participants in the cheque condition looked at the cheque. Those in the gun condition also remembered less information about the man, and were poorer at identifying him from a lineup subsequently.

The weapon focus effect is often small, and it is not always found. In Steblay's (1992) meta-analysis of 19 laboratory studies, only 6 showed a clear-cut effect. Some archival studies of real-life crimes have found evidence of a weapon focus effect, but others have not (e.g. Behrman and Davey, 2001). The effect tends to show up more in witnesses' descriptions than in identification parade performance.

Although the 'stress' explanation remains a popular explanation, a number of researchers have claimed that novelty may play a part. Pickel (1998, 1999) has argued that weapons may attract attention merely because they are unusual, unexpected objects. In one of her experiments (Pickel, 1998), participants saw a video of a man who approached a receptionist in a hair salon, took some money from her, and then left. While he did this, he held an object in his hand. This was either a pair of scissors (highly threatening, but not unusual in a hair salon); a wallet (unthreatening and not unusual); a gun (highly threatening and unusual); or a raw whole chicken (unthreatening, but highly unusual in a hair salon). Pickel found a significant 'weapon focus' effect, in that witnesses recalled fewer details about the man's physical characteristics when he held a gun than when he was empty-handed. However, similar effects were also obtained when he held the chicken. Pickel suggested that the 'weapon focus' effect might occur because a weapon attracts attention due to its unusualness, rather than because it is threatening.

In Pickel's (1999) study, participants saw different versions of a filmed interaction between a woman and a man holding a gun. The level of 'threat' was manipulated by changing the way in which the man behaved towards the woman (i.e. whether or not he pointed the gun at her). Weapon focus effects were obtained when the setting for the interaction was one in which guns might be unexpected (a baseball field), but not when the context was one in which guns might

be expected (a shooting range); participants provided more information about the man's appearance in the latter condition. Although participants in the 'threat' conditions interpreted the interaction correctly, the threat manipulation had no effect on their performance. In a second experiment, participants saw a video of a friendly (non-threatening) interaction between a man and a woman. He was carrying either a mobile phone or a gun, and was dressed as either a policeman or a priest. Participants remembered the 'policeman' equally well, regardless of whether he held a gun or a mobile phone; however, they produced significantly less information about the 'priest' if he held a gun rather than a phone. Pickel's interpretation is that policemen in the USA are expected to carry guns, and so the gun in this context is not novel; in contrast, it is unusual for a priest to carry a gun, and so the gun draws attention away from the person holding it.

Hope and Wright (2007) showed participants a series of slides depicting a man entering a grocery store and brandishing either a gun, a feather duster or a wallet (i.e. a threatening, novel or neutral object). The participants also performed a secondary task (pressing a button whenever an odd number appeared at the bottom of the display) so that the researchers could assess the extent to which attention was diverted to the object being held. Both the gun and the feather duster impaired performance on the secondary task to a similar extent, implying that they made similar demands on attentional resources. However, using a composite measure that took into account both recall performance and witness confidence, Hope and Wright found that recall for the man's appearance was worse for participants in the gun condition than for those who saw the feather duster. Their conclusion was that, although novelty may well be involved in the weapon focus effect, the emotive, threatening nature of weapons also has a role to play and should not be discounted.

One problem with investigating the effects of stress on eyewitness performance is that high stress levels are very difficult to simulate in experimental studies, for practical and ethical reasons. It has been claimed that this makes it difficult to generalize from laboratory studies to real life (Yuille, 1993). Tollestrup et al (1994) looked at suspect identification rates by real-life witnesses in relation to the type of crime in which they were involved. Identification rates were highest for victims of robbery (46%), lower for witnesses of robberies (33%), and lowest of all for victims of fraud (25%). Tollestrup et al's interpretation of these results is that stress at the time of the crime enhanced face recognition. They suggest that most of the laboratory research to date tells us something about 'unaffected witnesses' of crimes, but little about the eyewitness performance of victims of crime, who may process information rather differently due to their high stress levels.

Deffenbacher et al (2004) suggest that research has often confounded different phenomena under the single label of 'stress'. Their proposal is that stress affects the regulation of attention in two distinctly different ways. One is to produce an 'orienting' response that leads to attention being focused on the most informative aspects of the situation. In these circumstances, memory may be enhanced, especially for events in central vision. Alternatively, stress can elicit a 'defensive' response that involves physiological activation. Deffenbacher et al suggest that high stress levels can either impair or enhance eyewitness performance, depending on whether they provoke an 'orienting' response, a 'defensive' response, or both.

A meta-analysis confined to 63 studies involving only 'defensive' responses (Deffenbacher et al, 2004) found that high levels of stress impaired the accuracy of eyewitness identification performance, and also reduced the accuracy of recall of crime-related details. These effects were most pronounced in studies that used forensically relevant methods such as lineups and staged crimes. Deffenbacher et al suggest that many laboratory studies of 'high stress' that

find *enhanced* eyewitness performance have used manipulations (such as gory scenes) that encourage orienting responses. Real-life violent crimes are more likely to produce defensive stress responses, and these are likely to be much more pronounced than any that can be produced ethically in experiments. As a result, laboratory studies are likely to greatly underestimate how much eyewitness performance is impaired by stress.

Deffenbacher's model has recently been supported by the results of an ingenious study by Valentine and Mesout (2009). They examined the eyewitness performance of visitors to the 'Horror Labyrinth' at the London Dungeon (a horror museum full of shocks and scares). After visiting the exhibit, participants were given a surprise test; they were asked to identify one of the actors in the Labyrinth from a photospread lineup. Stress, as measured by heart rate and self-report during the visit, markedly affected recognition performance. Only 17% of participants who were highly stressed correctly identified the actor, compared with 75% of those who were low in stress. Like Deffenbacher, Valentine and Mesout concluded that laboratory research may have underestimated the effects of stress on eyewitness performance.

11.3.7 Previous encounters with the suspect

People are better at recognizing a face (getting a sense of familiarity from a face) than they are at knowing why that face seems familiar (remembering the circumstances in which the initial encounter took place). This can increase the risk of a misidentification in a lineup if a witness has seen the suspect's face before in some other context. One way this could happen is if the suspect's face was present amongst a set of mugshots that the witness had looked through previously. This might be enough for the suspect's face to evoke a feeling of familiarity in the witness when they come to inspect the lineup;

if the witness fails to identify the source of this feeling of familiarity accurately, they might well make a false identification of the suspect. (This issue will be returned to later, in the discussion of 'system variables'.) Similar effects can occur if the witness has encountered the suspect in some other context: perhaps the suspect was actually a bystander at the scene of the crime, or worked in a shop that was used by the witness.

These effects may be more pronounced when witnesses are asked to identify a suspect from a race different to their own. Horry and Wright (2008) showed White participants a series of photographs of White and Black faces. Each was superimposed on one of five different backgrounds: a photograph of a classroom, basketball court, prison, factory, or a uniform grey background. At test, participants were shown these faces on a plain white background, as well as distractor faces that they had never seen before. First the participants had to decide whether or not they had seen each face previously. If they thought they had, they were then asked to decide on which of the five backgrounds it had appeared originally. Participants made nearly twice as many more false alarms in response to the Black faces; in other words, they were more likely to decide mistakenly that Black distractor faces had been seen before. They were also poorer at remembering in which context they had seen the Black faces that they did identify correctly: only 52% of the background judgements for Black faces were correct, compared with 59% of the judgements for White faces.

11.3.8 Speed of recognition

Dunning and Perretta (2002) found that witnesses who made a positive identification from a lineup within 10–12 seconds were rarely inaccurate in their choices. Eighty-seven per cent of the correct identifications in their study were made within this amount of time. In contrast, only 10% of the inaccurate witnesses made an (incorrect) identification as quickly as this. One explanation

for this effect is that face recognition is fairly automatic; witnesses who take longer may be relying more on conscious deliberation in order to make their choice, and this takes time. Behrman and Richards (2005) obtained similar results in an archival study of real crimes; witnesses who made fast, confident identifications were more likely to be correct than those who were slow and deliberative.

At first sight, this looks like a promising diagnostic tool for evaluating the reliability of eyewitnesses. Unfortunately, however, the '10–12 seconds' rule cannot be regarded as invariant. For those participants who attempted a lineup identification in Sauerland and Sporer's (2007) study, 18 seconds was estimated to be the time interval that best differentiated accurate and inaccurate participants; 52% of correct decisions were made within this time, and 82% of misidentifications were made after it had elapsed. Although Brewer et al (2006) found a relationship between response time and accuracy, in their experiments the time that distinguished accurate from inaccurate witnesses varied from 5 to 36 seconds, depending on how much time elapsed between seeing a staged crime and seeing a lineup, and also depending on the size of the lineup that was used. Brewer et al suggest that the data are consistent with explanations other than Dunning and Perretta's. They favour an interpretation in terms of recognition memory being based on the degree of discriminability between the suspect and the distractors in the lineup. If a response is made once an individual has accumulated enough information to make a decision, then responses will be fast if the suspect and distractors are highly discriminable, and slower if they are not. Whatever the explanation, the variability in the amount of time that distinguishes accurate and inaccurate witnesses suggests that, although the basic finding is valid—that accurate witnesses tend to choose suspects more quickly than inaccurate ones—the '10–12 seconds' rule is unlikely to be useful in an applied context.

11.3.9 **Quality of the witness' description of the suspect**

Intuitively it seems plausible that if someone is able to describe a person in detail then they should also be good at recognizing them. This is another of the criteria that the US Supreme Court recommends jurors to use in order to evaluate the credibility of an eyewitness (*Neil versus Biggers* 1972). However, research suggests that there is virtually no relationship between the quality of witnesses' descriptions and their identification performance (review in Meissner et al, 2007[5]). Meissner et al suggest that this is because description and identification are based on quite different cognitive processes: description involves analysing the face in terms of constituent features that can be described verbally, whereas identification involves non-verbal processing of a more holistic nature.

The phenomenon of **verbal overshadowing** (Schooler and Engstler-Schooler, 1990) suggests that making a detailed verbal description of a face may impair subsequent recognition of it. In Schooler and Engstler-Schooler's original experiment, participants watched a video of a staged robbery. Those who were asked to describe the robber in detail were less likely to identify him correctly in a lineup than were participants who did not provide a description. Meissner and Brigham (2001b) performed a meta-analysis of 15 studies on overshadowing, and concluded that there was indeed a small but significant effect of verbal description on subsequent identification performance: producing a description increased the chances of making a false identification from a lineup.

There are several explanations of why overshadowing occurs (see Chin and Schooler [2007] for a recent review). Schooler and Engstler-Schooler's (1990) original explanation was in terms of **recoding interference**: when someone describes a face, they end up relying on this verbal description rather than on their (more accurate) visual memory for the face. Support for this explanation comes from studies by Meissner and his colleagues on **instructional bias**: witnesses were either encouraged to make very detailed descriptions of faces, or warned to confine their descriptions to details about which they were absolutely certain. Only the former condition produces verbal overshadowing effects (Meissner, 2002; Meissner et al, 2001). Meissner suggests that participants who produce very elaborate descriptions are more likely to include erroneous details as a result, which they come to believe are aspects of the face they saw originally. Support for this idea also comes from a study by Wogalter (1991), who asked participants to describe a face either by spontaneously supplying applicable adjectives (so that, for example, in response to the prompt 'nose?', they might write 'big') or by looking at a list of adjectives and ticking the ones that were applicable (so that they would be presented with 'nose?: big, small' and would tick the descriptor that best matched their memory of the facial feature in question). Participants in the latter condition were poorer at recognizing the face than those who came up with their own adjectives. Again, the suggestion is that perhaps

---

[5] A recent meta-analysis by Meissner et al (2008), based on 33 articles and 4,278 participants, did find some evidence of a relationship between description accuracy and identification accuracy. However, the relationship was very weak (*r* was generally 0.2 or less) and it was found only in studies within the 'pure' research tradition, using multiple target faces and short delays between presentation and testing, as opposed to studies using forensically relevant methods such as staged crimes followed by lineups. Meissner et al's conclusion is much the same as that of earlier studies: the quality of a witness' description of a face offers the legal system no reliable indication of whether or not that witness could actually recognize the face concerned.

the distracting adjectives contaminated the participants' memory for the original face.

This cannot be the entire explanation for verbal overshadowing effects, however, because there are some aspects to the phenomenon that cannot be easily explained by 'recoding interference' of this kind. For example, Dodson and colleagues (1997) showed that verbal overshadowing is not confined to the face that is described: describing one face impaired recognition for another one that had not been described. Brown and Lloyd-Jones (2003) showed participants a series of 12 faces, but asked them only to describe a 13th; this resulted in impaired recognition for *all* of the 12 faces in the set. Brown and Lloyd-Jones also showed that the effects of verbal overshadowing can extend from one stimulus type to another; describing a face impaired subsequent recognition of a series of photographs of cars (although describing a car did not affect face recognition).

An alternative explanation of verbal overshadowing that can account for these effects is in terms of **transfer-inappropriate processing shifts** (Schooler, 2002). The process of making a verbal description of a face may cause the witness to shift to a different mode of information processing from the one that they used to encode the face in the first place. This verbal processing mode is ill suited to the demands of a face recognition task, for which a configural processing mode would be more appropriate.

The results of Macrae and Lewis' (2002) study fit nicely with this kind of explanation. Participants saw a video of a staged robbery and then performed one of two versions of the **Navon task** (Navon, 1977). This task involves presenting participants with a series of large letters, each comprised of a different smaller letter (Fig. 11.3).

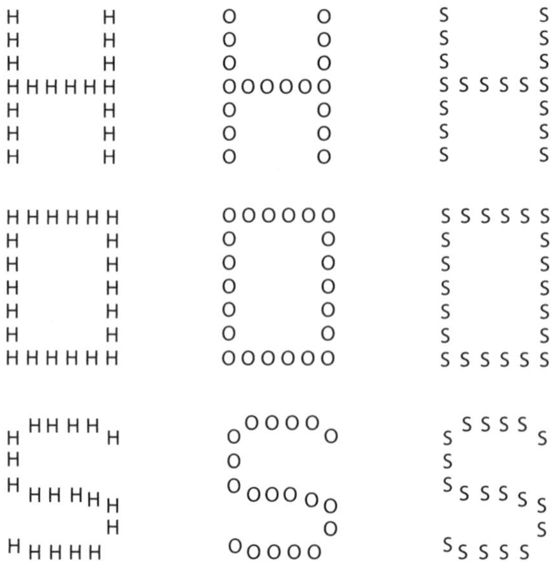

On each trial, one of these stimuli is shown. Participants either try to identify the large letter as quickly as possible, ignoring its constituent

FIGURE 11.3 Examples of Navon letters, as used by Macrae and Lewis (2002).

small letters, or try to identify the small letter on each trial, ignoring the large letter. In Macrae and Lewis' study, when presented with a lineup, only 30% of participants who had focused on the small letters correctly identified the 'robber' they had seen, compared with 83% of those who had concentrated on the large letters. Macrae and Lewis suggested that attending to the small letters encouraged participants to adopt an 'analytical' or 'featural' mode of processing, whereas attending to the larger letters encouraged a more 'holistic' processing style. The former processing mode is incompatible with how people normally process faces, and hence produces overshadowing effects. Perfect (2003) conducted a similar study, except that his participants performed both types of Navon task for five minutes each. Those who did the 'local' task second were worst at identification: only 43% of them recognized the target face, compared with 80% of those who did the 'global' task second.[6] It could be argued that both verbal

---

[6] Not all studies on the effects of the Navon tasks on face recognition have produced results as impressive as these; Lawson (2007) reported three studies in which she failed to induce processing biases by using Navon stimuli, and

overshadowing and the Navon effect are somehow related to the fact that both procedures use verbal stimuli. Hills and Lewis (2008) therefore replicated Perfect's procedure, but using non-verbal stimuli ('Navon symbols'—such as a large diamond comprised of small circles) and obtained similar results: improved recognition by those who identified the global shapes second, and impaired recognition by those who identified the local shapes second.

As well as explaining these findings, the processing shift explanation can also account for Meissner et al's (2001) 'instructional bias' effects mentioned above. Meissner et al interpreted their results as being due to a self-produced 'misinformation effect', but an alternative explanation is that asking participants to describe a face in exhaustive detail might have biased them towards a more 'piecemeal' and analytical mode of processing (Hunt and Carroll, 2008).

Fortunately, verbal overshadowing is probably not a problem for real-world witnesses. As well as the effect being quite weak, it also appears to be short-lived; although Schooler and Engstler-Schooler (1990) found that evidence of verbal overshadowing could be detected for up to two days after a description had been given, Meissner and Brigham (2001b) concluded the effects were strongest if identification was attempted within ten minutes of describing the face. In real life, there is normally a considerable delay between a witness supplying a description of a criminal and attempting to identify that person from a lineup, and so there is ample time for any effects of verbal overshadowing to dissipate. Meissner et al's (2001) study suggests that the effects can also be minimized if police interviewers encourage witnesses to confine their descriptions to what they genuinely remember about the criminal's face.

11.4 System variables

11.4.1 Prior exposure to mugshots

Following a crime, the police may ask a witness to look through a set of photographs of known criminals ('mugshots'), in the hope that the person that they saw already has a police record. Both the US Supreme Court and the UK Police and Criminal Evidence Act (PACE) guidelines recommend that a witness who has seen mugshots should not subsequently view a lineup, in case the witness' decision at the lineup stage is biased by their prior exposure to the mugshots. Some experiments by Brown et al (1977) showed the kinds of effects that exposure to mugshots might have. Participants saw a staged 'crime' and then looked through a set of mugshots. A face that was seen amongst the mugshots, and then encountered again as an innocent distractor in a lineup, was more likely to be falsely identified as the criminal in the staged event. It appeared that participants remembered seeing the innocent person's face before, but forgot the circumstances of this initial encounter. They wrongly attributed the feeling of familiarity to the fact that the face had been seen at the scene of the crime.

More recently, Deffenbacher, Bornstein and Penrod (2006) performed three meta-analyses of studies on the effects of mugshots. They concluded there is clear evidence that prior exposure to mugshots reduces performance with subsequent lineups: participants make fewer correct identifications and correct rejections, and are more likely to falsely identify an innocent person as the criminal. These effects are exacerbated if the witness positively identifies one of the mugshots as being the criminal that they saw; there may be a **commitment effect**,

---

concluded that these effects may be less robust than was hitherto believed. Weston et al (2008) point out that, although responding to Navon letters and verbally describing a face produce similar effects on face recognition performance, it is not a foregone conclusion that they are doing so for the same reasons: the processing orientation encouraged by describing a face may not necessarily be the same as that induced by Navon letters.

with the witness feeling under pressure to be consistent in their identifications at both the mugshot and lineup phases (e.g. Dysart et al, 2001; Gorenstein and Ellsworth, 1980). However, a reduction in accuracy may occur even if the witness does not make an identification at the time (i.e. even if they merely passively view a mugshot of someone who is seen again later in a lineup). Mugshot-induced biases may occur even if the viewings of the mugshots and the lineup are separated by as much as a fortnight.

Interestingly, Deffenbacher et al found that misidentifications were more likely if the witness looked through a few mugshots than if they looked through many. Deffenbacher and colleagues speculate that perhaps witnesses engage in deeper encoding of faces when they look through a small number of mugshots, because they believe that the police have some idea of the criminal's identity. In contrast, when witnesses look though a large number of mugshots, they may feel that they are merely searching in the remote hope that the criminal's face is present, and hence they may not encode the faces to the same extent.

Deffenbacher et al cite studies on **unconscious transference** which show that witnesses to a crime may subsequently identify an innocent bystander as the criminal, rather than the true culprit (e.g. Ross et al, 1994). Deffenbacher et al suggest that the mugshot-induced bias is an example of a more general psychological phenomenon: that memory for material (faces, objects or words) is better than memory for the context in which that material was originally encountered. However, Blunt and McAllister (2008) found no evidence of transference effects in their own study on mugshots, and suggest that the effects of viewing mugshots on subsequent lineup misidentifications are better explained in terms of witnesses feeling committed to be consistent in their choices. Whatever the true source of mugshot-induced biases turns out to be, the practical implication is the same: asking a witness to view an identification parade after exposure to mugshots increases the chances of that witness making a misidentification.

11.4.2 Composition of the lineup

If a lineup is 'fair', the suspect can be chosen only because the witness recognizes them, not on the basis of any other cues (Fig. 11.4).

With respect to producing a fair lineup, the choice of distractors is obviously very important. How does one decide whether or not a lineup is fair? Wells, Lieppe and Ostrom (1979) suggested that the important thing is the lineup's **functional size**: how many of the lineup members actually stand a good chance of being chosen instead of the suspect. This can be assessed as follows. Observers who have not seen the suspect but have seen only the witness' description of him or her are asked to pick the suspect from the lineup. If the lineup is fair, then everyone in the lineup should have an equal chance of being picked, and so choices should

FIGURE 11.4 Example of a biased lineup. Purely on the basis of the witness' description of the suspect ('tall, sallow, black cape, long incisors, no shadow') it would be possible to choose Dracula rather than any of the distractors.

be spread across all of the lineup members. In this situation, the functional size of the lineup is the same as its actual size. If, on the other hand, some people are picked frequently and others are chosen rarely, the lineup is not fair: its functional size is smaller than its actual size. Wells used this technique on data from a real-life case and found that, although the lineup contained six individuals, its functional size was only 1.6—close to the point where the lineup members other than the suspect could have been dispensed with!

How one constructs a fair lineup in practice turns out to be a complicated issue, as yet unresolved. There are two ways in which distractors can be chosen for a lineup. One way is to select distractors on the basis of their physical similarity to the suspect, so that the suspect is presented amongst a group of people who look like him or her. Another way is to choose the distractors on the basis of their similarity to the witness' initial *description* of the suspect. At present, UK police guidelines advocate using similarity-based lineups, while in the USA the Department of Justice recommends the use of description-based lineups.

Luus and Wells (1991) suggested that selection on the basis of similarity to the witness' description was the preferable method. However, if a lineup is constructed on the basis of similarity to the suspect, it is possible for the suspect to stand out because he or she effectively becomes the **prototype** from which all the other members of the lineup vary (Wogalter et al, 1992). Clark et al (2008) point out another potential problem with this method: it uses different criteria for including the suspect and the distractors in the lineup, and as a result could bias witnesses towards choosing the suspect. Suppose the police's suspect is actually innocent, but has been chosen to take part in a lineup because he or she fits the witness' description of the criminal. This person is the only one in the lineup who has been chosen on this basis; the other lineup members have been chosen because they resemble the suspect. Consequently

there is a risk that the person in the lineup who best matches the witness' memory of the criminal is the suspect—even if that suspect is in fact innocent.

With similarity-based lineup construction there is also the problem of how one assesses whether the degree of similarity is adequate; taken to its extreme, one could end up with a lineup in which the members were like 'clones', so similar to one another that there was no chance that even a highly reliable witness could tell which of them was the person they had originally seen. Earlier laboratory-based studies (e.g. Lindsay et al, Martin and Webber, 1994; Wells et al, 1993) found that lineups based on similarity to the witness' description produced more correct identifications. However, more recent research (Darling et al, 2008; Tunnicliff and Clark, 2000) has shown no difference between the two types of selection procedure. More research needs to be done in order to identify which of the many procedural differences between the earlier and later studies is responsible for this discrepancy. However, given that the later studies used procedures that were more similar to real-life police procedures (for example, in terms of the delay between witnesses' initial view of the suspect and seeing the lineup), Darling et al conclude that there is currently no sound scientific basis for recommending to UK police forces that they change their current practice of selecting lineup distractors on the basis of their similarity to the witness' description.

11.4.3 Sequential versus simultaneous presentation of lineup members

The traditional method of presenting a lineup to a witness has been to use simultaneous presentation: the lineup members are shown to the witness all at once, and the witness can look at any of them for as long as they want. An alternative method is to use sequential presentation, in which the witness sees the lineup members one at a time and decides for each person whether or not this is the person they saw. Rejection of a lineup member is final; the witness does not have the option of looking at earlier faces in the sequence again, and possibly reconsidering their earlier choices. If a positive identification is made, the process of inspecting lineup members stops, and any remaining lineup members (who may include the police's suspect) are not seen by the witness.

Comparisons of these two presentation methods suggest that they have different effects on witnesses' performance. When the culprit is actually present, witnesses are more likely to make a correct identification if the lineup is presented simultaneously than if it is presented sequentially. However, this effect is not as marked as the difference between the two methods when the culprit is absent from the lineup; under these conditions, sequential presentation reduces the chances of witnesses making a false identification of an innocent suspect (review in Steblay et al, 2001).

Wells (1984) suggested that these differences arise because the presentation methods have different effects on witnesses' decision-making processes. When lineup members are presented sequentially, the witness has to make an **absolute** decision about whether or not each person is the suspect before moving on to the next person in the lineup. In contrast, when the lineup members are presented simultaneously, the witness has the opportunity to make **relative** judgements. They can compare each lineup member with their memory of the person they saw, and end up picking the person who looks most like their memory.

While confirming the empirical finding that false identifications are somewhat less likely with sequential presentation, more recent research has suggested that Wells' 'relative/absolute' distinction may be an oversimplification. Witnesses' performance with sequential lineups can be influenced by the degree of similarity between the target and distractors, and by the target's position in the lineup (e.g. Clark and Davey, 2005; Flowe and Ebbesen, 2007). This implies that decision making with sequentially presented lineups may involve relative judgements about lineup members to a greater extent than was once thought. Following a critical review of research that has compared sequential and simultaneous lineups, McQuiston-Surrett et al (2006) argue that numerous procedural factors can influence whether or not sequential lineups are superior to the more traditional kind. McQuiston-Surrett and co-workers suggest that psychologists should not rush into advocating that law enforcement agencies abandon the use of simultaneous lineups until these factors have been fully explored, and until we know more about witnesses' decision-making processes in lineup situations.

11.4.4 'Target absent' warnings

As mentioned above, instructions to witnesses can affect their readiness to make false identifications in lineups. Witnesses are biased to identify someone in the lineup as being the suspect, even when the suspect is not actually there. This may be because they believe that the police have a good idea of who the suspect is, and wouldn't waste time setting up an identification parade if the suspect wasn't present in it. The chances of a false identification can be reduced by explicitly warning the witness that the suspect may not be present in the lineup (Clark, 2005; Malpass and Devine, 1981; Pozzulo and Dempsey, 2006; Steblay, 1997). This warning may discourage the witness from relying on a relative judgement strategy and choosing the person who looks most like the criminal (Wells, 1984).

11.4.5 'Changed appearance' warnings

If you think about it, it's somewhat strange that police descriptions of suspects often include details of their clothing. Wouldn't most criminals think of this, and change their clothes, and possibly their hairstyle? The US Department of Justice's Guide for lineups recommends that eyewitnesses should be warned that a suspect's appearance might have changed since the time of the crime. Surprisingly, there has been little research on the effects of this instruction on witnesses' behaviour. Charman and Wells (2007) looked at the effects of the 'appearance changed' warning and found that it failed to improve identification accuracy—on the contrary, it reduced it, as well as greatly increasing the number of false identifications. Charman and Wells suggest that one explanation for these effects is that the warning encourages witnesses with a poor memory for the criminal to try to make an identification anyway, instead of rejecting the lineup because none of its members matches their memory. Like simultaneous lineups, the 'appearance changed' instruction encourages witnesses to make relative judgements, which promote misidentification.

11.4.6 Moving or static lineups?

In the UK, traditional lineups, using physically present individuals, have largely been abandoned in favour of video-based lineups. The witness is presented with a series of video clips, one of which contains the suspect. There are a number of advantages to this procedure (e.g. Pike et al, 2002). Firstly, construction of lineups using real people is difficult, time consuming and expensive, especially if the suspect has an unusual appearance; in the past, the police needed to scour their local area to find enough volunteers to produce a lineup, and had to rely on all of these people turning up at the appointed time. Now, the police can access a central database of video clips produced from all over the country. In theory, at least, this should give them a greater choice in choosing distractors that match the suspect. An important issue, however, is whether using video affects the likelihood of witnesses making a correct identification. The PACE guidelines recommend the use of moving video lineups if practicable. As we saw in Chapter 1, studies of the role of motion in face recognition have found that it produces relatively small benefits to recognition. Applied studies are consistent with this conclusion: Valentine et al (2007) found that, although incorrect identifications were significantly less likely with moving target-absent video lineups than with static ones, the effect was small in practical terms.

11.4.7 Use of 'double-blind' procedures with lineups

The British Psychological Society document *Guidelines on Memory and the Law* has recommended to the police that they should use **double-blind** procedures when conducting lineups, similar to those routinely used in clinical medical trials. In other words, neither the witness nor the lineup administrator should know which member of the lineup is the person suspected by the police of being the criminal. There is a huge literature in psychology on **experimenter effects**, showing that the performance of participants in experiments can be influenced by the experimenter's expectations about how they are likely to perform. The influence of these expectations can be mediated by quite subtle and entirely unintentional cues that are given off by the experimenter and picked up by participants who are eager to please the experimenter.

Another advantage of 'double-blind' procedures is that they would reduce the chances of police officers unwittingly biasing not only the witness' decision-making process but also the witness' confidence in their decision. As we mentioned earlier, witnesses' confidence in their decisions can be affected by feedback, and comments (unintentional or otherwise) made by a police officer to a witness could potentially affect the latter's subsequent estimates of how confident they were when they made their selection from the lineup.

11.5 **Conclusion**

Despite the huge amount of research that has been conducted on unfamiliar face recognition, relatively few firm conclusions can be drawn, other than to say that people are not very good at it! Because unfamiliar face recognition is so poor, there is ample scope for all sorts of factors to affect eyewitness performance, individually and in interaction. Ultimately, a witness has to make a decision about whether or not the suspect is the person that they actually saw committing a crime. In the absence of a clear memory of the criminal's face, the witness may rely heavily on non-facial sources of information. These include social cues from the police officers administering the recognition test, the suspect's clothing, and a vague sense of familiarity (that may be misleading, if the witness fails to realize that it stems from having encountered the suspect's face in another context). Such effects may be stronger in witnesses who are poorer at recognizing faces in the first place, such as young children, elderly people, and adults trying to recognize a face from a different race.

What is clear is that the legal system's faith in the veracity of eyewitnesses is unjustified. Many of the criteria used to assess eyewitness reliability (such as the witness' level of confidence) have little or no empirical support.

The use of showups as an identification procedure seems to be particularly problematic (Dysart and Lindsay, 2007a,b). The main justifications for their use are that they are quick and easy for the police to administer and that they might enable the police to quickly eliminate potential suspects from their enquiries. However, showups tend to produce fewer correct identifications and more false identifications than lineups, and they appear to be more sensitive than lineups to the effects of delay between the initial encounter and subsequent recognition test.

One problem is that the legal system has sometimes seemed reluctant to take advice from psychologists. To some extent this is understandable: police officers, lawyers and judges would like clear, unambiguous, practical guidelines, but psychologists are unable to supply these because so many factors operate in interaction. What are the effects of delay on a witness' memory? It depends on so many other things that it is impossible to make general statements with any certainty. In addition, many psychological effects are real, but small in practical terms, so that their influence on real-life witnesses' performance might be minimal—or at least open to dispute by lawyers in adversarial legal systems such those of the UK and USA. Ultimately, too, there is the problem that the vast majority of applied research has been conducted on undergraduate students. These may constitute an adequate model for witnesses who experience crimes as disinterested bystanders, but not for highly stressed victims of violent crime (Tollestrup et al, 1994). This leaves lawyers and judges open to argue that such research has little or no relevance to real-life crimes.

These tensions between the scientific and legal communities are exemplified by the current controversy in the USA over the use of sequential versus simultaneous lineups. Although some State legislatures have adopted sequential lineups in response to psychologists' recommendations, a field study by the Illinois police that compared the two methods under real-life conditions concluded that sequential lineups were inferior to simultaneous lineups (Mecklenberg, 2006). Not only were there fewer identifications of the police's suspects when sequential lineups were used, but also—contrary to most of the psychological research findings—sequential presentations produced a *higher* rate of false identifications.

The reasons for the discrepancies between the Illinois study and the psychological research findings are unclear. However, Gary Wells (undated) has identified several methodological problems with the Illinois study. The most serious is that the sequential lineups were conducted 'blind' whereas the simultaneous lineups never were. This means that in the case of the simultaneous lineups, the police officers could 'steer' the witness away from identifying the foils and towards identifying the suspect. This may account for the extremely low foil identification rates for simultaneous lineups in the Illinois study (just 3% of lineups) compared with the field studies by Wright and McDaid (1996), Valentine et al (2003) and others, which report foil identification rates of around 22–24%. It may also be notable that the Illinois study failed to replicate other well-documented research findings, such as failing to find any evidence of an other-race effect in their data. Reading the Illinois report, one is also struck by the negative attitude towards the sequential lineup procedure by many of the police officers who were involved in the trial. Sequential lineups were time-consuming and awkward for them to implement,

and their supposed benefits were at odds with the officers' intuitions about what constituted a fair identification procedure.

Psychological research has the potential to make a significant contribution to the improvement of identification procedures in the USA and the UK. At the time of writing, the UK Police and Criminal Evidence Act is due for revision, and the British Psychological Society has made a number of suggestions for improvements to identification procedures. These include the use of 'double-blind' identification parades (also advocated in the USA by the American Psychological Association) and procedural changes to ensure that witnesses' ratings of their confidence are recorded at the time of the identification rather than at a later point. It will be interesting to see the UK Government's response to these proposals.

SUMMARY

- Eyewitness testimony is unreliable, and false identifications by eyewitnesses are a major factor in wrongful convictions.

- Factors that affect eyewitness performance can be divided into estimator variables (relating to the characteristics of the witness and the crime) and system variables (relating to the legal system's procedures for interviewing witnesses, staging lineups, etc.).

- Although individual differences in terms of sex, personality and intelligence affect face-processing performance in the laboratory, from an 'applied' point of view only age seems to make much practical difference to recognition performance.

- Eyewitnesses find it hard to recognize faces from other races (the 'other-race effect').

- Although difficult to simulate in the laboratory, stress may impair a witness' performance; there is some evidence that stress causes a narrowing of attention (such as in the 'weapons focus' effect, where witnesses focus on a weapon at the expense of attending to other aspects of the scene).

- There is no relationship between the quality of a witness' description of a suspect and their ability to recognize them. In fact, describing a face may temporarily impair recognition, as shown by the phenomenon of 'verbal overshadowing'.

- Witnesses are better at recognizing a face (i.e. sensing that it is somehow familiar) than at remembering the context in which they saw the face. This may lead to misidentifications (e.g. if a witness saw a suspect in a set of mugshots before taking part in an identity parade).

- Sequential lineups are generally found to be better than simultaneous lineups, as they tend to produce fewer misidentifications.

- Witnesses can be highly confident that they have identified a criminal, but completely mistaken. Not only is the relationship between confidence and accuracy weak, but witness confidence can also be affected by feedback about their performance.

- 'Double-blind' procedures are not used for lineups in either the UK or the USA, but would significantly reduce the opportunity for police officers to influence witnesses' identifications unintentionally.

FURTHER READING

Gary Wells' homepage: http://www.psychology. iastate.edu/~glwells/homepage.htm. Wells is a well-known researcher on factors affecting eyewitness performance. His website contains links to a wealth of useful information about the unreliability of eyewitness identifications: journal articles, newspaper reports, legal reports, case studies and more, albeit from a wholly US perspective. Highly recommended!

Lindsay, R. C. L., Ross, D. F., Read, J. D. and Toglia, M. P. (eds) (2007). *Handbook of Eyewitness Psychology, Vol. 2: Memory for People.* Mahwah, NJ: Erlbaum. This contains excellent reviews of many of the topics covered in this chapter, such as lineup construction, the other-race effect, the confidence–accuracy relationship in eyewitnesses, and so on.

Heaton-Armstrong, A., Shepherd, E., Gudjonsson, G. and Wolchover, D. (eds) (2006). *Witness Testimony: Psychological, Investigative and Evidential Perspectives.* Oxford: Oxford University Press. Although aimed slightly more at the legal profession than at psychologists, this book contains excellent reviews of some of the topics covered in this chapter (and many that are not, such as how easy it is to detect lying by witnesses and suspects).

Wilcox, R., Bull, R. and Milne, R. (2008). *Witness Identification in Criminal Cases: Psychology and Practice.* Oxford: Oxford University Press. Written by three longstanding experts in this area, this book focuses solely on the issue of identification. Useful for anyone who wants a deeper understanding of this area, although perhaps a little too detailed for undergraduate purposes.

12

OWN-GROUP BIASES IN FACE RECOGNITION

Although every face is unique, faces can be categorized into different types on the basis of properties such as gender, age and ethnic grouping ('race', for want of a better word), and this affects our ability to recognize them. It has been known for decades that people find it easier to recognize faces of their own race, but more recently it has become apparent that other **own-group biases** in performance exist too; there is some evidence for the existence of 'own-gender' and 'own-age' biases.

Understanding why such biases occur is important on both theoretical and practical grounds. On a theoretical level, they may provide some useful insights into how face recognition is achieved; for example, they show how experience affects face recognition, and they provide some clues about what information is being extracted from faces in order to achieve effective recognition. On a practical

level, own-group biases are very important because, as explained in Chapters 11 and 13, our ability to recognize unfamiliar faces is poor even when those faces have properties similar to our own. It is even worse with faces of other groups, which is worrying given that misidentification of suspects by eyewitnesses is such an important factor in miscarriages of justice. At the very least, research can demonstrate to the legal system that own-group biases exist and need to be taken into account when evaluating the reliability of eyewitnesses. Ideally, once we understand why own-group biases occur, we might be able to do something about them. For example, police officers, passport officials, diplomats and business people engaged in international commerce would all benefit from being better at recognizing other races, but no effective training in other-race recognition exists at present.

12.1 **The 'other-race effect'**

People are generally better at recognizing faces of their own race than those of another (Malpass and Kravitz, 1969; reviews in Brigham et al, 2007; Chance and Goldstein, 1996; Meissner and Brigham, 2001a; Sporer, 2001). Thus, Caucasians find it hard to distinguish between Black faces or between Asian faces.[1] These races also find it hard to recognize Caucasians, so the effect

---

[1] 'Asian' is an ambiguous term. In Britain, it usually refers to people from the Indian subcontinent. For most Australians, Americans and New Zealanders, it refers to South-East Asian people (Japanese, Korean, Chinese, etc.). Here it is used exclusively in the latter sense. 'Indian Asian' is used to refer to people from the Indian subcontinent.

does not occur merely because non-Caucasian faces really do all look alike. In any case, anthropometric analyses of Black, Caucasian and Asian faces suggest that these races all show similar amounts of facial variability (Goldstein, 1979a,b).

The other-race effect seems to stem from differences between races in terms of their facial features, rather than skin colour. Bar-Haim et al (2009) measured how well Caucasian students could recognize Caucasian and African faces whose skin colour had been altered digitally (Fig. 12.1). Caucasian faces were remembered better if they had white skin than if they appeared to have black skin. However, both types were remembered better than African faces, regardless of the latter's apparent skin colour, and 'white' African faces were recognized no better than 'black' African faces.

In an applied context, this **other-race effect** (also referred to as the **cross-race effect** or **own-race bias**) is likely to manifest itself in a number of ways. Witnesses are more likely to identify a face correctly if it is from the same race as themselves. They tend to be more confident about their decision for an own-race face than an other-race face, and for own-race faces this confidence is more diagnostic of whether they are actually correct in their judgement (Meissner et al, 2005). Importantly, witnesses are much more likely to make a false-positive identification when a lineup consists of faces of a different race to themselves (e.g. Meissner and Brigham, 2001a; Slone, Brigham and Meissner, 2000). Hence there is an increased risk of an innocent person being mistakenly identified as the criminal. Wells and Olson (2001) have suggested that the other-race effect might well be a factor in mistaken convictions in the USA; of the cases where DNA evidence has subsequently led to a conviction being overturned, a large proportion involved Black people who were convicted on the basis of misidentification by a Caucasian eyewitness.

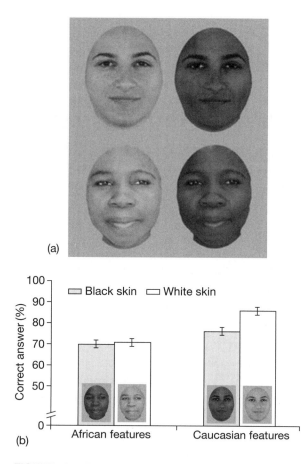

FIGURE 12.1 Effects of skin colour and facial features on the size of the 'other-race effect' for Caucasian participants in Bar-Haim et al's (2009) study. (a) Examples of digitally manipulated faces, whose skin colour is either original or swapped with that of the other race. (b) Mean percentage of correct identifications, in relation to face race and apparent skin colour. (Reprinted with permission from: Bar-Haim, Y., Saidel, T. & Yovel, G. (2009). The role of skin colour in face recognition. *Perception*, 38, 145–148. © Pion Limited, London)

12.2 The role of prejudice in the other-race effect

The most obvious explanation for the other-race effect is that it might reflect racial prejudice. However, explicit measures of prejudice (e.g. questionnaires that ask people directly how prejudiced they are) have failed to show any relationship between the size of the other-race effect and the degree of self-reported prejudice (review in Meissner and Brigham, 2001a). One problem with self-report measures is that questionnaire responses on such a sensitive subject might be distorted by 'social desirability' effects, with respondents trying to represent themselves as being less prejudiced than they actually are. To overcome this problem, Ferguson et al (2001) used an implicit test of prejudice originally devised by Fazio and colleagues (1995). Asian and Caucasian participants saw a list of adjectives, and decided as quickly as possible whether each word had positive or negative connotations. Each word was preceded by a picture of a face, which belonged either to the same race as the participant or to the other race. For prejudiced participants, the faces had a priming effect: the participants were quicker to decide that a word had positive connotations if it was preceded by an own-race face, and quicker to decide that a word had negative connotations if it was preceded by an other-race face. The Caucasian participants were also given a questionnaire to measure their degree of self-reported prejudice towards Asians. Ferguson et al found that the size of the other-race effect bore no relationship with either of these two measures of prejudice.

12.3 **The role of contact in the other-race effect**

Contact with other races seems to be quite influential in producing the other-race effect. A number of studies have shown that it tends to be more pronounced in groups that have had limited contact with the race in question. Ferguson et al's (2001) study, described in the previous section, showed a fairly typical result for research in this area: the difference in performance with Caucasian and Asian faces was greater for the Caucasian than for the Asian participants. Ferguson et al took no formal measure of degree of interracial contact, but their Asian participants were Chinese undergraduates living in Singapore. They were therefore likely to have had considerable contact with Westerners, whereas the Caucasians were likely to have had much less contact with Asians.

Chiroro and Valentine (1995) examined the other-race effect in Black and Caucasian students in Zimbabwe. For each race, there was a high-contact group (who had extensive contact with the other race, by virtue of attending a multiracial college) and a low-contact group (who attended a school or college in an area where there was minimal opportunity for contact with other races). The low-contact groups showed a clear other-race effect: the Black students performed better with Black faces than with Caucasian faces, and the Caucasian students showed the opposite pattern. The Black high-contact group performed equally well with both races of face, implying that contact with Caucasian faces had eliminated their own-race bias. However, this was not the case for the Caucasian high-contact group, who showed an other-race effect similar in magnitude to that of the Caucasian low-contact group. At first sight, this seems to contradict the notion that contact is important in the other-race effect. However, Zimbabwe was until comparatively recently a country that practised racial segregation. Perhaps the 'high-contact' Caucasian participants were in the presence of Black people but didn't pay much attention to them; in other words, the *quality* of the interaction may be an important factor in the other-race effect. It may not be enough merely to be surrounded by people from another race: perhaps one needs to interact with them, and be interested in trying to differentiate between them as individuals.

Wright, Boyd and Tredoux (2003) measured the other-race effect in three groups: Caucasian students from Bristol University in England, and Caucasian and Black students at the University of Cape Town in South Africa. The Caucasian students from both universities reported having had little contact with Black people. The South African Black students varied much more in terms of how much contact they had with Caucasian people. Each student saw 30 faces (15 Black and 15 Caucasian) for 3 seconds per face. They were then shown these faces mixed with 30 new faces, and asked to decide which ones they had seen before. Wright et al found that all three groups were better at recognizing Caucasian faces than Black faces, but there was a significant other-race effect because this effect was more pronounced for the two groups of Caucasian students than it was for the Black students. For the Black students, the amount of interracial contact was positively correlated with accuracy in recognizing Caucasian faces ($r = 0.41$, $p = 0.003$).

12.4 **Developmental studies of the other-race effect**

Studies of own- and other-race facial discrimination in infants and children suggest that early experience with faces may play a role in the development of the other-race effect. An early study by Chance and co-workers (1982) showed that by 6 years of age Caucasian children were better at recognizing faces of their own race than they were at recognizing Asian faces. Chance et al also reported a developmental trend, claiming that the other-race effect became more pronounced with increasing age, but this has not always been supported by subsequent studies. Pezdek et al (2003) found that the magnitude of the other-race effect in 5-year-old children was comparable to that shown by adults. Corenblum

and Meissner (2006) investigated the other-race effect in Caucasian Canadian children aged from 9 to 13 years, and in undergraduates; they too found little evidence of any developmental trends.

Even infants can show evidence of an other-race effect, as demonstrated by a series of studies by Kelly and his colleagues. Kelly et al (2005) presented infants with pairs of faces from different races (African, Middle Eastern, Asian or Caucasian) that were matched for gender, attractiveness and distinctiveness. Newborn Caucasian infants looked at each face in the pair equally, implying they had no spontaneous preference for any of the races concerned. (This is probably not because they were *unable* to discriminate between the faces, as there is evidence that newborns can discriminate between different faces of their own race; see Chapter 6.) In contrast, 3-month-old infants did prefer to look at faces of their own race. They spent about 60% of their time looking at own-race faces, compared with 40% looking at the other race (a pattern that was similar regardless of whether the other-race face was African, Asian or Middle-Eastern). This study suggests that by 3 months of age infants *prefer* to look at own-race faces.

Kelly et al (2007) investigated whether infants showed an own-race bias for *recognizing* faces. A visual paired-comparison (VPC) task was used. Each trial in the VPC task involves displaying a single face until the infant habituates to it and then showing this face again but paired with a novel face. If an infant looks longer at the novel face than at the previously seen face, this implies that he or she is able to discriminate between them. Kelly et al used this task with three different age groups of Caucasian babies (3-, 6- and 9-month-olds), looking at different permutations of Caucasian, Middle-Eastern, Asian and African faces in the habituation and test stages. The results suggested that there was a progressive narrowing of discrimination abilities with increasing age. Whereas the 3-month-old babies were able to discriminate between all racial groups,[2] this was not the case for the two older groups. The 6-month-old babies were able to discriminate only between Caucasian and Asian faces (but not Middle-Eastern or African faces), and the 9-month-old babies were able to discriminate only between faces of their own race.

Kelly et al's interpretation of their results is in terms of Nelson's (2001) idea of **perceptual narrowing** (i.e. that perceptual abilities become progressively more finely tuned with experience). Newborn infants arrive prepared to look at any face, regardless of race. However, in the normal course of events, they will mainly see own-race faces. This familiarity with own-race faces quickly produces an initial preference for looking at them. As a result, the infant effectively restricts its experience to own-race faces, even when other-race faces are available for scrutiny. This ultimately leads to greater expertise at processing own-race faces, at the expense of being able to do the same with other-race faces.

A recent study by Scott and Monesson (2009) is consistent with this idea. Three groups of 6-month-old infants were exposed to books containing six pictures of monkeys, for a period of three months. For one group, the monkeys had individual names; for the second group, they were all labelled 'monkey'; and the third group had no labels at all. A visual paired-comparison technique (see Chapter 5) showed that at the outset of the study all three groups could discriminate between the monkey faces. However, despite receiving roughly equivalent levels of exposure to the faces during the following three months, only those infants who learnt to individuate the monkey faces retained the ability to discriminate between them; the other two groups

developed the normal 'other species' effect. Scott and Monesson suggest that the own-race bias (or in this case, own-species bias) arises as a consequence of experience in individuating faces, obtained between 6 and 9 months of age. This experience allows the development of perceptual expertise for the set of faces that are being individuated. However, for groups of faces that are not being individuated, there is a loss of the ability to tell them apart.

If experience is important in producing these effects, then infants and children who have had prolonged exposure to other races should *not* show an other-race effect for them. There is some evidence that this is so. Sangrigoli et al (2005) found that 3 to 9-year-old Korean children who were adopted by Caucasian families in Europe showed an other-race effect but in the *opposite* direction to normal: these children found it harder to discriminate between Korean faces than between Caucasian faces. Overall, these developmental studies suggest that early experience with faces of a particular race normally produces an enduring bias towards better recognition for that race, although that bias can be eliminated or reversed given sufficient experience with other races.

Finally, as mentioned above in connection with other-race effects in adults, the *quality* of interaction with other races may be at least as important as the *quantity* (Chiroro and Valentine, 1995). Goodman et al (2007) performed a large multinational study to investigate the development of the other-race effect in Caucasian children in the USA, South Africa and Norway. The participants ranged in age from 5 years to adult, and their memory for pictures of faces of their own and other races was tested two days after they first saw the pictures. Goodman et al failed

---

[2] This is inconsistent with the results of Sangrigoli and de Schonen's (2004) study, which used a habituation paradigm. They reported that Caucasian infants as young as 3 months could discriminate between Caucasian and Asian faces, and showed evidence of better own-race recognition. More research needs to be done on this; the discrepancies might arise from methodological differences between the studies, but one possibility is that the other-race effect is simply rather fragile at this age.

to find any evidence of an other-race effect in 5 to 7-year-olds, but all of the older age-groups (9–10, 12–13 and undergraduates) were similar to one another in showing sizeable differences between their performance with own- and other-race faces. The other-race effect was as pronounced in the South African children as it was in the Norwegians, despite marked differences in the racial composition of the two countries. The South African children lived in a multiracial society (79% African, 10% Caucasian), whereas the Norwegians lived in an almost exclusively Caucasian country (94% Caucasian, 1% African). To ameliorate the other-race effect, it seems it is not enough to be surrounded by members of another race: one has to pay attention to them too.

An interesting aspect of the Goodman et al study is that it included a group of mixed-race (African/Caucasian) children who had experienced meaningful interactions with both of their parents' races. These children recognized Caucasian and African faces equally well, but showed an other-race effect for Asian faces that was as large as that found in the Caucasian children.

12.5 **Bias at the encoding or at the recall stage of visual processing?**

Most of the studies described so far have looked at recognition memory for own- and other-race faces, and found that the latter are recognized more poorly than the former. In principle, this could occur because other-race faces are not remembered as well, or because they are encoded less effectively in the first place.

Lindsay et al (1991) compared Caucasian and African-American participants on their ability to perform a delayed matching-to-sample task. On each trial, either a Caucasian or an African-American face was presented very briefly (for 120 milliseconds), followed by two faces side by side. One of these was the face that had just been shown and the other was a foil that was similar in appearance to it. Once again, the other-race effect occurred only amongst the Caucasian participants: they were more accurate at matching faces of their own race, whereas the African-Americans performed equally well with both races of face. (The Caucasians reported having much less other-race contact than did the African Americans.) Lindsay et al suggested that the other-race effect was attributable to differences in the efficiency of encoding faces.

Humphreys et al (2005) used a 'change blindness' technique to investigate whether there is an attentional bias to own-race faces. Caucasian and Indian Asian participants saw two photographs of scenes, in alternation. The scenes contained Caucasian and Indian Asian people, and were identical except for one change. This was either to a face, to body parts or to a background object. Both groups of participants were quicker to detect changes to faces than to body parts, and quicker to detect changes to body parts than to detect background changes. Both groups were also faster in detecting changes to own-race faces than to other-race faces. The fact that participants showed no difference in detecting own- and other-race body parts was taken to imply that both groups attended equally to both of the races in the pictures. Hirose and Hancock (2007) repeated Humphreys et al's study, using the same stimuli but also recording the participants' eye movements to test more directly where attention was allocated in each scene. For reasons that are unclear, Humphreys et al's study was not fully replicated, as only Hirose and Hancock's Caucasian participants demonstrated an own-race bias for detecting changes to faces; however, the eye movement recordings suggested that this did not occur because participants' attention was directed preferentially towards own-race faces. (In fact, both races looked longer and more often at the Caucasian faces.)

There is thus some evidence that participants can detect changes to own-race faces quicker and more easily than they can detect changes to other-race faces, and that this is not simply because people attend preferentially to faces of their own race. Humphreys et al (2005) speculate that we are more efficient at discriminating between own-race faces, and hence more likely to notice the differences if the face changes between the two photographs in a change-blindness trial.

12.6 **Theoretical explanations of the other-race effect**

12.6.1 **Contact and the 'perceptual expertise' hypothesis**

Clearly, the degree of contact with other races is influential in producing the other-race effect; by and large, people who have had limited experience with another race are less likely to be able to recognize individuals from that race. The precise mechanism by which contact exerts its effects remains elusive, however.

The most popular explanation has been in terms of **perceptual expertise**: perhaps we recognize faces of our own race better because extensive experience with them attunes us to the facial characteristics that are most effective for distinguishing between individual faces of that race (e.g. Brigham and Malpass, 1985; Chance and Goldstein, 1996). This hypothesis predicts that the magnitude of the other-race effect should be related to the amount of experience that people have had with the race in question; the effect should be shown most markedly by people who have had very limited contact with another race, and should be weak or non-existent in people

who have had extensive experience with that race. In a meta-analysis of 39 studies, Meissner and Brigham (2001a) found that there was a statistically significant correlation between the amount of self-reported contact with other races and the strength of the other-race effect, but it was a very weak relationship in absolute terms. However, this is not a strong argument against the perceptual expertise hypothesis, for two reasons. Firstly, estimates of self-reported contact may be fairly imprecise, and if there is sizeable error in one or both of the variables being correlated, the strength of the relationship between them may be underestimated. Secondly, a correlation test may not be the best way to measure the relationship between contact and the strength of the other-race effect; it presupposes that there is some kind of linear relationship between these variables, but it is quite possible that a certain threshold amount of contact with another race is sufficient to abolish the other-race effect, and that any further contact leads to minimal additional improvements in face recognition. Or, as suggested by Chiroro and Valentine (1995), it may be the *quality* of the contact that is important, rather than its quantity.

An alternative way to investigate the perceptual expertise hypothesis is to see whether own-race and other-race faces are processed in qualitatively different ways. Tanaka et al (2004) found evidence that Caucasian students engaged in more 'holistic' processing for faces of their own race, and more 'featural' processing of other-race faces (see Chapter 2, section 2.3.4). On each trial, participants saw a face followed by two test stimuli. On half of the trials, these stimuli consisted of isolated parts of faces (eyes, noses or mouths). On the remaining trials, the stimuli consisted of face parts embedded within a face (which was otherwise identical in both stimuli). The task was to decide which of the two test stimuli matched the face that preceded them. Caucasian participants were better at doing this when the face parts were embedded within a face, but only when they performed the task with own-race faces. The Asian students (who appear to have had reasonably extensive contact with Caucasians) showed a different pattern: they too were better at making matches between whole faces rather than between parts, but this was true regardless of whether the faces were Caucasian or Asian.

Michel et al (2006) used a different technique to examine whether other-race faces were processed less holistically than own-race faces. They measured the strength of the **Composite Face Effect** (CFE; see Chapter 2) in Caucasian and Asian participants. Each group was shown two unfamiliar faces in succession and asked to decide whether the top halves were the same or different. The second face was a composite face, comprised of the top of one face and the bottom of another. The top half of the second face was either the same as that of the first face or different, and it was either aligned or misaligned with the bottom half. The faces were either the same race as the participant or different (Fig. 12.2). Both races

showed a more pronounced CFE for faces of their own race. In other words, when shown a composite face comprised of aligned face-halves, participants were slower and less accurate at deciding that the composite's top matched that of the preceding face than when the face-halves were misaligned, and these effects were greatest when the stimuli were faces of their own race.

Michel et al interpret their results to mean that own-race faces are subjected to a greater degree of configural processing. However, some of their own data are at odds with this interpretation. For each participant, Michel et al subtracted the size of their CFE for other-race faces from their CFE for own-race faces, to obtain difference scores: the higher the score, the greater the discrepancy between a participant's CFE with own-race and other-race faces. If expertise with faces is responsible for the magnitude of the CFE, these scores might be expected to correlate with the size of the participant's own-race bias, but, in fact, no

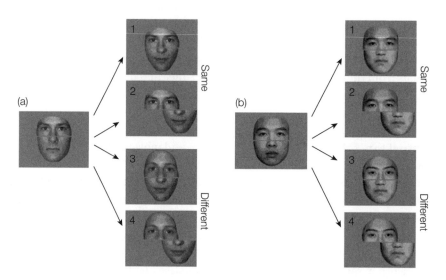

FIGURE 12.2 Examples of stimuli from Michel et al's (2006) experiment. On each trial, participants saw a pair of faces in rapid succession and decided whether the tops were the same or different. (The bottoms were always different.) The second face had either the same top as the first or a different one, and the halves were either aligned or misaligned. When the face-halves were aligned, participants were slower to decide that the tops were the same (the classic Composite Face Effect), an effect that was stronger for own-race faces.

such correlation was found. Another problem is that Michel et al's interpretation of their results relies on the assumption that the CFE is related to the processing of the subtle configural information that underlies face recognition—the so-called **second-order relational information**—whereas the CFE may in fact be driven by a different, coarser, kind of '**holistic**' processing that merely determines that the stimulus is a face, as opposed to something else (see Chapter 2 for a full discussion of these different types of processing).

Other researchers have examined whether another indicator of configural/holistic processing, the **Face Inversion Effect**, differs for own-race and other-race faces. We are much better at recognizing upright faces than upside-down ones (Yin, 1970). As discussed in Chapter 2 (section 2.3.1), it has been argued that the inversion effect is a byproduct of our expertise at discriminating between faces. With experience, we become adept at distinguishing between faces on the basis of comparatively subtle configural differences, but this ability comes at a cost: we need to see the face in its customary (upright) orientation. If people are more expert at recognizing own-race faces, then they might be expected to show a greater inversion effect for them, compared with other-race faces. Empirical evidence on this is mixed. An early study by Valentine and Bruce (1986c) found that Caucasian participants' recognition of both Caucasian and African faces was impaired by inversion, but that this effect was *worse* for African faces. However, interpretation of these results is complicated by the fact that Valentine and Bruce attempted to equate performance on the two types of stimulus by allowing their participants to see the African faces for longer than the Caucasian faces (for five seconds as opposed to two seconds).

Rhodes et al (1989) measured the strength of the inversion effect for own-race and other-race faces, using Chinese and Caucasian participants. In the study phase, each participant saw a series of unfamiliar upright faces. In the test phase, they were shown pairs of faces and asked to

decide which of the two they had seen earlier. Each participant performed this task for all permutations of orientation and race. The effects were somewhat weak and inconsistent across the two experiments performed by Rhodes et al; overall, however, the findings suggested that the inversion effect was more pronounced with own-race faces than with other-race faces, a result that Rhodes and colleagues claimed was consistent with the perceptual expertise account of the other-race effect.

More recently, Hancock and Rhodes (2008) performed a very similar experiment and obtained clearer results. They looked at the extent to which recognition memory performance was impaired by face inversion in Chinese and Caucasian participants, taking into account the quality and quantity of these participants' interactions with the other race, as measured by self-report. The usual other-race effect was obtained, with both races finding it easier to recognize faces of their own race. For both Caucasian and Chinese participants, recognition of own-race faces was affected more by inversion than was recognition of other-race faces. Both of these effects were influenced by contact: the greater the amount of self-reported contact with the other race, the smaller the other-race effect in recognition, and the smaller the difference between the effects of inversion for own-race and other-race faces. Hancock and Rhodes claim this demonstrates that configural coding is used to a greater extent with own-race faces, and that its use is affected by experience with a particular group of faces.

Hayward et al (2008) have demonstrated that not only do people process the configural information more effectively from own-race faces, but they also process the featural information better from these faces. Caucasian and Chinese participants were better at recognizing faces of their own race, regardless of whether these were heavily blurred (to remove featural information) or scrambled (to remove configural information).

The weight of evidence thus suggests that other-race faces may be processed less 'holistically' or 'configurally' than faces of one's own race. However, as McKone et al (2007a) point out, these studies all used wholly unfamiliar faces: what happens when an other-race face becomes familiar? To find out, McKone et al gave Caucasian (Australian) participants one hour of training with four own-race or four other-race (Chinese) faces. This amounted to 220 exposures to each face. This training was sufficient to eliminate the other-race effect: identification rates were comparable between the own-race and other-race faces, and holistic processing (as indexed by a modified version of the inversion effect) was as strong for the Asian faces as for the own-race faces. McKone et al's interpretation of their findings is that holistic processing is always potentially available for use with other-race faces, but is normally automatically 'turned off' in favour of classifying faces as own-race or other-race. (This idea fits in nicely with **social categorization** models of the other-race effect, which will be discussed later in this chapter.)

12.6.2 **Experience and the development of multidimensional face-space**

Valentine (1991) attempted to explain the own-race bias in terms of his **Multidimensional Face Space** model (see Chapter 1). Each face is represented as a unique point in a multidimensional space, where dimensions consist of factors such as eye separation, nose length, mouth width, and so on. The centre of the face space is the average on all these dimensions; typical faces form a dense cluster around this central point, whereas distinctive faces are located far away from the centre and have few neighbouring points. The other-race effect is explained by postulating that the dimensions of face space are developed via experience with faces, and hence are most appropriate for distinguishing between own-race faces. These dimensions are

not very useful for encoding faces from another race. For example, hair and eye colour might be useful for distinguishing between Caucasian faces, but they are not very helpful for distinguishing between two African faces. In addition, values on facial dimensions that are normal for one race may be unusual with respect to the norms of another race. For example, in relation to Asian facial norms, most Caucasians have unusually big noses; in relation to Caucasian norms, many Africans have unusually wide noses; and so on. Valentine's model thus accounts for the other-race effect by suggesting that other-race faces are encoded in relation to inappropriate (own-race) norms, and on dimensions that are not very useful for telling them apart. In effect, other-race faces form a dense cluster of 'distinctive' faces in face space (Fig. 12.3; see also Fig. 1.7).

In Valentine's model, faces that are close together in face space are difficult to tell apart. This would explain why faces from another race all look so similar to one another, as far as someone from a different race is concerned. In addition, because other-race faces form a cluster away from the own-race faces, the model accounts for another finding in this area: that participants are quicker to decide

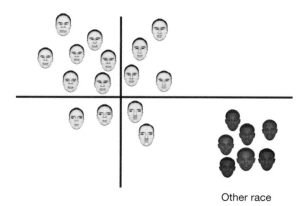

Own race

Other race

FIGURE 12.3 How own-race and other-race faces might be distributed in Valentine's (1991) Multidimensional Face Space. (© Graham Hole)

that a face belongs to another race than they are to decide it belongs to their own.

Byatt and Rhodes (2004) attempted to test the Multidimensional Face Space model using the statistical technique of **multidimensional scaling**, and found that human performance was in line with Valentine's model. Caucasian participants saw all possible pairings of 44 faces (22 Caucasian and 22 Chinese). For each pairing, they rated the faces' similarity to one another on a scale of one to seven, trying to ignore the race of the faces. These ratings showed that other-race faces were perceived to be more similar to each other than were own-race faces. Multidimensional scaling on these data produced six dimensions, one of which clearly separated the Chinese and Caucasian faces into two distinct clusters. (The other dimensions proved impossible to interpret.) A separate test of how well Caucasians could recognize Caucasian and Chinese faces produced the typical other-race effect, with higher hit rates and lower false alarms for Caucasian faces. Byatt and Rhodes' interpretation of their data was that both own-race and other-race faces are encoded using the same dimensions; experience with one's own race leads us to end up with a set of dimensions that are optimized for discriminating between own-race faces, but less effective for helping us to discriminate between other-race faces.

Byatt and Rhodes' interpretation is consistent with the results of an interesting study by Furl et al (2002). They examined the extent to which 13 different computational algorithms for face recognition adequately simulated the human other-race effect when they were tested with Caucasian and Asian faces. There were basically three types of algorithm. One type represented all faces in the same way, regardless of the race of the faces used in training. A second type used representations that were based on **Principal Component Analysis** (PCA), creating dimensions that accounted for most of the variation amongst faces. A third type also used PCA, but then

additionally 'warped' these dimensions in order to make individual faces more distinguishable from one another. A human-like other-race effect was exhibited only by algorithms of this third type. These results imply that contact *per se* might not be sufficient to produce the other-race effect; perhaps it will occur only in systems that are designed to group together images of the same person while emphasizing the differences between images from different individuals.

12.6.3 **The role of face categorization**

Differential perceptual expertise cannot be the entire explanation of the other-race effect, as shown by some ingenious experiments by MacLin and Malpass (2001, 2003). Using a computerized composite program, they produced a set of racially ambiguous faces. By giving the faces racially stereotypical hairstyles, MacLin and Malpass were able to bias Hispanic participants to see them as either Black or Hispanic (Fig. 12.4). This affected the participants' memory for the faces, in line with the other-race effect: when a face was categorized as 'Black', it was recognized less well than when it was categorized as 'Hispanic', even though it was the same face in both cases, apart from the

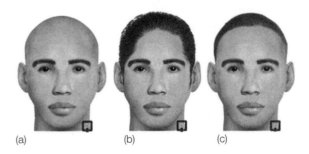

(a)   (b)   (c)

FIGURE 12.4 The ambiguous-race face illusion (MacLin and Malpass, 2001, 2003). By itself, the race of face (a) is ambiguous. The addition of an 'Hispanic' (b) or 'African' (c) hairstyle biases participants to perceive the face as Hispanic or African, affects perception of the face's characteristics (complexion, mouth width, etc.), and affects recognition in line with the other-race effect.

hairstyle. Consistent with more conventional studies of the other-race effect, MacLin and Malpass found an increase in false-positive responses for faces that were categorized as being 'Black'.

Not only memory but also *perception* of the faces appeared to be affected by the hairstyle manipulation. Once categorized as 'Black', faces appeared to be narrower, to have darker complexions, wider mouths and less protruding eyes than if they had been categorized as 'Hispanic'. The hairstyle also affected how the face was rated on various personality dimensions, such as 'suspiciousness', 'tenseness' and 'warmth'. MacLin and Malpass' findings show that the act of categorizing a face into one racial category or another affects how that face is processed perceptually, which in turn affects how well it can be remembered. Recently, Hilliar and Kemp (2008) have found that names produce similar effects on the perception of faces: racially ambiguous faces (morphs between European and Asian faces) were rated as appearing more European or more Asian according to whether they were presented in conjunction with stereotypical European or Asian names, respectively.

Shutts and Kinzler (2007) demonstrated that similar effects occur in children as young as 2.5 years of age. The children saw a series of pairs of faces. In each pair, one of the faces was an ambiguous-race face, produced by making a morph between a Caucasian face and a Black face. The other face in the pair was either the Caucasian face that had been used in the morph's construction, or the Black face. To encourage the children to categorize each morph as being 'Black' or 'White', they were told that the paired faces were siblings. As with MacLin and Malpass' studies, categorization produced other-race effects on memory for the faces; a morph was remembered better if it was thought to be 'White' than if it was thought to be 'Black'.

Bernstein et al (2007) showed that recognition performance for faces of one's own race can be influenced merely by categorizing them in terms of whether or not they belong to one's own group. In one study, Caucasian undergraduates saw a series of Caucasian faces. Each face was presented on either a red or a green background. The participants were either given no explanation for the background colour differences, or were told that the colours reflected the university to which the person belonged: faces on one colour were members of the participants' own university and the faces on the other colour came from a rival university. Participants who were led to believe that the background colours reflected university membership recognized the 'own-university' faces significantly better than the 'other-university' faces. Another group who were told that the background colour was irrelevant performed equally well with faces on either colour. In a second study, participants performed a bogus personality test that defined them as being either a 'red' or 'green' personality type, without any further explanation. Participants then saw a series of faces presented on red or green backgrounds, and subsequently recognized more of the faces from the background that fitted with their own 'personality type'. Thus, merely defining a face as being a member of an **in-group** or **out-group** can affect how well it is recognized subsequently, irrespective of its physical characteristics.

It seems that both cognitive and social–psychological processes are operating in the case of the other-race effect, and a number of researchers have proposed theories that attempt to integrate these. Levin (2000) has suggested that race is automatically taken into account when a face is encoded. Own-race face encoding emphasizes information about individual identity, whereas other-race encoding emphasizes information about race, at the expense of information about identity. The other-race effect thus arises, at least in part, from inappropriate allocation of attentional resources at the encoding stage: paying attention to encoding the face's race gets in the way of encoding information that would be useful in recognizing that particular face subsequently. Related to this is the concept of **cognitive disregard** (Rodin, 1987), which suggests that, if we categorize someone as being part of an 'out-group' because they are different to us in some way, that person becomes a representative of a stereotype and we fail to engage in any further processing of information about their individual attributes. Support for Levin's idea comes from experiments that require classification of faces by race (Levin, 1996, 2000). For example, when asked to decide whether faces are Caucasian or Black, people are *faster* to do this with other-race faces than with own-race faces. In a visual search task, they are quicker to detect a single Black face amongst an array of Caucasian distractors than to do the opposite.

A variant on Levin's idea is Sporer's (2001) **in-group/out-group model (IOM)**. This suggests that a face's race is taken into account when it is processed initially. If it is an own-race face, processing of the face's configural properties automatically takes place. In contrast, if the face is from a different race, it is categorized as belonging to an 'out-group'. Any further processing that occurs focuses on attending to the differences between the out-group face and one's own group, at the expense of concentrating on dimensions

that would aid differentiation between individual members of the out-group (Fig. 12.5).

Social categorization theories such as those of Levin and Sporer are quite compatible with demonstrations of reduced configural processing for other-race faces. They suggest that this occurs not because viewers are *unable* to use configural processing for these faces, but because they do not use it for strategic reasons; they use an alternative, feature-based processing strategy instead. This latter strategy is good for specifying the race of a face, but not so useful for remembering it. In effect, people encode the wrong facial characteristics for the task at hand (other-race face recognition).

According to social categorization theories, instructing participants to attend to the information that *individuates* other-race faces should reduce the other-race effect. Hugenberg et al (2007) found evidence that this was so. Before their Caucasian American participants engaged in an 'old/new' discrimination task with Caucasian and Black faces, they were warned of the existence of the own-race bias, and were asked to focus on whatever aspects of the faces they thought might serve to differentiate them from each other. These instructions—but not a simple exhortation to try as hard as possible—led to the virtual elimination of the other-race effect. These results are difficult to explain within straightforward 'perceptual expertise' accounts.

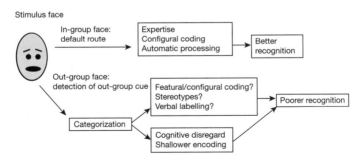

FIGURE 12.5 Sporer's (2001) 'in-group/out-group' model.

12.7 Other types of own-group bias: 'own gender', 'own age' and 'own species'

One virtue of theories such as Levin's and Sporer's, as opposed to ones based purely on perceptual expertise, is that they can account for other types of in-group bias as well as explaining the other-race effect. Wright and Sladden (2003) reported an 'own-gender bias', with both genders being better at recognizing faces of the same gender as themselves. There is also evidence of an **own-age bias**, a tendency for people to be better at recognizing faces similar in age to themselves. In general, undergraduates are better at recognizing faces of their own age than they are at recognizing elderly faces, and vice versa (Anastasi and Rhodes, 2005; Perfect and Moon, 2005; Wright and Stroud, 2002). As mentioned in Chapter 11, much of the apparent age-related decline in face recognition performance that was demonstrated in early studies might have arisen because young and elderly participants were tested only with photographs of young faces (see Lamont et al [2005] for a discussion of this issue). An own-age bias in these circumstances would favour the young participants. The elderly's 'deficit' often manifests itself in an elevated rate of false alarms (e.g. Bartlett and Leslie, 1986; Yarmey, 1984), which may be significant given that this is also a characteristic of the other-race effect.

In a series of experiments, Kuefner et al (2008) examined how well undergraduates could recognize upright and inverted faces of young adults, newborns and 3 to 4-year-old children, using a delayed matching-to-sample technique

(on each trial participants saw a face, followed by a pair of faces that consisted of the one just seen plus a same-aged distractor). Performance was better with the adult faces than with the children or infant faces. In addition, for the adult and child faces, but not for the infant faces, the participants showed an inversion effect: they performed better with upright faces than with inverted ones. Kuefner et al concluded that this showed that their participants were using configural processing with the upright adult faces, and to some extent with the children's faces. However, they could not use configural processing with infant faces, which is why inversion had no effect with this class of stimulus.

By analogy with the other-race effect, Kuefner et al suggested that their findings were consistent with an explanation in terms of perceptual expertise acquired through contact: most young adults have had little experience of seeing newborns, but older children are encountered to some extent in everyday life. They supported this explanation with a third experiment in which they showed that preschool teachers showed similar levels of recognition performance with children's faces as they did with adult faces, and a similarly sized inversion effect. Macchi Cassia et al (2009b) have recently reported similar effects with maternity-ward nurses and novices tested with newborn babies' faces.

However, as both Perfect and Moon (2005) and Anastasi and Rhodes (2005) point out, an explanation in terms of contact leading to perceptual expertise might explain why young people show an own-age bias for older faces, but it doesn't account for its existence in older people, as they have been members of the younger age groups at some point in their lives.[3] This argument applies even more forcefully in the case of the own-gender bias, because everyone[4]

---

[3] Actually, this is not quite fair on perceptual expertise models. If one assumes that it is only *recent* experience with faces that is important (as suggested by work on face adaptation effects; see Chapter 9), then perceptual expertise models can explain the existence of own-age biases, if not own-gender biases. In addition, own-age and own-gender biases pose problems for perceptual expertise models only if they are produced by the same mechanisms as the own-race bias, and that is not necessarily the case.

[4] With the possible exception of monks, nuns and lighthouse keepers.

has ample exposure to the opposite sex throughout life (Perfect and Moon, 2005). Whereas accounts based solely on perceptual expertise struggle to accommodate these findings, they are explicable in terms of in-group/out-group categorization.

A third factor may be at play: motivation to discriminate between faces of different groups, regardless of whether they are in-group or out-group members. Harrison and Hole (2009) compared two groups of similarly aged students (trainee teachers and undergraduates) in terms of their ability to recognize children's faces, and faces of adults similar in age to themselves. In-group/out-group models predict that both groups should perform similarly badly (because the children's faces constitute an 'out-group' for both groups of participants). In practice, the undergraduates showed an own-age bias, but—consistent with Kuefner et al's results— the trainee teachers were as good at recognizing the children's faces as they were at recognizing faces of their own age. Children are not part of the trainee teachers' in-group. However, trainee teachers are interested in children, and in order to do their job they are strongly motivated to be able to distinguish between them. Interest and/or motivation may have led to the development of enhanced processing for children's faces in the case of the trainee teachers.

Finally, some insight into own-group biases in recognition may be gained from looking at studies of cross-species recognition. Our primate relatives have faces with a roughly similar configuration to our own, and they live in social groups. How well can they recognize human faces (and how well can we recognize them)? Dufour et al (2006) used a visual paired-comparison task to investigate whether an own-species bias existed in humans, brown capuchin monkeys (*Cebus apella*) and Tonkean macaques (*Macaca tonkeana*). All of Dufour et al's participants (including the humans) had had minimal contact with the other species on which they were tested. Participants from each species were shown pictures of faces from their own species and from several other primate species, for three seconds per picture (Fig. 12.6).

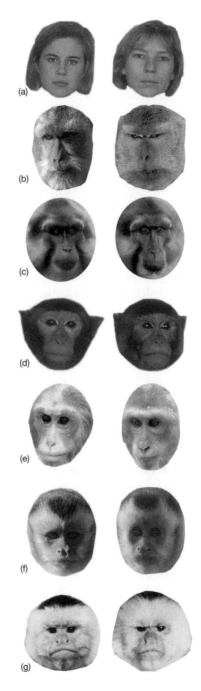

FIGURE 12.6 Examples of stimuli used by Dufour et al (2006) to investigate how well humans, Tonkean macaques and brown capuchin monkeys could discriminate between faces of different primate species. (a) *Homo sapiens*, (b) *Macaca fascicularis*, (c) *M. tonkeana*, (d) *M. mulatta*, (e) *M. arctoides*, (f) *Cebus apella*, (g) *C. capucinus*.

Immediately after each picture was displayed, it was presented again, but paired with a new picture of a face from the same species. Dufour et al measured the amount of time spent looking at each face in a pair.

The reasoning behind this study is that, if it is easy to discriminate between faces, the participants should show a preference for the novel face in each pair (because they have already looked at the 'old' face for some time). However, if participants find it hard to differentiate between the faces, they should look at both pictures fairly equally. The humans, capuchins and macaques all showed a similar pattern: a significant novelty preference only for faces of their own species. This implies that, for all three species, other-species faces look somewhat alike.

12.8 Conclusion

The existence of own-group biases is unarguable, but precisely why they occur is less well understood. For the most extensively researched of these biases—the other-race effect—contact is an important factor. Contact might exert its effects by increasing an individual's level of expertise in processing other-race faces. However, as we have

seen, social–psychological factors also play an important role. Merely by categorizing a face in terms of whether or not it belongs to one's own group affects how likely it is to be recognized subsequently.

There are two ways of looking at the research demonstrating differences in processing own-race and other-race faces. Studies showing apparently greater 'holistic' or 'configural' processing for own-race faces have often been interpreted as showing that we are 'face experts' for our own race, but not for others with which we have had little experience. The implication is that we have a skill (configural processing) whose use is confined to familiar (own-race) faces. An alternative interpretation of the same data is that they reflect the use of an encoding *strategy*, one that is habitually used with own-race faces but not with other-race faces, because we normally want to individuate the former but merely categorize the latter. The weight of evidence at present seems to favour the latter view. Certainly perceptual explanations alone are insufficient to account for the other-race effect.

An interesting issue for future research is to determine whether the own-race, own-gender and own-age biases have any deep underlying commonality: are they all reflections of the same process, or are they caused by different processes?

SUMMARY

- People find it hard to recognize faces from another race, a phenomenon variously referred to as the 'other-race effect', 'own-race bias' or 'cross-race effect'.

- The other-race effect has potentially serious legal implications, because it often manifests itself as a predisposition to make false identifications, for example from lineups.

- Lack of exposure to other races seems to be influential in the other-race effect, as contact seems to reduce the size of the effect. However, the quality of contact seems to be more important than its quantity.

- Developmental studies suggest there is a 'perceptual narrowing' in infancy: babies are initially able to discriminate between faces of all races, but lose this ability somewhere between 6 and 9 months of age. Experience with a particular race during infancy leads to expertise at processing faces of that race, and a loss of ability to process faces of other races.

- The most popular explanation for the other-race effect is that exposure to faces leads to the development of perceptual expertise at recognizing them, as shown by demonstrations of poorer configural processing with other-race effects.

- Valentine's (1991) Multidimensional Face Space model suggests that the difficulties in recognizing other-race faces arise from them being encoded with respect to inappropriate own-group norms, so that they form a tight cluster of 'distinctive' faces in face space.

- Studies of social categorization suggest that other non-perceptual factors must be involved too; simply labelling faces as 'in-group' or 'out-group' members affects how well they are recognized.

- Models such as Levin's and Sporer's suggest that an initial categorization of faces as in-group or out-group members has consequences for their subsequent processing; out-group faces are not processed in ways that would individuate them.

- 'Own-gender' and 'own-age' biases exist. Their relationship to the 'own-race' bias is uncertain. Teachers and nurses do not show an own-age bias for children, suggesting that the own-age bias, at least, may stem from a combination of exposure to faces of another group, plus motivation to individuate between them.

FURTHER READING

Brigham, J. C., Bennett, L. B., Meissner, C. A. and Mitchell, T. L. (2007). *The influence of race on eyewitness memory.* In: R. C. L. Lindsay, D. F. Ross, J. D. Read and M. P. Toglia (eds) *Handbook of Eyewitness Psychology, Vol. 2: Memory for People*, Ch. 11. Mahwah, NJ: Erlbaum. A good review of much of the literature on the own-race bias.

Meissner, C. A. and Brigham, J. C. (2001a). *Thirty years of investigating the own-race bias in memory for faces: a meta-analytic review.* Psychology and Public Policy Law, 7: 3–35. Again, a good review, albeit slightly dated now.

13

TECHNOLOGY AND FACIAL IDENTIFICATION

Your face is unique, and it's almost always on public display. As such, it is the most important guide to your identity that other people can use, and modern surveillance-obsessed societies rely heavily on this fact. CCTV cameras record the faces of commuters on public transport, drivers in petrol stations, shoppers in malls, and people walking around city centres. Go to the airport, and you will need to show your passport. Many organizations require employees to wear identity cards showing their photograph. If a crime occurs, the police may use a **face reconstruction system** such as E-FIT in order to generate a likeness of the criminal's face, an image that can be disseminated to the public in the hope of triggering recognition in someone who knows the person concerned.

All of these uses of faces have something in common: they require an observer to match two different images of an unfamiliar face. In the case of passports and identity cards, the observer merely

has to compare the photograph on the passport or ID card to the face of the person standing in front of them. Face reconstruction systems[1] require a witness to produce a likeness of the face that they saw—to make a match to their original memory of the suspect. If CCTV footage is used in court as evidence, jurors will be asked to decide whether the suspect in the dock and the person in the film are one and the same person.

All of these tasks are based on what at first sight seems a reasonable assumption, that people are competent at matching different views of unfamiliar faces. However, as we shall see, the evidence does not support this belief. Not only are people poor at *recognizing* unfamiliar faces, as shown by the research described in Chapter 11, but they also have great difficulty in *matching* two different images of the same unfamiliar face, even when these images are present in front of them.

---

[1] We use the term 'face reconstruction systems' here to refer to systems such as Photofit, Identi-Kit, E-FIT and EvoFIT that are used to produce a 'composite', a likeness of a suspect's face that can be publicized in the hope that someone who knows the suspect will recognize the composite and get in contact with the police. A reviewer pointed out to us that the same term has been used to describe a method of trying to produce a likeness of a face from a skull by estimating what it would look like with muscle, fat and skin added. They also pointed out that the terms 'facial composition system', a 'computerized method of synthesizing images' and 'facial identification software' have all been used to refer to the composite production systems that we are covering here.

13.1 **Face recognition from identity cards and CCTV**

Kemp et al (1997) looked at how well supermarket cashiers could match photographs on credit cards to the shopper standing in front of them. There were four conditions. In one, the shopper's appearance was similar to their photograph on the card. In another condition, the card showed a photograph of the shopper who was holding it, but with different clothes and minor changes in appearance, such as a different hairstyle. In a third condition, the photograph on the card was that of an entirely different person, but one whose appearance was matched to that of the person using the card. In the final condition, the photograph on the card was someone who looked completely different to the bearer; there was no attempt to match the two other than in terms of gender and race (Fig. 13.1).

There were individual differences in detection rates amongst the cashiers who took part in this study, but overall more than half of the fraudulent cards were mistakenly accepted and more than 10% of the legitimate ones were rejected. On average, cashiers incorrectly accepted a third of the cards for which no attempt had been made

(a) Unchanged apperance

(b) Changed apperance

(c) Matched foil

(d) Unmatched foil

FIGURE 13.1 Mean percentage of correct decisions in Kemp et al's (1997) study of how well supermarket cashiers could match photographs on credit cards to their bearers.

to match the photograph on the card to the appearance of the person using it. The cashiers also lacked insight into how poorly they had performed; they thought they had been very accurate and were surprised at the number of errors they had made. Pike et al (1998) suggest this may be because everyday experience at recognizing *familiar* faces fools people into thinking that they should also be good at recognizing *unfamiliar* ones.

More recently, Chiller-Glaus et al (2007) investigated how well people could be matched to their passport or ID-card photographs. Not only was matching performance highly error-prone, but performance was further worsened when participants were given only a few seconds to make their decisions—as might well happen in the case of passport checking at a busy airport, for example. Interestingly, like Kemp and colleagues, Chiller-Glaus et al found sizeable individual differences in performance. They speculated that participants might have varied in the strategies they used to perform the matching task, and that some strategies were better than others.

Comparable problems were found in a series of studies by Burton and his colleagues that looked at how well people can recognize faces from surveillance videos (Bruce et al, 1999b, 2001; Burton et al, 1999). Their participants had to judge whether faces in high-quality photographs had been seen before in video clips. Participants who were personally familiar with the faces in the videos performed very well (a demonstration of the robustness of familiar-face recognition), but participants who did not know them performed poorly.

In Henderson et al's (2001) study, participants saw a set of still images of a 'robber's' face, taken from a CCTV camera. They then had to try to identify the person from a lineup of eight faces. This was done with two different robbers. For the first robber, only 21% of participants made a correct identification; 21% decided incorrectly that he was not present in the lineup, and a whopping 58% picked a different face (i.e. they made a false

identification of what, in real life, would be an innocent person). For the second robber, 19% picked the right person from the lineup, 37% mistakenly decided that he was not in the lineup, and 43% picked someone else. Henderson et al wondered whether the results were due partly to the poor quality of the CCTV footage, so they repeated the experiment with high-quality full-face photographs of the two 'robbers' and TV broadcast-quality video. Similar results were obtained to those in the first study; for robber 1, only 16% of participants were able to pick the robber correctly from the lineup; 44% said he was absent from the lineup; and 40% picked someone else instead. The results were rather better in the case of the second robber, where 40% picked the right person from the lineup, 51% decided incorrectly that he was not present, and only 9% picked someone else. Overall, however, the results show clearly that people are very poor at matching two different images of the same person's face.

It may not help if the two images differ in quality or format (such as if one image is a poor-quality CCTV image and the other a high-quality photograph), but this is not the root cause of the difficulties because performance on matching images of the same face is poor even when both images are high quality (Bruce et al, 1999; Megreya and Burton, 2006b) (Fig. 13.2). In fact, there are some indications that improving image quality might even *worsen* performance. In a study of how well a face seen in CCTV footage could be identified afterwards from a lineup, Davies and Thasen (2000) found that the number of false identifications was actually *higher* for participants who saw colour CCTV video than for those who saw the same film in monochrome. Davies and Thasen suggest that the better quality of the colour footage might have increased participants' confidence, leading them to be more ready to make a decision irrespective of its accuracy.

In the studies mentioned above, participants tried to match either two static images, or a static image and a video. In courtroom settings, jurors

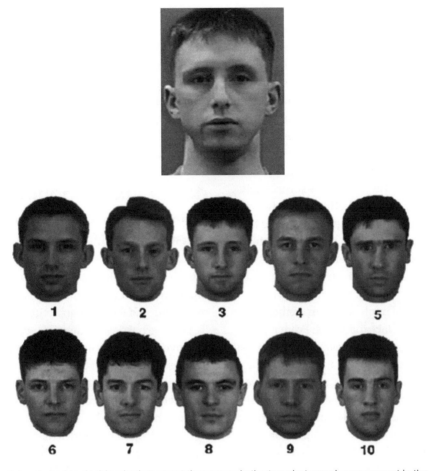

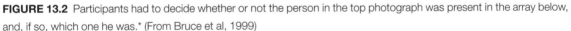

FIGURE 13.2 Participants had to decide whether or not the person in the top photograph was present in the array below, and, if so, which one he was.* (From Bruce et al, 1999)

   * It is number 3.

may often be asked to decide whether or not a criminal caught on CCTV is the same person as the defendant standing in front of them. Davis and Valentine (2009) investigated matching performance in this context. Participants first saw a video intended to simulate CCTV footage. It depicted a young man walking along, stopping and using a mobile phone. This was filmed from above, but provided good views of the actor's face from various angles, as well as of his whole body. After watching the video at least three times, participants decided whether or not a 'defendant' who was physically present in front of them was

the actor in the video. Eight different young men were used as 'defendants'. On half of the trials, the defendant was the person shown in the video; on the other half, they were different people, but similar in appearance. As in the Henderson et al (2001) study, participants' performance varied widely across different 'defendants', perhaps because they varied in facial distinctiveness. However, overall performance was poor. When the video showed the defendant, 22% of participants decided incorrectly that the person in front of them was not the man in the video. When the defendant was not in the video, 17% of participants decided incorrectly that he was. In another experiment, participants had to decide whether or not the defendant standing in front of them was the same person as shown in a video shot a year earlier. Overall, when the defendant was present in the video, 44% of participants decided incorrectly that he was not; and when the defendant was not in the video, 33% of participants mistakenly thought he was. Error rates were largely unaffected by giving participants a warning that the video was filmed a year earlier. They were also surprisingly little affected by disguise (whether or not the man in the video wore either dark glasses or a hat). Not only did Davis and Valentine's participants find it hard to make matches between individuals and video images, they were also often highly confident in their decisions, even when they were wrong.

There are several implications from these studies of unfamiliar face matching. From a theoretical point of view, they represent additional evidence that the poor performance of eyewitnesses is not due solely to memory limitations, because matching two faces that are physically present in front of you makes very little demand on memory. These studies also suggest that unfamiliar face recognition is 'image-based'—it is heavily tied to the particular view of the face that is being viewed, to the extent that changes in viewpoint, lighting conditions or expression are likely to cause recognition to fail. This suggests that face recognition may involve rather different cognitive systems depending on whether or not the face is known to the viewer. On a practical level, these studies indicate that attempts to identify criminals from CCTV footage may be highly unreliable. In particular, Henderson et al (2001) warn against the practice of inviting jurors to compare a CCTV image to a defendant in order to establish the latter's guilt. These studies on unfamiliar face matching also suggest that the UK government's plans to introduce compulsory identity cards for British citizens (now abandoned as a result of the economic recession) would have been an expensive waste of time. In fact, on the strength of Kemp et al's results, some banks dropped their plans to place photographs on cheque and credit cards.

13.2 Face recognition on the basis of composites (Photofit, Identi-Kit, E-FIT, etc.)

Witnesses to serious crimes are sometimes called upon to produce a likeness of a face that they saw, using a 'face reconstruction system' such as E-FIT.[2] Verbal descriptions of faces are usually too impoverished to be useful, so the idea is that the witness produces an external representation of their memory of the face they saw, a likeness that would hopefully be recognizable by anyone who knows the person depicted.

Identi-Kit is the oldest of these composite systems, introduced in 1959 by an American police officer, Hugh MacDonald (Davies and Valentine, 2007). Originally, Identi-Kit consisted of over 500 transparent acetate sheets, each containing a drawing of a facial feature. On the basis of a witness' initial description of each feature, the operator selects sheets and superimposes them to produce a **composite** face. The witness can then refine this by asking for features to be changed or altered. Figure 13.3 shows an early example of an Identi-Kit. On the basis of this composite, a policeman recognized Edwin Bush, and arrested him on suspicion of the murder of a London shopkeeper. Bush was subsequently identified in a lineup, convicted and executed for his crime.

---

[2] The police also sometimes use artists to produce a sketch of a face, working in interaction with a witness. However, face reconstruction systems are much more widely used, for reasons of cost and convenience.

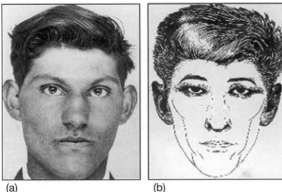

(a)   (b)

FIGURE 13.3 The first successful conviction using Identi-Kit in the UK: (a) Edwin Bush, who murdered a shopkeeper in 1961; (b) the Identi-Kit of him, produced by the shop's owner.

Photofit, invented by Penry (1971), consists of photographs of over 500 features. Features are printed on separate cards, which can be assembled in a frame, jigsaw-like, to form a composite face.

These older systems have been superseded by computerized systems. The most popular ones are **Identi-Kit 2000** and **FACES 3.0** in the USA, and **E-FIT** in the UK. FACES 3.0 (IQ Biometrix Ltd) uses more realistic facial features which can be resized, reshaped and moved around within the face outline to a much greater extent than is possible with non-computerized systems (Fig. 13.4).

E-FIT (Aspley Ltd, 1993)[3] uses photographic-quality features. On the basis of a '**cognitive interview**'[4] with the witness, the police operator creates an initial composite. This can then be

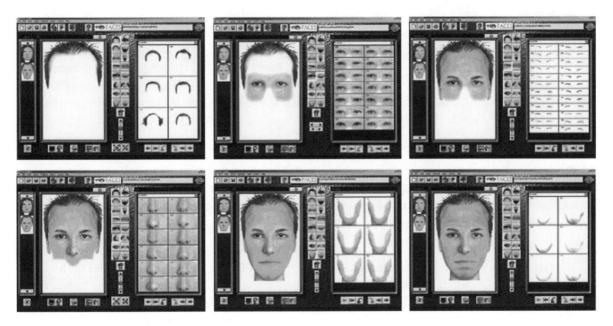

FIGURE 13.4 The process of building a composite using FACES 3.0. The witness can begin with any feature, and add others in any order. (From Wells and Hasel, 2007)

---

[3] E-FIT is now marketed by Visionmetric Ltd (http://www.visionmetric.com).

[4] The Cognitive Interview technique is the standard method for police interviews of witnesses in the UK, and is also widely used in the USA. Devised by Geiselman and his colleagues (e.g. Geiselman et al, 1985), it attempts to enhance a witness' recall of people and events by using techniques derived from psychological research on memory. For example, witnesses are encouraged to recall everything that they can, regardless of its apparent importance; to use context

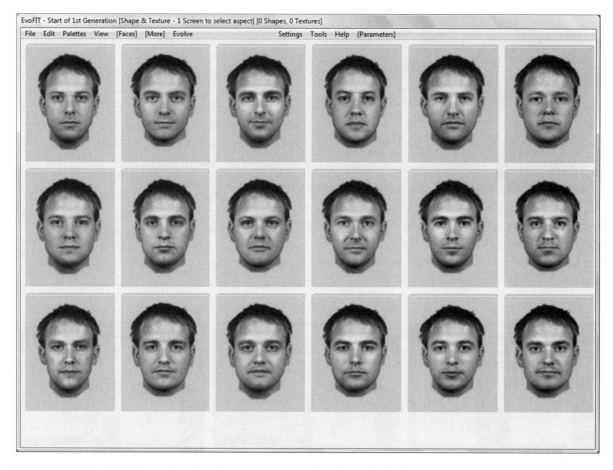

FIGURE 13.5 The EvoFIT procedure: the witness compares multiple faces with their memory of the face they saw. The ones most like the witness' memory are 'bred' together to form a new set of faces for evaluation, a process that is repeated until the witness is satisfied that a good likeness has been achieved (Frowd et al, 2007a). (Reproduced with kind permission of Charlie Frowd, University of Central Lancashire. © Charlie Frowd)

altered if necessary. One potential advantage of E-FIT is that it acknowledges that faces are processed configurally, as amended features are presented within the overall context of the face. Identi-Kit 2000 (Smith and Wesson Ltd) is somewhat similar to E-FIT, except that its features are more sketch-like in appearance, rather than of photographic quality.

EvoFIT and **EFIT-V** are examples of the very latest types of composite system to emerge. Like E-FIT, they attempt to take account of the configural nature of normal face processing, but take this one stage further: the witness never looks at individual facial features, only whole faces.

In EvoFIT, the witness is shown successive arrays of faces that are created from real faces using

reinstatement (e.g. mentally revisiting the scene of the crime); to recall events in varying temporal orders; and to try to recall events from perspectives other than their own. See Milne and Bull (2002) and Dando et al (2009) for details and reviews of the effectiveness of the Cognitive Interview.

a process called **Principal Components Analysis** (PCA[5]; Fig. 13.5; see Chapter 2, section 2.11, for more information). For each array, the witness picks the one face or several faces that most resemble the target face. Their selection influences the faces shown in the following array, as evolutionary algorithms narrow the variation within each successive array of faces. The process continues until it converges on a face that the witness considers is a very good likeness to the one that they saw originally.

EFIT-V uses broadly similar principles, but is more flexible. Again, the witness always sees whole faces, but they can employ both configural and featural processing modes as required. The witness begins by specifying overall face shape, age, gender, ethnicity and hairstyle. In its 'evolutionary' mode,

an array of faces is shown. Those that have some resemblance to the target face are retained, and morphed together; this morph acts as the basis for the next array of faces (Fig. 13.6). However, in contrast to EvoFIT, which is exclusively 'holistic' in nature, EFIT-V also gives the witness scope to engage in feature-based processing as well, if they wish. For example, individual features can be altered or retained, so that distinctive aspects of the face (such as a large nose) can be reproduced on all of the faces in the array. The faces can also be 'warped' or distorted, for example to make them thinner or fatter if necessary. Faces can also be 'aged' if required.

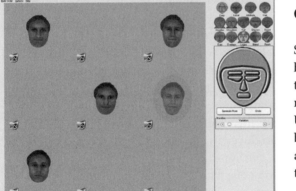

FIGURE 13.6 EFIT-V in its 'evolutionary' mode: some faces have been discarded, and the best match has been selected from the remainder. This face will be used to 'breed' another array of faces that are variants on the one selected. (Reproduced with kind permission of Chris Solomon. © Chris Solomon)

13.3 **Evaluations of facial composite systems**

Successful uses of composites tend to be publicized heavily in the media, giving the impression that these systems are highly successful in producing recognizable likenesses of criminals' faces. Unfortunately, this is far from the truth: it has long been apparent that there are serious limitations with all of the composite systems that have been devised to date (review in Davies and Valentine, 2007).

Ellis and co-workers performed a series of studies showing that Photofit produced very poor likenesses of faces. In one experiment (Ellis et al, 1978), they showed that Photofits were rated as poor likenesses when a photograph of the face—or even the person themselves—was in view during the process of construction, suggesting that it is hard to produce an accurate copy of a face with

---

[5] Principal Components Analysis is a statistical procedure that attempts to identify the main sources of variability in an image and reduce them to a few underlying factors (the principal components). The first factor accounts for most of the variability in the image; the second one accounts for most of whatever variability is left after the first factor has been removed; the third accounts for most of what's left after the first and second factors have been removed; and so on. In many respects, PCA is similar to the better-known procedure of Factor Analysis.

this system. This is supported by a study in which participants were asked simply to reconstruct two Photofit faces that were present in front of them throughout the composite production process (Ellis et al, 1975). Because the two faces were themselves Photofits, in theory it should have been possible to make perfect reproductions of them. In practice, the task proved to be very difficult. Participants were poor at selecting the correct features from the kit, especially in the case of noses and chins. Independent judges rated the degree of similarity between each target Photofit and its copies. On a seven-point scale, the average rating was only 4.5 (a 'moderate match').

In another experiment, Ellis et al (1975) asked participants to produce Photofits of six real faces from memory, immediately after seeing them. A second group tried to use these Photofits to identify the 6 original faces from a set of 36. Chance matching performance was 3% (1 in 36). The actual success rate was 12.5%—better than chance, but very poor. Ellis et al (1978) went on to show that the quality of the composite production was unaffected by variations in the duration of exposure to the face (15 seconds or 2.5 minutes) and whether or not participants attended to the face. In all cases, independent raters judged the resulting composites to be poor likenesses of the original faces. Laughery and Fowler (1980) reported that performance with the original version of Identi-Kit was similarly poor.

The problems with Photofit and Identi-Kit extend to the newer, more sophisticated, systems such as Mac-a-Mug Pro, E-FIT, Identi-Kit 2000 and EvoFIT. In a comparison between Photofit and E-FIT, Davies et al (2000) found that E-FIT produced good likenesses only when the face was in view at the time of construction; when faces were constructed from memory, E-FIT was no better than Photofit. Similar results have been found with Mac-a-Mug Pro; when any appreciable delay occurs between seeing a face and producing a composite of it, the resulting composites are a poor likeness of the target (Koehn and Fisher, 1997; Kovera et al, 1997).

Frowd et al (2005) compared the performance of a number of different composite systems, taking pains to reproduce the conditions under which these systems would be used by the police in real life. Thus, composite construction followed an initial interview; there was a realistic delay between the witness seeing the suspect and making a composite of them; the composite operators were highly experienced with the systems they were using; and each operator made only one composite in a session. Five different systems were evaluated. As well as Photofit, E-FIT, a system quite similar to E-FIT called PRO-Fit, and EvoFIT, Frowd et al looked at the performance of a skilled police sketch artist.

In Frowd et al's comparison of these systems, witnesses produced composites of faces of celebrities whom they did not know. Another group of participants, who were familiar with the celebrities concerned, then tried to identify these composites. This procedure attempted to simulate real life, where a composite of a criminal's face is produced by someone who does not know them, in the hope that recognition will be triggered in someone who *does* know the criminal. Frowd et al found significant effects of facial distinctiveness as well as the type of system being used to produce the composite. On average, E-FIT and PRO-Fit performed similarly, and were the best systems by far. However, even with these, fewer than 20% of the composites produced could be identified by the naive participants. Composites of highly distinctive celebrity faces were more recognizable than composites of undistinctive faces; for the latter, all of the systems produced recognition rates of around 5%.[6]

---

[6] Actually, PRO-Fit produced a recognition rate of 14% for undistinctive faces, but this was due to one 'outlier' face, that of the footballer Michael Owen.

Using similar methods, Frowd et al (2007d) evaluated the two systems most widely used in the USA, Identi-Kit 2000 and FACES 3.0, comparing each of them in turn to PRO-Fit. One set of participants produced composites of celebrity faces that were unfamiliar to them. Another group of participants, who were familiar with the celebrities concerned, tried to identify the composites. Figure 13.7 shows examples of composites made by the different systems for a single face, the British pop singer Noel Gallagher. Compared with FACES, PRO-Fit produced composites that were rated as better likenesses of the celebrities concerned. However, in absolute terms, the composites produced by both systems were rated as very poor. (The mean rating was 3.3 out of 7 for PRO-Fit and 2.5 for FACES, where a rating of 1 represented a 'poor likeness' and 7 was a 'good likeness'.) More importantly, both systems were similar in producing composites that were very difficult to recognize. Each of 12 participants produced 10 composites with PRO-Fit and 10 with FACES, and only *one* of these 240 composites was identified spontaneously. Similar results were obtained in the comparison between Identi-Kit 2000 and PRO-Fit; again, only 1 of 240 composites (one of the Identi-Kits) could be

(a) (b) (c)

(d) (e) (f)

FIGURE 13.7 (a) The pop-singer, Noel Gallagher; (b–f) Example composites of Gallagher from the study by Frowd et al (2005). (Gallagher was a 'highly distinctive' target face in this study.) Each composite was constructed by a different witness. (b) E-FIT, (c) EvoFIT, (d) Photofit, (e) sketch artist, (f) PRO-Fit.

recognized without any prompting. This time, the likeness ratings favoured Identi-Kit (3.1 for Identi-Kit and 2.6 for PRO-Fit).

13.4 Factors underlying the poor performance of composite systems

Why is performance with face reconstruction systems so disappointing? There seem to be a number of factors at work.

13.4.1 Restricted feature sets

In the early days of Photofit and Identi-Kit, there were limitations imposed by the systems themselves, in the sense that the feature sets were rather restricted and there were constraints on where features could be located within the face outline. However, this cannot be the whole explanation. As mentioned above, Ellis et al (1975) found that it was difficult to use Photofit to make a *copy* of a Photofit image, even when the latter was physically present throughout the construction process so that memory for the face was not required. Wells and Hryciw (1984) produced faces using Identi-Kit, and then asked participants to use Identi-Kit to recreate them. Thus, in theory, it should have been possible to make exact recreations of the original faces. In practice, independent judges rated the Identi-Kits as poor likenesses, giving them a mean rating of 2 on a seven-point scale, which ranged from 1 ('does not resemble') to 7 ('closely resembles').

Newer, computer-based systems such as E-FIT and FACES 3.0 have many more features at their disposal; there are no limits on where they can be positioned within the face outline, and subtle alterations can be made using paint software packages. E-FIT even has feature sets for different ethnic groups. These systems are much better than the early ones at producing realistic facial images, but even under optimal conditions they still struggle to produce recognizable likenesses. Frowd et al (2007a) asked operators to use PRO-Fit to make a copies of celebrity photographs that were continuously in view. Only 20% of the resulting composites could be named correctly by naive participants who were familiar with the celebrities concerned. In an evaluation of FACES 3.0, Oswald and Coleman (2007) produced composites from photographs that were continuously in view, and then presented each composite together with a five-photo lineup (a somewhat easier task than Frowd et al's). For each lineup, naive participants had to decide which face matched the composite. Under these ideal conditions, composites were matched correctly 62% of the time, well above chance performance but still quite poor.

13.4.2 Verbal mediation

Problems with composite systems might potentially stem from the fact that the witness produces the composite *indirectly*, via discussion with a trained police operative, rather than creating it themselves. One problem with this procedure is that languages are limited in terms of how many descriptive terms they contain for faces. Try describing a friend to someone who does not know them. Unless your friend has a particularly striking feature, you will find it difficult to come up with a description that could be used to discriminate your friend from other people of the same age, sex and ethnic grouping.

Brace et al (2006a) examined the effects of verbal mediation on the quality of E-FIT construction. Experienced police operators constructed composites of famous faces. There were two conditions in which the operator constructed the composite by themselves, either from memory or with the aid of a photograph of the face in question. There were a further two conditions in which the operator produced the composite indirectly, on the basis of another person's description of the face (without the operator knowing which famous face the person was attempting to describe). Again, this person either described the face from memory or used a photograph. All the composites were then shown to naive witnesses who tried to identify them. When the operators worked alone, there was little difference in how well their composites were recognized: 23% of those they produced from memory were identified, compared with 22% of those produced from a photograph. When the operators worked with someone who described the face to them, the composites were less recognizable: only 13% of the ones based on witnesses' memories were identified, compared with 18% of those based on witnesses' descriptions of photographs. Thus, whether or not the composite was made from memory, composite operators produced significantly more recognizable composites when they worked alone than when they worked with a 'witness' who described the face to them. These results suggest that the process of verbal mediation does indeed affect the quality of composites.

Another problem caused by the composite construction procedure is that the process of describing a face might interfere with the witness' original memory of it, due to the phenomenon of **verbal overshadowing**, described in Chapter 8.

13.4.3 **Feature-based construction methods**

The main problem with composite systems seems to be more fundamental: it is that they require a serial, feature-by-feature process of constructing a face that is at odds with the configural/holistic way in which people actually remember faces (Davies, 1983; Frowd et al, 2007a,b; see Chapter 2). Findings consistent with this view come from a study by Wells and Hryciw (1984). Participants saw a set of faces and were biased towards encoding them either **configurally** (by being asked to evaluate them on ten personality traits, such as honesty) or

featurally (by being asked to evaluate the face in terms of ten individual feature dimensions, such as nose size). The 'configural' encoders were better than the 'featural' encoders at identifying the faces in a lineup; however, the 'featural' encoders produced Identi-Kits that were better likenesses of the target faces. Similar effects of encoding strategy have been reported for PRO-Fit (Frowd et al, 2007a). Even composites produced using the more 'holistic' EvoFIT system are better when a feature-based strategy is used at the encoding stage (Frowd et al, 2007a).

The inventor of Photofit, Penry (1971), claimed that if you had the right features, in more or less the right positions, then you were guaranteed to get a good likeness of the face in question. However, everything we have learnt about face recognition since then suggests otherwise. As shown in Chapter 1, the spatial interrelationships between the features (a face's configural properties) play an extremely important role in face recognition. E-FIT, EFIT-V and EvoFIT are superior to Photofit and FACES in this respect, because any manipulations of features are always within the context of a whole facial configuration.

Another problem with composites may arise from differences in how familiar and unfamiliar faces are processed (see Chapter 2, section 2.9). Ellis et al (1979) showed that familiar faces are recognized better from their internal features (the region containing the eyes, nose and mouth), whereas unfamiliar faces are recognized better from their external features (face outline and hair). Because a composite is constructed by a witness who does not know the face, the composite's external features may be reconstructed more accurately than its internal features; however, it is the internal features that are most important, because they provide the best basis for triggering recognition of the composite in people who are familiar with the face. Frowd et al (2007b) compared the quality of the internal and external features of composites produced by various systems (a trained police sketch artist, E-FIT,

PRO-Fit and EvoFIT). The results were similar for all of the composite systems: external features were matched to photographs of the target faces about as accurately as whole composites (33% of matches correct), but internal features were matched significantly less accurately (less than 20% correct). Thus, all of the composites were better matches of the external facial features than they were of the internal ones.

Another experiment by Frowd et al showed that the superiority of external features over internal features persisted even when the composite constructors were familiar with the target faces; this implies that the problems in producing a good reconstruction of the internal facial region stem from some aspect of the composite construction process rather than from the external feature advantage for unfamiliar faces. Frowd et al speculate that the tendency for witnesses to select the external facial features first when constructing a composite might affect their ability to concentrate on the internal facial region subsequently; perhaps witnesses' attention to the internal features could be enhanced by blurring the external features until the internal features have been dealt with adequately.

13.5 Attempts at overcoming the limitations of composite systems

There have been attempts at trying to remedy the limitations of face reconstruction systems by combining the composites produced by different witnesses in various ways. In Bruce et al's (2002) study, 'witnesses' produced composites of a target

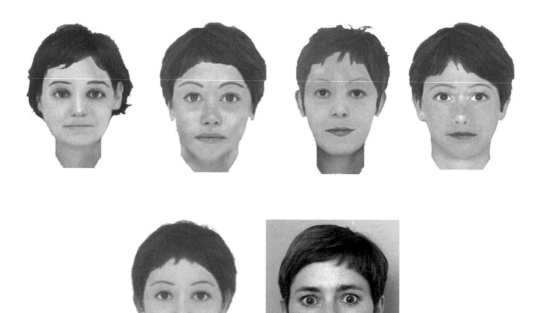

FIGURE 13.8 Examples of stimuli used in Bruce et al's (2002) study. Top row: four individual composites of the same face. Bottom row: four-face morph (left) and the original face (right).

face. Solely on the basis of these composites, another group of participants tried to identify the target face from a lineup. Performance on this task was better when these participants saw sets of four composites made by different witnesses, or morphs (blends) between four different witnesses' composites, rather than any single composite; they made more correct identifications and fewer false identifications (Fig. 13.8). Bruce et al suggest that morphing aids recognition because each person introduces errors into the composite that they construct, in the sense of deviations from the face's true appearance. These errors are unlikely to be the same for all participants, and so they cancel out, leaving in the averaged composite only those features that are actually correct. In effect, combining the individual composites produces a **prototype** of the target face. Similar results have been obtained by Hasel and Wells (2007) and Frowd et al (2007c).

Interestingly, Francis Galton anticipated this argument more than a century earlier. In 1879, he presented a paper to the Anthropological Institute of Great Britain and Ireland, in which he described a technique that he had devised to obtain an average face by means of optical superimposition of a number of images of individual faces. Galton's method was to use multiple exposures of appropriately aligned and resized faces on to a single photographic plate:

> [A]...use of this process is to obtain by photography a really good likeness of a living person. The inferiority of photographs to the best works of artists, so far as resemblance is concerned, lies in their catching no more than a single expression. If many photographs of a person were taken at different times, perhaps even years apart, their composite would possess that in which a single photograph is deficient.

Brace et al (2006b) have also found that presenting participants with multiple composites can lead to a higher rate of identification than when they are shown a single composite. In Brace et al's

study, eight 'witnesses' saw a staged crime involving a person who was unknown to them, and then made a composite with the aid of a police operator who was also unfamiliar with the target face (Fig. 13.9). These composites were presented in varying numbers to naive participants who attempted to use them in order to identify the 'criminal' from a lineup. Use of all eight composites produced a higher rate of identification than any single composite; however, the best identification rate was obtained by showing four composites, regardless of whether these were the four best, median or worst of the eight. Brace et al speculate that this is because using four composites enables participants to extract the similarities and differences between them; eight may be too many to keep in memory in order to do this.

As both Bruce et al (2002) and Brace et al (2006b) point out, UK law currently precludes techniques that involve combining data from witnesses, or allowing one witness to see another's attempt at a composite. In fact, according to Bruce et al, current UK police guidelines stipulate that only one of the witnesses to a particular crime should produce a composite. Brace et al therefore examined the effectiveness of an alternative method to the one used in their first study. Independent judges who were unfamiliar with the targets were shown the eight composites and asked to pick the four that looked most alike. From their selections, it was possible to work out which four composites were chosen most often, and also which single composite was chosen most often. A separate group of participants, each of whom was familiar with the target face, was then shown either all eight composites, the four that had been chosen most often, or the single most frequently selected composite. Showing participants the latter did not elicit as many correct identifications as the technique used in the first study, but was still as good as showing the naive participants the single 'best' composite. Brace et al's interpretation of these results is similar to Bruce

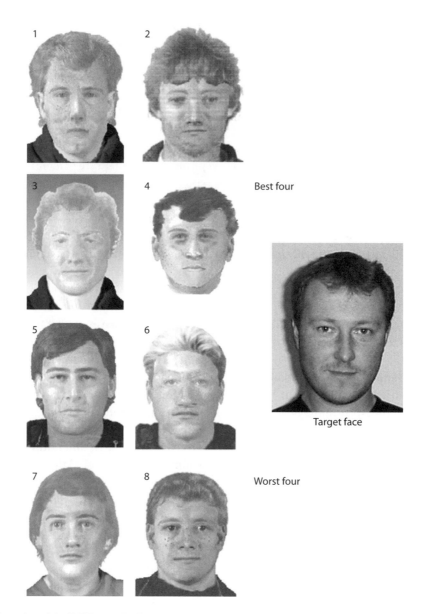

Best four

Target face

Worst four

FIGURE 13.9 Examples of the E-FITs used in Brace et al's (2006b) study, together with the original face on which they were based. (The eight composites are arranged in order of rated likeness to the face: 1 = best, 8 = worst.)

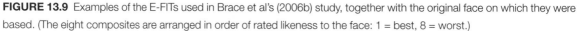

et al's explanation for their morphing study: the composite that is rated as most similar to all of the other composites effectively acts as a prototype of the target face. Brace et al suggest that if the police wished to publicize only one image of a suspect then they could use this method in order to select the one that was most likely to be recognized.

Frowd et al (2007c) performed a series of experiments to investigate whether caricature could be used to improve performance with composites. Taking E-FIT, PRO-Fit and

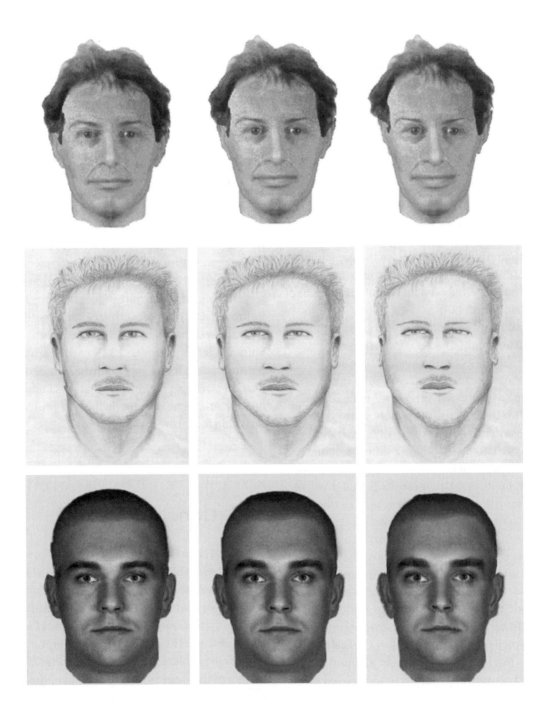

FIGURE 13.10 Examples of the composite caricatures used by Frowd et al (2007c). Central column: original images (top: E-FIT of Tony Blair; centre: sketch of Brad Pitt; bottom: EvoFIT of Robbie Williams). Left column: 50% caricatures; right column: +50% caricatures.

EvoFIT composites from their previous research, together with drawings by a police sketch artist, they used a computer program to produce a series of **caricatures** of these images. Some were '**positive**' caricatures, in which the differences between the composite and an 'average' face were exaggerated to varying degrees. Others were **anti-caricatures**, in which the differences were reduced, so that the composite looked more like the average face (Fig. 13.10). Previous research has shown that mild levels of positive caricature enhance face recognition; compared with the original pictures, these caricatures are recognized better, and are rated as being better likenesses of the person that they depict. Anti-caricaturing impairs recognition (see Chapter 1 for a fuller discussion of caricaturing effects).

Frowd et al's original expectation was that caricaturing might make a composite more recognizable by exaggerating its differences from the average face, effectively drawing attention to whatever aspects make the original face distinctive. In fact, the results showed the opposite: for individual composites, participants generally selected an anti-caricature as being the best likeness of the person concerned. Frowd et al's explanation of their results is that positive caricaturing of a composite exaggerates the distinctiveness of a face, but it also exaggerates the errors in the composite that are produced by the participant's poor memory of the facial features and their configuration. An anti-caricature may decrease the distinctiveness of a face, but it also reduces the magnitude of the errors. On balance, the anti-caricatures end up as more recognizable composites. Consistent with this interpretation, Frowd et al found that morphed composites, similar to those used in Bruce et al's (2002) study, were *less* recognizable following anti-caricaturing; because the errors in the composite have already been minimized by the process of averaging that is inherent in the morphing process, anti-caricaturing serves only to impair recognition by reducing the face's distinctiveness.

Frowd et al found that there were large individual differences between composite faces in terms of how much caricaturing was preferred. Therefore, they examined the effects on recognition of presenting participants with a series of caricatures of each face, rather than a single image that represented a particular level of caricature. The series was presented to participants either as an animation that repeatedly varied from extreme anti-caricature through to extreme positive caricature, or as a static photospread of the images that were used to produce the animation. In both cases, spontaneous naming of the faces was markedly improved. Only 29% of veridical composites were named, compared with 42% of the animated composites and 37% of the caricature photospreads. It remains to be determined why presenting a range of caricatures has such beneficial effects, but clearly this is a promising direction for future research.

13.6 **Conclusion**

The research in Chapter 11 highlighted how poor we are at recognizing unfamiliar faces—at trying to decide whether someone we are seeing now (perhaps in a set of mugshots or in an identity parade) is the same person that we saw at some previous time. The research in this chapter shows that these problems extend to *matching* different images of the same person, even when those images are both in view at the same time, as in the case of identity cards, passports and the like. As Burton and his colleagues have emphasized, familiar face recognition seems to be qualitatively different from unfamiliar face recognition.

Familiar face recognition seems to be based more on 'abstractive' representations that respond to many different views of a known face. As a result, it is highly tolerant of changes in viewpoint, illumination, etc. In contrast, unfamiliar face recognition is more 'image based', tied closely to the original view of the face that was encountered (Hancock et al, 2000). Almost inevitably, the view of a face that is depicted on an identity card or recorded on CCTV will differ from the view of that face that is currently being seen by an observer. These differences defeat the observer's attempts at making reliable matches between the two images.

We are also very poor at making reconstructions of unfamiliar faces using composite systems such as Photofit, Identi-Kit and E-FIT. As we have seen, at best composites are identified only about 20% of the time, even when they are produced soon after seeing the target face (Frowd et al, 2005, 2007a,d). The problems arise from limitations in the witness, rather than the composite construction systems. It is true that the early systems, such as Photofit and Identi-Kit, were limited both technologically and conceptually; they struggled to produce truly face-like images, and were based on inappropriate (feature-based) models of how humans normally process faces. The latest systems (EvoFIT and EFIT-V) are much better in both respects. They can produce extremely lifelike images, and they have been designed on sound psychological principles, encouraging witnesses to use configural processing throughout the composite construction procedure. Even so, formal evaluations of EvoFIT have shown that EvoFITs are only marginally better than the composites produced by the older systems. EvoFIT's superiority over PRO-Fit and E-FIT does seem to increase with longer time delays between inspecting the face and producing a composite of it, however. After a delay of two days, Frowd et al (2005) found that nearly three times more EvoFITs could be named than PRO-Fits. Frowd et al suggest that this reflects the way in which a witness' memory of a face changes over time: as time passes, a face memory becomes more of a holistic impression, and the ability to recall its individual features is progressively lost. Feature-based composite systems should therefore function most effectively immediately after the face is seen, whereas holistic systems like EvoFIT might work best later on.[7]

As Hasel and Wells (2007) point out, our face-processing systems are designed for recognition on the basis of holistic representations, rather than recall on the basis of individual facial features. For early humans, living in relatively small and tightly knit groups, there must have been strong selection pressures for recognizing familiar faces. However, unfamiliar face processing would presumably not have needed to extend beyond detecting that a face was that of a stranger. Remembering a face that was encountered only once is probably a highly unnatural task for us, let alone constructing a composite of it!

---

[7] Before you get too depressed, we should point out that psychological research probably overemphasizes the deficiencies of composite systems. In practice, the police generally publicize composites in the hope that they will trigger recognition in someone who knows the person depicted. And, of course, they need this to happen in only one person for the composite to have been a success (N. A. Brace, personal communication). Although even the latest composite systems leave a lot of room for improvement, they are still much better than nothing—and indeed they have produced some spectacular successes in terms of solving crimes.

SUMMARY

- People find it difficult to match two different views of the same unfamiliar face: this has serious implications for the effectiveness of ID cards, passports and driving licences as a means of verifying someone's identity.

- Identifications of unfamiliar people from CCTV footage are similarly unreliable.

- A number of 'face reconstruction systems' have been devised. Their aim is to enable a witness to produce a representation of the suspect's face, one that is good enough to trigger recognition in someone who knows the suspect.

- Early composite systems, such as Photofit and Identi-Kit, were based on the idea that faces were merely collections of isolated features. More recent systems, such as PRO-Fit, E-FIT and EvoFIT, acknowledge the fact that people process faces in a more 'holistic' way, with reference to the target face's 'configural' properties.

- Despite their technological sophistication, even the most modern systems struggle to produce recognizable likenesses.

- The limitations on composites probably now stem more from limitations in the witness' memory than from problems with the technology.

FURTHER READING

Keval, H. U. and Sasse, M. A. (2008). *Can we ID from CCTV? Image quality in digital CCTV and face identification performance.* In: S. S. Agaian and S. A. Jassim (eds) *SPIE Mobile Multimedia/ Image Processing, Security, and Applications*. Proceedings of SPIE series. SPIE. Available online from: http://hornbeam.cs.ucl.ac.uk/hcs/people/ documents/Angela%20Publications/2008/ CanweIDfromCCTV_HK.pdf (accessed 24 November 2009). This contains an interesting discussion of how CCTV image quality affects identification performance.

Lindsay, R. C. L., Ross, D. F., Read, J. D. and Toglia, M. P. (eds) (2007). *Handbook of Eyewitness Psychology, Vol. 2: Memory for People*. Mahwah, NJ: Erlbaum. This contains excellent reviews of some of the topics covered in this chapter, such as composite construction and the effectiveness of mugshots.

Hopefully, this book has given you an idea of the breadth of interest in face processing. We have divided research into 'psychological', 'neuropsychological' and 'applied' sections largely for convenience of exposition. However, interdisciplinary work that bridges these areas is becoming increasingly common, particularly within the field of neuropsychology. For example, affective neuroscience and social neuroscience are rapidly developing areas of study. Within the field of face processing, examples of such research includes recent attempts to understand the neuropsychological basis of own-group biases, facial emotion and the semantic information associated with faces.

Nevertheless, in spite of the huge amount of research on face processing that has been conducted, there are still many questions that either are not yet fully resolved or have barely been addressed yet. For the remainder of this chapter, we will highlight some of these outstanding issues. We don't have a crystal ball, so it's quite possible that any or all of these questions may no longer be interesting by the time that this book finds itself in a 'remainders' bin, but here goes...

How do faces become familiar?

We've seen throughout this book that there are important differences between the processing of familiar and unfamiliar faces: not only are we much better at recognizing faces that we know well, compared with faces we've seen only once or twice, but we seem to process them in rather different ways. One big question is: what happens as faces become familiar? How often do you have to see a face before it becomes a 'familiar' face, and what changes in processing accompany this transition? Is familiar face recognition really qualitatively different from unfamiliar face recognition? Burton et al's 'shape averaging' model, discussed in Chapter 2, provides a nice way of bridging the gap between the two. It shows how what *look* like qualitative differences between familiar and unfamiliar face recognition (in terms of 'robustness' with respect to lighting and expression changes) could be produced by a *quantitative* change in the amount of experience with a given face. Clearly our ability to learn faces is pretty fundamental to our social interactions. Although we currently have little understanding of this process, hopefully this will change over the next few years.

Can people be trained to recognize faces better?

An important issue is how best to train people to recognize faces. This is particularly important from an 'applied' perspective. We have evolved to recognize a relatively limited number of faces belonging to members of our own tribe, but we now live in an increasingly multicultural world and come into contact with hundreds of faces. What are the most effective forms of training for teaching people how to recognize faces of other races, for example? Can police officers, security guards and passport officials be trained to encode and remember faces better than the general public? As we saw in Chapters 8 and 9, there is some evidence that training can improve the face-processing skills of various special groups. For example, children's abilities to recognize emotional expressions can be improved with training, and improved face-processing skills following training have also been reported in patients with congenital prosopagnosia, autistic spectrum disorders and schizophrenia. But overall, the effects of training have been comparatively under-researched and represent an interesting and important area for future study.

Can face reconstruction systems be improved any further?

Face reconstruction systems such as E-FIT and EvoFIT are far more sophisticated than the original versions of Photofit and Identi-Kit: long gone are the days when the attempts to construct composites were hampered by 'mechanical' limitations such as having only a limited number of features and strong constraints on their location within the face. However, as we saw in Chapter 13, even the best composite systems still produce rather poor likenesses of the target face in many cases. As Graham Pike (personal communication) has observed, the problems now seem to lie in the witnesses rather than in the technology; composite construction systems are probably as good as they are going to get, and the limiting factor on performance is the witnesses themselves. What we need is more research on how witnesses try to remember a face; which ways are effective at producing a good likeness, and which ways are not; and whether there are any factors that can reliably predict whether or not a person is likely to be able to produce a recognizable composite.

What exactly is configural processing?

Probably the most frequently recurring theme in this book has been the relative importance of configural and featural information for face processing. This was one of the main themes in Chapter 2, and it was also discussed in detail in several other chapters. As we saw in Chapter 3, as well as being important for the processing of facial identity, configural and featural facial information have been shown to be important for processing facial emotion. In Chapters 7 and 8 we saw that impaired face processing often results from deficits in configural processing, and in Chapter 9 we saw that these two types of information are processed in different parts of the brain. In Chapter 10, we discussed evidence suggesting that there may be face-specific forms of configural processing that are not used for processing other types of stimulus. However, we still know comparatively little about the nature of configural processing.

The consensus is that faces are recognized primarily on the basis of their configural properties, and that we are highly sensitive to these. As we saw in Chapter 2, this view has been supported by research demonstrating that we are more sensitive to configural properties of faces when they are displayed upright; by studies showing that we are quite good at detecting configural changes to faces produced by feature displacements; and by studies showing that we are not very good at recognizing 'scrambled' faces in which the facial features have been rearranged. All of this evidence has led to the assumption that face recognition is based on a high level of sensitivity to the configural properties of a face. This may be so, but we also have to account for findings suggesting that the precise details of facial configurations are *not* apparently critical for successful recognition. Faces can be recognized easily despite major changes to their normal configuration: stretching, squashing and shearing produce no detectable effects on face recognition (Hole et al, 2002), and distorting faces to a standard configuration (as in Burton et al's [2005] shape-free averaging model) also has little effect on recognition. Consider also the fact that facial resemblance between related individuals can be detected at levels well above chance, even when the faces are very different ages and hence quite different in configuration. 'Configural' processing involves the detection of some property from the entire face; but, contrary to what our conscious perception of faces might lead us to think, it does not consist of a simple aggregation of facial measurements. The time has come to move away from demonstrating that configural processing is important, to elucidating exactly what it involves. The next few years are likely to be very exciting from this point of view.

To what extent do different face processes interact?

By simply looking at a face we can tell its sex, age, race, emotional expression, how attractive we think they are, and we may attribute certain characteristics to them (such as whether they are trustworthy, intelligent, etc.). We can also tell whether the person is familiar or unfamiliar to us. If the person is familiar we have loads of additional information associated with them, such as their name, occupation, what their hobbies are, how we know them and how other people that we know are associated with them. One issue that is still very unclear is how much these various processes and types of information interact with one another.

According to the Bruce and Young (1986) model, the various components of face processing are independent of each other: identity, sex and expression are handled by separate processes. Apart from the theoretical justification for

this, it has suited researchers to treat them as independent, and investigate them in isolation. (It's hard enough studying just one aspect of face processing in an experiment, let alone several.) However, within this book we have discussed a few sources of evidence that do not entirely support the idea of independence. In Chapter 1 we discussed evidence suggesting that the processing of identity and sex interact to some degree. In Chapter 3 we discussed whether the processing of identity and of emotional expression are independent. Here the evidence was not quite so clear. The behavioural psychological experiments suggest that there is interdependence between identity and emotional expression, although this relationship may be asymmetrical. However, the neuropsychological evidence suggests that quite distinct brain regions are involved in the processing of identity and emotional expression. Tackling the issue of independence is likely to be difficult, but needs to be done in the future, not just for theoretical purposes but because such interactions may have important consequences from an 'applied' standpoint, if they affect the memorability of faces.

To what extent do we underestimate children's face-processing abilities?

Psychological research has often underestimated what children are capable of; for example, Piaget's research on children's cognitive abilities used complicated tasks that made little sense to his child participants. More 'child-friendly' testing techniques by later researchers showed that children had greater cognitive skills than Piaget originally thought. This trend has been repeated in research on children's face recognition abilities. As we saw in Chapters 5 and 11, conventional laboratory experiments paint a poorer picture of children's abilities than do 'applied' studies. Although no one is denying that very young children are probably not as good as adults at recognizing faces, the research reviewed in Chapters 5 and 6 suggests that neither are children quite as incompetent at face processing as was once believed. Increasingly ingenious techniques are showing that even very young infants are surprisingly sophisticated face processors, and that older children differ from adults only in quantitative terms. One group that has been under-researched is the toddler age-range. This is primarily for practical reasons, because they are 'difficult' participants to work with. However, interesting things probably occur in the development of face processing between 2 and 4 years of age, and as yet we know little about them.

What do laboratory studies really tell us about our ability to process faces?

In Parts I and II of this book, the research that we discussed was conducted almost entirely within a laboratory setting. In Part III we discussed applied aspects of face processing; some of this research has been performed in naturalistic settings, but much has taken place in the psychology laboratory. It is a concern that so much of our knowledge comes from laboratory experiments. To what extent does this research really tell us about how we process faces in the real world? Perhaps laboratory studies tell us more about how our face-processing skills cope when pushed to their limits. For example, since Haig (1984), various studies have provided information on how well people can detect small displacements of facial

features. It remains unclear whether this tells us much about normal, everyday, face processing. How 'precise' does sensitivity to facial configurations have to be, in real life, for us to be able to discriminate between individuals? We suspect the answer is 'probably not so much as you might think': everyday recognition is aided by contextual cues, such as clothing, gait, and the probability of encountering someone in a specific location. In Chapter 4 we mentioned the idea of 'cognitive ethology': research that attempts to investigate how cognition occurs in real-life situations. We need more information on what people really do with faces, rather than on what they *can* do with them. To find out how people normally process faces is going to be difficult; however, because humans are frustratingly adaptable, give them a task and they are likely to use all sorts of strategies to solve it.

Related to this, we need to know more about face processing in age groups other than children and young adults. Cognitive psychology is still very much the study of information processing in undergraduates (and mostly psychology undergraduates at that). It has been assumed that findings on this group can simply be extrapolated to other groups in the population, but the existence of own-age and own-gender biases suggests this is not necessarily true.

Having said all this, we certainly do not want to claim that laboratory work on face processing tells us nothing useful! On the contrary, as we have seen in this book, experimental studies have provided a wealth of insight into our ability to process faces—knowledge that we could never have gained in any other way. However, perhaps it is time to start moving out of the laboratory a bit more, in a bid to discover how much of what we have found out about face processing applies to the real world, as opposed to it merely reflecting what our amazing face-processing abilities are capable of when stretched to their limits.

Are faces special?

Given that we devoted an entire chapter to this question, you would have thought we might have a clear answer to it! Unfortunately, we do not. As we saw in Chapter 10, some researchers have claimed vehemently that faces are processed by dedicated mechanisms that have evolved to process faces. Others have claimed equally vehemently that they are not special, and that any differences between the processing of faces and other objects occur merely as a consequence of the extensive practice that we obtain with faces throughout life. Phrased in these terms, this is an insoluble question. Ultimately, advocates of the 'expertise' argument can always explain away any evidence presented by the 'faces are special' camp simply by claiming that we get so much more experience with faces than with any other type of object. The strongest evidence for faces being 'special' is the evolutionary argument: the importance of faces for social interaction must have exerted strong selection pressures on our ancestors. Those individuals who could quickly identify their kin, allies and enemies in a crowd, and who could discern those people's moods from the subtleties of their facial expressions, would have been at a considerable advantage. However, even this is open to an 'expertise' counter-argument. There would also have been strong evolutionary pressures on humans to be able to learn to make subtle discriminations between non-face objects; for example, many nutritious and poisonous plants look very similar to one another, and can be differentiated only by subtle configural differences between them. One thus comes back to the issue of whether face processing is truly unique to faces, or uses types of processing that can be extended to other types of object if necessary.

One way to resolve the argument is to take a middle ground, and to consider whether we actually have *two* mechanisms that are able to process faces, as implied by the 'dual route' hypothesis described in Chapter 2. One mechanism might be especially dedicated to face processing, and the other might consist of more generic processes that are used primarily for processing non-face stimuli, but that can be co-opted to process faces if necessary. If this were the case, it might explain why the evidence on both sides of the argument seems so strong. Perhaps the people in support of faces being 'special' are focusing on the specialized face-processing mechanism, whereas the people who argue against faces being special are focusing on the more generalized object-processing mechanism.

In Chapter 7 we discussed how patients with prosopagnosia tend to be impaired at processing configural facial information and that their residual abilities tend to involve the processing of featural information. It is possible that in these patients the specialized face-processing mechanism has been damaged and therefore the processing of faces is dependent upon the generalized object-processing mechanisms. This may also explain why patients with unilateral brain lesions tend to suffer from only selective impairments to face processing, whereas those with bilateral lesions are more likely to suffer from more extensive impairments. Perhaps the specialized face-processing mechanism and the generalized object-processing mechanism are located in different parts of the brain. This possibility is supported by the evidence from both clinical and non-clinical samples showing that configural processing is lateralized to the right hemisphere, whereas featural processing is lateralized to the left hemisphere.

When looked at in combination, all of this evidence points towards an interesting possibility. Maybe we have two distinct mechanisms that contribute to face processing: a specialized mechanism in the right hemisphere that processes configural facial information and a generalized mechanism in the left hemisphere that processes featural information. Although this idea is purely speculative, it does provide a nice account for some of the findings reported throughout this book.

The argument over whether or not faces are 'special' is reminiscent of similar arguments in psychology's past, such as the 'nature/nurture' debate. 'Either/or' stances are generally misconceived, and the arguments end up becoming rather sterile. Fundamentally, all biological properties are inherently the outcome of interplay between a set of genes and the environment within which those genes find themselves. As we saw in Chapter 5, the face-processing system may start out with little more than a basic predisposition to attend to top-heavy patterns. This predisposition guarantees that, in the normal course of events, faces are attended to more than other types of object, and expertise for faces starts to develop. This expertise continues to be fine-tuned by the environment throughout life, as shown by the adaptation studies described in Chapters 1 and 9, and by the existence of the various 'own-group' biases discussed in Chapter 8. From this viewpoint, both camps are right: the expertise in face processing shown by adults *is* the outcome of experience with faces, but faces end up being a very special kind of visual stimulus because, at the outset of development, there was a bias towards attending to patterns that happen to be rather face-like.

We have ended this book with a lot of questions and speculation, but that's in the nature of scientific research. Questions tend to generate more questions, and we progress to a state of ever more enlightened ignorance. However, as shown by the research described in this book, we already know a great deal about face processing. We began this book with a reference to Humpty Dumpty's complaint about the essential difficulty raised by faces: that they are all basically just variations on a theme. Nevertheless, these small variations between faces are immensely important to us, given that they provide us with so much information about their owners. Faces are fascinating on so many different levels that it is clear that the intensive research on face processing is likely to continue unabated for the next few decades!

THE METHODS USED TO INVESTIGATE FACE PROCESSING

The scientific study of face processing has benefited greatly from the fact that researchers from a wide variety of backgrounds have been interested in faces. Face processing has been studied by cognitive psychologists, social psychologists, developmental psychologists, evolutionary psychologists, neuropsychologists, neurophysiologists, anthropologists and computer scientists, to name but a few. One advantage of this is that a diversity of techniques has been used to investigate face processing. However, this also means that there are lots of different techniques to understand! In this appendix we give a little more detail on some of the key methodologies discussed throughout this book.

Behavioural methods for investigating face processing

Explicit measures of face recognition: old/new discrimination

One of the oldest and most widely used methods of investigating face recognition has involved testing people's ability to make 'old/new' discriminations. They first see a set of faces and are then presented with these faces again, but mixed in with other faces that they have never seen before. The task is to identify which faces were seen before. On each trial, the participant presses one of two keys: one if he or she remembers having seen the face in the original sequence of faces, and the other key if he or she thinks the face is one that wasn't seen before.

Sometimes participants are given a set of pictures of faces to remember and are then shown exactly the same images in the test phase, mixed in with new faces. A better procedure is to use two different images of each to-be-remembered face in the two phases of the study (e.g. two views of each face that differ in pose and/or expression). This is because, if identical images are shown in the learning and test phases, it is impossible to know to what extent participants' performance reflects memory for the picture, as opposed to the person depicted in the picture (Bruce, 1986). By using two different images of each face, we can be sure that participants are remembering the face as opposed to the picture of it, and hence that we are testing face recognition rather than picture memory.

The old/new discrimination procedure generates two measures: response time and accuracy (the number of trials on which the participant was correct in their judgement).

Often accuracy data will be converted into a measure called d' (d-prime). This is a measure of discriminability. It is intuitively less easy to understand than 'number correct', but it has the big advantage of taking into account the participant's errors as well as their correct responses. Suppose we showed someone ten faces, and then tested them to see whether they could remember these faces when they were mixed together with ten new faces. Someone who responded 'seen' to all ten of the faces that they saw before would get a score of 100% correct. However, so too would someone who simply responded 'seen' to all 20 of the faces! These two individuals are clearly performing very differently: the first is showing perfect discrimination between the new and old faces, whereas the second is effectively showing no discrimination whatsoever. Whereas their 'number correct' scores would be identical, their d' scores would be very different. (Sometimes you may see references to A' (A-prime). This is an alternative version of d', based on much the same logic. For those of you who are familiar with statistics, A' is a 'non-parametric' measure of sensitivity; compared with d', it makes fewer assumptions about the characteristics of the data on which it is based.)

'Applied' research on face recognition commonly uses a variant on the old/new discrimination task that involves showing participants only one face, and then asking them to decide whether or not this face is present in a lineup of half a dozen or more faces. Researchers in this area use this method because they want to be able to apply their findings to real-world police identification procedures. For the same reason, applied researchers tend to focus more on accuracy as a measure (typically reporting the number of correct identifications, and misidentifications) rather than response times, although this is not invariably the case.

Implicit measures of face recognition

The techniques just described require participants to make a conscious decision about whether or not they remember having seen a face before. This involves the use of explicit memory. However, there are other methods that can show that someone has retained some information about a face, without them necessarily being aware of having done so. Such methods test implicit memory for faces: they do not require the person to try consciously to access information.

'Priming' tasks tap into implicit memory. 'Repetition priming' refers to the fact that, having seen a face once, people are faster at responding to it when they see it again (Fig. A1, (a)). The nervous system seems to be in a state of readiness to respond to that face. Repetition priming effects can be very long-lived, and persist even if other faces are seen in the interval between the two exposures to the target face. 'Semantic priming' effects can also be found; after exposure to a face, people are quicker to respond to other faces that are related to it by virtue of properties such as occupation (Fig. A1, (b)). So, for example, seeing Brad Pitt would prime recognition of his partner, Angelina Jolie.[1] Semantic priming effects are generally quite weak and short-lived; for example, they are not seen if an unrelated face is shown in between the two semantically related ones. Implicit recognition can also be demonstrated in various physiological measures, such as the electrical conductance of the skin (the galvanic skin response [GSR], which forms the basis of police lie detectors) or pupil size.

---

[1] For those people who have bought a faded, yellow-paged copy of this book in a charity shop in 2015, Brad Pitt and Angelina Jolie were both famous American film stars at the time we wrote this.

(a) Repetition priming:

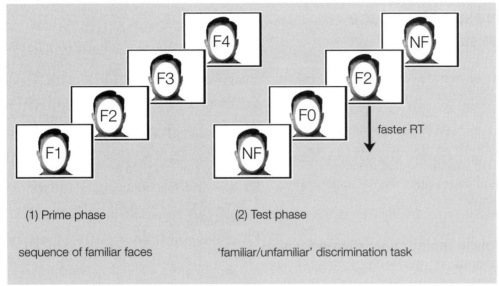

(1) Prime phase

sequence of familiar faces

(2) Test phase

'familiar/unfamiliar' discrimination task

(b) Semantic priming:

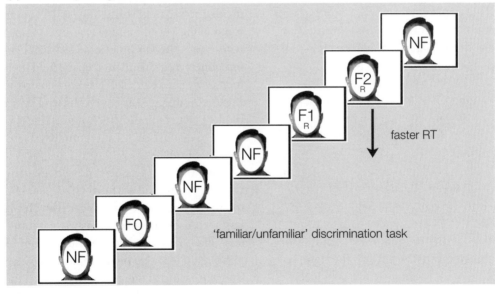

'familiar/unfamiliar' discrimination task

FIGURE A1 (a) Repetition priming procedure: as a result of having been seen previously in the prime phase, responses to familiar face F2 are quicker than to other familiar faces (such as F0) that were not seen in the prime phase. (b) Semantic priming: the response time to familiar face F2 is faster because it was preceded immediately by another, closely related, familiar face.

Neuropsychological methods for investigating face processing

In order to examine the neuropsychological processing of information (not just faces!) within the normal population, a range of methods have been developed that allow us to discover what is going on in the brain. These methods fall into three different categories: behavioural, electrophysiological and metabolic neuroimaging.

Behavioural techniques: divided visual field studies

One of the earliest neuropsychological techniques to be used on individuals without brain damage was the 'divided visual field' paradigm. This developed out of research on 'split brain' patients (see Chapter 7), which showed that information presented in one visual field feeds through to the opposite hemisphere, and at least initially, is processed there (see Fig. 7.8). This paradigm requires very strict methodological controls (see Bourne, 2006), but when used properly it can be very informative about patterns of lateralization.

In a divided visual field experiment, stimuli are presented very briefly in either the extreme left or the extreme right visual field, while the participant is looking at a central fixation point. Within a series of trials, each stimulus is presented randomly to the left and the right, so that the participant cannot predict on which side it will appear. If the stimulus is presented for less than about 200 milliseconds, there isn't time for the participant to move their eyes to it, and so the stimulus is effectively presented only to the opposite hemisphere. When presented to the left visual field, the stimulus is initially received and processed by the right hemisphere. When presented to the right visual field, the stimulus is initially received and processed by the left hemisphere. The experimenter then compares performance, normally both speed and accuracy of responding, across the two visual field presentations. If responses are faster and more accurate in one visual field condition than the other, this suggests a hemispheric bias or specialization for processing that type of information. For example, if faces presented to the left visual field were processed faster and more accurately than faces presented to the right visual field, this would suggest that the right hemisphere is better at processing faces than the left hemisphere.

This method doesn't actually enable us to 'see' what is going on in the brain, we just get to estimate which hemisphere is more proficient. However, it provided a number of valuable insights into the lateralization of face processing before neuroimaging techniques were developed, and divided visual field studies are still frequently used today. (One big advantage over neuroimaging techniques such as functional magnetic resonance imaging is that the divided visual field technique is incredibly cheap to use!) It is particularly nice that this methodology has been validated by the more modern neuroimaging techniques that we are about to discuss (e.g. Hunter and Brysbaert, 2008; Yovel et al, 2008).

One test that has been developed using the same rationale as the divided visual field technique is the chimeric faces test. This test has been used most frequently to examine lateralization for processing facial emotion, although it has also been employed to investigate the processing of facial identity, gender and age. In this test, vertically split chimeric faces are made where the left and right half-faces differ. If we were interested in lateralization for processing the facial emotion of happiness, one half of the face would be happy and the other half would be neutral. This face would then be presented with its mirror image either above or below it (Fig. A2). The participant then needs to decide,

FIGURE A2 Chimeric face stimuli. This example uses positive facial emotion. In the top face, the left half-face is expressing happiness whereas in the bottom face the right half-face is expressing happiness. Which face do you personally think looks happier? (From Bourne, 2008)

Adaptation effects

A relatively new addition to the gamut of behavioural neuropsychological techniques comes from research on face adaptation effects. Essentially, viewing a face for a prolonged period (say, 30 seconds or 1 minute) affects the appearance of that face, and sometimes other faces too, by desensitizing participants to certain aspects of the face that is being used as the adapting stimulus. For example, Webster and MacLin (1999) showed that staring at a distorted face causes a normally proportioned face to appear distorted in the opposite direction; thus, for example, staring at a vertically stretched face makes a normal face appear squashed (see Fig. 9.11). Leopold et al (2001) showed that adaptation to one facial identity resulted in participants becoming temporarily less sensitive to that particular identity but not others. Because the findings of adaptation studies are so intrinsically related to the methods that they employ, we will not discuss them any further here. See Chapter 1 (section 1.3.2) for an explanation of Leopold et al's original study; Chapter 2 (section 2.10) for a review of adaptation effects in connection with the controversy over whether or not face recognition shows viewpoint independence; and Chapter 9 (section 9.5) for a detailed discussion of adaptation effects in general. Suffice it to say that adaptation techniques provide a very powerful addition to our set of techniques for studying face recognition.

in this example, which face looks happier. If the participant chooses the face with happiness expressed in their left visual field, this indicates right-hemisphere dominance for processing happiness (remember that information from the left visual field goes first to the right hemisphere, and vice versa). If the participant chooses the face with happiness expressed in their right visual field, this indicates left-hemisphere dominance for processing happiness.

Electrophysiological techniques: event-related potentials

Event-related potentials (ERPs) were initially developed from another methodology: electroencephalography (EEG). If a particular part of the brain is busy processing information, it will generate lots of electrical activity, because neurones communicate with one another by transmitting electrochemical signals. This activity

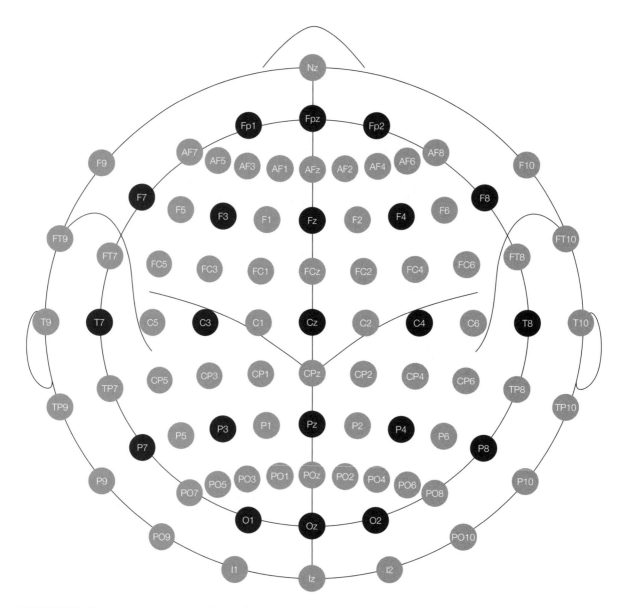

FIGURE A3 Electrode placement according to the International 10–20 system (black circles) and the International 10–10 system (gray circles), which includes more electrodes. (From Oostenveld and Praamstra, 2001).

can be recorded from electrodes placed on the scalp. To record the EEG the participant wears a cap and the electrodes are attached to it in a standardized configuration. The exact number of channels recorded from (or number of electrodes attached to) the cap varies between experiments, but most use the International 10–20 system which specifies the placement of the electrodes (Fig. A3). Each channel is coded according to its placement over the brain: there are frontal (F), temporal (T), parietal (P), occipital (O) and central (C) channels.

As you can see in Fig. A4, the EEG changes when something happens. In psychological research, experimenters record the EEG whilst showing stimuli to participants. The EEG activity changes after an event has occurred, such as a face being presented. This small segment of EEG around the event is the 'event-related potential' (also sometimes known as the 'evoked response potential'), or ERP. The problem is that random neural activity makes it hard to see the brain's response to the stimulus on a single trial. Usually a large number of trials are conducted and the ERPs across all these trials are averaged. The principle is simple: over trials, random activity at any given instant is as likely to produce a positive signal as it is to produce a negative one. However, the brain's response to a stimulus should be much the same on every trial. Therefore, if ERPs from a number of trials are averaged together, the random activity should all cancel out, making it easier to see the brain's response to the stimulus that was

presented. ERPs are described on the basis of two properties: whether the change in potential is positive (P) or negative (N), and the latency (the time between the onset of the stimulus and the peak of the ERP, measured in milliseconds). A number of ERP components can be found in response to a stimulus (Fig. A4) and the ERPs can also vary a great deal across the different recording sites.

Although ERPs are widely used in face-processing research and have greatly advanced our understanding of the neuropsychological processes underlying face processing, it is important to be aware of the advantages and disadvantages of this technique. Perhaps its biggest advantage is that it measures brain activity in a non-invasive manner that is not uncomfortable or potentially distressing to participants—ERPs can even be used with infants! ERPs also have excellent temporal resolution: they can record very rapid changes in electrical activity in the brain,

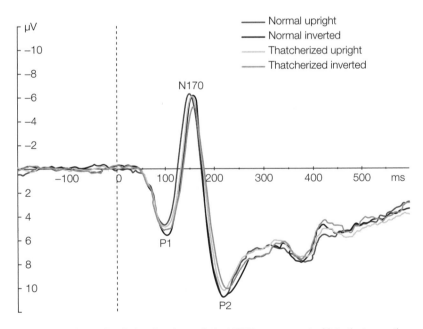

FIGURE A4 ERPs to a range of face stimuli showing three distinct ERP components. Note that sometimes, as in this figure, the *y*-axis is plotted with the negative potentials going upwards and the positive potentials going downwards. Keep an eye out for this when looking at ERPs. (From Boutsen et al, 2006)

lasting in the order of milliseconds. However, there are disadvantages. It can be relatively difficult to isolate the ERP in response to the stimulus that is presented from other changes in the EEG. Artefacts such as eye blinks, eye movements, even feeling a bit sleepy, can change the EEG. However, there are established algorithms to remove these artefacts. The ERP technique is also limited in how much it can tell you about where in the brain particular processes take place. The International 10–20 system was established to standardize the placement of electrodes, but all skulls and brains vary slightly. This can cause some variability in recording site between individuals. Additionally, because the ERP is taken from changes in electrical activity across the scalp, it is limited to measuring changes in brain activity from regions of the brain close to the scalp and cannot be used to examine activity from areas deeper into the brain.

Magnetoencephalography (MEG) is a more recently developed technique that works by measuring the magnetic field generated by electrical activity in the brain. The rationale behind the methodology is similar to that of ERPs. When a part of the brain is used there is electrical activity, which then generates magnetic fields. By seeing how the magnetic fields change between control and experimental conditions, it is possible to measure where in the brain processing occurs. MEG retains the temporal resolution advantage of ERPs and is able to measure activity with an accuracy of about 1 ms. Unlike ERPs, MEG also has good spatial resolution and has an accuracy of about 2 mm. It is also able to scan activity in any part of the brain and is not limited to recording activity near to the scalp.

Metabolic neuroimaging techniques

One of the most recently developed, and now widely used, methods of neuroimaging is functional magnetic resonance imaging (fMRI). When a brain region processes information, the neurones in that area are more active and hence require more oxygen. To provide this oxygen, more blood flows to that area—there is increased cerebral blood flow (CBF). This variability in blood flow and oxygen consumption is known as the 'blood oxygenation level dependent (BOLD)' effect, and it is measured using fMRI. Because oxygenated and deoxygenated blood contain different amounts of haemoglobin, they have different magnetic properties, and an fMRI scanner detects these differences. By measuring the BOLD effect under different conditions (e.g. when processing faces as opposed to some other kind of stimulus), it is possible to see which parts of the brain have become active. These patterns of activation are then superimposed onto an image of the physical structure of the brain to inform us where the patterns of activation are occurring in the brain (Fig. A5).

Another neuroimaging method that has been widely used is positron emission tomography (PET). For a PET scan, participants are injected with a short-lived radioactive isotope that tags itself to a particular chemical in the blood—usually glucose in the case of neuroscience research. When you process information, blood flows to that area of the brain and glucose is consumed by the metabolically active neurones in that region. The PET scan detects the positrons given off by the isotope that is tagged to the glucose. In a similar way to fMRI, the consumption of energy in the brain is compared between resting or control conditions and the processing of the stimuli that you are interested in.

Methods such as fMRI and PET offer great advantages over behavioural and electrophysiological techniques in terms of being able to show us where in the brain processing occurs. However, both techniques also have some disadvantages. Although fMRI has no known side-effects or risks, PET is rarely used with healthy participants because it involves injecting radioactive substances into the bloodstream (albeit in tiny amounts that are probably quite safe). From a research point of view, although both PET and fMRI have much better spatial resolution than electrophysiological methods, they are still

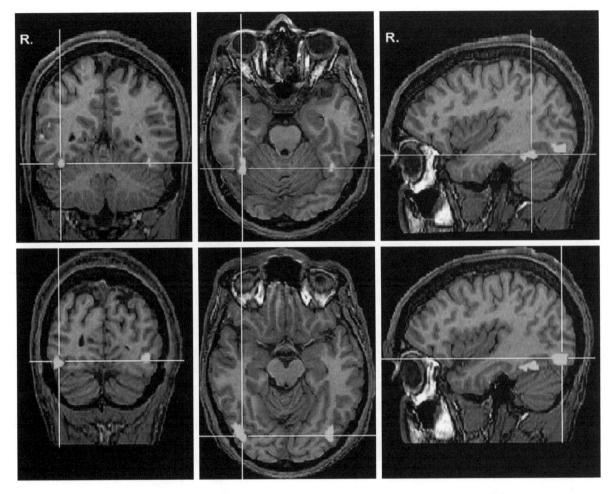

FIGURE A5 Areas of the brain found to respond to faces, over and above the activation found in response to non-face stimuli, as revealed through fMRI scans. Note that the right hemisphere is shown on the left of the image (i.e. the image is mirror-reversed). This is a convention with radiological images, so watch out for this when looking at PET, MRI and fMRI scans. (From Schiltz and Rossion, 2006)

fairly coarse in absolute terms. PET scanners typically have a resolution of 5–7 mm. The spatial resolution of fMRI depends on the strength of the magnets in the scanner, but even the best scanners cannot distinguish between areas of activity that are smaller than about 1–2 mm. This might sound pretty good, but it's not that great when one takes into account how small neurones are; much of the cortex seems to be organized into columns of neurones with common functional properties, and each column is only about half a millimetre wide.

At its very best, fMRI can never do better than measure the activity of millions of neurones!

Another problem is that the areas of activation are overlaid on to images of the underlying brain structure. In the past, they have been overlaid on to an 'average' brain. Given that all brains vary slightly in their structure, this introduces additional imprecision into the process of identifying whereabouts activity has occurred. However, one advantage of fMRI is that it is possible to use the same scanner to produce both 'functional' and 'structural' images of the same individual's brain, within the same experimental session.

Probably the biggest limitation of the metabolic neuroimaging methods is the poor temporal resolution. The change in blood supply to parts of the brain in response to stimuli is relatively slow—in some situations slower than our ability to process the stimuli. This can make it difficult to distinguish between different stages of processing. Take, for example, the recognition of a face as 'familiar'. At best, fMRI has a temporal resolution of about a second. However, within that amount of time, we can identify the stimulus as a face, structurally encode that information, identify who the person is and retrieve semantic information about them, including their name. The temporal resolution of PET is even worse, in the order of minutes. Therefore, it is difficult to distinguish between different stages of processing by using fMRI and PET, and we rely mainly on clever experimental design and different experimental conditions to enable us to make such distinctions.

Electrophysiological methods and imaging techniques thus have complementary advantages and disadvantages. Functional neuroimaging is spatially fine-grained but sluggish, whereas ERP and MEG techniques are spatially coarse but capable of tracking fast-changing patterns of neural activity. Only by examining the neuropsychology of face processing with a range of techniques will we be able to obtain a clear and accurate idea of the brain structures that underlie face processing.

A basic guide to neuroanatomy

Although neuropsychology has some daunting terminology, it is not quite as difficult as it may seem to work out what it actually means. This section is intended to give you a brief guide to the brain to help you in the various sections of this book that discuss neuropsychological evidence.

Probably the most obvious features of the human brain are the two hemispheres. These sit on top of the *cerebellum* and *brain stem* (Fig. A6).

The brainstem and cerebellum are, evolutionarily speaking, very old parts of the brain which deal with basic survival process such as temperature regulation, hunger and thirst, and coordination of complex motor movements. In contrast, the *hemispheres* (the *cerebral cortex* or neocortex) evolved relatively recently and this is where the more recently evolved higher cognitive functions, such as language and face processing, occur.

There are two hemispheres, the left and the right hemisphere. They are connected by the *corpus callosum* which allows information to be passed between the hemispheres. Each hemisphere is made up of four lobes: the *frontal* lobe, the *parietal* lobe, the *temporal* lobe and the *occipital* lobe (see Fig. A6). This is usually the most basic level at which the areas of brain are described. For example, a patient might have a lesion in the right temporal lobe. Sometimes these terms are combined when the area of interest straddles two lobe of the brain. Thus, an occipitotemporal lesion would be damage to the part of the brain where the occipital and temporal lobes meet. It is even possible to make these combinations to describe the junctions between three lobes, such as the occipital–temporal–parietal junction. Whenever you see two or three lobes mentioned in the description of a brain area, this simply means you should look at where those areas meet.

When you look at the human brain, one obvious feature is that it is covered in lumps and bumps. Essentially, as humans evolved their brains became too big for the skull, so the surface crumpled up to allow more surface area within a confined space. Consequently, the human brain comprises a number of *gyri* (the lumps; singular, *gyrus*) and *sulci* (the crevices in between the gyri; singular, *sulcus*). For example, if you look at the temporal lobe, you can see that it is formed from three distinct gyri: the superior temporal gyrus, the middle temporal gyrus and the inferior temporal gyrus. The temporal lobe also has two sulci: the superior temporal sulcus and the middle temporal sulcus. Which leads us onto our next point…

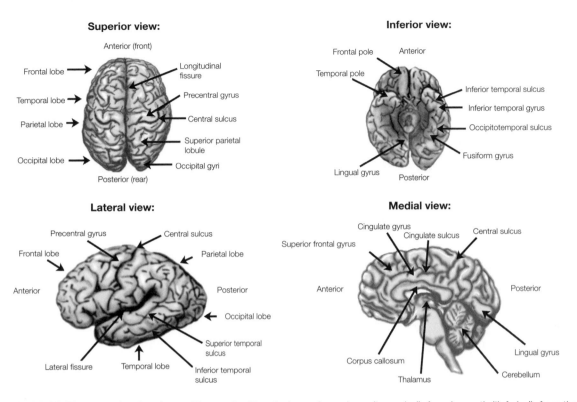

FIGURE A6 Diagrams showing views of the cerebral hemispheres from above ('superior'), from beneath ('inferior'), from the left side ('lateral') and in the middle, between the hemispheres ('medial'). The four lobes plus various gyri (bumps) and sulci (clefts) are shown—this is not an exhaustive list!

Up to this point, we would know how to describe a particular location in the brain by describing whether it is in the left or right hemisphere, which lobe it is in, and which gyrus or sulcus it is located at. However, we can take it down to a finer level of detail than that. Again, there is particular terminology to describe this level of detail. It is easiest just to present these in a glossary format:

- Anterior: towards the front
- Posterior: towards the back
- Superior: towards the top
- Inferior: towards the bottom
- Medial: towards the middle
- Lateral: towards the outside.

Consequently, the term 'inferior temporal lobe' does not mean that it's a somewhat rubbish temporal lobe: it is referring to the lower section of the temporal lobe. Similarly, 'medial occipital lobe' means 'towards the middle of the occipital lobe'. Whenever you come across a scarily long description of a part of the brain, just try to break it down using the following questions:

- Left hemisphere, right hemisphere or bilateral (both hemispheres)?
- Which lobe? Or is the area at the junction between two or three lobes?
- Are particular gyri or sulci identified?
- Is the location further specified in terms of anterior/posterior, superior/inferior or medial/lateral?

references

Addington, J., Saeedi, H. & Addington, D. (2006). Facial affect recognition: a mediator between cognitive and social functioning in psychosis? *Schizophrenia Research*, 85(1–3), 142–150.

Adolphs, R., Jansari, A. & Tranel, D. (2001). Hemispheric perception of emotional valence from facial expressions. *Neuropsychology*, 15(4), 516–524.

Adolphs, R., Tranel, D., Damasio, H., et al. (1994). Impaired recognition of emotion in facial expressions following bilateral damage to the human amygdala. *Nature*, 372(6507), 669–672.

Afraz, S. R. & Cavanagh, P. (2008). Retinotopy of the face aftereffect. *Vision Research*, 48(1), 42–54.

Akechi, H., Senju, A., Kikuchi, Y., et al. (2009). Does gaze direction modulate facial expression processing in children with autism spectrum disorder? *Child Development*, 80(4), 1134–1146.

Alley, T. R. & Cunningham, M. R. (1991). Averaged faces are attractive, but very attractive faces are not average. *Psychological Science*, 2, 123–125.

Allison, T., Puce, A., Spencer, D. D., et al. (1999). Electrophysiological studies of human face perception. I: Potentials generated in occipitotemporal cortex by face and non-face stimuli. *Cerebral Cortex*, 9(5), 415–430.

Allwood, C. M., Knutsson, J. & Granhag, P. A. (2006). Eyewitnesses under influence: how feedback affects the realism in confidence judgements. *Psychology, Crime and Law*, 12(1), 25–38.

Alvergne, A., Faurie, C. & Raymond, M. (2007). Differential facial resemblance of young children to their parents: who do children look like more? *Evolution and Human Behavior*, 28(2), 135–144.

Alvergne, A., Huchard, E., Caillaud, D., et al. (2009). Human ability to visually recognize kin within primates. *International Journal of Primatology*, 30, 199–210.

Alves, N. T., Aznar-Casanova, J. A. & Fukusima, S. S. (2009). Patterns of brain asymmetry in the perception of positive and negative facial expressions. *Laterality*, 14(3), 256–272.

Anaki, D., Zion-Golumbic, E. & Bentin, S. (2007). Electrophysiological neural mechanisms for detection, configural analysis and recognition of faces. *Neuroimage*, 37(4), 1407–1416.

Anastasi, J. S. & Rhodes, M. G. (2005). An own-age bias in face recognition for children and older adults. *Psychonomic Bulletin and Review*, 12(6), 1043–1047.

Anastasi, J. S. & Rhodes, M. G. (2006). Evidence for an own-age bias in face recognition. *North American Journal of Psychology*, 8, 237–253.

Anderson, N. D. & Wilson, H. R. (2005). The nature of synthetic face adaptation. *Vision Research*, 45(14), 1815–1828.

Andrews, T. J. & Ewbank, M. P. (2004). Distinct representations for facial identity and changeable aspects of faces in human visual cortex, *NeuroImage*, 23, 905–913.

Andrews, T. J. & Schluppeck, D. (2004). Neural responses to Mooney images reveal a modular representation of faces in human visual cortex. *Neuroimage*, 21(1), 91–98.

Andrews, T. J., Schluppeck, D., Homfray, D., et al. (2002). Activity in the fusiform gyrus predicts conscious perception of Rubin's vase–face illusion. *Neuroimage*, 17, 890–901.

Anes, M. D. & Kruer, J. L. (2004). Investigating hemispheric specialization in a novel face–word stroop task. *Brain and Language*, 89(1), 136–141.

Anilkumar, A. P. P., Kumari, V., Mehrotra, R., et al. (2008). An fMRI study of face encoding and recognition in first-episode schizophrenia. *Acta Neuropsychiatrica*, 20(3), 129–138.

Annaz, D., Karmiloff-Smith, A., Johnson, M. H., et al. (2009). A cross-syndrome study of the development of holistic face recognition in children with autism, Down syndrome, and Williams syndrome. *Journal of Experimental Child Psychology*, 102(4), 456–486.

Apicella, C. L., Little, A. C. & Marlowe, F. W. (2007). Facial averageness and attractiveness in an isolated population of hunter-gatherers. *Perception*, 36, 1813–1820.

Ashley, V., Vuilleumier, P. & Swick, D. (2004). Time course and specificity of event-related potentials to emotional expressions. *Neuroreport*, 15(1), 211–216.

Ashwin, C., Baron-Cohen, S., Wheelwright, S., et al. (2007). Differential activation of the amygdala and the 'social brain' during fearful face-processing in Asperger syndrome. *Neuropsychologia*, 45(1), 2–14.

Ashwin, C., Wheelwright, S. & Baron-Cohen, S. (2005). Laterality biases to chimeric faces in Asperger syndrome: what is 'Right' about face-processing? *Journal of Autism and Developmental Disorders*, 35(2), 183–196.

Aslin, R. N. (1981). Development of smooth pursuit in human infants. In: D. F. Fisher, R. A. Monty & J. W. Senders (eds), *Eye movements: Cognition and Visual Perception*, pp 31–41. Hillsdale, NJ: Lawrence Erlbaum Associates.

Aslin, R. N. & Salapatek, P. (1975). Saccadic localization of visual targets by the very young human infant. *Perception & Psychophysics*, 17, 293–302.

Assal, G., Favre, C. & Anderes, J. P. (1984). Non-Recognition of familiar animals by a farmer—zooagnosia or prosopagnosia for animals. *Revue Neurologique*, 140(10), 580–584.

Austin, E. J. (2005). Emotional intelligence and emotional information processing. *Personality and Individual Differences*, 39(2), 403–414.

Avidan, G., Hasson, U., Malach, R., et al. (2005). Detailed exploration of face-related processing in congenital prosopagnosia: 2. Functional neuroimaging findings. *Journal of Cognitive Neuroscience*, 17(7), 1150–1167.

Back, E., Ropar, D. & Mitchell, P. (2007). Do the eyes have it? Inferring mental states from animated faces in autism. *Child Development*, 78(2), 397–411.

Baenninger, M. (1994). The development of face recognition: featural or configural processing? *Journal of Experimental Child Psychology*, 57(3), 377–396.

Bahrick, L. E. & Newell, L. C. (2008). Infant discrimination of faces in naturalistic events: actions are more salient than faces. *Developmental Psychology*, 44(4), 983–996.

Bahrick, L. E., Gogate, L. J. & Ruiz, I. (2002). Attention and memory for faces and actions in infancy: the salience of actions over faces in dynamic events. *Child Development*, 73, 1629–1643.

Balas, B., Cox, D. A. & Conwell, E. (2006). The effect of personal familiarity on the speed of face recognition. In: R. Sun & N. Miyake (eds), *Proceedings of the 28th Annual Meeting of the Cognitive Science Society*. Vancouver, BC: Cognitive Science Society.

Banks, M. S. & Salapatek, P. (1981). Infant pattern vision: a new approach based on the Contrast Sensitivity Function. *Journal of Experimental Child Psychology*, 31, 1–45.

Bar-Haim, Y., Saidel, T. & Yovel, G. (2009). The role of skin colour in face recognition. *Perception*, 38, 145–148.

Bar-Haim, Y., Ziv, T., Lamy, D., et al. (2006). Nature and nurture in own-race face processing. *Psychological Science*, 17(2), 159–163.

Baron-Cohen, S. (1994). How to build a baby that can read minds: cognitive mechanisms in mindreading. *Cahiers de Psychologie Cognitive/ Current Psychology of Cognition*, 13, 513–552.

Baron-Cohen, S. (1995). *Mindblindness: An Essay on Autism and Theory of Mind*. Cambridge, MA: MIT Press/Bradford Books.

Barrett, S. E. & O'Toole, A. J. (2009). Face adaptation to gender: does adaptation transfer across age categories? *Visual Cognition*, 17(5), 700–715.

Bartlett, J. C. & Leslie, J. E. (1986). Aging and memory for faces versus single views of faces. *Memory and Cognition*, 14, 371–381.

Bartlett, J. C. & Searcy, J. (1993). Inversion and configuration of faces. *Cognitive Psychology*, 25, 281–316.

Bartlett, J. C., Searcy, J. H. & Abdi, H. (2003). What are the routes to face recognition? In: M. Peterson & G. Rhodes (eds), *Perception of F, Objects, and Scenes: Analytic and Holistic Processes*, pp 21–52. Oxford: Oxford University Press.

Barton, J. J. S. (2003). Disorders of face perception and recognition. *Neurologic Clinics*, 21(2), 521–548.

Barton, J. J. S. (2008). Prosopagnosia associated with a left occipitotemporal lesion. *Neuropsychologia*, 46(8), 2214–2224.

Barton, J. J. S., Cherkasova, M. V. & Hefter, R. (2004). The covert priming effect of faces in prosopagnosia. *Neurology*, 63(11), 2062–2068.

Barton, J., Keenan, J. & Bass, T. (2001). Discrimination of spatial relations and features in faces: effects of inversion and viewing duration. *British Journal of Psychology*, 92, 527–549.

Barton, J. J. S., Press, D. Z., Keenan, J. P., et al. (2002). Lesions of the fusiform face area impair perception of facial configuration in prosopagnosia. *Neurology*, 58(1), 71–78.

Barton, J. J. S., Radcliffe, N., Cherkasova, M. V. et al. (2006). Information processing during face recognition: the effects of familiarity, inversion, and morphing on scanning fixations. *Perception*, 35, 1089–1105.

Barton, J. J. S., Zhao, J. H. & Keenan, J. P. (2003). Perception of global facial geometry in the inversion effect and prosopagnosia. *Neuropsychologia*, 41(12), 1703–1711.

Bartrip, J., Morton, J. & de Schonen, S. (2001). Responses to mother's face in 3-week to 5-month-old infants. *British Journal of Developmental Psychology*, 19, 219–232.

Basu, A. & Mandal, M. K. (2004). Visual-field superiority as a function of stimulus type and content: further evidence. *International Journal of Neuroscience*, 114(7), 833–839.

Batki, A., Baron-Cohen, S., Wheelwright, S., et al. (2000). Is there an innate gaze module? Evidence from human neonates. *Infant Behavior & Development*, 23, 223–229.

Batty, M. & Taylor, M. J. (2003). Early processing of the six basic facial emotional expressions. *Cognitive Brain Research*, 17(3), 613–620.

Baudouin, J. Y. & Humphreys, G. W. (2006). Compensatory strategies in processing facial emotions: evidence from prosopagnosia. *Neuropsychologia*, 44(8), 1361–1369.

Baudouin, J. Y. & Tiberghien, G. (2002). Gender is a dimension of face recognition. *Journal of Experimental Psychology: Learning, Memory, and Cognition*, 28(2), 362–365.

Baudouin, J. Y., Vernet, M. & Franck, N. (2008). Second-order facial information processing in schizophrenia. *Neuropsychology*, 22(3), 313–320.

Bauer, R. M. (1984). Autonomic recognition of names and faces in prosopagnosia—a neuropsychological application of the Guilty Knowledge Test. *Neuropsychologia*, 22(4), 457–469.

Bava, S., Ballantyne, A. O., May, S. J., et al. (2005). Perceptual asymmetry for chimeric stimuli in children with early unilateral brain damage. *Brain and Cognition*, 59(1), 1–10.

Bayer, U. & Erdmann, G. (2008). The influence of sex hormones on functional cerebral asymmetries in postmenopausal women. *Brain and Cognition*, 67(2), 140–149.

Begeer, S., Rieffe, C., Terwogt, M. M., et al. (2006). Attention to facial emotion expressions in children with autism. *Autism*, 10(1), 37–51.

Begleiter, H., Porjesz, B. & Wang, W. (1995). Event-related potentials differentiate priming and recognition to familiar and unfamiliar faces. *Electroencephalography and Clinical Neurophysiology*, 94, 41–49.

Behrman, B. W. & Davey, S. L. (2001). Eyewitness identification in actual criminal cases: an archival analysis. *Law and Human Behavior*, 25(5), 475–491.

Behrman, B. W. & Richards, R. E. (2005). Suspect/foil identification in actual crimes and in the laboratory: a reality monitoring analysis. *Law and Human Behavior*, 29(3), 279–301.

Behrmann, M., Avidan, G., Gao, F., et al. (2007). Structural imaging reveals anatomical alterations in inferotemporal cortex in congenital prosopagnosia. *Cerebral Cortex*, 17(10), 2354–2363.

Behrmann, M., Marotta, J., Gauthier, I., et al. (2005). Behavioral change and its neural correlates in visual agnosia after expertise training. *Journal of Cognitive Neuroscience*, 17(4), 554–568.

Bellugi, U., Lichtenberger, L., Jones, W., et al. (2000). The neurocognitive profile of Williams syndrome: a complex pattern of strengths and weaknesses. *Journal of Cognitive Neuroscience*, 12, 7–29.

Benke, T. (1988). Visual agnosia and amnesia from a left unilateral lesion. *European Neurology*, 28(4), 236–239.

Benson, P. J. & Perrett, D. I. (1991). Perception and recognition of photographic quality facial caricatures: implication for the recognition of natural images. *European Journal of Cognitive Psychology*, 3, 105–135.

Benson, P. & Perrett, D. I. (1994). Visual processing of facial distinctiveness. *Perception*, 23, 75–93.

Bentin, S. & Deouell, L. Y. (2000). Structural encoding and identification in face processing: ERP evidence for separate mechanisms. *Cognitive Neuropsychology*, 17(1–3), 35–54.

Bentin, S., Allison, T., Puce, A., et al. (1996). Electrophysiological studies of face perception in humans. *Journal of Cognitive Neuroscience*, 8(6), 551–565.

Benton, C. P., Jennings, S. J. & Chatting, D. J. (2006). Viewpoint dependence in adaptation to facial identity. *Vision Research*, 46, 3313–3325.

Bernstein, M. J., Young, S. G. & Hugenberg, K. (2007). The cross-category effect. Mere social categorization is sufficient to elicit an own-group bias in face recognition. *Psychological Science*, 706–712.

Bestelmeyer, P. E. G., Jones, B. C., DeBruine, L. M., et al. (2008). Sex-contingent face aftereffects depend on perceptual category rather than structural encoding. *Cognition*, 107(1), 353–365.

Bestelmeyer, P. E. G., Jones, B. C., DeBruine, L. M., et al. (2009). Face aftereffects suggest interdependent processing of expression and sex and of expression and race. *Visual Cognition*, 18(2), 255–274.

Bi, T., Su, J., Chen, J., et al. (2009). The role of gaze direction in face viewpoint aftereffect. *Vision Research*, 49(18), 2322–2327.

Biederman, I. & Kalocsai, P. (1997). Neurocomputational bases of object and face recognition. *Philosophical Transactions of the Royal Society of London. Biological Sciences*, 352, 1203–1219.

Biederman, I., Subramaniam, S., Bar, M., et al. (1999). Subordinate-level object classification re-examined. *Psychological Research*, 62, 131–153.

Bindemann, M., Scheepers, C. & Burton, A. M. (2009). Viewpoint and center of gravity affect eye movements to human faces. *Journal of Vision*, 9(2), 1–16.

Birmingham, E., Bischof, W. F., & Kingstone, A. (2009). Get real! Resolving the debate about equivalent social stimuli. *Visual Cognition*, 17(6/7), 904–924.

Blaney, R. N. & Winograd, E. (1978). Developmental differences in children's memory for faces. *Developmental Psychology*, 14, 441–442.

Blass, E. M. & Camp, C. A. (2004). The ontogeny of face identity I. Eight- to 21-week-old infants use internal and external face features in identity. *Cognition*, 92, 305–327.

Blau, V. C., Maurer, U., Tottenham, N., et al. (2007). The face-specific N170 component is modulated by emotional facial expression. *Behavioral and Brain Functions*, 3, 7.

Bliem, H. R. (1998). Experimental and clinical exploration of a possible neural subsystem underlying configurational face processing. *Brain and Cognition*, 37(1), 16–18.

Blunt, M. R. & McAllister, H. A. (2008). Mug shot exposure effects: does size matter? *Law and Human Behaviour*, 33, 175–182.

Bobes, M. A., Lopera, F., Comas, L. D., et al. (2004). Brain potentials reflect residual face processing in a case of prosopagnosia. *Cognitive Neuropsychology*, 21(7), 691–718.

Bobes, M. A., Lopera, F., Garcia, M., et al. (2003). Covert matching of unfamiliar faces in a case of prosopagnosia: an ERP study. *Cortex*, 39(1), 41–56.

Bobes, M. A., Martin, M., Olivares, E., et al. (2000). Different scalp topography of brain potentials related to expression and identity matching of faces. *Cognitive Brain Research*, 9(3), 249–260.

Boehm, S. G. & Sommer, W. (2005). Neural correlates of intentional and incidental recognition of famous faces. *Cognitive Brain Research*, 23(2–3), 153–163.

Boeri, R. & Salmaggi, A. (1994). Prosopagnosia—commentary. *Current Opinion in Neurology*, 7(1), 61–64.

Bolte, S. & Poustka, F. (2003). The recognition of facial affect in autistic and schizophrenic subjects and their first-degree relatives. *Psychological Medicine*, 33(5), 907–915.

Bonner, L. & Burton, A. M. (2004). 7–11-year-old children show an advantage for matching and recognizing the internal features of familiar faces: evidence against a developmental shift. *Quarterly Journal of Experimental Psychology*, 57A(6), 1019–1029.

Bookheimer, S. Y., Wang, A. T., Scott, A., et al. (2008). Frontal contributions to face processing differences in autism: evidence from fMRI of inverted face processing. *Journal of the International Neuropsychological Society*, 14(6), 922–932.

Booth, M. C. A. & Rolls, E. T. (1998). View-invariant representations of familiar objects by neurons in the inferior temporal visual cortex. *Cerebral Cortex*, 8, 510–523.

Bornstein, M. H. & Arterberry, M. E. (2003). Recognition, discrimination and categorization of smiling by 5-month-old infants. *Developmental Science*, 6(5), 585–599.

Bornstein, R. F. (1989). Exposure and affect: overview and meta-analysis of research, 1968–1987. *Psychological Bulletin*, 106, 265–289.

Bothwell, R. K., Deffenbacher, K. A. & Brigham, J. C. (1987). Correlation of eyewitness accuracy and confidence: optimality hypothesis revisited. *Journal of Applied Psychology*, 72, 691–695.

Bourne, V. J. (2005). Lateralised processing of positive facial emotion: sex differences in strength of hemispheric dominance. *Neuropsychologia*, 43(6), 953–956.

Bourne, V. J. (2006). The divided visual field paradigm: methodological considerations. *Laterality*, 11(4), 373–393.

Bourne, V. J. (2008). Examining the relationship between degree of handedness and degree of cerebral lateralization for processing facial emotion. *Neuropsychology*, 22(3), 350–356.

Bourne, V. J. (2009). How are emotions lateralised in the brain? Contrasting existing hypotheses using the chimeric faces test. *Cognition & Emotion*, in press.

Bourne, V. J. & Gray, D. L. (2009). Hormone exposure and functional lateralisation: examining the contributions of prenatal and later life hormonal exposure. *Psychoneuroendocrinology*, 34(8), 1214–1221.

Bourne, V. J. & Hole, G. J. (2006). Lateralized repetition priming for familiar faces: evidence for asymmetric interhemispheric cooperation. *Quarterly Journal of Experimental Psychology*, 59(6), 1117–1133.

Bourne, V. J., Vladeanu, M. & Hole, G. J. (2009). Lateralised repetition priming for featurally and configurally manipulated familiar faces: evidence for differentially lateralised processing mechanisms. *Laterality*, 14(3), 287–299.

Boutsen, L. & Humphreys, G. W. (2002). Face context interferes with local part processing in a prosopagnosic patient. *Neuropsychologia*, 40(13), 2305–2313.

Boutsen, L. & Humphreys, G. W. (2003). The effect of inversion on encoding of normal faces and the Thatcher illusion. *Quarterly Journal of Experimental Psychology*, 56A, 955–975.

Boutsen, L., Humphreys, G. W., Praamstra, P., et al. (2006). Comparing neural correlates of configural processing in faces and objects: an ERP study of the Thatcher illusion. *Neuroimage*, 32, 352–367.

Box, O., Laing, H. & Kopelman, M. (1999). The evolution of spontaneous confabulation, delusional misidentification and a related delusion in a case of severe head injury. *Neurocase*, 5(3), 251–262.

Boyce, M., Beaudry, J. L. & Lindsay, R. C. L. (2007). Belief of eyewitness identification evidence. In: R. C. L. Lindsay, D. F. Ross, J. D. Read & M. P. Toglia (eds), *Handbook of Eyewitness Psychology, Vol. 2: Memory for People*, pp 501–525. Mahwah, NJ: Erlbaum.

Brace, N. A., Hole, G. J., Kemp, R. I., et al. (2001). Developmental changes in the effect of inversion: using a picture book to investigate face recognition. *Perception*, 30, 85–94.

Brace, N. A., Pike, G. E., Allen, P., et al. (2006a). Identifying composites of famous faces: investigating memory, language and system issues. *Psychology, Crime and Law*, 12(4), 351–366.

Brace, N., Pike, G., Kemp, R., et al. (2006b). Does the presentation of multiple facial composites improve suspect identification? *Applied Cognitive Psychology*, 20, 213–226.

Bradshaw, J. L. & Sherlock, D. (1982). Bugs and faces in the two visual fields: the analytic/holistic processing dichotomy and task sequencing. *Cortex*, 18, 211–226.

Brédart, S. & Devue, C. (2006). The accuracy of memory for faces of personally known individuals. *Perception*, 35, 101–106.

Brédart, S. & French, R. M. (1999). Do babies resemble their fathers more than their mothers? A failure to replicate Christenfeld & Hill (1995). *Evolution and Human Behavior*, 20, 129–135.

Breen, N., Caine, D. & Coltheart, M. (2000). Models of face recognition and delusional misidentification: a critical review. *Cognitive Neuropsychology*, 17(1–3), 55–71.

Breiter, H. C., Etcoff, N. L., Whalen, P. J., et al. (1996). Response and habituation of the human amygdala during visual processing of facial expression. *Neuron*, 17(5), 875–887.

Bressan, P. & Dal Martello, M. F. (2002). Talis pater, talis filius: perceived resemblance and the belief in genetic relatedness. *Psychological Science*, 13, 213–218.

Bressan, P. & Grassi, M. (2004). Parental resemblance in one-year-olds and the Gaussian curve. *Evolution and Human Behavior*, 25, 133–141.

Bressan, P. & Zucchi, G. (2009). Human kin recognition is self- rather than family-referential. *Biology Letters*, 5, 336–338.

Brewer, N. & Wells, G. L. (2006). The confidence–accuracy relationship in eyewitness identification: effects of lineup instructions, foil similarity, and target-absent base rates. *Journal of Experimental Psychology: Applied*, 17(1), 11–30.

Brewer, N., Caon, A., Tod, C., et al. (2006). Eyewitness identification accuracy and response latency. *Law and Human Behavior*, 30(1), 31–50.

Brigham J. C. & Malpass R. S. (1985). The role of experience and contact in the recognition of faces of own- and other-race persons. *Journal of Social Issues*, 41, 139–155.

Brigham, J. C., Bennett, L. B., Meissner, C. A., et al. (2007). The influence of race on eyewitness memory. In: R. C. L. Lindsay, D. F. Ross, J. D. Read & M. P. Toglia (eds), *Handbook of Eyewitness Psychology*, pp 257–281. Mahwah, NJ: Erlbaum.

British Psychological Society Research Board (2008). *Guidelines on Memory and the Law: Recommendations from the Scientific Study of Human Mmemory*. Leicester: British Psychological Society. (Available online at http://www.bps.org.uk/the-society/ organisation-and-governance/research-board/ steering-groups-and-working-parties/ memory-and-the-law-working-party.cfm)

Bronson, G. W. (1990). Changes in infants' visual scanning across the 2- to 14-week age period. *Journal of Experimental Child Psychology*, 49, 101–125.

Brooks, B. E. & Cooper, E. E. (2006). What types of visual recognition tasks are mediated by the neural subsystem that subserves face recognition? *Journal of Experimental Psychology: Learning Memory and Cognition*, 32(4), 684–698.

Brooks, K. R. & Kemp, R. I. (2007). Sensitivity to feature displacement in familiar and unfamiliar faces: beyond the internal/external feature distinction. *Perception*, 36, 1646–1659.

Brown, C. & Lloyd-Jones, T. J. (2003). Verbal overshadowing of multiple face and car recognition: effects of within- versus across-category verbal descriptions. *Applied Cognitive Psychology*, 17, 183–201.

Brown, E. & Perrett, D. I. (1993). What gives a face its gender? *Perception*, 22, 829–840.

Brown, E. L., Deffenbacher, K. A. & Sturgill, W. (1977). Memory for faces and the circumstances of encounter. *Journal of Applied Psychology*, 62, 311–318.

Bruce, V. (1982). Changing faces: visual and non-visual coding processes in face recognition. *British Journal of Psychology*, 73, 105–116.

Bruce, V. (1986). Influences of familiarity on the processing of faces. *Perception*, 15, 387–397.

Bruce, V. (1988). *Recognising Faces*. London: Erlbaum.

Bruce, V. & Valentine, T. (1985). Identity priming in face recognition. *British Journal of Psychology*, 76, 373–383.

Bruce, V. & Young, A. (1986). Understanding face recognition. *British Journal of Psychology*, 77, 305–327.

Bruce, V. & Young, A. W. (1998). *In the Eye of the Beholder: The Science of Face Perception*. Oxford: Oxford University Press.

Bruce, V., Burton, A. M. & Dench, N. (1994). What's distinctive about a distinctive face? *Quarterly Journal of Experimental Psychology*, 47A, 119–141.

Bruce, V., Campbell, R. N., Doherty-Sneddon, G., et al. (2000). Testing face processing skills in children. *British Journal of Developmental Psychology*, 18, 319–333.

Bruce, V., Doyle, T., Dench, N., et al. (1991). Remembering facial configurations. *Cognition*, 38, 109–144.

Bruce, V., Hanna, E., Dench, N., et al. (1992). The importance of 'mass' in line drawings of faces. *Applied Cognitive Psychology*, 6, 619–628.

Bruce, V., Henderson, Z., Greenwood, K., et al. (1999). Verification of face identities from images captured on video. *Journal of Experimental Psychology: Applied*, 5, 339–360.

Bruce, V., Henderson, Z., Newman, C., et al. (2001). Matching identities of familiar and unfamiliar faces caught on CCTV images. *Journal of Experimental Psychology: Applied*, 7(3), 207–218.

Bruce, V., Ness, H., Hancock, P. J. B., et al. (2002). Four heads are better than one: combining face composites yields improvements in face likeness. *Journal of Applied Psychology*, 87, 894–902.

Bruce, V., Valentine, T. & Baddeley, A. (1987). The basis of the three-quarters view advantage in face recognition. *Applied Cognitive Psychology*, 1, 109–120.

Brunas-Wagstaff, J., Young, A. W. & Ellis, A.W. (1992). Repetition priming follows spontaneous but not prompted recognition of familiar faces. *Quarterly Journal of Experimental Psychology: Human Experimental Psychology*, A44, 423–454.

Brune, M. (2005). Emotion recognition, 'theory of mind,' and social behavior in schizophrenia. *Psychiatry Research*, 133(2–3), 135–147.

Bruyer, R. & Crispeels, G. (1992). Expertise in person recognition. *Bulletin of the Psychonomic Society*, 30(6), 501–504.

Bruyer, R., Laterre, C., Seron, X., et al. (1983). A case of prosopagnosia with some preserved covert remembrance of familiar faces. *Brain and Cognition*, 2(3), 257–284.

Bucks, R. S., Garner, M., Tarrant, L., et al. (2008). Interpretation of emotionally ambiguous faces in older adults. *Journal of Gerontology Series B: Psychological Sciences and Social Sciences,* 63(6), P337–P343.

Bukach, C. M., Gauthier, I. & Tarr, M. J. (2006). Beyond faces and modularity: the power of an expertise framework. *Trends in Cognitive Science*, 10(40), 159–166.

Burnham, H. & Hogervorst, E. (2004). Recognition of facial expressions of emotion by patients with dementia of the Alzheimer type. *Dementia and Geriatric Cognitive Disorders*, 18(1), 75–79.

Burriss, R. P., Little, A. C. & Nelson, E. C. (2007). 2D : 4D and sexually dimorphic facial characteristics. *Archives of Sexual Behavior*, 36(3), 377–384.

Burt, D. M. & Perrett, D. I. (1995). Perception of age in adult Caucasian male faces: computer graphic manipulation of shape and colour information. *Proceedings of the Royal Society of London. Series B*, 259, 137–143.

Burton, A. M. (1998). A model of human face recognition. In: J. Grainger & A. M. Jacobs (eds), *Localist Connectionist Approaches to Human Cognition*, pp 75–100. Hillsdale, NJ: Erlbaum.

Burton, A. M. & Bruce, V. (1993). Naming faces and naming names: exploring an interactive activation model of person recognition. *Memory*, 83, 457–480.

Burton, A. M., Bindemann, M., Langton, S. R. H., et al. (2009). Gaze perception requires focused attention: evidence from an interference task. *Journal of Experimental Psychology: Human Perception & Performance*, 35, 108–118.

Burton, A. M., Bruce, V. & Dench, N. (1993). What's the difference between men and women? Evidence from facial measurement. *Perception*, 22, 153–176.

Burton, A. M., Bruce, V. & Hancock, P. J. B. (1999a). From pixels to people: a model of familiar face recognition. *Cognitive Science*, 23(1), 1–31.

Burton, A. M., Bruce, V. & Johnston, R. A. (1990). Understanding face recognition with an interactive activation model. *British Journal of Psychology*, 81, 361–380.

Burton, A. M., Jenkins, R., Hancock, P. B. J., et al. (2005). Robust representations for face recognition. *Cognitive Psychology*, 51, 256–284.

Burton, A. M., Kelly, S. W. & Bruce, V. (1998). Cross-domain repetition priming in person recognition. *Quarterly Journal of Experimental Psychology*, 51A, 515–529.

Burton, A. M., Wilson, S., Cowan, M., et al. (1999b). Face recognition in poor quality video: evidence from security surveillance. *Psychological Science*, 10, 243–248.

Bushnell, I. W. R. (1998). The origins of face perception. In: F. Simion and G. Butterworth (eds), *The Development of Sensory, Motor and Cognitive Capacities in Early Infancy*, pp 69–86. Hove: Psychology Press.

Bushnell, I. W. R. (2001). Mother's face recognition in newborn infants: learning and memory. *Infant and Child Development*, 10, 67–74.

Bushnell, I. W. R., Sai, F. & Mullin, J. T. (1989). Neonatal recognition of the mother's face. *British Journal of Developmental Psychology*, 7, 3–15.

Butler, A., Oruc, I., Fox, C. J., et al. (2008). Factors contributing to the adaptation aftereffects of facial expression. *Brain Research*, 1191, 116–126.

Buttle, H. & Raymond, J. E. (2003). High familiarity enhances visual change detection for face stimuli. *Perception & Psychophysics*, 65(8), 1296–1306.

Byatt, G. & Rhodes, G. (1998). Recognition of own-race and other-race caricatures: implications for models of face recognition. *Vision Research*, 38(15–16), 2455–2468.

Byatt, G. & Rhodes, G. (2004). Identification of own-race and other-race faces: implications for the representation of race in face space. *Psychonomic Bulletin and Review*, 11(4), 735–741.

Cabeza, R. & Kato, T. (2000). Features are also important: contributions of featural and configural processing to face recognition. *Psychological Science*, 11(5), 429–433.

Cain, W. J., Baker-Ward, L. & Eaton, K. L. (2005). A face in the crowd: the influences of familiarity and delay on preschoolers' recognition. *Psychology, Crime and Law*, 11(3), 315–327.

Caldara, R., Seghier, M. L., Rossion, B., et al. (2006). The fusiform face area is tuned for curvilinear patterns with more high-contrasted elements in the upper part. *NeuroImage*, 31, 313–319.

Calder, A. J., Lawrence, A. D. & Young, A. W. (2001). Neuropsychology of fear and loathing. *Nature Reviews Neuroscience*, 2(5), 352–363.

Calder, A. J., Young, A. W., Keane, J., et al. (2000). Configural information in facial expression perception. *Journal of Experimental Psychology: Human Perception and Performance*, 26(2), 527–551.

Calder, A. J., Young, A. W., Rowland, D., et al. (1996). Facial emotion recognition after bilateral amygdala damage: differentially severe impairment of fear. *Cognitive Neuropsychology*, 13(5), 699–745.

Calvert, G. A., Bullmore, E. T., Brammer, M. J., et al. (1997). Activation of auditory cortex during silent lipreading. *Science*, 276(5312), 593–596.

Calvo, M. G. & Lundqvist, D. (2008). Facial expressions of emotion (KDEF): identification under different display-duration conditions. *Behavior Research Methods*, 40(1), 109–115.

Campanella, S., Quinet, P., Bruyer, R., et al. (2002). Categorical perception of happiness and fear facial expressions: an ERP study. *Journal of Cognitive Neuroscience*, 14(2), 210–227.

Campbell, D. W., Sareen, J., Paulus, M. P., et al. (2007). Time-varying amygdala response to emotional faces in generalized social phobia. *Biological Psychiatry*, 62(5), 455–463.

Campbell, R. & Tuck, M. (1995). Recognition of parts of famous-face photographs by children: an experimental note. *Perception*, 24, 451–456.

Campbell, R., Benson, P. J., Wallace, S. B., et al. (1999a). More about brows: how poses that change brow position affect perceptions of sex. *Perception*, 28, 489–504.

Campbell, R., Coleman, M., Walker, J., et al. (1999b). When does the inner-face advantage in familiar face recognition arise and why? *Visual Cognition*, 6(2), 197–216.

Campbell, R., Heywood, C. A., Cowey, A., et al. (1990). Sensitivity to eye gaze in prosopagnosic patients and monkeys with superior temporal sulcus ablation. *Neuropsychologia*, 28, 1123–1142.

Campbell, R., Landis, T. & Regard, M. (1986). Face recognition and lipreading: a neurological dissociation. *Brain*, 109, 509–521.

Campbell, R., Walker, J. & Baron-Cohen, S. (1995). The development of differential use of inner and outer face features in familiar face identification. *Journal of Experimental Child Psychology*, 59, 196–210.

Canli, T., Cooney, R. E., Goldin, P., et al. (2005). Amygdala reactivity to emotional faces predicts improvement in major depression. *Neuroreport*, 16(12), 1267–1270.

Carbon, C. C. (2008). Famous faces as icons. The illusion of being an expert in the recognition of famous faces. *Perception*, 37, 801–806.

Carbon, C. C. & Leder, H. (2005). When feature information comes first! Early processing of inverted faces. *Perception*, 34, 1117–1134.

Carbon, C. C., Schweinberger, S. R., Kaufmann, J. M., et al. (2005). The Thatcher illusion seen by the brain: an event-related brain potentials study. *Cognitive Brain Research*, 24(3), 544–555.

Carbon, C. C., Strobach, T., Langton, S. R. H., et al. (2007). Adaptation effects of highly familiar faces: immediate and long lasting. *Memory and Cognition*, 35(8), 1966–1976.

Carey, S. (1981). The development of face perception. In: G. Davies, H. Ellis and J. Shepherd (eds), *Perceiving and Remembering Faces*, pp 9–38. London: Academic Press.

Carey, S. & Diamond, R. (1977). From piecemeal to configurational representation of faces. *Science*, 195, 312–314.

Carey, S. & Diamond, R. (1994). Are faces perceived as configurations more by adults than by children? *Visual Cognition*, 1, 253–274.

Carey, S., Diamond, R. & Woods, B. (1980). Development of face recognition: a maturational component? *Developmental Psychology*, 16(4), 257–269.

Carmel, D. & Bentin, S. (2002). Domain specificity versus expertise: factors influencing distinct processing of faces. *Cognition*, 83(1), 1–29.

Carroll, L. (1871). *Through the Looking Glass, and What Alice Found There*. London: MacMillan.

Cassia, V. M., Turati, C. & Simion, F. (2004). Can a nonspecific bias toward top-heavy patterns explain newborns' face preference? *Psychological Science*, 15(6), 379–383.

Castelli, F. (2005). Understanding emotions from standardized facial expressions in autism and normal development. *Autism*, 9(4), 428–449.

Cavanagh, J. & Geisler, M. W. (2006). Mood effects on the ERP processing of emotional intensity in faces: A P3 investigation with depressed students. *International Journal of Psychophysiology*, 60(1), 27–33.

Cellerino, A., Borghetti, D. & Sartucci, C. (2004). Sex differences in face gender recognition in humans. *Brain Research Bulletin*, 63(6), 443–449.

Chambon, V., Baudouin, J. Y. & Franck, N. (2006). The role of configural information in facial emotion recognition in schizophrenia. *Neuropsychologia*, 44(12), 2437–2444.

Chan, S. W. Y., Norbury, R., Goodwin, G. M., et al. (2009). Risk for depression and neural responses to fearful facial expressions of emotion. *British Journal of Psychiatry*, 194(2), 139–145.

Chance, E. & Goldstein, A. G. (1996). The other-race effect and eyewitness identification. In: S. L. Sporer, R. S. Malpass & G. Koehnken (eds), *Psychological Issues in Eyewitness Identification*, pp 153–176. Mahwah, NJ: Erlbaum.

Chance, J. E., Turner, A. L. & Goldstein, A. G. (1982). Development of differential recognition for own- and other-race faces. *Journal of Psychology*, 112, 29–37.

Chang, P. P. W., Levine, S. C. & Benson, P. J. (2002). Children's recognition of caricatures. *Developmental Psychology*, 38(6), 1038–1051.

Charcot, J. M. (1883). Un cas de suppression brusque et isolee de la vision mentale des signes et des objets (formes et couleurs). *Progres Medical*, 11, 568–571.

Charman, S. D. & Wells, G. L. (2007). Eyewitness lineups: is the appearance-change instruction a good idea? *Law and Human Behavior*, 31(6), 3–22.

Chen, C. C., Kao, K. L. C. & Tyler, C. W. (2007). Face configuration processing in the human brain: the role of symmetry. *Cerebral Cortex*, 17(6), 1423–1432.

Chen, W. & Liu, C. H. (2009). Transfer between pose and expression training in face recognition. *Vision Research*, 49, 368–373.

Chen, Y., Norton, D., McBain, R., et al. (2009). Visual and cognitive processing of face information in schizophrenia: detection, discrimination and working memory. *Schizophrenia Research*, 107(1), 92–98.

Cheung, O. S., Richler, J. J., Palmeri, T. J., et al. (2008). Revisiting the role of spatial frequencies in the holistic processing of faces. *Journal of Experimental Psychology: Human Perception and Performance*, 34(6), 1327–1336.

Chiller-Glaus, S. D., Schwaninger, A. & Hofer, F. (2007). Identity verification from photographs in travel documents: the role of display duration and orientation on performance. *Proceedings of the Human Factors and Ergonomics Society 51st Annual Meeting, 2007,* 1327–1330.

Chin, J. M. & Schooler, J. W. (2007). Why do words hurt? Content, process, and criterion shift accounts of verbal overshadowing. *European Journal of Cognitive Psychology*, 20(3), 396–413.

Chiroro, P. & Valentine, T. (1995). An investigation of the contact hypothesis of the own-race bias in face recognition. *Quarterly Journal of Experimental Psychology A*, 48, 879–894.

Christianson, S. A. (1992). Emotional stress and eyewitness memory: a critical review. *Psychological Bulletin*, 112(2), 284–309.

Christman, S. D. & Hackworth, M. D. (1993). Equivalent perceptual asymmetries for free viewing of positive and negative emotional expressions in chimeric faces. *Neuropsychologia*, 31(6), 621–624.

Chung, M.-S. & Thomson, D. M. (1995). The development of face recognition. *British Journal of Psychology*, 86(1), 55–87.

Clark, S. E. (2005). A re-examination of the effects of biased lineup instructions in eyewitness identification. *Law and Human Behavior*, 29, 395–424.

Clark, S. E. & Davey, S. L. (2005). The target-to-foils shift in simultaneous and sequential lineups. *Law and Human Behavior*, 29(2), 151–172.

Clark, S. E., Howell, R. T. & Davey, S. L. (2008). Regularities in eyewitness identification. *Law and Human Behavior*, 32, 187–218.

Clark, T. F., Winkielman, P. & McIntosh, D. N. (2008). Autism and the extraction of emotion from briefly presented facial expressions: stumbling at the first step of empathy. *Emotion*, 8(6), 803–809.

Clifford, C. W. G. & Rhodes, G. (2005). *Fitting the Mind to the World: Adaptation and Aftereffects in High-level Vision*. Oxford: Oxford University Press.

Cloutier, J., Turk, D. J. & Macrae, C. N. (2008). Extracting variant and invariant information from faces: the neural substrates of gaze detection and sex categorization. *Social Neuroscience*, 3(1), 69–78.

Clutterbuck, R. & Johnston, R. A. (2002). Exploring levels of face familiarity by using an indirect face-matching measure. *Perception*, 31, 985–994.

Clutterbuck, R. & Johnston, R. A. (2004). Matching as an index of face familiarity. *Visual Cognition*, 11, 857–869.

Clutterbuck, R. & Johnston, R. A. (2005). Demonstrating how unfamiliar faces become familiar using a face matching task. *European Journal of Cognitive Psychology*, 17(1), 97–116.

Cohen, L. B. & Cashon, C. H. (2001). Do 7-month-old infants process independent features or facial configurations? *Infant and Child Development*, 10, 83–92.

Coleman, S. R. & Grover, R. (2006). The anatomy of the aging face: volume loss and changes in 3-dimensional topography. *Aesthetic Surgery Journal*, 26(Suppl), S4–S9.

Collishaw, S. M. & Hole, G. J. (2000). Featural and configurational processes in the recognition of faces of different familiarity. *Perception*, 29, 893–909.

Collishaw, S. M. & Hole, G. J. (2002). Is there a linear or a nonlinear relationship between rotation and configural processing of faces? *Perception*, 31, 287–296.

Compton, R. (2002). Inter-hemispheric interaction facilitates face processing. *Neuropsychologia*, 40, 2409–2419.

Compton, R. J., Feigenson, K. & Widick, P. (2005). Take it to the bridge: an interhemispheric processing advantage for emotional faces. *Cognitive Brain Research*, 24(1), 66–72.

Compton, R. J., Fisher, L. R., Koenig, L. M., et al. (2003). Relationship between coping styles and perceptual asymmetry. *Journal of Personality and Social Psychology*, 84(5), 1069–1078.

Conway, C. A., Jones, B. C., DeBruine, L. M., et al. (2008). Evidence for adaptive design in human gaze preference. *Proceedings of the Royal Society of London. Series B*, 275, 63–69.

Cooney, R. E., Atlas, L. Y., Joormann, J., et al. (2006). Amygdala activation in the processing of neutral faces in social anxiety disorder: Is neutral really neutral? *Psychiatry Research: Neuroimaging*, 148(1), 55–59.

Cooper, T. J., Harvey, M., Lavidor, M., et al. (2007). Hemispheric asymmetries in image-specific and abstractive priming of famous faces: evidence from reaction times and event-related brain potentials. *Neuropsychologia*, 45, 2910–2921.

Corballis, M. C. (1998). Interhemispheric neural summation in the absence of the corpus callosum. *Brain*, 121, 1795–1807.

Corcoran, K. M., Woody, S. R. & Tolin, D. F. (2008). Recognition of facial expressions in obsessive-compulsive disorder. *Journal of Anxiety Disorders*, 22(1), 56–66.

Corenblum, B. & Meissner, C. A. (2006). Recognition of faces of ingroup and outgroup children and adults. *Journal of Experimental Child Psychology*, 93, 187–206.

Costafreda, S. G., Khanna, A., Mourao-Miranda, J., et al. (2009). Neural correlates of sad faces predict clinical remission to cognitive behavioural therapy in depression. *Neuroreport*, 20(7), 637–641.

Costen, N. P., Parker, D. M. & Craw, I. (1994). Spatial content and spatial quantization effects in face recognition. *Perception*, 23, 129–146.

Costen, N. P., Parker, D. M. & Craw, I. (1996). Effects of high-pass and low-pass spatial filtering on face identification. *Perception and Psychophysics*, 58, 602–612.

Creswell, C., Woolgar, M., Cooper, P., et al. (2008). Processing of faces and emotional expressions in infants at risk of social phobia. *Cognition & Emotion*, 22(3), 437–458.

Crookes, K. & McKone, E. (2009). Early maturity of face recognition: no childhood development of holistic processing, novel face encoding, or face-space. *Cognition*, 111, 219–247.

Csukly, G., Czobor, P., Szily, E., et al. (2009). Facial expression recognition in depressed subjects: the impact of intensity level and arousal dimension. *Journal of Nervous and Mental Disease*, 197(2), 98–103.

Cunningham M. R. (1986). Measuring the physical in physical attractiveness. Quasiexperiments on the sociobiology of female facial beauty. *Journal of Personality and Social Psychology*, 50, 925–935.

da Costa, A. P., Leigh, A. E., Man, M. S., et al. (2004). Face pictures reduce behavioural, autonomic, endocrine and neural indices of stress and fear in sheep. *Proceedings of the Royal Society of London. Series B, Biological Sciences,* 271(1552), 2077–2084.

Dakin, S. C. & Watt, R. J. (2009). Biological 'bar codes' in human faces. *Journal of Vision*, 9(4), 1–10.

Dal Martello, M. F. & Maloney, L. T. (2006). Where are kin recognition signals in the human face? *Journal of Vision*, 6, 1356–1366.

Dalton, K. M., Nacewicz, B. M., Johnstone, T., et al. (2005). Gaze fixation and the neural circuitry of face processing in autism. *Nature Neuroscience*, 8(4), 519–526.

Damasio, A. R., Damasio, H. & VanHosen, G. W. (1982). Prosopagnosia: anatomic basis and behavioural mechanisms. *Neurology*, 32, 321–341.

Dando, C., Wilcock, R., Milne, R., et al. (2009). A modified Cognitive Interview procedure for frontline police investigators. *Applied Cognitive Psychology*, 23, 698–716.

D'Argembeau, A. & Van der Linden, M. (2007). Facial expressions of emotion influence memory for facial identity in an automatic way. *Emotion*, 7(3), 507–515.

D'Argembeau, A., Van der Linden, M., Etienne, A. M., et al. (2003). Identity and expression memory for happy and angry faces in social anxiety. *Acta Psychologica*, 114(1), 1–15.

Darling, S., Valentine, T. & Memon, A. (2008). Selection of lineup foils in operational contexts. *Applied Cognitive Psychology*, 22, 159–169.

Darlington, C. L. (2002). *The Female Brain*. London: Taylor and Francis.

Darwin, C. R. (1872). *The Expression of the Emotions in Man and Animals*. London: John Murray.

Darwin, C. R. (1874). *The Descent of Man*. London: John Murray.

Davidoff, J. and Donnelly, N. (1990). Object superiority: a comparison of complete and part probes. *Acta Psychologia*, 73, 225–243.

Davidson, R. J. (1992). Anterior cerebral asymmetry and the nature of emotion. *Brain and Cognition*, 20(1), 125–151.

Davies, G. (1983), The recognition of persons from drawings and photographs. *Human Learning*, 2, 237–249.

Davies, G. (1991). Children on trial? Psychology, videotechnology and the law. *The Howard Journal*, 30(3), 177–191.

Davies, G. (1993). Children's memory for other people: an integrative review. In: C. A. Nelson (ed.), *Memory and Affect in Development: The Minnesota Symposia on Child Psychology*, Vol. 26, pp 123–157. London: Lawrence Erlbaum Associates.

Davies, G. & Thasen, S. (2000). Closed-circuit television: how effective an identification aid? *British Journal of Psychology*, 91, 411–426.

Davies, G. M. & Valentine, T. (2007). Facial composites: forensic utility and psychological research. In: R. C. L. Lindsay, D. F. Ross, J. D. Read & M. P. Toglia (eds), *Handbook of Eyewitness Psychology, Vol. 2: Memory for People*, pp 59–83. Mahwah, NJ: Lawrence Erlbaum Associates.

Davies, G., Ellis, H. & Shepherd, J. (1978). Face recognition as a function of mode of representation. *Journal of Applied Psychology*, 63, 180–187.

Davies, G., Stevenson-Robb, Y. & Flin, R. (1988). Tales out of school: children's memory for an unexpected incident. In: M. Gruneberg, P. E. Morris and R. N. Sykes (eds), *Practical Aspects of Memory: Current Research and Theory*, pp 122–127. Chichester: Wiley.

Davies, G. M., van der Willik, P. & Morrison, L. (2000). Facial composite production: a comparison of mechanical and computer-driven systems. *Journal of Applied Psychology*, 85, 119–124.

Davis, J. P. & Valentine, T. (2009). CCTV on trial: matching video images with the defendant in the dock. *Applied Cognitive Psychology*, 23, 482–505.

Dawkins, R. (1976). *The Selfish Gene*. Oxford: Oxford University Press.

Dawson, G., Carver, L., Meltzoff, A. N., et al. (2002). Neural correlates of face and object recognition in young children with autism spectrum disorder, developmental delay, and typical development. *Child Development*, 73(3), 700–717.

Dawson, G., Webb, S. J. & McPartland, J. (2005). Understanding the nature of face processing impairment in autism: insights from behavioral and electrophysiological studies. *Developmental Neuropsychology*, 27(3), 403–424.

de Gelder, B. & Rouw, R. (2000a). Structural encoding precludes recognition of face parts in prosopagnosia. *Cognitive Neuropsychology*, 17(1–3), 89–102.

de Gelder, B. & Rouw, R. (2000b). Paradoxical configuration effects for faces and objects in prosopagnosia. *Neuropsychologia*, 38(9), 1271–1279.

de Gelder, B. & Rouw, R. (2001). Beyond localisation: a dynamical dual route account of face recognition. *Acta Psychologica*, 107(1–3), 183–207.

de Gelder, B., Bachoud-Levi, A. C. & Degos, J. D. (1998). Inversion superiority in visual agnosia may be common to a variety of orientation polarised objects besides faces. *Vision Research*, 38(18), 2855–2861.

de Haan, E. H. & Campbell, R. (1991). A fifteen year follow-up of a case of developmental prosopagnosia. *Cortex*, 27, 489–509.

de Haan, E. H., Young, A. W. & Newcombe, F. (1987). Face recognition without awareness. *Cognitive Neuropsychology*, 4, 385–415.

de Haan, E. H. F., Young, A. W. & Newcombe, F. (1991). A dissociation between the sense of familiarity and access to semantic information concerning familiar people. *European Journal of Cognitive Psychology*, 3, 51–67.

de Haan, M., Johnson, M. H., Maurer, D., et al. (2001). Recognition of individual faces and average face prototypes by 1- and 3-month-old infants. *Cognitive Development*, 16, 659–678.

de Haan, M., Pascalis, O. & Johnson, M. H. (2002). Specialization of neural mechanisms underlying face recognition in human infants. *Journal of Cognitive Neuroscience*, 14(2), 199–209.

de Heering, A., Houthuys, S. & Rossion, B. (2007). Holistic face processing is mature at 4 years of age: evidence from the composite face effect. *Journal of Experimental Child Psychology*, 96, 57–70.

de Heering, A., Turati, C., Rossion, B., et al. (2008). Newborns' face recognition is based on spatial frequencies below 0.5 cycles per degree. *Cognition*, 106, 444–454.

De Renzi, E. & di Pellegrino, G. (1998). Prosopagnosia and alexia without object agnosia. *Cortex*, 34(3), 403–415.

De Renzi, E., Faglioni, P., Grossi, D., et al. (1991). Apperceptive and associative forms of prosopagnosia. *Cortex*, 27(2), 213–221.

De Renzi, E., Faglioni, P. & Scotti, G. (1968). Tactile spatial impairment and unilateral cerebral damage. *Journal of Nervous and Mental Disorders*, 146(6), 468–475.

De Renzi, E., Perani, D., Carlesimo, G. A., et al. (1994). Prosopagnosia can be associated with damage confined to the right hemisphere: an MRI and PET study and a review of the literature. *Neuropsychologia*, 32(8), 893–902.

De Renzi, E., Zambolin, A. & Crisi, G. (1987). The pattern of neuropsychological impairment associated with left posterior cerebral artery infarcts. *Brain*, 110(5), 1099–1116.

de Schonen, S. & Mathivet, E. (1990). Hemispheric-asymmetry in a face discrimination task in infants. *Child Development*, 61(4), 1192–1205.

De Souza, W. C., Eifuku, S., Tamura, R., et al. (2005). Differential characteristics of face neuron responses within the anterior superior temporal sulcus of macaques. *Journal of Neurophysiology*, 94, 1252–1266.

de Wit, T. C. J., Falck-Ytter, T. & von Hofsten, C. (2008). Young children with autism spectrum disorder look differently at positive versus negative emotional faces. *Research in Autism Spectrum Disorders*, 2(4), 651–659.

DeBruine, L. M. (2004). Facial resemblance increases the attractiveness of same-sex faces more than other-sex faces. *Proceedings of the Royal Society of London. Series B*, 271(1552), 2085–2090.

DeBruine, L. M., Jones, B. C., Unger, L., et al. (2007). Dissociating averageness and attractiveness: attractive faces are not always average. *Journal of Experimental Psychology: Human Perception and Performance*, 33(6), 1420–1430.

DeBruine, L. M., Smith, F. G., Jones, B. C., et al. (2009). Kin recognition signals in adult faces. *Vision Research*, 49, 38–43.

Deeley, Q., Daly, E. M., Surguladze, S., et al. (2007). An event related functional magnetic resonance imaging study of facial emotion processing in Asperger syndrome. *Biological Psychiatry*, 62(3), 207–217.

Deffenbacher, K. A., Bornstein, B. H., McGorty, E. K., et al. (2008). Forgetting the once-seen face: estimating the strength of an eyewitness's memory representation. *Journal of Experimental Psychology: Applied*, 14(2), 139–150.

Deffenbacher, K. A., Bornstein, B. H., Penrod, S. D., et al. (2004). A meta-analytic review of the effects of high stress on eyewitness memory. *Law and Human Behavior*, 28(6), 687–706.

Deffenbacher, K. A., Bornstein, B. H. & Penrod, S. D. (2006). Mugshot exposure effects: retroactive interference, mugshot commitment, source confusion, and unconscious transference. *Law and Human Behavior*, 30(3), 287–307.

Deffke, I., Sander, T., Heidenreich, J., et al. (2007). MEG/EEG sources of the 170-ms response to faces are co-localized in the fusiform gyrus. *Neuroimage*, 35(4), 1495–1501.

DeGutis, J. M., Bentin, S., Robertson, L. C., et al. (2007). Functional plasticity in ventral temporal cortex following cognitive rehabilitation of a congenital prosopagnosic. *Journal of Cognitive Neuroscience*, 19(11), 1790–1802.

Dekowska, M., Kuniecki, M. & Jaskowski, P. (2008). Facing facts: neuronal mechanisms of face perception. *Acta Neurobiologiae Experimentalis*, 68(2), 229–252.

Denkova, E., Botzung, A. & Manning, L. (2006). Neural correlates of remembering/knowing famous people: an event-related fMRI study. *Neuropsychologia*, 44(14), 2783–2791.

Derntl, B., Windischberger, C., Robinson, S., et al. (2008). Facial emotion recognition and amygdala activation are associated with menstrual cycle phase. *Psychoneuroendocrinology*, 33(8), 1031–1040.

Deruelle, C. & Santos, A. (2009). Happy, sad or angry? What strategies do children with Williams syndrome use to recognize facial expressions of emotion? *Evolution Psychiatrique*, 74(1), 55–63.

Deruelle, C., Mancini, J., Livet, M. O., et al. (1999). Configural and local processing of faces in children with Williams syndrome. *Brain and Cognition*, 41(3), 276–298.

Deruelle, C., Rondan, C., Gepner, B., et al. (2004). Spatial frequency and face processing in children with autism and Asperger syndrome. *Journal of Autism and Developmental Disorders*, 34(2), 199–210.

Deruelle, C., Rondan, C., Salle-Collemiche, X., et al. (2008). Attention to low- and high-spatial frequencies in categorizing facial identities, emotions and gender in children with autism. *Brain and Cognition*, 66(2), 115–123.

Desimone, R., Albright, T. D., Gross, C. G., et al. (1984). Stimulus-selective properties of inferior temporal neurons in the macaque. *Journal of Neuroscience*, 4(8), 2051–2062.

Devue, C., Collette, F., Balteau, E., et al. (2007). Here I am: the cortical correlates of visual self-recognition. *Brain Research*, 1143, 169–182.

Diamond, R. & Carey, S. (1977). Developmental changes in the representation of faces. *Journal of Experimental Child Psychology*, 23, 1–22.

Diamond, R. & Carey, S. (1986). Why faces are and are not special: an effect of expertise. *Journal of Experimental Psychology: General*, 115(2), 107–117.

Dobel, C., Bolte, J., Aicher, M., et al. (2007). Prosopagnosia without apparent cause: overview and diagnosis of six cases. *Cortex*, 43(6), 718–733.

Dobel, C., Geiger, L., Bruchmann, M., Putsche, C., et al. (2008). On the interplay between familiarity and emotional expression in face perception. *Psychological Research*, 72(5), 580–586.

Dodson, C. S., Johnson, M. K. & Schooler, J. W. (1997). The verbal overshadowing effect: why descriptions impair face recognition. *Memory and Cognition*, 25, 129–139.

Doherty, M. J. (2006). The development of mentalistic gaze understanding. *Infant and Child Development*, 15, 179–186.

Doherty, M. J., Anderson, J. R. & Howieson, L. (2009). The rapid development of explicit gaze judgment ability at 3 years. *Journal of Experimental Child Psychology*, 104, 296–312.

Dolan, M. & Fullam, R. (2006). Face affect recognition deficits in personality-disordered offenders: association with psychopathy. *Psychological Medicine*, 36(11), 1563–1569.

Donnelly, N. & Hadwin, J. A. (2003). Children's perception of the Thatcher illusion: evidence for development in configural face processing. *Visual Cognition*, 10(8), 1001–1017.

Douglass, A. M. & Steblay, N. (2006). Memory distortion in eyewitnesses: a meta-analysis of the Post-identification Feedback Effect. *Applied Cognitive Psychology*, 20, 859–869.

Drebing, C. E., Federman, E. J., Edington, P., et al. (1997). Affect identification bias demonstrated with individual chimeric faces. *Perceptual and Motor Skills*, 85(3), 1099–1104.

Driver, J., Davis, G., Ricciardelli, P., et al. (1999). Gaze perception triggers visuospatial orienting by adults in a reflexive manner. *Visual Cognition*, 6, 509–540.

Duchaine, B. C. (2000). Developmental prosopagnosia with normal configural processing. *Neuroreport*, 11(1), 79–83.

Duchaine, B. C. (2006). Prosopagnosia as an impairment to face-specific mechanisms: elimination of the alternative hypotheses in a developmental case. *Cognitive Neuropsychology*, 23(5), 714–747.

Duchaine, B. C. & Weidenfeld, A. (2003). An evaluation of two commonly used tests of unfamiliar face recognition. *Neuropsychologia*, 41(6), 713–720.

Duchaine, B. C., Dingle, K., Butterworth, E., et al. (2004). Normal greeble learning in a severe case of developmental prosopagnosia. *Neuron*, 43(4), 469–473.

Duchaine, B., Germine, L. & Nakayama, K. (2007). Family resemblance: ten family members with prosopagnosia and within-class object agnosia. *Cognitive Neuropsychology*, 24(4), 419–430.

Duchaine, B. C., Parker, H. & Nakayama, K. (2003). Normal recognition of emotion in a prosopagnosic. *Perception*, 32(7), 827–838.

Duchaine, B., Yovel, G., Butterworth, E., et al. (2006). Prosopagnosia as an impairment to face-specific mechanisms: elimination of the alternative hypotheses in a developmental case. *Cognitive Neuropsychology*, 23(5), 714–747.

Dufour, V., Pascalis, O. & Petit, O. (2006). Face processing limitation to own species in primates: a comparative study in brown capuchins, Tonkean macaques and humans. *Behavioural Processes*, 73, 107–113.

Dunning, D. & Perretta, S. (2002). Automaticity and eyewitness accuracy: a 10–12 second rule for distinguishing accurate from inaccurate positive identifications. *Journal of Applied Psychology*, 87, 951–962.

Durand, K., Gallay, M., Seigneuric, A., et al. (2007). The development of facial emotion recognition: the role of configural information. *Journal of Experimental Child Psychology*, 97(1), 14–27.

Dysart, J. E. & Lindsay, R. C. L. (2007a). Show-up identifications: suggestive technique or reliable method? In: R. C. L. Lindsay, D. F. Ross, J. D. Read & M. P. Toglia (eds), *Handbook of Eyewitness Psychology, Vol. 2: Memory for People*, pp 137–154. Mahwah, NJ: Erlbaum.

Dysart, J. E. & Lindsay, R. C. L. (2007b). The effects of delay on eyewitness identification accuracy: should we be concerned? In: R. C. L. Lindsay, D. F. Ross, J. D. Read & M. P. Toglia (eds), *Handbook of Eyewitness Psychology, Vol. 2: Memory for People*, pp 361–376. Mahwah, NJ: Erlbaum.

Dysart, J., Lindsay, R. C. L., Hammond, R., et al. (2001). Mug shot exposure prior to lineup identification: interference, transference, and commitment effects. *Journal of Applied Psychology*, 86, 1280–1284.

Easterbrook, J. A. (1959). The effect of emotion on cue utilization and the organization of behavior. *Psychological Review*, 66, 183–201.

Easterbrook, M. A., Kisilevsky, B. S., Hains, S. M. J., et al. (1999). Faceness or complexity: evidence from newborn visual tracking of facelike stimuli. *Infant Behavior and Development*, 22(1), 17–35.

Ebner, N. C. & Johnson, M. K. (2009). Young and older emotional faces: are there age group differences in expression identification and memory? *Emotion*, 9(3), 329–339.

Edelstyn, N. M. J., Oyebode, F. & Barrett, K. (2001). The delusions of Capgras and intermetamorphosis in a patient with right-hemisphere white-matter pathology. *Psychopathology*, 34(6), 299–304.

Edmonds, A. J. & Lewis, M. B. (2007). The effect of rotation on configural encoding in a face-matching task. *Perception*, 36, 446–460.

Edwards, J., Pattison, P. E., Jackson, H. J., et al. (2001). Facial affect and affective prosody recognition in first-episode schizophrenia. *Schizophrenia Research*, 48(2–3), 235–253.

Egan, V. & Cordan, G. (2009). Barely legal: is attraction and estimated age of young female faces disrupted by alcohol use, make up, and the sex of the observer? *British Journal of Psychology*, 100, 415–427.

Eger, E., Schweinberger, S. R., Dolan, R. J., et al. (2005). Familiarity enhances invariance of face representations in human ventral visual cortex: fMRI evidence. *NeuroImage*, 26(4), 1128–1139.

Eimer, M. (2000). Effects of face inversion on the structural encoding and recognition of faces—evidence from event-related brain potentials. *Cognitive Brain Research*, 10(1–2), 145–158.

Eimer, M. & Holmes, A. (2002). An ERP study on the time course of emotional face processing. *Neuroreport*, 13(4), 427–431.

Ekman, P. (1972). Universals and cultural differences in facial expressions of emotion. In: J. Cole (ed.), *Nebraska Symposium on Motivation, 1971*, Vol. 19, pp 207–282. Lincoln: University of Nebraska Press.

Ekman, P. & Friesen, W. V. (1971). Constants across cultures in the face and emotion. *Journal of Personality and Social Psychology*, 17, 124–129.

Ekman, P. & Friesen, W. V. (1976). Measuring facial movement. *Environmental Psychology and Nonverbal Behavior*, 1(1), 56–75.

Ekman, P., Sorenson, E. R. & Friesen, W. V. (1969). Pan-cultural elements in facial displays of emotions. *Science*, 164(3875), 86–88.

Elfenbein, H. A. & Ambady, N. (2002). On the universality and cultural specificity of emotion recognition: a meta-analysis. *Psychological Bulletin*, 128(2), 203–235.

Elfenbein, H. A. & Ambady, N. (2003). Universals and cultural differences in recognizing emotions. *Current Directions in Psychological Science*, 12(5), 159–164.

Elfenbein, H. A., Beaupre, M., Levesque, M., et al. (2007). Toward a dialect theory: cultural differences in the expression and recognition of posed facial expressions. *Emotion*, 7(1), 131–146.

Elfgren, C., van Westen, D., Passant, U., et al. (2006). fMRI activity in the medial temporal lobe during famous face processing. *Neuroimage*, 30(2), 609–616.

Ellis, A. W. & Young, A. W. (1990). Accounting for delusional misidentifications. *British Journal of Psychiatry*, 157, 239–248.

Ellis, A. W., Flude, B. M., Young, A., et al. (1996). Two loci of repetition priming in the recognition of familiar faces. *Journal of Experimental Psychology: Learning, Memory, and Cognition*, 22(2), 295–308.

Ellis, A. W., Young, A. W., Flude, B. M., et al. (1987). Repetition priming of face recognition. *Quarterly Journal of Experimental Psychology*, 39A, 193–210.

Ellis, A. W., Young, A. W. & Flude, B. M. (1990). Repetition priming and face processing: priming occurs within the system that responds to the identity of a face. *Quarterly Journal of Experimental Psychology: Human Experimental Psychology*, 42(A), 495–512.

Ellis, H. D. (1992). The development of face processing skills. *Philosophical Transactions of the Royal Society of London. Series B*, 335, 105–111.

Ellis, H. D. (1994). The role of the right-hemisphere in the Capgras delusion. *Psychopathology*, 27(3–5), 177–185.

Ellis, H. D. & Flin, R. H. (1990). Encoding and storage effects in 7-year-olds' and 10-year-olds' memory for faces. *British Journal of Developmental Psychology*, 8, 77–92.

Ellis, H. D. & Florence, M. (1990). Bodamer (1947) paper on prosopagnosia. *Cognitive Neuropsychology*, 7(2), 81–105.

Ellis, H. D. & Lewis, M. B. (2001). Capgras delusion: a window on face recognition. *Trends in Cognitive Sciences*, 5(4), 149–156.

Ellis, H. D. & Shepherd, J. W. (1975). Recognition of upright and inverted faces presented in the left and right visual fields. *Cortex*, 11, 3–7.

Ellis, H., Davies, G. & Shepherd, J. (1978). A critical examination of the Photofit system for recalling faces. *Ergonomics*, 21(4), 297–307.

Ellis, H. D., Depauw, K. W., Christodoulou, G. N., et al. (1993a). Responses to facial and non-facial stimuli presented tachistoscopically in either or both visual-fields by patients with the Capgras delusion and paranoid schizophrenics. *Journal of Neurology Neurosurgery and Psychiatry*, 56(2), 215–219.

Ellis, H. D., Ellis, D. M. & Hosie, J. A. (1993b). Priming effects in children's face recognition. *British Journal of Psychology*, 84, 101–110.

Ellis, H., Shepherd, J. & Davies, G. (1975). An investigation of the use of the Photofit technique for recalling faces. *British Journal of Psychology*, 66(1), 29–37.

Ellis, H. D., Shepherd, J. W. & Davies, G. M. (1979). Identification of familiar and unfamiliar faces from internal and external features: some implications for theories of face recognition, *Perception*, 8, 431–439.

Ellis, H. D., Young, A. W., Quayle, A. H., et al. (1997). Reduced autonomic responses to faces in Capgras delusion. *Proceedings of the Royal Society of London. Series B, Biological Sciences*, 264(1384), 1085–1092.

Emery, N. J. (2000). The eyes have it: neuroethology, function and evolution of social gaze. *Neuroscience and Biobehavioral Reviews*, 24(6), 581–604.

Engell, A. D. & Haxby, J. V. (2007). Facial expression and gaze-direction in human superior temporal sulcus. *Neuropsychologia*, 45(14), 3234–3241.

Enlow, D. (1982). *Handbook of Facial Growth*. Philadelphia: W. B. Saunders.

Etcoff, N. L. & Magee, J. J. (1992). Categorical perception of facial expressions. *Cognition*, 44(3), 227–240.

Evans, J. J., Heggs, A. J., Antoun, N., et al. (1995). Progressive prosopagnosia associated with selective right temporal-lobe atrophy—a new syndrome. *Brain*, 118, 1–13.

Ewbank, M. P., Lawrence, A. D., Passamonti, L., et al. (2009). Anxiety predicts a differential neural response to attended and unattended facial signals of anger and fear. *Neuroimage*, 44(3), 1144–1151.

Fagot, B. I. & Leinbach, M. D. (1993). Gender-role development in young-children—from discrimination to labeling. *Developmental Review*, 13(2), 205–224.

Fairweather, H., Brizzolara, D., Tabossi, P., et al. (1982). Functional cerebral lateralization—dichotomy or plurality. *Cortex*, 18(1), 51–65.

Faja, S., Aylward, E., Bernier, R., et al. (2008). Becoming a face expert: a computerized face-training program for high-functioning individuals with autism spectrum disorders. *Developmental Neuropsychology*, 33(1), 1–24.

Fakra, E., Salgado-Pineda, P., Delaveau, P., et al. (2008). Neural bases of different cognitive strategies for facial affect processing in schizophrenia. *Schizophrenia Research*, 100(1–3), 191–205.

Fallshore, M. & Bartholow, J. (2003). Recognition of emotion from inverted schematic drawings of faces. *Perceptual and Motor Skills*, 96(1), 236–244.

Fang, F. & He, S. (2005). Viewer-centered object representation in the human visual system revealed by viewpoint aftereffects. *Neuron*, 45(5), 793–800.

Fang, F., Ijichi, K. & He, S. (2007). Transfer of the face viewpoint aftereffect from adaptation to different and inverted faces. *Journal of Vision*, 7(13), 1–9.

Farah, M. J. (1990). *Visual Agnosia: Disorders of Object Recognition and What They Tell Us About Normal Vision*. Cambridge, MA: MIT Press.

Farah, M. J. (1995). Dissociable systems for visual recognition: a cognitive neuropsychology approach. In: **S. M. Kosslyn & D. N. Osherson (eds)**, *An Invitation to Cognitive Science* (2nd edn), pp 101–119. Cambridge, MA: MIT Press.

Farah, M. J., Rabinowitz, C., Quinn, G. E., et al. (2000). Early commitment of neural substrates for face recognition. *Cognitive Neuropsychology*, 17(1–3), 117–123.

Farah, M. J., Wilson, K. D., Drain, H. M., et al. (1995). The inverted face inversion effect in prosopagnosia—evidence for mandatory, face-specific perceptual mechanisms. *Vision Research*, 35(14), 2089–2093.

Farroni, T., Csibra, G., Simion, F., et al. (2002). Eye contact detection in humans from birth. *Proceedings of the National Academy of Sciences of the United States of America*, 99, 9602–9605.

Farroni, T., Johnson, M. H., Menon, E., et al. (2005). Newborns' preference for face-relevant stimuli: effects of contrast polarity. *Proceedings of the National Academy of Sciences*, 102(47), 17245–17250.

Fazio, R. H., Jackson, J. R., Dunton, B. C., et al. (1995). Variability in automatic activation as an unobstrusive measure of racial attitudes: a bona fide pipeline? *Journal of Personality and Social Psychology*, 69, 1013–1027.

Feinberg, D. R., Jones, B. C., Law-Smith, M. J., et al. (2006). Menstrual cycle, trait estrogen level, and masculinity preferences in the human voice. *Hormones and Behavior*, 49(2), 215–222.

Feinberg, T. E., Eaton, L. A., Roane, D. M., et al. (1999). Multiple Fregoli delusions after traumatic brain injury. *Cortex*, 35(3), 373–387.

Feinberg, T. E., Schindler, R. J., Ochoa, E., et al. (1994). Associative visual agnosia and alexia without prosopagnosia. *Cortex*, 30(3), 395–411.

Feinman, S. & Entwistle, D. R. (1976). Children's ability to recognize other children's faces. *Child Development*, 47(2), 506–510.

Ferguson, D. P., Rhodes, G., Lee, K., et al. (2001). 'They all look alike to me': prejudice and cross-race face recognition. *British Journal of Psychology*, 92, 567–577.

Field, T. M., Cohen, D., Garcia, R., et al. (1984). Mother–stranger face discrimination by the newborn. *Infant Behavior & Development*, 7(1), 19–25.

Fink, B., Grammer, K. & Matts, P. J. (2006). Visible skin color distribution plays a role in the perception of age, attractiveness, and health in female faces. *Evolution and Human Behavior*, 27, 433–442.

Fink, B., Grammer, K. & Thornhill, R. (2001). Human (*Homo sapiens*) facial attractiveness in relation to skin texture and color. *Journal of Comparative Psychology*, 115(1), 92–99.

Fink, B., Manning, J. T., Neave, N., et al. (2004). Second to fourth digit ratio and hand skill in Austrian children. *Biological Psychology*, 67(3), 375–384.

Fiorentini, A., Maffei, L. & Sardini, G. (1983). The role of high spatial frequencies in face perception. *Perception*, 12, 195–201.

Fiser, J., Biederman, I. & Cooper, E. E. (1996). To what extent can matching algorithms based on direct outputs of low level generic descriptors account for human object recognition. *Spatial Vision*, 10(3), 237–271.

Fitzgerald, D. A., Angstadt, M., Jelsone, L. M., et al. (2006). Beyond threat: amygdala reactivity across multiple expressions of facial affect. *Neuroimage*, 30(4), 1441–1448.

Fleuaris, A. V., Robertson, L. C. & Bentin, S. (2008). Using spatial frequency scales for processing face features and face configuration: an ERP analysis. *Brain Research*, 1194, 100–109.

Flin, R. H. (1980). Age effects in children's memory for unfamiliar faces. *Developmental Psychology*, 16, 373–374.

Flin, R. H. (1985). Development of face recognition: an encoding switch? *British Journal of Psychology*, 76, 123–134.

Flin, R. & Dzurawiec, S. (1989). Developmental factors in face perception. In: **A. W. Young & H. D. Ellis (eds)**, *Handbook of Research on Face Processing*, pp 335–378. Amsterdam: Elsevier/North Holland.

Flin, R., Boon, J., Knox, A., et al. (1992). The effect of a five month delay on children's and adults' eyewitness memory. *Journal of Psychology*, 83, 323–336.

Flowe, H. D. & Ebbesen, E. B. (2007). The effect of lineup member similarity on recognition accuracy in simultaneous and sequential lineups. *Law and Human Behaviour*, 31, 33–52.

Flude, B. M., Ellis, A. W. & Kay, J. (1989). Face processing and name retrieval in an anomic aphasic—names are stored separately from semantic information about familiar people. *Brain and Cognition*, 11(1), 60–72.

Fox, C. J. & Barton, J. J. S. (2007). What is adapted in face adaptation? The neural representations of expression in the human visual system. *Brain Research*, 1127(1), 80–89.

Fox, C. J., Moon, S. Y., Iaria, G., et al. (2009). The correlates of subjective perception of identity and expression in the face network: an fMRI adaptation study. *Neuroimage*, 44(2), 569–580.

Fox, C. J., Oruc, I. & Barton, J. J. S. (2008). It doesn't matter how you feel. The facial identity aftereffect is invariant to changes in facial expression. *Journal of Vision*, 8(3), 1–13.

Freire, A. & Lee, K. (2001). Face recognition in 4- to 7-year-olds: processing of configural, featural, and paraphernalia information. *Journal of Experimental Child Psychology*, 80, 347–371.

Freire, A., Lee, K. & Symons, L. A. (2000). The face-inversion effect as a deficit in the encoding of configural information: direct evidence. *Perception*, 29(2), 159–170.

Frenkel, T. I., Lamy, D., Algom, D., et al. (2009). Individual differences in perceptual sensitivity and response bias in anxiety: evidence from emotional faces. *Cognition & Emotion*, 23(4), 688–700.

Friesen, C. K. & Kingstone, A. (1998). The eyes have it: reflexive orienting is triggered by nonpredictive gaze. *Psychonomic Bulletin and Review*, 5, 490–493.

Friesen, C. K., Moore, C. & Kingstone, A. (2005). Does gaze direction really trigger a reflexive shift of spatial attention? *Brain & Cognition*, 57, 66–69.

Frigerio, E., Burt, D. M., Gagliardi, C., et al. (2006). Is everybody always my friend? Perception of approachability in Williams syndrome. *Neuropsychologia*, 44(2), 254–259.

Frommann, N., Streit, M. & Wolwer, W. (2003). Remediation of facial affect recognition impairments in patients with schizophrenia: a new training program. *Psychiatry Research*, 117(3), 281–284.

Frost, P. (1994). Preference for darker faces in photographs at different phases on the menstrual cycle: preliminary assessment of evidence for a hormonal relationship. *Perceptual and Motor Skills*, 79, 507–514.

Frowd, C. D., Bruce, V., Ness, H., et al. (2007a). Parallel approaches to composite production: interfaces that behave contrary to expectation. *Ergonomics*, 50(4), 562–585.

Frowd, C., Bruce, V., Ross, D., et al. (2007b). The relative importance of external and internal features of facial composites. *British Journal of Psychology*, 98, 61–77.

Frowd, C., Bruce, V., Ross, D., et al. (2007c). An application of caricature: how to improve the recognition of facial composites. *Visual Cognition*, 15(8), 954–984.

Frowd, C. D., Carson, D., Ness, H., et al. (2005). Contemporary composite techniques: the impact of a forensically-relevant target delay. *Legal and Criminological Psychology*, 10, 63–81.

Frowd, C. D., McQuiston-Surrett, D., Anandaciva, S., et al. (2007d). An evaluation of US systems for facial composite production. *Ergonomics*, 50(12), 1987–1998.

Fu, C. H. Y., Mourao-Miranda, J., Costafrecla, S. G., et al. (2008a). Pattern classification of sad facial processing: toward the development of neurobiological markers in depression. *Biological Psychiatry*, 63(7), 656–662.

Fu, C. H. Y., Williams, S. C. R., Brammer, M. J., et al. (2007). Neural responses to happy facial expressions in major depression following antidepressant treatment. *American Journal of Psychiatry*, 164(4), 599–607.

Fu, C. H. Y., Williams, S. C. R., Cleare, A. J., et al. (2008b). Neural responses to sad facial expressions in major depression following cognitive behavioral therapy. *Biological Psychiatry*, 64(6), 505–512.

Furl, N., Phillips, P. J. & O'Toole, A. J. (2002). Face recognition algorithms as models of the other-race effect. *Cognitive Science*, 96, 1–19.

Furl, N., van Rijsbergen, N. J., Treves, A., et al. (2007). Face adaptation aftereffects reveal anterior medial temporal cortex role in high level category representation. *Neuroimage*, 37(1), 300–310.

Gagliardi, C., Frigerio, E., Burt, D. M., et al. (2003). Facial expression recognition in Williams syndrome. *Neuropsychologia*, 41(6), 733–738.

Galper, R. E. (1970). Recognition of faces in photographic negative. *Psychonomic Science*, 19, 207–208.

Galton, F. (1879). Composite portraits, made by combining those of many different persons into a single resultant figure. *Journal of the Anthropological Institute of Great Britain and Ireland*, 8, 132–144.

Ganel, T. & Goshen-Gottstein, Y. (2002). Perceptual integrality of sex and identity of faces: further evidence for the single-route hypothesis. *Journal of Experimental Psychology: Human Perception and Performance*, 28(4), 854–867.

Ganel, T. & Goshen-Gottstein, Y. (2004). Effects of familiarity on the perceptual integrality of the identity and expression of faces: the parallel-route hypothesis revisited. *Journal of Experimental Psychology: Human Perception and Performance*, 30(3), 583–597.

Gao, X. Q. & Maurer, D. (2009). Influence of intensity on children's sensitivity to happy, sad, and fearful facial expressions. *Journal of Experimental Child Psychology*, 102(4), 503–521.

Garcia-Rodriguez, B., Ellgring, H., Fusari, A., et al. (2009). The role of interference in identification of emotional facial expressions in normal ageing and dementia. *European Journal of Cognitive Psychology*, 21(2–3), 428–444.

Garner, M., Baldwin, D. S., Bradley, B. P., et al. (2009). Impaired identification of fearful faces in generalised social phobia. *Journal of Affective Disorders*, 115(3), 460–465.

Gasbarri, A., Pompili, A., d'Onofrio, A., et al. (2008). Working memory for emotional facial expressions: role of the estrogen in young women. *Psychoneuroendocrinology*, 33(7), 964–972.

Gauthier, I. & Bukach, C. (2007). Should we reject the expertise hypothesis? *Cognition*, 103(2), 322–330.

Gauthier, I. & Tarr, M. J. (1997). Becoming a 'greeble' expert: exploring mechanisms for face recognition. *Vision Research*, 37(12), 1673–1682.

Gauthier, I., Behrmann, M. & Tarr, M. J. (1999a). Can face recognition really be dissociated from object recognition? *Journal of Cognitive Neuroscience*, 11(4), 349–370.

Gauthier, I., Klaiman, C. & Schultz, R. T. (2009). Face composite effects reveal abnormal face processing in autism spectrum disorders. *Vision Research*, 49(4), 470–478.

Gauthier, I., Skudlarski, P., Gore, J. C., et al. (2000). Expertise for cars and birds recruits brain areas involved in face recognition. *Nature Neuroscience*, 3(2), 191–197.

Gauthier, I., Tarr, M. J., Anderson, A. W., et al. (1999b). Activation of the middle fusiform 'face area' increases with expertise in recognizing novel objects. *Nature Neuroscience*, 2(6), 568–573.

Gauthier, I., Williams, P., Tarr, M. J., et al. (1998). Training 'greeble' experts: a framework for studying expert object recognition processes. *Vision Research*, 38(15–16), 2401–2428.

Gazzaniga, M. S. & Smylie, C. S. (1983). Facial recognition and brain asymmetries: clues to underlying mechanisms. *Annals of Neurology*, 13, 536–540.

Ge, L., Anzures, G., Wang, Z., et al. (2008). An inner face advantage in children's recognition of familiar peers. *Journal of Experimental Child Psychology*, 101, 124–136.

Ge, L., Luo, J., Nishimura, M. & Lee, K. (2003). The lasting impression of Chairman Mao: hyperfidelity of familiar-face memory. *Perception*, 32, 601–614.

Geiselman, R. E., Fisher, R. P., MacKinnon, D. P., et al. (1985). Eyewitness memory enhancement in the police interview. *Journal of Applied Psychology*, 27, 358–418.

Geldart, S., Mondloch, C. J., Maurer, D., et al. (2002). The effect of early visual deprivation on the development of face processing. *Developmental Science*, 5(4), 490–501.

Gentili, C., Gobbini, M. I., Ricciardi, E., et al. (2008). Differential modulation of neural activity throughout the distributed neural system for face perception in patients with social phobia and healthy subjects. *Brain Research Bulletin*, 77(5), 286–292.

George, N., Dolan, R. J., Fink, G. R., et al. (1999). Contrast polarity and face recognition in the fusiform gyrus. *Nature Neuroscience*, 2(6), 574–580.

George, N., Jemel, B., Fiori, N., et al. (2005). Electrophysiological correlates of facial decision: insights from upright and upside-down Mooney-face perception. *Cognitive Brain Research*, 24(3), 663–673.

George, P. A. & Hole, G. J. (1995). Factors influencing the accuracy of age estimates of unfamiliar faces. *Perception*, 24, 1059–1073.

George, P. A. & Hole, G. J. (2000). The role of spatial and surface cues in the age-processing of unfamiliar faces. *Visual Cognition*, 7(4), 485–509.

George, P. A., Hole, G. J. & Scaife, M. (2000). Factors influencing young children's ability to discriminate unfamiliar faces by age. *International Journal of Behavioural Development*, 24(4), 480–491.

Geschwind, N. & Galaburda, A. M. (1985). Cerebral lateralization—biological mechanisms, associations, and pathology. 1. A hypothesis and a program for research. *Archives of Neurology*, 42(5), 428–459.

Gilboa-Schechtman, E., Ben-Artzi, E., Jeczemien, P., et al. (2004). Depression impairs the ability to ignore the emotional aspects of facial expressions: evidence from the Garner task. *Cognition & Emotion*, 18(2), 209–231.

Gobbini, M. I. & Haxby, J. V. (2007). Neural systems for recognition of familiar faces. *Neuropsychologia*, 45(1), 32–41.

Goffaux, V. & Rossion, B. (2006). Faces are 'spatial': holistic face perception is supported by low spatial frequencies. *Journal of Experimental Psychology: Human Perception and Performance*, 32, 1023–1039.

Goffaux, V., Hault, B., Michel, C., et al. (2005). The respective role of low and high spatial frequencies in supporting configural and featural processing of faces. *Perception*, 34, 77–86.

Going, M. & Read, J. D. (1974). The effect of uniqueness, sex of subject and sex of photograph on facial recognition. *Perceptual and Motor Skills,* 39, 109–110.

Golby, A. J., Gabrieli, J. D. E., Chiao, J. Y., et al. (2001). Differential responses in the fusiform region to same-race and other-race faces. *Nature Neuroscience*, 4(8), 845–850.

Goldstein, A. G. (1979a). Race-related variation of facial features: anthropometric data I. *Bulletin of the Psychonomic Society*, 13, 187–190.

Goldstein, A. G. (1979b). Facial feature variation: anthropometric data II. *Bulletin of the Psychonomic Society*, 13, 191–193.

Goldstein, A. G. & Chance, J. F. (1964). Recognition of children's faces. *Child Development*, 35, 129–136.

Goldstein, A. G. & Mackenberg, E. J. (1966). Recognition of human faces from isolated facial features: a developmental study. *Psychonomic Science*, 6, 149–150.

Goodman, G. S., Liat Sayfan, L., Lee, J. S., et al. (2007). The development of memory for own- andother-race faces. *Journal of Experimental Child Psychology*, 98, 233–242.

Goren, C. C., Sarty, M. & Wu, P. Y. K. (1975). Visual following and pattern discrimination of face-like stimuli by newborn infants. *Pediatrics*, 56(4), 544–549.

Gorenstein, G. W. & Ellsworth, P. C. (1980). Effect of choosing an incorrect photograph on a later identification by an eyewitness. *Journal of Applied Psychology*, 65, 616–622.

Gorno Tempini, M. L., Price, C. J., Josephs, O., et al. (1998). The neural systems sustaining face and proper name processing. *Brain*, 121, 2103–2118.

Goshen-Gottstein, Y. & Ganel, T. (2000). Repetition priming for familiar and unfamiliar faces in a sex-judgment task: evidence for a common route for the processing of sex and identity. *Journal of Experimental Psychology: Learning, Memory, and Cognition*, 26, 1198–1214.

Gosselin, F. & Schyns, P. G. (2001). Bubbles: a technique to reveal the use of information in recognition tasks. *Vision Research*, 41, 2261–2271.

Gosselin, P., Perron, M., Legault, M. & Campanella, P. (2002). Children's and adults' knowledge of the distinction between enjoyment and nonenjoyment smiles. *Journal of Nonverbal Behavior*, 26(2), 83–108.

Graham, R., Devinsky, O. & LaBar, K. S. (2007). Quantifying deficits in the perception of fear and anger in morphed facial expressions after bilateral amygdala damage. *Neuropsychologia*, 45(1), 42–54.

Greene, D. J., Mooshagian, E., Kaplan, J. T., et al. (2009). The neural correlates of social attention: automatic orienting to social and nonsocial cues. *Psychological Research*, 73(4), 499–511.

Grill-Spector, K., Knouf, N. & Kanwisher, N. (2004). The fusiform face area subserves face perception, not generic within-category identification. *Nature Neuroscience*, 7(5), 555–562.

Grinspan, D., Hemphill, A. & Nowicki, S. (2003). Improving the ability of elementary school-age children to identify emotion in facial expression. *Journal of Genetic Psychology*, 164(1), 88–100.

Gross, C. G. (2002). Genealogy of the 'grandmother cell'. *Neuroscientist*, 8(5), 512–518.

Grueter, M., Grueter, T., Bell, V., et al. (2007). Hereditary prosopagnosia: the first case series. *Cortex*, 43(6), 734–749.

Gur, R. E., McGrath, C., Chan, R. M., et al. (2002). An fMRI study of facial emotion processing in patients with schizophrenia. *American Journal of Psychiatry*, 159(12), 1992–1999.

Haas, B. W., Mills, D., Yam, A., et al. (2009). Genetic influences on sociability: heightened amygdala reactivity and event-related responses to positive social stimuli in Williams syndrome. *Journal of Neuroscience*, 29(4), 1132–1139.

Habel, U., Windischberger, C., Derntl, B., et al. (2007). Amygdala activation and facial expressions: explicit emotion discrimination versus implicit emotion processing. *Neuropsychologia*, 45(10), 2369–2377.

Hadjikhani, N., Hoge, R., Snyder, J., et al. (2008). Pointing with the eyes: the role of gaze in communicating danger. *Brain and Cognition*, 68(1), 1–8.

Hadjikhani, N., Joseph, R. M., Snyder, J., et al. (2004). Activation of the fusiform gyrus when individuals with autism spectrum disorder view faces. *Neuroimage*, 22(3), 1141–1150.

Hadjikhani, N., Joseph, R. M., Snyder, J., et al. (2007). Abnormal activation of the social brain during face perception in autism. *Human Brain Mapping*, 28(5), 441–449.

Hadjikhani, N., Kveraga, K., Naik, P., et al. (2009). Early (M170) activation of face-specific cortex by face-like objects. *Neuroreport*, 20(4), 403–407.

Hagenbeek, R. E. & Van Strien, J. W. (2002). Left–right and upper–lower visual field asymmetries for face matching, letter naming, and lexical decision. *Brain and Cognition*, 49, 34–44.

Haig, N. D. (1984). The effect of feature displacement on face recognition. *Perception*, 13, 505–512.

Haig, N. D. (1985). How faces differ: a new comparative technique. *Perception*, 14, 601–615.

Haig, N. D. (1986). Exploring recognition with interchanged facial features. *Perception*, 15, 235–247.

Halberstadt, J. & Rhodes, G. (2000). The attractiveness of non-face averages: implications for an evolutionary explanation of the attractiveness of average faces. *Psychological Science*, 11, 285–289.

Halberstadt, J. & Rhodes, G. (2003). It's not just average faces that are attractive: computer-manipulated averageness makes birds, fish, and automobiles attractive. *Psychonomic Bulletin & Review*, 10(1), 149–156.

Halgren, E., Raij, T., Marinkovic, K., et al. (2000). Cognitive response profile of the human fusiform face area as determined by MEG. *Cerebral Cortex*, 10(1), 69–81.

Hall, D. A., Fussell, C. & Summerfield, A. Q. (2005). Reading fluent speech from talking faces: typical brain networks and individual differences. *Journal of Cognitive Neuroscience*, 17(6), 939–953.

Hall, J., Whalley, H. C., McKirdy, J. W., et al. (2008). Overactivation of fear systems to neutral faces in schizophrenia. *Biological Psychiatry*, 64(1), 70–73.

Halpern, D. F. (2000). *Sex differences in cognitive abilities* (3rd edn). Mahwah, NJ: Lawrence Earlbaum Associates.

Hamilton, W. D. (1964). The genetical evolution of social behaviour, I. *Journal of Theoretical Biology*, 7, 1–16.

Hampson, E., van Anders, S. M. & Mullin, L. I. (2006). A female advantage in the recognition of emotional facial expressions: test of an evolutionary hypothesis. *Evolution and Human Behavior*, 27(6), 401–416.

Hamsher, K., Levin, H. S. & Benton, A. L. (1979). Facial recognition in patients with focal brain lesions. *Archives of Neurology*, 36(13), 837–839.

Hancock, K. J. & Rhodes, G. (2008). Contact, configural coding and the other-race effect in face recognition. *British Journal of Psychology*, 99, 45–56.

Hancock, P. J. B., Bruce, V. & Burton, A. M. (1998). A comparison of two computer-based face identification systems with human perceptions of faces. *Vision Research*, 38, 2277–2288.

Hancock, P. J. B., Bruce, V. & Burton, A. M. (2000). Recognition of unfamiliar faces. *Trends in Cognitive Sciences*, 4, 330–337.

Harris, A. M. & Aguirre, G. K. (2008). The effects of parts, wholes, and familiarity on face-selective responses in MEG. *Journal of Vision*, 8(10), 1–12.

Harris, A. M., Duchaine, B. C. & Nakayama, K. (2005). Normal and abnormal face selectivity of the M170 response in developmental prosopagnosics. *Neuropsychologia*, 43(14), 2125–2136.

Harrison, D. W. & Gorelczenko, P. M. (1990). Functional asymmetry for facial affect perception in high and low hostile men and women. *International Journal of Neuroscience*, 55(2–4), 89–97.

Harrison, V. & Hole, G. J. (2009). Evidence for a contact-based explanation of the own-age bias in face recognition. *Psychonomic Bulletin and Review*, 16, 264–269.

Hasel, L. E. and Wells, G. L. (2007). Catching the bad guy: morphing composite faces helps. *Law and Human Behavior*, 31(2), 193–207.

Hasselmo, M. E., Rolls, E. T. & Baylis, G. C. (1989). The role of expression and identity in the face-selective responses of neurons in the temporal visual cortex of the monkey. *Behavioural Brain Research*, 32(3), 203–218.

Hasson, U., Avidan, G., Deouell, L. Y., et al. (2003). Face-selective activation in a congenital prosopagnosic subject. *Journal of Cognitive Neuroscience*, 15(3), 419–431.

Hausmann, M. (2005). Hemispheric asymmetry in spatial attention across the menstrual cycle. *Neuropsychologia*, 43(11), 1559–1567.

Hausmann, M. & Gunturkun, O. (2000). Steroid fluctuations modify functional cerebral asymmetries: the hypothesis of progesterone-mediated interhemispheric decoupling. *Neuropsychologia*, 38(10), 1362–1374.

Hausmann, M., Becker, C., Gather, U., et al. (2002). Functional cerebral asymmetries during the menstrual cycle: a cross-sectional and longitudinal analysis. *Neuropsychologia*, 40(7), 808–816.

Haxby, J. V., Hoffman, E. A. & Gobbini, M. I. (2000). The distributed human neural system for face perception. *Trends in Cognitive Sciences*, 4(6), 223–233.

Haxby, J. V., Ungerleider, L. G., Clark, V. P., et al. (1999). The effect of face inversion on activity in human neural systems for face and object perception. *Neuron*, 22(1), 189–199.

Hay, D. C. & Cox, R. (2000). Developmental changes in the recognition of faces and facial features. *Infant and Child Development*, 9, 199–212.

Hay, D. C. & Young, A. W. (1982). The human face. In: A. W. Ellis (ed.), *Normality and Pathology in Cognitive Functions*, pp 173–202. London: Academic Press.

Hayden, A., Bhatt, R. S., Reed, R., et al. (2007). The development of expert face processing: are infants sensitive to normal differences in second-order relational information? *Journal of Experimental Child Psychology*, 97, 85–98.

Hayward, W. G., Rhodes, G. & Schwaninger, A. (2008). An own-race advantage for components as well as configurations in face recognition. *Cognition*, 106, 1017–1027.

Heath, R. L., Rouhana, A. & Ghanem, D. A. (2005). Asymmetric bias in perception of facial affect among Roman and Arabic script readers. *Laterality*, 10(1), 51–64.

Hécaen, H. & Angelergues, R. (1962). Agnosia for faces (prosopagnosia). *Archives of Neurology*, 7, 92–100.

Henderson, Z., Bruce, V. & Burton, A. M. (2001). Matching the faces of robbers captured on video. *Applied Cognitive Psychology*, 15, 445–464.

Henke, K., Schweinberger, S. R., Grigo, A., et al. (1998). Specificity of face recognition: recognition of exemplars of non-face objects in prosopagnosia. *Cortex*, 34(2), 289–296.

Henry, J. D., Ruffman, T., McDonald, S., et al. (2008). Recognition of disgust is selectively preserved in Alzheimer's disease. *Neuropsychologia*, 46(5), 1363–1370.

Herba, C. M., Benson, P., Landau, S., et al. (2008). Impact of familiarity upon children's developing facial expression recognition. *Journal of Child Psychology and Psychiatry*, 49(2), 201–210.

Herlitz, A. & Yonker, J. E. (2002). Sex differences in episodic memory: the influence of intelligence. *Journal of Clinical and Experimental Neuropsychology*, 24(1), 107–114.

Hernandez, N., Metzger, A., Magne, R., et al. (2009). Exploration of core features of a human face by healthy and autistic adults analyzed by visual scanning. *Neuropsychologia*, 47(4), 1004–1012.

Herridge, M. L., Harrison, D. W., Mollet, G. A., et al. (2004). Hostility and facial affect recognition: effects of a cold pressor stressor on accuracy and cardiovascular reactivity. *Brain and Cognition*, 55(3), 564–571.

Herrmann, M. J., Aranda, D., Ellgring, H., et al. (2002). Face-specific event-related potential in humans is independent from facial expression. *International Journal of Psychophysiology*, 45(3), 241–244.

Herrmann, M. J., Ehlis, A. C., Ellgring, H., et al. (2005). Early stages (P100) of face perception in humans as measured with event-related potentials (ERPs). *Journal of Neural Transmission*, 112(8), 1073–1081.

Herrmann, M. J., Schreppel, T., Jager, D., et al. (2007). The other-race effect for face perception: an event-related potential study. *Journal of Neural Transmission*, 114(7), 951–957.

Herzmann, G. & Sommer, W. (2007). Memory-related ERP components for experimentally learned faces and names: characteristics and parallel-test reliabilities. *Psychophysiology*, 44(2), 262–276.

Hetzroni, O. & Oren, B. (2002). Effects of intelligence level and place of residence on the ability of individuals with mental retardation to identify facial expressions. *Research in Developmental Disabilities*, 23(6), 369–378.

Heuer, K., Rinck, M. & Becker, E. S. (2007). Avoidance of emotional facial expressions in social anxiety: the approach-avoidance task. *Behaviour Research and Therapy*, 45(12), 2990–3001.

Heywood, C. A. & Cowey, A. (1992). The role of the 'face-cell' area in the discrimination and recognition of faces by monkeys. *Philosophical Transactions of the Royal Society of London. Series B, Biological Sciences*, 335(1273), 31–38.

Hill, H. & Bruce, V. (1996). Effects of lighting on the perception of facial surfaces. *Journal of Experimental Psychology: Human Perception & Performance*, 22(4), 986–1004.

Hill, H. & Johnston, A. (2001). Categorizing sex and identity from the biological motion of faces. *Current Biology*, 11, 880–885.

Hilliar, K. F. & Kemp, R. I. (2008). Barack Obama or Barry Dunham? The appearance of multiracial faces is affected by the names assigned to them. *Perception*, 37(10), 1605–1608.

Hillger, L. A. & Koenig, O. (1991). Separable mechanisms in face processing: evidence for hemispheric specialisation. *Journal of Cognitive Neuroscience*, 3(1), 42–58.

Hills, P. J. & Lewis, M. B. (2008). Testing alternatives to Navon letters to induce a transfer-inappropriate processing shift in face recognition. *European Journal of Cognitive Psychology*, 20(3), 561–576.

Hippolyte, L., Barisnikov, K., Van der Linden, M., et al. (2009). From facial emotional recognition abilities to emotional attribution: a study in Down syndrome. *Research in Developmental Disabilities*, 30(5), 1007–1022.

Hirose, Y. & Hancock, P. J. B. (2007). Equally attending but still not seeing: an eye-tracking study of change detection in own and other-race faces. *Visual Cognition*, 15(6), 647–660.

Hobson, R. P., Ouston, J. & Lee, A. (1988). What's in a face—the case of autism. *British Journal of Psychology*, 79, 441–453.

Hoehl, S., Reid, V. M., Parise, E., et al. (2009). Looking at eye gaze processing and its neural correlates in infancy—implications for social development and autism spectrum disorder. *Child Development*, 80(4), 968–985.

Hoffman, E. A. & Haxby, J. V. (2000). Distinct representations of eye gaze and identity in the distributed human neural system for face perception. *Nature Neuroscience*, 3, 80–84.

Hofmann, S. G., Suvak, M. & Litz, B. T. (2006). Sex differences in face recognition and influence of facial affect. *Personality and Individual Differences*, 40(8), 1683–1690.

Hole, G. J. (1994). Configurational factors in the perception of unfamiliar faces. *Perception*, 23, 65–74.

Hole, G. J., George, P. A. & Dunsmore, V. (1999). Evidence for holistic processing of faces viewed as photographic negatives. *Perception*, 28, 341–359.

Hole, G. J., George, P. A., Eaves, K., et al. (2002). Effects of geometric distortions on face-recognition performance. *Perception*, 31(10), 1221–1240.

Holt, D. J., Kunkel, L., Weiss, A. P., et al. (2006). Increased medial temporal lobe activation during the passive viewing of emotional and neutral facial expressions in schizophrenia. *Schizophrenia Research*, 82(2–3), 153–162.

Hooker, C. & Park, S. (2002). Emotion processing and its relationship to social functioning in schizophrenia patients. *Psychiatry Research*, 112(1), 41–50.

Hope, L. & Wright, D. (2007). Beyond unusual? Examining the role of attention in the Weapon Focus effect. *Applied Cognitive Psychology*, 21, 951–961.

Horley, K., Williams, L. M., Gonsalvez, C., et al. (2004). Face to face: visual scanpath evidence for abnormal processing of facial expressions in social phobia. *Psychiatry Research*, 127(1–2), 43–53.

Horry, R. & Wright, D. B. (2008). I know your face but not where I saw you: context memory is impaired for other race faces. *Psychonomic Bulletin and Review*, 15, 610–614.

Hoss, R. A., Ramsey, J. L., Griffin, A. M., et al. (2005). The role of facial attractiveness and facial masculinity/femininity in sex classification of faces. *Perception*, 34(12), 1459–1474.

Hubl, D., Bolte, S., Feineis-Matthews, S., et al. (2003). Functional imbalance of visual pathways indicates alternative face processing strategies in autism. *Neurology*, 61(9), 1232–1237.

Hugenberg, K., Miller, J. & Claypool, H. M. (2007).Categorization and individuation in the cross-race recognition deficit: toward a solution to an insidious problem. *Journal of Experimental Social Psychology*, 43(2), 334–340.

Hughlings Jackson, J. (1876). Case of large cerebral tumour without optic neuritis and left hemiplegia and imperception. *Royal London Ophthalmic Hospital Reports*, 8, 434.

Humphreys, G. W., Hodsoll, J. & Campbell, C. (2005). Attending but not seeing: the 'other race' effect in face and person perception studied through change blindness. *Visual Cognition*, 12(1), 249–262.

Humphreys, K., Gosselin, F., Schyns, P. G., et al. (2006). Using 'Bubbles' with babies: a new technique for investigating the informational basis of infant perception. *Infant Behavior and Development*, 29(3), 471–475.

Humphreys, K., Minshew, N., Leonard, G. L., et al. (2007). A fine-grained analysis of facial expression processing in high-functioning adults with autism. *Neuropsychologia*, 45(4), 685–695.

Hunnius, S., & Geuze, R. H. (2004). Developmental changes in visual scanning of dynamic faces and abstract stimuli in infants: a longitudinal study. *Infancy*, 6(2), 231–255.

Hunt, C. & Carroll, M. (2008). Verbal Overshadowing Effect: how temporal perspective may exacerbate or alleviate the processing shift. *Applied Cognitive Psychology*, 22, 85–93.

Hunter, Z. R. & Brysbaert, M. (2008). Visual half-field experiments are a good measure of cerebral language dominance if used properly: evidence from fMR1. *Neuropsychologia*, 46(1), 316–325.

Innocence Project News and Information. http://www.innocenceproject.org (accessed 11 February 2010).

Inoue, S., Kondoh, T., Nishihara, M., et al. (2008). Transient prosopagnosia after removal of a tumor in the right occipito-temporal cortex: a case report. *Neurological Surgery, 36*(11), 1023–1027.

Isaacowitz, D. M., Lockenhoff, C. E., Lane, R. D., et al. (2007). Age differences in recognition of emotion in lexical stimuli and facial expressions. *Psychology and Aging,* 22(1), 147–159.

Ishi, H., Gyoba, J., Kamachi, M., et al. (2004). Analyses of facial attractiveness on feminised and juvenilised faces. *Perception*, 33, 135–145.

Ishizu, T., Ayabe, T., & Kojima, S. (2008). Configurational factors in the perception of faces and non-facial objects: an ERP study. *International Journal of Neuroscience*, 118(7), 955–966.

Itier, R. J. & Taylor, M. J. (2002a). Inversion and contrast polarity reversal affect both encoding and recognition processes of unfamiliar faces: a repetition study using ERPs. *Neuroimage*, 15(2), 353–372.

Itier, R. J. & Taylor, M. J. (2002b). Sufficient encoding eliminates performance decrements with inverted and contrast-reversed faces: can ERPs explain why? *Journal of Cognitive Neuroscience*, C85.

Itier, R. J. & Taylor, M. J. (2004a). Effects of repetition and configural changes on the development of face recognition processes. *Developmental Science*, 7(4), 469–487.

Itier, R. J. & Taylor, M. J. (2004b). Effects of repetition learning on upright, inverted and contrast-reversed face processing using ERPs. *Neuroimage*, 21(4), 1518–1532.

Itier, R. J. & Taylor, M. J. (2004c). Face recognition memory and configural processing: a developmental ERP study using upright, inverted, and contrast-reversed faces. *Journal of Cognitive Neuroscience*, 16(3), 487–502.

Itier, R. J. & Taylor, M. J. (2004d). Source analysis of the N170 to faces and objects. *Neuroreport*, 15(8), 1261–1265.

Itier, R. J. & Taylor, M. J. (2004e). N170 or N1? Spatiotemporal differences between object and face processing using ERPs. *Cerebral Cortex*, 14(2), 132–142.

Itier, R. J., Alain, C., Sedore, K., et al. (2007). Early face processing specificity: it's in the eyes! *Journal of Cognitive Neuroscience*, 19(11), 1815–1826.

Itier, R. J., Herdman, A. T., George, N., et al. (2006a). Inversion and contrast-reversal effects on face processing assessed by MEG. *Brain Research*, 1115, 108–120.

Itier, R. J., Latinus, M. & Taylor, M. J. (2006b). Face, eye and object early processing: what is the face specificity? *Neuroimage*, 29(2), 667–676.

Izard, C. E. (1968). Cross-cultural research findings on development in recognition of facial behaviour. *Proceedings of the 76th Annual Convention of the American Psychological Association*, 3, 727.

Izard, C. E. (1971). *The Face of Emotion*. New York: Appleton Century Crofts.

Jacques, C. & Rossion, B. (2006). The speed of individual face categorization. *Psychological Science*, 17(6), 485–492.

Jacques, C. & Rossion, B. (2007). Early electrophysiological responses to multiple face orientations correlate with individual discrimination performance in humans. *Neuroimage*, 36(3), 863–876.

Jacques, C., d'Arripe, O. & Rossion, B. (2007). The time course of the inversion effect during individual face discrimination. *Journal of Vision*, 7(8), 1–9.

Jansari, A., Tranel, D. & Adolphs, R. (2000). A valence-specific lateral bias for discriminating emotional facial expressions in free field. *Cognition & Emotion*, 14(3), 341–353.

Jaquet, E., Rhodes, G. & Hayward, W. G. (2008). Race-contingent aftereffects suggest distinct perceptual norms for different race faces. *Visual Cognition*, 16(6), 734–753.

Jeffery, L., Rhodes, G. & Busey, T. (2006). View-specific coding of face shape. *Psychological Science*, 17(6), 501–505.

Jemel, B., Mottron, L. & Dawson, M. (2006). Impaired face processing in autism: fact or artifact? *Journal of Autism and Developmental Disorders*, 36(1), 91–106.

Jiang, F., Blanz, V. & O'Toole, A. J. (2006). Probing the visual representation of faces with adaptation—a view from the other side of the mean. *Psychological Science*, 17(6), 493–500.

Jiang, F., Blanz, V. & O'Toole, A. J. (2007). The role of familiarity in three-dimensional view-transferability of face identity adaptation. *Vision Research*, 47(4), 525–531.

Jiang, F., Blanz, V. & O'Toole, A. J. (2009). Three-dimensional information in face representations revealed by identity aftereffects. *Psychological Science*, 20(3), 318–325.

Johnson, B., McKenzie, K. & Hamm, J. (2002). Cerebral asymmetry for mental rotation: effects of response hand, handedness and gender. *Neuroreport*, 13(15), 1929–1932.

Johnson, M. H. (2001). The development and neural basis of face recognition: comment and speculation. *Infant and Child Development*, 10, 31–33.

Johnson, M. H. (2005). Subcortical face processing. *Nature Reviews Neuroscience*, 6, 766–774.

Johnson, M. H. & de Haan, M. (2001). Developing cortical specialization for visual–cognitive function: the case of face recognition. In: J. L. McClelland & R. S. Seigler (eds). *Mechanisms of Cognitive Development: Behavioral and Neural Perspectives*, pp 253–270. Mahwah, NJ: Lawrence Erlbaum Associates.

Johnson, M. H. & Humphreys, K. (2007). The development of 'face-space' in infancy. *Visual Cognition*, 15(5), 578–598.

Johnson, M. H. & Morton, J. (1991). *Biology and Cognitive Development: The Case of Face Recognition*. Oxford: Basil Blackwell.

Johnson, M. H., Dziurawiec, S., Ellis, H., et al. (1991). Newborns' preferential tracking of face-like stimuli and its subsequent decline. *Cognition*, 40(1–2), 1–19.

Johnston, A., Hill, H. & Carman, N. (1992). Recognizing faces: effects of lighting direction, inversion and brightness reversal. *Cognition*, 40, 1–19.

Johnston, R. A. & Ellis, H. D. (1995). Age effects in the processing of typical and distinctive faces. *Quarterly Journal of Experimental Psychology*, 48A, 447–465.

Johnston, V. S., Hagel, R., Franklin, M., et al. (2001). Male facial attractiveness—evidence for hormone-mediated adaptive design. *Evolution and Human Behavior*, 22(4), 251–267.

Jokela, M. (2009). Physical attractiveness and reproductive success in humans: evidence from the late 20th century United States. *Evolution and Human Behavior*, 30, 342–350.

Jones, B. C., DeBruine, L. M., Perrett, D. I., et al. (2008). Effects of menstrual cycle phase on face preferences. *Archives of Sexual Behavior*, 37(1), 78–84.

Jones, B. C., Little, A. C., Boothroyd, L., et al. (2005a). Commitment to relationships and preferences for femininity and apparent health in faces are strongest on days of the menstrual cycle when progesterone level is high. *Hormones and Behavior*, 48(3), 283–290.

Jones, B. C., Little, A. C., Burt, D. M., et al. (2004). When facial attractiveness is only skin deep. *Perception*, 33(5), 569–576.

Jones, B. C., Perrett, D. I., Little, A. C., et al. (2005b). Menstrual cycle, pregnancy and oral contraceptive use alter attraction to apparent health in faces. *Proceedings of the Royal Society of London. Series B, Biological Sciences*, 272(1561), 347–354.

Jones, D. (1995). Sexual selection, physical attractiveness, and facial neoteny: cross-cultural evidence and implications. *Current Anthropology*, 36, 723–748.

Jones, G. & Smith, P. K. (1984). The eyes have it: young children's discrimination of age in masked and unmasked facial photographs. *Journal of Experimental Child Psychology*, 38, 328–337.

Joormann, J. & Gotlib, I. H. (2006). Is this happiness I see? Biases in the identification of emotional facial expressions in depression and social phobia. *Journal of Abnormal Psychology*, 115(4), 705–714.

Joseph, R. M. & Tanaka, J. (2003). Holistic and part-based face recognition in children with autism. *Journal of Child Psychology and Psychiatry and Allied Disciplines*, 44(4), 529–542.

Joshua, N. & Rossell, S. (2009). Configural face processing in schizophrenia. *Schizophrenia Research*, 112(1–3), 99–103.

Joubert, S., Felician, O., Barbeau, E., et al. (2003). Impaired configurational processing in a case of progressive prosopagnosia associated with predominant right temporal lobe atrophy. *Brain*, 126, 2537–2550.

Kampf, M., Nachson, I. & Babkoff, H. (2002). A serial test of the laterality of familiar face recognition. *Brain and Cognition*, 50(1), 35–50.

Kan, Y., Mimura, M., Kamijima, K., et al. (2004). Recognition of emotion from moving facial and prosodic stimuli in depressed patients. *Journal of Neurology Neurosurgery and Psychiatry*, 75(12), 1667–1671.

Kanwisher, N. & Yovel, G. (2006). The fusiform face area: a cortical region specialized for the perception of faces. *Philosophical Transactions of the Royal Society of London. Series B, Biological Sciences*, 361(1476), 2109–2128.

Kanwisher, N., McDermott, J. & Chun, M. M. (1997). The fusiform face area: a module in human extrastriate cortex specialized for face perception. *Journal of Neuroscience*, 17(11), 4302–4311.

Kanwisher, N., Stanley, D. & Harris, A. (1999). The fusiform face area is selective for faces not animals. *Neuroreport*, 10(1), 183–187.

Kanwisher, N., Tong, F. & Nakayama, K. (1998). The effect of face inversion on the human fusiform face area. *Cognition*, 68(1), B1–B11.

Karmiloff-Smith, A., Thomas, M., Annaz, D., et al. (2004). Exploring the Williams syndrome face-processing debate: the importance of building developmental trajectories. *Journal of Child Psychology and Psychiatry*, 45(7), 1258–1274.

Karpov, B. A., Meerson, Y. A. & Tonkonogh, I. M. (1979). On some peculiarities of the visuomotor system in visual agnosia. *Neuropsychologia*, 17, 281–294.

Katsyri, J., Saalasti, S., Tiippana, K., et al. (2008). Impaired recognition of facial emotions from low-spatial frequencies in Asperger syndrome. *Neuropsychologia*, 46(7), 1888–1897.

Kaufmann, J. M. & Schweinberger, S. R. (2004). Expression influences the recognition of familiar faces. *Perception*, 33(4), 399–408.

Kaufmann, J. M. & Schweinberger, S. R. (2008). Distortions in the brain? ERP effects of caricaturing familiar and unfamiliar faces. *Brain Research,* 1228, 177–188.

Kaufmann, J. M., Schweinberger, S. R. & Burton, A. M. (2009). N250 ERP correlates of the acquisition of face representations across different images. *Journal of Cognitive Neuroscience*, 21(4), 625–641.

Kee, K. S., Horan, W. P., Wynn, J. K., et al. (2006). An analysis of categorical perception of facial emotion in schizophrenia. *Schizophrenia Research*, 87(1–3), 228–237.

Keenan, J. P., Wheeler, M., Platek, S. M., et al. (2003). Self-face processing in a callosotomy patient. *European Journal of Neuroscience*, 18(8), 2391–2395.

Keightley, M. L., Winocur, G., Burianova, H., et al. (2006). Age effects on social cognition: faces tell a different story. *Psychology and Aging*, 21(3), 558–572.

Kelly, D. J., Quinn, P. C., Slater, A. M., et al. (2005). Three-month-olds, but not newborns, prefer own-race faces. *Developmental Science*, 8(6), F31–F36.

Kelly, D. J., Quinn, P. C., Slater, A. M., et al. (2007). The other-race effect develops during infancy: evidence of perceptual narrowing. *Psychological Science*, 18(12), 1084–1089.

Kemp, R., McManus, C. & Pigott, T. (1990). Sensitivity to the displacement of facial features in negative and inverted images. *Perception*, 19, 531–543.

Kemp, R., Pike, G., White, P. & Musselman, A. (1996). Perception and recognition of normal and negative faces: the role of shape from shading and pigmentation. *Perception*, 25, 37–52.

Kemp, R., Towell, N. & Pike, G. (1997). When seeing should not be believing: photographs, credit cards and fraud. *Applied Cognitive Psychology*, 11(3), 211–222.

Kessler, R. C., Demler, O., Frank, R. G., et al. (2005). Prevalence and treatment of mental disorders, 1990 to 2003. *New England Journal of Medicine*, 352(24), 2515–2523.

Kiffel, C., Campanella, S. & Bruyer, R. (2005). Categorical perception of faces and facial expressions: ehe age factor. *Experimental Aging Research*, 31(2), 119–147.

Killgore, W. D. S. & Yurgelun-Todd, D. A. (2005). Social anxiety predicts amygdala activation in adolescents viewing fearful faces. *Neuroreport*, 16(15), 1671–1675.

Kim, J. S., Yoon, H. W., Kim, B. S., et al. (2006). Racial distinction of the unknown facial identity recognition mechanism by event-related fMRI. *Neuroscience Letters*, 397(3), 279–284.

Kingstone, A. (2009). Taking a real look at social attention. *Current Opinion in Neurobiology*, 19, 52–56.

Klein, S. B., Gabriel, R. H., Gangi, C. E., et al. (2008). Reflections on the Self: a case study of a prosopagnosic patient. *Social Cognition*, 26(6), 766–777.

Kleiner, K. A. (1987). Amplitude and phase spectra as indices of infants' pattern preferences. *Infant Behavior and Development*, 10, 49–59.

Kleiner, K. A. (1990). Models of neonates' preferences for facelike patterns: a response to Morton, Johnson, and Maurer. *Infant Behavior and Development*, 13, 105–108.

Kleiner, K. A. & Banks, M. S. (1987). Stimulus energy does not account for 2-month-old's preferences. *Journal of Experimental Psychology: Human Perception and Performance*, 13, 594–600.

Kloth, N., Dobel, C., Schweinberger, S. R., et al. (2006). Effects of personal familiarity on early neuromagnetic correlates of face perception. *European Journal of Neuroscience*, 24(11), 3317–3321.

Knight B. & Johnston, A. (1997). The role of movement in face recognition. *Visual Cognition*, 4, 265–273.

Kobayashi, H. & Kohshima, S. (1997). Unique morphology of the human eye. *Nature*, 387, 767–768.

Kobayashi, H. & Kohshima, S. (2001). Unique morphology of the human eye and its adaptive meaning: comparative studies on external morphology of the primate eye. *Journal of Human Evolution*, 40, 419–435.

Koehn, C. E. & Fisher, R. P. (1997). Constructing facial composites with the Mac-a-Mug Pro system. *Psychology, Crime and Law*, 3, 215–224.

Kolassa, I. T., Kolassa, S., Musial, F., et al. (2007). Event-related potentials to schematic faces in social phobia. *Cognition & Emotion*, 21(8), 1721–1744.

Kolassa, I. T. & Miltner, W. H. R. (2006). Psychophysiological correlates of face processing in social phobia. *Brain Research*, 1118, 130–141.

Koster, E. H. W., Leyman, L., De Raedt, R., et al. (2006). Cueing of visual attention by emotional facial expressions: the influence of individual differences in anxiety and depression. *Personality and Individual Differences*, 41(2), 329–339.

Kotsoni, E., de Haan, M. & Johnson, M. H. (2001). Categorical perception of facial expressions by 7-month-old infants. *Perception*, 30(9), 1115–1125.

Kouider, S., Eger, E., Dolan, R., et al. (2009). Activity in face-responsive brain regions is modulated by invisible, attended faces: evidence from masked priming. *Cerebral Cortex*, 19(1), 13–23.

Kovacs, G., Gulyas, B., Savic, I., et al. (2004). Smelling human sex hormone-like compounds affects face gender judgment of men. *Neuroreport*, 15(8), 1275–1277.

Kovera, M. B., Penrod, S. D., Pappas, C., et al. (1997). Identification of computer generated facial composites. *Journal of Applied Psychology*, 82, 235–246.

Kracke, I. (1994). Developmental prosopagnosia in Asperger syndrome—presentation and discussion of an individual case. *Developmental Medicine and Child Neurology*, 36(10), 873–886.

Krolak-Salmon, P., Fischer, C., Vighetto, A., et al. (2001). Processing of facial emotional expression: spatio-temporal data as assessed by scalp event-related potentials. *European Journal of Neuroscience*, 13(5), 987–994.

Krolak-Salmon, P., Henaff, M. A., Isnard, J., et al. (2003). An attention modulated response to disgust in human ventral anterior insula. *Annals of Neurology*, 53(4), 446–453.

Kucharska-Pietura, K. & David, A. S. (2003). The perception of emotional chimeric faces in patients with depression, mania and unilateral brain damage. *Psychological Medicine*, 33(4), 739–745.

Kucharska-Pietura, K., David, A. S., Masiak, M., et al. (2005). Perception of facial and vocal affect by people with schizophrenia in early and late stages of illness. *British Journal of Psychiatry*, 187, 523–528.

Kuczaj, S. A. & Lederberg, A. R. (1976). Height, age, and function: differing influences on children's comprehension of 'younger' and 'older'. *Journal of Child Language*, 4, 395–416.

Kuefner, D., Macchi Cassia, V., Picozzi, M., et al. (2008). Do all kids look alike? Evidence for an other-age effect in adults. *Journal of Experimental Psychology: Human Perception and Performance*, 34(4), 811–817.

Kuhn, G. & Kingstone, A. (2009). Look away! Eyes and arrows engage oculomotor responses automatically. *Perception and Psychophysics*, 71(2), 314–327.

Kuhn, G. & Land, M. F. (2006). There's more to magic than meets the eye! *Current Biology*, 16(22), R950–R951.

Kuhn, G. & Tatler, B. W. (2005). Magic and fixation: now you don't see it, now you do. *Perception*, 34(9), 1155–1161.

Kuhn, G., Amlani, A. A. & Rensink, R. R. (2008). Towards a science of magic. *Trends in Cognitive Sciences*, 12, 349–354.

Kuhn, G., Tatler, B. W. & Cole, G. G. (2009). You look where I look! Effect of gaze cues on overt and covert attention in misdirection. *Visual Cognition*, 17(6), 925–944.

Kuhn, G., Tatler, B. W., Findlay, J. M., et al. (2008). Misdirection in magic: implications for the relationship between eye gaze and attention. *Visual Cognition*, 16(2/3), 391–405.

Kylliainen, A., Braeutigam, S., Hietanen, J. K., et al. (2006). Face- and gaze-sensitive neural responses in children with autism: a magnetoencephalographic study. *European Journal of Neuroscience*, 24(9), 2679–2690.

Lacreuse, A., Martin-Malivel, J., Lange, H. S., et al. (2007). Effects of the menstrual cycle on looking preferences for faces in female rhesus monkeys. *Animal Cognition*, 10(2), 105–115.

Lacroix, A., Guidetti, M., Roge, B., et al. (2009). Recognition of emotional and nonemotional facial expressions: a comparison between Williams syndrome and autism. *Research in Developmental Disabilities*, 30(5), 976–985.

Lades, M., Vortbrüggen, J. C., Buhmann, J., et al. (1993). Distortion invariant object recognition in the dynamic link architecture. *IEEE Transactions on Computers*, 42, 300–311.

Lahaie, A., Mottron, L., Arguin, A., et al. (2006). Face perception in high-functioning autistic adults: evidence for superior processing of face parts, not for a configural face-processing deficit. *Neuropsychology*, 20(1), 30–41.

Lamont, A. V., Stewart-Williams, S. & Podd, J. (2005). Face recognition and aging: effects of target age and memory load. *Memory and Cognition*, 33(6), 1017–1024.

Lander, K. & Bruce, V. (2000). Recognizing famous faces: exploring the benefits of facial motion. *Ecological Psychology*, 12, 259–272.

Lander, K. & Bruce, V. (2003). The role of motion in learning new faces. *Visual Cognition*, 10, 897–912.

Lander, K. & Bruce, V. (2004). Repetition priming from moving faces. *Memory and Cognition*, 32, 640–647.

Lander, K. & Chuang, L. (2005). Why are moving faces easier to recognize? *Visual Cognition*, 12, 429–442.

Lander, K. & Metcalfe, S. (2007). The influence of positive and negative facial expressions on face familiarity. *Memory*, 15(1), 63–69.

Lander, K., Bruce, V. & Hill, H. (2001). Evaluating the effectiveness of pixelation and blurring on masking the identity of familiar faces. *Applied Cognitive Psychology*, 15, 101–116.

Lander, K., Christie, F. & Bruce, V. (1999). The role of movement in the recognition of famous faces. *Memory and Cognition*, 27, 974–985.

Landis, T., Regard, M., Bliestle, A., et al. (1988). Prosopagnosia and agnosia for noncanonical views—an autopsied case. *Brain*, 111, 1287–1297.

Langenecker, S. A., Bieliauskas, L. A., Rapport, L. J., et al. (2005). Face emotion perception and executive functioning deficits in depression. *Journal of Clinical and Experimental Neuropsychology*, 27(3), 320–333.

Langlois, J. H. & Roggman, L. A. (1990). Attractive faces are only average. *Psychological Science*, 1(2),115–121.

Langlois, J. H., Kalakanis, L., Rubenstein, A. J., et al. (2000). Maxims or myths of beauty? A meta-analytic and theoretical review. *Psychological Bulletin*, 126, 390–423.

Langlois J. H., Roggman, L. A., Casey, R. J., et al. (1987). Infant preferences for attractive faces: rudiments of a stereotype? *Developmental Psychology*, 23, 363–369.

Langton, S. R. H. (2000). The mutual influence of gaze and head orientation in the analysis of social attention direction. *Quarterly Journal of Experimental Psychology Series A*, 53, 825–845.

Langton, S. R. H. & Bruce, V. (1999). Reflexive visual orienting in response to the social attention of others. *Visual Cognition*, 6, 541–568.

Langton, S. R. H., Watt, R. J. & Bruce, V. (2000). Do the eyes have it? Cues to the directionof social attention. *Trends in Cognitive Sciences*, 4(2), 50–59.

Large, M. E., Cavina-Pratesi, C., Vilis, T., et al. (2008). The neural correlates of change detection in the face perception network. *Neuropsychologia*, 46(8), 2169–2176.

Larner, A. J. (2004). Lewis Carroll's Humpty Dumpty: an early report of prosopagnosia? *Journal of Neurology, Neurosurgery, and Psychiatry*, 75, 1063.

Latinus, M. & Taylor, M. J. (2006). Face processing stages: impact of difficulty and the separation of effects. *Brain Research*, 1123, 179–187.

Laughery, K. & Fowler, R. (1980). Sketch artist and Identikit procedures for recalling faces. *Journal of Applied Psychology*, 65, 307–316.

Lawrence, K., Bernstein, D., Pearson, R., et al. (2008). Changing abilities in recognition of unfamiliar face photographs through childhood and adolescence: performance on a test of non-verbal immediate memory (Warrington RMF) from 6 to 16 years. *Journal of Neuropsychology*, 2, 27–45.

Lawson, R. (2007). Local and global processing biases fail to influence face, object, and word recognition. *Visual Cognition*, 15(6), 710–740.

Le Grand, R., Mondloch, C. J., Maurer, D., et al. (2001). Neuroperception—early visual experience and face processing. *Nature*, 410(6831), 890.

Le Grand, R., Mondloch, C. J., Maurer, D., et al. (2004). Impairment in holistic face processing following early visual deprivation. *Psychological Science*, 15(11), 762–768.

Leber, S., Heidenreich, T., Stangier, U., et al. (2009). Processing of facial affect under social threat in socially anxious adults: mood matters. *Depression and Anxiety*, 26(2), 196–206.

Leder, H. (1996). Line drawings of faces reduce configural processing. *Perception*, 25, 355–366.

Leder, H. & Bruce, V. (2000). When inverted faces are recognised: the role of configural information in face recognition. *Quarterly Journal of Experimental Psychology: Human Experimental Psychology*, 53, 513–536.

Lederman, S. J., Kilgour, A., Kitada, R., et al. (2007). Haptic face processing. *Canadian Journal of Experimental Psychology*, 61(3), 230–241.

Lee, C. U., Shenton, M. E., Salisbury, D. F., et al. (2002). Fusiform gyrus volume reduction in first-episode schizophrenia—a magnetic resonance imaging study. *Archives of General Psychiatry*, 59(9), 775–781.

Leehey, S. C. & Cahn, A. (1979). Lateral asymmetries in the recognition of words, familiar faces and unfamiliar faces. *Neuropsychologia*, 17, 619–627.

Leehey, S. C., Carey, S., Diamond, R., et al. (1978). Upright and inverted faces: the right hemisphere knows the difference. *Cortex*, 14, 411–419.

Leo, I. & Simion, F. (2009). Face processing at birth: a Thatcher illusion study. *Developmental Science*, 12(3), 492–498.

Leopold, D. A., O'Toole, A. J., Vetter, T., et al. (2001). Prototype-referenced shape encoding revealed by high-level after effects. *Nature Neuroscience*, 4(1), 89–94.

Leppänen, J. M., Kauppinen, P., Peltola, M. J., et al. (2007). Differential electrocortical responses to increasing intensities of fearful and happy emotional expressions. *Brain Research*, 1166, 103–109.

Leppänen, J. M., Milders, M., Bell, J. S., et al. (2004). Depression biases the recognition of emotionally neutral faces. *Psychiatry Research*, 128(2), 123–133.

Letourneau, S. M. & Mitchell, T. V. (2008). Behavioral and ERP measures of holistic face processing in a composite task. *Brain and Cognition*, 67(2), 234–245.

Leveroni, C. L., Seidenberg, M., Mayer, A. R., et al. (2000). Neural systems underlying the recognition of familiar and newly learned faces. *Journal of Neuroscience*, 20(2), 878–886.

Levin D. T. (1996). Classifying faces by race: the structure of face categories. *Journal of Experimental Psychology: Learning, Memory, & Cognition*, 22, 1364–1382.

Levin, D. T. (2000). Race as a visual feature: using visual search and perceptual discrimination tasks to understand face categories and the cross-race recognition deficit. *Journal of Experimental Psychology: General*, 129, 559–574.

Levy, Y. & Bentin, S. (2008). Interactive processes in matching identity and expressions of unfamiliar faces: evidence for mutual facilitation effects. *Perception*, 37(6), 915–930.

Levy, J., Heller, W., Banich, M. T., et al. (1983). Asymmetry of perception in free viewing of chimeric faces. *Brain and Cognition*, 2, 404–419.

Levy, J., Trevarthen, C. & Sperry, R. W. (1972). Perception of bilateral chimeric figures following hemispheric disconnection. *Brain*, 95, 61–78.

Lewin, C. & Herlitz, A. (2002). Sex differences in face recognition—women's faces make the difference. *Brain and Cognition*, 50(1), 121–128.

Lewin, C., Wolgers, G. & Herlitz, A. (2001). Sex differences favoring women in verbal but not in visuospatial episodic memory. *Neuropsychology*, 15(2), 165–173.

Lewis, M. B. (2001). The Lady's not for turning. Rotation of the Thatcher illusion. *Perception*, 30, 769–774.

Lewis, M. B. & Johnston, R. A. (1998). Understanding caricatures of faces. *Quarterly Journal of Experimental Psychology*, 50A, 321–346.

Lewis, M. B. & Johnston, R. A. (1999a). A unified account of the effects of caricaturing faces. *Visual Cognition*, 6(1), 1–41.

Lewis, M. B. & Johnston, R. A. (1999b). Are caricatures special? Evidence of peak shift in face recognition. *European Journal of Cognitive Psychology*, 11(1), 105–117.

Lieberman, D., Tooby, J. & Cosmides, L. (2007). The architecture of human kin detection. *Nature*, 445, 727–731.

Light, L. L., Hollander S. & Kayra-Stuart, F. (1981). Why attractive people are harder to remember. *Personaity and Social Psychology Bulletin*, 7, 269–276.

Lindsay, D. S., Jack, P. C. & Christian, M. A. (1991). Other-race face perception. *Journal of Applied Psychology*, 76(4), 587–589.

Lindsay, R. C. L., Martin, R. & Webber, L. (1994). Default values in eyewitness descriptions: a problem for the match-to-description lineup foil selection strategy. *Law and Human Behavior*, 18, 527–541.

Lipp, O. V., Price, S. M. & Tellegen, C. L. (2009). No effect of inversion on attentional and affective processing of facial expressions. *Emotion*, 9(2), 248–259.

Lippa, R. A. (2007). The preferred traits of mates in a cross-national study of heterosexual and homosexual men and women: an examination of biological and cultural influences. *Archives of Sexual Behavior*, 36, 193–208.

Little, A. C. & Hancock, P. J. B. (2002). The role of masculinity and distinctiveness in judgments of human male facial attractiveness. *British Journal of Psychology*, 93, 451–464.

Little, A. C. & Perrett, D. I. (2007). Using composite images to assess accuracy in personality attribution to faces. *British Journal of Psychology*, 98, 111–126.

Little, A. C., DeBruine, L. M. & Jones, B. C. (2005). Sex-contingent face after-effects suggest distinct neural populations code male and female faces. *Proceedings of the Royal Society of London. Series B: Biological Sciences*, 272(1578), 2283–2287.

Little, A. C., DeBruine, L. M., Jones, B. C., et al. (2008a). Category contingent aftereffects for faces of different races, ages and species. *Cognition*, 106(3), 1537–1547.

Little, A. C., Jones, B. C. & Burriss, R. P. (2007a). Preferences for masculinity in male bodies change across the menstrual cycle. *Hormones and Behavior*, 51(5), 633–639.

Little, A. C., Jones, B. C. & DeBruine, L. M. (2008b). Preferences for variation in masculinity in real male faces change across the menstrual cycle: women prefer more masculine faces when they are more fertile. *Personality and Individual Differences*, 45(6), 478–482.

Little, A. C., Jones, B. C., Burt, D. M., et al. (2007b). Preferences for symmetry in faces change across the menstrual cycle. *Biological Psychology*, 76(3), 209–216.

Little, A. C., Jones, B. C., Waitt, C., et al. (2008c). Symmetry is related to sexual dimorphism in faces: data across culture and species. *PLoS ONE*, 3(5), 1–8.

Liu, C. H. & Chaudhuri, A. (2002). Reassessing the 3/4 view effect in face recognition. *Cognition*, 83(1), 31–48.

Liu, C. H., Bhuiyan, Md. A.-A., Ward, J., et al. (2009). Transfer between pose and illumination training in face recognition. *Journal of Experimental Psychology: Human Perception and Performance*, 39, 939–947.

Liu, C. H., Seetzen, H., Burton, A. M., et al. (2003). Face recognition is robust with incongruent image resolution. *Journal of Experimental Psychology: Applied*, 9(1), 33–41.

Lobmaier, J. S., Klaver, P., Loenneker, T., et al. (2008). Featural and configural face processing strategies: evidence from a functional magnetic resonance imaging study. *Neuroreport*, 19(3), 287–291.

Loftus, E. F., Loftus, G. R. & Messo, J. (1987). Some facts about 'weapon focus'. *Law and Human Behavior*, 11, 55–62.

Loftus, E. F., Schooler, J. W., Boone, S. M., et al. (1987). Time went by so slowly: overestimation of event duration by males and females. *Applied Cognitive Psychology*, 1, 3–13.

Losh, M., Bellugi, U., Reilly, J., et al. (2000). Narrative as a social engagement tool: the excessive use of evaluation in narratives from children with Williams syndrome. *Narrative Inquiry*, 10(2), 265–290.

Loughland, C. M., Williams, L. M. & Gordon, E. (2002). Visual scanpaths to positive and negative facial emotions in an outpatient schizophrenia sample. *Schizophrenia Research*, 55(1–2), 159–170.

Lutchmaya, S., Baron-Cohen, S., Raggatt, P., et al. (2004). 2nd to 4th digit ratios, fetal testosterone and estradiol. *Early Human Development*, 77(1–2), 23–28.

Luus, C. A. E. & Wells, G. L. (1991). Eyewitness identification and the selection of distracters for lineups. *Law and Human Behavior*, 15, 43–57.

Luus, C. A. E. & Wells, G. L. (1994). Determinants of eyewitness confidence. In: D. F. Ross, J. D. Read & M. P. Toglia (eds), *Adult Eyewitness Testimony: Current Trends and Developments*, pp 348–362. New York: Cambridge University Press.

Lynn, S. K. & Salisbury, D. F. (2008). Attenuated modulation of the N170 ERP by facial expressions in schizophrenia. *Clinical EEG and Neuroscience*, 39(2), 108–111.

McAnany, J. J. & Levine, M. W. (2007). Magnocellular and parvocellular visual pathway contributions to visual field anisotropies. *Vision Research*, 47, 2327–2336.

McBain, R., Norton, D. & Chen, Y. (2009). Females excel at basic face perception. *Acta Psychologica*, 130(2), 168–173.

McCarthy, G., Puce, A., Gore, J. C., et al. (1997). Face-specific processing in the human fusiform gyrus. *Journal of Cognitive Neuroscience*, 9(5), 605–610.

Macchi Cassia, V., Picozzi, M., Kuefner, D., et al. (2009a). Holistic processing for faces and cars in preschool-aged children and adults: evidence from the composite effect. *Developmental Science*, 12(2), 236–248.

Macchi Cassia, V., Picozzi, M., Kuefner, D., et al. (2009b). Why mix-ups don't happen in the nursery: evidence for an experience-based interpretation of the other-age effect. *Quarterly Journal of Experimental Psychology*, 62(6), 1099–1107.

Macchi Cassia, V., Turati, C. & Simion, F. (2004). Can a non specific bias toward top-heavy patterns explain newborns' face preference? *Psychological Science*, 15, 379–383.

McCarthy, G., Puce, A., Belger, A., et al. (1999). Electrophysiological studies of human face perception. II: Response properties of face-specific potentials generated in occipitotemporal cortex. *Cerebral Cortex*, 9(5), 431–444.

McClure, E. B. (2000). A meta-analytic review of sex differences in facial expression processing and their development in infants, children, and adolescents. *Psychological Bulletin*, 126(3), 424–453.

McCrae, R. R. & Costa, P. T. (1997). Personality trait structure as a human universal. *American Psychologist*, 52(5), 509–516.

McCullough, S. & Emmorey, K. (2009). Categorical perception of affective and linguistic facial expressions. *Cognition*, 110, 208–221.

Macefield, V. G. (2009). Developments in autonomic research: a review of the latest literature. *Clinical Autonomic Research*, 19(3), 133–136.

McGivern, R. F., Andersen, J., Byrd, D., et al. (2002). Cognitive efficiency on a match to sample task decreases at the onset of puberty in children. *Brain and Cognition*, 50, 73–89.

McKone, E. (2004). Isolating the special component of face recognition: peripheral identification and a Mooney face. *Journal of Experimental Psychology: Learning, Memory, and Cognition*, 30, 181–197.

McKone, E. (2008). Configural processing and face viewpoint. *Journal of Experimental Psychology: Human Perception and Performance*, 34(2), 310–327.

McKone, E. & Robbins, R. (2007). The evidence rejects the expertise hypothesis: reply to Gauthier & Bukach. *Cognition*, 103(2), 331–336.

McKone, E., Brewer, J. L., MacPherson, S., et al. (2007a). Familiar other-race faces show normal holistic processing and are robust to perceptual stress. *Perception*, 36, 224–248.

McKone, E., Kanwisher, N. & Duchaine, B. C. (2007b). Can generic expertise explain special processing for faces? *Trends in Cognitive Sciences*, 11(1), 8–15.

MacLin, O. H. & Malpass, R. S. (2001). Racial categorization of faces: the ambiguous-race face effect. *Psychology, Public Policy and Law*, 7, 98–118.

MacLin, O. H. & Malpass, R. S. (2003). Last but not least: the ambiguous-race face illusion. *Perception*, 32, 249–252.

McMullen, P. A., Fisk, J. D., Phillips, S. J., et al. (2000). Apperceptive agnosia and face recognition. *Neurocase*, 6(5), 403–414.

McNeil, J. E. & Warrington, E. K. (1993). Prosopagnosia: a face-specific disorder. *Quarterly Journal of Experimental Psychology: Human Experimental Psychology*, 46A(1), 1–10.

McPartland, J., Dawson, G., Webb, S. J., et al. (2004). Event-related brain potentials reveal anomalies in temporal processing of faces in autism spectrum disorder. *Journal of Child Psychology and Psychiatry*, 45(7), 1235–1245.

MacPherson, S. E., Phillips, L. H. & Della Sala, S. (2006). Age-related differences in the ability to perceive sad facial expressions. *Aging Clinical and Experimental Research*, 18(5), 418–424.

McQuiston-Surrett, D., Malpass, R. S. & Tredoux, C. G. (2006). Sequential vs. simultaneous lineups: a review of methods, data, and theory. *Psychology, Public Policy, and Law*, 12(2), 137–169.

Macrae, C. N. & Lewis, H. L. (2002). Do I know you? Processing orientation and face recognition. *Psychological Science*, 13(2), 194–196.

Macrae, C. N. & Martin, D. (2007). A boy primed Sue: feature-based processing and person construal. *European Journal of Social Psychology*, 37(5), 793–805.

Macrae, C. N., Alnwick, K. A., Milne, A. B., et al. (2002). Person perception across the menstrual cycle: hormonal influences on social-cognitive functioning. *Psychological Science*, 13(6), 532–536.

Malhi, G. S., Lagopoulos, J., Sachdev, P. S., et al. (2007). Is a lack of disgust something to fear? A functional magnetic resonance imaging facial emotion recognition study in euthymic bipolar disorder patients. *Bipolar Disorders*, 9(4), 345–357.

Malone, D. R., Morris, H. H., Kay, M. C., et al. (1982). Prosopagnosia: a double dissociation between the recognition of familiar and unfamiliar faces. *Journal of Neurology, Neurosurgery and Psychiatry*, 45, 820–822.

Maloney, L. T. & Dal Martello, M. F. (2006). Kin recognition and the perceived facial similarity of children. *Journal of Vision*, 6(10), 1047–1056.

Malpass, R. S. & Devine, P. G. (1981). Eyewitness identification: lineup instructions and the absence of the offender. *Journal of Applied Psychology*, 66, 482–489.

Malpass, R. S. & Kravitz, J. (1969). Recognition for faces of own and other-race. *Journal of Personality and Social Psychology*, 13, 300–334.

Manning, J. T., Scutt, D., Wilson, J., et al. (1998). The ratio of 2nd to 4th digit length: a predictor of sperm numbers and concentrations of testosterone, luteinizing hormone and oestrogen. *Human Reproduction*, 13(11), 3000–3004.

Mark, L. S. & Todd, J. T. (1983). The perception of growth in three dimensions. *Perception and Psychophysics*, 33(2), 193–196.

Mark, L. S. & Todd, J. T. (1985). Describing perceptual information about human growth in terms of geometric invariants. *Perception and Psychophysics*, 37(3), 245–256.

Mark, L. S., Pittenger, J. B., Hines, H., et al. (1980). Wrinkling and head shape as coordinated sources of age-level information. *Perception and Psychophysics*, 27(2), 117–124.

Marotta, J. J., Genovese, C. R. & Behrmann, M. (2001). A functional MRI study of face recognition in patients with prosopagnosia. *Neuroreport*, 12(8), 1581–1587.

Marotta, J. J., McKeeff, T. J. & Behrmann, M. (2002). The effects of rotation and inversion on face processing in prosopagnosia. *Cognitive Neuropsychology,* 19(1), 31–47.

Marotta, J. J., Voyvodic, J. T., Gauthier, I., et al. (1999). A functional MRI study of face recognition in patients with prosopagnosia. *Cognitive Neuroscience Society*, 83.

Marr, D. (1982). *Vision*. New York: W. H. Freeman.

Marsh, A. A., Kozak, M. N. & Ambady, N. (2007). Accurate identification of fear facial expressions predicts prosocial behavior. *Emotion*, 7(2), 239–251.

Marsh, P. J. & Williams, L. M. (2006). ADHD and schizophrenia phenomenology: visual scanpaths to emotional faces as a potential psychophysiological marker? *Neuroscience and Biobehavioral Reviews*, 30(5), 651–665.

Martens, M. A., Wilson, S. J. & Reutens, D. C. (2008). Research Review: Williams syndrome: a critical review of the cognitive, behavioral, and neuroanatomical phenotype. *Journal of Child Psychology and Psychiatry*, 49(6), 576–608.

Martin, F., Baudouin, J. Y., Tiberghien, G., et al. (2005). Processing emotional expression and facial identity in schizophrenia. *Psychiatry Research*, 134(1), 43–53.

Marwick, K. & Hall, J. (2008). Social cognition in schizophrenia: a review of face processing. *British Medical Bulletin*, 88(1), 43–58.

Marzi, T. & Viggiano, M. P. (2007). Interplay between familiarity and orientation in face processing: an ERP study. *International Journal of Psychophysiology*, 65(3), 182–192.

Masten, C. L., Guyer, A. E., Hodgdon, H. B., et al. (2008). Recognition of facial emotions among maltreated children with high rates of post-traumatic stress disorder. *Child Abuse & Neglect*, 32(1), 139–153.

Mattson, A. J., Levin, H. S. & Graman, J. (2000). A case of prosopagnosia following moderate closed head injury with left hemisphere focal lesion. *Cortex*, 36, 125–137.

Maurer, D. (1985). Infants' perception of facedness. In: T. M. Field and N. Fox (eds), *Social Perception in Infants*, pp 73–100. Norwood, NJ: Ablex Publishing.

Maurer, D. & Barrera, M. (1981). Infants' perception of natural and distorted arrangements of a schematic face. *Child Development*, 52(1), 196–202.

Maurer, D. and Salapatek, P. (1976). Developmental changes in the scanning of faces by young infants. *Child Development*, 47, 523–527.

Maurer, D. & Young, R. E. (1983). Newborns' following of natural and distorted arrangements of facial features. *Infant Behavior & Development*, 6(1), 127–131.

Maurer, D., Le Grand, R. & Mondloch, C. J. (2002). The many faces of configural processing. *Trends in Cognitive Sciences*, 6, 255–260.

Maurer, D., Mondloch, C. J. & Lewis, T. L. (2007). Effects of early visual deprivation on perceptual and cognitive development. *From Action to Cognition*, 164, 87–104.

Meadows, J. C. (1974). The anatomical basis of prosopagnosia. *Journal of Neurology, Neurosurgery and Psychiatry*, 37(5), 489–501.

Mecklenberg, S. H. (2006). Report to the legislature of the State of Illinois: the Illinois Pilot Program on sequential double-blind identification procedures. http://www. chicagopolice.org/IL%20Pilot%20on%20 Eyewitness%20ID.pdf (accessed 28 September 2009).

Megreya, A. M. & Burton, A. M. (2006a). Recognising faces seen alone or with others: when two heads are worse than one. *Applied Cognitive Psychology*, 20, 957–972.

Megreya, A. M. & Burton, A. M. (2006b). Unfamiliar faces aren't faces: evidence from a matching task. *Memory and Cognition*, 34(4), 865–876.

Megreya, A. M. & Burton, A. M. (2007). Hits and false positives in face matching: a familiarity based dissociation. *Perception and Psychophysics*, 69, 1175–1184.

Megreya, A. M. & Burton, A. M. (2008). Matching faces to photographs: poor performance in eyewitness memory (without the memory). *Journal of Experimental Psychology: Applied*, 14(4), 364–372.

Meissner, C. A. (2002). Applied aspects of the instructional bias effect in verbal overshadowing. *Applied Cognitive Psychology*, 16, 911–928.

Meissner, C. A. & Brigham, J. C. (2001a). Thirty years of investigating the own-race bias in memory for faces: a meta-analytic review. *Psychology, Public Policy, and Law*, 7, 335.

Meissner, C. A. & Brigham, J. C. (2001b). A meta-analysis of the verbal overshadowing effect in face identification. *Applied Cognitive Psychology*, 15, 603–616.

Meissner, C. A., Brigham, J. C. & Butz, D. A. (2005). Memory for own- and other-race faces: a dual-process approach. *Applied Cognitive Psychology*, 19, 545–567.

Meissner, C. A., Brigham, J. C. & Kelley, C. M. (2001). The influence of retrieval processes in verbal overshadowing. *Memory and Cognition*, 29(1), 176–186.

Meissner, C. A., Sporer, S. L. & Schooler, J. W. (2007). Person descriptions as eyewitness evidence. In: R. C. L. Lindsay, D. F. Ross, J. D. Read & M. P. Toglia (eds), *Handbook of Eyewitness Psychology: Memory for People*, pp 3–34. Mahwah, NJ: Erlbaum.

Meissner, C. A., Sporer, S. L. & Susa, K. J. (2008). A theoretical review and meta-analysis of the description-identification relationship in memory for faces. *European Journal of Cognitive Psychology*, 20(3), 414–455.

Melfsen, S. & Florin, I. (2002). Do socially anxious children show deficits in classifying facial expressions of emotions? *Journal of Nonverbal Behavior*, 26(2), 109–126.

Memon, A., Bartlett, J., Rose, R., et al. (2003a). The aging eyewitness: effects of age on face, delay, and source-memory ability. *The Journals of Gerontology Series B: Psychological Sciences and Social Sciences*, 58, 338–345.

Memon, A., Hope, L. & Bull, R. (2003b). Exposure duration: effects on eyewitness accuracy and confidence. *British Journal of Psychology*, 94, 339–354.

Mendlewicz, L., Linkowski, P., Bazelmans, C., et al. (2005). Decoding emotional facial expressions in depressed and anorexic patients. *Journal of Affective Disorders*, 89(1–3), 195–199.

Meyer, M. B. & Kurtz, M. M. (2009). Elementary neurocognitive function, facial affect recognition and social-skills in schizophrenia. *Schizophrenia Research*, 110(1–3), 173–179.

Meyer-Lindenberg, A., Hariri, A. R., Munoz, K. E., et al. (2005). Neural correlates of genetically abnormal social cognition in Williams syndrome. *Nature Neuroscience*, 8(8), 991–993.

Miall, R. C., Gowen, E. & Tchalenko, J. (2009). Drawing cartoon faces—a functional imaging study of the cognitive neuroscience of drawing. *Cortex*, 45(3), 394–406.

Michalopoulou, P. G., Surguladze, S., Morley, L. A., et al. (2008). Facial fear processing and psychotic symptoms in schizophrenia: functional magnetic resonance imaging study. *British Journal of Psychiatry*, 192(3), 191–196.

Michel, C., Rossion, B., Han, J., et al. (2006). Holistic processing is finely tuned for faces of one's own race. *Psychological Science*, 17(7), 608–615.

Miles, L. & Johnston, L. (2007). Detecting happiness: perceiver sensitivity to enjoyment and non-enjoyment smiles. *Journal of Nonverbal Behavior*, 31(4), 259–275.

Mills, D. L., Alvarez, T. D., St George, M., et al. (2000). Electrophysiological studies of face processing in Williams syndrome. *Journal of Cognitive Neuroscience*, 12, 47–64.

Milne, R. & Bull, R. (2002). Back to basics: a componential analysis of the original cognitive interview mnemonics with three age groups. *Applied Cognitive Psychology*, 16, 743–753.

Minnebusch, D. A. & Daum, I. (2009). Neuropsychological mechanisms of visual face and body perception. *Neuroscience and Biobehavioral Reviews*, 33(7), 1133–1144.

Mohlman, J., Carmin, C. N. & Price, R. B. (2007). Jumping to interpretations: social anxiety disorder and the identification of emotional facial expressions. *Behaviour Research and Therapy*, 45(3), 591–599.

Mondloch, C. J., Dobson, K. S., Parsons, J., et al. (2004). Why 8-year-olds cannot tell the difference between Steve Martin and Paul Newman: factors contributing to the slow development of sensitivity to the spacing of facial features. *Journal of Experimental Child Psychology*, 89, 159–181.

Mondloch, C. J., Le Grand, R. & Maurer, D. (2002). Configural face processing develops more slowly than featural face processing. *Perception*, 31, 553–566.

Mondloch, C. J., Lewis, T. L., Budreau, D. R., et al. (1999). Face perception during early infancy. *Psychological Science*, 10, 419–422.

Monk, C. S. (2008). The development of emotion-related neural circuitry in health and psychopathology. *Development and Psychopathology*, 20(4), 1231–1250.

Montagne, B., Kessels, R. P. C., De Haan, E. H. F., et al. (2007). The emotion recognition task: a paradigm to measure the perception of facial emotional expressions at different intensities. *Perceptual and Motor Skills*, 104(2), 589–598.

Montepare, J. M. & McArthur, L. Z. (1986). The influence of facial characteristics on children's age perceptions. *Journal of Experimental Child Psychology*, 42, 303–314.

Moore, C. D., Cohen, M. X. & Ranganath, C. (2006). Neural mechanisms of expert skills in visual working memory. *Journal of Neuroscience*, 26(43), 11187–11196.

Morel, S., Ponz, A., Mercier, M., et al. (2009). EEG–MEG evidence for early differential repetition effects for fearful, happy and neutral faces. *Brain Research*, 1254, 84–98.

Morris, J. P., Pelphrey, K. A. & McCarthy, G. (2007). Face processing without awareness in the right fusiform gyrus. *Neuropsychologia*, 45(13), 3087–3091.

Morris, J. S., Friston, K. J., Buchel, C., et al. (1998). A neuromodulatory role for the human amygdala in processing emotional facial expressions. *Brain*, 121, 47–57.

Morris, J. S., Frith, C. D., Perrett, D. I., et al. (1996). A differential neural response in the human amygdala to fearful and happy facial expressions. *Nature*, 383(6603), 812–815.

Morrison, D. J. & Schyns, P. G. (2001).Usage of spatial scales for the categorization of faces, objects, and scenes. *Psychonomic Bulletin and Review*, 8(3), 454–469.

Morrison, E. R., Gralewski, L., Campbell, N., et al. (2007). Facial movement varies by sex and is related to attractiveness. *Evolution and Human Behavior*, 28(3), 186–192.

Morton, J. & Johnson, M. H. (1991). CONSPEC and CONLERN: a two-process theory of infant face recognition. *Psychological Review*, 98(2), 164–181.

Moscovitch, M. & Moscovitch, D. A. (2000). Super face-inversion effects for isolated internal or external features, and for fractured faces. *Cognitive Neuropsychology*, 17(1–3), 201–219.

Moscovitch, M., Winocur, G. & Behrmann, M. (1997). What is special about face recognition? Nineteen experiments on a person with visual object agnosia and dyslexia but normal face recognition. *Journal of Cognitive Neuroscience*, 9(5), 555–604.

Mouchetant-Rostaing, Y., Giard, M. H., Bentin, S., et al. (2000). Neurophysiological correlates of face gender processing in humans. *European Journal of Neuroscience*, 12(1), 303–310.

Muhlberger, A., Wieser, M. J., Herrmann, M. J., et al. (2009). Early cortical processing of natural and artificial emotional faces differs between lower and higher socially anxious persons. *Journal of Neural Transmission*, 116(6), 735–746.

Mullins, D. T. & Duke, M. P. (2004). Effects of social anxiety on nonverbal accuracy and response time I: Facial expressions. *Journal of Nonverbal Behavior*, 28(1), 3–33.

Münte, T. F., Brack, M., Grootheer, O., et al. (1998). Brain potentials reveal the timing of face identity and expression judgments. *Neuroscience Research*, 30(1), 25–34.

Murray, J. E., Yong, E. & Rhodes, G. (2000). Revisiting the perception of upside-down faces. *Psychological Science*, 11, 498–502.

Nakamura, M., Watanabe, S., Gunji, A., et al. (2006). The magnetoenceph-alographic response to upright and inverted face stimuli in a patient with Williams syndrome. *Pediatric Neurology*, 34(5), 412–414.

Namiki, C., Hirao, K., Yamada, M., et al. (2007). Impaired facial emotion recognition and reduced amygdalar volume in schizophrenia. *Psychiatry Research: Neuroimaging*, 156(1), 23–32.

Natale, M., Gur, R. E. & Gur, R. C. (1983). Hemispheric asymmetries in processing emotional expressions. *Neuropsychologia*, 21(5), 555–565.

Navon, D. (1977). Forest before the trees: the precedence of global features in visual perception. *Cognitive Psychology*, 9, 353–383.

Nelson, C. A. (2001). The development and neural bases of face recognition. *Infant and Child Development,* 10, 3–18.

Newell, F. N., Chiroro, P. & Valentine, T. (1999). Recognizing unfamiliar faces: the effects of distinctiveness and view. *Quarterly Journal of Experimental Psychology A: Human Experimental Psychology,* 52, 509–534.

Nkengne, A., Bertin, C., Stamatas, G. N., et al. (2008). Influence of facial skin attributes on the perceived age of Caucasian women. *Journal of the European Academy of Dermatology and Venereology,* 22, 982–991.

Norton, D., McBain, R., Holt, D. J., et al. (2009). Association of impaired facial affect recognition with basic facial and visual processing deficits in schizophrenia. *Biological Psychiatry*, 65(12), 1094–1098.

Nunn, J. & Peters, E. (2001). Schizotypy and patterns of lateral asymmetry on hemisphere-specific language tasks. *Psychiatry Research*, 103(2–3), 179–192.

Nunn, J. A., Postma, P. & Pearson, R. (2001). Developmental prosopagnosia: should it be taken at face value? *Neurocase*, 7, 15–27.

O'Connor, K., Hamm, J. P. & Kirk, I. J. (2005). The neurophysiological correlates of face processing in adults and children with Asperger's syndrome. *Brain and Cognition*, 59(1), 82–95.

O'Donnell, C. & Bruce, V. (2001). Familiarisation with faces selectively enhances sensitivity to changes made to the eyes. *Perception*, 30, 755–764.

O'Hearn, K., Courtney, S., Street, W., et al. (2009). Working memory impairment in people with Williams syndrome: effects of delay, task and stimuli. *Brain and Cognition*, 69(3), 495–503.

Oinonen, K. A. & Mamanian, D. (2007). Facial symmetry detection ability changes across the menstrual cycle. *Biological Psychology*, 75(2), 136–145.

Okada, K. & Hickok, G. (2009). Two cortical mechanisms support the integration of visual and auditory speech: a hypothesis and preliminary data. *Neuroscience Letters*, 452(3), 219–223.

Oliva, A. & Schyns, P. G. (1997). Coarse blobs or fine edges? Evidence that information diagnosticity changes the perception of complex visual stimuli. *Cognitive Psychology*, 34, 72–107.

Olivares, E. I. & Iglesias, J. (2008). Brain potentials and integration of external and internal features into face representations. *International Journal of Psychophysiology*, 68(1), 59–69.

Onitsuka, T., Niznikiewicz, M. A., Spencer, K. M., et al. (2006). Functional and structural deficits in brain regions subserving face perception in schizophrenia. *American Journal of Psychiatry*, 163(3), 455–462.

Oostenveld, R. & Praamstra, P. (2001). The five percent electrode system for high-resolution EEG and ERP measurements. *Clinical Neurophysiology*, 112, 713–719.

Orgeta, V. & Phillips, L. H. (2008). Effects of age and emotional intensity on the recognition of facial emotion. *Experimental Aging Research*, 34(1), 63–79.

Oswald, K. M. & Coleman, M. J. (2007). Memory demands on facial composite identification. *Applied Cognitive Psychology*, 21, 345–360.

O'Toole, A. J., Deffenbacher, K. A., Valentin, D., et al. (1998). The perception of face gender: the role of stimulus structure in recognition and classification. *Memory & Cognition*, 26(1), 146–160.

O'Toole, A. J., Price, T. Vetter, T., et al. (1999). 3D shape and 2D surface textures of human faces: the role of 'averages' in attractiveness and age. *Image and Vision Computing*, 18, 9–19.

O'Toole, A. J., Roark, D. A. & Abdi, H. (2002). Recognizing moving faces: a psychological and neural synthesis. *Trends in Cognitive Sciences*, 6, 261–266.

Palermo, M. T., Pasqualetti, P., Barbati, G., et al. (2006). Recognition of schematic facial displays of emotion in parents of children with autism. *Autism*, 10(4), 353–364.

Paller, K. A., Gonsalves, B., Grabowecky, M., et al. (2000). Electrophysiological correlates of recollecting faces of known and unknown individuals. *Neuroimage*, 11(2), 98–110.

Parker, D. M. & Costen, N. P. (1999). One extreme or the other or perhaps the golden mean? Issues of spatial resolution in face processing. *Current Psychology*, 18, 118–127.

Parkin, A. J. & Williamson, P. (1987). Cerebral lateralisation at different stages of facial processing. *Cortex*, 23, 99–110.

Parr, L. A. & Heintz, M. (2009). Facial expression recognition in rhesus monkeys, Macaca mulatta. *Animal Behaviour*, 77(6), 1507–1513.

Pascalis, O. & Kelly, D. J. (2009). The origins of face processing in humans: phylogeny and ontogeny. *Perspectives on Psychological Science*, 4(2), 200–209.

Pascalis, O., de Haan, M. & Nelson, C. A. (2002). Is face processing species-specific during the first year of life? *Science*, 296, 1321–1323.

Pascalis, O., de Schonen, S., Morton, J., et al. (1995). Mother's face recognition by neonates: a replication and an extension. *Infant Behavior and Development*, 18(1), 79–85.

Pascalis, O., Scott, L. S., Kelly, D. J., et al. (2005). Plasticity of face processing in infancy. *Proceedings of the National Academy of Sciences of the United States of America*, 102, 5297–5300.

Pasley, B. N., Mayes, L. C. & Schultz, R. T. (2004). Subcortical discrimination of unperceived objects during binocular rivalry. *Neuron*, 42(1), 163–172.

Passarotti, A. M., Smith, J., DeLano, M. & Huang, J. (2007). Developmental differences in the neural bases of the face inversion effect show progressive tuning of face-selective regions to the upright orientation. *Neuroimage*, 34(4), 1708–1722.

Paterson, H. M. & Kemp, R. I. (2006). Co-witnesses talk: a survey of eyewitness discussion. *Psychology, Crime, and Law*, 12, 181–191.

Patterson, K. & Bradshaw, J. L. (1975). Differential hemispheric mediation of nonverbal visual stimuli. *Journal of Experimental Psychology: Human Perception and Performance*, 1(3), 246–252.

Pawlowski, B. & Jasienska, G. (2005). Women's preferences for sexual dimorphism in height depend on menstrual cycle phase and expected duration of relationship. *Biological Psychology*, 70(1), 38–43.

Peace, V., Miles, L. & Johnston, L. (2006). It doesn't matter what you wear: the impact of posed and genuine expressions of happiness on product evaluation. *Social Cognition*, 24(2), 137–168.

Pearson, R. & Lewis, M. B. (2005). Fear recognition across the menstrual cycle. *Hormones and Behavior*, 47(3), 267–271.

Pedelty, L., Levine, S. C. & Shevell, S. K. (1985). Developmental changes in face processing: results from multidimensional scaling. *Journal of Experimental Child Psychology*, 39, 421–436.

Peelen, M. V. & Downing, P. E. (2005). Selectivity for the human body in the fusiform gyrus. *Journal of Neurophysiology*, 93(1), 603–608.

Pegna, A. J., Landis, T. & Khateb, A. (2008). Electrophysiological evidence for early non-conscious processing of fearful facial expressions. *International Journal of Psychophysiology*, 70(2), 127–136.

Pellicano, E. & Rhodes, G. (2003). Holistic processing of faces in preschool children and adults. *Psychological Science*, 14(6), 618–622.

Pellicano, E., Rhodes, G. & Peters, M. (2006). Are preschoolers sensitive to configural information in faces? *Developmental Science*, 9(3), 270–277.

Pelphrey, K. A., Morris, J. P., McCarthy, G., et al. (2007). Perception of dynamic changes in facial affect and identity in autism. *Social Cognitive and Affective Neuroscience*, 2(2), 140–149.

Pelphrey, K. A., Sasson, N. J., Reznick, J. S., et al. (2002). Visual scanning of faces in autism. *Journal of Autism and Developmental Disorders*, 32(4), 249–261.

Peltola, M., Leppanen, J. M. & Hietanen, J. K. (2008). Modulation of attention by emotional faces in 7-month-old infants. *International Journal of Psychology*, 43(3–4), 72.

Penn, D. L., Combs, D. R., Ritchie, M., et al. (2000). Emotion recognition in schizophrenia: further investigation of generalized versus specific deficit models. *Journal of Abnormal Psychology*, 109(3), 512–516.

Penrod, S. & Bornstein, B. (2007). Generalizing eyewitness reliability research. In: R. C. L. Lindsay, D. F. Ross, J. D. Read & M. P. Toglia (eds), *Handbook of Eyewitness Psychology, Vol. 2: Memory for People*, pp 529–556. Mahwah, NJ: Erlbaum.

Penrod, S. & Cutler, B. (1995). Witness confidence and witness accuracy: assessing their forensic relation. *Psychology, Public Policy, and Law*, 1, 817–845.

Penry, J. (1971). *Looking at Faces and Remembering Them: A Guide to Facial Identification*. London: Elek Books.

Penton-Voak, I. S. & Chen, J. Y. (2004). High salivary testosterone is linked to masculine male facial appearance in humans. *Evolution and Human Behavior*, 25(4), 229–241.

Penton-Voak, I. S. & Perrett, D. I. (2000). Female preference for male faces changes cyclically: further evidence. *Evolution and Human Behavior*, 21(1), 39–48.

Penton-Voak, I. S., Perrett D. I., Castles, D. L., et al. (1999). Menstrual cycle alters face preference. *Nature*, 399, 741–742.

Perfect, T. J. (2003). Local processing bias impairs line-up performance. *Psychological Reports*, 93, 393–394.

Perfect, T. J. & Moon, H. C. (2005). The own-age effect in face recognition. In: J. Duncan, L. Phillips & P. McLeod (eds), *Measuring the Mind: Speed, Control, and Age*, pp 317–340. Oxford: Oxford University Press.

Perrett, D. I., Burt, D. M., Penton-Voak, I. S., et al. (1999). Symmetry and human facial attractiveness. *Evolution and Human Behavior*, 20, 295–307.

Perrett, D. I., Hietanen, J. K., Oram, M. W., et al. (1992). Organisation and functions of cells responsive to faces in the temporal cortex. *Philosophical Transactions of the Royal Society of London. Series B*, 335, 23–30.

Perrett, D. I., Lee, K. J., Penton-Voak, I., et al. (1998a). Effects of sexual dimorphism on facial attractiveness. *Nature*, 394, 884–887.

Perrett, D. I., May, K. A. & Yoshikawa, S. (1994). Facial shape and judgments of female attractiveness. *Nature*, 368, 239–242.

Perrett, D. I., Oram, M. W. & Ashbridge, E. (1998b). Evidence accumulation in cell populations responsive to faces: an account of generalisation of recognition without mental transformations. *Cognition*, 67, 111–145.

Perrett, D. I., Oram, M. W., Harries, M. H., et al. (1991). Viewer-centred and object-centred coding of heads in the macaque temporal cortex. *Experimental Brain Research*, 86(1), 159–173.

Perrett, D. I., Smith, P. A. J., Potter, D. D., et al. (1985). Visual cells in the temporal cortex sensitive to face view and gaze directions. *Proceedings of the Royal Society of London. Series B, Biological Sciences*, 223, 293–317.

Peskin, M. & Newell, F. N. (2004). Familiarity breeds attraction: effects of exposure on the attractiveness of typical and distinctive faces. *Perception*, 33, 147–157.

Pessoa, L., McKenna, M., Gutierrez, E., et al. (2002). Neural processing of emotional faces requires attention. *Proceedings of the National Academy of Sciences of the United States of America*, 99(17), 11458–11463.

Pezdek, K. & Arredondo, P. (2007). The development of memory for own- and other-race faces. *Journal of Experimental Child Psychology*, 98, 233–242.

Pezdek, K., Blandon-Gitlin, I. & Moore, C. (2003). Children's face recognition memory: more evidence for the Cross-Race Effect. *Journal of Applied Psychology*, 88(4), 760–763.

Pezzini, G., Vicari, S., Volterra, V., et al. (1999). Children with Williams syndrome: is there a single neuropsychological profile? *Developmental Neuropsychology*, 15(1), 141–155.

Pfutze, E. M., Sommer, W. & Schweinberger, S. R. (2002). Age-related slowing in face and name recognition: evidence from event-related brain potentials. *Psychology and Aging*, 17, 140–160.

Phan, K. L., Fitzgerald, D. A., Nathan, P. J., et al. (2006). Association between amygdala hyperactivity to harsh faces and severity of social anxiety in generalized social phobia. *Biological Psychiatry*, 59(5), 424–429.

Phillips, L. H. & Allen, R. (2004). Adult aging and the perceived intensity of emotions in faces and stories. *Aging Clinical and Experimental Research*, 16(3), 190–199.

Phillips, M. L. & David, A. S. (1997). Viewing strategies for simple and chimeric faces: an investigation of perceptual bias in normals and schizophrenic patients using visual scan paths. *Brain and Cognition*, 35(2), 225–238.

Phillips, M. L., Williams, L. M., Heining, M., et al. (2004). Differential neural responses to overt and covert presentations of facial expressions of fear and disgust. *Neuroimage*, 21(4), 1484–1496.

Phillips, M. L., Young, A. W., Senior, C., et al. (1997). A specific neural substrate for perceiving facial expressions of disgust. *Nature*, 389(6650), 495–498.

Pickel, K. L. (1998). Unusualness and threat as possible causes of 'weapon focus'. *Memory*, 6(3), 277–295.

Pickel, K. L. (1999). The influence of context on the 'Weapon Focus' Effect. *Law and Human Behavior*, 23(3), 299–311.

Picozzi, M., Macchi Cassia, V., Turati, C., et al. (2009). The effect of inversion on 3- to 5-year-olds' recognition of face and nonface visual objects. *Journal of Experimental Child Psychology*, 102, 487–502.

Pierce, K., Haist, F., Sedaghat, F., et al. (2004). The brain response to personally familiar faces in autism: findings of fusiform activity and beyond. *Brain*, 127, 2703–2716.

Pierce, K., Muller, R. A., Ambrose, J., et al. (2001). Face processing occurs outside the fusiform 'face area' in autism: evidence from functional MRI. *Brain*, 124, 2059–2073.

Pigott, M., Brigham, J. C. & Bothwell, R. K. (1990). A field study of the relationship between description accuracy and identification accuracy. *Journal of Police Science and Administration*, 17, 84–88.

Pike, G., Brace, N. & Kynan, S. (2002). The visual identification of suspects: procedures and practice. Home Office Briefing Note 2/02. http://www.homeoffice.gov.uk/rds/pdfs2/brf202.pdf (accessed 15 September 2008).

Pike, G., Kemp, R. and Towell, N. (1998) The face of identity checking, *Forensic Update*, 52, 8–13.

Pike, G. E., Kemp, R. I., Towell, N. A., et al. (1997). Recognizing moving faces: the relative contribution of motion and perspective view information. *Visual Cognition*, 4, 409–437.

Pillay, S. S., Rogowska, J., Gruber, S. A., et al. (2007). Recognition of happy facial affect in panic disorder: an fMRI study. *Journal of Anxiety Disorders*, 21(3), 381–393.

Pittenger, J. B. & Shaw, R. E. (1975). Ageing faces as visceral-elastic events: implications for a theory of nonrigid shape perception. *Journal of Experimental Psychology: Human Perception and Performance*, 1(4), 374–482.

Pittenger, J. B., Shaw, R. E. & Mark, L. S. (1979). Perceptual information for the age-level of faces as a higher-order invariant of growth. *Journal of Experimental Psychology: Human Perception and Performance*, 5, 478–493.

Platek, S. M. & Kemp, S. M. (2009). Is family special to the brain? An event-related fMRI study of familiar, familial, and self-face recognition. *Neuropsychologia*, 47, 849–858.

Platek, S. M., Wathne, K., Tierney, N. G., et al. (2008). Neural correlates of self-face recognition: an effect-location meta-analysis. *Brain Research*, 1232, 173–184.

Plesa-Skwerer, D., Faja, S., Schofield, C., et al. (2006). Perceiving facial and vocal expressions of emotion in individuals with Williams syndrome. *American Journal on Mental Retardation*, 111(1), 15–26.

Pocock, G. & Richards, C. D. (2006). *Human Physiology: The Basis of Medicine*. Oxford: Oxford University Press.

Pollak, S. D. & Sinha, P. (2002). Effects of early experience on children's recognition of facial displays of emotion. *Developmental Psychology*, 38(5), 784–791.

Pollatos, O., Herbert, B. M., Schandry, R., et al. (2008). Impaired central processing of emotional faces in anorexia nervosa. *Psychosomatic Medicine*, 70(6), 701–708.

Porter, S. & ten Brinke, L. (2008). Reading between the lies: identifying concealed and falsified emotions in universal facial expressions. *Psychological Science*, 19(5), 508–514.

Posner, M. I. (1980). Orienting of attention. *Quarterly Journal of Experimental Psychology*, 32, 3–25.

Pourtois, G., Schwartz, S., Seghier, M. L., et al. (2005a). View-independent coding of face identity in frontal and temporal cortices is modulated by familiarity: an event-related fMI study. *Neuroimage*, 24(4), 1214–1224.

Pourtois, G., Schwartz, S., Seghier, M. L., et al. (2005b). Portraits or people? Distinct representations of face identity in the human visual cortex. *Journal of Cognitive Neuroscience*, 17(7), 1043–1057.

Pozzulo, J. D. & Dempsey, J. (2006). Biased lineup instructions: examining the effect of pressure on children's and adults' eyewitness identification accuracy. *Journal of Applied Social Psychology*, 36(6), 1381–1394.

Pozzulo, J. D. & Lindsay, R. C. L. (1998). Identification accuracy of children versus adults: a meta-analysis. *Law and Human Behavior*, 22, 549–570.

Prkachin, G. C. (2003). The effects of orientation on detection and identification of facial expressions of emotion. *British Journal of Psychology*, 94, 45–62.

Puce, A., Allison, T., Asgari, M., et al. (1996). Differential sensitivity of human visual cortex to faces, letterstrings, and textures: a functional magnetic resonance imaging study. *Journal of Neuroscience*, 16(16), 5205–5215.

Puce, A., Allison, T., Bentin, S., et al. (1998). Temporal cortex activation in humans viewing eye and mouth movements. *Journal of Neuroscience*, 18(6), 2188–2199.

Pulvermuller, F. (1999). Words in the brain's language. *Behavioral and Brain Sciences*, 22(2), 253–336.

Pulvermuller, F. & Mohr, B. (1996). The concept of transcortical cell assemblies: a key to the understanding of cortical lateralization and interhemispheric interaction. *Neuroscience and Biobehavioral Reviews*, 20(4), 557–566.

Quinn, P. C. & Slater, A. (2003). Face perception at birth and beyond. In: O. Pascalis & A. Slater (eds), *The Development of Face Processing in Infancy and Early Childhood: Current Perspectives*, pp 3–12. Huntington, NY: Nova Science.

Quinn, P. C., Yahr, J., Kuhn, A., et al. (2002). Representation of the gender of human faces by infants: a preference for female. *Perception*, 31, 1109–1121.

Rahman, R. A., Sommer, W. & Schweinberger, S. R. (2002). Brain-potential evidence for the time course of access to biographical facts and names of familiar persons. *Journal of Experimental Psychology: Learning, Memory, and Cognition*, 28(2), 366–373.

Ramanathan, N. & Chellappa, R. (2006). Modeling age progression in young faces. *IEEE Computer Vision and Pattern Recognition (CVPR)*, 1, 387–394.

Ramanathan, N., Chellappa, R. & Biswas, S. (2009). Computational methods for modelling facial aging: a survey. *Journal of Visual Languages and Computing*, 20, 131–144.

Rapaczynski, W. & Ehrlichman, H. (1979). Opposite visual hemifield superiorities in face recognition as a function of cognitive style. *Neuropsychologia*, 17, 645–652.

Rapaczynski, W. & Ehrlichman, H. (1979). Opposite visual hemifield superiorities in face recognition as a function of cognitive style. *Neuropsychologia*, 17, 645–652.

Rapcsak, S. Z., Polster, M. R., Comer, J. F., et al. (1994). False recognition and misidentification of faces following right hemisphere damage. *Cortex*, 30, 565–583.

Rasmjou, S., Hausmann, M. & Gunturkun, O. (1999). Hemispheric dominance and gender in the perception of an illusion. *Neuropsychologia*, 37(9), 1041–1047.

Read, J. D. (1995). The availability heuristic in person identification—the sometimes misleading consequences of enhanced contextual information. *Applied Cognitive Psychology*, 9, 91–121.

Rehnman, J. & Herlitz, A. (2006). Higher face recognition ability in girls: magnified by own-sex own-ethnicity bias. *Memory*, 14(3), 289–296.

Reilly, J. S., McIntire, M. & Bellugi, U. (1990). The acquisition of conditionals in American Sign Language—grammaticized facial expressions. *Applied Psycholinguistics*, 11(4), 369–392.

Renault, B., Signoret, J. L., Debruille, B., et al. (1989). Brain potentials reveal covert facial recognition in prosopagnosia. *Neuropsychologia*, 27(7), 905–912.

Rhodes, G. (1988). Looking at faces. First-order and second-order features as determinants of facial appearance. *Perception*, 17, 43–63.

Rhodes, G. (1993). Configural coding, expertise, and the right hemisphere advantage for face recognition. *Brain and Cognition*, 22, 19–41.

Rhodes, G. (1996). *Superportraits: Caricatures and Recognition*. Hove: Psychology Press.

Rhodes, G. (2006). The evolutionary psychology of facial beauty. *Annual Review of Psychology*, 57, 199–236.

Rhodes, G. & Tremewan, T. (1994). Understanding face recognition: caricature effects, inversion, and the homogeneity problem. *Visual Cognition*, 1, 275–311.

Rhodes, G. & Tremewan, T. (1996). Averageness, exaggeration, and facial attractiveness. *Psychological Science*, 7, 105–110.

Rhodes, G., Brake, K. & Atkinson, A. (1993). What's lost in inverted faces? *Cognition*, 47, 25–57.

Rhodes, G., Brake, S., Taylor, K., et al. (1989). Expertise and configural coding in face recognition. *British Journal of Psychology*, 80, 313–331.

Rhodes, G., Brennan, S. & Carey, S. (1987). Identification and ratings of caricatures: implications for mental representations of faces. *Cognitive Psychology*, 19, 473–497.

Rhodes, G., Byatt, G., Michie, P. T., et al. (2004a). Is the fusiform face area specialized for faces, individuation, or expert individuation? *Journal of Cognitive Neuroscience*, 16(2), 189–203.

Rhodes, G., Hickford, C. & Jeffery, L. (2000). Sextypicality and attractiveness: are supermale and superfemale faces super-attractive? *British Journal of Psychology*, 91, 125–140.

Rhodes, G., Jeffery, L., Watson, T. L., et al. (2003). Fitting the mind to the world: face adaptation and attractiveness aftereffects. *Psychological Science*, 14(6), 558–566.

Rhodes, G., Jeffery, L., Watson, T. L., et al. (2004b). Orientation-contingent face aftereffects and implications for face-coding mechanisms. *Current Biology*, 14(23), 2119–2123.

Rhodes, G., Proffitt, F., Grady, J. M., et al. (1998). Facial symmetry and the perception of beauty. *Psychonomic Bulletin and Review*, 5, 659–669.

Rhodes, G., Roberts, J. & Simmons, L. (1999a). Reflections on symmetry and attractiveness. *Psychology, Evolution and Gender*, 1, 279–295.

Rhodes, G., Simmons, L. & Peters, M. (2005). Attractiveness and sexual behaviour: does attractiveness enhance mating success? *Evolution and Human Behavior*, 26, 186–201.

Rhodes, G., Sumich, A. & Byatt, G. (1999b). Are average facial configurations attractive only because of their symmetry? *Psychological Science*, 10, 52–58.

Rhodes, D. M. G. (2009). Age estimation of faces: a review. *Applied Cognitive Psychology*, 23, 1–12.

Riby, D. M. & Hancock, P. J. B. (2008). Viewing it differently: social scene perception in Williams syndrome and autism. *Neuropsychologia*, 46(11), 2855–2860.

Riby, D. & Hancock, P. J. B. (2009a). Looking at movies and cartoons: eye-tracking evidence from Williams syndrome and autism. *Journal of Intellectual Disability Research*, 53, 169–181.

Riby, D. M. & Hancock, P. J. B. (2009b). Do faces capture the attention of individuals with Williams syndrome or autism? Evidence from tracking eye movements. *Journal of Autism and Developmental Disorders*, 39(3), 421–431.

Riddoch, M. J., Johnston, R. A., Bracewell, R. M., et al. (2008). Are faces special? A case of pure prosopagnosia. *Cognitive Neuropsychology*, 25(1), 3–26.

Ridout, N., Dritschel, B., Matthews, K., et al. (2009). Memory for emotional faces in major depression following judgement of physical facial characteristics at encoding. *Cognition & Emotion*, 23(4), 739–752.

Riesenhuber, M., Jarudi, I., Gilad, S., et al. (2004). Face processing in humans is compatible with a simple shape-based model of vision. *Proceedings in Biological Sciences*, 271(Suppl 6), S448–S450.

Rizzolatti, G., Umilta, C. & Berlucchi, G. (1971). Opposite superiorities of the right and left cerebral hemispheres in discriminative reaction time to physiognomical and alphabetical material. *Brain*, 94(3), 431–442.

Roark, D. A., Barrett, S. E., Spence, M. J., et al. (2003). Psychological and neural perspectives on the role of motion in face recognition. *Behavioral and Cognitive Neuroscience Reviews*, 2, 15–46.

Robbins, R. & McKone, E. (2007). No face-like processing for objects-of-expertise in three behavioural tasks. *Cognition*, 103(1), 34–79.

Robbins, R., McKone, E. & Edwards, M. (2007). Aftereffects for face attributes with different natural variability: adapter position effects and neural models. *Journal of Experimental Psychology: Human Perception and Performance*, 33(3), 570–592.

Roberson, D., Damjanovic, L. & Pilling, M. (2007). Categorical perception of facial expressions: evidence for a 'category adjustment' model. *Memory & Cognition*, 35(7), 1814–1829.

Rocca, C. C. D., van den Heuvel, E., Caetano, S. C., et al. (2009). Facial emotion recognition in bipolar disorder: a critical review. *Revista Brasileira De Psiquiatria*, 31(2), 171–180.

Rock, I. (1988). On Thompson's inverted-face phenomenon. *Perception*, 17, 815–817.

Rodin, M. J. (1987). Who is memorable to whom: a study of cognitive disregard. *Social Cognition*, 5, 144–165.

Rodway, P., Wright, L. & Hardie, S. (2003). The valence-specific laterality effect in free viewing conditions: the influence of sex, handedness, and response bias. *Brain and Cognition*, 53(3), 452–463.

Rose, S. A., Jankowski, J. J. & Feldman, J. F. (2008). The inversion effect in infancy: the role of internal and external features. *Infant Behavior and Development*, 31, 470–480.

Ross, D. F., Ceci, S. J., Dunning, D., et al. (1994). Unconscious transference and mistaken identity: when a witness misidentifies a familiar but innocent person. *Journal of Applied Psychology*, 79, 918–930.

Rossion, B. (2002). Is sex categorization from faces really parallel to face recognition? *Visual Cognition*, 9(8), 1003–1020.

Rossion, B. (2008). Picture–plane inversion leads to qualitative changes of face perception. *Acta Psychologica*, 128, 274–289.

Rossion, B., Caldara, R., Seghier, M., et al. (2003a). A network of occipito-temporal face-sensitive areas besides the right middle fusiform gyrus is necessary for normal face processing. *Brain*, 126, 2381–2395.

Rossion, B., Campanella, S., Gomez, C. M., et al. (1999a). Task modulation of brain activity related to familiar and unfamiliar face processing: an ERP study. *Clinical Neurophysiology*, 110(3), 449–462.

Rossion, B., Delvenne, J. F., Debatisse, D., et al. (1999b). Spatio-temporal localisation of the face inversion effect: an event-related potentials study. *Biological Psychology*, 50(3), 173–178.

Rossion, B., Dricot, L., Devolder, A., et al. (2000a). Hemispheric asymmetries for whole-based and part-based face processing in the human fusiform gryus. *Journal of Cognitive Neuroscience*, 12(5), 793–802.

Rossion, B., Gauthier, I., Goffaux, V., et al. (2002). Expertise training with novel objects leads to left-lateralized facelike electrophysiological responses. *Psychological Science*, 13(3), 250–257.

Rossion, B., Gauthier, I., Tarr, M. J., et al. (2000b). The N170 occipito-temporal component is delayed and enhanced to inverted faces but not to inverted objects: an electrophysiological account of face-specific processes in the human brain. *Neuroreport*, 11(1), 69–74.

Rossion, B., Schiltz, C. & Crommelinck, M. (2003b). The functionally defined right occipital and fusiform 'face areas' discriminate novel from visually familiar faces. *Neuroimage*, 19(3), 877–883.

Rotshtein, P., Geng, J. J., Driver, J., et al. (2007). Role of features and second-order spatial relations in face discrimination, face recognition, and individual face skills: behavioral and functional magnetic resonance imaging data. *Journal of Cognitive Neuroscience*, 19(9), 1435–1452.

Rouw, R. & de Gelder, B. (2002). Impaired face recognition does not preclude intact whole face perception. *Visual Cognition*, 9(6), 689–718.

Rovee-Collier, C. & Cuevas, K. (2009). Multiple memory systems are unnecessary to account for infant memory development: an ecological model. *Developmental Psychology*, 45(1), 160–174.

Rubenstein, A. J., Langlois, J. H. & Roggman, L. A. (2002). What makes a face attractive and why: the role of averageness in defining facial beauty. In: G. Rhodes and L. Zebrowitz (eds), *Facial Attractiveness: Evolutionary, Cognitive, and Social Perspectives*, pp 1–34. Westport, CT: Ablex.

Ruffman, T., Henry, J. D., Livingstone, V., et al. (2008). A meta-analytic review of emotion recognition and aging: implications for neuropsychological models of aging. *Neuroscience and Biobehavioral Reviews*, 32(4), 863–881.

Ruiz-Soler, M. & Beltran, F. S. (2006). Face perception: an integrative review of the role of spatial frequencies. *Psychological Research*, 70, 273–292.

Rupp, H. A., James, T. W., Ketterson, E. D., et al. (2009). Neural activation in women in response to masculinized male faces: mediation by hormones and psychosexual factors. *Evolution and Human Behavior*, 30(1), 1–10.

Russell, R. & Sinha, P. (2007). Real-world face recognition: the importance of surface reflectance properties. *Perception*, 36, 1368–1374.

Russell, R., Sinha, P., Biederman, I., et al. (2006). Is pigmentation important for face recognition? Evidence from contrast negation. *Perception*, 35, 749–759.

Russell, T. A., Green, M. J., Simpson, I., et al. (2008). Remediation of facial emotion perception in schizophrenia: concomitant changes in visual attention. *Schizophrenia Research*, 103(1–3), 248–256.

Ryu, J. J. & Chaudhuri, A. (2006). Representations of familiar and unfamiliar faces as revealed by viewpoint-aftereffects. *Vision Research*, 46(23), 4059–4063.

Sachs, G., Steger-Wuchse, D., Kryspin-Exner, I., et al. (2004). Facial recognition deficits and cognition in schizophrenia. *Schizophrenia Research*, 68(1), 27–35.

Sagiv, N. & Bentin, S. (2001). Structural encoding of human and schematic faces: holistic and part-based processes. *Journal of Cognitive Neuroscience*, 13(7), 937–951.

Samuels, C. A. & Ewy, R. (1985). Aesthetic perception of faces during infancy. *British Journal of Developmental Psychology*, 3, 221–228.

Sangrigoli, S. & de Schonen, S. (2004). Effect of visual experience on face processing: a developmental study of inversion and non-native effects. *Developmental Science*, 7, 74–87.

Sangrigoli, S., Pallier, C., Argenti, A.-M., et al. (2005). Reversibility of the other-race effect in face recognition during childhood. *Psychological Science*, 16, 440–444.

Sato, W., Kochiyama, T., Uono, S., et al. (2008). Time course of superior temporal sulcus activity in response to eye gaze: a combined fMRI and MEG study. *Social Cognitive and Affective Neuroscience*, 3(3), 224–232.

Sauerland, M. & Sporer, S. S. (2007). Post-decision confidence, decision time, and self-reported decision processes as postdictors of identification accuracy. *Psychology, Crime and Law*, 13(6), 611–625.

Saumier, D., Arguin, M. & Lassonde, M. (2001). Prosopagnosia: a case study involving problems in processing configural information. *Brain and Cognition*, 46(1–2), 255–259.

Schattmann, L. & Sherwin, B. B. (2007). Testosterone levels and cognitive functioning in women with polycystic ovary syndrome and in healthy young women (vol 51, pg 587, 2007). *Hormones and Behavior*, 52(2), 280 [Erratum].

Scherf, K. S., Behrmann, M., Minshew, N., et al. (2008). Atypical development of face and greeble recognition in autism. *Journal of Child Psychology and Psychiatry*, 49(8), 838–847.

Schiltz, C. & Rossion, B. (2006). Faces are represented holistically in the human occipito-temporal cortex. *Neuroimage*, 32(3), 1385–1394.

Schiltz, C., Sorger, B., Caldara, R., et al. (2006). Impaired face discrimination in acquired prosopagnosia is associated with abnormal response to individual faces in the right middle fusiform gyrus. *Cerebral Cortex*, 16(4), 574–586.

Schooler, J. W. (2002). Verbalization produces a transfer inappropriate processing shift. *Applied Cognitive Psychology*, 16, 979–989.

Schooler, J. W. & Engstler-Schooler, T. Y. (1990). Verbal overshadowing of visual memories: some things are better left unsaid. *Cognitive Psychology*, 22, 36–71.

Schultz, R. T., Gauthier, I., Klin, A., et al. (2000). Abnormal ventral temporal cortical activity during face discrimination among individuals with autism and Asperger syndrome. *Archives of General Psychiatry*, 57(4), 331–340.

Schwaninger, A. & Mast, F. (1999). Why is face recognition so orientation-sensitive? Psychophysical evidence for an integrative model. *Perception*, 28(Suppl), 116 (Abstract).

Schwaninger, A., Lobmeier, J. S. & Collishaw, S. M. (2002). The role of featural and configural information in familiar and unfamiliar face recognition. *Lecture Notes in Computer Science*, 2525, 643–650.

Schwaninger, A., Ryf, S. & Hofer, F. (2003). Configural information is processed differently in perception and recognition of faces. *Vision Research*, 43, 1501–1505.

Schwarzer, G. & Zauner, N. (2003). Face processing in 8-month-old infants: evidence for configural and analytical processing. *Vision Research*, 43, 2783–2793.

Schwarzlose, R. F., Baker, C. I. & Kanwisher, N. (2005). Separate face and body selectivity on the fusiform gyrus. *Journal of Neuroscience*, 25(47), 11055–11059.

Schweinberger, S. R. (1996). How Gorbachev primed Yeltsin: analyses of associative priming in person recognition by means of reaction times and event-related brain potentials. *Journal of Experimental Psychology: Learning Memory and Cognition*, 22(6), 1383–1407.

Schweinberger, S. R. & Burton, A. M. (2003). Covert recognition and the neural system for face processing. *Cortex*, 39(1), 9–30.

Schweinberger, S. R. & Soukup, G. R. (1998). Asymmetric relationships among perceptions of facial identity, emotion, and facial speech. *Journal of Experimental Psychology: Human Perception and Performance*, 24, 1748–1765.

Schweinberger, S. R., Baird, L. M., Blumler, M., et al. (2003). Interhemispheric cooperation for face recognition but not for affective facial expressions. *Neuropsychologia*, 41, 407–414.

Schweinberger, S. R., Burton, A. M. & Kelly, S. W. (1999). Asymmetric dependencies in perceiving identity and emotion: experiments with morphed faces. *Perception & Psychophysics*, 61(6), 1102–1115.

Schweinberger, S. R., Kaufmann, J. M., Moratti, S., et al. (2007). Brain responses to repetitions of human and animal faces, inverted faces, and objects—an MEG study. *Brain Research*, 1184, 226–233.

Schweinberger, S. R., Landgrebe, A., Mohr, B., et al. (2002a). Personal names and the human right hemisphere: an illusory link? *Brain and Language*, 80(2), 111–120.

Schweinberger, S. R., Pfutze, E. M. & Sommer, W. (1995). Repetition priming of face recognition: evidence from event-related potentials. *Journal of Experimental Psychology: Learning, Memory and Cognition*, 21, 722–736.

Schweinberger, S. R., Pickering, E. C., Burton, A. M., et al. (2002b). Human brain potential correlates of repetition priming in face and name recognition. *Neuropsychologia*, 40, 2057–2073.

Schyns, P. G. & Oliva, A. (1994). From blobs to boundary edges: evidence for time and spatial scale-dependent scene recognition. *Psychological Science*, 5, 195–200.

Schyns, P. G. & Oliva, A. (1999). Dr. Angry and Mr. Smile: when categorization flexibly modifies the perception of faces in rapid visual presentations. *Cognition*, 69, 243–265.

Scott, L. S. and Monesson, A. (2009). The origin of biases in face perception. *Psychological Science*, 20(6), 676–680.

Scott, L. S. & Nelson, C. A. (2006). Featural and configural face processing in adults and infants: a behavioral and electrophysiological investigation. *Perception*, 35(8), 1107–1128.

Searcy, J. H. & Bartlett, J. C. (1996). Inversion and processing of component and spatial-relational information in faces. *Journal of Experimental Psychology: Human Perception and Performance*, 22, 904–915.

Seiferth, N. Y., Pauly, K., Kellermann, T., et al. (2009). Neuronal correlates of facial emotion discrimination in early onset schizophrenia. *Neuropsychopharmacology*, 34(2), 477–487.

Seitz, K. (2002). Parts and wholes in person recognition: developmental trends. *Journal of Experimental Child Psychology*, 82, 367–381.

Sekuler, A. B., Gaspar, C. M., Gold, J. M., et al. (2004). Inversion leads to quantitative, not qualitative, changes in face processing. *Current Biology*, 14, 391–396.

Sergent, J. (1982). About face—left-hemisphere involvement in processing physiognomies. *Journal of Experimental Psychology: Human Perception and Performance*, 8(1), 1–14.

Sergent, J. (1984). An investigation into component and configural processes underlying face perception. *British Journal of Psychology*, 75, 221–242.

Sergent, J. (1986). Microgenesis of face perception. In: H. D. Ellis, M. A. Jeeves, F. Newcombe & A. M. Young (eds), *Aspects of Face Processing*, pp 17–33. Dordrecht: Martinus Nijhoff.

Sergent, J. & Signoret, J. L. (1992). Varieties of functional deficits in prosopagnosia. *Cerebral Cortex*, 2(5), 375–388.

Sergent, J. & Villemure, J. G. (1989). Prosopagnosia in a right hemispherectomized patient. *Brain*, 112, 975–995.

Sergent, J., Ohta, S. & Macdonald, B. (1992). Functional neuroanatomy of face and object processing—a positron emission tomography study. *Brain*, 115, 15–36.

Sergerie, K., Chochol, C. & Armony, J. L. (2008). The role of the amygdala in emotional processing: a quantitative meta-analysis of functional neuroimaging studies. *Neuroscience and Biobehavioral Reviews*, 32(4), 811–830.

Shapiro, P. N. & Penrod, S. (1986). Meta-analysis of facial identification studies. *Psychological Bulletin*, 100, 139–156.

Shaw, J. S. I., Garcia, L. A. & McClure, K. A. (1999). A lay perspective on the accuracy of eyewitness testimony. *Journal of Applied Social Psychology*, 29, 52–71.

Shearer, D. & Mikulka, P. (1996). Effect of facial familiarity and task requirement on electrodermal activity. *American Journal of Psychology*, 109(1), 131–137.

Sheline, Y. I., Barch, D. M., Donnelly, J. M., et al. (2001). Increased amygdala response to masked emotional faces in depressed subjects resolves with antidepressant treatment: an fMRI study. *Biological Psychiatry*, 50(9), 651–658.

Shepherd, J. W., Davies, G. M. & Ellis, A. W. (1981). Studies of cue saliency. In: G. Davies, H. Ellis & J. Shepherd (eds), *Perceiving and Remembering Faces*, pp 105–131. New York: Academic Press.

Sherwin, B. B. (2003). Estrogen and cognitive functioning in women. *Endocrine Reviews*, 24(2), 133–151.

Shimojo, S., Simion, C., Shimojo, E., et al. (2003). Gaze bias both reflects and influences preference. *Nature Neuroscience*, 6, 1317–1322.

Shin, Y. W., Na, M. H., Ha, T. H., et al. (2008). Dysfunction in configural face processing in patients with schizophrenia. *Schizophrenia Bulletin*, 34(3), 538–543.

Shuttleworth, E. C., Jr., Syring, V. & Allen, N. (1982). Further observations on the nature of prosopagnosia. *Brain and Cognition*, 1(3), 307–322.

Shutts, K. & Kinzler, K. D. (2007). An ambiguous-race illusion in children's face memory. *Psychological Science*, 18(9), 763–767.

Sigala, N. (2004). Visual categorization and the inferior temporal cortex. *Behavioural Brain Research*, 149(1), 1–7.

Silver, H., Goodman, C., Bilker, W., et al. (2006). Impaired error monitoring contributes to face recognition deficit in schizophrenia patients. *Schizophrenia Research*, 85(1–3), 151–161.

Silver, H., Goodman, C., Knoll, G., et al. (2004). Brief emotion training improves recognition of facial emotions in chronic schizophrenia. A pilot study. *Psychiatry Research*, 128(2), 147–154.

Silvia, P. J., Allan, W. D., Beauchamp, D. L., et al. (2006). Biased recognition of happy facial expressions in social anxiety. *Journal of Social and Clinical Psychology*, 25(6), 585–602.

Simion, F., Macchi Cassia, V., Turati, C., et al. (2001). The origins of face perception: specific versus non-specific mechanisms. *Infant and Child Development*, 10, 59–65.

Simion, F., Valenza, E., Macchi Cassia, V., et al. (2002). Newborns' preference for up-down asymmetrical configurations. *Developmental Science*, 5(4), 427–434.

Simonian, S. J., Beidel, D. C., Turner, S. M., et al. (2001). Recognition of facial affect by children and adolescents diagnosed with social phobia. *Child Psychiatry & Human Development*, 32(2), 137–145.

Skagerberg., E. M. (2007). Co-witness feedback in line-ups. *Applied Cognitive Psychology*, 21, 489–497.

Slater, A., Bremner, G., Johnson, S. P., et al. (2000a). Newborn infants' preference for attractive faces: the role of internal and external facial features. *Infancy*, 1(2), 265–274.

Slater, A., Quinn, P. C., Hayes, R. A., et al. (2000b). The role of facial orientation in newborn infants' preference for attractive faces. *Developmental Science*, 3, 181–185.

Slater, A., von der Schulenburg, C., Brown, E., et al. (1998). Newborn infants prefer attractive faces. *Infant Behavior and Development*, 21, 345–354.

Slone, A. E., Brigham, J. C. & Meissner, C. A. (2000). Social and cognitive factors affecting the own-race bias in Whites. *Basic and Applied Social Psychology*, 22, 71–84.

Snowden, P. T. & Schyns, P. G. (2006). Channel surfing in the visual brain. *Trends in Cognitive Science*, 10(12), 538–545.

Soppe, H. J. G. (1986). Children's recognition of unfamiliar faces: developments and determinants. *International Journal of Behavioral Development*, 9, 219–233.

Sorger, B., Goebel, R., Schiltz, C., et al. (2007). Understanding the functional neuroanatomy of acquired prosopagnosia. *Neuroimage*, 35(2), 836–852.

Sörqvist, P. & Eriksson, M. (2007). Effects of training on age estimation. *Applied Cognitive Psychology*, 21, 131–135.

Speer, L. L., Cook, A. E., McMahon, W. M., et al. (2007). Face processing in children with autism—effects of stimulus contents and type. *Autism*, 11(3), 265–277.

Spezio, M. L., Adolphs, R., Hurley, R. S. E., et al. (2007). Abnormal use of facial information in high-functioning autism. *Journal of Autism and Developmental Disorders*, 37(5), 929–939.

Spiridon, M. & Kanwisher, N. (2002). How distributed is visual category information in human occipito-temporal cortex? An fMRI study. *Neuron*, 35(6), 1157–1165.

Sporer, S. L. (2001). Recognizing faces of other ethnic groups: an integration of theories. *Psychology, Public Policy and Law*, 7, 36–97.

Sprengelmeyer, R. & Jentzsch, I. (2006). Event related potentials and the perception of intensity in facial expressions. *Neuropsychologia*, 44(14), 2899–2906.

Sprengelmeyer, R., Perrett, D. I., Fagan, E. C., et al. (2009). The cutest little baby face: a hormonal link to sensitivity to cuteness in infant faces. *Psychological Science*, 20(2), 149–154.

Sprengelmeyer, R., Rausch, M., Eysel, U. T., et al. (1998). Neural structures associated with recognition of facial expressions of basic emotions. *Proceedings of the Royal Society of London. Series B, Biological Sciences*, 265(1409), 1927–1931.

Steblay, N. M. (1992). A meta-analytic review of the weapon focus effect. *Law and Human Behavior*, 16, 413–424.

Steblay, N. M. (1997). Social influence in eyewitness recall: a meta-analytic review of lineup instruction effects. *Law and Human Behavior*, 21, 283–297.

Steblay, N., Dysart, J. E., Fulero, S., et al. (2001). Eyewitness accuracy rates in sequential and simultaneous line-up presentations: a meta-analytic comparison. *Law and Human Behavior*, 25, 459–473.

Steblay, N., Dysart, S., Fulero, S., et al. (2003). Eyewitness accuracy rates in police showup and lineup presentations: a meta-analytic comparison. *Law and Human Behavior*, 27(5), 523–540.

Steede, L. & Hole, G. J. (2006). Repetition priming and recognition of dynamic and static chimeras. *Perception*, 35, 1367–1382.

Steede, L. L., Tree, J. J. & Hole, G. J. (2007). I can't recognize your face but I can recognize its movement. *Cognitive Neuropsychology*, 24(4), 451–466.

Steeves, J. K. E., Culham, J. C., Duchaine, B. C., et al. (2006). The fusiform face area is not sufficient for face recognition: evidence from a patient with dense prosopagnosia and no occipital face area. *Neuropsychologia*, 44(4), 594–609.

Stein, M. B., Goldin, P. R., Sareen, J., et al. (2002). Increased amygdala activation to angry and contemptuous faces in generalized social phobia. *Archives of General Psychiatry*, 59(11), 1027–1034.

Stephan, B. C. M. & Caine, D. (2007). What is in a view? The role of featural information in the recognition of unfamiliar faces across viewpoint transformation. *Perception*, 36, 189–198.

Stephan, B. C. M., Breen, N. & Caine, D. (2006). The recognition of emotional expression in prosopagnosia: decoding whole and part faces. *Journal of the International Neuropsychological Society*, 12(6), 884–895.

Sterling, L., Dawson, G., Webb, S., et al. (2008). The role of face familiarity in eye tracking of faces by individuals with autism spectrum disorders. *Journal of Autism and Developmental Disorders*, 38(9), 1666–1675.

Sterzer, P., Jalkanen, L. & Rees, G. (2009). Electromagnetic responses to invisible face stimuli during binocular suppression. *Neuroimage*, 46(3), 803–808.

Stevenage, S. V. & Osborne, C. D. (2006). Making heads turn: the effect of familiarity and stimulus rotation on a gender-classification task. *Perception*, 35, 1485–1494.

Stevenage, S. V., Lee, E. A. & Donnelly, N. (2005). The role of familiarity in a face classification task using Thatcherized faces. *Quarterly Journal of Experimental Psychology*, 58A(6), 1103–1118.

Stone, A. & Valentine, T. (2005). Strength of visual percept generated by famous faces perceived without awareness: effects of affective valence, response latency, and visual field. *Consciousness and Cognition*, 14(3), 548–564.

Stormark, K. M. (2004). Skin conductance and heart-rate responses as indices of covert face recognition in preschool children. *Infant and Child Development*, 13, 42–433.

Sturzel, F. & Spillmann, L. (2000). Thatcher illusion: dependence on angle of rotation. *Perception*, 29, 937–942.

Sugase, Y., Yamane, S., Ueno, S., et al. (1999). Global and fine information coded by single neurons in the temporal visual cortex. *Nature*, 400(6747), 869–873.

Sugiura, M., Sassa, Y., Jeong, H., et al. (2008). Face-specific and domain-general characteristics of cortical responses during self-recognition. *Neuroimage*, 42(1), 414–422.

Sullivan, S., Ruffman, T. & Hutton, S. B. (2007). Age differences in emotion recognition skills and the visual scanning of emotion faces. *Journals of Gerontology Series B: Psychological Sciences and Social Sciences*, 62(1), P53–P60.

Surakka, V. & Hietanen, J. K. (1998). Facial and emotional reactions to Duchenne and non-Duchenne smiles. *International Journal of Psychophysiology*, 29(1), 23–33.

Surguladze, S., Brammer, M. J., Keedwell, P., et al. (2005). A differential pattern of neural response toward sad versus happy facial expressions in major depressive disorder. *Biological Psychiatry*, 57(3), 201–209.

Surguladze, S. A., Brammer, M. J., Young, A. W., et al. (2003). A preferential increase in the extrastriate response to signals of danger. *Neuroimage*, 19(4), 1317–1328.

Surguladze, S. A., Young, A. W., Senior, C., et al. (2004). Recognition accuracy and response bias to happy and sad facial expressions in patients with major depression. *Neuropsychology*, 18(2), 212–218.

Susac, A., Ilmoniemi, R. J., Pihko, E., et al. (2009). Early dissociation of face and object processing: a magnetoencephalographic study. *Human Brain Mapping*, 30(3), 917–927.

Tager-Flusberg, H., Plesa-Skwerer, D., Faja, S., et al. (2003). People with Williams syndrome process faces holistically. *Cognition*, 89(1), 11–24.

Takahashi, N., Kawamura, M., Hirayama, K., et al. (1995). Prosopagnosia: a clinical and anatomic study of four patients. *Cortex*, 31, 317–329.

Talarovicova, A., Krskova, L. & Blazekova, J. (2009). Testosterone enhancement during pregnancy influences the 2D:4D ratio and open field motor activity of rat siblings in adulthood. *Hormones and Behavior*, 55, 235–239.

Tamietto, M., Adenzato, M., Geminiani, G., et al. (2007). Fast recognition of social emotions takes the whole brain: interhemispheric cooperation in the absence of cerebral asymmetry. *Neuropsychologia*, 45(4), 836–843.

Tamietto, M., Corazzini, L. L., de Gelder, B., et al. (2006). Functional asymmetry and interhemispheric cooperation in the perception of emotions from facial expressions. *Experimental Brain Research*, 171(3), 389–404.

Tanaka, J. W. & Curran, T. (2001). A neural basis for expert object recognition. *Psychological Science*, 12(1), 43–47.

Tanaka, J. W. & Farah, M. J. (1993). Parts and whole in face recognition. *Quarterly Journal of Experimental Psychology: Human Experimental Psychology*, 46A(2), 225–245.

Tanaka, J. & Porterfield, A. (2002). The own-face effect as an electrophysiological marker of self. *Journal of Cognitive Neuroscience*, B105.

Tanaka, J. & Sengco, J. A. (1997). Features and their configuration in face recognition. *Memory and Cognition*, 25(5), 583–592.

Tanaka, J. W., Curran, T., Porterfield, A. L., et al. (2006). Activation of preexisting and acquired face representations: the N250 event-related potential as an index of face familiarity. *Journal of Cognitive Neuroscience*, 18(9), 1488–1497.

Tanaka, J., Giles, M., Kremen, S., et al. (1998). Mapping attractor fields in face space: the atypicality bias in face recognition. *Cognition*, 68, 199–220.

Tanaka, J. W., Kiefer, M. & Bukach, C. M. (2004). A holistic account of the own-race effect in face recognition: evidence from a cross-cultural study. *Cognition*, 93, B1–B9.

Tanskanen, T., Nasanen, R., Ojanpaa, H., et al. (2007). Face recognition and cortical responses: effect of stimulus duration. *Neuroimage*, 35(4), 1636–1644.

Tantam, D., Monaghan, L., Nicholson, H., et al. (1989). Autistic children's ability to interpret faces: a research note. *Journal of Child Psychology, Psychiatry and Allied Disciplines*, 30(4), 623–630.

Tardif, C., Laine, F., Rodriguez, M., et al. (2007). Slowing down presentation of facial movements and vocal sounds enhances facial expression recognition and induces facial–vocal imitation in children with autism. *Journal of Autism and Developmental Disorders*, 37(8), 1469–1484.

Tarr, M. J. & Gauthier, I. (2000). FFA: a flexible fusiform area for subordinate-level visual processing automatized by expertise. *Nature Neuroscience*, 3(8), 764–769.

Tate, A. J., Fischer, H., Leigh, A. E., et al. (2006). Behavioural and neurophysiological evidence for face identity and face emotion processing in animals. *Philosophical Transactions of the Royal Society of London. Series B, Biological Sciences*, 361(1476), 2155–2172.

Taylor, M. J., Edmonds, G. E., McCarthy, G., et al. (2001). Eyes first! Eye processing develops before face processing in children. *Neuroreport*, 12(8), 1671–1676.

Teunisse, J. P. & de Gelder, B. (2001). Impaired categorical perception of facial expressions in high-functioning adolescents with autism. *Child Neuropsychology*, 7(1), 1–14.

Thibault, P., Gosselin, P., Brunel, M. L., et al. (2009). Children's and adolescents' perception of the authenticity of smiles. *Journal of Experimental Child Psychology*, 102(3), 360–367.

Thomas, L. A., De Bellis, M. D., Graham, R., et al. (2007). Development of emotional facial recognition in late childhood and adolescence. *Developmental Science*, 10(5), 547–558.

Thompson, P. (1980). Margaret Thatcher: a new illusion. *Perception*, 9, 483–484.

Thompson, P. (2002). Eyes wide apart: overestimating interpupillary distance. *Perception*, 31(6), 651–656.

Thornhill, R. & Gangestad, S. W. (1999). Facial attractiveness. *Trends in Cognitive Sciences*, 3, 452–460.

Thornton, I. M. & Kourtzi, Z. (2002). A matching advantage for dynamic human faces. *Perception*, 31, 113–132.

Tollestrup, P. A., Turtle, J. W. & Yuille, J. C. (1994). Actual victims and witnesses to robbery and fraud: an archival analysis. In: D. F. Ross, J. D. Read & M. P. Toglia (eds), *Adult Eyewitness Testimony: Current Trends and Developments*, pp 144–160. Cambridge: Cambridge University Press.

Tong, F. & Nakayama, K. (1999). Robust representations for faces: evidence from visual search. *Journal of Experimental Psychology: Human Perception and Performance*, 25(4), 1016–1035.

Tong, F., Nakayama, K., Moscovitch, M., et al. (2000). Response properties of the human fusiform face area. *Cognitive Neuropsychology*, 17(1–3), 257–279.

Tranel, D. & Damasio, A. R. (1988). Non-conscious face recognition in patients with face agnosia. *Behavioural Brain Research*, 30(3), 235–249.

Tranel, D., Damasio, A. R. & Damasio, H. (1988). Intact recognition of facial expression, gender, and age in patients with impaired recognition of face identity. *Neurology*, 38(5), 690–696.

Trivers, R. L. (1971). The evolution of reciprocal altruism. *Quarterly Review of Biology*, 46, 35–57.

Troje, N. F. & Bülthoff, H. H. (1998). How is bilateral symmetry of human faces used for recognition of novel views. *Vision Research*, 38, 79–89.

Tsao, D. Y., Freiwald, W. A., Knutsen, T. A., et al. (2003). Faces and objects in macaque cerebral cortex. *Nature Neuroscience*, 6(9), 989–995.

Tsao, D. Y., Freiwald, W. A., Tootell, R. B. H., et al. (2006). A cortical region consisting entirely of face-selective cells. *Science*, 311(5761), 670–674.

Tsoi, D. T., Lee, K. H., Khokhar, W. A., et al. (2008). Is facial emotion recognition impairment in schizophrenia identical for different emotions? A signal detection analysis. *Schizophrenia Research*, 99(1–3), 263–269.

Tsukiura, T., Mochizuki-Kawai, H. & Fujii, T. (2006). Dissociable roles of the bilateral anterior temporal lobe in face-name associations: an event-related fMRI study. *Neuroimage*, 30(2), 617–626.

Tsukiura, T., Suzuki, C., Shigemune, Y., et al. (2008). Differential contributions of the anterior temporal and medial temporal lobe to the retrieval of memory for person identity information. *Human Brain Mapping*, 29(12), 1343–1354.

Tsunoda, T., Yoshino, A., Furusawa, T., et al. (2008). Social anxiety predicts unconsciously provoked emotional responses to facial expression. *Physiology & Behavior*, 93(1–2), 172–176.

Tunnicliff, J. L. & Clark, S. E. (2000). Selecting foils for identification lineups: matching suspects or descriptions. *Law and Human Behavior*, 24, 231–258.

Turati, C., Bulf, H. & Simion, F. (2008). Newborns' face recognition over changes in viewpoint. *Cognition*, 106(3), 1300–1321.

Turati, C., Sangrigoli, S., Ruel, J., et al. (2004). Evidence of the face inversion effect in 4-month-old infants. *Infancy*, 6(2), 275–297.

Turati, C., Simion, F., Milani, I., et al. (2002). Newborns' preference for faces: what is crucial? *Developmental Psychology*, 38(6), 875–882.

Turati, C., Valenza, E., Leo, I., et al. (2005). Three-month-olds' visual preference for faces and its underlying visual processing mechanisms. *Journal of Experimental Child Psychology*, 90(3), 255–273.

Turetsky, B. I., Kohler, C. G., Indersmitten, T., et al. (2007). Facial emotion recognition in schizophrenia: when and why does it go awry? *Schizophrenia Research*, 94(1–3), 253–263.

Turk, D. J., Heatherton, T. F., Kelley, W. M., et al. (2002). Mike or me? Self-recognition in a split-brain patient. *Nature Neuroscience*, 5(9), 841–842.

Turk, D. J., Rosenblum, A. C., Gazzaniga, M. S., et al. (2005). Seeing John Malkovich: the neural substrates of person categorization. *Neuroimage*, 24(4), 1147–1153.

Turton, D. (2004). Lip-plates and the people who take photographs. Uneasy encounters between Mursi and tourists in southern Ethiopia. *Anthropology Today*, 20(3), 3–8.

Uddin, L. Q., Rayman, J. & Zaidel, E. (2005). Split-brain reveals separate but equal self-recognition in the two cerebral hemispheres. *Consciousness and Cognition*, 14(3), 633–640.

Utama, N. P., Takemoto, A., Koike, Y., et al. (2009). Phased processing of facial emotion: an ERP study. *Neuroscience Research*, 64(1), 30–40.

Uttner, I., Bliem, H. & Danek, A. (2002). Prosopagnosia after unilateral right cerebral infarction. *Journal of Neurology*, 249(7), 933–935.

Valentine, T. (1991). A unified account of the effects of distinctiveness, inversion, and race in face recognition. *Quarterly Journal of Experimental Psychology*, 43A(2), 161–204.

Valentine, T. (2006). Forensic facial identification. In: A. Heaton-Armstrong, E. Shepherd, G. Gudjonsson & D. Wolchover (eds), *Witness Testimony: Psychological, Investigative and Evidential Perspectives*, pp 281–308. Oxford: Oxford University Press.

Valentine, T. & Bruce, V. (1986a). Recognizing familiar faces: the role of distinctiveness and familiarity. *Canadian Journal of Psychology*, 40, 300–305.

Valentine, T. & Bruce, V. (1986b). The effect of distinctiveness in recognizing and classifying faces. *Perception*, 15, 525–535.

Valentine, T. & Bruce, V. (1986c). The effect of race, inversion and encoding activity upon face recognition. *Acta Psychologica*, 61, 259–273.

Valentine, T. & Bruce, V. (1988). Mental rotation of faces. *Memory and Cognition*, 16, 556–566.

Valentine, T. & Endo, M. (1992). Towards an exemplar model of face processing: the effects of race and distinctiveness. *Quarterly Journal of Experimental Psychology*, 44A(4), 671–703.

Valentine, T. & Mesout, J. (2009). Eyewitness identification under stress in the London Dungeon. *Applied Cognitive Psychology*, 23(2), 151–161.

Valentine, T., Darling, S. & Donnelly, M. (2004). Why are average faces attractive? The effect of view and averageness on the attractiveness of female faces. *Psychonomic Bulletin and Review*, 11, 482–487.

Valentine, T., Darling, S. & Memon, A. (2007). Do strict rules and moving images increase the reliability of sequential identification procedures? *Applied Cognitive Psychology*, 21, 933–949.

Valentine, T., Pickering, A. & Darling, S. (2003). Characteristics of eyewitness identification that predict the outcome of real lineups. *Applied Cognitive Psychology*, 17, 969–993.

Valenza, E., Simion, F., Macchi Cassia, V., et al. (1996). Face preference at birth. *Journal of Experimental Psychology: Human Perception and Performance*, 22(4), 892–903.

van Beek, Y. & Dubas, J. S. (2008). Decoding basic and non-basic facial expressions and depressive symptoms in late childhood and adolescence. *Journal of Nonverbal Behavior*, 32(1), 53–64.

van der Gaag, C., Minderaa, R. B. & Keysers, C. (2007). The BOLD signal in the amygdala does not differentiate between dynamic facial expressions. *Social Cognitive and Affective Neuroscience*, 2(2), 93–103.

van't Wout, M., Aleman, A., Kessels, R. P. C., et al. (2007a). Exploring the nature of facial affect processing deficits in schizophrenia. *Psychiatry Research*, 150(3), 227–235.

van't Wout, M., van Dijke, A., Aleman, A., et al. (2007b). Fearful faces in schizophrenia—the relationship between patient characteristics and facial affect recognition. *Journal of Nervous and Mental Disease*, 195(9), 758–764.

Varendonck, M. J. (1911). Les témoignages d'enfants dans un procès retentissant. *Archives de Psychologie*, 11(42), 128–171.

Vermeire, B. A. & Hamilton, C. R. (1998). Inversion effect for faces in split-brain monkeys. *Neuropsychologia*, 36(10), 1003–1014.

Vestlund, J., Langeborg, L., Sörqvist, P., et al. (2009). Experts on age estimation. *Scandinavian Journal of Psychology*, 50, 301–307.

Vladeanu, M. & Bourne, V. J. (2009). Examining the hemispheric distribution of semantic information using lateralised priming of familiar faces. *Brain and Cognition*, 69(2), 420–425.

Vokey, J. R. & Read, J. D. (1992). Familiarity, memorability, and the effect of typicality on the recognition of faces. *Memory and Cognition*, 20, 291–302.

Vokey, J. R., Rendall, D., Parr, L. A., et al. (2004). Visual kin recognition and family resemblance in chimpanzees. *Journal of Comparative Psychology*, 118, 194–199.

Vuilleumier, P., Armony, J. L., Driver, J., et al. (2001). Effects of attention and emotion on face processing in the human brain: an event-related fMRI study. *Neuron*, 30(3), 829–841.

Wada, Y. & Yamamoto, T. (2001). Selective impairment of facial recognition due to a haematoma restricted to the right fusiform and lateral occipital region. *Journal of Neurology, Neurosurgery and Psychiatry*, 71(2), 254–257.

Wallace, S., Coleman, M. & Bailey, A. (2008). An investigation of basic facial expression recognition in autism spectrum disorders. *Cognition & Emotion*, 22(7), 1353–1380.

Wallace, S., Coleman, M., Pascalis, O., et al. (2006). A study of impaired judgment of eye-gaze direction and related face-processing deficits in autism spectrum disorders. *Perception*, 35(12), 1651–1664.

Walther, S., Federspiel, A., Horn, H., et al. (2009). Encoding deficit during face processing within the right fusiform face area in schizophrenia. *Psychiatry Research: Neuroimaging*, 172(3), 184–191.

Walton, G. E. & Bower, T. G. R. (1993). Newborns form 'prototypes' in less than 1 minute. *Psychological Science*, 4(3), 203–205.

Wang, P. P., Doherty, S., Rourke, S. B., et al. (1995). Unique profile of visuo-perceptual skills in a genetic syndrome. *Brain and Cognition*, 29(1), 54–65.

Want, S. C., Pascalis, O., Coleman, M., et al. (2003). Recognizing people from the inner or outer parts of their faces: developmental data concerning 'unfamiliar' faces. *British Journal of Developmental Psychology*, 21, 125–135.

Warrington, E. K. & James, M. (1967). An experimental investigation of facial recognition in patients with unilateral cerebral lesions. *Cortex*, 3, 317–326.

Warrington, E. K. & Taylor, A. M. (1978). Two categorical stages of object recognition. *Perception*, 7(6), 695–705.

Watson, T. L. & Clifford, C. W. G. (2003). Pulling faces: an investigation of the face-distortion aftereffect. *Perception*, 32(9), 1109–1116.

Webster, M. A. & MacLin, O. H. (1999). Figural aftereffects in the perception of faces. *Psychonomic Bulletin & Review*, 6(4), 647–653.

Webster, M. A., Kaping, D., Mizokami, Y., et al. (2004). Adaptation to natural facial categories. *Nature*, 428(6982), 557–561.

Weissman, D. H. & Banich, M. T. (2000). The cerebral hemispheres cooperate to perform complex but not simple tasks. *Neuropsychology*, 14(1), 41–59.

Welling, L. L. M., Jones, B. C., DeBruine, L. M., et al. (2008). Men report stronger attraction to femininity in women's faces when their testosterone levels are high. *Hormones and Behavior*, 54(5), 703–708.

Wells, G. L. (1978). Applied eyewitness testimony research: system variables and estimator variables. *Journal of Personality and Social Psychology*, 36, 1546–1557.

Wells, G. L. (1984). The psychology of lineup identifications. *Journal of Applied Social Psychology*, 14, 89–103.

Wells, G. L. (undated) Gary L. Wells' comments on the Mecklenburg Report. http://www.psychology.iastate.edu/~glwells/Illinois_Project_Wells_comments.pdf (accessed 28 January 2009).

Wells, G. L. & Bradfield, A. L. (1998). 'Good, you identified the suspect': feedback to eyewitnesses distorts their reports of the witnessing experience. *Journal of Applied Psychology*, 83, 360–376.

Wells, G. L. & Bradfield, A. L. (1999). Distortions in eyewitnesses' recollections: can the postidentification feedback effect be moderated? *Psychological Science*, 10, 138–144.

Wells, G. L. & Hasel, L. E. (2007). Facial composite production by eyewitnesses. *Current Directions In Psychological Science*, 16(1), 6–10.

Wells, G. L. & Hryciw, B. (1984). Memory for faces: encoding and retrieval operations. *Memory and Cognition*, 12, 338–344.

Wells, G. L. & Olson, E. A. (2001). The other-race effect in eyewitness identification: what do we do about it? *Psychology, Public Policy, and Law*, 7(1), 230–246.

Wells, G. L. & Olson, E. (2003). Eyewitness identification. *Annual Review of Psychology*, 54, 277–295.

Wells, G. L., Leippe, M. R. & Ostrom, T. M. (1979). Guidelines for empirically assessing the fairness of a lineup. *Law and Human Behavior*, 3, 285–293.

Wells, G. L., Olson, E. A. & Charman, S. D. (2003). Distorted retrospective eyewitness reports as functions of feedback and delay. *Journal of Experimental Psychology: Applied*, 9(1), 42–52.

Wells, G. L., Rydell, S. M. & Seelau, E. P. (1993). On the selection of distractors for eyewitness lineups. *Journal of Applied Psychology*, 78, 835–844.

Weniger, G., Lange, C., Ruther, E., et al. (2004). Differential impairments of facial affect recognition in schizophrenia subtypes and major depression. *Psychiatry Research*, 128(2), 135–146.

Werker, J. F. & Tees, R. C. (2005). Speech perception as a window for understanding plasticity and commitment in language systems of the brain. *Developmental Psychobiology*, 46, 233–251.

Weston, N. J., Perfect, T. J., Schooler, J. W., et al. (2008). Navon processing and verbalisation: a holistic/featural distinction. *European Journal of Cognitive Psychology*, 20(3), 587–611.

Whiteley, A. M. & Warrington, E. K. (1977). Prosopagnosia: a clinical, psychological, and anatomical study of three patients. *Journal of Neurology, Neurosurgery and Psychiatry*, 40(4), 395–403.

Whittaker, J. F., Deakin, J. F. W. & Tomenson, B. (2001). Face processing in schizophrenia: defining the deficit. *Psychological Medicine*, 31(3), 499–507.

Wickline, V. B., Bailey, W. & Nowicki, S. (2009). Cultural in-group advantage: emotion recognition in African American and European American faces and voices. *Journal of Genetic Psychology*, 170(1), 5–28.

Wiese, H. & Schweinberger, S. R. (2008). Event-related potentials indicate different processes to mediate categorical and associative priming in person recognition. *Journal of Experimental Psychology: Learning Memory and Cognition*, 34(5), 1246–1263.

Wiese, H., Schweinberger, S. R. & Hansen, K. (2008). The age of the beholder: ERP evidence of an own-age bias in face memory. *Neuropsychologia*, 46(12), 2973–2985.

Wigan, A. L. (1844). *A New View of Insanity: The Duality of Mind*. London: Longman, Brown, Green and Longmans.

Wilbrand, H. (1892). Ein Fall von Seelenblindheit und Hemianopsie mit Sectionsbefund. *Deutsche Zeitschrift für Nervenheilkunde*, 2, 361–387.

Wild, H. A., Barrett, S. E., Spence, M. J., et al. (2000). Recognition and sex categorization of adults' and children's faces: examining performance in the absence of sex-stereotyped cues. *Journal of Experimental Child Psychology*, 77(4), 269–291.

Wild-Wall, N., Dimigen, O. & Sommer, W. (2008). Interaction of facial expressions and familiarity: ERP evidence. *Biological Psychology*, 77(2), 138–149.

Williams, L. M., Senior, C., David, A. S., et al. (2001). In search of the 'Duchenne smile': evidence from eye movements. *Journal of Psychophysiology*, 15(2), 122–127.

Willner, P. & Rowe, G. (2001). Alcohol servers' estimates of young people's ages. *Drugs: Education, Prevention, and Policy*, 8, 375–383.

Wilson, R. R., Blades M. & Pascalis, O. (2007a). What do children look at in an adult face with which they are personally familiar? *British Journal of Developmental Psychology*, 25, 375–382.

Wilson, R., Pascalis, O. & Blades, M. (2007b). Familiar face recognition in children with autism: the differential use of inner and outer face parts. *Journal of Autism and Developmental Disorders*, 37(2), 314–320.

Winkielman, P., Halberstadt, J., Fazendeiro, T., et al. (2006). Prototypes are attractive because they are easy on the mind. *Psychological Science*, 17, 799–806.

Winston, J. S., Henson, R. N. A., Fine-Goulden, M. R., et al. (2004). fMRI-adaptation reveals dissociable neural representations of identity and expression in face perception. *Journal of Neurophysiology*, 92(3), 1830–1839.

Wirth, M. M. & Schultheiss, O. C. (2007). Basal testosterone moderates responses to anger faces in humans. *Physiology & Behavior*, 90(2–3), 496–505.

Wiscott, L., Fellous, J.-M., Krüger, N., et al. (1997). Face recognition by elastic graph matching. *IEEE Pattern Recognition and Machine Intelligence*, 19, 775–779.

Wogalter, M. S. (1991). Effects of post-exposure description and imaging on subsequent face recognition performance. *Proceedings of the Human Factors Society*, 35, 575–579.

Wogalter, M. S., Marwitz, D. B. & Leonard, D. C. (1992). Suggestiveness in photo spread line-ups: similarity induces distinctiveness. *Applied Cognitive Psychology*, 5, 443–453.

Wollaston, W. H. (1824). On the apparent direction of eyes in a portrait. *Philosophical Transactions of the Royal Society of London, Series B*, 114, 247–256.

Wolwer, W., Frommann, N., Halfmann, S., et al. (2005). Remediation of impairments in facial affect recognition in schizophrenia: efficacy and specificity of a new training program. *Schizophrenia Research*, 80(2–3), 295–303.

World Health Organization (2001). *The World Health Report 2001. Mental Health: New Understanding, New Hope*. Geneva: World Health Organization.

Wright, C. I., Martis, B., Schwartz, C. E., et al. (2003). Novelty responses and differential effects of order in the amygdala, substantia innominata, and inferior temporal cortex. *Neuroimage*, 18(3), 660–669.

Wright, D. B. & McDaid, A. T. (1996). Comparing system and estimator variables using data from real line-ups. *Applied Cognitive Psychology*, 10(1), 75–84.

Wright, D. B. & Sladden, B. (2003). An own gender bias and the importance of hair in face recognition. *Acta Psychologica*, 114(1), 101–114.

Wright, D. B. & Stroud, J. N. (2002). Age differences in lineup identification accuracy: people are better with their own age. *Law and Human Behavior*, 26(6), 641–654.

Wright, D. B., Boyd, C. E. & Tredoux, C. (2003). Inter-racial contact and the own-race bias for face recognition in South Africa and England. *Applied Cognitive Psychology*, 17, 365–373.

Wright, H., Wardlaw, J., Young, A. W., et al. (2006). Prosopagnosia following nonconvulsive status epilepticus associated with a left fusiform gyrus malformation. *Epilepsy & Behavior*, 9(1), 197–203.

Wynn, J. K., Lee, J., Horan, W. P., et al. (2008). Using event related potentials to explore stages of facial affect recognition deficits in schizophrenia. *Schizophrenia Bulletin*, 34(4), 679–687.

Yamashita, J. A., Hardy, J. L., De Valois, K. K., et al. (2005). Stimulus selectivity of figural aftereffects for faces. *Journal of Experimental Psychology: Human Perception and Performance*, 31(3), 420–437.

Yarmey, A. D. (1984). Age as a factor in eyewitness memory. In: G. L. Wells & E. F. Loftus (eds), *Eyewitness Testimony: Psychological Perspectives*, pp 142–154. Cambridge: Cambridge University Press.

Yin, R. K. (1969). Looking at upside-down faces. *Journal of Experimental Psychology*, 81(1), 141–145.

Yin, R. K. (1970). Face recognition by brain injured patients: a dissociable ability? *Neuropsychologia*, 8, 395.

Yoon, J. H., D'Esposito, M. & Carter, C. S. (2006). Preserved function of the fusiform face area in schizophrenia as revealed by fMRI. *Psychiatry Research: Neuroimaging*, 148(2–3), 205–216.

Yoon, K. L. & Zinbarg, R. E. (2007). Threat is in the eye of the beholder: social anxiety and the interpretation of ambiguous facial expressions. *Behaviour Research and Therapy*, 45(4), 839–847.

Yoon, K. L., Fitzgerald, D. A., Angstadt, M., et al. (2007). Amygdala reactivity to emotional faces at high and low intensity in generalized social phobia: a 4-Tesla functional MRI study. *Psychiatry Research: Neuroimaging*, 154(1), 93–98.

Yoon, K. L., Joormann, J. & Gotlib, I. H. (2009). Judging the intensity of facial expressions of emotion: depression-related biases in the processing of positive affect. *Journal of Abnormal Psychology*, 118(1), 223–228.

Young, A. W. (1998). Covert face recognition in prosopagnosia. In: A. W. Young (ed.), *Face and Mind*, pp 282–312. Oxford: Oxford University Press.

Young, A. W., Hay, D. C. & Ellis, A. W. (1985a). The faces that launched a thousand slips: everyday difficulties and errors in recognising people. *British Journal of Psychology*, 76, 495–523.

Young, A. W., Hay, D. C., McWeeny, K. H., et al. (1985b). Familiarity decisions for faces presented to the left and right cerebral hemispheres. *Brain and Cognition*, 4(4), 439–450.

Young, A. W., Hay, D. C., McWeeny, K. H., et al. (1985c). Matching familiar and unfamiliar faces on internal and external features. *Perception*, 14(6), 737–746.

Young, A. W., Hellawell, D. & de Haan, E. H. F. (1988). Cross-domain semantic priming in normal subjects and a prosopagnosic patient. *Quarterly Journal of Experimental Psychology Section A: Human Experimental Psychology*, 40(3), 561–580.

Young, A., Hellawell, D. & Hay, D. C. (1987). Configurational information in face perception. *Perception*, 16, 737–759.

Young, A. W., McWeeny, K. H., Ellis, A. W., et al. (1986a). Naming and categorization latencies for faces and written names. *Quarterly Journal of Experimental Psychology*, 38A, 297–318.

Young, A. W., McWeeny, K. H., Hay, D. C., et al. (1986b). Access to identity-specific semantic codes from familiar faces. *Quarterly Journal of Experimental Psychology. A, Human Experimental Psychology*, 38(2), 271–295.

Young, A. W., Newcombe, F., de Haan, E. H. F., et al. (1993). Face perception after brain injury: selective impairments affecting identity and expression. *Brain*, 116, 941–959.

Young, A. W., Perrett, D. I., Calder, A. J., et al. (2002). *Facial Expressions of Emotion: Stimuli and Tests (FEEST)*. Bury St Edmunds: Thames Valley Test Company.

Young, A. W., Rowland, D., Calder, A. J., et al. (1997). Facial expression megamix: tests of dimensional and category accounts of emotion recognition. *Cognition*, 63(3), 271–313.

Yovel, G. & Kanwisher, N. (2004). Face perception: domain specific, not process specific. *Neuron*, 44(5), 889–898.

Yovel, G. & Kanwisher, N. (2005). The neural basis of the behavioral face-inversion effect. *Current Biology*, 15(24), 2256–2262.

Yovel, G., Tambini, A. & Brandman, T. (2008). The asymmetry of the fusiform face area is a stable individual characteristic that underlies the left-visual-field superiority for faces. *Neuropsychologia*, 46(13), 3061–3068.

Yuill, N. & Lyon, J. (2007). Selective difficulty in recognising facial expressions of emotion in boys with ADHD—general performance impairments or specific problems in social cognition? *European Child & Adolescent Psychiatry*, 16(6), 398–404.

Yuille, J. C. (1993). We must study forensic eyewitnesses to know about them. *American Psychologist*, 48, 572–573.

Yuodelis, C. & Hendrickson, A. (1986). A qualitative and quantitative analysis of the human fovea during development. *Vision Research*, 26(6), 847–855.

Zajonc, R. B. (1968) Attitudinal effects of mere exposure. *Journal of Personality and Social Psychology*, 9, 1–27.

Zhao, L. & Chubb, C. (2001). The size-tuning of the face-distortion after-effect. *Vision Research*, 41(23), 2979–2994.

Zhao, W., Chellappa, R., Phillips, P. J., et al. (2003). Face recognition: a literature survey. *ACM Computing Surveys*, 35(4), 399–458.

index